D1271563

An Unconventional History of Western Philosophy

An Unconventional History of Western Philosophy

Conversations between Men and Women Philosophers

EDITED BY KAREN J. WARREN

With the research assistance of Audun Solli

ROWMAN & LITTLEFIELD PUBLISHERS, INC.
Lanham • Boulder • New York • Toronto • Plymouth, UK

ROWMAN & LITTLEFIELD PUBLISHERS, INC.

Published in the United States of America
by Rowman & Littlefield Publishers, Inc.
A wholly owned subsidiary of The Rowman & Littlefield Publishing Group, Inc.
4501 Forbes Boulevard, Suite 200, Lanham, Maryland 20706
www.rowmanlittlefield.com

Estover Road
Plymouth PL6 7PY
United Kingdom

British Library Cataloguing in Publication Information Available

Library of Congress Cataloging-in-Publication Data

Warren, Karen, 1947-
  An unconventional history of Western philosophy : conversations between men and women philosophers / edited by Karen J. Warren.
     p. cm.
  ISBN-13: 978-0-7425-5923-3 (cloth : alk. paper)
  ISBN-10: 0-7425-5923-8 (cloth : alk. paper)
  ISBN-13: 978-0-7425-5924-0 (pbk. : alk. paper)
  ISBN-10: 0-7425-5924-6 (pbk. : alk. paper)
  eISBN-13: 978-0-7425-6460-2
  eISBN-10: 0-7425-6460-6
1. Philosophy. I. Title.
  BD21.W355 2008
  190—dc22
                                                                                    2008014126

Printed in the United States of America

∞ ™ The paper used in this publication meets the minimum requirements of American National Standard for Information Sciences—Permanence of Paper for Printed Library Materials, ANSI/NISO Z39.48-1992.

DEDICATED
to my mother, Marge Warren Bails, and
to the memory of my special friend George Anton Christiansen

Contents

Foreword

INCLUDING WOMEN IN "ANCIENT AND MEDIEVAL PHILOSOPHIES"

Henry R. West

I cotaught Ancient and Medieval Philosophies for ten years (1993–2002) in collaboration with Jeremiah Reedy, a member of the Macalester College Classics Department. We used standard textbooks: *Philosophical Classics, Volume 1: Ancient Philosophy*, edited by Forrest E. Baird and Walter Kaufmann with selections from *Volume 2: Medieval Philosophy*; Frederick Copleston's *History of Philosophy, Volume 1: Greece and Rome—From the Pre-Socratics to Plotinus*, with selections from *Volume 2: Medieval Philosophy*. There were no women in our reading list. Copleston has no women in the index to volume 1. Baird and Kaufmann had no women in their anthology from 1961 to 1997, when selections from Hildegard of Bingen and Catherine of Siena were introduced in the second edition of *Volume II, Medieval Philosophy*. In 2000, four pages on Aspasia were included in the third edition of Baird and Kaufmann's *Volume I: Ancient Philosophy*. Reedy and I, with our male bias, did not include either Hildegard or Catherine in our reading assignments. In the medieval period, we concentrated on the issue of faith and reason, the problem of universals, and arguments for the existence of God. We did not read any writings by women.

In fall 2003, after Reedy's retirement, I cotaught the course with Karen J. Warren. We included readings from women philosophers in the ancient and medieval periods: women Pythagoreans (including Aesara of Lucania and others), Aspasia, Diotima (treated as a real person, not as a figment of the imagination of Socrates), Julia Domna, Hildegaard, Heloise, Mechtild of Magdeburg, and Christine de Pisan. These are philosophers well worthy of study. Baird and Kaufmann say: "In fact, the whole of Plato's thought, from his earliest to his latest works, can be understood as a gradual and sustained departure from the heritage of Socrates to that of Pythagoras" (Vol. 1, 4th ed., 1). This is an obscure statement unless one reads not just the sayings attributed to Pythagoras but those attributed to Pythagoreans, some of whom were women philosophers. Among my discoveries was that the Pythagorean Aesara of Lucania, evidently earlier than Plato (ca. 400–300 B.C.E.), put forward a tripartite theory of the psyche—basically the same theory Plato stated in the *Republic*. When Diotima is treated as a historical person, rather than as a figure by which Socrates can put forward positive views while claiming that he knows nothing, her vision of eternal and unchangeable Beauty can be seen as a forerunner of the Socratic/Platonic theory of the Forms. Similarly, her claim that people seek their immortality in bearing children can be seen as a challenge to which Plato's theory of the immortal soul, which exists before birth and continues to exist after death, is viewed as an alternative theory of immortality. As a last example, the ethical theory of Abelard and Heloise is more clearly stated and practiced by Heloise than by Abelard.

Why have these women not received recognition as women philosophers? One explanation is that they wrote in literary forms such as letters, visions, and allegories, or only carried on conversations without writing. But that is true of Epicurus, whose surviving works are letters, and Socrates, who wrote nothing. Plato's allegories are among his most quoted works. Another explanation is that we usually have only fragments of their writings, but that is true of all the pre-Socratics, who are considered philosophers. A third is that the history of philosophy has been preserved as the work of a few great philosophers. And I would not claim that any of these early women have the rank of Plato, Aristotle, or Augustine.

But the best explanation for why these women have been omitted from the history of philosophy or, if included, not recognized as philosophers, is male bias. When male pre-Socratics are quoted by Aristotle, their work, although only fragments, is attended to. When Socrates says that Aspasia was his teacher of rhetoric and that Diotima taught him the Ladder of Love, these statements are dismissed without attention.

In the class with Karen J. Warren, we felt that some students did not take the women philosophers as seriously as they did the philosophers in the textbooks. They had to read them from handouts or had to print them from electronic communication. That made it inconvenient. But I believe that another factor was that the assignments did not have the authority of being in the textbooks. In the opinion of some students, if a reading is in the textbook, it must be objectively important. If it is not, it is just important in the subjective judgment of the instructors. This anthology, edited by Karen J. Warren, will correct that.

Preface

Karen J. Warren

This book is an outgrowth of what has come to be known as "the recovery project" in philosophy. "The recovery project" refers primarily to those efforts to rediscover the names, identities, and philosophical contributions of women philosophers whose existence has been virtually overlooked, neglected, ignored, or lost in the traditional or canonical account of the history of Western philosophy, especially from 600 B.C.E. to 1600 C.E. It was initiated by philosophers who raised a simple but basic question that, at the time, had mostly not been asked (despite how obvious the question seems now): "Could there really have been no women philosophers throughout the history of Western philosophy?" They knew there had to have been women philosophers, but who were they?

Rediscovering these women philosophers has been a labor-intensive effort, undertaken by a handful of dedicated people. Mary Ellen Waithe's pioneering work in the already classic four volume set, *A History of Women Philosophers*, was a decisive turning point in the generation of the names, lives, and writings of many forgotten women philosophers[1] (see introduction to chapter 4). Many of the commentators in this textbook provided early translations or commentaries on texts in Waithe's series; others published articles and books on individual women philosophers as part of the recovery project.[2] Their recovery work has generated an ever-burgeoning scholarly literature on women philosophers who currently are absent in the history of Western philosophy (see appendix A). This recovery work in philosophy also continues to be important and actively engaged in by scholars. That this book focuses on filling a critical gender omission in the history of Western philosophy by including women alongside their historical male philosopher contemporaries neither diminishes the significance of the on-going recovery project work nor overrides the gratitude and admiration due those scholars who are continuing the work, especially in this historically gender-exclusive field, philosophy, to which all contributors to this book have dedicated our professional lives.

This book builds on the success of the recovery project by extending it to the inclusion of women philosophers with their historical male philosopher contemporaries in each of the four main historical periods in the history of Western philosophy: ancient, medieval, modern, and contemporary philosophy. With the publication of this book it is no longer scholarly accurate, appropriate, acceptable, or necessary to describe, conceptualize, or teach the history of Western philosophy *without women.*

The publication of this book, *An Unconventional History of Western Philosophy: Conversations between Men and Women Philosophers,* reflects the contributions of many people. The most important are the chapter commentators: their philosophical expertise, willingness to accept my editorial decisions, choice of primary texts for their philosophical pairs, and perseverance made possible an account of the history of Western philosophy *with women included.* It is the commentators who make the case here—and in their writings elsewhere—that these recovered historical women deserve to take their rightful and neglected place in the history of Western philosophy *as* philosophers. They are the ones who interpret the writings and philosophical positions of their philosophical pair; recommend new or different ways to think about what makes someone a philosopher; and address the issue whether gender figures in an understanding of the positions, methodologies, or philosophical stature of each philosophical pair. None of these commentators needed to augment their curricula vitae by writing the essays they did. I am convinced that they stayed with the project through its unanticipated vicissitudes in large part because they are consummate professionals who understand how the publication of this book is a timely service to the profession they love.

As a philosophy professor at a small liberal arts college, there are precious few opportunities to engage in funded collaborative research with students. So, I am especially grateful to Macalester College and Macalester's Center for Scholarship and Teaching (CST) for providing me with grants to help fund Audun Solli and Melissa Anderson as summer student researchers on the book project, and additional grant money to hire Audun as my research assistant for nearly four years. Audun is a wonderfully bright, patient, highly self-motivated, and self-directed person who successfully juggled many responsibilities without complaint as my research assistant (see appendix B). His supererogatory efforts included providing extensive written feedback to all the commentators on their commentaries from the perspective of an introductory philosophy student—one of the intended audiences of the book. He vigilantly monitored the allotted word counts for each chapter (12,500 combined words for the primary texts and 6,250 words for each commentary) and proposed that a glossary be included in the text after keeping a list of terms used in each chapter whose meanings were unclear. For all Audun is and does, I borrow from Tina Turner: Audun is "simply the best . . . better than all the rest!" For his hard work, humor, and irrepressible spirit, I say to Audun, simply, "Tusen takk!"

On the publishing side, I am profoundly grateful to Ross H. Miller, Ph.D., previously senior acquisitions editor, Philosophy and Religion at Prentice-Hall (where this project began) and currently senior editor at Rowman & Littlefield Publishers, Sheed & Ward Catholic Books/Philosophy & Religion Division. Ross believed in me and the idea of the book from the moment I proposed it to him over breakfast at an American Philosophical Association (APA) meeting. Ross has provided endless patience and compassion that I did not know I would need as seven unexpected surgeries interfered with my ability to produce the book within the timeframe we both wanted. This book may never have been finished had Ross not trusted his own judgment about the significance and promise of this badly needed book. Ross was the one person of authority on the publisher side who knew that if he remained supportive and kept the faith, I would persist until the manuscript was finished. So, I thank Ross for staying with me and this unique book until it reached the market. As the managing editor, I hope Ross believes it was worth the wait.

I also want to thank Wendy Yurash, assistant editor, Philosophy and Religion at Prentice-Hall, and Ruth Gilbert, editorial assistant, Rowman & Littlefield, who kindly answered the myriad of questions directed to them about style and formatting, reprint permissions, and publishing information; the Association of Marquette University Women (AMUW), who hosted me as the occupant of the 2004 Woman's Chair in Humanistic Studies and provided the financial means for me to have the research assistance of Rebecca Lloyd while I was at Marquette; Dr. John Jones, then chair of Marquette's Philosophy Department, who provided me with office space and protected time to work on the book; the students in my Macalester College course, the history of Western women philosophers, especially Joshua Fogt, Audun Solli, and Sara Oviatt; Dr. Michael Nelson, who taught my students how to create web sites on key women philosophers; former provost and dean of the faculty at Macalester College, Dan Hornbach, who did not simply make possible necessary medical leaves, but did so in ways that clearly communicated the college's commitment to protect, support, and keep its best faculty; the Macalester Philosophy Department, its administrative assistant, Toni Schrantz, student staff (particularly Jamie Schmeits), and especially my colleague Professor Henry West. Henry was the most involved with this book project. He invited me to classroom test some of the material in the book by coteaching Ancient and Medieval Philosophies; more important, he provided the collegial support and friendship I needed during the more difficult stages of writing this book.

On the more personal side, I want to thank the two people to whom this book is dedicated: my mother, Marge Warren Bails, and my recently deceased friend, George Anton Christiansen. The book is dedicated to them because, more than any other persons, they provided the consistent, positive, unwavering encouragement I needed to keep this book project afloat when umpteen challenges—including self-doubt—threatened to derail it. They did so largely by reminding me of what motivated me to initiate and design the project and thereby urging me to complete this book *for my sake.* My mother's and Anton's love and financial assistance made it possible for me to hire staff who turned out to be necessary to the completion of this book. There was never a question in my mind about the people to whom I would dedicate this book. With gratitude and love beyond expression, I dedicate this book to them.

During the final year on this book, I was quite literally rescued from overwhelming administrative tasks by my sister Barbara Warren, who took over all desktop publishing aspects of the manuscript, applications for reprint permissions, and correspondence so that I could just focus on writing, revising, and editing all substantive parts of the book. Just as important, Barbara helped normalize my life by providing structure and stability to my daily regimen. Whether it was bringing me cappuccino in the morning, restocking my supply of firewood, running umpteen errands for whatever I needed, fixing a meal, or . . . Barbara's distinctive humor and acts of sisterly love kept my spirits afloat and my attention focused on writing. Finishing the final manuscript turned out to be a team effort by the two Warren sisters.

My sister Jan is the calm in the middle of a storm, the peaceful presence that fills a room with the unspoken message, I am here, with you. Everything is okay. Jan helped me nurture the courage to say what I wanted to say and sustain the mental acuity to pick up and work on the book project for as many times as I stumbled or fell.

My daughter, Cortney S. Warren, helped me in ways that only a daughter can. During the year that ended with her receiving her Ph.D. in psychology, Cortney spent her days doing intensive work at Harvard's McLean Hospital, only to go home exhausted each night with a dissertation to write. Cortney's diligence and ways to manage her overwhelming schedule helped me finish this book project in two distinct ways. When Cortney was home, necessity dictated that we spent much of our time together working on our own scholarly projects, typically in front of a blazing fire. The intimacy and comfort of being with someone who understood that the work simply needed to be done, and that it could only be done by "keeping at it" in a regimented way each day, created a way for us to be together lovingly and supportively; that was the first gift only Cortney could give me. The second was that she phoned or emailed me frequently the last several months, sending encouraging and upbeat messages to help me with the final push to finish the manuscript. One e-mail was a list of one-liners to tell myself daily (some of which I recognized as ones I had given her at various times in her developing career): "Sit down and stay seated until you have written at least two pages; just write: empty your mind. Don't revise or edit; Let yourself write as if you were giving a lecture or explaining it to me [a good idea since Cortney has never taken a philosophy course]; you know these philosophers. You may not be an expert on each—nor should you be since that is why you have the commentators—but you are schooled enough to write about them all; set a schedule for yourself and don't deviate; stay in the present and stay positive; and my two favorites: the book does not define you. It is a scholarly project; and, You can do this, mom!" These things to remember and phone calls that began with a cheery and hope-filled, "Hi, mama. How's the book project going today?" always came at just the right time and in just the right way (as Aristotle might put it) to enable me to finish the book. Cortney was both an inspiration and a help; that she is my daughter makes my gratitude for her contributions inexpressible.

My loyal and patient friend Bruce Nordstrom-Loeb, himself an academic (sociologist), was often the first person I turned to when my writing hit substantive snags. After talking with him, I usually saw the way "to show the fly out of the fly bottle" (Wittgenstein). Bruce was always available to listen even though I often simply repeated myself until I (or Bruce) figured out how to fix what was broken, to say what I wanted to say, and to write in my own voice. As a great editor who also knows me so well, he sometimes worked magic on drafts of my writing. I am blessed to have Bruce as a friend.

I also want to thank Charme Davidson for nudging me to keep writing, get a schedule going and sticking to it, and to tell myself whenever I doubted that I was up to the task, that "not finishing the book is not an option"; Jennie Whitehouse, for typing a handful of primary texts so they were in digital form; Jane Hallas, simply for being my friend; and Michelle Bailey, for her loyalty and willingness to keep my surroundings fresh and neat—conditions I accept as a necessary part of my writing ritual. I want to acknowledge the help I received from several health care professionals: my primary care physician, Dr. Steven Cytrynowicz; my back surgeon, Dr. Manuel Pinto; my orthopedic surgeon, Dr. Thomas Nelson; my case manager, Elizabeth Betz Ulrich, RN; and my home health care professionals Lori Freagon, Dian Doss, Nadine Miller, Diane Windey, and Shelly Heinen.

As I reflect on this book at the end of the writing process, I am struck by three things: First, this book was the most difficult scholarly project I have ever undertaken; it required more of me at times then I thought I had to give. Second, this book was a labor of commitment—a commitment to the project, to the commentators, to myself, and to the discipline of philosophy. That commitment motivated me to finish the book when my desire and best intentions were not enough. Third, I could not have written this book very much earlier in my career. Nothing in my graduate training as an analytic philosopher, my initial years as a philosopher teaching as and what she had been taught, or my early beginnings as a feminist philosopher prompted me to ever think to ask the most obvious question, Who are the women philosophers in the history of Western philosophy? As unbelievable as it may seem, even to myself now, I simply did not notice the absence of women philosophers until the late 1970s. It was another fifteen years before I began to educate myself about who these neglected women philosophers were. It was not until the turn of the century, when I first taught a course (eventually twice) on the history of Western women philosophers, that I really appreciated the need for a book that provided a gender-inclusive account of that history.

That span of thirty or so years since I received my Ph.D., I now know, was a necessary part of an evolutionary process that led me—reluctantly and sometimes in nonextinguishable fear—from competent and comfortable analytic philosopher to uncomfortable novice in this relatively new and unchartered terrain of gendered analyses and approaches to philosophy. I felt the way I did as a philosophy professor taking an introductory Spanish class along with many of my own students, finding the learning of a new language a taxing and awkward process that required acceptance of my elementary, at best, foreign language skills, grammar and vocabulary. But it was just this unfolding process over a thirty-year time span that provided the time and experience to know that a gender-inclusive account of the history of Western philosophy was no longer a luxury that philosophers could ignore. It was a scholarly necessity and a matter of truth in advertising that, like any evolutionary process, leads one eventually to a place where one can no longer turn back and engage in "business as usual." Once one is willing to have one's most cherished beliefs about philosophy and philosophers open to criticism as male biased, the only direction forward is to identify the bias and begin to take steps to eliminate it. It was at that point that the need, design, and objectives of this book became an irrevocable scholarly and personal undertaking. The book's primary objective was unalterably clear: to provide an account of the history of Western philosophy that includes women philosophers. All other questions were secondary—choosing the female (and male) philosophers to include, determining the "pairs" of men and women philosophers, choosing primary texts by each on a topic of mutual interest, selecting the commentators (the easiest part). All such choices ultimately were answered by how well they achieved the goal of providing a user-friendly, scholarly book on men and women philosophers, in paired conversations, from 400 B.C.E. to the present. It is up to you, the reader, to decide whether this book accomplishes its goal.

Notes

1. See references to Mary Ellen Waithe in lead essay, note 3.
2. See resources in lead essay, note 3.

Lead Essay: 2,600 Years of the History of Western Philosophy *Without Women*

THIS BOOK AS A UNIQUE, GENDER-INCLUSIVE ALTERNATIVE

Karen J. Warren

Introduction

Gender scholarship in academia during the past four decades has shown that the exclusion of women's voices and perspectives has male-gender biased and diminished academic disciplines in important ways. Traditional scholarship in philosophy, especially the history of Western philosophy, is no different. The "recovery project" in philosophy is engaged in rediscovering the names, lives, texts, and perspectives of women philosophers from roughly the sixth century B.C.E. to the present. It has unearthed hundreds of names of Western women philosophers who lived and wrote during the past 2,600 years (see appendix A). With this material readily available, any scholarship or curriculum that provides an account of the history of Western philosophy without women philosophers is seriously outdated and inaccurate.

This book is an outgrowth of the successes of the recovery project. Many of the women philosophers whose writings are excerpted in this book were "lost" or neglected until "recovery" scholars rediscovered them.[1] But this book goes beyond the recovery project by including women philosophers alongside men philosophers in the history of Western philosophy. As such, this book is more aptly described an "inclusion project." Its primary objective is to eliminate the gender exclusivity of traditional accounts of the history of Western philosophy—what I refer to as "the philosophical canon" or simply "the canon" (defined below)—by providing an account of that history that includes the contributions of women philosophers without abandoning the canonical account.

The need for a book of this kind has been clear to me on numerous occasions. One occurred when I was occupant of the Woman's Chair in Humanistic Studies at Marquette University during the spring of 2004. Toward the end of the semester I was invited to give a talk on a topic of my choosing. I decided that this was a wonderful opportunity for me to both describe what it is that I do as a feminist philosopher, while also testing some of the material I was working on for this book. The talk I chose to give was titled, "What Is Wrong with Traditional Philosophy Anyway? Why Do We Need Feminist Philosophy?"

1

The turnout for the talk was approximately eighty philosophy faculty and students. After I had addressed the two questions in the title of my talk, I ended my presentation by saying, "There is one final remark I want to make about 'what is wrong with traditional philosophy.' It concerns the gender exclusivity of traditional accounts of the history of Western philosophy." I then proceeded by asking, "How many of you can give the name of at least one woman philosopher who lived during the time frame 600 B.C.E. to 300 C.E. and make one true claim about her philosophical views?" No hands went up. I then asked, "How many of you can give the name of at least two women philosophers during the timeframe 500–1500 C.E. and state at least one true claim about each of their philosophical views?" One hand went up. I proceeded to ask the same question about the modern period, roughly 1600–1900 C.E., raising the number to at least three, and about contemporary women philosophers in the twentieth century who were no longer alive, raising the number to five. In each case, few hands were raised.

I then distributed a handout that gave the names of eighty women philosophers, divided into each of the four historical time periods that I had just asked them about (see appendix A). What followed surprised me. The room remained eerily silent for what felt like an unusually long time. Finally, a stately, charismatic looking man in the back of the room, sitting at a dining table in a pose much like Rodin's famous sculpture *The Thinker*, slowly stood up. He turned toward me, stood still for a few moments, and then began to speak, carefully choosing his words. He stated his name, identified himself as a Jesuit priest and emeritus faculty member of the Marquette Philosophy Department, and, in a voice both kind and rich with conviction, said simply, "Thank you." After a few seconds, he spoke again: "Thank you. Although I am retired, I teach medieval philosophy occasionally. When I leave here I am going home. I will look up these medieval women on your sheet. And I will learn about them and teach them the next time I teach."

This senior male philosopher's openness to what I had said and his public commitment to learn about medieval women philosophers and to teach his area of expertise differently—with women in it—were profoundly moving for me. It was as if he had taken a stand and laid down the gauntlet for every other faculty member in the room, inviting—even challenging them—to do likewise. In response, I found myself drawn to him as if pulled by an invisible cord. Saying nothing, I weaved among tables until I finally arrived at where he stood. I then simply extended my hand and said, "Hello. My name is Karen Warren. I am delighted to meet you. I want to say how deeply touched I am by your response to my questions." I saw this person about two weeks later. He told me that he had begun reading some of the writings of the medieval women philosophers whose names were on my handout. He just wanted me to know "I am rediscovering medieval philosophy through these women philosophers and the result is just plain fun."

As I reflect on the Marquette audience's deer-staring-in-the-headlights response to the handout with the names of women philosophers since 600 B.C.E., I am reminded of my own response, about thirty years earlier, when I participated in a workshop by Peggy McIntosh on five phases of gender curricular integration (discussed later in this essay). I was having difficulty understanding how gender could play an important role in the discipline of philosophy, since it was dedicated to the objective and rational pursuit of Truth. I was like the majority of the Marquette audience who, staring at the handout, were being asked to rethink their conception of the history of Western philosophy to ensure that their curriculum included some of these unknown women.

The Main Objective of the Book

The main objective of this book is to provide a gender-inclusive account of the history of Western philosophy that avoids the so-called "add-women-and-stir" problem in a way that does not require abandoning canonical accounts of that history. The primary question that drives the design and content of this book is straightforwardly simple: "How does one accomplish this objective?" Answering the question, however, is more complicated: Who are these neglected (omitted, forgotten, overlooked) women philosophers? How does one decide which women are (really) philosophers? Does the inclusion of women philosophers in the history of Western philosophy change the conception of philosophy or who qualifies as a philosopher? Which features of traditional accounts of the history of Western philosophy survive a gendered critique and which do not? How are the main areas of philosophy (e.g., ethics, epistemology, metaphysics, logic, the history of philosophy) changed by the inclusion of women philosophers? Given the success of inclusion projects in so many other academic disciplines, why are history of Western philosophy courses still mostly taught without women? [2]

That these questions have only been raised recently—during the third quarter of the twentieth century—is paradoxical. Until gender became a legitimate category of philosophical analysis, the basic assumptions of Western philosophy—e.g., assumptions about the objectivity, impartiality, and gender neutrality of philosophy—actually blinded philosophy and traditionally trained philosophers like myself from recognizing philosophy's male-gender biases. Philosophy's attachment to its illusions of gender-neutrality functioned like Narcissus's perception of himself when he looked at his image in the lake: he saw only what he wanted to see. Analogously, canonical Western philosophy has historically "seen" only what its illusions permitted it to see. Any gender scholarship that challenged those illusions initially was—and, in some philosophical circles, continues to be—simply invisible, dismissed as not worth considering, or deemed merely a political, not philosophical, issue.

Canonical philosophy's long-standing comfort with such illusions comes at a high price. The discipline of philosophy is in serious jeopardy if its practitioners choose not to confront its illusions. This book begins to correct that complicity by including women philosophers in the account one gives of the history of Western philosophy.

Sixteen Distinctive Features of This Book

The Marquette story is just one person's account of a familiar, initial response when the names and writings of women philosophers are made available to philosophy teachers, students, and interested lay people. It invites philosophers to rewrite that history and to create curricula that include these overlooked women philosophers. This anthology, *An Unconventional History of Western Philosophy: Conversations between Men and Women Philosophers* (henceforth referred to as *An Unconventional History of Western Philosophy*) begins that rewriting.

There are sixteen distinctive features of the book. [3] (1) The book's most striking feature is its status (as far as I know) as the first book in any language to include in one text women philosophers alongside their historical male philosopher contemporaries. The significance of "being the first" is inextricably connected to (2) the way this book dissolves the add-women-and-stir problem that has stymied scholarly development and curricular integration projects since the 1970s (described below). (3) The women philosophers are included by being paired with canonical male contemporaries with whom they share an interest in a common topic or area. (4) The (roughly) fifteen pairs of philosophers include at least two from each of the four major historical time periods: ancient, medieval, modern, and contemporary philosophy. (5) The primary texts of the "philosopher pairs"[4] address topics or positions in philosophy that, (6) when taken together, are best read as a philosophical conversation between each chapter's philosopher pairs.

These six features share a characteristic that deserves special mention: the pairing of women philosophers with men philosophers could only occur after I had selected the men philosophers for inclusion in the anthology. Then I could construct a short list of women who would fit with the selected men philosophers. To decide which women best fit with their male contemporaries I felt a need to develop, if only for myself, criteria for determining whether or not a woman was a philosopher.[5]

Ultimately I developed six criteria, with the more criteria that fit, the stronger the case:

(i)   The woman was engaged with the philosophical ideas of the time.
(ii) There is reference to the woman as a philosopher, or to her ideas or writings as philosophical, by a canonically recognized male philosopher or historian of philosophy.
(iii) The woman's biography, including her education, scholarship, and teaching, is sufficiently similar to that of other philosophers (especially of her era) to qualify her as a philosopher.
(iv) The woman's writing style is consonant with acceptable philosophical methodologies or writing styles by male philosophers of the time period in which she lived.
(v)   The woman was interested in the sorts of philosophical questions, issues, and problems that interested men philosophers, especially those of her era.
(vi) The omission of a particular women from the history of Western philosophy would maintain and perpetuate, not help remedy, the exclusivist male-gender bias of that history.

Of course, any of these six criteria for saying a woman is a philosopher may be challenged and reasonable people may disagree about what a particular criterion means. Furthermore, the fourth criterion concerning philosophical methodology is a contentious one, especially in light of twentieth-century emphases on philosophical methodologies that advance arguments through critical thinking, symbolic logic, or even syllogistic logic. Last, the final criterion, (vi), is not actually about the woman *per se*, but about the importance of having a woman's work acknowledged as deserving inclusion or scholarly attention.

These six criteria—understood as useful heuristic devices or guidelines—were the ones I used to develop my short list of women philosophers. This short list permitted me to explore different possible combinations of male-female philosopher pairs, decide on my "dream team" of commentators, and jump-start conversations about the question, "Is she a philosopher?" that always arise regarding some of the women (and perhaps some of the men) included in this book (more on this later).

We now resume the discussion of the remaining ten distinctive features of the book. (7) Each chapter has a commentary on the chapter's philosophical pair that is written by a contemporary expert. (8) Each commentary addresses the same four issues: the area or topic of philosophy addressed by the pair; each philosopher's basic position as articulated in the primary texts; the basic similarities and dissimilarities between their philosophers' positions; and the role (if any) gender plays for understanding or appreciating the positions of each philosophical pair or for assessing whether a particular women is a philosopher.

This book is designed to be user-friendly. (9) Major sections of it have been class-room tested in my History of Women Philosophers course (taught twice), and the first four chapters were assigned readings in ancient and medieval philosophy when I cotaught the course. (10) The inclusion of chapter introductions contributes to the accessibility of the primary texts and the historical philosophical context in which the philosophers wrote in two explicit ways: they provide a basic story line that threads traditional accounts of the history of Western philosophy from chapter to chapter, thereby ensuring that key features of the philosophical canon are available to those who want to adopt or read this book without thereby abandoning traditional accounts, and they provide informative biographical material that situates the philosophical pair and their positions within a specific historical context in a way that also sets up the primary texts and commentaries that follow. (11) The three questions for reflection at the end of each chapter contribute to the accessibility of the text by encouraging readers to reflect on specific features of the chapter's primary texts and commentaries. (12) A list of names of women philosophers (appendix A) is provided for those who are interested in learning more about other women philosophers and their philosophical positions. (13) The Foreword by Henry West provides a brief testimonial on the difference it made to his Ancient and Medieval Philosophies course to include women philosophers. (14) The short essay (appendix B) by my undergraduate research assistant, Audun Solli, describes both his research responsibilities and, as an introductory philosophy student, his reflections on what he learned by studying these (and other) women philosophers. (15) This lead essay, which describes the main goals, organizational structure, substantive content, and scholarly challenges of producing this book helps the reader understand the distinctive philosophical and pedagogical challenges of producing a first-of-its-kind gender-inclusive history of Western philosophy. (16) Last, the book offers a solution to the curricular and scholarly challenges of producing a book that avoids the (soon to be described) add-women-and-stir problem without forfeiting canonical accounts of the history of Western philosophy.

The Western Philosophical Canon

As I use the expression, "the Western philosophical canon" (or "the canon") does not refer to all philosophers, all philosophical texts, all philosophical methodologies, all philosophy departments and curricula, all descriptions of the history of Western philosophy, or all aspects of the discipline of philosophy. Nor does it assume that an account of the history of Western philosophy is monolithic, uniform, without dissenters from mainstream views, or hopelessly male biased. Rather, by "the Western philosophical canon" I am referring to six features of traditional accounts of the history of Western philosophy: first, the depiction of the Western philosophical tradition as traceable to ancient Greece, beginning with the pre-Socratics (who lived around 600–400 B.C.E.) and emerging as a discipline with Socrates, Plato, and Aristotle; second, reference to those philosophers who are commonly taught, and those texts that are commonly read, in history of (Western) philosophy courses at the majority of colleges and universities throughout the English-speaking Western world, with more consensus about who those philosophers are through the nineteenth century than since. These philosophers have been almost exclusively male. In fact, it is precisely because there is such conformity about which male philosophers and texts are taught with regularity that one can identify a traditional account as the Western philosophical canon and that reference to it as the dominant tradition—not the only tradition—is appropriate.

Who are these male philosophers? They include the following, with the bracketed names indicating male philosophers who are currently studied with increasing frequency but without consensus about their place in historical accounts of the Western philosophy: the pre-Socratics; the Pythagoreans; Epicurus and the Epicureans; the Cynics and Stoics; Socrates, Plato, and Aristotle; [Plotinus], Augustine, Anselm, Abelard, and Aquinas; [Bacon], Descartes, Hobbes, Spinoza, Leibniz, Locke, Berkeley, Hume, Rousseau, and Kant; [Hegel, Schopenhauer, Nietzsche, Marx]; Mill; [Frege, Heidegger, and Whitehead]; Russell and Wittgenstein; James, [Peirce], Dewey; [Derrida, Sartre], and Quine.

A third feature of canonical philosophy is its focus on distinctively "philosophical questions" (defined below). Fourth, there is also a striking degree of agreement about basic assumptions, concepts, values, beliefs, definitions, and distinctions (including dualisms) that are and belong at the center or core of Western philosophy. The fifth element is an on-going concern with so-called problems of philosophy (see the glossary), and the sixth is a strong methodological preference for an argument-based style of analysis (described variously as logical reasoning, rhetorical reasoning, critical thinking, and analytical reasoning) that often involves explicit use of syllogistic or symbolic logic.

The Metaphor of Building a House

One way to illustrate these six features of the philosophical canon is through the metaphor of building a house and the visual image of the house that is built. When one builds a traditional house, the first step is to pour (or lay) the foundation; the foundation must be in place before building the rest of the house. The next construction piece is to frame in the house, usually by putting in place upright posts (such as two by fours), insulation, and sheetrock, the walls, the floor, and roof—the framework of the house. When the framework is external, it encloses the house, giving it its basic structure, size, and shape. The internal framework sometimes shares a common wall with the external framework, but other times frames in rooms and other structural features of the interior of the house (e.g., the placement of various rooms within the house). The framework of the house, then, consists of external and internal walls or structures. The houses that result may vary in their aboveground structures, making different houses look and be different structurally (in contrast, say, to being different aesthetically).

The development of the Western philosophical canon is like building a house. It begins with the laying of a foundation, followed by the "framing in" of both the external and internal framework of the house. The structural features of the house that are built represent the Western philosophical canon, characterized by the six features described above—what I call "The Canonical House" or simply "The House." A diagram of The House, shown here, is useful both for illustrating the six basic features of the Western philosophical canon and for providing an image that is easy to recall and visualize when generalized references are made to the Western philosophical canon.

There are several noteworthy things to say about The House. First, it includes the three necessary structural features involved in the construction of any house—the foundation, the external framework, and internal framework (represented by the triangle and oval shapes). Second, these three structural features do not themselves identify this house as The Canonical House. To do that, the six substantive features of the philosophical canon—its foundation and interior features—must be "filled in." Third, the substantive features of the external framework of The House are intentionally left open since canonical philosophers offer different views about the nature of the external framework (an issue addressed later).

Diagram 1. The House

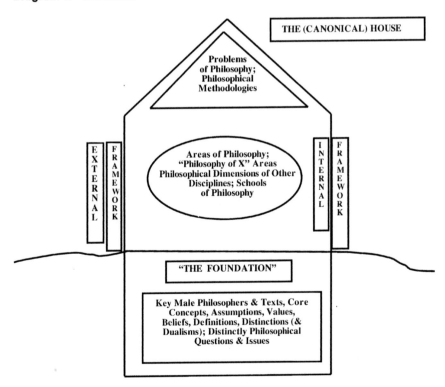

Two more features of The House deserve notice. One concerns the use of the term "framework." Talk of the external and internal framework of a house is analogous to talk about the outside and inside of a box. In a four-sided box, the sides are the upright dividers that delineate both the inside and the outside of the box. While the inside and the outside of the box share a common side (wall, divider), the inside also refers to any features—structural or substantive—of the interior space. Analogously, the framework of The House consists in the upright dividers that delineate both its inside (internal framework) and outside (external framework). On the diagram of The House, structural features are represented by the lines and shapes (rectangles, ovals, and triangles); substantive (content) features are represented within those lines and shapes. What is not represented on the diagram is the way any particular male philosopher fits within The House. As is the case with visual inspections of actual houses, in order to see the philosophical positions of individual male philosophers within The House, one must do a walk-through of his version of The House, its interior structure and content.

The second feature that deserves mention is the issue of male bias. Inclusion projects assume that the exclusivity of women from the philosophical canon is a form of male bias. However, this form of male bias is not represented explicitly anywhere on the diagram. That is because it is implied (or represented implicitly) by feature (2) of The House.

The Problem That Simply Would Not Go Away

The problem that simply would not go away—as hard and as often as I worked on it since I participated in Peggy McIntosh's workshops on five phases of integrative curricular development—is the add-women-and-stir problem. It is a sufficiently troublesome problem—one that has interfered with effective gender integration in the classroom and with the development of scholarly materials for more than three decades—that resolving it is crucial for successful gender-inclusion projects (such as this book).

What is the add-women-and-stir problem and why has solving it been so difficult in philosophy—especially for curricular and scholarly inclusion projects (including this book)? Philosopher Charlotte Bunch named the add-women-and-stir problem when she claimed that one cannot "just add women and stir" them into an otherwise unchanged conception and curriculum of philosophy.[6] Bunch's remark is a criticism of Phase 3 of Peggy McIntosh's five-phase integrative model of gender curricular development projects.[7] Using philosophy to illustrate McIntosh's five-phase model, Phase 1 is "The History of Western Philosophy without Women" and Phase 2 is "The History of Western Philosophy with Exceptional Women." Sadly, Phases 1 and 2 are the status quo for mainstream history of Western philosophy courses and texts. This status quo is unnecessary and unacceptable—given the current availability of material on women philosophers throughout the history of Western philosophy.

Phase 3 is "The History of Western Philosophy with Ordinary Women." If one could do the history of Western philosophy at Phase 3, we would have a gender-inclusive account of that history. So what has prevented Phase 3 inclusion projects from succeeding? In large part, the failure of Phase 3 integration efforts turns on the myriad difficulties with attempts to add women and stir. As Elizabeth Minnich succinctly states the problem, "We cannot simply add the idea that the world is round to the conviction that the world is flat."[8] Attempts to include women through an add-women-and-stir strategy fail when the basic philosophical claims, positions, or methodologies of the women added are logically incompatible with those of The House. In such cases, attempts to add women and stir produce something more like an explosion than an integrated mixture.

The curricular challenges for those attempting to teach Phase 3 courses are often daunting. Phase 3 courses may seem disorganized, lacking a coherent theme or direction, confused and confusing. For students it is like watching a ping-pong match, where the professor is constantly moving back and forth between sides, positions, and issues, saying things like "The canonical view here is A; but this woman philosopher asserts B, thereby rejecting the canonical view, claiming not simply *not-A*, but that the basic assumptions and distinctions on which A is based—indeed, the foundational assumptions of The House—are problematic, mistaken, false, or logically inconsistent with the claim, B, she is defending." The canonical thinker then replies by defending claim B or defending claim A against the woman philosopher's objections, often quickly creating a sort of philosophical "tug of war." And so it goes, back and forth. Watching the match as a student raises its own challenges; being the professor who is the sole ping-pong player—serving from one end of the table and running to return the serve from the other end, back and forth, back and forth—is exhausting.[9]

Difficulties with trying to teach Phase 3 courses has moved many philosophers to skip Phase 3 altogether and develop Phase 4 courses and scholarly materials. Phase 4 is "Women's Philosophy or Philosophy by Women." There are a plethora of Phase 4 philosophy courses, with such titles as feminist philosophy, ecofeminist philosophy, feminist ethics, feminist epistemology, feminist philosophy of science, and the history of Western women philosophers. McIntosh assumes (incorrectly, I think) that once Phase 4 curricular development projects have succeeded, philosophy will arrive at the final phase, Phase 5: Philosophy that includes us all.[10]

My Personal Journey with the Add-Women-and-Stir Problem

The challenge of resolving the Phase 3 add-women-and-stir problem is conceptual as well as pedagogical. The problem began for me in the late 1970s to early 1980s, when I attended two Peggy McIntosh workshops on her five-phase model of integrated curricular development. I struggled to figure out what her five-phase model had to do with philosophy. All her explanations used examples from art, biology, history, psychology—never philosophy. During the question-and-answer session, I asked her about what was troubling me: "I see how this phase model works in the academic disciplines you discussed—in fact, for most academic disciplines. But I don't see how it works in philosophy. Since philosophy is the impartial pursuit of Truth and Wisdom—Moses-like truths carved in stone "from on high"—how is it ever possible that the inclusion of women philosophers could actually produce an add-women-and-stir problem at the foundational level of the discipline? That problem could arise only if the women "added" were not really philosophers, were not doing philosophy, or were not making true philosophical claims. But if one knew that about a particular woman's views, why would one include them as philosophers in a philosophy course anyway?"

I remember exactly what McIntosh said in response: "Whenever I do these work-shops and a philosopher is in attendance, I get basically the same questions. I just don't know what to say to you philosophers. Philosophy is a difficult case."

That was almost thirty years ago. I did not know then and do not know now what McIntosh intended when she said "philosophy is a difficult case." But I remember what I thought about her reply: "If the time-honored conception of philosophy is false or illusory—no more reliable than Narcissus's self-reflection—then what is philosophy, who am I as a professional philosopher, and what does it mean to be a philosophy teacher?" The implications of adding women who challenged the fundamental foundation and framework of The House were very unsettling to me.

I tell this story to illustrate two points about the add-women-and-stir problem in philosophy. First, thirty or more years ago, many of the women philosophers working in academia (myself included) were trained within the Western analytical tradition of philosophy—The House. Although politically I (like others) supported the women's movement, I had difficulty seeing its profound significance to philosophy. Even when I began to teach Phase 4 courses, I had not really *abandoned* The House or rejected all aspects of Phase 3 inclusion projects. I just stopped trying to *integrate* perspectives of women philosophers that challenged or conflicted with House views by adding and stir-ring them into otherwise unchanged mainstream courses. As incredulous as it may seem today to lay people and academics from other disciplines—many academic professional women philosophers schooled in the analytic tradition during the 1960s and early 1970s really had to work hard to imagine a conception and practice of philosophy that might be radically altered by taking seriously considerations of gender. If the addition of women philosophers meant that The House was flawed in fundamental ways, then wouldn't The House collapse, like a house of cards?

The story also is intended to convey the confusion and ambivalence many (mostly women) philosophers felt about whether there could be a plausible conception of philoso-phy other than the canonical one. Paradoxically, in the end it was my deep philosophical commitment to "the search for truths" and my emotional temperament to "overturn ev-ery stone" until I found what survived gender (and other) criticisms of The House—that is, doing philosophy in the spirit of Socrates—that made me push through my discomfort and explore ways to include women philosophers in philosophy courses, even if "philoso-phy is a difficult case."

Dissolution of the Add-Women-and-Stir Problem

Even though almost all my scholarship as a professional philosopher has been from a gen-dered perspective, I did not know how to solve the add-women-and-stir problem when I began this book project. Just at the point when I thought I had reached a dead end on what to say about the add-women-and-stir problem and how to ensure that classroom use of this book did not create the problem, I had an epiphany: The solution to the problem was staring right at me! The epiphany was simple: the problem with the add-women-and-stir problem is that it is *misnamed*. Phase 3 is not, or not necessarily, an addition issue;

it is an *inclusion* issue. This book is about the inclusion—not the addition—of women philosophers in the account one gives of the history of Western philosophy. So, if there is a problem, it is an inclusion, not an addition, problem. Furthermore, misnaming the problem an "addition" problem is critically important since how one names a problem—what one takes to be the problem—will effect what solutions one offers.

The misnaming of Phase 3 as an addition problem involves a genuine—not merely semantic—issue. A merely semantic issue is resolvable by agreement about the facts (e.g., that women have been excluded from House accounts of the history of philosophy—a factual claim I think any reasonable person should agree is true). A genuine semantic issue will not go away simply when there is agreement about the facts. The add-women-and-stir problem assumes that inclusion of women is (always) an *additive* process when it is not. Once the addition-inclusion distinction is made, one begins to ask very different questions: "Are there different ways to include women in philosophy—ways that never give rise to the add-women-and-stir problem? Can one include in one history of Western philosophy women (and men) philosophers who represent a range of positions—from those whose views may be compatible with, and those whose views may be incompatible with, foundation-level features of The House while also producing a clear, coherent account of that history? This book is set up to do just that.

Different Sorts of Inclusion

There are at least seven different ways to "include" something—through

- addition,
- revision (or reform),
- integration,
- radicalization,
- a combination of some revision and some radicalization,
- transformation, and
- an altogether different starting point or (conceptual) framework.

Consider an example of each, setting aside for now the question of *how* to accomplish the inclusion of women in a book also designed to preserve fundamental features of The House.[11]

If the inclusion of women in the history of Western philosophy is a case of mere addition, then their inclusion would not really be logically possible. This is because one of the distinguishing features of The House is its exclusion of women philosophers. So, any inclusion-as-addition will always involve some revision of The House. Stated differently, when the inclusion of women philosophers is a genuine case of addition, the women must be canonical thinkers whose inclusion is accomplished by reforming The House through an integration process that eliminates the second feature of The House, namely that only men philosophers are read or taught. One then has a Revised House. In this book, the inclusion of the women philosophers Elisabeth, Macaulay, Conway, van Schurman, and Anscombe, as well as the late Pythagorean women, Diotima's "voice," Hildegard, and

Heloise as philosophers, especially during the periods of ancient and medieval philosophy, are arguably such cases. The inclusion of canonical women thinkers through reform and integration does not give rise to the add-women-and-stir problem.

Some contemporary "radical feminist" philosophers find The House hopelessly patriarchal. The inclusion of these women philosophers would be a case of radicalization; the proposed solution would be akin to bulldozing The House and replacing it with something else, minimally a reconception of the nature and practice of philosophy. The inclusion of male philosopher-economist Karl Marx, Marxist philosopher Angela Davis, and radical feminist philosopher Mary Daly would be cases of radicalization.[12]

Some women philosophers regard The House as deeply rooted in objectionable forms of male-gender bias that must be eliminated by some radical changes, while also claiming that other features of The House should be retained in some form (a combination of some revision and some radicalization). Arguably, this book's inclusion of Masham, Wollstonecraft, and Taylor, whose "radical" views about the equality of women and advocacy for changes in institutions in both the so-called private, domestic sphere and the public economic, political sphere are examples of inclusion as a combination of some revision and some radicalization. Inclusion of some contemporary academic ecofeminist philosophers, feminist ethicists, and feminist epistemologists in the history of Western philosophy would also provide some examples of the "reform and radical" combination of curricular inclusion.[13]

Inclusion of women philosophers whose views are transformative (provide an alternative starting point or reflecting altogether a different conceptual framework), are more difficult to illustrate in terms of The House. This is because both involve either moving beyond The House—for example, by rejecting its foundation-level features—or offering an entirely different starting point. Inclusion as transformation (or a transformative process) might be illustrated by the popular children's toys called Transformers. The toy begins as one thing (say, a robot) and, with some manipulation, can be turned ("transformed") into a second thing (say, an airplane), and then again into a third thing (say, a butterfly), where the morphed items bear little or no resemblance to each other. The inclusion of women philosophers whose views about the nature and practice of philosophy are transformative, may begin with The House (the robot), which is then transformed into something else, say a reformed and radicalized version of The House (the airplane), and ends up with an altogether different conception of philosophy and philosophical methodology (the butterfly). Commentator Elizabeth Minnich is a philosopher whose inclusion in the history of Western philosophy would offer a transformative view of philosophy and philosophical methodology. Minnich describes philosophical methodology as "philosophical fieldwork" (or, "fieldwork philosophizing"); it is neither objective nor subjective, universal nor particular, absolutist nor relativist (familiar House concepts and dualisms that she rejects). Philosophical fieldwork is

> thinking with others out and about in the *agora* and then reflecting in solitude with them in mind. . . . It is neither deductive nor inductive, nor is it held within any other single logic. Rather, it is about listening and hearing, looking and seeing, taking in and trying to comprehend without rushing to interpret, to translate into familiar terms, to explain. In Simone Weil's sense, it is about being attentive . . . it entails listening for meanings, and, as philosophers do,

for moves—for what is being done conceptually, as well as for what someone is wanting to mean.[14]

The transformation may be a process whereby a philosopher advocates positions later in life that contradict positions advocated earlier. For example, Wittgenstein's philosophical views about language were transformed significantly from the early Wittgenstein of *The Tractaetus* to the later Wittgenstein of the *Philosophical Investigations*. Or the transformation may enable new conceptions of philosophy to emerge that transcend their initial starting points. One might argue that Arendt (a phenomenologist and political philosopher), Addams (a classical American pragmatist), and Beauvoir (a French feminist existentialist) be understood as women philosophers whose inclusion in the history of Western philosophy provides transformative accounts of philosophy. Arendt provides a now classic analysis of totalitarianism and the banality of evil, arguments about the dangers of thinking divorced from public life, a new term, "natality," to describe the human condition for action, and criticizes the masculinized nature of the history of Western philosophy. Addams provides a pragmatic conception of philosophy as a way of life, located in activities of social reform and political action; and whose philosophical analyses are assessed by how well they capture the significance of the concrete, felt, lived realities from which it emerges. Beauvoir's existentialist philosophy rejects the Cartesian legacy in favor of a conception of philosophy that focuses on new concepts as the Self, the Other, and the Look; it also offers a classic feminist statement of the subordination of women in *The Second Sex*.

The inclusion of a woman philosopher whose philosophical positions are self-described as articulated from the starting point (or through the lens) of a Chicana, feminist, an Afrocentric, or Native American perspective could be a case of providing an altogether different starting point or (conceptual) framework. A similar case could be made for the "philosophy is dead" perspective or Richard Rorty's conception of philosophy as "edifying conversation," where the job of the professional philosopher (especially in the classroom) is to facilitate discussions of "the great books," not to discover alleged truths that "mirror nature." The philosopher-as-facilitator role reflects Rorty's view that the philosopher is the one most likely to be familiar with the contents and issues of "the great books;" it is *not* the philosopher's job to defend as true or correct any philosophical position since there are no correct or incorrect positions to defend.[15] Heidegger's call for philosophy to return to the fundamental philosophical question "What is Being?" is offered in tandem with his view that philosophy should return to the sort of thinking Socrates represents: "pure" thinking itself that is based in wonder and puzzlement, not thinking that is instrumental, goal directed, and aimed at reaching some conclusion or developing a theory. Heidegger's "hermeneutical phenomenology" could be interpreted as a starting over or a new starting point—one Heidegger believed has not been practiced since Socrates.

A different sort of case of inclusion could occur when the women philosophers included provide an altogether different account of the history of philosophy than any provided by the ways listed above. This may be one currently beyond comprehension—philosophy in 3000. But there are some historical precedents, such as Howard Zinn's *A People's History of the United States*[16]—history as conceptualized from the perspective of the common or ordinary person. Western women philosophers who offer feminist perspectives through the lens of interconnected "positionalities" of gender, race/ethnicity, socioeconomic status, or sexual orientation may ultimately provide altogether different accounts of philosophy.

To summarize, there are seven ways women philosophers could be *included* in the history of Western philosophy, only one of which involves addition and none of which gives rise to the add-women-and-stir problem. This is important for inclusion projects such as this book for three reasons. Most obviously, it means that the problem with Phase 3 curricular development projects has been eliminated, since one can provide a gender-inclusive Revised House account of philosophy that is neither additive nor integrative, except in the one case where the women included are canonical thinkers whose exclusion was based on gender and not on any main philosophical difference with House positions. Reforming The House to permit their inclusion involves no more than removing men-only restrictions. Second, the seven different ways to include women philosophers do not require *foreknowledge* of the compatibility or incompatibility of their views with House or Revised House accounts. That is as it should be: it should be an open, legitimate philosophical issue whether a woman's views are or are not compatible with House views—not something one simply assumes and certainly not something one must know before one is willing to include women in Revised House accounts of the history of Western philosophy. Last—and this takes us back to where we began—the inclusion-addition distinction helps to explain *how* one can accomplish the inclusion of women philosophers in the history of Western philosophy even if their views are in fundamental conflict with House features. The rest of this section describes how this book makes that happen.

This book accomplishes the inclusion of women philosophers, independent of how close to or far from The House their views are, in a way that is coherent, user-friendly, and teachable. The key lies in the three-part organizational structure of each chapter, the stand-alone nature of each chapter, and the clearly identified and different contributions each of the three parts plays in the integrity and coherence of the book as a whole. In short, the three-part design and three goals of each part permit a canonical *and* an inclusive account of the history of Western philosophy to be presented, taught together, and accomplish the gender inclusion that is the main goal of the project.

The three-part structure consists of a chapter introduction, primary texts, and a commentary. The chapter introductions begin with a discussion of the canonical male philosopher's biography and main philosophical positions. That is intentional, since it is through the opening descriptions of the traditionally taught male philosopher that the chapter introductions are able to preserve a canonical account of the history of Western philosophy even in cases where a philosophical pair is challenging, sometime denying, the basic foundational features of House accounts. The second part of each chapter introduction focuses similarly on the women philosophers' biographies and basic philosophical positions. When helpful, comments are made about the extent to which a particular woman philosopher articulates views, uses a writing style, or participates in philosophical discussions in ways that are, or are not, typical of The House. Each chapter introduction ends by stating how the material presented in the introduction sets up the primary texts and commentary that follow.

The way the women philosophers are included (not added and stirred except in the cases where particular women philosophers endorse The House) is by pairing them with men philosophers of the same historical time period—philosophers who were their historical contemporaries. The selected primary texts for each pair were chosen in part because they genuinely can be read as if the philosophical pair were engaged in a conversation with *each other* on a topic of mutual interest. In fact, it is precisely this pairing structure that makes the inclusion of women philosophers into historical accounts of philosophy not a case of addition. Addition attempts to integrate (assimilate) women philosophers *within* the philosophical canon and to recognize *as* women philosophers only those whose philosophical views are compatible with House views; inclusion efforts (such as this book) pair women philosophers with historical men philosopher contemporaries, and that inclusion process occurs separately from, and yet *in tandem with*, the canon. It is as if one were in a large room—the history of Western philosophy room—where what one sees and hears when one steps back are conversations on a variety of topics between pairs of men and women philosophers with no one conversation having *a priori* privilege or status over others.

This leads to comments about the primary texts in each chapter. Selected by the commentators, these texts constitute the "conversations" between the philosophical pairs. They may be read, described, interpreted, understood, and evaluated in terms of their content vis-à-vis each other or vis-à-vis other paired conversations in the room. One might well imagine a sign overhead designating the room as "The History of Western Philosophy Room: All Philosophers Welcome." Anyone (a teacher, student, interested lay person) may enter the room and join a conversation in progress (including those between House philosophers) or initiate a new conversation *without* thereby having to decide which conversations belong in The House and which do not. After all, the large room is the History of Western Philosophy Room, not The House Room. Like real-life conversations between people, the substantive content of conversations can be described, understood, studied, taught, and evaluated on their own merit rather than for their compatibility with House positions.

With the primary texts serving as the conversations between pairs of philosophers, the commentaries in each chapter describe, compare, and critique the philosophical content and form (methodology) of their pair's conversation. They present, describe, interpret, understand, challenge, and raise critical issues concerning not only the views of their pair, but their pair's views in light of traditional canonical views.

Taken together, the tripartite chapter design—introductions, primary texts, and commentaries—provides the organizational structure and substantive content that makes possible the inclusion of women philosophers in a book on the history of Western philosophy that is capable of both preserving and/or critiquing the canonical account of the last 2,600 years. When the primary texts are treated as conversations between historical men and women philosopher contemporaries, they can be read, described, interpreted, understood, and questioned in terms of the content of the conversations. The inclusion of women and men philosophers is accomplished without giving rise to the treacherous add-women-and-stir problem.

The Main Features of The House as Exemplified by the Philosophers in This Book

In this section, the six key features of The House or, if canonical women thinkers are included, The Revised House (without feature 2) are illustrated briefly by appeals to the philosophical positions of the philosophers in this book.

FOUNDATIONALISM

This feature of The House is represented on the diagram of The House simply as The Foundation. For Plato (chapter 1) the foundation of philosophy is given by his metaphysical Theory of Forms, where Forms are the eternal, unchanging Absolute Essences of such things as mathematical objects and particular objects in the world of sense perception. For Descartes (chapter 5), in his two most frequently read books, *Discourse on Method* and *Meditations,* his method of systematically doubting everything that is capable of being doubted in order to arrive at some *epistemologically* (rather than merely *psychologically*) certain, indubitable claim is designed to produce some claim that serves as the unshakeable foundation for philosophy. The claim Descartes offers as one that survives the method of systematic doubt is "I [Descartes] exist." It is the axiomatic, epistemologically certain, foundational truth that grounds the other claims of philosophy. For Kant (chapter 10), in his *Groundwork of the Metaphysic of Morals,* the foundational claim of ethics is provided through three versions of what he defends as the supreme, absolute principle of morality, The Categorical Imperative.

Wittgenstein (chapter 14) is a more controversial case since one of Wittgenstein's widely accepted views is that once philosophy shows us the futility of looking for Cartesian foundations or of attempting to resolve canonical problems of philosophy (such as the problem of the existence of the external world), then philosophy will simply go away. Philosophy will be left out in the cold; there will be nothing for (Cartesian-like) philosophy to do. Yet Wittgenstein is included as a canonical philosopher in this book. In what sense could he be if foundationalism is a characteristic of The House?

The simplest answer for Wittgenstein's inclusion—as well as that of the male philosophers Heidegger, Dewey, and Sartre—is primarily that his writings are studied with increasing frequency in Western philosophy, (feature 2 of The House), rather than because he is an exemplar of The House. The more complicated answer turns on the question whether Wittgenstein subscribes to some form of foundationalism even if he denies Cartesian foundationalism—the position that philosophy has an epistemologically certain, bedrock foundation. Wittgenstein rejects a Cartesian foundationalism for philosophy. But he defends the view that our practices (forms of life) show that certain propositions are presupposed by what we say and do—what Wittgenstein calls "framework propositions" (see chapter 14). It is in this sense that Wittgenstein is committed to a non-Cartesian foundationalism: he is committed to fundamental framework propositions and forms of life, rather than to philosophy itself as foundational.

THE DISTINCTIVENESS AND SIGNIFICANCE OF PHILOSOPHICAL QUESTIONS

A foundational feature of The House is that distinctly philosophical questions are key to the conception and practice of philosophy. According to The House, a philosophical question typically has five features. It is:

basic (fundamental, presupposed by other philosophical questions or positions),
general (not about an individual or "particular" thing),

at the level of either *conceptual* analysis (what is meant by a term or claim), or *logical* analysis (e.g., how one claim implies another), and calls for some form of *proof* or *justification* for the answers one gives or positions one holds.

Because of the centrality of philosophical questions to philosophy, they are represented as part of the foundation of The House. But they also contribute to how one "frames in" the exterior and interior of The House, since the questions one asks affect both one's understanding or interpretation of a philosophical issue and the answers one gives. In fact, philosophical questions are so significant to philosophy that they constitute one major difference between philosophy and other academic disciplines. The question "What is philosophy?" is itself a philosophical question, which reasonable people will answer differently. It is a self-reflective question, since, once asked, the question turns in upon itself: sincere attempts to answer the question engage one in the very activity (doing philosophy) that one is seeking to define (philosophy).

This is not true of definitional questions asked about or within other disciplines. "What is art?" and "What is economics?" are not art (artistic, aesthetics) or economics questions. They are philosophical questions about art and economics. Artists and economists may and do ask these questions. When they do, they are asking philosophical questions about the nature (definition) of the disciplines of art and economics.

What all the texts in this anthology have in common is that they raise distinctively philosophical questions. Plato (chapter 1) asks, "What is love?" and "What is beauty?" in the *Symposium* and *Phaedrus*, respectively. Aristotle (chapter 2) asks, "In what does *eudaimonia* (human well-being or flourishing) consist?" and the late Pythagorean women are concerned with the meaning and application of the Pythagorean principle of *harmonia* to the "domestic sphere." Augustine and Hildegard (chapter 3) are concerned with the question, "What is the relationship between humans and God?"—a question that led each to raise a range of other questions: "What is it to be human and to live an ethical life?" "How should one understand the struggle between good and evil?" "What is the nature and relationship between the body and soul?" "How does the human relationship to God help one understand human knowledge?"

The correspondence between Heloise and Abelard (chapter 4) raises the philosophical questions, "What is friendship?" and "What is love?" Descartes and Elizabeth (chapter 5) ask "How is it possible for nonextended minds to casually interact with extended bodies?" Macaulay (chapter 6) asks, "What is the role of sympathy in the development of virtue?" Unlike Hobbes, Macaulay claims that sympathy (benevolent action) is necessary and ultimately the foundation of all human virtue. Locke and Masham (chapter 7) ask, "What is the relationship of religion to philosophy, particularly ethics?" opening a discussion of the Divine Command Theory of Ethics. Both argue that religion ought to be rational, and to the extent that religious claims or revelations can be shown to be rational, they are philosophically legitimate.

Although some find an important similarity between Conway and Leibniz (chapter 8) in their mutual use of the term "monads" to denote individual substances, their answers to the questions, "What is the nature of individual substances?" and "How do substances causally interact?" reveal that their similarities may be more apparent than real. Rousseau and Wollstonecraft (chapter 9) talk about freedom but neither provides an answer to the main question, "What is freedom?" Underlying Kant's concern with the question, "What is knowledge?" and van Schurman's concern with the question, "What is a woman scholar?" (chapter 10) is an implicit shared concern with the question, "What is the role of experience in knowledge?" Taking one step backward, the question, "What is meant by 'experience'?" is a fundamental philosophical question that one needs to answer to understand their views.

Mill and Taylor (chapter 11) provide a negative answer to the question, "Are there any legitimate grounds for the subordination and disenfranchisement of women?" The writings by Heidegger and Arendt (chapter 12) and Arendt's criticism of Heidegger for his support of the Nazis raise the question, Does a person's philosophical views, especially when that person's philosophical position is about "authentic" existence involving practical engagement with everyday life, have less merit when the person's own life arguably contradicts the person's teachings? Arendt is concerned with this question, especially as it affects her relationship to, and scholarly divergences from, Heidegger.

In contrast to Heidegger, the two American pragmatist philosophers Dewey and Addams (chapter 13) lived a "public philosophy" that is testimony to their philosophical pragmatism. Dewey's answer to the question, "How do we know when philosophy is doing its job?" is that the abstractions of philosophy are warranted if we can use them to return to everyday experience with a richer, fuller, understanding of our experiences.

The French existentialists Beauvoir and Sartre (chapter 15) and phenomenologists Heidegger and Arendt (chapter 12), are probably the pairs whose philosophical positions depart most from The House. Beauvoir and Sartre rejected the Cartesian notion of the disembodied, mental self that exists separately from the material world. Although both embraced the ideas of embodiment, temporality, the Other, and intersubjectivity, in her student diaries and her metaphysical novel, *She Came to Stay*, Beauvoir offers formulations of these notions that seem quite different from Sartre's. In Beauvoir's case, the reader is encouraged to raise the question, What role does gender play in the development, presentation, and reception of Sartre's and Beauvoir's alternative formulations of these concepts, as well as ascription of their proper authorship?

Wittgenstein (chapter 14) asks, "What is the nature of language?" and Anscombe (also chapter 14) asks three different, interrelated basic questions about intentions and their role in ethics: "What is an intentional act?, What is the role of a theory of intentionality to moral philosophy? and, in the context of World War II and the just war theory, What is an 'intentional bombing' and when, if ever, does a just war justify intentional killings?" Her answer makes a theory of intentions essential to moral theory.

Philosophical questions are so basic to philosophy that Bertrand Russell describes the value of philosophy in terms of them. In his book *The Problems of Philosophy*, Russell wrote:

> Thus, to sum up our discussion of the value of philosophy; [sic] Philosophy is to be studied, not for the sake of any definite answers to its questions, since no definite answers can, as a rule, be known to be true, but rather for the sake of the questions themselves; because these questions enlarge our conception of what is possible, enrich our intellectual imagination and diminish the dogmatic assurance which closes the mind against speculation; but above all because, through the greatness of the universe which philosophy contemplates, the mind also is rendered great, and becomes capable of that union with universe which constitutes its highest good.[17]

THE CENTRAL ROLES PLAYED BY DUALISMS

Dualisms, especially mutually exclusive dualisms, are a mainstay of the philosophical canon. Among the most common are the dualisms reason versus emotion, mind versus body, culture versus nature, public versus private, objective versus subjective, and absolutism versus relativism. But many philosophers worry that these dualisms have neither functioned historically in gender-innocent or neutral ways nor accurately represented reality.

Consider the two related dualisms reason versus emotion and mind versus body. These dualisms have been criticized as having functioned historically in The House as mutually exclusive, oppositional, gender-valued dualisms that assign higher status, value, and prestige to that disjunct (reason, mind) that has historically—and stereotypically—been identified with males and male-gender traits in Western societies, while assigning lower status, value, and prestige to the other disjunct (emotion, body) that has historically—and stereotypically—been identified with females and female-gender traits. One important critique of The House proceeds this way in that the reason versus emotion and mind versus body dualisms have functioned as premises in arguments for a host of objectionable, false conclusions, such as the claims that: women are naturally inferior to men; the rights of citizenship, such as the right to vote or the right to an education, are justifiably denied to women; and the relegation of women to the domestic sphere and men to the public sphere is not a case of an unjustified gendered division of labor. The missing premises needed to validly argue from claims about the gender-valued nature of these dualisms to any of these false conclusions have roughly the same form: Since women are less rational and more emotional than men, more closely identified with the body than the mind, with nature than with culture, and with the private than the public sphere, one can infer that women are naturally inferior to men, lack the requisite amount of rationality to be granted the rights of full citizenship, and are best suited for work in the domestic or "private" sphere. The exclusion of women from the canonical history of Western philosophy has historically functioned as an expression and perpetuation of these false, gender-biased dualisms about women's "natural" inferiority.

FIVE ASSUMPTIONS

The last foundational feature of The House discussed concerns its basic assumptions. Consider five of them:

(1) *Rationalism*: the assumption that reason (rationality) is both the hallmark of being human and what distinguishes (some) humans from nonhuman animals and nature. There are four important concerns about rationalism. First, different philosophers (e.g., Kant and Mill) understand the concept of reason/rationality differently. Mill understands the concept of reason *instrumentally*, as the ability to anticipate and calculate the consequences of actions, while Kant understands the concept of reason as the ability to entertain and act in accordance with abstract, objective, universalizable principles. Second, as we have seen, rationalism presupposes—in practice, if not in theory—the reason versus emotion dualism that has functioned historically

in two important ways to rule out rational or moral emotions (such as the ability to care), which are central to ethical reasoning and decision making and that support other problematic gender-valued dualisms (such as the culture versus nature, mind versus body, and public versus private dualisms), which have functioned historically to justify the subordination of women. As a related third point, rationalism has been applied historically to those humans who are or will become adults with full cognitive capacities in the course of their normal development. The majority of well-known canonical male philosophers have argued that women lack the full capacity to reason. The implication is that, at least historically, women have been conceived as neither fully human not fully capable of doing philosophy.

Last, historically rationalism has placed a firm ontological divide between rational humans and nonrational animals and nature. But historically not all humans (e.g., women, or all except the "women worthies") have been considered rational. Reason/rationality, coupled with the problematic interrelated gendered dualisms described above, have functioned historically in arguments for the superiority of men, inferiority of women, and the moral justification for the subordination of women—and people of color, poor people, children, nonhuman animals, and nature. By extension, one can derive the views that the naturalization of women and feminization of nature have historically played a significant role in justifying the exclusion of women from the conception and practice of Western philosophy.[18]

Paradoxically, one challenge to rationalism is conceptually incompatible with rationalism. The challenge is from those philosophers who argue that what makes humans distinctive is a function of culture—socially constructed identities that reflect historical location, gender, race/ethnicities, sexual orientation and lifestyle, geographic location, age—rather than reason or rationality. Arguments against rationalism that are based on the claim that culture is what makes humans distinctive may be viewed as not rational.

(2) *Essentialism*: the assumption that things, including human beings, have properties (essences) that make them what they are and distinguish them from what they are not. For Plato, essentialism underlies his description of the Theory of Forms: Forms are the essences of all objects that exist. For Aristotle, things have essences but not Platonic essences; the essence of a thing—its form that identifies what a thing is meant to be—is located in the thing itself. For example, the form of a statue exists in the clay or marble—the matter—out of which a thing becomes a statue. For still others, such as the early Sartre, essentialism, whether Platonic or Aristotelian, is false in the case of humans though true in the case of other beings or objects.[19] If essentialism is the position that essence precedes existence, then for Sartre, essentialism is false in the case of humans. For humans, the converse is true—existence precedes essence. Humans are born totally free, without a predetermined essence (essential nature); humans create their essence every moment of their lives by the choices they make. One implication of this view is that, for Sartre, humans are "condemned to be free": we are born in a state of total freedom (without an essence) and have no choice but to take responsibility for who we are by the choices we make.

Marx argued against most of the key assumptions of the Western philosophical canon. (His "bracketed" inclusion in feature 2 of The House signifies that he is read with increasing frequency, not that he endorses foundational features of The House.) Marx claims that humans have no Platonic essence, but that they have an essence in the sense of *praxis*, where *praxis* is defined as the conscious ability to transform nature to meet human material needs. Human *praxis* changes, depending on the social relationships of production that characterize the economic or material base of a society in any given historical time period. As such, human essences are not fixed, abstract, or transcendental; they are historically located, economically embedded, and socially constructed—a view that conflicts with the canonical notion of essentialism.

Some feminist philosophers argue that, in contemporary society, there is no such being as a woman or human *simpliciter*. All humans are socially constructed beings, whose multiple identities reflect their gender, race/ethnicities, sexual orientations, geographic location, and other factors. This position is the denial of *conceptual* essentialism, which is distinguished from *strategic* essentialism. The distinction is based on the assumption that there is a difference between an essentialism based on the notion of some necessary and sufficient conditions or properties that identify something as what it is and an essentialism that collectivizes a group for practical, political, or strategic reasons. Strategic essentialism is based on the assumption that one wants to be able to make some true generalizations. In fact, to do philosophy or theory at all, one must make *some* generalizations—for example, generalizations about the exclusion of women from canonical accounts of the history of Western philosophy. But strategic essentialism does *not* commit one to conceptual essentialism.

There are three reasons for introducing the conceptual versus strategic essentialism distinction here. First, the distinction clarifies that it is conceptual essentialism that is a foundational assumption of The House. Second, the distinction is useful for clarifying that historical bases for the exclusion of women philosophers from the history of Western philosophy often have been based on false, conceptually essentialist claims about women—for example, that women's inferiority to men is based on women's lack of full rationality. Third, the distinction reinforces the view that when one talks (generalizes) about women one is not entitled to assume that there are necessary and sufficient conditions that identify all and only women as women—an assumption made by many House philosophers.

(3) *Objectivism*: the assumption that the basic, true claims of philosophy are impartial, detached, and disinterested (in contrast to being subjective, partial, attached, and interested). In the objective versus subjective dualism, objectivism and subjectivism are assumed to be mutually exclusive, incompatible concepts. Again the objective versus subjective dualism has functioned historically as a gender-valued dualism, whereby women, at least in Western societies, have been identified with the less-valued trait of subjectivity. Many women philosophers who warrant inclusion in the history of Western philosophy claim this is a false male-gender biased dichotomy.

(4) *Universalism and* (5) *Absolutism*: The House assumes that basic, true philosophical principles apply cross-culturally (*universalism*) and are absolute in the sense of being either *prima facie* binding or never overridable (*absolutism*).[20] These assumptions are often mistakenly used interchangeably. The main distinction is that universalism is about the nature and scope of true principles (rules, rights): they apply cross-culturally, independent of historical, cultural, gender, race/ethnic, and similar conditions. Absolutism is about the degree to which those principles (rules, rights) are binding on individuals and groups of individuals

There are three senses in which a principle (rule, right) could be absolute. In the weakest sense, a principle (rule, right) is absolute within a well-defined scope. This is the sense of "absolute" in which the rule, It is wrong to yell "Fire!" in a crowded theater, is absolute: it holds within the well-defined context of a crowded theater. In the second sense, a principle (rule, right) is *prima facie* absolute when there must be very strong and compelling reasons to override it; it is absolute all other things being equal. This is, I think, the sense of "absolute" in which the right to liberty—to free bodily movement—is absolute: it is only overriddable in very stringent conditions, such as an imminent public-health risk that could harm whole populations of innocent people. In the third, strongest sense, a principle (rule, right) is absolute when it is *never* justifiably overridden. This is, I think, the sense of "absolute" in which a right not to be exploited or tortured is absolute.[21]

Since "absolute" has these three meanings, absolutism *could* be understood in any of these three senses. Minimally, universalism and absolutism claim that the main principles of philosophy apply cross-culturally (their scope is universal) and they are binding absolutely—in at least the first two senses of "absolute." The third sense is more controversial.

"Absolutism" also is used in the context of the absolutism versus relativism dualism. Is this a true dualism? Many women scholars, particularly in the fields of ethics and epistemology, would answer no. In her commentary in chapter 2, for example, Vicki Harper goes between the horns of the dilemma and argues that Aristotle's virtue-based ethic is a *contextual* ethic—neither absolute nor relativist. Elizabeth Minnich (commentator, chapter 12) holds that since knowledge is transformative, it is neither absolute nor relative, objective nor subjective. Commitments to contextual ethics and transformative knowledge hold that absolutism versus relativism is neither a mutually exclusive dualism nor an accurate representation of reality—or knowledge.

Conclusion

This essay was designed to show five things: First, it showed how and why the exclusion of women from the history of Western philosophy is the unacceptable status quo of canonical accounts of that history. Second, it described the add-women-and-stir problem and claimed that a long-standing inability to resolve it is due to its having been misnamed. Third, by distinguishing addition from inclusion, it offered seven possible ways to include women philosophers in the history of Western philosophy that neither inherit the add-women-and-stir problem, nor require foreknowledge of the compatibility or incompatibility of the views of the women philosophers with key claims of The House account of the history of Western philosophy. Fourth, this essay showed how the organizational division of the book into fifteen self-contained chapters, each of which has a three-part structure that is key to the successful inclusion of women philosophers of every philosophical persuasion in an account of the history of Western philosophy. Fifth, it draws on the philosophical perspectives of the men and women philosophers in this book to illustrate key features of the foundation of The House: foundationalism; the importance of philosophical questions; the role of dualisms; and five common House assumptions—rationalism, essentialism, objectivism, universalism, and absolutism.

The main goal of this book is to correct the gender exclusivity of canonical accounts of the history of Western philosophy. This book provides the scholarship, organizational structure, and user-friendly features that make it possible for philosophers to redesign their history of Western philosophy courses to include women and for other readers to learn a more accurate, gender inclusive, account of that history. With the publication of this book, there is no defensible reason for anyone to continue to conceive or teach the history of philosophy as if there were no women philosophers.

That this book is the first of its kind is both good and bad news: The good news is that there is now a single book that corrects the male gender bias of texts of the history of Western philosophy that exclude women. The bad news is that it is not until now—the beginning of the twenty-first century—that there is such a book. Sadly, this book's status as the first is a stain on the discipline of philosophy, since it is evidence that neither canonical Western philosophy nor the curriculum that reflects it has progressed very far since the early 1970s, when recovery and inclusion projects were gaining momentum.

For all the contemporary philosophers who unearthed neglected, forgotten, or omitted women philosophers in the history of Western philosophy; for all the students and teachers who do not know but want to learn who the women philosophers were in the history of Western philosophy; for all the readers who purchase this book for their personal use or school libraries; for all the teachers who adopt this book for their college and university courses; for professional philosophers everywhere who read this book because they want to learn the who, what, where, when, and how of a scholarly accurate, *gender-inclusive* account of the history of Western philosophy; and for anyone who is just curious about what a gender-inclusive history of Western philosophy since 400 B.C.E. might be—this book is for you.

Notes

1. The startling exception to the absence of material on women philosophers until recently is Gilles Ménage, a seventeenth-century classical scholar, who claimed to have "discovered sixty-five women scholars of antiquity." He published the results in his *Historia Mulierum Philosopharum*, published in 1690 and 1692. His efforts are published in a complete modern English translation, with aids to the reader (e.g., an introduction, an index of Ménage's sources) in Gilles Ménage, *The History of Women Philosophers*, trans. Beatrice H. Zedler (Lanham, MD: University Press of America, 1984). (See also introduction to chapter 4.)

2. Race/ethnicity and gay and lesbian studies, especially queer theory, remind us that gender includes more than the female/male or man/woman binary. But this wider project of gender inclusion is beyond the scope of this book.

3. Four types of source materials were used or consulted for those portions of the book I wrote:

(1) Lecture notes from more than thirty years of teaching, primarily for the lead essay, on almost all the men and women philosopher pairs in each chapter and for background philosophical content of the chapter introductions; (2) "recovery project" texts, primarily to learn about the women philosophers in each chapter (and others in the history of Western philosophy), to write the biographies of the women philosophers and to generate the list of women philosophers in appendix A; (3) Internet web sites, primarily for biographical information for the chapter introductions and the glossary; and (4) some secondary source material on or in the history of Western philosophy, primarily for those philosophers whom I have not taught.

(2) The "recovery project "material includes the following:

Alic, Margaret. *Hypatia's Heritage: A History of Women in Science From Antiquity Through the Nineteenth Century* (Boston: Beacon Press, 1986).
Allen, Sister Prudence RSM. *The Concept of Woman: The Aristotelian Revolution, 750 B.C.–A.D. 1250* (Grand Rapids, MI: William B. Freedman Publishing Co., 1985).

Allen, Sister Prudence RSM. *The Concept of Woman*, vol. 2, *The Early Humanist Revolution, 1250–1500* (Grand Rapids, MI: William B. Freedman Publishing Co., 2002).

Atherton, Margaret, ed. *Women Philosophers of the Early Modern Period* (Indianapolis, IN: Hackett Publishing Co., 1994).

Barth, Else M. *Women Philosophers: A Bibliography of Books Through 1990* (Bowling Green, OH: Philosophy Documentation Center, 1992).

Broad, Jacqueline. *Women Philosophers of the Seventeenth Century* (New York: Cambridge University Press, 2002).

Dykeman, Therese Boos, ed. *American Women Philosophers, 1650–1930: Six Exemplary Thinkers* (Lewiston, NY: Edwin Mellen Press, 1993).

Dykeman, Therese Boos, ed. *The Neglected Canon: Nine Women Philosophers* (Boston: Kluwer Academic Publishers, 1999).

Gardner, Catherine Villanueva. *Rediscovering Women Philosophers: Philosophical Genre and the Boundaries of Philosophy* (Boulder, CO: Westview, 2000).

Gould, Vivian. *Daughters of Time, 2000 Notable Women: Antiquity to 1800* (North Charleston, SC: Book Surge, 2005).

Kersey, Ethel M. *Women Philosophers: A Bio-Critical Source Book* (New York: Greenwood Press, 1989).

McAlister, Linda Lopez, ed. *Hypatia: A Journal of Feminist Philosophy, Special Issue on the History of Women in Philosophy* 4, no. 1 (Spring 1989).

Ménage, Gilles. *The History of Women Philosophers* trans. Beatrice H. Zedler (Lanham, MD: University Press of America, 1984).

Rogers, Dorothy, and Therese Boos Dykeman, eds. *Hypatia: A Journal of Feminist Philosophy, Special Issue on Women in the American Philosophical Tradition, 1800–1930* 19, no. 2 (Spring 2004).

Simons, Margaret A., ed. *Hypatia: A Journal of Feminist Philosophy, Special Issue on the Philosophy of Simone de Beauvoir* 14, no. 2 (Fall 1999).

Tougas, Cecile T., and Sara Ebenreck, eds. *Presenting Women Philosophers* (Philadelphia, PA: Temple University Press, 2000).

Waithe, Mary Ellen, ed. *A History of Women Philosophers*, vol. 1, *Ancient Women Philosophers 600 BC–500 AD* (Dordrecht, The Netherlands: Martinus Nijholf Publishers, 1987). Excerpts are published with kind permission of Springer Science and Business Media.

Waithe, Mary Ellen, ed. *A History of Women Philosophers*, vol. 2, *Medieval, Renaissance and Enlightenment Women Philosophers 500–1600 AD* (Dordrecht, The Netherlands: Kluwer Academic Publisher, 1989). Excerpts are published with kind permission of Springer Science and Business Media.

Waithe, Mary Ellen, ed., *A History of Women Philosophers*, vol. 3, *Modern Women Philosophers 1600–1900* (Dordrecht, The Netherlands: Kluwer Academic Publisher, 1991). Excerpts are published with kind permission of Springer Science and Business Media.

Waithe, Mary Ellen, ed., *A History of Women Philosophers*, vol. 4, *Contemporary Women Philosophers 1900–Present* (Dordrecht, The Netherlands: Kluwer Academic Publisher, 1995). Excerpts are published with kind permission of Springer Science and Business Media.

Warnock, Mary, ed. *Women Philosophers* (London: Orion Publishing Group, 1997).

Women Philosophers web site, from 2500 B.C.E.–500 C.E., www.women-philosophers.com

(3) The Internet sites I consulted were:

About.com: Women's History, Philosophy & Philosophers, http://womenshistory.about.com/od/philosophy/Philosophy_Philosophers.htm

Assembled Western Philosophers, www.philosophypages.com/ph/index.htm

Biography, www.biography.com/search/

David Nash Ford's Royal Berkshire History, Biographies, www.berkshirehistory.com/index.html

A Dictionary of Philosophical Terms and Names, www.philosophypages.com/dy/

Episteme Links: Philosophical Resources on the Internet, www.epistemelinks.com/Main/MainPers.aspx

Glossary of Philosophical Terms, www.filosofia.net/materiales/rec/glosaen.htm

Guide to Philosophy on the Internet, www.earlham.edu/~peters/gpi/dicts.htm

The Internet Encyclopedia of Philosophy, www.iep.utm.edu/

Mythos and Logos, www.mythosandlogos.com/

Philosophers A–Z, http://users.ox.ac.uk/~worc0337/phil-1.html

Philosophy Pages, www.philosophypages.com/ph/index.htm

Spartacus Educational, www.spartacus.schoolnet.co.uk/
Stanford On-Line Encyclopedia, http://plato.stanford.edu/entries/plato/
Sunshine for Women: www.pinn.net/~sunshine/main.html
Wikipedia: The Free Encyclopedia: http://en.wikipedia.org/wiki/

(4) The secondary sources included:

Ayer, A. J., and Raymond Winch, eds. *British Empirical Philosophers: Locke, Berkeley, Hume, Reid and J. S. Mill* (New York: Simon & Schuster, 1968).

Baird, Forrest E., and Walter Kaufmann. *Twentieth-Century Philosophy*, vol. 5 (Upper Saddle River, NJ: Prentice Hall, 1997).

Copleston, Frederick, SJ. *A History of Philosophy*, vols. 1–9 (New York: Doubleday, 1993).

Edwards, Paul, ed. *The Encyclopedia of Philosophy*, vols. 1–8 (New York: Macmillan Publishing Co., 1967).

Hornblower, Simon, and Anthony Spawforth, eds. *Oxford Classical Dictionary*, 3rd ed. (Cambridge, UK: Cambridge University Press, 1996).

Lloyd, Genevieve, ed. *Feminism & History of Philosophy* (New York: Oxford University Press, 2002).

Popkin, Richard H., ed. *This Philosophy of the Sixteenth and Seventeenth Centuries* (New York: Free Press, 1966).

Russell, Bertrand. *A History of Western Philosophy* (New York: Simon & Schuster, 1972).

Solomon, Robert C. *Introducing Philosophy: A Text with Integrated Readings*, 8th ed. (New York: Oxford University Press, 2005).

Ward, Julie K. ed. *Feminism and Ancient Philosophy* (New York: Routledge, 1996).

Weitz, Morris, ed. *Twentieth-Century Philosophy: The Analytic Tradition* (New York: Free Press, 1966).

4. Diotima is the only case of a member of a philosophical pair (Plato and Diotima) for whom there is no primary text.

5. As we shall see, the question "What makes someone a philosopher?" is itself a philosophical question that will engage people in debates about both the conception and practice of philosophy. It was not a question I set out to resolve. I simply wanted guidelines for choosing the women candidates for inclusion in this book.

6. According to Elizabeth Minnich, "This line spread primarily through conversations: when asked, Bunch said that the idea . . . was developed in conversations with Mary E. Hunt." Minnich, *Transforming Knowledge*, 2nd ed. (Philadelphia, PA: Temple University Press, 2005), chapter 2, note 22. See also Charlotte Bunch, *Passionate Politics: Essays (1968–1986)* (New York: St. Martin's Press, 1987), 140.

7. Peggy McIntosh's five-phase interactive model of curricular development was first presented by her in the early 1970s and revised twice, in 1983 and 1991, as "Interactive Phases of Personal and Curricular Re-Vision"; all three published by the Center for Women at the Wellesley Center for Women.

8. Elizabeth Minnich originated the line quoted in the early 1970s. It appears in print in her "Conceptual Errors Across the Curriculum: Towards a Transformation of the Tradition," in *The Research Clearinghouse and Curriculum Integration Project*, Center for Research on Women, Memphis State University, 1986: 1. But she provides a much more expansive and in-depth account of the conceptual roots of additive, rather than transformative, nature of thinking, knowledge, meaning, construction, and gender-inclusive curriculum projects in her book, *Transforming Knowledge*, 2nd edition.

9. In a personal conversation, Joy Laine described similar challenges and frustrations that she experiences when she tries to integrate (Asian) Indian philosophical views into her mainstream Western courses through an add-and-stir approach.

10. I have many philosophical difficulties with the McIntosh model, particularly its failure to recognize that claims about women (or men) must also involve claims about such identity-formative traits as race/ethnicity, socioeconomic status, affectional orientation, dominant/subordinate, and colonizer/colonized status. Furthermore, there are many ways of accomplishing inclusion projects other than simply focusing on women. For a description and defense of the strengths and weaknesses of the McIntosh model, see my essay, "Re-Writing the Future: The Feminist Challenge to the Malestream Curriculum," *Feminist Teacher* 4, no. 2/3 (Fall 1989), 46–52.

11. This list of possible meanings of "inclusion" is not intended to be exhaustive. Discussion of the inclusion/addition distinction, and possible meanings of "inclusion" is intended to illustrate that gender inclusion projects come in various forms and that inclusion projects need not ever encounter the hitherto crippling add-women-and-stir problem.

12. Many ecofeminist philosophers, for example, claim that The House is inescapably committed to unacceptable views about nonhuman animals and "nature" (e.g., that both have only instrumental value as mere property or as the means of production of commodity goods for humans). At the same time, many argue for retaining but reforming some House concepts (e.g., the notions of intrinsic value, respect for others, rights) in ways suitable for their application to nonhuman animals and perhaps even what Aldo Leopold calls "the land."

13. In the case of Marx and Angela Davis, philosophy of The House is a reflection of the social relationships between those who own the means of production (the bourgeoisie) and those who do not (the proletariat or workers). Marx argued that in a preindustrial, capitalist economic organization of society, society's superstructure (its law, philosophy, religion, art, history, culture—anything that was not part of the society's material or economic base—is nothing more than an expression of the values and interests of the ruling class. Philosophy as conceptualized and practiced within The House is simply a case of liberal "ideology." Marx was critical of "armchair philosophy." He claimed that "philosophers have only interpreted the world, in various ways; the point, however, is to change it." (This quotation is from Robert C. Tucker, ed., *The Marx-Engels Reader*, 2nd ed. (New York: W.W. Norton, 1978):145.

14. Minnich, *Transforming Knowledge*, 2nd ed., 4.

15. See Richard Rorty, *Philosophy as the Mirror of Nature* (Princeton, NJ: Princeton University Press, 1979).

16. Howard Zinn, *People's History of the United States: 1492 to Present* (New York: HarperCollins, 2005).

17. Bertrand Russell, *The Problems of Philosophy* (New York: Oxford University Press, 1997), 155–156, 161.

18. Ecofeminist philosophy and queer theory are just two (of many) theoretical positions that reject the gender dualisms of male versus female and man versus woman not having functioned historically in innocent or neutral ways. I am well aware of the irony that this book uses—though it does not embrace—the very dualisms it challenges. It does so for practical or strategic reasons: to make some true generalizations about the exclusion of women philosophers from the philosophical canon of the last 2,600 years. For a fuller discussion of the biased nature of canonical dualisms, see Karen J. Warren, *Ecofeminist Philosophy: A Western Perspective on What It Is and Why It Matters* (Lanham, MD: Rowman & Littlefield, 2000).

19. Jean Paul Sartre, "Existentialism as a Humanism" (1946) in *Existentialism from Dostoyevsky to Sartre*, ed. Walter Kaufman, trans. Philip Mairet (New York: Meridian Publishing Co., 1989), (first published by World Publishing Co. in 1956).

20. One more paradox is that if universalism and objectivism were true characteristics of philosophy, then "Western philosophy" would be misnamed. Any genuine or real philosophy would not need the qualifier "Western"; it would just be "philosophy." At best, we might refer to the historical tradition traceable back from the present to the pre-Socratics as philosophy as developed by Western thinkers.

21. See Joel Feinberg, *Social Philosophy* (Englewood Cliffs, NJ: Prentice-Hall, 1973).

CHAPTER 1

Plato and Diotima

Introduction by *Karen J. Warren*

The twentieth-century philosopher Alfred North Whitehead once said, "The safest characterization of the philosophical tradition is that it consists in a series of footnotes to Plato."[1] Whether or not one agrees with Whitehead, his remark highlights the significance of Plato's philosophy as a defining framework (lens or starting point) for conceptualizing and practicing Western philosophy—what I have called "canonical Western philosophy" ("traditional philosophy," "the canon," or "The House") (see lead essay). This is the tradition whose lineage is traceable to classical Greece, which scholars identify as beginning either around 800 B.C.E. or with the writings of the pre-Socratics around 600 B.C.E. It gains full expression in the philosophical views of Socrates (469–399 B.C.E.), his student Plato (427–347 B.C.E.), and Plato's student Aristotle (384–322 B.C.E.).

The tradition of canonical Western philosophy probably peaked with Immanuel Kant at the beginning of the nineteenth century. Since Kant, Western philosophy is more aptly characterized as a set of different, often competing, philosophical positions, some more closely tied to the traditional philosophical canon than others. These alternative positions all engage canonical philosophy in one way or another. Some are best understood as providing critiques of it (e.g., some feminist philosophies and existentialism), while other positions are best understood as continuing it (e.g., analytical philosophy and logical positivism).

Given the central role Platonic philosophy plays in constructing the foundation and framework (both external and internal) of The House, this introduction is different from subsequent ones. It provides a relatively lengthy discussion of central Platonic doctrines that are featured in this chapter's primary texts and commentary and are discernable in subsequent chapters. To understand the canonical importance of Plato's philosophy, one must go back to the pre-Socratics and ancient Greece (*Hellas*).

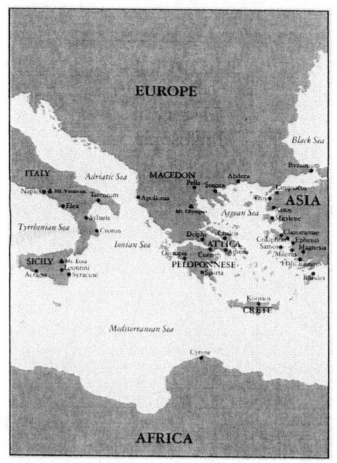

The Greek World. The "Greek World" map is published with the permission of Harcourt Brace Jovanovich.

THE PRE-SOCRATICS

The pre-Socratics flourished in Miletus (in Asia Minor) and Hellas (Greece) between the end of the seventh century B.C.E. and the middle of the fourth century B.C.E. (see map of Greece above). This timeframe means that some pre-Socratics were actually contemporaries of Socrates.

Historians often divide the pre-Socratic philosophers into four groups[2]: (1) the three well-known Milesians from the Greek colony of Miletus, Thales, Anaximander, and Anaximenes; (2) the three great independent thinkers who came from different places and stood for quite different principles, Pythagoras, Xenophanes, and Heraclitus; (3) the three great Eleatics, Parmenides, Zeno of Elea, and Melissus; and (4) the three great pluralists, Empedocles, Anaxagoras, and Democritus.

There is relatively little known about the pre-Socratics, since only fragments (apothegms) of their writings survive. What is known reveals that they were interested primarily in identifying the different substances (substrata) that constituted the metaphysical explanations of the world's existence and nature. Some pre-Socratics turned to the natural elements of water (Thales), air (Anaximenes), and fire (Heraclitus) as the stuff (substratum) of which the earth was made. Anaximander and Pythagoras believed that the ultimate substratum of the world could not be reduced to one of its natural elements: for Anaximander it consisted of the *apeiron*—the unobservable, indeterminate, boundless, or unlimited; for Pythagoras, the world consists of numbers (see chapter 2).

Despite such differences, the pre-Socratics represent a philosophical and epistemological departure from other Mediterranean cultures by their use of observation and reason to think about the world and provide theories about the ultimate stuff (substratum) of reality. Their focus moved away from issues of *cosmogony*—theories and supernatural explanations about the origins of the world (*kosmos*), transmitted through stories of a poetic or literary nature (*mythos*)—to issues of *cosmology*—theories and empirical explanations of the essence or nature of the world, transmitted through logical reasoning (*logos*). *Logos* provides a rational account of what is perceptible through observation and knowable through reason. What is known through *logos* may lead to wisdom (*sophia*). Those who, like the pre-Socratics, had a love (*philo*) of wisdom (*sophia*) and dedicated their lives to the pursuit of wisdom were called philosophers (*philosophia*). It is this shift from *mythos* to *logos* that characterizes the emergence of Western philosophy.

This sketch of the pre-Socratics is important for three reasons. First, it helps to establish when, where, and why Western philosophy began when it did (between 800 and 600 b.c.e.). Second, it provides the historical context for the early pre-Socratic definition of philosophy as the pursuit of wisdom, accomplished through thinking based on *logos* rather than *mythos*. Third, it explains why the turn from *mythos* to *cosmos* through *logos* helped establish the beginnings of Western philosophy.

While the pre-Socratics represent the beginning of Western philosophy, it is in the conception and practice of philosophy, attributed to the historical Socrates and to his pupil Plato, that the major themes of Western philosophy took hold. What characterizes this transition from the pre-Socratics to Socrates and Plato?

THE TRANSITION FROM THE PRE-SOCRATICS TO SOCRATES AND PLATO

During the time of the early pre-Socratics, there were no sciences (e.g., physics, astronomy, biology, botany, psychology) separate from philosophy. One might be tempted to describe contemporary philosophy as what remains after these various sciences splintered off from philosophy and, over the centuries, became distinct disciplines with their own methodologies, interests, and research projects. As one writer puts it, "the theories put forth in Ancient Greece could be called the origins of Western science with as much justification as they can be called the origins of Western philosophy, even though at that early period, no such distinctions could be made."[3]

However, even if true, this conception of philosophy fails to capture the distinctive nature of philosophical inquiry and to explain the central place of philosophy in "the academy" and a liberal arts education. To capture that one needs to remember that the type of question canonical philosophy asks is not only uniquely philosophical but also foundational. To review from the lead essay, a philosophical question is: (1) basic;

(2) general; (3) about conceptual analysis and/or (4) logical analysis; and (5) requires some form of proof or justification. The question, What is philosophy? unlike the questions, What is economics? or What is history? is itself a philosophical question.

We are now in a position to see why Socratic inquiry and Platonic doctrines have been identified as quintessentially philosophical—they asked distinctly philosophical questions and, unlike most of their predecessors, asked them about a different set of topics than those of cosmology and cosmogony—topics such as the nature of the human self, knowledge, ethics, justice, beauty, love, reality, and language. They did so through the use of a question-answer approach (the Socratic method) and a dialogic (conversational) form. Like the pre-Socratics, Socrates and Plato conceived of philosophy as a love of wisdom (*philo-sophia*) and the genuine (not sophist) pursuit of truth. The philosopher's job is to scrutinize any view, no matter how commonly held, through asking and attempting to answer distinctly philosophical questions. As such, their thinking and questioning was original in kind, groundbreaking in scope, and enduring in influence throughout the history of canonical Western philosophy.

SOCRATES

The historical man Socrates lived all his life in Athens. If he actually wrote anything, that writing has not survived. Most of what we know about him and his philosophical views come to us through the early writings of Plato and the General Xenophon. The Socrates who appears as a main character and interlocutor in Plato's early dialogues (e.g., *Euthyphro*, *Apology*, *Crito*, and *Meno*) probably represents the actual views of the historical Socrates, while the Socrates who appears in somewhat later dialogues (e.g., the *Symposium* and *Menexenus*), and some of Plato's middle dialogues (e.g., the *Republic*), probably represents the Platonic Socrates—a spokesperson for distinctly Platonic views. Distinguishing between the two—the historical and the Platonic Socrates—is often a matter of scholarly debate.

What is not controversial is that the primary role of each Socrates in Plato's dialogues is to engage others in inquiry about the answers to key philosophical questions. For example, the central question in *Euthyphro* is What is piety?, in *Meno*, What is knowledge?, in *Republic*, What is justice?, and in the *Symposium* and *Phaedrus*, What is love? and What is beauty?, respectively. The historical Socrates described himself both as a gadfly—getting people to challenge their own thoughts—and a midwife—helping people remember (recollect, rebirth) what their souls once knew but forgot when they were born. Here the historical Socrates and Plato share the view that knowledge is recollection. Socrates helps in this recollection by engaging others in the Socratic method: Socrates poses a philosophical question (e.g., What is love?). He then proceeds meticulously to draw answers from his pupils—typically answers in the form of definitions—that Socrates then shows untenable. The conversation usually ends with Socrates noting that neither he nor his pupils know the answer. The open questioning and continuing inquiry is what matters.

Socrates's incessant philosophical inquiry with the ordinary citizens of Athens made him unpopular among the ruling elite. When he was about seventy years old, Socrates was charged with two crimes: corrupting Athenian youth and believing in false gods. Because of the amnesty rule implemented after the Peloponnesian War, the Athenians could not accuse him of any acts covered by the amnesty rules. So the two accusations of Socrates's wrongdoing are based on clearly trumped up charges.

Plato documented the famous accusation, trial, and death of Socrates in his trilogy *Euthyphro, Apology,* and *Crito,* and the death scene in *Phaedo.* Socrates was found guilty on both charges. Although Socrates remained steadfast in his claims of innocence, he refused to escape his death sentence when his friends made the opportunity available. His reasoning was that by living all his life in Athens, never challenging its laws, he had, in effect, tacitly consented to obey its rules, including the decisions of its courts. Leaving Athens would be a violation of that duty and, hence, wrong. This line of reasoning is an early statement of the social contract theory that, in modern philosophy, is a commonly offered moral basis for the legitimacy of a government (i.e., its right to rule) and the correlative obligation or duty of citizens to obey (see chapters 6 and 9).

PLATO

Plato was one of the most powerful thinkers of all time. To discuss Plato's philosophy today is to be immersed in some of the most significant, enduring, and perhaps irresolvable debates in Western philosophy. In the remainder of this introduction, I discuss ten Platonic doctrines—only a fraction of the positions for which he is known. These ten doctrines are chosen for their relevance to the excerpted texts in this and subsequent chapters.

A cornerstone of Plato's philosophy is his Theory of Forms, the metaphysical *sine qua non* of Plato's other major doctrines. Plato's description of the Theory of Forms is illustrated through two well-known examples, what Plato calls the simile of "the divided line" and "the allegory of the cave," both given in the *Republic.* (I discuss only the former here.) The traditional interpretation and visual representation of the divided line is one I adapted to develop a visual image of Plato's theory in diagram 1.1.

The "divided line" diagram represents the Theory of Forms as a metaphysical doctrine that is intimately linked with Plato's theories in ontology, ethics, epistemology, psychology, aesthetics, and politics. Plato's divided line also sets up key features of the Western philosophical canon that are recognizable in one way or another in nearly all the writings of the other male philosophers in this book.

Traditionally, Plato's simile of the divided line has been interpreted as illustrating two different worlds: the visible, perceptible, changing, earthly world of space and time—the World of Particulars—and the invisible, unchanging, eternal, nonspatial, nontemporal world of the most real "things"—the World of Forms or Ideas.[4] This traditional interpretation is bolstered by Plato's own description and image of two worlds divided by a horizontal line.

But Plato did not stop there. Plato also held that within each world, there are two kinds of objects that are themselves both different in kind (ontologically different) and in degrees of reality (metaphysically different). In the World of Forms, the two kinds of objects are mathematical objects or concepts—such as triangularity—and the really real Forms themselves—Platonic essences, eternal realities, or Ideas (not "ideas," which are

PLATO'S THEORY OF THE FORMS

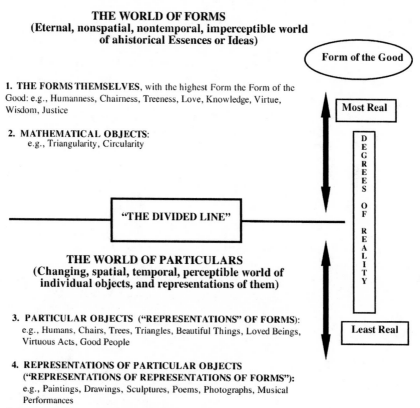

THE WORLD OF FORMS
(Eternal, nonspatial, nontemporal, imperceptible world
of ahistorical Essences or Ideas)

Form of the Good

1. **THE FORMS THEMSELVES**, with the highest Form the Form of the
Good: e.g., Humanness, Chairness, Treeness, Love, Knowledge, Virtue,
Wisdom, Justice

Most Real

2. **MATHEMATICAL OBJECTS**:
    e.g., Triangularity, Circularity

"THE DIVIDED LINE"

THE WORLD OF PARTICULARS
(Changing, spatial, temporal, perceptible world of
individual objects, and representations of them)

DEGREES OF REALITY

3. **PARTICULAR OBJECTS ("REPRESENTATIONS" OF FORMS)**:
    e.g., Humans, Chairs, Trees, Triangles, Beautiful Things, Loved Beings,
    Virtuous Acts, Good People

Least Real

4. **REPRESENTATIONS OF PARTICULAR OBJECTS**
("REPRESENTATIONS OF REPRESENTATIONS OF FORMS"):
    e.g., Paintings, Drawings, Sculptures, Poems, Photographs, Musical
    Performances

Diagram 1.1.   The Divided Line.

human cognitions), such as Humanness, Chairness, Tableness, Love, Beauty, and the most real Form, the Form of the Good. Similarly, in the world of particulars, there are two sorts of objects: individual objects, such as humans, chairs, triangles, or animals, and representations (images, copies) of particular objects, such as paintings or sculptures of humans, chairs, and triangles as well as poems about such objects.

Plato held that there is an important ontological relationship between the two worlds: objects in both worlds—particular objects in the spatiotemporal world and mathematic objects in the world of Forms—are "instantiations" (instances, reflections, copies) of the corresponding Forms that are their essences. For example, humans are instantiations of the Form Humanness, which not only captures the essential characteristics of what it is to be human but the existence of which is necessary in order for any actual humans to exist.

Furthermore, the Forms are more real than any of their instantiations, with the degrees of reality in descending order, from the most real Forms (Beauty, the Good) to the (slightly) less real mathematical objects, to particular objects, and ultimately to the least real things, representations of particular objects. The ontological status of the latter three kinds of objects—how real they are—depends upon how closely or distantly related they are to the most real objects, the Forms.

Plato's Theory of Forms is intimately connected to other Platonic doctrines, also represented by the divided line. A second such doctrine is Plato's *conceptual essentialism*, the position that there is a set of properties that defines concepts and objects, that makes them what they are rather than something else. These properties constitute the essence of the concept or thing. All objects and concepts have an essence, which is its corresponding Form. In this way, Plato's essentialism presupposes his Theory of Forms. Without the Form of a particular thing, that thing could not exist as the kind of thing it is, with the defining properties it has. Only by appeal to Forms can one know the essence, or defining properties, of something.

Plato's essentialism is connected to a third doctrine, Plato's *definitional thesis*: one cannot truly know the meaning of a term (e.g., the meaning of love or beauty) unless one can define it. The definitional thesis is so central to Plato's writing that many of his dialogues are known as "definitional dialogues": they are designed to provide a definition for (typically) one basic philosophical concept. When Plato asks, "What is love?" in the *Symposium* or "What is beauty?" in the *Phaedrus*, he assumes that definitions of love and beauty are possible and will provide the essence (or meaning) of Love or Beauty (the Forms of Love, Beauty or The Beautiful).

In turn, the definitional thesis is closely connected to a fourth Platonic doctrine, the *one-over-many principle*. Simplifying a complex thesis, this principle asserts that one may properly call many particular things (a, b, and c) by the same name (x) if and only if that name (x) applies to all and only the particulars things that are called by that name (a, b, and c). For example, one may call many particular chairs "chairs" if and only if the word chair properly applies to all and only those things are called chairs. In the context of the *Symposium*, the one-over-many principle asserts that many things are properly called "love" (a linguistic interpretation of the one-over-many principle) and are genuine examples of love (a metaphysical interpretation of the principle) if and only if there exists one essence, the Form Love, which provides the meaning and true nature of "love." The one Form is necessary for both naming different kinds of love (e.g., filial, parental, erotic love) and for the many kinds of love to exist. For Plato, an answer to the question, "What is the meaning or essence of love?" presupposes the one-over-many principle, which, in turn, presupposes the definitional thesis, conceptual essentialism and, ultimately, the Theory of Forms.

Fifth, the divided line also illustrates the basics of Plato's *ethics*: the Form of the Good is the most real Form (see diagram 1.1.) Plato's views about the Form of the Good and its relation to the Form of Beauty is a subject of scholarly debate. But whatever else he meant, Plato's ethical views about The Good are intimately tied to a sixth area of Plato's thought, his *epistemology*: one must go beyond mere opinion or judgment (*dôxa*) of the observable world of particulars to gain knowledge (*epistême*, the Greek root for "epistemology") of the Forms, including, ultimately, the Form of the Good. Genuine knowledge of the Form of the Good is incorrigible (a point I return to shortly).

How does one know what is good? Plato's answer is that to know the Good is to become good. Here Plato endorses the seventh Socratic view that *akrasia*—a term used for weakness of the will or acting against one's own better judgment—is impossible. This is because, for Plato, no one does wrong knowingly, willingly, or intentionally;

any wrongdoing is done involuntarily or out of ignorance. As counterintuitive as Plato's denial of *akrasia* may seem, it is based in his epistemological view that if one really knew—saw and understood—the Good—one would become good. So, one cannot genuinely *know* The Good and act unethically (do wrong). Plato's denial of *akrasia* is important for understanding how Diotima's account of Eros in the *Symposium* is related to the Platonic account of how one knows what is good.

Plato's view that to know the Good is to become good is connected to an eighth doctrine that is identified as originating with Plato, the *psychological* theory of "the tripartite notion of the soul." The view that the doctrine of the three parts of the soul originated with Plato historically has been so often repeated that it is identified as one of Plato's most famous philosophical positions. (Is Plato the author of the doctrine? See the Foreword.) The doctrine asserts that the soul or self consists of reason (the rational part), spirit (the spirited part), and appetite (the appetitive part). Furthermore, each part of the self is associated with an *ethical virtue*: wisdom, the virtue associated with reason; courage, the virtue associated with appetite; and moderation, the virtue associated with the appetitive part. A harmonious self is one where each part of the self exercises its proper virtue; when there is conflict between them, reason must rule over the other two through the exercise of the virtue wisdom.

According to Plato's psychology (above), individuals achieve happiness, or *harmonia*, when the soul (a) aims at recollecting lost knowledge through the use of reason (*epistême*) and (b) seeks to understand the virtue wisdom in order to become wise. These two happiness-producing activities of reason, (a) and (b), are necessary for individuals to become both harmonious and wise selves—that is, for the three parts of the soul to exhibit their proper virtues.

There are two additional Platonic doctrines that are related to Plato's psychology. One is Plato's (ninth) doctrine that *knowledge is recollection* (a position mentioned earlier). This doctrine asserts that we are each born with all knowledge, but we lose it at birth. In order to (re)gain knowledge, we must remember what we lost at birth. The other is Plato's (tenth) *political* position on the nature of a just society. It is based on an analogy between the harmonious self and the just society or state (given in the *Republic*). A just state is achieved when the three parts of the state do what they are best suited for: the rulers (philosopher kings) exercise reason through the virtue wisdom; the soldiers exercise their spirited part through the virtue courage; and the workers exercise their appetites through the virtue moderation.

This overview of the pre-Socratics, Socrates, and ten Platonic doctrines does three things: it provides the historical context in which the foundation of canonical Western philosophy—The House—formed; it sets up (or frames) the trajectory of philosophical thinking that characterizes much of canonical Western philosophy during the past 2,600 years; last, it enables the reader to better understand and discuss key Platonic doctrines that arise in the *Symposium* and *Phaedrus*.

DIOTIMA: HER HISTORICITY

Most scholars who discuss Diotima of Matinea begin by addressing her historicity: Was Diotima an actual person who lived during the 400s B.C.E., as Mary Ellen Waithe claims[5] or a fictional, though important, female character in Plato's *Symposium*, as Eve Browning argues in her commentary in this chapter? Browning's main claim is that the evidence for authenticating her existence is inconclusive but that, nonetheless, Diotima should be considered as a "woman's voice," which defends an important position on the nature of love that is endorsed in her name and endorsed by Socrates.[6]

Suppose the historicity of Diotima can never be proven. Does this mean that the character, Diotima, and the speech she gives on love in Plato's *Symposium*, ought to be discarded either as not philosophically significant or as simply a fictitious female philosopher's voice on love in the *Symposium*? One way to think about this two-part question comes in the form of an analogy. Consider characters in a great fictional novel or classic fictional movie. These characters do not really exist in the spatiotemporal world in the way actual humans do. But the characters make memorable speeches or provide distinct, new points of view or become spokespersons for a certain perspective or historical time period—such as Scarlett O'Hara in *Gone with the Wind*, Willy Loman in *Death of a Salesman*, or the figure E. T. in the movie by that name. Their lack of "historicity" does not imply anything about the significance of what they say, whether their speeches have philosophical importance, or whether their gender is relevant to the nature of what they say or represent in the context of the larger story or play.

Should the same be said of Diotima, treating her speech on love, delivered by the character Socrates in *Symposium*, as not simply an important philosophical position but one attributed to a female character or represented as a woman's voice? First, she is answering a distinctly philosophical question, "What is love?," in a way Socrates finds fully acceptable in the context of a traditional Platonic dialogue. Second, the answer attributed to Diotima is one Socrates finds fully acceptable. Diotima is a woman whose views are defended by Socrates at a dinner party of men only, during a time (ancient Greece) when women tended not to be included in public philosophical discussions. In fact, in all of Plato's writings there are only two women—Diotima in *Symposium* and Aspasia in *Menexenus*—who appear as female characters; in both cases, their position is "impersonated" or articulated in absentia by Socrates.[7] As such, and if for no other reason, Socrates's attribution to a woman, Diotima, a philosophical view on love that he says he accepts and to which he has nothing significant to add makes her voice and gender significant—whether or not she was a historical person.

Third, Diotima's gender is noteworthy in that, for Plato, as for most philosophers throughout Western philosophy, the reason versus emotion dualism historically identified women, in contrast to (at least dominant-group) men, with the less valued trait of emotion. That it is a woman, Diotima, who has given a philosophical view on love (Eros) is an interesting twist of gender identity: the topic, love, is about an emotion, but Diotima's speech, as articulated by Socrates, is rationally defended. So Socrates provides an interesting gender role reversal in saying that he has nothing to add to what Diotima has said.

For at least these three reasons, Diotima's speech on love warrants philosophical consideration as a woman's voice on an important and distinctly philosophical topic, love, in the familiar and accepted format of a Platonic dialogue. In addition, the question "What is love?" is presented and answered in a way that uses *logos* and conceptual analysis. Does this historically gender-identified perspective on love, given by Diotima through Socrates, warrant calling Diotima a woman philosopher, whether she is a historical person or not—insofar as Diotima's voice represents that of a woman philosopher? Though she believes Diotima's historicity will never be conclusively established, in either case commentator Eve Browning's answer is "Yes."

BROWNING'S COMMENTARY

After a brief discussion of the historicity of Diotima, Browning presents two accounts of the relation of Eros to philosophical wisdom in Plato's *Symposium*. Browning then contrasts these two accounts in the *Symposium* with those in the *Phaedrus*. She uses Plato's image of the chariot with two horses to show that Socrates's view in the *Phaedrus* portrays erotic love as "characterized by inevitable conflict and division." Browning ends by comparing the similarities and differences between Eros (or erotic love) as provided by Socrates in the *Phaedrus* and by Diotima in the *Symposium*, construing the characters Socrates and Diotima as examples of two Platonic theoreticians offering different views on love and wisdom. The reader is left to decide which Platonic view is more compelling.

Excerpts of Writings by Plato and Speech Attributed to Diotima

I. EXCERPTS FROM PLATO'S *SYMPOSIUM*[8]

d   Now I let you go. I shall try to go through for you the speech about Love I once heard from a woman of Mantinea, Diotima—a woman who was wise about many things besides this: once she even put off the plague for ten years by telling the Athenians what sacrifices to make. She is the one who taught me the art of love, and I shall go through her speech as best I can on my own, using what Agathon and I have agreed to as a basis.

Following your lead, Agathon, one should first describe who Love is and what he is like, and afterwards describe his works—I think it will be easiest for me to proceed the way Diotima did and tell you how she questioned me.

You see, I had told her almost the same things Agathon told me just now: that Love is a great god and that he belongs to beautiful things. And she used the very same arguments against me that I used against Agathon; she showed how, according to my very own speech, Love is neither beautiful nor good.

So I said, "What do you mean, Diotima? Is Love ugly, then, and bad?" But she said, "Watch your tongue! Do you really think that, if a thing is not beautiful, it has to be ugly?"

"I certainly do."

"And if a thing's not wise, it's ignorant? Or haven't you found out yet that there's something in between wisdom and ignorance?"

"What's that?"

e

"It's judging things correctly without being able to give a reason. Surely you see that this is not the same as knowing—for how could knowledge be unreasoning? And it's not ignorance either—for how could what hits the truth be ignorance? Correct judgment, of course, has this character: it is in between understanding and ignorance."

"True," said I, "as you say."

"Then don't force whatever is not beautiful to be ugly, or whatever is not good to be bad. It's the same with Love: when you agree he is neither good nor beautiful, you need not think he is ugly and bad; he could be something in between," she said.

"Yet everyone agrees he's a great god," I said.

"Only those who don't know?" she said. "Is that how you mean 'everyone'? Or do you include those who do know?"

"Oh, everyone together."

And she laughed. "Socrates, how could those who say that he's not a god at all agree that he's a great god?"

"Who says that?" I asked.

"You, for one," she said, "and I for another."

"How can you say this!" I exclaimed.

"That's easy," said she. "Tell me, wouldn't you say that all gods are beautiful and happy? Surely you'd never say a god is not beautiful or happy?"

"Zeus! Not I," I said.

"Well, by calling anyone happy, don't you mean they possess good and beautiful things?"

"Certainly."

"What about Love? You agreed he needs good and beautiful things, and that's why he desires them—because he needs them."

"I certainly did."

"Then how could he be a god if he has no share in good and beautiful things?"

"There's no way he could, apparently."

"Now do you see? You don't believe Love is a god either!"

"Then, what could Love be?" I asked. "A mortal?"

"Certainly not."

"Then, what is he?"

"He's like what we mentioned before," she said. "He is in between mortal and immortal."

"What do you mean, Diotima?"

"He's a great spirit, Socrates. Everything spiritual, you see, is in between god and mortal."

"What is their function?" I asked.

"They are messengers who shuttle back and forth between the two, conveying prayer and sacrifice from men to gods, while to men they bring commands from the gods and gifts in return for sacrifices. Being in the middle of the two, they round out the whole and bind fast the all to all.

"Through them all divination passes, through them the art of priests in sacrifice and ritual, in enchantment, prophecy, and sorcery. Gods do not mix with men; they mingle and converse with us through spirits instead, whether we are awake or asleep. He who is wise in any of these ways is a man of the spirit, but he who is wise in any other way, in a profession or any manual work, is merely a mechanic. These spirits are many and various, then, and one of them is Love."

b   "Who are his father and mother?" I asked.

"That's rather a long story," she said. "I'll tell it to you, all the same."

"When Aphrodite was born, the gods held a celebration. Poros, the son of Metis, was there among them. When they had feasted, Penia came begging, as poverty does when there's a party, and stayed by the gates. Now Poros got drunk on nectar (there was no wine yet, you see) and, feeling drowsy, went into the garden of Zeus, where he fell

c   asleep. Then Penia schemed up a plan to relieve her lack of resources: she would get a child from Poros. So she lay beside him and got pregnant with Love. That is why Love was born to follow Aphrodite and serve her: because he was conceived on the day of her birth. And that's why he is also by nature a lover of beauty, because Aphrodite herself is especially beautiful.

"As the son of Poros and Penia, his lot in life is set to be like theirs. In the first place,

d   he is always poor, and he's far from being delicate and beautiful (as ordinary people think he is); instead, he is tough and shriveled and shoeless and homeless, always lying on the dirt without a bed, sleeping at people's doorsteps and in roadsides under the sky, having his mother's nature, always living with Need. But on his father's side he is a schemer after the beautiful and the good; he is brave, impetuous, and intense, an awesome hunter, always weaving snares, resourceful in his pursuit of intelligence, a lover of wisdom through all his life, a genius with enchantments, potions, and clever pleadings.

e   "He is by nature neither immortal nor mortal. But now he springs to life when he gets his way; now he dies—all in the very same day. Because he is his father's son, however, he keeps coming back to life, but then anything he finds his way to always slips away, and for this reason Love is never completely without resources, nor is he ever rich.

204   "He is in between wisdom and ignorance as well. In fact, you see, none of the gods loves wisdom or wants to become wise—for they are wise—and no one else who is wise already loves wisdom. On the other hand, no one who is ignorant will love wisdom or want to become wise. For what's especially difficult about being ignorant is that you are content with yourself, even though you're neither beautiful and good nor intelligent. If you don't think you need anything, of course you won't want what you don't think you need."

b   "In that case, Diotima, who are the people who love wisdom, if they are neither wise nor ignorant?"

"That's obvious," she said. "A child could tell you. Those who love wisdom fall in between those two extremes. And Love is one of them, because he is in love with what is beautiful, and wisdom is extremely beautiful. It follows that Love must be a lover of wisdom and, as such, is in between being wise and being ignorant. This, too, comes to him from his parentage, from a father who is wise and resourceful and a mother who is not wise and lacks resource.

c   "My dear Socrates, that then is the nature of the Spirit called Love. Considering what you thought about Love, it's no surprise that you were led into thinking of Love as you did. On the basis of what you say, I conclude that you thought Love was being loved, rather than being a lover. I think that's why Love struck you as beautiful in every way: because it is what is really beautiful and graceful that deserves to be loved, and this is perfect and highly blessed; but being a lover takes a different form, which I have just described."

d   So I said, "All right then, my friend. What you say about Love is beautiful, but if you're right, what use is Love to human beings?"

"I'll try to teach you that, Socrates, after I finish this. So far, I've been explaining the character and the parentage of Love. Now, according to you, he is love for beautiful things. But suppose someone asks us, 'Socrates and Diotima, what is the point of loving beautiful things?'

"It's clearer this way: 'The lover of beautiful things has a desire; what does he desire?'"

"That they become his own," I said.

"But that answer calls for still another question, that is, 'What will this man have, when the beautiful things he wants have become his own?'"

e   I said there was no way I could give a ready answer to that question.

Then she said, "Suppose someone changes the question, putting 'good' in place of 'beautiful,' and asks you this: 'Tell me, Socrates, a lover of good things has a desire; what does he desire?'"

"That they become his own," I said.

"And what will he have, when the good things he wants have become his own?"

05   "This time it's easier to come up with the answer," I said. "He'll have happiness."

"That's what makes happy people happy, isn't it—possessing good things. There's no need to ask further, 'What's the point of wanting happiness?' The answer you gave seems to be final."

"True," I said.

"Now this desire for happiness, this kind of love—do you think it is common to all human beings and that everyone wants to have good things forever and ever? What would you say?"

"Just that," I said. "It is common to all."

b   "Then, Socrates, why don't we say that everyone is in love," she asked, "since everyone always loves the same things? Instead, we say some people are in love and others not; why is that?"

"I wonder about that myself," I said.

"It's nothing to wonder about," she said, "It's because we divide out a special kind of love, and we refer to it by the word that means the whole—'love'; and for the other kinds of love we use other words."

"What do you mean?" I asked.

"Well, you know, for example, that 'poetry' has a very wide range. After all, everything that is responsible for creating something out of nothing is a kind of poetry; and c   so all the creations of every craft and profession are themselves a kind of poetry, and everyone who practices a craft is a poet."

"True."

"Nevertheless," she said, "as you also know, these craftsmen are not called poets. We have other words for them, and out of the whole of poetry we have marked off one part, the part the Muses give us with melody and rhythm, and we refer to this by the word that means the whole. For this alone is called 'poetry,' and those who practice this part of poetry are called poets."

d   "True"

"That's also how it is with love. The main point is this: every desire for good things or for happiness is 'the supreme and treacherous love' in everyone. But those who pursue this along any of its many other ways—through making money, or through the love of sports, or through philosophy—we don't say that these people are in love, and we don't call them lovers. It's only when people are devoted exclusively to one special kind of love that we use these words that really belong to the whole of it: 'love' and 'in love' and 'lovers.'"

"I am beginning to see your point," I said.

e   "Now there is a certain story," she said, "according to which lovers are those people who seek their other halves. But according to my story, a lover does not seek the half or the whole, unless, my friend, it turns out to be good as well. I say this because people are even willing to cut off their own arms and legs if they think they are diseased. I don't think an individual takes joy in what belongs to him personally unless by 'belonging to me' he means 'good' and by 'belonging to another' he means 'bad.' Do you disagree?"

"Zeus, not I," I said.

"Now, then," she said, 'Can we simply say that people love the good?"

"Yes," I said.

"But shouldn't we add that, in loving it, they want the good to be theirs?"

"We should."

"And not only that," she said. "They want the good to be theirs forever, don't they?"

"We should add that too."

"In a word, then, love is wanting to possess the good forever."

b   "That's very true," I said.

"This, then, always is the object of love," she said. "In view of that, how do people pursue it if they are truly in love? What do they do with the eagerness and zeal we call love? What is the real purpose of love? Can you say?"

"If I could," I said, "I wouldn't be your student, filled with admiration for your wisdom, and trying to learn these very things."

c   "Well, I'll tell you," she said. "It is giving birth in beauty whether in body or in soul."

"It would take divination to figure out what you mean. I can't."

"Well I'll tell you more clearly," she said. "All of us are pregnant, Socrates, both in body and in soul, and, as soon as we come to a certain age, we naturally desire to give birth. Now no one can possibly give birth in anything ugly; only in something beautiful. That's because when a man and a woman come together in order to give birth, this is a

d   godly affair. Pregnancy, reproduction—this is an immortal thing for a mortal animal to do, and it cannot occur in anything that is out of harmony, but ugliness is out of harmony with all that is godly. Beauty, however, is in harmony with the divine. Therefore the goddess who presides at childbirth—she's called Moira or Eilithuia—is really Beauty. That's why, whenever pregnant animals or persons draw near to beauty, they become gentle and joyfully disposed and give birth and reproduce; but near ugliness they are foul faced and draw back in pain; they turn away and shrink back and do not reproduce, and because they hold on to what they carry inside them, the labor is painful. This is the source of the

e   great excitement about beauty that comes to anyone who is pregnant and already teeming with life: beauty releases them from their great pain. You see, Socrates," she said, "what Love wants is not beauty, as you think it is."

"Well, what is it, then?"

"Reproduction and birth in beauty."

"Maybe," I said.

"Certainly," she said. "Now, why reproduction? It's because reproduction goes on
207 forever; it is what mortals have in place of immortality. A lover must desire immortality
along with the good, if what we agreed earlier was right, that Love wants to possess the
good forever. It follows from our argument that Love must desire immortality."

All this she taught me, on those occasions when she spoke on the art of love. And
once she asked, "What do you think causes love and desire, Socrates? Don't you see what
b an awful state a wild animal is in when it wants to reproduce? Footed and winged animals
alike, all are plagued by the disease of Love. First they are sick for intercourse with each
other, then for nurturing their young—for their sake the weakest animals stand ready to
do battle against the strongest and even to die for them, and they may be racked with
famine in order to feed their young. They would anything for their sake. Human beings,
you'd think, would do this because they understand the reason for it; but what causes
wild animals to be in such a state of love? Can you say?"

And I said again that I didn't know.

So she said, "How do you think you'll ever master the art of love, if you don't know
that?"

"But that's why I came to you, Diotima, as I just said. I knew I needed a teacher. So
tell me what causes this, and everything else that belongs to the art of love."

"If you really believe that Love by its nature aims at what we have often agreed it
d does, then don't be surprised at the answer," she said. "For among animals the principle
is the same as with us, and mortal nature seeks so far as possible to live forever and be
immortal. And this is possible in one way only: by reproduction, because it always leaves
behind a new young one in place of the old. Even while each living thing is said to be
alive and to be the same—as a person is said to be the same from childhood till he turns
into an old man—even then he never consists of the same things, though he is called the
e same, but he is always being renewed and in other respects passing away, in his hair and
flesh and bones and blood and his entire body. And it's not just in his body, but in his
soul, too, for none of his manners, customs, opinions, desires, pleasures, pains, or fears
ever remains the same, but some are coming to be in him while others are passing away.
208 And what is still far stranger than that is that not only does one branch of knowledge
come to be in us while another passes away and that we are never the same even in respect
of our knowledge, but that each single piece of knowledge has the same fate. For what we
call studying exists because knowledge is leaving us, because forgetting is the departure
of knowledge, while studying puts back a fresh memory in place of what went away,
thereby preserving a piece of knowledge, so that it seems to be the same. And in that way
b everything mortal is preserved, not, like the divine, by always being the same in every way,
but because what is departing and aging leaves behind something new, something such
as it had been. By this device, Socrates," she said, "what is mortal shares in immortality,
whether it is a body or anything else, while the immortal has another way. So don't be
surprised if everything naturally values its own offspring, because it is for the sake of immortality that everything shows this zeal, which is 'Love.'"

c Yet when I heard her speech I was amazed, and spoke: "Well," said I, "Most wise
Diotima, is this really the way it is?"

And in the manner of a perfect Sophist she said, "Be sure of it, Socrates. Look, if
you will, at how human beings seek honor. You'd be amazed at their irrationality, if you
didn't have in mind what I spoke about and if you hadn't pondered the awful state of

love they're in, wanting to become famous and 'to lay up glory immortal forever,' and how they're ready to brave any danger for the sake of this, much more than they are for their children; and they are prepared to spend money, suffer through all sorts of ordeals,

d   and even die for the sake of glory. Do you really think that Alcestis would have died for Admetus," she asked, "or that Achilles would have died after Patroclus, or that your Codrus would have died so as to preserve the throne for his sons, if they hadn't expected the memory of their virtue—which we still hold in honor—to be immortal? Far from it,"

e   she said. "I believe that anyone will do anything for the sake of immortal virtue and the glorious fame that follows; and the better the people, the more they will do, for they are all in love with immortality.

"Now, some people are pregnant in body, and for this reason turn more to women and pursue love in that way, providing themselves through childbirth with immortality and remembrance and happiness, as they think, for all time to come; while others are pregnant in soul—because there surely are those who are even more pregnant in their souls than in their bodies, and these are pregnant with what is fitting for a soul to bear and bring to birth. And what is fitting? Wisdom and the rest of virtue, which all poets beget, as well as all the craftsmen who are said to be creative. But by far the greatest and most beautiful part of wisdom deals with the proper ordering of cities and households, and that

b   is called moderation and justice. When someone has been pregnant with these in his soul from early youth, while he is still a virgin, and, having arrived at the proper age, desires to beget and give birth, he too will certainly go about seeking the beauty in which he would beget; for he will never beget in anything ugly. Since he is pregnant, then, he is much more drawn to bodies that are beautiful than to those that are ugly; and if he also has the luck to find a soul that is beautiful and noble and well-formed, he is even more drawn to

c   this combination; such a man makes him instantly teem with ideas and arguments about virtue—the qualities a virtuous man should have and the customary activities in which he should engage; and so he tries to educate him. In my view, you see, when he makes contact with someone beautiful and keeps company with him, he conceives and gives birth to what he has been carrying inside him for ages. And whether they are together or apart, he remembers that beauty. And in common with him he nurtures the newborn; such people, therefore, have much more to share than do the parents of human children, and have a firmer bond of friendship, because the children in whom they have a share

d   are more beautiful and more immortal. Everyone would rather have such children than human ones, and would look up to Homer, Hesiod, and the other poets with envy and admiration for the offspring they have left behind—offspring, which, because they are immortal themselves, provide their parents with immortal glory and remembrance. For example," she said, "those are the sort of children Lycurgus left behind in Sparta as the saviors of Sparta and virtually all of Greece.

e   "Among you the honor goes to Solon for his creation of your laws. Other men in other places everywhere Greek or barbarian, have brought a host of beautiful deeds into the light and begotten every kind of virtue. Already many shrines have sprung up to honor them for their immortal children, which hasn't happened yet to anyone for human offspring.

210   "Even you, Socrates, could probably come to be initiated into these rites of love. But as for the purpose of these rites when they are done correctly—that is the final and highest

mystery, and I don't know if you are capable of it. I myself will tell you," she said, "and I won't stint any effort. And you must try to follow if you can.

"A lover who goes about this matter correctly must begin in his youth to devote himself to beautiful bodies. First, if the leader leads aright, he should love one body and beget
b beautiful ideas there; then he should realize that the beauty of any one body is brother to the beauty of any other and that if he is to pursue beauty of form he'd be very foolish not to think that the beauty of all bodies is one and the same. When he grasps this, he must become a lover of all beautiful bodies, and he must think that this wild gaping after just one body is a small thing and despise it.

"After this he must think that the beauty of people's souls is more valuable than the
c beauty of their bodies, so that if someone is decent in his soul, even though he is scarcely blooming in his body, our lover must be content to love and care for him and to seek to give birth to such ideas as will make young men better. The result is that our lover will be forced to gaze at the beauty of activities and laws and to see that all this is akin to itself, with the result that he will think that the beauty of bodies is a thing of no importance.
d After customs he must move on to various kinds of knowledge. The result is that he will see the beauty of knowledge and be looking mainly not at beauty in a single example—as a servant who favored the beauty of a little boy or a man or a single custom (being a slave, of course, he's low and small minded)—but the lover is turned to the great sea of beauty, and, gazing upon this, he gives birth to many gloriously beautiful ideas and theories, in unstinting love of wisdom, until, having grown and been strengthened there, he catches sight of such knowledge, and it is the knowledge of such beauty.

"Try to pay attention to me," she said, "as best you can. You see, the man who has been thus far guided in matters of Love, who has beheld beautiful things in the right order and correctly, is coming now to the goal of Loving: all of a sudden he will catch
11 sight of something wonderfully beautiful in its nature; that, Socrates, is the reason for all his earlier labors:

"First, it always is and neither comes to be nor passes away, neither waxes nor wanes. Second, it is not beautiful this way and ugly that way, nor beautiful at one time and ugly at another, nor beautiful in relation to one thing and ugly in relation to another; nor is it beautiful here but ugly there, as it would be if it were beautiful for some people and ugly for others. Nor will the beautiful appear to him in the guise of a face or hands or anything else that belongs to the body. It will not appear to him as one idea or one kind of knowledge.
b "It is not anywhere in another thing, as in an animal, or in earth, or in heaven, or in anything else, but itself by itself with itself, it is always one in form; and the other beautiful things share in that, in such a way that when those others come to be or pass away, this does not become the least bit smaller or greater nor suffer any change. So when someone rises
c by these stages through loving boys correctly, and begins to see this beauty, he has almost grasped his goal. This is what it is to go aright, or be led by another, into the mystery of Love: one goes always upward for the sake of this Beauty, starting out from beautiful things and using them like rising stairs: from one body to two and from two to all beautiful bodies, then from beautiful bodies to beautiful customs, and from customs to learning beautiful things, and from these lessons he arrives in the end at this lesson, which is learning of
d this very Beauty, so that in the end he comes to know just what it is to be beautiful.

"And there in life, Socrates, my friend," said the woman from Mantinea, "there if anywhere should a person live his life, beholding that Beauty. If you once see that, it won't occur to you to measure beauty by gold or clothing or beautiful boys and youths—who, if you see them now, strike you out of your senses, and make you, you and many others, eager to be with the boys you love and look at them forever, if there were any way to do that, forgetting food and drink, everything but looking at them and being with them. But how would it be, in our view," she said, "if someone got to see the Beautiful itself, absolute, pure, unmixed, not polluted by human flesh or colors or any other great nonsense of mortality, but if he could see the divine Beauty itself in its one form? Do you think it would be a poor life for a human being to look there and to behold it by that which he ought, and to be with it? Or haven't you remembered," she said, "that in that life alone, when he looks at Beauty in the only way that Beauty can be seen—only then will it become possible for him to give birth not to images of virtue (because he's in touch with no images), but to true virtue (because he is in touch with the true Beauty). The love of the gods belongs to anyone who has given birth to true virtue and nourished it, and if any human being could become immortal, it would be he."

This, Phaedrus and the rest of you, was what Diotima told me. I was persuaded. And once persuaded, I try to persuade others too that human nature can find no better workmate for acquiring this than Love. That's why I say that every man must honor Love, why I honor the rites of Love myself and practice them with special diligence, and why I commend them to others. Now and always I praise the power and courage of Love so far as I am able. Consider this speech, then, Phaedrus, if you wish, a speech in praise of Love. Or if not, call it whatever and however you please to call it.

II. EXCERPTS FROM PLATO'S *PHAEDRUS*[9]

Phaedrus: He is here, always right by your side, whenever you want him. Socrates: You'll have to understand, beautiful boy, that the previous speech was by Phaedrus, Pythocles's son, from Myrrhinus, while the one I am about to deliver is by Stesichorus Euphemus's son, from Himera. And here is how the speech should go:

"There's no truth to that story—that when a lover is available you should give your favors to a man who doesn't love you instead, because he is in control of himself while the lover has lost his head. That would have been fine to say if madness were bad, pure and simple; but in fact the best things we have come from madness, when it is given as a gift of the god.

"The prophetess of Delphi and the priestesses at Dodona are out of their minds when they perform that fine work of theirs for all of Greece, either for an individual person or for a whole city, but they accomplish little or nothing when they are in control of themselves. We will not mention the Sybil or the others who foretell many things by means of god-inspired prophetic trances and give sound guidance to many people—that would take too much time for a point that's obvious to everyone. But here's some evidence worth adding to our case: The people who designed our language in the old days never thought of madness as something to be ashamed of or worthy of blame; otherwise they would not have used the word 'manic' for the finest experts of all—the ones who tell the future—thereby weaving insanity into prophesy. They thought it was wonderful when it came as a gift of the gods, and that's why they gave its name to prophesy; but nowadays people don't know the fine points, so they stick in a 't' and call it 'mantic.' Similarly, the clear-headed study of the future, which uses birds and other signs, was originally called *oionoistic*, since it uses reasoning to bring intelligence (*nous*) and learning (*historia*) into human thought; but now modern speakers call it oionistic, putting on airs with their long 'o.' To the extent, then, that prophesy, mantic, is more perfect and more admirable than sign-based prediction, oionistic, in both name and achievement, madness (mania) from a god is finer than self-control of human origin, according to the testimony of the ancient language givers.

"Next, madness can provide relief from the greatest plagues of trouble that beset certain families because of their guilt for ancient crimes: it turns up among those who need a way out; it gives prophesies and takes refuge in prayers to the gods and in worship, discovering mystic rites and purifications that bring the man it touches through to safety for this and all time to come. So it is that the right sort of madness finds relief from present hardships for a man it has possessed.

"Third comes the kind of madness that is possession by the Muses, which takes a tender virgin soul and awakens it to a Bacchic frenzy of songs and poetry that glorifies the achievements of the past and teaches them to future generations. If anyone comes to the gates of poetry and expects to become an adequate poet by acquiring expert knowledge of the subject without the Muses' madness, he will fail, and his self-controlled verses will be eclipsed by the poetry of men who have been driven out of their minds.

"There you have some of the fine achievements—and I could tell you even more—that are due to god-sent madness. We must not have any fear on this particular point, then, and we must not let anyone disturb us or frighten us with the claim that you should prefer a friend who is in control of himself to one who is disturbed. Besides proving that point, if he is to win his case, our opponent, then this sort of madness is given us by the gods to ensure our greatest good fortune. It will be a proof that convinces the wise if not the clever.

"Now we must first understand the truth about the nature of the soul, divine or human, by examining what it does and what is done to it. Here begins the proof:

"Every soul is immortal. That is because whatever is always in motion is immortal, while what moves, and is moved by, something else stops living when it stops moving. So it is only what moves itself that never desists from motion, since it does not leave off being itself. In fact, this self-mover is also the source and spring of motion in everything else that moves: and a source has no beginning. That is because anything that has a beginning comes from some source, but there is no source for this, since a source that got its start from something else would no longer be the source. And since it cannot have a beginning, then necessarily it cannot be destroyed. That is because if a source were destroyed it could never get started again from anything else and nothing else could get started from it—that is, if everything gets started from a source. This then is why a self-mover is a source of motion.

"And that is incapable of being destroyed or starting up; otherwise all heaven and everything that has been started up would collapse, come to a stop, and never have cause to start moving again. But since we have found that a self-mover is immortal, we should have no qualms about declaring that this is the very essence and principle of a soul, for every bodily object that is moved from outside has no soul, while a body whose motion comes from within, from itself, does have a soul; that being nature of a soul; and if this is so—that whatever moves itself is essentially a soul—then it follows necessarily that soul should have neither birth nor death.

246   "That, then, is enough about the soul's immortality. Now here is what we must say about its structure. To describe what the soul actually is would require a very long account, altogether a task for a god in every way; but to say what it is like is humanly possible and takes less time. So let us do the second in our speech. Let us then liken the soul to the natural union of a team of winged horses and their charioteer. The gods' horses and charioteers that are themselves all good and come from good stock besides, while everyone

b   else has a mixture. To begin with, our driver is in charge of a pair of horses; second, one of his horses is beautiful and good and from stock of the same sort, while the other is the opposite and has the opposite sort of bloodline. This means that chariot driving in our case is inevitably a painfully difficult business.

"And now I should try to tell you why living things are said to include both mortal

c   and immortal beings. All souls look after all that lacks a soul, and patrol all of heaven, taking different shapes at different times. So long as its wings are in perfect condition it flies high, and the entire universe is its dominion; but a soul that sheds its wings wanders until it lights on something solid, where it settles and takes on an earthly body, which then, owing to the power of this soul, seems to move itself. The whole combination of soul and body is called a living thing, or animal, and has the designation 'mortal' as well. Such a combination cannot be immortal, not on any reasonable account. In fact it is

d   pure fiction, based neither on observation nor on adequate reasoning, that a god is an immortal living thing which has a body and a soul, and that these are bound together by nature for all time—but of course we must let this be as it may please the gods, and speak accordingly.

"Let us turn to what causes the shedding of the wings, what makes them fall away from a soul. It is something of this sort: By their nature wings have the power to lift up heavy things and raise them aloft where the gods all dwell and so, more than anything

e   that pertains to the body, they are akin to the divine, which has beauty, wisdom, goodness, and everything of that sort. These nourish the soul's wings, which grow best in their presence; but foulness and ugliness make the wings shrink and disappear.

"Now Zeus, the great commander in heaven, drives his winged chariot first in the procession, looking after everything and putting all things in order. Following him is an

247   army of gods and spirits arranged in eleven sections. Hestia is the only one who remains at the home of the gods; all the rest of the twelve are lined up in formation, each god in command of the unit to which he is assigned. Inside heaven are many wonderful places from which to look and many aisles which the blessed gods take up and back, each seeing to his own work, while anyone who is able and wishes to do so follows along, since jealousy has no place in the gods' chorus. When they go to feast at the banquet they have

b   a steep climb to the high tier at the rim of heaven; on this slope the gods' chariots move easily, since they are balanced and well under control, but the other chariots barely make it. The heaviness of the bad horse drags its charioteer toward the earth and weighs him down if he has failed to train it well, and this causes the most extreme toil and struggle that a soul will face. But when the souls we call immortals reach the top, they move out-

c   ward and take their stand on the high ridge of heaven, where its circular motion carries them around as they stand while they gaze upon what is outside heaven.

"The place beyond heaven—none of our earthly poets has ever sung or ever will sing its praises enough! Still, this is the way it is—risky as it may be, you see, I must attempt to speak the truth, especially since the truth is my subject. What is in this place is without color and without shape and without solidity, a being that really is what it is, the subject of all true knowledge, visible only to intelligence, the soul's steersman. Now a god's mind is nourished by intelligence and pure knowledge, as is the mind of any soul that is concerned to take in what is appropriate to it, and so it is delighted at last to be seeing what is real and watching what is true, feeding on all this and feeling wonderful, until the circular motion brings it around to where it started. On the way around it has a view of Justice as it is; it has a view of Self-control; it has a view of Knowledge—not the knowledge that is close to change, that becomes different as it knows the different things that we consider real down here. No, it is the knowledge of what really is what it is. And when the soul has seen all the things that are as they are and feasted on them, it sinks back inside heaven and goes home. On its arrival the charioteer stables the horses by the manger, throws in ambrosia, and gives them nectar to drink besides.

"Now that is the life of the gods. As for the other souls, one that follows a god most closely, making itself most like that god, raises the head of its charioteer up to the place outside and is carried around in the circular motion with the others. Although distracted by the horses, this soul does have a view of Reality, just barely. Another soul rises at one time and falls at another, and because its horses pull it violently in different directions, it sees some real things and misses others. The remaining souls are all eagerly straining to keep up, but are unable to rise; they are carried around below the surface, trampling and striking one another as each tries to get ahead of the others. The result is terribly noisy, very sweaty, and disorderly. Many souls are crippled by the incompetence of the drivers, and many wings break much of their plumage. After so much trouble, they all leave the sight of reality unsatisfied, and when they have gone they will depend on what they think is nourishment—their own opinions.

"The reason there is so much eagerness to see the plain where truth stands is that this pasture has the grass that is the right food for the best part of the soul, and it is the nature of the wings that lift up the soul to be nourished by it. Besides, the law of Destiny is this: If any soul becomes a companion to a god and catches sight of any true thing, it will be unharmed until the next circuit; and if it is able to do this every time, it will always be safe. If, on the other hand, it does not see anything true because it could not keep up, and by some accident takes on a burden of forgetfulness and wrongdoing, then it is weighed down, sheds its wings and falls to earth. At that point, according to the law, the soul is not born into a wild animal in its first incarnation; but a soul that has seen the most will be planted in the seed of a man who will become a lover of wisdom or of beauty, or who will be cultivated in the arts and prone to erotic love. The second sort of soul will be put into someone who will be a lawful king or warlike commander; the third, a statesman, a manager of a household, or a financier; the fourth will be a trainer who loves exercise or a doctor who cures the body; the fifth will lead the life of a prophet or priest of the mysteries. To the sixth the life of a poet or some other representational artist is properly assigned; to the seventh the life of a manual labor or farmer; to the eighth the career of a sophist or demagogue, and to the ninth a tyrant.

"Of all these, any who have led their lives with justice will change to a better fate, and any who have led theirs with injustice, to a worse one. In fact, no soul returns to

249   the place from which it came for ten thousand years, since its wings will not grow before then, except for the soul of a man who practices philosophy without guile or who loves boys philosophically. If, after the third cycle of one thousand years, the last-mentioned souls have chosen such a life three times in a row, they grow their wings back, and they depart in the three thousandth year. As for the rest, once their first life is over, they come to judgment; and, once judged, some are condemned to go to places of punishment beneath the earth and pay the full penalty for their injustice, while the others are lifted up

b   by justice to a place in heaven where they live in the manner the life they led in human form has earned them. In the thousandth year both groups arrive at a choice and allotment of second lives, and each soul chooses the life it wants. From there, a human soul can enter a wild animal, and a soul that was once human can move from an animal to a human being again. But a soul that never saw the truth cannot take a human shape, since

c   a human being must understand speech in terms of general forms, proceeding to bring many perceptions together into a reasoned unity. That process is the recollection of the things our soul saw when it was traveling with god, when it disregarded the things we now call real and lifted up its head to what is truly real instead.

"For just this reason it is fair that only a philosopher's mind grows wings, since its memory always keeps it as close as possible to those realities by being close to which the gods are divine. A man who uses reminders of these things correctly is always at the highest, most perfect level of initiation, and he is the only one who is perfect as perfect can

d   be. He stands outside human concerns and draws close to the divine; ordinary people think he is disturbed and rebuke him for this, unaware that he is possessed by god. Now this takes me to the whole point of my discussion of the fourth kind of madness—that which someone shows when he sees the beauty we have down here and is reminded of true beauty; then he takes wing and flutters in his eagerness to rise up, but is unable to do so; and he gazes aloft, like a bird, paying no attention to what is down below—and that

e   is what brings on him the charge that he has gone mad. This is the best and noblest of all the forms that possession by god can take for anyone who has it or is connected to it, and when someone who loves beautiful boys is touched by this madness he is called a lover. As I said, nature requires that the soul of every human being has seen reality; otherwise,

250   no soul could have entered this sort of living thing. But not every soul is easily reminded of the reality there by what it finds here—not souls that got only a brief glance at the reality there, not souls who had such bad luck when they fell down here that they were twisted by bad company into lives of injustice so that they forgot the sacred objects they had seen before. Only a few remain whose memory is good enough; and they are startled when they see an image of what they saw up there. Then they are beside themselves, and

b   their experience is beyond their comprehension because they cannot fully grasp what it is that they are seeing.

"Justice and self-control do not shine out through their images down here, and neither do the other objects of the soul's admiration; the senses are so murky that only a few people are able to make out, with difficulty, the original of the likenesses they encounter here. But beauty was radiant to see at that time when the souls, along with the glorious chorus (we were with Zeus, while others followed other gods), saw that blessed and spectacular vision and were ushered into the mystery that we may rightly call the blessed of

c   all. And we who celebrated it were wholly perfect and free of all the troubles that awaited us in time to come, and we gazed at sacred revealed objects that were perfect, and simple, and unshakeable and blissful. That was the ultimate vision, and we saw it in pure light because we were pure ourselves, not buried in this thing we are carrying around now, which we call a body, locked in it like an oyster in its shell.

"Well, all that was for love of a memory that made me stretch out my speech in longing for the past. Now beauty, as I said, was radiant among the other objects; and now that we have come down here we grasp it sparkling through the clearest of our senses. Vision, of course, is the sharpest of our bodily senses, although it does not see wisdom. It would awaken a terribly powerful love if an image of wisdom came through our sight as clearly as beauty does, and the same goes for the other objects of inspired love. But now beauty alone has this privilege, to be the most clearly visible and the most loved. Of course a man who was initiated long ago or who has become defiled is not to be moved abruptly from here to a vision of beauty itself, when he sees what we call beauty here; so instead of gazing at the latter reverently, he surrenders to pleasure and sets out in the manner of a four-footed beast, eager to make babies; and, wallowing in vice, he goes after unnatural pleasure too, without a trace of fear or shame. A recent initiate, however, one who has seen much in heaven—when he sees a godlike face or bodily form that has captured Beauty well, first he shudders and the fear comes over him like those he felt at the earlier time; then he gazes at him with the reverence due a god, and if he weren't afraid people would think him completely mad, he'd even sacrifice to his boy as if he were the image of a god. Once he has looked at him, his chill gives way to sweating and a high fever, because the stream of beauty that pours into him through his eyes warms him up and waters the growth of his wings. Meanwhile, the heat warms him and melts the places where the wings once grew, places that were long ago closed off with hard scabs to keep the spells from coming back; but as nourishment flows in, the feather shafts swell and rush to grow from their roots beneath every part of the soul. (Long ago, you see, the entire soul had wings.) Now the whole soul seethes and throbs in this condition. Like a child whose teeth are just starting to grow in, and its gums are all aching and itching—that is exactly how the soul feels when it begins to grow wings. It swells up and with aches and tingles as it grows them. But when it looks upon the beauty of the boy it takes in the stream of particles flowing into it from his beauty (that is why this is called 'desire'), when it is watered and warmed by this, then all its pain subsides and is replaced by joy. When, however, it is separated from the boy and runs dry, then the openings of the passages in which the feathers grow are dried shut and keep the wings from sprouting. Then the stump of each feather is blocked in its desire and it throbs like a pulsing artery while the feather pricks at its passageway, with the result that the whole soul is stung all around, and the pain simply drives it wild—but then, when it remembers the boy in his beauty, it recovers its joy. From the outlandish mix of these two feelings—pain and joy—comes anguish and helpless raving: in its madness the lover's soul cannot sleep at night or stay put by day; it rushes, yearning, wherever it expects to see the person who has that beauty. When it does see him, it opens the sluice gates of desire and sets free the parts that were blocked up before. And now that the pain and the goading have stopped, it can catch its breath and once more suck in for the moment, this sweetest of all pleasures. This it is not at all willing to give up, and no one is more important to it than the beautiful boy. It forgets mother and brothers and friends entirely and doesn't care at all if it loses its wealth through neglect. And as for proper and decorous behavior, in which it used to take pride, the soul despises the whole business. Why, it is even willing to sleep like a slave, anywhere,

b

as near to the object of its longing as it is allowed to get! That is because in addition to its reverence for one who has such beauty, the soul has discovered that the boy is the only doctor for all that terrible pain.

"This is the experience we humans call love, you beautiful boy (I mean the one to whom I am making this speech). You are so young that what the gods call it is likely to strike you as funny. Some of the successors of Homer, I believe, report two lines from the less well-known poems, of which the second is quite indecent and does not scan very well. They praise love this way:

> Yes, mortals call him powerful winged 'Love';
> But because of his need to thrust out the wings,
> the gods call him 'Shove.'

c

"You, may believe this or not as you like. But, seriously, the cause of love is as I have said, and this is how lovers really feel.

"If the man who is taken by love used to be an attendant on Zeus, he will be able to bear the burden of this feathered force with dignity. But if it is one of Ares' troops who has fallen prisoner of love—if that is the god with whom he took the circuit—then if he has the slightest suspicion that the boy he loves has done him wrong, he turns murderous, and he is ready to make a sacrifice of himself as well as the boy.

d

"So it is with each of the gods: everyone spends his life honoring the god in whose chorus he danced, and emulates that god in every way he can, so long as he remains undefiled and in his first life down here. And that is how he behaves with everyone at every turn, not just with those he loves. Everyone chooses his love after his own

e

fashion from among those who are beautiful and then treats the boy like his very own god, building him up and adorning him as an image to honor and worship. Those who followed Zeus, for example, choose someone to love who is Zeus himself in the nobility of his soul. So they make sure he has a talent for philosophy and the guidance of others, and once they have found him and are in love with him they do everything to develop that talent. If any lovers have not yet embarked on this practice, then they start to learn, using any source they can and also making progress on their own. They are

253

well equipped to track down their god's true nature with their own resources because of their driving need to gaze at the god, and as they are in touch with the god by memory they are inspired by him and adopt his customs and practices, so far as a human being can share a god's life. For all of this they know they have the boy to thank, and so they love him all the more; and if they draw their inspiration from Zeus, then, like the Bacchants, they pour it into the soul of the one they love in order to help him take

b

on as much of their own god's qualities as possible. Hera's followers look for a kingly character, and once they have found him they do all the same things for him. And so it is for followers of Apollo or any other god: They take their god's path and seek for their own a boy whose nature is like the god's; and when they have got him they emulate the god, convincing the boy they love and training him to follow their god's pattern and

c

way of life, so far as is possible in each case. They show no envy, no mean-spirited lack of generosity, toward the boy, but make every possible effort to draw him into being totally like themselves and the god to whom they are devoted. This, then, is any true lover's heart's desire: if he follows that desire in the manner I described, this friend who has been driven mad by love will secure a consummation for the one he has befriended that is as beautiful and blissful as I said—if, of course, he captures him. Here, then, is how the captive is caught:

"Remember how we divided each soul in three at the beginning of our story—two parts in the form of horses and the third in that of a charioteer? Let us continue with that. One of the horses, we said, is good, the other not; but we did not go into the details of the goodness of the good horse or the badness of the bad. Let us do that now. The horse that is on the right, or nobler, side is upright in frame and well jointed, with a high neck and a regal nose; his coat is white, his eyes are black, and he is a lover of honor with modesty and self-control; companion to true glory, he needs no whip, and is guided by verbal commands alone. The other horse is a crooked great jumble of limbs with a short bull-neck, a pug nose, black skin, and bloodshot white eyes; companion to wild beasts and indecency, he is shaggy around the ears—deaf as a post—and just barely yields to horsewhip and goad combined. Now when the charioteer looks in the eye of love, his entire soul is suffused with a sense of warmth and starts to fill with tingles and the goading of desire. As for the horses, the one who is obedient to the charioteer is still controlled, then as always, by its sense of shame, and so prevents itself from jumping on the boy. The other one, however, no longer responds to the whip or the goad of the charioteer; it leaps violently forward and does everything to aggravate its yokemate and its charioteer, trying to make them go up to the boy and suggest to him the pleasures of sex. At first the other two resist, angry in their belief that they are being made to do things that are dreadfully wrong. At last, however, when they see no end to their trouble, they are led forward, reluctantly agreeing to do as they have been told. So they are close to him now, and they are struck by the boy's face as if by a bolt of lightning. When the charioteer sees that face, his memory is carried back to the real nature of Beauty, and he sees it again where it stands on the sacred pedestal next to Self-control. At the sight he is frightened, falls over backward awestruck, and at the same time has to pull the reins back so fiercely that both horses are set on their haunches, one falling back voluntarily with no resistance, but the other insolent and quite unwilling. They pull back a little further; and while one horse drenches the whole soul with sweat out of shame and awe, the other—once it has recovered from the pain caused by the bit and its fall—bursts into a torrent of insults as soon as it has caught its breath, accusing its charioteer and yokemate of all sorts of cowardice and unmanliness for abandoning their position and their agreement. Now once more it tries to make its unwilling partners advance, and gives in grudgingly only when they beg it to wait till later. Then, when the promised time arrives, and they are pretending to have forgotten, it reminds them; it struggles, it neighs, it pulls them forward and forces them to approach the boy again with the same proposition; and as soon as they are near, it drops its head, straightens its tail, bites the bit, and pulls without any shame at all. The charioteer is now struck with the same feelings as before, only worse, and he's falling back as he would from a starting gate; and he violently yanks the bit back out of the teeth of the insolent horse, only harder this time, so that he bloodies its foul-speaking tongue and jaws, sets its legs and haunches firmly on the ground, and 'gives it over to pain.' When the bad horse has suffered this same thing time after time, it stops being so insolent; now it is humble enough to follow the charioteer's warnings, and when it sees the beautiful boy it dies of fright, with the result that now at last the lover's soul follows its boy in reverence and awe.

255   "And because he is served with all the attentions due a god by a lover who is not pretending otherwise but is truly in the throes of love, and because he is by nature disposed to be a friend of the man who is serving him (even if he has already been set against love by school friends or others who say that it is shameful to associate with a lover, and initially rejects the lover in consequence), as time goes forward he is brought by his ripening

b   age and a sense of what must be to a point where he lets the man spend time with him. It is a decree of fate, you see, that bad is never friends with bad, while good cannot fail to be friends with good. Now that he allows his lover to talk and spend time with him, and the man's good will is close at hand, the boy is amazed by it as he realizes that all the friendship he has from his other friends and relatives put together is nothing compared to that of this friend who is inspired by a god.

"After the lover has spent some time doing this, staying near the boy (and even

c   touching him during sports and on other occasions), then the spring that feeds the stream Zeus named 'Desire' when he was in love with Ganymede begins to flow mightily in the lover and is partly absorbed by him, and when he is filled it overflows and runs away outside him. Think how a breeze or an echo bounces back from a smooth solid object to its source; that is how the stream of beauty goes back to the beautiful boy and sets him a

d   flutter. It enters through his eyes, which are its natural route to the soul; there it waters the passages for the wings, starts the wings growing, and fills the soul of the loved one with love in return. Then the boy is in love, but has no idea what he loves. He does not understand, and cannot explain, what has happened to him. It is as if he had caught an eye disease from someone else, but could not identify the cause; he does not realize that he is seeing himself in the lover as in a mirror. So when the lover is near, the boy's pain is relieved just as the lover's is, and when they are apart he yearns as much as he is yearned

e   for, because he has a mirror image of love in him—'backlove'—though he neither speaks nor thinks of it as love, but as friendship. Still, his desire is nearly the same as the lover's, though weaker: he wants to see, touch, kiss, and lie down with him; and of course, as you might expect, he acts on these desires soon after they occur.

"When they are in bed, the lover's undisciplined horse has a word to say to the

256   charioteer—that after all its sufferings it is entitled to a little fun. Meanwhile, the boy's bad horse has nothing to say, but swelling with desire, confused, it hugs the lover and kisses him in delight at his great good will. And whenever they are lying together it is completely unable, for its own part, to deny the lover any favor he might beg to have. Its yokemate, however, along with its charioteer, resists such requests with modesty and reason. Now if the victory goes to the better elements in both their minds, which lead

b   them to follow the assigned regimen of philosophy, their life here below is one of bliss and shared understanding. They are modest and fully in control of themselves now that they have enslaved the part that brought trouble into the soul and set free the part that gave it virtue. After death, when they have grown wings and become weightless, they have won the first of three rounds in these, the true Olympic Contests. There is no greater good than this that either human self-control or divine madness can offer a man. If, on

c   the other hand, they adopt a lower way of living, with ambition in place of philosophy, then pretty soon when they are careless because they have been drinking or for some other reason, the pair's undisciplined horses will catch their souls off guard and together bring them to commit that act which ordinary people would take to be the happiest choice d of all; and when they have consummated it once, they go on doing this for the rest of their lives, but sparingly, since they have not approved of what they are doing with their whole minds. So these two also live in mutual friendship (though weaker than that of the philosophical pair), both while they are in love and after they have passed beyond it, because they realize they have exchanged such firm vows that it would be forbidden for them ever to break them and become enemies. In death they are wingless when they leave the body, but their wings are bursting to sprout, so the prize they have won from the madness of love is considerable, because those who have begun the sacred journey in

e lower heaven may not by law be sent into darkness for the journey under the earth; their lives are bright and happy as they travel together, and thanks to their love they will grow wings together when the time comes.

"These are the rewards you will have from a lover's friendship, my boy, and they are as great as divine gifts should be. A nonlover's companionship, on the other hand, is diluted by human self-control; all it pays are cheap, human dividends, and though the slavish attitude it engenders in a friend's soul is widely praised as virtue, it tosses the soul

57 around for nine thousand years on the earth and leads it, mindless, beneath it.

"So now, dear Love, this is the best and most beautiful palinode we could offer as payment for our debt, especially in view of the rather poetical choice of words Phaedrus made me use.

"Forgive us our earlier speeches in return for this one; be kind and gracious toward my expertise at love, which is your own gift to me: do not, out of anger, take it away

b or disable it; and grant that I may be held in higher esteem than ever by those who are beautiful. If Phaedrus and I said anything that shocked you in our earlier speech, blame it on Lysias, who was its father, and put a stop to his making speeches of this sort; convert him to philosophy like his brother Polemarchus so that his lover here may no longer play both sides as he does now, but simply devote his life to Love through philosophical discussions."

Commentary by *Eve A. Browning*, Diotima and Plato: On Love, Desire, and Wisdom

INTRODUCTION

Is there a relationship between Eros and enlightenment? As desiring and loving beings, humans are also seekers of wisdom. Desire or love, *philos*, goes together with its object wisdom, *sophia*, to give philosophy its very name. Yet human desire and human love are also notorious distractions and obstacles in the path of wisdom's attainment.

No Western philosopher has written more beautifully and passionately about this constellation of topics than Plato. In the opening scene of his great moral work *Republic*, Plato describes an encounter among friends, one of whom is advanced in years.

A brash and relatively youthful Socrates asks this aged man, whose name is Cephalus, how it feels to be old—and specifically, how he is faring in the sexual desire department. Cephalus responds that old age brings a freedom, like being freed from "many and mad masters," with its lightening of the burden of desire. Under the lash of lust, a human soul can appear to be driven along helplessly, toward good or evil. Age brings a welcome respite from this slavery.

Yet Plato's works also strongly stress a quite different way of understanding the relationship between desire, virtue, and understanding. In the *Phaedrus* and the *Symposium*, two works in which the topic of Eros is of focal importance, desire can draw the soul upward, so to speak, in a dynamic process of yearning for, seeking, and ultimately finding the transcendent reality in which alone it can truly rest. That Eros has this power to inspire and direct us in our search for wisdom is a doctrine that is one of Plato's most original and striking contributions to the development of Western philosophy. Plato is acutely aware of the distraction potential of lust and love as ordinarily experienced. Yet he also strenuously maintains that these very experiences, which can be so devastating to our rational plans, can also be indispensable steps to achieving the very highest order mental states available to humans in this lifetime.

EROS PRESENTS A PARADOX

The paradox deepens when we look more closely at the way the key discussions of Eros are presented in Plato's dialogues. In one of these discussions (in the *Phaedrus*), the character Socrates is the main speaker and sole apparent source of the ideas presented. Yet in the other (*Symposium*) a rather mysterious woman named Diotima is credited by Socrates as the sole source of the ideas, and Socrates actually impersonates Diotima when he presents the view of Eros that he attributes to her. Was Diotima a real person? Did the historical Socrates study under her direction, as the character Socrates asserts in this dialogue? These are questions that cannot be answered with certainty. But we will explore them briefly for what they recommend about gender in the context of discussions of Eros, before turning to a comparison between the two sets of views on Eros in relation to philosophical wisdom that can be derived from *Symposium* and *Phaedrus*.

First, it must be noted as important that Plato's philosophical works are not written in the first person. That is, Plato's own views are not directly expressed in any dialogue. These works consist of conversations among other persons, with typically no single set of views or viewpoint being labeled as the correct one. In most of Plato's works, Socrates is a leading character. Since we know that Socrates was a real historical person and also that Plato knew and followed this historical Socrates, it is overwhelmingly tempting to infer that whatever the character Socrates says in any dialogue represents Plato's own views and also the ones we readers should assume are the most nearly correct views. But this would be a mistake.

Plato could certainly have written philosophical essays if his interest had been in presenting and arguing for a single viewpoint. Plato's contemporaries in the field of rhetoric had perfected the argumentative essay as a literary form. Isocrates, Demosthenes, Lysias, and many others show great skill at arguing a viewpoint, supporting their claims with subsidiary arguments and examples. This type of writing was a known form and thus readily available to Plato had he been inclined toward such a purpose.

Instead, however, Plato chooses (and perfects) a quite different philosophical writing format. The medium is pure conversation (dialogue), and no accompanying or concluding essay ever appears to render the often-inconclusive exchanges more fixed and stable. Plato's works depict questions being asked and not answered; questions being transformed into quite different questions and left dangling; powerful arguments beautifully developed and imaginatively presented before they are abandoned. In a Platonic dialogue, the conclusion of the argument is often treated as the least interesting aspect of all the great conversation that transpires.

Thus it is not really possible to identify Plato (the author) with the views of any character in his dialogues; nor does it seem like a correct understanding of Plato's philosophical aims to attempt to do so. When we read a quite different philosopher such as Aristotle, who is close to Plato temporally but a world away stylistically, we are involved in a very different type of philosophical activity. In Aristotle's works, Aristotle is the speaker and he wants us to listen to him. In Plato's works, there are a plurality of speakers and it appears that we must not only listen, but also participate. Issues are not decided for us, but rather placed in a certain light for our consideration.

One of these issues revolves around the possibility that there was a historical person, a wise woman named Diotima from Mantinea, who taught the historical Socrates his most important lessons about the relationship between Eros and wisdom. This is a remarkable and very exciting possibility. The general absence of women's voices and authorship, of women's perspectives and involvement, in the project of philosophy in the ancient world is a disappointing fact. We listen mostly in vain for any of that warm tone we so appreciate in the voices of women today, that connection and instant communication. The women of the ancient intellectual world are present mostly only as men have deigned to describe them, or are absent insofar as men ignored them. How refreshing and rare it would be to have Plato's character Diotima confidently identified as a solid personage in the ancient philosophical milieu.

Some of the characters in Plato's dialogues are thus confidently identified; Socrates is the preeminent example. A man named Socrates was born 470 b.c.e. and died in 399 b.c.e. of drinking hemlock. He apparently lived a life that included marriage, children, military service, intellectual conversation, and a brief stint in public office. But did he hold the views he is made to advance in Plato's works? In other words, is Plato's Socrates identical to the historical Socrates?

Several arguments lead us to answer no. First, it is highly unlikely that any historical person would have advanced all the views, in precisely all these details, that are included in Plato's massive philosophical output. Even if Plato's main interest were in capturing all and only the actual sayings of Socrates (and this is in itself doubtful), it would be physically impossible for Plato to have written them all down as spoken, or remembered them accurately to write down later. Therefore an inevitable straying from and spinning upon the historical original would have to have taken place.

Second, it is highly unlikely that Plato did merely desire to be Socrates's "recording angel." While such master-servant relationships do seem to happen now and then in human history (think of Boswell and Johnson), Plato's originality as a writer is such that it is overwhelmingly probable that he would have added significant original touches to the conversations as he developed them into written works.

Third, Plato's writing career went on for another fifty years after Socrates was executed. During this time, the views his dialogue character Socrates was advancing, the methods he was pursuing, and the problems he was exploring, all changed and developed. Since the historical Socrates was no longer alive, it is only reasonable to infer that Plato is himself orchestrating a process that (perhaps increasingly) disconnects from the historical Socrates's actual views. Perhaps Plato's work preserves Socrates's spirit, perhaps it remains within some of his parameters. But Plato's work can hardly be considered Socrates's philosophical biography taken as a whole.

Return now to the problem of the historicity of Diotima. It can immediately be seen that, just as the historical Socrates is both more and less than the Platonic dialogue character Socrates, so also is the hypothetical historical Diotima. No solid evidence exists to show that a real woman named Diotima existed in the historical period that would have allowed her to meet and instruct the historical Socrates. But on the other hand, since it is logically impossible to prove a negative, it will never be demonstrated that no such real Diotima existed. Historical Diotima remains, and will always remain, a tantalizing possibility on the horizon of our fragmentary knowledge of the classical past.

However, the Platonic character Diotima is as real as the Platonic character Socrates, and as such she is a striking and thought-provoking individual. It is for this reason that Diotima is included in this anthology. Considered as an authoritative character in an ancient dialogue about Eros and wisdom, Diotima is eminently deserving of our study. The literary-philosophical space she inhabits is absolutely unique, since she is given the credit for creating one of the grandest visions of love's spiritual possibilities to be found in Western literature. And that vision has some very interesting ramifications, as we shall soon see.

DIOTIMA, "THE STRANGE WOMAN," ON EROS

Plato's *Symposium* has as its dramatic setting one of the most paradigmatically male of all ancient social scenes. The classical Greek symposium was a formal men's gathering with conversation, drinking, and often also fornicating as its central themes. At this particular men's party, most of those present are suffering such severe hangovers that they propose to drink moderately and take turns giving speeches, with each man "praising Love as beautifully as he can"(177D). Eros or Love is introduced as a personal deity who has received an inadequate share of praise in hymns and poems, according to at least two of the guests, Phaedrus and Erixymachus: "So great a god, and so neglected!" (177C). Socrates approves this choice of topic; how could he do otherwise, since, as he claims, "I set up to understand nothing but love matters" (ta erotica, 177E)? He worries only that the speakers who take their turns later, those at the bottom of the table near and including himself, will be at a disadvantage.

While every aspect of this beautiful dialogue is rewarding to study, and every speech in praise of Eros gives us a wealth of food for thought, we are interested particularly in the contribution of Diotima, the last formal speech of the work. Into the all-male atmosphere of this abstemious drinking party, from which even the flute-playing slave girl had been ejected as too distracting (176E), a philosophical woman's presence makes itself decisively manifest.

In a very real sense, Diotima takes Socrates's turn in the round of speeches about Eros. Socrates states that he heard a discourse about Eros "one day from a Mantinean woman named Diotima; in this subject she was skilled" (201D). He proposes to narrate to his fellow guests, "as well as I am able, the speech she delivered to me." Diotima, on that unnamed day, spoke to Socrates (and others?) about "Who and what sort of being is Eros, and . . . of his works." The form of her discourse is said to have been question and answer.

Diotima's indirect presence in the dialogue constitutes a counterbalance and a correction to what has preceded [it] in several ways: Most obviously, the dialogue so far has been an all-male conversation. This tacit presumption of male authority about Eros is tacitly challenged by the abrupt introduction of Diotima and her Socratically certified expertise. It is well known that Socrates (both the historical man and the Platonic character) professed to know nothing; it is in this epistemic humility that Socrates believes his only wisdom consists. Diotima is quoted as an expert and master of her subject. Thus, she is to be understood not only as wise, but at least on a par with, if not more knowledgeable than Socrates himself on the philosophical topic of love.

Diotima proceeds to develop a conception of Eros that is thoroughly dynamic in nature. While the preceding speeches had variously addressed Eros as the oldest of the gods, the most delicate of the gods, the bringer of the greatest blessings to humankind, and so forth (all stable qualities), Diotima maintains that Eros is a process and a dynamic ongoing synthesis. She will describe its awakening in our lives as the beginning of a spiritual journey that properly understood has no end. Thus Diotima decisively shifts the ground of the conversation, from the rather conservative and often platitudinous praises of the previous speakers, to a conceptually more complex and shifting higher ground.

Diotima will also transform the object of Eros in a way that is surprising: from the level on which Eros is understood as defining a relationship between individual human beings, she will develop the object into The Beautiful Itself, a rarified and sublime entity whose nature none of us will ever fully comprehend. Thus Diotima moves Eros from the mundane to the transcendent.

In summary, Diotima's speech in Plato's *Symposium* introduces a voice of a wise woman, Eros, into a living and dynamic psychological process, and translates the object of Eros from the human to the sublime. Throughout his narration and impersonation of Diotima's analysis, Socrates expresses not the slightest shadow of doubt as to its philosophical value. While many readers have taken this as evidence that Diotima represents "Socrates's view, ironically presented by a woman," or "Plato's own view," or even "the true view," we have already seen that such guesses rest on an incorrect reading of Plato's philosophical works and mistake his method. Diotima's interpretation of Eros and its relation to the higher human possibilities is set before the reader as a challenge to the reader's independent mind: could it be that love and desire draw the eye of the soul upward, purifying and rarefying us, transforming us and informing us, rendering us sublime? Is this the true meaning of the human drives and appetites and yearnings that begin at a humbler level, the level of an attraction to a beautiful body? Is the horizon of our desire really so vast, and so perfectly beautiful, when understood in all its fullness by Diotima?

The vision of Eros that Diotima expresses is one of the most sublime in all Western literature, and yet it is not without problems. The careful reader will perhaps wonder whether Eros in Diotima's account too quickly becomes impersonal, too readily leaves the actual human love object behind for a higher and more intellectually exciting abstraction.

This reader may also question whether an Eros, which is so completely self-driven, can ever ultimately satisfy. A skeptical reader may even ask whether, at the end of her account, Diotima is really still talking about love and desire as experienced by ordinary mortals at all. If not, has she changed the subject? If so, she has done this in an undoubtedly fascinating manner, and careful study of her account will be repaid with a rich set of challenges to our thinking about this, arguably the most important topic in human experience.

PLATO'S SOCRATES ON LOVE, DESIRE, AND WISDOM

The dramatic setting of Plato's dialogue *Phaedrus* is very different from that of the *Symposium*: the conversation of the former takes place only between two characters (Socrates and Phaedrus); it is situated outdoors and outside the walls of Athens—a situation that Socrates emphasizes is unusual for him. In the *Phaedrus*, a manuscript is read, the topic of which is a sustained argument that a "beloved" should grant sexual favors to one who is not loved, but who has some other material advantages to offer. Socrates then criticizes the argument and compositional style of this piece of rhetoric, offering an alternative speech from the hypothetical standpoint of one who loves but chooses to conceal that fact from the beloved; weirdly, this speech is delivered while Socrates's head is covered by his cloak.

Finally, an uncovered Socrates gives another speech, in which the true philosophical lover is described and genuine Eros appropriately praised. He begins (244C–D) with an argument for the immortality of the soul. "Every soul is immortal. That is because whatever is always in motion is immortal, while what moves, and is moved by, something else stops living when it stops moving." The soul is a "self-mover" (245D), having its own internal source of energy and direction; therefore "it follows necessarily that soul should have neither birth nor death."

There then follows an account of soul's nature in terms of an extended simile: "Let us . . . liken the soul to the natural union of a team of winged horses and their charioteer" (246A). One of the horses in the team is beautiful, well bred, and obedient; the other is surly, willful, and almost impossible to control.

In what follows, the linked philosophical and erotic adventures of the human soul are described within the terms of this image. The soul chariot makes a lengthy journey around the heavens and catches glimpses of reality on the "plain of truth" as it follows the chariot of some chosen god. This heavenly circuit is fraught with danger, however, since many charioteers can't keep their unruly horse in line. Many souls are injured and fall to earth to commence human life as we know it. Those who have seen much reality in their journeys will become philosophers, or lovers of beauty, or "will be cultivated in the arts and prone to erotic love" (248D). Souls that have seen less on the Plain of Truth will have lower lives: kings, commanders, statesmen, household managers, and so forth on down to the lowest type of soul: the tyrant (248E).

While living a human life, the basic division within the soul—unruly horse, biddable horse, charioteer in charge—still obtains. According to Plato's Socrates in this dialogue, the soul is a theater of division, and not a peaceful division either. Love for this soul, intrinsically divided against itself, is always to some degree a struggle among nobler and baser desires. The unruly horse represents physical desire in a low and urgent form; the nobler horse is also a figure of desire but of a loftier emotional type. The charioteer represents a rational element that has the responsibility of mediating the desires of the horses and integrating them into a rational life plan.

This process of integration can be quite a violent struggle. In the presence of an object of desire and erotic love, the charioteer wishes to hang back and admire beauty from a respectful distance, but the unruly horse drags the whole soul chariot forward with brutish lust. At this point the charioteer "violently yanks the bit back out of the teeth of the insolent horse, only harder this time, so that he bloodies its foul-speaking tongue and jaws, sets its legs and haunches firmly on the ground, and 'gives it over to pain'" (255E). After repeatedly experiencing this harsh restraint, the unruly horse develops a kind of traumatized response to its own impulses of desire, and "dies of fright" whenever it sees a love object. The soul-chariot then is able to safely approach the beloved with no danger of an excessively physical encounter. The beauty of the beloved object will remind the lover's soul of that other purer Beauty that it glimpsed in its lengthy previous lifetime(s). When equally high-minded lovers meet and study philosophy together, they literally earn their wings and will eventually be rewarded with a return to the celestial band of chariots from which they have fallen. Socrates says, "There is no greater good than this that either human self-control or divine madness can offer a man."

So far, the character Socrates in Plato's *Phaedrus*, has described erotic love in terms of conflict and struggle. A stable and valuable love relationship can only be achieved after the brutal subjugation of one of the soul's three principle elements, namely, reason, spirit, and appetite. Only after the "dark horse" of the soul has been repeatedly bloodied and traumatized into submission can a peaceful love relationship be commenced. Eros is founded upon struggle and hard-won renunciation of desires, and its stability seems always somewhat precarious as long as the dark horse survives.

This is a fascinating and turbulent view of Eros. Readers may recognize, in the three-part model of the soul, an important precursor vision to that of Sigmund Freud centuries later. Freud, too, will situate human psychological life in the midst of a precarious and costly internal struggle between dark impulses and higher-order imperatives. Freud, too, will describe psychological stability (such as it is) as founded upon the renunciation of powerful instincts.

The celestial flight of the winged souls envisioned here by Socrates presents a beautiful and imaginative picture, and it well explains our vague and occasional sense of having "once upon a time" perhaps caught a glimpse of higher realities. As loving desire can make us feel captured and bound to temporality and finitude, so also it can draw us out of ourselves and upward, in an ascending path of spiritual expansion. Socrates ends with a direct prayer to "Dear Eros" (257A), in which he dedicates his speech to the god and prays for blessings for himself and his friends.

COMPARISON OF DIOTIMA AND SOCRATES

How do Diotima and Socrates compare as Platonic theoreticians of Eros and wisdom? There are several important conceptual similarities between their accounts. Both maintain that Eros can be a source of intellectual energy and enlightenment; loving desire leads us to insight and confirms us in our philosophical quest. Thus for both accounts, the intellectual and the emotional/sexual aspects of human life are interrelated in ways that few other philosophers have acknowledged. Also for both, the intellectual trumps the emotional/sexual side in the end. At the height of the spiritual journey described by Diotima, we seem to find a purely intellectual or spiritual experience, which even a hypothetical disembodied spirit could have; and the perfect philosophical lovers of Socrates's chariot simile lie side by side in chaste conversation. In other words, sexual desire may play a role in the search for wisdom but it is not present on stage at the finale.

But there are also some interesting contrasts between their accounts. While Diotima argues for a relatively smooth linear progression from the particular love to the general, Socrates figuratively describes a bloody struggle that appears to end only in an uneasy and coercive truce. No reader of the *Phaedrus* can ever forget the violence of the psychic struggle it describes, with its image of the bloody-mouthed rebellious horse of lust and desire dragged back repeatedly until its spirit is broken and it is afraid to move on its own. This paints a dark picture of human sexual nature. Diotima's philosophical psychology is much less conflict ridden and much more harmonious. The reader herself must decide which is more grounded in reality.

In addition, while Diotima sees the Beautiful Itself as the ultimate object of all our real love and desire, in the *Phaedrus* Socrates seems to find in the experience of sexual sublimation some kind of indirect intellectual fuel for the remembrance of (logically) prior insights—the beloved is a source of energized reminders. Thus, on Socrates's account, truth and beauty are in a sense forever distant: glimpsed at best from a flying chariot across a panoramic sky, and hardly glimpsed at all most of the time. On Diotima's account, the things of this world, even in their humblest particularity, contain an imminent and indwelling spark of the divine; they can draw the mind's eye upward because of qualities they genuinely if only incompletely possess.

Readers will certainly notice many other points of comparison and difference between these two beautiful philosophical accounts of Eros and wisdom. Both challenge us to think of our lives as desiring and inquiring beings in new ways. Both make actual sexuality a promising and also problematic aspect of human experience. And in accordance with Plato's general philosophical aims, both invite the reader to enter the conversation as the most important unheard voice so far.

Questions for Reflection

According to Diotima, what is the relationship between love or Eros and wisdom?

How does Diotima support the view that love is a crucial component of the philosophical life?

What does Diotima mean by "The Beautiful Itself" and how is this the ultimate goal of philosophical lovers?

Notes

1. Alfred North Whitehead, *Process and Reality* (New York: Free Press, 1929), 39.

2. Forrest E. Baird and Walter Kaufmann, *Ancient Philosophy*, 4th ed. (Upper Saddle River, NJ: Prentice Hall, 2003), 3.

3. Donald Palmer, *Looking at Philosophy: The Unbelievable Heaviness of Philosophy Made Lighter*, 3rd ed. (Mountain View, CA: Mayfield Publishing Co., 2001), 8.

4. In her comments on an early draft of this introduction, Vicki Harper notes that although this is the common interpretation, "not all Plato scholars think Plato wanted separately existing Forms for everything, and not all accept the two-worlds, degrees of reality view of his metaphysics, even for the middle dialogues." I offer here only the common view, leaving more sophisticated scholarly debates to the discretion of the teacher or reader.

5. Mary Ellen Waithe, *A History of Women Philosophers*, vol. 1, *600 B.C. to 500 A.D.* (Dordrecht, The Netherlands: Martin Nijhoff Publishers, 1987), 5.

6. Browning takes a similar position with Aspasia, treating the Aspasia section of Plato's *Menexenus* as a woman's voice only.

7. Aspasia gives a speech about those who have died in war. The *Menexenus* is a seldom-studied minor dialogue whose authenticity has sometimes been disputed.

8. Plato, *Symposium*, in *Plato: The Collected Dialogues*, trans. by Alexander Nehamas and Paul Woodruff (Indianapolis, IN: Hackett Publishing, 1989), 45–60. Excerpts reprinted by permission of Hackett Publishing Company, Inc. All rights reserved.

9. Plato, *Phaedrus*, in *Plato: The Collected Dialogues*, trans. by Alexander Nehamas and Paul Woodruff (Indianapolis, IN: Hackett Publishing, 1989), 522–33. Excerpts reprinted by permission of Hackett Publishing Company, Inc. All rights reserved.

CHAPTER 2

Aristotle and the Late Pythagorean Women Periktione and Theano

Introduction by *Karen J. Warren*

This introduction, like the subsequent thirteen ones, are shorter in length, narrower in scope, and designed to accomplish a different objective than the introduction to chapter 1. They identify the topic of the chapter, provide brief biographies, and describe the basic positions of the chapters' philosophical pairs in order to set up the commentaries that follow. The chapter introductions are designed to answer four questions:

(1) What is key or interesting about the philosophers' lives?
(2) Is there historical information that would be helpful to understanding the pairs' philosophical positions?
(3) What are the key elements of their positions in the chapters?
(4) What are the main claims of the chapter commentary?

The common topic of this chapter is ethics. It begins with information on Pythagoreanism; it provides the historical and philosophical context that situates the ethical views of Aristotle and, especially, the Late Pythagorean women.

PYTHAGORAS, PYTHAGOREANISM, AND ARISTOTLE

Very little is known about Pythagoras (ca. 572–500 B.C.E.) since, if he wrote anything, those works have perished. He was an Ionian Greek from the island of Samos, near Miletus (see Greek map at the beginning of chapter 1). Pythagoras founded the School of Pythagoreans, a religious, political, and philosophical school that lasted about four hundred years. During at least the sixth and fifth centuries B.C.E., followers of Pythagoras are known as "Pythagoreans." Pythagoreanism refers to two distinct forms of Pythagorean philosophy: a philosophical and scientific form (*mathematikoi*) that uses mathematical principles to explain reality, and a religious form (*akousmatikoi*) that is concerned with such issues as the transmigration of souls, burial rites, and special vegetarian dietary restrictions. "Neo-Pythagoreanism" refers to the version of Pythagoreanism that was revived as a way of life before the first century B.C.E. and lasted through the first and second centuries C.E.

Sometimes it is difficult to identify the date, origin, and authorship of Pythagorean texts since the authors wrote pseudonymously. This is especially true of Neo-Pythagorean *pseudepigrapha*—spurious writings—works thought not to be written by the authors to whom they are attributed. Their date and origin are a matter of scholarly debate.

Some classical Greek scholars who were attracted to Pythagorean ideas (e.g., Plato and Aristotle) contributed to the longevity of Pythagoreanism. Unlike the Milesians, who sought to define the ultimate nature of things by positing a single element as the basic essence of the *kosmos*, Pythagoras thought the world consisted in patterns that are given by numerical formulae. Pythagoras' signature doctrine is "the world consists of numbers." Some interpret this claim to mean that everything in the cosmos and the cosmos itself is describable by mathematical laws and formulas, proportions and ratios. Sister Prudence Allen interprets it to mean that numbers and numerical relationships are the determining essences of things (i.e., the original forms of which all corporeal things are copies), not that corporeal objects consist of or are caused by noncorporeal numbers.[1] Some women Pythagoreans held that "things are numbers" means that things had to be numbered to be counted. But none of these claims really clarifies *how* the world consists of numbers. They describe the role of numbers in counting (presumably an uncontroversial claim) and in providing the metaphysical and ontological status of objects in the world.

One way to decipher what Pythagoras may have meant that addresses how the world consists of numbers is through an example. Consider the movie *A Beautiful Mind* about the brilliant and eccentric mathematician Robert Nash. In an early scene Nash is in Harvard University's courtyard attending a reception for new graduate students. He becomes distracted by the behaviors of pigeons running about. He takes out a pad and pen and, with singular focus, carefully observes their behavior while rapidly scribbling numbers on paper. Nash's behavior takes the viewer into a different world—one in which Nash seems to be frantically trying to record and represent the pigeon's patterns of movement and spatiotemporal relationships to each other through numbers. The impression is that Nash is using numbers—symbols, mathematical theorems, algorithms, proportions, and ratios—in an attempt to describe, represent, and even predict the behavior of the pigeons. This is, I think, an example of what Pythagoras meant by "the world consists of numbers."

One of the most important Pythagorean doctrines is the principle of *harmonia* ("fitting together"). Set in the context of the view that the world consists of numbers and that numbers consist of the opposites of odd and even, this principle states that, ideally, the world consists of "the concordant fitting together of opposites." In *Metaphysics*, Aristotle constructed a table of opposites—odd and even, one and many, right and left, male and female, the limited and unlimited—attributed to the Pythagoreans.[2] Ethically, the principle of *harmonia* asserts that humans ought to strive to live well-ordered, appropriate, "harmonious" lives.

In order for the world to be a harmonious whole, all opposites must be reconciled. *Harmonia* is about the world as an ideal, organic whole—an orderly, morally appropriate, nonconflictual set of arrangements that is also an expression of beauty. One important connection between Pythagoras' number theory and the principle of *harmonia* is that both appeal to the theory of numbers to claim that harmonious actions and a flourishing soul function in right proportion.

ARISTOTLE'S BIOGRAPHY AND ETHICS

Aristotle (384–322 B.C.E.) was born in Stagira, in northern Greece. When seventeen he traveled to Athens and entered Plato's Academy, remaining for forty years, until Plato's death in 348/7 B.C.E. Plato's philosophical influence is evident in all of Aristotle's work. As Martha Nussbaum writes, "Even when he is critical (a great part of the time) he expresses deep respect for Plato's genius." Continuing, she says that one ought not assume that Aristotle's criticisms occurred after Plato's death; rather "an attractive possibility is that the arguments of his brilliant pupil were among the stimuli that led Plato to rethink his cherished positions."[3]

When Plato died in 347 B.C.E., Aristotle went to Assos, on the coast of Asia Minor, where he married Pythias, and then to Mytilene, Island of Lesbos, where he tutored Alexander, the son of Philip II, king of Macedon. Aristotle returned to Athens in 335 B.C.E. and founded the Lyceum—the "Peripatetic" School, allegedly because Aristotle liked to discuss philosophy while walking. He retired to Chalchis, where he died in 322 of a digestive illness.[4]

The extant works by Aristotle (probably lecture notes) are often classified according to three categories: (1) logic and metaphysics; (2) nature, biology (life), and psychology (mind); and (3) ethics, politics, and art. It is his work on ethics that is the subject of this chapter.

Aristotle's ethics is an *aretaic* ethic—a virtue or character-based ethics. First, *aretaic* ethics require the development of the virtues and human excellences that are necessary for a sound disposition and the ability to respond appropriately. For Aristotle, goodness of character has to be developed by practice, by doing virtuous acts, which will then develop into a habitual sound disposition.

Aristotle's *aretaic* ethic is intimately connected with other Aristotelian doctrines: the second is that human life has a *telos* (goal, function, purpose), which is the "excellence" (*arête*) of being human. The *telos* of human life is *eudaimonia*—human flourishing—rather than human happiness, as it is often defined. As such, Aristotle's ethics is teleological rather than deontological. Third, there are two main ways to fulfill our human function (*telos*), two kinds of human excellence: moral excellence—a character trait or settled disposition—and intellectual excellence, which is either the use of theoretical wisdom, *sophia*, or practical wisdom, *phronesis*. Practical wisdom is knowing how to make applied value judgments in order to achieve virtue. Fourth, virtue is about having the right amount of something (e.g., the right amount of fear, the right amount of anger). Virtue is a means between two extremes, each of which are vices—one an excess and one a defect—either in regard to a feeling or in regard to an action.

Aristotle's *aretaic* ethic based on virtue presupposes a fifth position, Aristotle's Doctrine of the Mean; this doctine clarifies what the "right amount" of something is: morally appropriate action and emotional responses avoid excess and defect and "act in accordance with the mean." The Doctrine of the Mean thereby functions as a guide to right conduct, where human excellence is a state between the extremes of excess and deficiency.

Aristotle would say that one could give away too much money and impoverish oneself, which is a defect of character, or one could give away too little money, and be a miser, which is also a defect of character. So, as a sixth point, the virtue of exercising generosity is a practical judgment using our reason to determine the appropriate means. When one lives in accordance with the mean, the soul achieves its excellence, *eudaimonia*, which is an outgrowth of the mutual interaction of theoretical and practical wisdom. According to *eudiamonia*, all good actions have a certain order or proportion (akin to Pythagoras's "numbers"?). So, one comes around full circle: the Pythagorean principle of *harmonia* is thus comparable to Aristotle's *aretaic* ethics: ethics is doing or acting in accordance with what is appropriate or fitting in concrete situations.

THE LATE PYTHAGOREAN WOMEN: PERIKTIONE AND THEANO

According to Sister Prudence Allen, key Pythagorean themes include the special significance of the principle of *harmonia*; the separate education of men and women, the virtue of obedience of wives to their husbands (with the proviso that the virtue of temperance or moderation is more common to women, while courage and justice are common to both); the importance of modesty; and the need for everyone to study philosophy and to seek wisdom. Although women's nature and morally appropriate tasks are different from men's, women are not of lesser value; women and men are morally equal and both should be educated. Pythagoreans also believed that the soul is immortal; it transmigrates and may be reincarnated as bodies with very different lives (humans, nonhuman animals, and in some cases plants)—a view rejected by Aristotle. Last, to actualize the principle of *harmonia*, the universe needs to function as an organic, harmonious whole, where all opposites are reconciled. This requires acting temperately, moderately, and in ethically fitting ways.[5]

For our purposes, there are two groups of Pythagorean women philosophers: the Early Pythagorean women, who lived during the sixth and fifth centuries B.C.E., and the Late Pythagoreans, who lived during the fourth and third centuries B.C.E.[6] The Early Pythagoreans include Themistoclea (Theoclea or Aristoclea) and, according to some sources, Theano of Crotona, most famous of the women Pythagoreans who was the wife of Pythagoras, a teacher in Pythagoras's school, and later its director. The Early Pythagoreans also include the three daughters of Pythagoras and Theano—Arignote, Myia, and Damo—who were educated in their parents' school and accepted the Pythagorean belief about the mathematical nature of the cosmos. Myia's "Letter to Phyllis," for example, discusses the harmonious care and rearing of newborns—and other aspects of domestic living—in terms of what Aristotle would call moderation, the virtue of the mean.[7]

The pairing of Aristotle with the writings of the two Late Pythagorean women Periktione and Theano is based on four considerations: (1) They are roughly Aristotle's historical contemporaries whose ethical views are greatly influenced by Pythagorean doctrines. (2) These Late Pythagorean women apply the Pythagorean principle of *harmonia* to such practical matters as how to run a harmonious household. (3) Their writings reveal a conception of human excellence (*arête*), as expressed through Aristotelian-identified themes of moral and intellectual excellences. Last, (4) the concept of *eudaimonia*, central to Aristotle's ethics, is expressed in the letters of Periktione and Theano.

HARPER'S COMMENTARY

In her commentary, Vicki Harper compares Aristotle's Doctrine of the Mean and the Pythagorean principle of *harmonia*. Both concern the idea of appropriate or fitting ways of living and are intended as guides for moral action—to help us respond in ways that are fitting or appropriate to variable contexts by avoiding excess and deficiency.

Harper discusses four similarities and two dissimilarities between Aristotle's ethics and the ethics of the two Late Pythagorean women. Her helpful, clear account illustrates these comparisons by appealing to some doctrines not discussed in this introduction, such as Pythagorean metaphysics with regard to human nature and the soul, the immortality of the soul, and its transmigration. Appeal to them helps account for the Pythagorean women's views about sex-gender roles, perceived injustices, and such practical matters as dietary restrictions in raising children. After describing dissimilarities between their views and Aristotle's metaphysics, Harper ends by considering whether the Late Pythagorean women are, and should properly be called, philosophers whose writings are philosophical texts. This question is raised throughout the book about other philosophical pairs in other commentaries.

Excerpts of Writings by Aristotle and the Late Pythagorean Women

I. EXCERPTS FROM ARISTOTLE'S *NICOMACHEAN ETHICS* (NE)[8]

1. NE Book II Chapter 1 (Excerpts 1103a–1103b)

Virtue, then, is of two kinds: that of the intellect and that of character. Intellectual virtue owes its origin and development mainly to teaching, for which reason its attainment requires experience and time; virtue of character (êthos) is a result of habituation (ethos, for which reason it has acquired its name through a small variation on "ethos." From this it is clear that none of the virtues of character arises in us by nature. For nothing natural can be made to behave differently by habituation. For example, a stone that naturally falls downward could not be made by habituation to rise upward, not even if one tried to habituate it by throwing it up ten thousand times; nor can fire be habituated to burn downward, nor anything else that naturally behaves in one way be habituated to behave differently. So virtues arise in us neither by nature nor contrary to nature, but nature gives us the capacity to acquire them, and completion comes through habituation.

Again, in all cases where something arises in us by nature, we first acquire the capacities and later exhibit the activities. This is clear in the case of the senses, since we did not acquire them by seeing often or hearing often; we had them before we used them, and did not acquire them by using them. Virtues, however, we acquire by first exercising them. The same is true with skills, since what we need to learn before doing, we learn by doing; for example, we become builders by building, and lyre players by playing the lyre. So too we become just by doing just actions, temperate by temperate actions, and courageous by courageous actions. What happens in cities bears this out as well, because legislators make the citizens good by habituating them, and this is what every legislator intends. Those who do not do it well miss the target; and it is in this respect that a good political system differs from a bad one.

Again, as in the case of a skill, the origin and means of the development of each virtue are the same as those of its corruption; it is from playing the lyre that people become good and bad lyre players. And it is analogous in the case of builders and all the rest, since from building well, people will be good builders, from building badly, bad builders. If this were not so, there would have been no need of a person to teach them, but they would all have been born good or bad at their skill.

It is the same, then, with the virtues. For by acting as we do in our dealings with other men, some of us become just, others unjust; and by acting as we do in the face of danger, and becoming habituated to feeling fear or confidence, some of us become courageous, others cowardly. The same goes for cases of appetites and anger; by conducting themselves in one way or the other in such circumstances, some become temperate and even tempered, others intemperate and bad tempered. In a word, then, like states arise from like activities. This is why we must give a certain character to our activities, since it is on the differences between them that the resulting states depend. So it is not unimportant how we are habituated from our early days; indeed it makes a huge difference—or rather all the difference.

2. NE Book II Chapter 2 (Excerpts 1103b–1104b)

The branch of philosophy we are dealing with at present is not purely theoretical like the others, because it is not in order to acquire knowledge that we are considering what virtue is, but to become good people—otherwise there would be no point in it. So we must consider the matter of our actions, and in particular how they should be performed, since, as we have said, they are responsible for our states developing in one way or another.

The idea of acting in accordance with right reason is a generally accepted one. Let us take it for granted—we shall discuss it later, both what right reason is and how it is related to the other virtues. But this we must agree on before we begin: that the whole account of what is to be done ought to be given roughly and in outline. As we said at the start, the accounts we demand should be appropriate to their subject matter; and the spheres of actions and of what is good for us, like those of health, have nothing fixed about them.

Since the general account lacks precision, the account at the level of particulars is even less precise. For they do not come under any skill or set of rules; agents must always look at what is appropriate in each case as it happens, as do doctors and navigators. But, though our present account is like this, we should still try to offer some help.

First, then, let us consider this—the fact that states like this are naturally corrupted by deficiency and excess, as we see in the cases of strength and health (we must use clear examples to illustrate the unclear); for both too much exercise and too little ruin one's strength, and likewise too much food and drink and too little ruin one's health, while the right amount produces, increases, and preserves it. The same goes, then, for temperance, courage, and the other virtues: the person who avoids and fears everything, never standing his ground, becomes cowardly, while he who fears nothing, but confronts every danger, becomes rash. In the same way, the person who enjoys every pleasure and never restrains himself becomes intemperate, while he who avoids all pleasure—as boors do—becomes, as it were, insensible. Temperance and courage, then, are ruined by excess and deficiency, and preserved by the mean.

Not only are virtues produced and developed from the same origins and by the same means as those from which and by which they are corrupted, but the activities that flow from them will consist in the same things. For this is also true in other more obvious cases, like that of strength. It is produced by eating a great deal and going through a great deal of strenuous exercise, and it is the strong person who will be most able to do these very things. The same applies to virtues. By abstaining from pleasures we become temperate, and having become so we are most able to do these very things. Similarly with courage: by becoming habituated to make light of what is fearful and to face up to it, we become courageous; and when we are, we shall be the most able to face it.

3. NE Book II Chapter 3 (Excerpts 1104b–1105a)

We must take as an indication of a person's states the pleasure or pain consequent on what he does, because the person who abstains from bodily pleasure and finds his enjoyment in doing just this is temperate, while the person who finds doing it oppressive is intemperate, and the person who enjoys facing up to danger, or at least does not find it painful to do so, is courageous, while he who does find it painful is a coward. For virtue of character is concerned with pleasures and pains: it is because of pleasure that we do bad actions, and pain that we abstain from noble ones. It is for this reason that we need to have been brought up in a particular way from our early days, as Plato says, so we might find enjoyment or pain in the right things; for the right education is just this.

Again, if the virtues are to do with actions and situations of being affected, and pleasure and pain follow from every action and situation of being affected, then this is another reason why virtue will be concerned with pleasures and pains.

Again, as we said recently, every state of the soul is naturally related to, and concerned with, the kind of things by which it is naturally made better or worse. It is because of pleasures and pains that people become bad—through pursuing or avoiding the wrong ones, or at the wrong time, or in the wrong manner, or in any other of the various ways distinguished by reason. This is why some have classified virtues as forms of insensibility or states of rest; but this is wrong, because they speak without qualification, without saying "in the right way" and "in the wrong way," "at the right time" and "at the wrong time," and the other things one can add.

We assume, then, that virtue will be the sort of state to do the best actions in connection with pleasures and pains, and vice the contrary. The following considerations should also make it plain to us that virtue and vice are concerned with the same things.

There are three objects of choice—the noble, the useful, and the pleasant—and three of avoidance—their contraries, the shameful, the harmful, and the painful. In respect of all of these, especially pleasure, the good person tends to go right, and the bad person to go wrong. For pleasure is shared with animals, and accompanies all objects of choice, because what is noble and what is useful appear pleasant as well.

Again, pleasure has grown up with all of us since infancy and is consequently a feeling difficult to eradicate, ingrained as it is in our lives. And, to a greater or lesser extent, we regulate our actions by pleasure and pain. Our whole inquiry, then, must be concerned with them, because whether we feel enjoyment and pain in a good or bad way has great influence on our actions.

Again, as Heraclitus says, it is harder to fight against pleasure than against spirit. But both skill and virtue are always concerned with what is harder, because success in what is harder is superior. So this is another reason why the whole concern of virtue and political science is pleasures and pains; the person who manages them well will be good, while he who does so badly will be bad.

Let it be taken as established, then, that virtue is to do with pleasures and pains, that the actions which produce it also increase it, or, if they assume a different character, corrupt it; and that the sphere of its activity is the actions that themselves give rise to it.

4. NE II Chapter 5 (Excerpts 1105b–1106a)

Next we must consider what virtue is. There are three things to be found in the soul—feelings, capacities, and states—so virtue should be one of these. By feelings, I mean appetite, anger, fear, confidence, envy, joy, love, hate, longing, emulation, pity, and in general things accompanied by pleasure or pain. By capacities, I mean the things on the basis of which we are described as being capable of experiencing these feelings—on the basis of which, for example, we are described as capable of feeling anger, fear, or pity. And by states I mean those things in respect of which we are well or badly disposed in relation to feelings. If, for example, in relation to anger, we feel it too much or too little, we are badly disposed; but if we are between the two, then [we are] well disposed. And the same goes for the other cases.

Neither the virtues nor the vices are feelings, because we are called good or bad on the basis not of feelings, but of our virtues and vices; and also because we are neither praised nor blamed on the basis of our feelings (the person who is afraid or angry is not praised, and the person who is angry without qualification is not blamed but rather the person who is angry in a certain way), but we are praised or blamed on the basis of our virtues and vices. Again, we become angry or afraid without rational choice, while the virtues are rational choices or at any rate involve rational choice. Again, in respect of our feelings, we are said to be moved, while in respect of our virtues and vices we are said not to be moved but to be in a certain state.

For these reasons they are not capacities either. For we are not called either good or bad, nor are we praised or blamed, through being capable of experiencing things, without qualification. Again, while we have this capacity by nature, we do not become good or bad by nature; we spoke about this earlier.

So if the virtues are neither feelings nor capacities, it remains that they are states. We have thus described what virtue is generically.

5. NE Book II Chapter 6 (Excerpts 1106a–1107a)

But we must say not just that virtue is a state, but what kind of state. We should mention, then, that every virtue causes that of which it is a virtue to be in a good state, and to perform its characteristic activity well. The virtue of the eye, for example, makes it and its characteristic activity good, because it is through the virtue of the eye that we see well. Likewise, the virtue of the horse makes a horse good—good at running, or carrying its rider, and at facing the enemy. If this is so in all cases, then the virtue of a human being too will be the state that makes a human being good and makes him perform his characteristic activity well.

We have already said how this will happen, and it will be clear also from what follows, if we consider what the nature of virtue is like.

In everything continuous and divisible, one can take more, less, or an equal amount and each either in respect of the thing itself or relative to us; and the equal is a sort of mean between excess and deficiency. By the mean in respect of the thing itself I mean that which is equidistant from each of the extremes, this being one single thing and the same for everyone, and by the mean relative to us I mean that which is neither excessive nor deficient—and this is not one single thing, nor is it the same for all. If, for example, ten are many and two are few, six is the mean if one takes it in respect of the thing, because it is by the same amount that it exceeds the one number and is exceeded by the other. This is the mean according to the arithmetic progression. The mean relative to us, however, is not to be obtained in this way. For if ten pounds of food is a lot for someone to eat, and two pounds a little, the trainer will not necessarily prescribe six; for this may be a lot or a little for the person about to eat it—for Milo, a little, for a beginner at gymnastics, a lot. The same goes for running and wrestling. In this way every expert in a science avoids excess and deficiency, and aims for the mean and chooses it—the mean, that is, not in the thing itself but relative to us.

If, then, every science does its job well in this way, with its eye on the mean and judging its products by this criterion (which explains why people are inclined to say of successful products that nothing can be added or taken away from them, implying that excess and deficiency ruin what is good in them, while the mean preserves it, and why those who are good at the skills have their eye on this, as we say, in turning out their products) and if virtue, like nature, is more precise and superior to any skill, it will also be the sort of thing that is able to hit the mean.

I am talking here about virtue of character, since it is this that is concerned with feelings and actions, and it is in these that we find excess, deficiency, and the mean. For example, fear, confidence, appetite, anger, pity, and in general pleasure and pain can be experienced too much or too little, and in both ways not well. But to have them at the right time, about the right things, toward the right people, for the right end, and in the right way, is the mean and best; and this is the business of virtue. Similarly, there is an excess, a deficiency, and a mean in actions. Virtue is concerned with feelings and actions, in which excess and deficiency constitute misses of the mark, while the mean is praised and on target, both of which are characteristics of virtue. Virtue, then, is a kind of mean, at least in the sense that it is the sort of thing that is able to hit a mean.

Again, one can miss the mark in many ways (since the bad belongs to the unlimited, as the Pythagoreans portrayed it, and the good to the limited), but one can get things right in only one (for which reason one is easy and the other difficult—missing the target easy, hitting it difficult). For these reasons as well, then, excess and deficiency are characteristics of vice, the mean characteristic of virtue: a state involving rational choice, consisting in a mean relative to us and determined by reason—the reason, that is, by reference to which the practically wise person would, for good people are just good, while bad people are bad in all sorts of ways. Virtue, then, is a determinant. It is a mean between two vices, one of excess, the other of deficiency. It is a mean also in that some vices fall short of what is right in feelings and actions, and others exceed it, while virtue both attains and chooses the mean. So, in respect of its essence and the definition of its substance, virtue is a mean, while with regard to what is best and good it is an extreme.

But not every action or feeling admits of a mean. For some have names immediately connected with depravity, such as spite, shamelessness, envy, and, among actions, adultery, theft, homicide. All these, and others like them, are so called because they themselves, and not their excesses or deficiencies, are bad. In their case, then, one can never hit the mark, but always misses. Nor is there a good or bad way to go about such things—committing adultery, say, with the right woman, at the right time, or in the right way. Rather, doing one of them, without qualification, is to miss the mark.

It would be equally wrong, therefore, to expect there to be a mean, an excess, and a deficiency in committing injustice, being a coward, and being intemperate, since then there would be a mean of excess and a mean of deficiency, an excess of excess and a deficiency of deficiency. Rather, just as there is no excess or deficiency of temperance and courage, because the mean is, in a sense, an extreme, so too there is no mean, excess, or deficiency in the cases above. However they are done, one misses the mark, because, generally speaking, there is neither a mean of excess or deficiency, nor an excess or deficiency of a mean.

6. NE Book VIII Chapter 10 (Excerpts 1160a–1160b)

There are three species of polity, and an equal number of deviations from them—corruptions of them, so to speak. The three are kingship, aristocracy, and a third based on ownership of property (*timema*), which it seems proper to call timocratic, though most people usually call it a polity. The best of these is kingship, the worst timocracy.

The deviation from kingship is tyranny. Though both are monarchic, there is a very great difference between them: the tyrant looks to his own advantage, the king to that of his subjects. For a person is not a king unless he is self-sufficient and superior in all that is good; such a person needs nothing further, so he will look not to his own interests but to that of his subjects. A king who is not like this would be a king in name only.

Oligarchy emerges from aristocracy though the vice of the rulers, who distribute what belongs to the city contrary to merit—to themselves, all or most of what is good, and offices always to the same people, regarding wealth as the most important factor. So it is a few bad people who rule, and the wicked instead of the best.

Democracy emerges from timocracy, since they have the same boundary. For timocracy too is meant to be rule by the majority, and everyone with property is equal. . . . One can also find in households resemblances to these political systems and, as it were, models of them. The community of a father and his sons has the form of a kingship, since the father cares for his children. . . .

The community constituted by man and woman appears aristocratic, since the man rules in accordance with merit and in those areas in which a man should rule; but whatever befits a woman, he places in her hands. If, however, the man is in charge of everything, the relation changes into oligarchy; for he does this contrary to merit and not in so far as he is superior. Sometimes, however, women rule, because they are heiresses; their rule is thus not in accordance with virtue, but due to wealth and power, as in oligarchies.

The community constituted by brothers is a timocracy, since they are equal, except in so far as they differ in age; so if their ages vary greatly, the friendship is no longer fraternal.

Democracy is found most of all in households lacking a master, since everyone there is on an equal footing, and in those where the person in charge is weak and everyone can do as he likes.

7. NE Book VIII Chapter 11 (Excerpts 1161a–1161b)

In a tyranny, there is little or no friendship. For when ruler and ruled have nothing in common, since there is no justice, there is no friendship either. Take, for example, the relation of craftsman to tool, and soul to body. The latter in each pair is benefited by its user, but there is neither friendship nor justice toward soulless things. Nor is there any toward an ox, or even a slave, in so far as he is a slave; for master and slave have nothing in common since a slave is a tool with a soul, while a tool is a slave without one. In so far as he is a slave, then, there cannot be friendship with him.

But there can be friendship in so far as he is a human being, since there does seem to be justice of some kind between any human and any other capable of community in law and agreement. So there can also be friendship, in so far as he is a human being.

8. NE Book VIII Chapter 12 (Excerpt 1162a)

The friendship of man and woman also seems natural. For human beings naturally tend to form couples more than to form cities, in as much as the household is antecedent to the city, and more necessary, and reproduction is more widely shared with animals.

With other animals, the community extends only to this point, but human beings live together not only for reproductive purposes but also to supply what they need for life. For from the start their characteristic activities are divided, those of the man being different from those of the woman. They supply one another's needs, therefore, by putting their own talents to the common good. These reasons explain why this friendship seems to include both utility and pleasure. But it may also be a friendship for virtue, if they are good, since each has his or her own virtue, and can find enjoyment in this. Children seem to be another bond, which is why childless people separate more quickly: children are a good, which is common to both, and what is common holds things together.

9. NE Book IX Chapter 3 (Excerpts 1165a–1165b)

Another puzzle that arises is whether or not to break off friendships with those who do not remain the same. Presumably there is nothing odd in breaking off friendships based on utility or pleasure when our friends no longer have these qualities. For it was the qualities we loved, and when they disappear, not loving is reasonable. . . .

But if we accept another person as good, and he turns out to be an obvious villain, should we continue to love him? Or is that not impossible, if not everything is worthy of love, but only what is good? What is bad is not worthy of love nor should it be loved; we should not love what is bad, nor act like someone shameful, and we have already said that like is friendly to like.

Should it then be dissolved immediately? Or is this required not in all cases, but only when they are incurably wicked? If they could be reformed, we should save their character more than their property in so far as character is better and more a part of friendship. But someone who does dissolve such a friendship would not seem to be doing anything odd, because he did not become a friend of a person like this. So if his friend has altered, and he cannot redeem him, he gives up.

II. EXCERPT FROM ARISTOTLE'S *METAPHYSICS*[9]

The Pythagoreans, as they are called, devoted themselves to mathematics; they were the first to advance this study, and having been brought up in it they thought its principles were the principles of all things . . . and in numbers they seemed to see many resemblances to the things that exist and come into being—more than in fire and earth and water (such a modification of numbers being justice, another being soul and reason, another being opportunity—and similarly almost all other things being numerically expressible); since, again, they saw that the attributes and the ratios of the musical scales were expressible in numbers; since, then, all other things seemed in their whole nature to be modeled after numbers, and numbers seemed to be the first things in the whole of nature, they supposed the elements of numbers to be the elements of all things, and the whole heaven to be a musical scale and a number.

Other members of this same school say there are ten principles, which they arrange in two columns of cognates—limit and unlimited, odd and even, one and plurality, right and left, male and female, resting and moving, straight and curved, light and darkness, good and bad, square and oblong.

III. EXCERPT FROM PORPHYRY[10]

First he [Pythagoras] declares that the soul is immortal; then that it changes into other kinds of animals; in addition that things that happen recur at certain intervals, and nothing is absolutely new; and that all things that come to be must be thought akin.

IV. EXCERPTS FROM THE LATE PYTHAGOREAN WOMEN TEXTS[11]

Dates and places of origin of these texts are uncertain and highly controversial. However, on philological and other grounds we know that the letters attributed to Theano were not written by Pythagoras' wife (or daughter) Theano. The Theano letters must be Hellenistic or later; that is, not earlier than the fourth century B.C.E. It also was an established convention for later Pythagoreans to attribute their works to well-known Early Pythagoreans. These pseudepigrapha were not forgeries in a modern sense; nor were they intended to deceive. Moreover, even in antiquity, more than one person could have the same name.[12]

Theano's letters are written in Attic Greek (Letters to Kallisto and Nikostrate) and Attic Koine (Letter to Euboule). Periktione's *On the Harmony of Women* is written in Ionic Greek, with a few Doric touches. Thesleff suggests a date of fourth-to-third century B.C. for the Periktione text. Plato's mother, who lived during the fifth-to-fourth centuries B.C., was named Periktione.

1. Letter from Theano to Euboule[13]

Theano to Euboule: Greetings. I hear that you are raising your children in luxury. The mark of a good mother is not attention to the pleasure of her children but education with a view to temperance. Look out lest you accomplish not the work of a loving mother, but that of a doting one. When pleasure and children are brought up together, it makes the children undisciplined. What is sweeter to the young than familiar pleasure? One must take care, my friend, lest the upbringing of one's children become their downfall. Luxury perverts nature when children become lovers of pleasure in spirit and sensualists in body, mentally afraid of toil and physically soft. Indeed, a mother must exercise her charges in the things they dread, even if this causes them some pain and distress, so that they shall not become slaves of their feelings—greedy for pleasure and shrinking from pain—but, rather, shall honor virtue above everything and be able to abstain from pleasure and to withstand pain.

Don't let them be sated with nourishment, nor gratified in their every pleasure. Such lack of restraint in childhood makes them unbridled. It lets them say anything and try everything; especially if you take alarm every time they cry out, and always take pride in their laughter, smiling indulgently even if they strike their nurse or taunt you; and if you insist on keeping them unnaturally cool in summer and warm in winter, giving them every luxury. Poor children have no experience of these things; yet they grow up readily enough—they grow no less and become stronger by far. But you nurse your children like the scions of Sardanapallos, enfeebling their manly natures with pleasures. What would you make of a child who, if he does not eat sooner, clamors; who, whenever he eats, craves the delights of delicacies; who wilts in the heat and is felled by the cold; who, if someone finds fault with him, strikes back; who, if one does not cater to his every pleasure, is aggrieved; who, if he does not chew on something, is discontent; who gets into mischief just for the fun of it, and stutters about, perplexed?

Take care, my friend—conscious of the fact that children who live licentiously become slaves when they blossom to manhood—to deprive them of such pleasures. Make their nourishment austere rather than sumptuous, let them endure both hunger and thirst, both cold and heat, and even shame, whether before their peers or their overseers. This is how they turn out to be brave in spirit no matter whether they are exalted or tormented. Hardships, my dear, serve as a hardening-up process for children, a process by which virtue is perfected. Those who have been dipped sufficiently in hardships bear the tempering bath of virtue as a more natural thing. So look out, dear, lest—just as vines that have been improperly tended are deficient in fruit—your children produce the evil fruit of licentiousness and worthlessness, all because of luxury. Farewell.

2. Letter from Theano to Kallisto[14]

Theano to Kallisto: To you younger women, just as soon as you are married, authority is granted by law to govern the household. But, to do well, instruction about household management is needed from older women: a continual source of advice. It is well to learn what you do not know ahead of time and to deem most proper the advice of older women; in these matters a young soul must be brought up from girlhood. The primary authority of women in the household is authority over the servants. And the greatest thing, my dear, is good will on the slave's part. For this possession is not bought along with their bodies; rather, intelligent mistresses bring it about in time. Just usage is the cause of this—seeing to it that they are neither worn out by toil nor incapacitated because of deprivation.

For they are human in nature. There are some women who suppose the profitable to be what is most unprofitable: maltreatment of their servants, overburdening them with tasks to be done, and depriving them of the things they need. And then, having made much of an obol's profit,[15] they pay the price in enormous damages: ill will and the worst treacheries. As for you, let there be ready at hand a measure of food that is proportionate to the amount of wool work produced by a day's labor. With respect to the diet of your servants, this will suffice. As for undisciplined behavior, one must assist to the utmost what is fitting for you not what is advantageous to them. For it is necessary to estimate one's servants at their proper worth. On the one hand, cruelty will not bring proper gratitude to a soul; on the other hand, reasoning, no less than righteous indignation is an effective means of control. But if there should be too much unconquerable vice on the part of the servants, one must send them away to be sold. Let what is alien to the needs [of the house] be estranged from its mistress as well.

Let proper judgment of this take precedence so that you will determine the true facts of wrongdoing in keeping with the justice of the condemnation, and the magnitude of wrongdoing in proportion to the proper punishment. But sometimes the mistress's forgiveness and kindness toward those who have erred will release them from penalties. In this way, too, you will preserve a fitting and appropriate mode of life. There are some women, my dear, who because they are cruel—brutalized by jealousy or anger—even whip the bodies of their servants as if they were inscribing the excess of their bitterness as a memorandum. In time, some of these [female servants] are used up, utterly worked out; others procure safety by escaping; but some stop living, withdrawing into death by their own hands. In the end, the isolation of the mistress, bewailing her lack of consideration, finds desolate repentance. But, my dear, likening yourself to musical instruments, know what sounds they make when [their strings] are loosened too much, but that they are snapped asunder when stretched too tight. It is the same way for your servants. Too much license creates dissonance in the matter of obedience, but the stretching of forceful necessity causes the dissolution of nature itself. One must meditate upon this: "Right measure is best in everything." Farewell.

3. Letter from Theano to Nikostrate[16]

Theano to Nikostrate: Greetings. I hear repeatedly about your husband's madness: he has a courtesan; also that you are jealous of him. My dear, I have known many men with the same malady. It is as if they are hunted down by these women and held fast, as if they had lost their minds. But you are dispirited by night and by day; you are sorely troubled and contrive things against him. Don't you, at least, be that way, my dear. For the moral excellence of a wife is not surveillance of her husband but companionable accommodation; it is in the spirit of accommodation to bear his folly.

If he associates with the courtesan with a view toward pleasure, he associates with his wife with a view toward the beneficial. It is beneficial not to compound evils with evils, not to augment folly with folly. Some faults, dear, are stirred up all the more when they are condemned, but cease when they are passed over in silence, much as they say fire quenches itself if left alone. Besides, though it seems that you wish to escape notice yourself, by condemning him you will take away the veil that covers your own condition.

Then you will manifestly err. You are not convinced that love of one's husband resides in conduct that is noble and good. For this is the grace of marital association. Recognize the fact that he goes to the courtesan in order to be frivolous but that he abides with you in order to live a common life; that he loves you on the basis of good judgment, but her on the basis of passion. The moment for this is brief; it almost coincides with its own satisfaction. In a trice it both arises and ceases. The time for a courtesan is of brief duration for any man who is not excessively corrupt. For what is emptier than desire whose benefit of enjoyment is unrighteousness?. Eventually, he will perceive that he is diminishing his life and slandering his good character.

No one who understands persists in self-chosen harm. Thus, being summoned by his just obligation toward you and perceiving the diminution of his livelihood [he will take notice of you]; unable to bear the outrage of moral condemnation, he will soon repent. My dear, this is how you must live: not defending yourself against courtesans, but distinguishing yourself from them by your orderly conduct toward your husband, by your careful attention to the house, by the calm way in which you deal with the servants, and by your tender love for your children. You must not be jealous of that woman (for it is good to extend your emulation only to women who are virtuous); rather, you must make yourself fit for reconciliation. Good character brings regard even from enemies, dear, and esteem is the product of nobility and goodness alone. In this way it is even possible for the power of a woman to surpass that of a man. It is possible for her to grow in his esteem instead of having to serve one who is hostile toward her.

If he has been properly prepared for it by you, he will be all the more ashamed; he will wish to be reconciled sooner and, because he is more warmly attached to you, he will love you more tenderly. Conscious of his injustice toward you, he will perceive your attention to his livelihood, and make trial of your affection toward himself. Just as bodily illnesses make their cessations sweeter, so also do differences between friends make their reconciliation more intimate. As for you, do resist passionate resolutions of your suffering. Because he is not well, he excites you to share in his plight; because he himself misses the mark of decency, he invites you to fail in decorum; having damaged his own life, he invites you to harm what is beneficial to you. Consequently you will seem to have conspired against him, and in reproving him will appear to reprove yourself.

If you divorce yourself from him and move on, you will change your first husband only to try another and, if he has the same failings, you will resort to yet another (for the lack of a husband is not bearable for young women); or else you will abide alone without any husband like a spinster. Do you intend to be negligent of the house and to destroy your husband? Then you will share the spoils of an anguished life. Do you intend to avenge yourself upon the courtesan? Being on her guard, she will circumvent you; but if she actively wards you off, a woman who has no tendency to blush is formidable in battle. Is it good to fight with your husband day after day? To what advantage? The battles and reproaches will not stop his licentious behavior, but they will increase the dissension between you by their escalations. Don't do it, my dear. Tragedy teaches us to conquer jealousy, encompassing a systematic treatise on the actions by which Medea was led to the commission of outrage. Just as it is necessary to keep one's hands away from a disease of the eyes, so must you separate your pretension from your pain. By patiently enduring you will quench your suffering sooner.

V. EXCERPTS FROM PERIKTIONE'S *ON THE HARMONY OF WOMEN*[17]

With respect to her own husband a woman must thus live lawfully and honorably: not considering anything privately, but preserving and guarding her marriage. For in this is everything. A woman must bear everything on the part of her husband, even if he should be unfortunate, or fail on account of ignorance or illness or drink, or cohabit with other women. For this transgression is forgiven in the case of men; for women, never. Rather, retribution is imposed. Therefore she must keep the law and not be envious. She must bear anger and stinginess, fault finding, jealousy and abuse, and any other natural bent he may have. Being discreet, she must handle all of his traits in a way pleasing to him. When a woman is loving toward her husband, and acts agreeably to him, harmony reigns; she loves the entire household and makes outsiders well-disposed toward the house.

But when she is not loving, she wishes to see safe and sound neither the house nor her own children, nor the servants, nor any of the property but—as if she were an enemy—invokes and prays for total ruin. She even prays for her husband to die, on the grounds that he is hateful, in order that she may cohabit with other men; and whoever pleases him, she hates. But I think a woman is harmonious in the following way: if she becomes full of wisdom and self-control. For this benefits not only her husband, but also the children, relatives, slaves, the whole house, including possessions and friends, both fellow citizens and foreign guest friends. Artlessly, she will keep their house, speaking and hearing fair things, and obeying her husband in the unanimity of their common life, attending upon relatives and friends whom he extols, and thinking the same things sweet and bitter as he—lest she be out of tune in relation to the whole.

Commentary by *Vicki Lynn Harper*, The Late Pythagorean Women and Aristotle: Contextual Ethics

INTRODUCTION

A brief overview of Pythagoreanism and the philosophy of Aristotle were given in the chapter introduction. Since the common topic in this chapter is ethics, Late Pythagorean works attributed to women are analyzed in comparison to selections from Aristotle's ethical works.

As noted in the chapter introduction, the date and origin of these Late Pythagorean works are highly controversial. However, there is a general consensus among scholars that they are no earlier than Hellenistic times, that is, no earlier than the fourth century B.C.E. Thus, although we cannot know for certain who wrote these works, the Theano who wrote the "Letter to Kallisto" cannot be Pythagoras' wife or daughter, who lived in the late sixth century B.C.E. Nevertheless, gender is relevant for at least two reasons: first, there are good reasons for supposing that these works were written by women; second, the Pythagorean works discuss ethics from the standpoint of gendered roles, for example, the role of mistress of a household, and utilize gendered forms of writing, as in Theano's letter of advice to a young woman on the eve of her marriage.

The main focus of the chapter is a comparison of Aristotle's Doctrine of the Mean and a Pythagorean principle of harmony (*harmonia*), each of which concerns the idea of appropriate or fitting ways of living. Both the Doctrine of the Mean and Pythagorean concepts of harmony are explained in detail later (in the section of this commentary subtitled "Ethics: Providing Flexible Guidelines for Variable Contexts"). As we shall see, Aristotle's Doctrine of the Mean is intended as a guide for moral action to help us respond in ways that are fitting or appropriate to variable contexts by avoiding excess and deficiency. This is also true of the Pythagorean principle of harmony (*harmonia*, the Greek word, basically means "fitting together"). The Pythagorean principle, however, is set in the context of Pythagorean metaphysics and connects moral action with the idea of being in tune with the beauty and order of the cosmos as a whole.

This is one example of some important differences in the metaphysical views of Aristotle and the Pythagoreans, especially with respect to human nature and the soul. For example, Aristotle views the soul as an integral aspect of the living body. In contrast, Pythagoreans view the soul as immortal and separable from the body and believe in reincarnation.

Despite such differences in their overall worldviews, Aristotle and the Late Pythagorean women authors included in this chapter have many points of agreement in their approaches to ethics and living well as good human beings. First, all of them reflect upon human experience and are vitally concerned with the application of philosophical insights to practice. As Aristotle remarks, "It is not in order to acquire knowledge that we are considering what virtue is, but to become good people—otherwise there would be no point in it" (NE II.2). Practicability is often seen as a criterion for the adequacy of ethical theory; all of the authors studied in this chapter would seem to agree. For example, in her remarks, Theano has given considerable thought to the question of how the Pythagorean principle of *harmonia* is to be applied to the practical role of mistress of a household, and both Theano and Periktione reflect upon the implications of this principle in the context of less than ideal human relationships such as institutionalized slavery or abusive marriages.

Second, connected with the idea of practicability is a common concern for moral psychology. As Aristotle notes, if one wishes to help people become good, one "must consider the soul (psyche), and consider it with a view to understanding virtue" (NE I.13 1102a). Since virtue is primarily excellence of character—a settled disposition to act rightly and to respond with morally perceptive sensitivity—an understanding of human psychology is also important for understanding character development.

A third similarity between Aristotle and the Late Pythagorean women authors included in this chapter is that all stress the role of character, recognizing the all-too-human stumbling blocks to the development and preservation of moral character and integrity. A fourth and final point of agreement concerns the importance of context. As I shall show, Aristotle's Doctrine of the Mean is explicitly contextual. Still, all of these authors are sensitive to the variability of concrete relationships and situations. As Theano suggests to Kallisto (in the text included here), sometimes kindness and forgiveness are more fitting than the requirements of strict justice. This is because, in some contexts, reconciliation and the preservation of relationships are seen as more important than retaliation for perceived wrongs.

In the following comments on the specific texts, I shall elaborate on these four similarities, but I shall also highlight two important differences. First, the Late Pythagorean women speak from the standpoint of their subordinate social position and gender, while Aristotle speaks from a position of class and gender privilege. Second, given the differences in their metaphysical views of the soul, Aristotle presupposes that we each have one finite life to live, while Pythagoreans presuppose the immortality of the soul and the possibilities of future reincarnations. Pythagorean metaphysics can affect Pythagorean responses to apparent injustice: Pythagoreans believe that one's current reincarnation is a result of one's conduct in past lives, and that, if one lives virtuously this time, current misfortunes can be rectified in future reincarnations. Thus, as we shall see, the Pythagorean authors included here are more likely to advocate fortitude than indignation or retaliation for the wrongs one suffers at the hands of another.

HUMAN NATURE AND THE DEVELOPMENT OF CHARACTER

Aristotle does not believe people are good by nature, but he doesn't believe they are naturally bad either. As such, he does not hold anything analogous to the doctrine of original sin (or, that humans are born sinful or, in the Christian tradition, become sinful as the result of the acts of Adam and Eve). Humans have the capacity for good and evil, either of which can be realized and habituated through human choice and environmental influences. As he puts it succinctly in NE II.1, "Virtues arise in us neither by nature nor contrary to nature, but nature gives us the capacity to acquire them, and completion comes through habituation." Our characters are shaped by the way we live. By habitually acting in certain ways we develop settled dispositions or states of character (NE II.5 and 6). Thus, for Aristotle, it matters a great deal how we are brought up and what habits we cultivate to the character and virtues we acquire

Similarly, Aristotle also believes it is possible for us to shape our feelings. "Feeling" (*pathos*) includes both emotion (*thumos*) and appetite (*epithumia*): "By feelings I mean appetite, anger, fear, confidence, envy, joy, love, hate, longing, emulation, pity, and in general things accompanied by pleasure or pain" (NE II.5 1105b 21–23). According to Aristotle, both types of feeling have a cognitive aspect: to have an appetite for something is to regard it as pleasant. In the case of emotions, the cognitive aspect involves a belief that something is good or bad (NE VII.6 1149a30–1149b1). This point can be illustrated by Aristotle's definition of anger in the *Rhetoric*: "Anger is a desire, coupled with pain, for retaliation against what appears to be an unjustified slight against oneself or one's friends"

(*Rhet.* II.21378a30–32). Thus the belief that one has been maltreated—the cognitive or intentional object of our anger—is a factor in being angry at someone.

According to Aristotle, our emotional dispositions and our tendencies to respond to pleasures and pains can be shaped by altering our perceptions. As Aristotle puts it in Book VI of the *Nicomachean Ethics*, we should heed practically wise people "because their experienced eye enables them to see correctly" (NE VI.11 1143b12–14). The key to shaping the cognitive aspect of feelings is habit, or our habitual patterns of responses: "The same goes for appetites and anger; by conducting themselves in one way or another in such circumstances, some become temperate and even tempered, others intemperate and bad tempered" (NE II.1). He sees a connection between feelings and patterns of action: "By acting as we do in the face of danger, and becoming habituated to feeling fear or confidence, some of us become courageous, others cowardly" (NE II.1). One might think there is a kind of catch-22 paradox here: Must one not already be courageous to face up to danger in fearful situations? For Aristotle, by repeatedly choosing to act as if we were not afraid—to act courageously—we can cultivate feelings of confidence: "By becoming habituated to make light of what is fearful and to face up to it, we become courageous; and when we are, we shall be most able to face it" (NE II.2). When we are able to "make light" of what is fearful, we no longer see it in the same way. Thus, for Aristotle the development of good habits and character involves not merely acting in accordance with right reason (NE II.2), but with rational choice as well (NE II.5 and 6). As such, we are responsible for the characters we develop (or become).[18]

Aristotle's approach to ethics is *aretaic*, or virtue based. The Greek word *arête* means excellence. Virtue, or moral excellence, is one kind of human excellence. Moral excellence, or excellence of character (*êthos*), is related to the intellectual excellence or practical wisdom (*phronesis*) (NE I.13 1103a). Aretaic approaches to ethics focus on the role of moral character rather than on the stipulation of moral rules.

Aristotle gives extra attention to the topic of pleasure in his discussion of human nature and character. "Pleasure has grown up with all of us since infancy and is consequently a feeling difficult to eradicate, ingrained as it is in our lives. And, to a greater or lesser extent, we regulate our actions by pleasure or pain" (NE II.3). The question, then, is how do Aristotle's views on pleasure relate to the ideas discussed above, especially to the idea that virtue and human character involve rational choice?

Here one might distinguish first-order desires (e.g., an immediate desire to pursue or avoid something one finds pleasurable or painful) from second-order desires to have desires of a certain kind (e.g., the desire to become a certain kind of person, such as one who takes pleasure in what is good, rather than in things that are harmful or bad). This distinction is most obvious in cases of *akrasia*, or weakness of the will. (Plato uses a similar term, *akrateia*, to denote a lack of self-control in general.) An example of weakness of the will can be seen in the case of people who give in to their immediate desire for a cigarette, even though they desire not to have such a desire. Aristotle's optimistic idea is that we can shape our desires; we can control what we find pleasurable. As such, we can eradicate harmful or bad first-order desires. Aristotle does not think this is easy: "As Heraclitus says, it is harder to fight against pleasure than spirit" (NE II.3). In this quotation from the pre-Socratic philosopher, the term "spirit" (*thumos*) probably means an emotion such as anger. Only by repeatedly choosing to act as if one did not have the desire can one come not to have it. This does not mean that a virtuous person must eradicate all pleasure—insensible boors who avoid all pleasure (NE II.2) are not virtu-ous. But what we find pleasurable is a mark of our character. And for Aristotle, the most virtuous character is one who enjoys doing the right thing.

Theano's letter to Euboule is consonant with these Aristotelian philosophical insights on the role of pleasure in human nature and character development. First, Theano makes clear that she shares Aristotle's view that it matters a great deal how we are brought up, that our characters develop in accordance with our habits, and that exposure to hardship can aid the development of character. Secondly, she also recognizes unrestrained pleasure as a formidable stumbling block on the road to virtue: "What is sweeter to the young than familiar pleasure?" "But you nurse your children like the scions of Sardanapollos, enfeebling their manly natures with pleasures."[19] In addition, her letter illuminates the difference between living solely in accordance with immediate first-order desires, and an articulate life shaped by reflective second-order desires, and rational choice. In the section of her letter that begins "What would you make of a child who, if he does not eat sooner, clamors," Theano paints a vivid picture of a child wholly governed by immediate first-order desires. Immediate gratification and unreflective response to stimuli ("if someone finds fault with him, fight back") determine this child's behavior. Theano characterizes this as "slavish." Such children "become slaves of their feelings."

Aristotle would agree with Theano's assessment of childlike and children's unre-flective desire for immediate gratification as slavish behavior. In the first book of the *Nicomachean Ethics*, Aristotle labels a life devoted to immediate gratification as slavish, citing Sardanapollos as a negative role model (NE I.5). For Aristotle, as for Theano, true freedom is not simply being able to do whatever one wants. For no one who unreflectively lives a life of immediate gratification is autonomous or self-governing. These people are simply affected and moved by their feelings (rather than their cognitions). According to Theano, such a person "stutters about, perplexed." The Greek word *periagomenon*, which I have translated by its metaphorical meaning of "perplexed," literally means "led round and round"—and so—"going nowhere." The reference to stuttering (*battalizetai*) here invokes a contrast to articulate speech—the successful use of linguistic structure to convey meaning. A life devoted to the immediate gratification of first-order desires is not articulate or meaningful. For both Theano and Aristotle, free people are not those who simply do whatever they do or may happen to want, but those who deliberately structure their lives and priorities by rational choice.

ETHICS: PROVIDING FLEXIBLE GUIDELINES FOR VARIABLE CONTEXTS

Aristotle insists that there cannot be an exact science of ethics. A general account of what is to be done "ought to be given roughly and in outline" and "the account at the level of particulars is even less precise. For they do not come under any skill or set of rules; agents must always look at what is appropriate in each case as it happens, as do doctors and navi-gators" (NE II.2). As the reference here to doctors and navigators suggests, this does not mean that there are no guidelines at all, or that what "ought to be done" is reducible to purely subjective preference. Rather, given his famous Doctrine of the Mean, Aristotle's general account is that what is appropriate in a particular situation must avoid excess and deficiency (NE II.2 and 6). As such, "right reason" and rational choice involve careful attention to the variable details of concrete situations. In this way Aristotle's Doctrine of the Mean (which he explains in chapter 6) is explicitly contextual.

What is this Doctrine of the Mean? Aristotle distinguishes a fixed mean "in respect of a thing itself"; for example, six as the mean between two and ten, from a mean that is "relative to us." He first illustrates the kind of relativity he has in mind by pointing out that it is not appropriate for everyone to eat as much as an Olympic wrestler. Not eating what Olympic wrestlers eat is not an example of a simple or unqualified, noncontextual doctrine of moderation, since it is appropriate for the wrestler to eat quite a lot. Rather, it is about what is appropriate for different people under different conditions and in different situations. Moreover, the relativity of the mean does not simply concern differences in facts about particular agents; it extends to all the relevant contextual details of concrete situations, including both human actions and feelings. Achieving the (relative) mean with respect to feelings entails a disposition "to have them at the right time, about the right things, toward the right people, for the right end, and in the right way." Achieving the (relative) mean with respect to action entails a disposition to do the right thing at the right time, toward the right people, for the right end, and in the right way. In other words, the (relative) mean is an appropriate, *contextual* response to the variable particulars of concrete situations, and virtue is a disposition or state of character that "both attains and chooses the mean."

Although the mean cannot be reduced to a fixed set of rules, one can point to specific details of concrete situations in order to explain why particular actions or emotional responses are appropriate or inappropriate. Sometimes anger can be unreasonable (e.g., furious indignation over a trivial offense), but at other times it can be unreasonable not to be indignant (e.g., about flagrant violations of justice). As Elizabeth Spelman's memorable translation of a line from Book IV of Aristotle's *Nicomachean Ethics* states it, "[Anyone] who does not get angry when there is reason to be angry, or does not get angry in the right way at the right time with the right people, is a dolt" (NE IV.5 1126a4–6).[20]

Like Aristotle, Theano, in her letter to Kallisto, recommends flexible guidelines for assessing human character and action, emphasizing "right measure" and proper judgment as appropriately proportionate to context. She cautions Kallisto to "determine the true facts of wrongdoing in keeping with the justice of the condemnation" and to avoid excessive punishment. She reminds her that "reasoning no less than righteous indignation is an effective means of control." And she adds that sometimes it is appropriate to override strict justice in favor of kindness and forgiveness.

But the subtleties of the text suggest an extra dimension, one that may reflect distinctively Pythagorean views. Theano's musical analogy and her understanding of "right measure" are illuminated by an appeal to the principle of *harmonia*, which is accepted by all Pythagoreans. As we noted earlier, this principle applies not just to music, but also to the entire cosmos and everything in it. According to Pythagoreans, a cosmos is an ordered world system, and all order is defined by the delineation of limit in the unlimited, or, definition of what was indefinite. For example, the Pythagoreans noted that in a range of sound rising in pitch, the limits imposed by the musical intervals of the octave, the fifth and the fourth are defined by the specific ratios of 2:1, 4:3, and 3:2, respectively. That is, if the strings of a musical instrument are tightened to the same tension, then if one string is twice as long as another, the notes they sound will be precisely an octave apart. From measured (limited) intervals, harmonious music is produced.

Pythagoreans often use analogies to music in discussing ethical concerns. All coherent structure, whether it is musical, ethical, social, or cosmological, is preserved by the delineation of differences. Order is a relation among things that are distinct from one another: without the definition of different entities, there is only an indefinite, undifferentiated mass. What is indefinite is "unlimited" (*apeiron*), or "without boundary." The word is probably formed from an alpha privative *a*, meaning "without," plus *peiras*, "limit" or "boundary." (An alternative etymology for the word suggests the root of the verb *perao*, "to traverse," rather than the noun *peiras*.) But all differences are a part of the same coherent whole. Thus, according to the Pythagoreans, "all nature is akin" (or the same) even though there are differences within nature that are ethically significant.

The idea that all nature is akin is even more obviously reflected in the Pythagorean doctrine of reincarnation and the transmigration of souls. The same soul that is incarnated as an animal in one life can reappear as a human being in another. For individual souls, hierarchy is not immutably fixed, and the manner in which one leads one's current life can affect one's future reincarnations. In this respect, a sincere belief in the doctrine of reincarnation might very well extend one's imaginative appreciation of other living creatures and people. The thought that "I" could be a different kind of animal, or a human being of an opposite gender, or of a different social status should alter one's perspective on social justice or the exploitation of animals. (As a matter of fact, Pythagoreans advocated vegetarianism. I shall pursue this theme in the following section.[21])

SUBJECTS AND OBJECTS

On the eve of Kallisto's marriage, Theano's letter to the prospective bride does not mention the bridegroom at all. Instead, it focuses on Kallisto's new job as mistress of the household and its attendant role of authority in relation to the household maidservants (slaves). Theano uses the inclusive term *oiketai*, "household inmates," that would apply to everyone living in the household, regardless of status; she uses the term almost interchangeably with the terms for servants and slaves. This is true even though, where the text explicitly acknowledges that the servants are slaves, she does not mince words: "goodwill on the slave's part, for this possession is not bought along with their bodies." But the letter opens with the inclusive term and, as I will now argue, ends with a simile that, by the logical principle of transitivity, articulates a significant likeness between the mistress and her slaves.

In the first part of the letter, Theano talks as if responsibility to one's servants is analogous to cost-effective maintenance of inanimate tools by keeping them in good working order: the mistress of the household should control potentially recalcitrant slaves just as one would draft animals. This would be to treat them as objects, rather than as subjects whose desires, needs, and interests are worthy of consideration in their own right. Theano does not question the justice of the servants' subordinate role, and she insists that, if they display "unconquerable vice," one must "send them away to be sold."

Nor does Theano question the idea that individuals should be subordinated to the welfare of the community. In this respect, she shares antiquity's most prevalent attitude toward "enemies of the house." But the relevant question here is not whether Theano is an abolitionist, but whether her letter to Kallisto urges any kind of sympathetic acknowledgement of the slaves' humanity and subjectivity. As I will now argue, I think the answer is yes.

The tale of the brutal mistresses, which builds up to the crescendo and finale of the letter, deserves close study. There are several textual details that may bear on the answer to our question whether Theano acknowledges the slaves' humanity and subjectivity. At first there is a plurality of brutal mistresses: the passage begins with "some women." So when the reader comes to the feminine plural article "some (females)" at the beginning of the next sentence, one expects to hear more about the mistresses. Yet, without using any noun to mark the shift, the author has turned her attention from mistresses to slaves. Her shift of attention to the abused slaves is especially poignant here, in that it suggests an increasingly sympathetic awareness of the slaves' feelings: "Some are used up, utterly worked out." Although this sentence could be compatible with a mere concern for cost-effectiveness of mere objects (not subjects), it also seems to convey some sensitivity to the slaves' fatigue.

When Theano writes, "Others procure safety by escaping," is this merely analogous to noting that a valuable draft horse may bolt? Or, does it convey a sense of the slaves' desperate desire for safety? And finally, when Theano writes "but some stop living, withdrawing into death by their own hands," is she suggesting that suicide, as an individual and deliberate act, is distinctively human, thereby acknowledging the slaves' humanity?

At this point in the text, the discussion returns to the mistresses, but with a subtle shift in focus. Not only is the term "mistress" now in the singular but, grammatically, the subject of the sentence is not the mistress herself, but the isolation of the mistress. The syntactical construction no longer presents the mistress directly to us as a subject. It is as if Theano is arguing that by denying the subjectivity of her servants, the brutal mistress has erased her own.

The finale is the simile to musical instruments: "likening yourself to musical instruments, know what sounds they make when they are loosened too much, but that they are snapped asunder when stretched too tight. It is the same way for your servants." But, if I am like something in some respect, and if my servants are like the same thing in the same respect, it follows that I am like my servants in that respect. Since resemblance is a symmetrical relationship, if my servant resembles a lyre in being breakable under too much tension, then a lyre resembles my servant in this respect. Thus, by the logical principle of transitivity, since I resemble a lyre in this respect, and a lyre resembles my servant in the same respect, it follows that I resemble my servant: we are both vulnerable; both of us can be strained past the breaking point.

The analogy suggests a significant likeness between the mistress and her servants. The subordination of the servants' role is mirrored in the subordination of the social role of the mistress, for the mistress of a household is subordinate to its master; both servant and mistress are instrumental to the maintenance of social order. Both must stay in tune; but in both cases the intimate concern is that, if the string is stretched too tightly, it will snap asunder. If the strings are broken, it is difficult to see just what kind of harmony—the desired social end—is possible. Thus, although Theano does not reject the institution of slavery as such, or question the subordination of women, the nuances of the text suggest a sympathetic awareness of the slaves' humanity and subjectivity, inviting Kallisto to compare her servants to herself.

What does Aristotle have to say about relationships between masters and slaves? In his discussion of friendship, he notes that, in so far as the relationship is that of master to slave, it is like the relationship between user and tool, which is incompatible with both friendship and the subjectivity of slaves. But, he hastens to add, "There can be friendship in so far as he is a human being" (NE XIII.11). Aristotle does not condemn the institution of slavery in itself; he even claims that some people are naturally fitted to be slaves (*Politics* I.5), though he acknowledges that, as a result of political strife and warfare, people who are not slavish by nature can become enslaved (*Politics* I.6). His belief that some people are natural slaves seems incompatible with his insistence elsewhere that one human being cannot be more or less a human being than another (see *Categories*, chapter 5, 3.b32 ff.). But, despite such apparent inconsistencies in his writings, his remarks in the *Nicomachean Ethics* about slavery and friendship are consonant with an important moral insight: to treat someone simply as a tool is to treat that someone as less than human, as less subject than object.

COMMUNITY AND RELATIONSHIPS

According to Aristotle, human beings are social beings by nature (NE I.7 1097b). In Book of the *Nicomachean Ethics*, Aristotle stresses the idea that the good for human beings is to be found in a context of political, social, and familial relations. In Book VIII he notes that justice and friendship are to be found in the context of community (NE VII. 9–11). Aristotle says that familial relations within a household either resemble political systems or serve as models of them: both are examples of communities. The community of a father and his son resembles kingship, that of husband and wife an aristocracy, a community of brothers a timocracy (NE VIII.10).

Furthermore, according to Aristotle, just as political systems (large communities) can become perverted, so too can family relationships (small communities). An unhealthy father-son relationship can resemble tyranny rather than kingship; with respect to husbands and wives, if "the man is in charge of everything, the relation changes into oligarchy" (NE VIII.10).

In Aristotle's discussion of kingship, the self-sufficiency of the true king seems oddly overstated: he must be "superior in all that is good; and such a person needs nothing further." This seems incongruent with the idea that human beings are naturally social, thereby needing a great many things. Nonetheless, it is clear that, for Aristotle, the true king is supposed to be paternalistic; he will look not to his own interests but to that of his subjects. This reflects Aristotle's general view that the superior benefits the inferior, rather than vice-versa. The rule of a genuine king must be good for his subjects. At times one may well ask from whose point of view the benefit is construed. An answer is suggested in his remarks about what makes a horse good: "the virtue of a horse makes a horse good—good at running, at carrying its rider and at facing the enemy" (NE II.6 1106a). This view of what makes a horse good is presented from the point of view of the horse's master and looks to the master's benefit. But, if one could show that the relationship between a king and his subjects is not really good for the subjects, Aristotle would say it is tyranny, not kingship.

The case is somewhat similar for women. Although Aristotle does believe that men are superior to women (see, for example, *Politics* I, 5), he characterizes a relationship in which a man grants no autonomy at all to his wife, who is viewed as deviant and contrary to merit. Aristotle further analyzes the relationship between husband and wife in NE VIII.12, bringing in the distinctions he introduced at the beginning of the book concerning three forms of friendship based, respectively, on utility, pleasure, or virtue. Presumably, even friendships based on utility are not supposed to involve treating the other person simply or merely as a tool (as a mere means to an end). Here one might compare successful commercial transactions, in which there are congruent needs or interests, and exchanges to mutual advantage. Aristotle says that the relationship between husband and wife can exhibit features of all three forms of friendship. By investing their individual talents in the common good, husband and wife can supply one another's needs. Children provide another bond; indeed, marriages were generally arranged with a view to the production of legitimate heirs. Moreover, if both spouses are good, each can find enjoyment in the exercise of their individual virtues. Thus, although Aristotle has neither an egalitarian nor romantic view of the marriage relationship, he does think that a good marriage involves enjoyment, as well as mutual appreciation and advantage. One might say that Aristotle's views on women is that while (superior) men/husbands must rule (inferior) women, they must do so in ways that are good for women/the wife.

NONIDEAL MARRIAGES: THE STRAINS OF COMMITMENT

Theano's letter to Nikostrate, and the selection from Periktione, both confront the plight of women in less-than-ideal marriages. Theano's letter is addressed to a woman whose husband has taken up with a courtesan; Periktione addresses a variety of ills. Both reflect a Pythagorean concern for harmony in the household, though there is a difference in tone. Theano is optimistic about the possibility of the husband's repentance and reformation; she focuses on ways to mend the fabric of a torn relationship that may be basically sound. Periktione, on the other hand, speaks of virtuous endurance of the status quo rather than mutual reciprocity. In Periktione's text, the required effort seems wholly one-sided.

When one compares Theano's letter to Aristotle's thoughts about disillusionment with a friend whom one had esteemed, there is consonance. Aristotle writes, "But if we accept another person as good, and he turns out to be an obvious villain, should we continue to love him?" (NE IX.3). Aristotle's answer is yes, unless he has become incurably wicked. Although Aristotle does regard adultery as a serious moral failure (NE II.6), if one's friend is not "incurably wicked," he thinks there is an obligation to aid in the redemption of his character (NE IX.3). Similarly, Theano stresses the more promising aspects of the errant husband's character: "He abides with you in order to live a common life. . . . He loves you on the basis of good judgment." "Eventually he will perceive that he is diminishing his life and slandering his good character." Since, according to Theano, "No one who understands persists in self-chosen harm," the errant husband will become "conscious of his injustice toward you" and "soon repent." For this reason, Theano portrays Nikostrate's husband as suffering from weakness of the will (*akrasia*) rather than incurable vice. He has been "hunted down" and enticed into a trap of frivolously lustful first-order desire; it is as if he has temporarily lost his mind. At the same time, Theano is acutely aware of the hazards to Nikostrate's own character. The temptation to retaliate is all too human, and the desire to lash out in some way can become oddly displaced. (Remember the letter to Kallisto, which tells the cautionary tale of women who, "brutalized by jealousy or anger, even whip the bodies of their servants as if they were inscribing the excesses of their bitterness as a memorandum.) Theano even points out that, in his current state, Nikostrate's husband might find malicious satisfaction in Nikostrate's damaging of her own character: "Because he is not well, he excites you to share in his plight; because he himself misses the mark, he invites you to fail in decorum." Although this does not present an admirable side of Nikostrate's husband's character, it is a shrewd way to harness Nikostrate's rage and direct her energy in more beneficial directions. In reminding Nikostrate of the tragic excesses of Medea, who, in Euripides' classic drama, "was led" by jealous rage at her husband to the slaughter of her own children, Theano encourages Nikostrate to view her own jealousy and anger with horror.

Remember that the basic meaning of *harmonia*, the highest Pythagorean virtue, is "fitting together." (The related verb even applies to the construction of joints in carpentry.) Periktione's text strikes a pragmatic note in the face of entrenched social facts. It acknowledges the limited scope for women's practical application of the principle of *harmonia*—in the author's current social context. Given the actual structure of her society, and given that the highest virtue is harmony, a woman must act in certain prescribed ways in order to act harmoniously within that society. Otherwise she will not fit in; she will be out of tune with the whole. Like a legal realist who holds that the key to jurisprudence is what the courts actually do (rather than what they should do), Periktione points to the judgments that society actually makes; she asserts that these are the rules in accordance with which a woman must live. For example, she notes that the transgression of adultery "is forgiven in the case of men; for women, never. Rather, retribution is imposed."

In response to this social fact about what we might now call "the status of women," Periktione merely comments that women must uphold this law "and not be envious." Since the exact date and place of origin of Periktione's text is uncertain, we cannot know exactly what the ramifications of this "retribution" might have been. But it is worth mentioning that, in classical Athens, during the fifth to fourth centuries B.C.E., the husband of an adulterous wife was required by law to divorce her. As such, divorced women faced some legal restrictions, as well as social disgrace. However, the laws were not designed to make divorce easy or painless, even for aggrieved husbands. In the case of well-born women, the dissolution of marriage meant that not only the bride, but her dowry as well, must be returned to her family. Not even the children of the dissolved marriage had a legal claim to the dowry as inheritance.[22]

Periktione's conservative pragmatism, embedded as it is in a graphic description of the abuses with which women might have to contend, might strike one, as it initially struck me, as merely repellant. I would have liked more thought, for example, about what harmony could be in an ideal society. Upon reflection, however, it impressed me as clear-eyed recognition of brute fact—namely, the fact that her actual social context limits and restricts the ways in which women can embody the principle of harmony. Rather than speculating about what harmony could be in some hypothetical society, she considers what a woman must do to fit into her actual social world—in Periktione's case, classical antiquity in the fourth century B.C.E, or somewhat later. For Pythagorean women of Periktione's time, "fitting in"—commitment to the principle of *harmonia*—could be a strain. The subordination of wives to husbands left women vulnerable to abuse. What consolation can there be for a woman who "must bear everything on the part of her husband," including "anger and stinginess, fault-finding, jealousy and abuse?" Perhaps Pythagorean metaphysical and religious beliefs are a factor here. Periktione's concession to the status quo could be mitigated by a belief in the immortality of the soul and the doctrine of reincarnation. Fortitude in present adversity can help to purify one's soul, and the wrongs one has suffered in this life can be rectified in a future reincarnation.

Conclusion

In this comparison of Late Pythagorean texts attributed to women with selections from Aristotle's works, the common topic was ethics. Despite differences in their overall metaphysical views, we have found four similarities between Aristotle's ethical views and those of the Late Pythagorean authors included in this chapter. First, all of them are vitally concerned with the application of philosophical theory to practice. With a view to the practicability of their ethical views, they reflect carefully upon human experience. Second, in keeping with their concern for practicability, they all pay considerable attention to the analysis of moral psychology. A third similarity is that all stress the role of moral character in human excellence and identify obstacles to the development and preservation of moral character and integrity. The fourth and final similarity concerns their contextual approach to ethics. Rather than stipulating abstract principles or rules for conduct, they all stress the discernment of what is fitting in variable concrete relationships and situations.

We also highlighted two important differences. First, while Aristotle speaks from a position of class and gender privilege, the Late Pythagorean women speak from the standpoint of the subordinate social position of their gender. This is shown in their acknowledgment of the strains of commitment to a social order than leaves them vulnerable to abuse, and (in her letter to Kallisto) in Theano's sympathetic acknowledgment of the feelings of servants and slaves. Second, we saw that Pythagorean metaphysical and religious beliefs—especially with respect to their doctrine of reincarnation and the immortality of the soul—might affect Pythagorean responses to apparent injustice. The Pythagorean authors tended to advocate fortitude for women, rather than indignation at a lack of reciprocity or retaliation for unfairness or abuse. From a Pythagorean point of view, such fortitude can contribute to the purification of one's soul and offer hope for future reincarnations.

Finally, there is the question, are these Late Pythagorean works that are attributed to women philosophical? The format of most of these works—letters of advice—may not fit what we are accustomed to think of as philosophy today. But such an objection would apply to the works of other philosophers in antiquity, such as the pre-Socratic Parmenides, who wrote in verse, or Plato, who wrote in dialogue form, or Socrates, who apparently wrote no philosophical works, but relied on living dialogue. In terms of content, the Pythagorean works' concern for practicability and interest in moral psychology should not count against them. Practicability is a generally recognized criterion for the adequacy of moral theories, and some analysis of moral psychology is essential to this end. Moreover, the similarities to Aristotle's *aretaic,* or virtue-based, approach to ethics are striking. Philosophers may disagree about whether deontological (duty-based) or *aretaic* (virtue-based) approaches to ethics yield more adequate ethical theories. But anyone who regards *aretaic* ethics as philosophy should concede that these Late Pythagorean works count as philosophy too. Finally, these Late Pythagorean works offer something that is missing from Aristotle's works: an appreciation of the strains of commitment from the standpoint of subordinate social roles. Philosophers concerned with social justice should consider this a plus for philosophical analysis.[23]

Questions for Reflection

In what ways are both Aristotelian and Late Pythagorean ethics contextual? If moral rightness is relative to context, does this mean that whatever anyone thinks is right, is right for him or her?

What role does moral psychology play in Aristotelian and Late Pythagorean ethics? Should philosophers advocate moral ideals without regard to human psychology?

How do the various authors included in this chapter treat differences with respect to gender and social status? Do you think any of these philosophers are especially open to ideas of social change?

Notes

1. Sister Prudence Allen, *The Concept of Woman: The Aristotelian Revolution, 750 B.C.–C.E. 1250* (Grand Rapids, MI: William B. Freedman Publishing Co., 1985), 142.

2. Allen, *The Concept of Woman*, 21–24.

3. Martha Craven Nussbaum, "Aristotle," *Oxford Classical Dictionary*, 3rd ed., eds. Simon Hornblower and Anthony Spawforth (Cambridge, UK: Cambridge University Press, 1996), 165.

4. Nussbaum, "Aristotle," 166.

5. Allen, *The Concept of Woman*, 19.

6. There is also a third group, "Neo-Pythagorean" women of the first century B.C.E. through (perhaps) the third century C.E. Mary Ellen Waithe, *A History of Women Philosophers*, vol. 1, *600 B.C. to 500 C.E.* (Dordrecht, The Netherlands: Martin Nijhoff Publishers, 1987), 11–12.

7. Waithe, *A History of Women Philosophers*, vol. 1, 56.

8. Aristotle, *Nicomachean Ethics*, trans. Roger Crisp (Cambridge, UK: Cambridge University Press, 2001), 23–27, 29–31, 155–60, 167–68. Excerpts reprinted wih the permission of Cambridge University Press.

9. Aristotle, *Metaphysics*, in *The Complete Works of Aristotle: The Revised Oxford Translation*, vol. 2, ed. Jonathan Barnes, Bollingen Series (Princeton, NJ: Princeton University Press, 1984), 1:985b–986a.

10. Porphyry, *Life of Pythagoras*, in *Philosophy Before Socrates*, trans. Richard D. Mckirahan Jr. (Indianapolis, IN: Hackett Publishing Co., 1994), 84. Excerpts reprinted by permission of the publisher. All rights reserved.

11. *Late Pythagorean Texts*, trans. Vicki Lynn Harper, first printed in *A History of Women Philosophers*, vol. 1, 34, 42–48.

12. A detailed discussion of controversies concerning the chronology of these texts is found in Holger Thesleff, *An Introduction to the Pythagorean Writings of the Hellenistic Period* (Abo, Finland: Abo Akademi, 1961).

13. *Late Pythagorean Texts*, 42–43.

14. *Late Pythagorean Texts*, 47–48.

15. An obol is a small Greek coin, one-sixth of a drachma. The sense is "a small amount," "nickels and dimes," according to Vicki Harper, personal communication with editor, July 29, 2007.

16. *Late Pythagorean Texts*, 44–46.

17. *Late Pythagorean Texts*, 34.

18. Readers might reflect upon their own experience in considering whether they agree with Aristotle on these points. Readers might also reflect on the key existentialist claim, made by both Jean-Paul Sartre and Simone de Beauvoir—the philosophical pair in chapter 15 of this anthology—that we are all born "radically free" and are who we are solely by the free, individual choices we make at each moment in our lives.

19. Sardanapollos is the Greek name for the seventh century B.C.E. Assyrian king Ashurbanipal, who was legendary for indulgence in luxury.

20. Elizabeth Spelman, "Anger and Insubordination," in *Women, Knowledge and Reality*, eds. Ann Gary and Marilyn Pearsall (New York: Routledge, 1992), 263.

21. That discussion draws on my analysis of Theano's letter to Kallisto in *A History of Women Philosophers*, vol. 1, 49–52.

22. See, for example, Elaine Fantham et al., *Women in the Classical World* (New York: Oxford University Press, 1994).

23. I have borrowed the phrase "the strains of commitment" from John Rawls, *A Theory of Justice* rev. ed. (Cambridge, MA: Belknap Press of Harvard University Press, 1971 and 1999). See especially, pages 153–54. My use of this phrase differs from Rawls' in that, as a part of his abstract theoretical analysis, he considers only a general knowledge of human psychology, while I apply it to Late Pythagorean texts, which take a specifically contextual, rather than an abstract, approach to analysis.

CHAPTER 3

Augustine and Hildegard

Introduction by *Karen J. Warren*

Judith Stark's commentary treats Augustine of Hippo (354–430) and Hildegard of Bingen (1098–1179) as "eternal contemporaries": different thinkers from different historical cultures and contexts who are presented together in order to enrich one's understanding of each in a way that studying them separately does not. This introduction follows Stark's lead: it provides a glimpse of Augustine's and Hildegard's biographies and philosophical perspectives that complements Stark's commentary.

AUGUSTINE

When Constantine, the newly converted Roman emperor, issued the Edict of Milan in 313 C.E., Christianity suddenly became a powerful force in the Mediterranean world.[1] Even prior to this event early church fathers sought in Neoplatonism a philosophical foundation for the religious doctrines of Christianity. This required translating Greek works into Latin and providing commentaries on Platonic and Aristotelian writings—activities that helped bridge Ancient Philosophy and the Middle Ages. No longer the object of scorn or the target of persecutions, Christianity became the dominant religion under the protection of Emperor Constantine.

Augustine was born just a few decades after these momentous events. He, like other Christian writers and teachers, began to rethink and reconstruct their religion's relationship to society in the late imperial world. Although earlier Christians had used philosophical tools and methods in their writings, including the works of Plato and the Neoplatonists, Augustine was the major architect who designed the synthesis between Christianity and Neoplatonism that prevailed in the West for almost a millennium. Vocationally, Augustine taught rhetoric; in 395 he became the Bishop of Hippo, a position he held until his death.

93

Among Augustine's major works are the *Confessions*, *The City of God*, and *The Trinity*. In *Confessions* Augustine describes the philosophical and theological preoccupations of his young adulthood and his spiritual journey to becoming a Christian in 386 C.E. This work is generally regarded as the first autobiography in Western literature. In *The City of God* (a total of twenty-two books, written between 413–427) Augustine, inspired to defend Christianity against the charge that the Roman empire's adoption of Christianity caused the sack of Rome in 410 C.E., explored Christianity's relationship with competing religions and philosophies. It was written largely to console Christians by revealing the ultimate triumph of Christianity in "the city of God." *The Trinity* (written 399–417) is an exploration of the Trinitarian view of three persons in one God—the Father, the Son (Jesus), and the Holy Spirit. Here Augustine argues for the link between the divine and human through the notion of humans as created in the image and likeness of God.

Certain themes emerge in these three writings that are characteristic of Augustine's philosophy. One is Augustine's epistemology. Augustine holds that knowledge is a function of the mind or soul, defined as a "substance endowed with reason and fitted to rule a body." He claims that there are two kinds of knowledge, rational thinking (faith and belief) and understanding. Sometimes Augustine describes them by distinguishing between believing and seeing, respectively. Believing—associated with rational thinking—is an act of thinking whose object remains unreliable and changeable. Believing provides an inferior kind of knowledge than that provided by seeing—associated with understanding; it is acquired directly either through visions, illuminations, or conversion experiences or through logical reasoning and sense perception. For Augustine, some claims may only be believed. Other claims, such as God exists, may be first believed but subsequently understood (e.g., when one knows—"sees"—that God exists).

One feature of Augustine's epistemology is historically significant: Descartes's arguments against skepticism (see chapter 5) are similar in their starting points to Augustine's. Augustine argues that if one doubts, or if one doubts and knows that one doubts, then one knows one truth—one exists—and skepticism is false. Furthermore, one knows that "either A or not A" is true and that "A and not-A" is false. Again, skepticism is false. Since there must be a ground (justification) for this knowledge, that ground is God. The mind of God illuminates one's mind with knowledge. However, unlike Descartes, Augustine claims that the fact that one's senses have sometimes deceived one is not grounds for not trusting one's senses altogether (looking forward, it is not ground for Descartes's "systematic doubt" of all sense perception). One can be deceived by the testimony of another but that does not mean that one should never believe another person's word.

A second theme that emerges is that morality is of central importance for Augustine's philosophy. For Augustine—and Hildegard—philosophy is a way of life, one devoted to the search for truth and wisdom with the aim of achieving human happiness (blessedness, beatitude) through right living. The job of philosophers is to show the way to wisdom and, ultimately, human happiness. Disagreements among philosophers are understood as disagreements about how to achieve the ways of life that lead to genuine human happiness.

Morality is also intimately connected to Augustine's views about God, order, free will, and virtue. Augustine's Christian worldview assumes God's presence in the world; the right order of things is testimony to God's presence. The moral notion of right living involves both virtue and free will—humans voluntarily undertake right action by setting things in their right order according to their worth. But since free will implies human capacity to do evil, Augustine needed to solve the problem of evil; he needed an account of evil that was compatible with free will and God's nature as a benevolent, omnipotent, omniscient being.

Augustine's resolution of the problem was that evil is a privation, a lack or deficiency in an otherwise good substance. This theory reflects Plato's metaphysical views, as given by the simile of the divided line (chapter 1). Since degrees of reality are correlated to degrees of goodness, and ultimate reality is the immaterial good, evil is viewed as a privation or lack of both goodness and reality. Moral evil occurs as the result of freely chosen human action, not God's will. Furthermore, goodness is the will turning toward God, made possible by divine grace, whereas evil is the will turning away from God, the fallen state of humanity without the grace of God. By accepting God's grace, one can choose to do no evil by directing the will toward virtue and the right objects of human use.

HILDEGARD

Hildegard of Bingen, the youngest of ten children, was born into a noble and well-established family in Germany. Even as a young girl, she claimed to have visionary experiences—illuminations that came from God, since only God can illumine. At the age of eight she entered the Benedictine Abbey of Disibodenburg, where she was tutored by the nun Jutta. At around age seventeen Hildegard became a member of the Benedictine Order. When Jutta died in 1136, she became the leader of that community and later of the monastery she founded in 1150. She continued there as abbess until her death in 1179.

Hildegard's most important works dealt with philosophical issues of her time: In *Scivias* (written between 1147–1157) she describes and interprets a series of visions from God; in the *Book of Life's Merits* (1158–1163) she develops the themes of human vices and the need for repentance; in the *Book of Divine Works* (1163–1173) she explores the nature of virtues and vices and develops a cosmological position whereby both women and men are co-workers with God in the ongoing task of creation. She also wrote *Natural History* and *Causes and Cures*, a description of illnesses and herbal remedies. In total, Hildegard wrote nine books, more than seventy-two songs and seventy poems, and an assortment of letters. Hildegard's extraordinary knowledge spanned music and drama, language and philosophical psychology, theology, science, medicine, and philosophy. In the late 1150s, Hildegard embarked on preaching tours, typically undertaken by men, particularly priests and monks. She was sought out for her counsel as a religious leader—an abbess, visionary, teacher, preacher, writer, composer, healer, and spiritual guide. As a woman of the twelfth century, Hildegard's stature was remarkable.

Hildegard's views about how to live ethically are contextual: she claims that to know what ought to be done in any given circumstance or situation, one needs to have knowledge of the people involved.[2] Her ethical views include her claims about women. She claims that women ought to obey men, but since obedience is a virtue that is practiced by choice, there are times when other virtues override the duty to obey. She also claims that although women are the weaker sex, women are superior to men by God's grace. These claims seem conflicting; they are, at least, confusing. How might one understand them?

Sister Prudence Allen explains these seemingly conflicting views as an example of a "theory of sex complementarity." According to Allen, this theory is one of three alternative theories that emerged historically to explain the concept of woman in relation to the concept of man with respect to two different philosophical criteria: equality and differentiation. The issue of equality "concerns whether women and men are considered to be equal in human dignity and worth"; the issue of differentiation "concerns whether there are any philosophically significant differences between women and men." The theory of sex complementarity claims that women and men are significantly different *and* that they are equal.[3] Allen claims that Hildegard was "the first philosopher to articulate a complete theory of sex complementarity. Although some earlier Christian philosophers, including Augustine, had defended a vew of sex complementarity, they did not accord women full equality with men."[4]

Some debate concerns whether Hildegard is a philosopher. Ethel Kersey claims she is. Kersey writes that Hildegard "was one of the most influential philosophers of her time and for centuries afterward, distinguished by the breadth and diversity of the subject matter of her writings."[5] Margaret Alic agrees, confirming the assessment of the historian George Sarton, who called Hildegard "the most distinguished naturalist and the most original twelfth-century philosopher in Western Europe."[6] Sister Prudence Allen calls Hildegard a philosopher, claiming that "the intellectual breadth and diversity of her writings address some of the most important issues of medieval philosophy."[7]

Helen John agrees with these three scholars but for different reasons. She claims that Hildegard has been omitted from histories of medieval philosophy for three reasons: her remarkable intellectual achievements were based on revealed Christian doctrines rather than human reasoning; Hildegard describes her intellectual approach and ways of knowing as grounded in visions and illuminations, not philosophical reasoning; and Hildegard's claims that her writings and visions were based in divine inspiration and are not compatible with the writings and kind of reasoning that characterized male medieval philosophers.[8] John then counters each reason: first, Hildegard integrated a Christian worldview with human reason in ways that "characterized the spirit of medieval philosophy"; second, Hildegard enhances the philosophical heritage of her time; and, third, Hildegard's appeal to divine inspiration "occurs in ways that are compatible with the exercise of philosophical wisdom," understood as grounded in human reason and common human experience—typical of male philosophers of the medieval period.[9] She concludes:

> I would contend that she belongs among the philosophers as a powerful exemplar—of the range and authority of women's vision and experience. Her approach to human generation, her development of the concept of "*viriditas*" [verdancy] and her portrayal of Divine Love in feminine form are strong contributions to the medieval philosophical tradition. The task of finding a place for her will be as rewarding as it is strenuous.[10]

Other scholars are not so sure. Elisabeth Gossman claims, "It is problematic to refer to Hildegard of Bingen as a philosopher, even though she was familiar with the philosophical currents of her time and could animatedly and competently take a stand on them." Gossman thinks it more appropriate to call her a theologian. Unlike philosophers, Hildegard grounds her claims in her visionary experiences, which she offers as a "philosophical-theological view of the world."[11]

STARK'S COMMENTARY

Stark's commentary provides four reasons for regarding Hildegard as a philosopher. She also raises the issue of what is at stake by *not* considering Hildegard a philosopher: Is a double standard being applied, one that uses one set of characteristics to identify men as philosophers but ignores those or provides others to identify women as philosophers? The issue of a possible double standard is not simply a question about Hildegard as a philosopher; it is about the basic question, "What *is* philosophy and philosophical methodology, and what makes someone a philosopher?" With Augustine as an example of a late Roman philosopher, what should one say about Hildegard's status as a philosopher?

Excerpts of Writings by Augustine and Hildegard

I. EXCERPTS FROM AUGUSTINE'S *CONFESSIONS*[12]

i (1) "You, are great, Lord, and highly to be praised" (Ps. 47:2); "great is your power and your wisdom is immeasurable" (Ps. 146:5). Man, a little piece of your creation, desires to praise you, a human being "bearing his mortality with him" (2 Cor. 4:10), carrying with him the witness of his sin and the witness that you "resist the proud" (1 Pet. 5:5). Nevertheless, to praise you is the desire of man, a little piece of your creation. You stir man to take pleasure in praising you, because you have made us for yourself, and our heart is restless until it rests in you.

"Grant me Lord to know and understand" (Ps. 118:34, 73, 144) which comes first—to call upon you or to praise you, and whether knowing you precedes calling upon you. But who calls upon you when he does not know you? For an ignorant person might call upon someone else instead of the right one. But surely you may be called upon in prayer that you may be known. Yet "how shall they call upon him in whom they have not believed? And how shall they believe without a preacher?" (Rom. 10:14). "They will praise the Lord who seek for him" (Ps. 21:27).

In seeking him they find him, and in finding they will praise him. Lord, I would seek you, calling upon you—and calling upon you is an act of believing in you. You have been preached to us. My faith, Lord, calls upon you. It is your gift to me. You breathed it into me by the humanity of your son, by the ministry of your preacher.

ii (2) How shall I call upon my God, my God and Lord? Surely when I call on him, I am calling on him to come into me. But what place is there in me where my God can enter into me? "God made heaven and earth" (Gen. 1:1). Where may he come to me? Lord my God, is there any room in me which can contain you? Can heaven and earth, which you have made and in which you have made me, contain you? Without you, whatever exists would not exist. Then can what exists contain you? I also have being. So why do I request you to come to me when, unless you were within me, I would have no being at all? I am not now possessed by Hades; yet even there are you (Ps. 138:8): for "even if I were to go down to Hades, you would be present." Accordingly, my God, I would have no being, I would not have any existence, unless you were in me. Or rather, I would have no being if I were not in you "of whom are all things, through whom are all things, in whom are all things" (Rom. 11:36). Even so, Lord, even so. How can I call on you to come if I am already in you? Or where can you come from so as to be in me? Can I move outside heaven and earth so that my God may come to me from there? For God has said "I fill heaven and earth" (Jer. 23:24).

x (16) By the Platonic books I was admonished to return into myself. With you as my guide I entered into my innermost citadel, and was given power to do so because you had become my helper (Ps. 29:11). I entered and with my soul's eye, such as it was, saw above that same eye of my soul the immutable light higher than my mind—not the light of every day, obvious to anyone, nor a larger version of the same kind which would, as it were, have given out a much brighter light and filled everything with its magnitude. It was not that light, but a different thing, utterly different from all our kinds of light. It transcended my mind, not in the way that oil floats on water, nor as heaven is above earth. It was superior because it made me, and I was inferior because I was made by it. The person who knows the truth knows it, and he who knows it knows eternity. Love knows it. Eternal truth and true love and beloved eternity: you are my God. To you I sigh "day and night" (Ps: 42:2). When I first came to know you, you raised me up to make me see that what I saw is Being, and that I who saw am not yet Being. And you gave a shock to the weakness of my sight by the strong radiance of your rays, and I trembled with love and awe. And I found myself far from you "in the region of dissimilarity," and heard as it were your voice from on high. "I am the food of the fully grown; grow and you will feed on me. And you will not change me into you like the food your flesh eats, but you will be changed into me."

xi (17) And I considered the other things below you, and I saw that neither can they be said absolutely to be or absolutely not to be. They are because they come from you. But they are not because they are not what you are. That which truly is is that which unchangeably abides. But "it is good for me to stick fast to God" (Ps. 72:28); for if I do not abide in him, I can do nothing (John 15:5). But he "abiding in himself makes all things new" (Wisdom 7:27). "You are my Lord because you have no need of my goodness" (Ps. 15:2).

xii (18) It was obvious to me that things which are liable to corruption are good. If they were the supreme goods, or if they were not good at all, they could not be corrupted. For if they were supreme goods, they would be incorruptible. If there were no good in them, there would be nothing capable of being corrupted. Corruption does harm and unless it diminishes the good, no harm would be done. Therefore either corruption does not harm, which cannot be the case, or (which is wholly certain) all things that are corrupted suffer privation of some good. If they were to be deprived of all good, they would not exist at all. If they were to exist and to be immune from corruption, they would be superior because they would be permanently incorruptible. What could be more absurd than to say that by losing all good, things are made better? So then, if they are deprived of all good, they will be nothing at all. Therefore as long as they exist, they are good. Accordingly, whatever things exist are good, and the evil into whose origins I was inquiring is not a substance, for if it were a substance, it would be good. Either it would be an incorruptible substance, a great good indeed, or a corruptible substance, which could be corrupted only if it were good. Hence I saw and it was made clear to me that you made all things good, and there are absolutely no substances which you did not make. As you did not make all things equal, all things are good in the sense that taken individually they are good, and all things taken together are very good. For our God has made "all things very good" (Gen. 1:31).

xiii (19) For you evil does not exist at all, and not only for you but for your created universe, because there is nothing outside it which could break in and destroy the order which you have imposed upon it. But in the parts of the universe, there are certain elements which are thought evil because of a conflict of interest. These elements are congruous with other elements and as such are good, and are also good in themselves. All these elements which have some mutual conflict of interest are congruous with the inferior part of the universe which we call earth. Its heaven is cloudy and windy, which is fitting for it.

It is far from my mind now to say, "Would that those things did not exist!" If I were to regard them in isolation, I would indeed wish for something better; but now even when they are taken alone, my duty is to praise you for them. That you are to be praised is shown by dragons on earth and all deeps, fire, hail, snow, ice, the hurricane and tempest, which perform your word—mountains and all hills, fruitful trees and all cedars, beasts and all cattle, reptiles and winged birds; kings of the earth and all peoples, princes and all judges of the earth, young men and maidens, old men with younger: let them praise your name (Ps. 148:7–12). Moreover, let these from the heavens praise you: let all your angels praise you in the height, our God all your powers, sun and moon, all stars and light, the heaven of heavens and the waters that are above the heavens: let them praise your name (Ps. 148:1–5).

I no longer wished individual things to be better, because I considered the totality. Superior things are self-evidently better than inferior. Yet with a sounder judgment I held that all things taken together are better than superior things by themselves.

xvii (23) I was astonished to find that already I loved you, not a phantom surrogate for you. But I was not stable in the enjoyment of my God. I was caught up to you by your beauty and quickly torn away from you by my weight. With a groan I crashed into inferior things. This weight was my sexual habit. But with me there remained a memory of you. I was in no kind of doubt to whom I should attach myself, but was not yet in a state to be able to do that. "The body, which is corruptible, weighs down the soul, and our earthly habitation drags down the mind to think many things" (Wisdom 9:15). Moreover, I was wholly certain that your invisible nature "since the foundation of the world is understood from the things which are made, that is your eternal power and divinity" (Rom. 1:20).

I asked myself why I approved of the beauty of bodies, whether celestial or terrestrial, and what justification I had for giving an unqualified judgment on mutable things, saying "This ought to be thus, and that ought not to be thus." In the course of this inquiry why I made such value judgments as I was making, I found the unchangeable and authentic eternity of truth to transcend my mutable mind. And so step by step I ascended from bodies to the soul which perceives through the body, and from there to its inward force, to which bodily senses report external sensations, this being as high as the beasts go. From there again I ascended to the power of reasoning to which is to be attributed the power of judging the deliverances of the bodily senses. This power, which in myself I found to be mutable, raised itself to the level of its own intelligence, and led my thinking out of the ruts of habit. It withdrew itself from the contradictory swarms of imaginative fantasies, so as to discover the light by which it was flooded. At that point it had no hesitation in declaring that the unchangeable is preferable to the changeable, and that on this ground it can know the unchangeable, since, unless it could somehow know this, there would be no certainty in preferring it to the mutable. So in the flash of a trembling glance it attained to that which is. At that moment I saw your "invisible nature understood through the things which are made" (Rom. 1:20). But I did not possess the strength to keep my vision fixed. My weakness reasserted itself, and I returned to my customary condition. I carried with me only the loving memory and a desire for that of which I had the aroma but which I had not yet the capacity to eat.

vii (16) This was the story Ponticianus told. But while he was speaking, Lord, you turned my attention back to myself. You took me up from behind my own back where I had placed myself because I did not wish to observe myself (Ps. 20:13), and you set me before my face (Ps. 49:21) so that I should see how vile I was, how twisted and filthy, covered in sores and ulcers. And I looked and was appalled, but there was no way of escaping from myself. If I tried to avert my gaze from myself, his story continued relentlessly, and you once again placed me in front of myself; you thrust me before my own eyes so that I should discover my iniquity and hate it. I had known it, but deceived myself, refused to admit it, and pushed it out of my mind.

(17) But at that moment the more ardent my affection for those young men of whom I was hearing, who for the soul's health had given themselves wholly to you for healing, the more was the detestation and hatred I felt for myself in comparison with them. Many years of my life had passed by—about twelve—since in my nineteenth year I had read Cicero's *Hortensius*, and had been stirred to a zeal for wisdom. But although I came to despise earthly success, I put off giving time to the quest for wisdom. For "it is not the discovery but the mere search for wisdom which should be preferred even to the discovery of treasures and to ruling over nations and to the physical delights available to me at a nod." But I was an unhappy young man, wretched as at the beginning of my adolescence when I prayed you for chastity and said: "Grant me chastity and continence, but not yet." I was afraid you might hear my prayer quickly, and that you might too rapidly heal me of the disease of lust which I preferred to satisfy rather than suppress. I had gone along "evil ways" (Eccles. 2:10) with a sacrilegious superstition, not indeed because I felt sure of its truth but because I preferred it to the alternatives, which I did not investigate in a devout spirit but opposed in an attitude of hostility.

viii (19) Then in the middle of that grand struggle in my inner house, which I had vehemently stirred up with my soul in the intimate chamber of my heart, distressed not only in mind but in appearance, I turned on Alypius and cried out: "What is wrong with us? What is this that you have heard? Uneducated people are rising up and capturing heaven (Matt. 11:12), and we with our high culture without any heart—see where we roll in the mud of flesh and blood. Is it because they are ahead of us that we are ashamed to follow? Do we feel no shame at making not even an attempt to follow?" That is the gist of what I said, and the heat of my passion took my attention away from him as he contemplated my condition in astonished silence. For I sounded very strange. My uttered words said less about the state of my mind than my forehead, cheeks, eyes, color, and tone of voice.

Our lodging had a garden. We had the use of it as well as of the entire house, for our host, the owner of the house, was not living there. The tumult of my heart took me out into the garden where no one could interfere with the burning struggle with myself in which I was engaged, until the matter could be settled. You knew, but I did not, what the outcome would be. But my madness with myself was part of the process of recovering health, and in the agony of death I was coming to life. I was aware how ill I was, unaware how well I was soon to be. So I went out into the garden. Alypius followed me step after step. Although he was present, I felt no intrusion on my solitude. How could he abandon me in such a state? We sat down as far as we could from the buildings. I was deeply disturbed in spirit, angry with indignation and distress that I was not entering into my pact and covenant with you, my God, when all my bones (Ps. 34:10) were crying out that I should enter into it and were exalting it to heaven with praises. But to reach that destination one does not use ships or chariots or feet. It was not even necessary to go the distance I had come from the house to where we were sitting. The one necessary condition, which meant not only going but at once arriving there, was to have the will to go—provided only that the will was strong and unqualified, not the turning and twisting first this way, then that, of a will half-wounded, struggling with one part rising up and the other part falling down.

xii (28) From a hidden depth a profound self-examination had dredged up a heap of all my misery and set it "in the sight of my heart" (Ps. 18:15). That precipitated a vast storm bearing a massive downpour of tears. To pour it all out with the accompanying groans, I got up from beside Alypius (solitude seemed to me more appropriate for the business of weeping), and I moved further away to ensure that even his presence put no inhibition upon me. He sensed that this was my condition at that moment. I think I may have said something which made it clear that the sound of my voice was already choking with tears. So I stood up while in profound astonishment he remained where we were sitting. I threw myself down somehow under a certain fig tree, and let my tears flow freely. Rivers streamed from my eyes, a sacrifice acceptable to you (Ps. 50:19), and (though not in these words, yet in this sense) I repeatedly said to you: "How long, O Lord? How long, Lord, will you be angry to the uttermost? Do not be mindful of our old iniquities" (Ps. 6:4). For I felt my past to have a grip on me. It uttered wretched cries: "How long, how long is it to be?" "Tomorrow, tomorrow." "Why not now? Why not an end to my impure life in this very hour?"

(29) As I was saying this and weeping in the bitter agony of my heart, suddenly I heard a voice from the nearby house chanting as if it might be a boy or a girl (I do not know which), saying and repeating over and over again "Pick up and read, pick up and read." At once my countenance changed, and I began to think intently whether there might be some sort of children's game in which such a chant is used. But I could not remember having heard of one. I checked the flood of tears and stood up. I interpreted it solely as a divine command to me to open the book and read the first chapter I might find. For I had heard how Antony happened to be present at the gospel reading, and took it as an admonition addressed to himself when the words were read: "Go, sell all you have, give to the poor, and you shall have treasure in heaven; and come, follow me" (Matt. 19:21). By such an inspired utterance he was immediately "converted to you" (Ps. 50:15). So I hurried back to the place where Alypius was sitting. There I had put down the book of the apostle when I got up. I seized it, opened it, and in silence read the first passage on which my eyes lit: "Not in riots and drunken parties, not in eroticism and indecencies, not in strife and rivalry, but put on the Lord Jesus Christ and make no provision for the flesh in its lusts" (Rom. 13:13–14).

I neither wished nor needed to read further. At once, with the last words of this sentence, it was as if a light of relief from all anxiety flooded into my heart. All the shadows of doubt were dispelled.

(30) Then I inserted my finger or some other mark in the book and closed it. With a face now at peace I told everything to Alypius. What had been going on in his mind, which I did not know, he disclosed in this way. He asked to see the text I had been reading. I showed him, and he noticed a passage following that which I had read. I did not know how the text went on; but the continuation was "Receive the person who is weak in faith" (Rom. 14:1). Alypius applied this to himself, and he made that known to me. He was given confidence by this admonition. Without any agony of hesitation he joined me in making a good resolution and affirmation of intention, entirely congruent with his moral principles in which he had long been greatly superior to me. From there we went in to my mother, and told her. She was filled with joy. We told her how it had happened. She exulted, feeling it to be a triumph, and blessed you who "are powerful to do more than we ask or think" (Eph. 3:20). She saw that you had granted her far more than she had long been praying for in her unhappy and tearful groans.

The effect of your converting me to yourself was that I did not now seek a wife and had no ambition for success in this world. I stood firm upon that rule of faith on which many years before you had revealed me to her. You "changed her grief into joy" (Ps. 29:12) far more abundantly than she desired, far dearer and more chaste than she expected when she looked for grandchildren begotten of my body.

Book IX Cassiciacum: To Monica's Death

x (23) The day was imminent when she was to depart this life (the day which you knew and we did not). It came about, as I believe by your providence through your hidden ways, that she and I were standing leaning out of a window overlooking a garden. It was at the house where we were staying at Ostia on the Tiber, where, far removed from the crowds, after the exhaustion of a long journey, we were recovering our strength for the voyage.

Alone with each other, we talked very intimately. "Forgetting the past and reaching forward to what lies ahead" (Phil. 3:13), we were searching together in the presence of the truth which is you yourself. We asked what quality of life the eternal life of the saints will have, a life which "neither eye has seen nor ear heard, nor has it entered into the heart of man" (1 Cor. 2:9). But with the mouth of the heart wide open, we drank in the waters flowing from your spring on high, "the spring of life" (Ps. 35:10) which is with you. Sprinkled with this dew to the limit of our capacity, our minds attempted in some degree to reflect on so great a reality.

(24) The conversation led us toward the conclusion that the pleasure of my bodily senses, however delightful in the radiant light of this physical world, is seen by comparison with the life of eternity to be not even worth considering. Our minds were lifted up by an ardent affection toward eternal being itself. Step by step we climbed beyond all corporeal objects and the heaven itself, where sun, moon, and stars shed light on the earth. We ascended even further by internal reflection and dialogue and wonder at your works, and we entered into our own minds. We moved up beyond them so as to attain to the region of inexhaustible abundance where you feed Israel eternally with truth for food. There life is the wisdom by which all creatures come into being, both things which were and which

will be. But wisdom itself is not brought into being but is as it was and always will be. Furthermore, in this wisdom there is no past and future, but only being, since it is eternal. For to exist in the past or in the future is no property of the eternal. And while we talked and panted after it, we touched it in some small degree by a moment of total concentration of the heart. And we sighed and left behind us "the first fruits of the Spirit" (Rom. 8:23) bound to that higher world, as we returned to the noise of our human speech where a sentence has both a beginning and an ending. But what is to be compared with your word, Lord of our lives? It dwells in you without growing old and gives renewal to all things.

xvii (26) Great is the power of memory, an awe-inspiring mystery, my God, a power of profound and infinite multiplicity. And this is mind, this is I myself. What then am I, my God? What is my nature? It is characterized by diversity, by life of many forms, utterly immeasureable. See the broad plains and caves and caverns of my memory. The varieties there cannot be counted, and are, beyond any reckoning, full of innumerable things. Some are there through images, as in the case of all physical objects, some by immediate presence like intellectual skills, some by indefinable notions or recorded impressions, as in the case of the mind's emotions, which the memory retains even when the mind is not experiencing them, although whatever is in the memory is in the mind. I run through all these things, I fly here and there, and penetrate their working as far as I can. But I never reach the end. So great is the power of memory, so great is the force of life in a human being whose life is mortal.

xxvii (38) Late have I loved you, beauty so old and so new: late have I loved you. And see, you were within and I was in the external world and sought you there, and in my unlovely state I plunged into those lovely created things which you made. You were with me, and I was not with you. The lovely things kept me far from you, though if they did not have their existence in you, they had no existence at all. You called and cried out loud and shattered my deafness. You were radiant and resplendent, you put to flight my blindness. You were fragrant, arid I drew in my breath and now pant after you. I tasted you, and I feel but hunger and thirst for you. You touched me, and I am set on fire to attain the peace which is yours.

II. EXCERPTS FROM AUGUSTINE'S *LITERAL COMMENTARY ON GENESIS*[13]

But in the ordinary course of our daily life there are other objects that arise in various ways from our spirit itself or are, after a fashion, suggested to the spirit by the body, according as we have been influenced by the flesh or by the mind. Thus men in their waking hours think of their troubles, turning over in their minds the likenesses of bodily things; and so in their sleep, too, they frequently dream of something they need. The reason for this is that greed is the motive force of their business dealings; and when they happen to go to sleep hungry and thirsty, they are often after food and drink with open mouth. Now, in my opinion, when these objects are compared with the revelations of angels, they ought to be assigned the same relative value that we give, in the corporeal order, to earthly bodies in comparison with celestial bodies.

So also among the objects of the intellect; there are some that are seen in the soul itself: for example, the virtues (to which the vices are opposed), either virtues which will endure, such as piety, or virtues that are useful for this life and not destined to remain in the next, as faith, by which we believe what we do not see, and hope, by which we await with patience the life that shall be, and patience itself, by which we bear every adversity until we arrive at the goal of our desires. These virtues, of course, and other similar ones, which are quite necessary for us now in living out our exile, will have no place in the blessed life, for the attainment of which they are necessary. And yet even they are seen with the intellect; for they are not bodies, nor have they forms similar to bodies. But distinct from these objects is the light by which the soul is illumined, in order that it may see and truly understand everything, either in itself or in the light. For the light is God himself, whereas the soul is a creature; yet since it is rational and intellectual, it is made in his image. And when it tries to behold the Light, it trembles in its weakness and finds itself unable to do so. Yet from this source comes all the understanding it is able to attain. When, therefore, it is thus carried off and after being withdrawn from the senses of the body, is made present to this vision in a more perfect manner (not by a spatial relation, but in a way proper to its being), it also sees above itself that Light in whose illumination it is enabled to see all the objects that it sees and understands in itself.

III. EXCERPTS FROM AUGUSTINE'S *THE TRINITY*[44]

Book 10, Chapter 5

(7) Why, then, was it commanded to know itself? It was, I believe, that it might consider itself and live according to its nature, that is, that it might desire to be ruled according to its nature, namely, under Him to whom it must be brought into subjection, and above those to whom it must be preferred; under Him by whom it must be governed, above those whom it must govern. For it does many things through evil desires, as though it had forgotten itself.

The force of love is so great that the mind draws in with itself those things upon which it has long reflected with love, and to which it has become attached by its devoted care, even when it returns in some way to think of itself. And because they are bodies which it has loved outside of itself through the senses of the body, and with which it has become entangled by a kind of daily familiarity, it cannot bring them into itself as though into a country of incorporeal nature, and, therefore, it fastens together their images, which it has made out of itself. For in forming them it gives them something of its own essence, but it also keeps something by which it may freely judge of the species of these images; this is what is called more precisely the mind, namely, the rational understanding which is kept in order to pass judgment. For we perceive that we have, in common with the beasts, those parts of the soul that are informed by the images of bodies.

Book 12, Chapter 7

(9) We ought, therefore, not to understand man as made to the image of the exalted Trinity, that is, to the image of God, in such a way that the same image is understood to be in three human beings; especially since the Apostle says that the man is the image of God, and consequently should remove the covering from his head, which he warns the woman

to use, when he speaks as follows: "A man indeed ought not to cover his head, because he is the image and glory of God. But the woman is the glory of the man" (1 Cor. 11:7).

What, then, is to be said about this? If the woman according to her own person completes the image of the Trinity, why is the man still called that image when she has been taken from his side? Or if even one human person out of three can be called the image of God, as each person in the exalted Trinity itself is also God, why is not the woman also the image of God? For this is also the reason why she is commanded to cover her head which he is forbidden to do because he is the image of God.

(10) But we must see how the words spoken by the Apostle, that not the woman but the man is the image of God, are not contrary to that which is written in Genesis: "God made man, to the image of God he made him; male and female he made them and blessed them" (Gen. 1:27). For he says that human nature itself, which is complete in both sexes, has been made to the image of God, and he does not exclude the woman from being understood as the image of God. For after he had said that God made man to the image of God, he went on to say: "He made him male and female," or at any rate (if we punctuate this passage differently) "male and female he made them." In what sense, therefore, are we to understand the Apostle, that the man is the image of God, and consequently is forbidden to cover his head, but the woman is not, and on this account is commanded to do so? The solution lies, I think, in what I already said when discussing the nature of the human mind, namely, that the woman together with her husband is the image of God, so that that whole substance is one image. But when she is assigned as a helpmate, a function that pertains to her alone, then she is not the image of God; but as far as the man is concerned, he is by himself alone the image of God, just as fully and completely as when he and the woman are joined together into one.

IV. EXCERPTS FROM HILDEGARD OF BINGEN'S *SCIVIAS*[15]

Declaration

10 *These Are True Visions Flowing from God*

And behold! In the forty-third year of my earthly course, as I was gazing with great fear and trembling attention at a heavenly vision, I saw a great splendor in which resounded a voice from Heaven, saying to me,

"O fragile human, ashes of ashes, and filth of filth! Say and write what you see and hear. But since you are timid in speaking, and simple in ex-pounding, and untaught in writing, speak and write these things not by a human mouth, and not by the understanding of human invention, and not by the requirements of human composition, but as you see and hear them on high in the heavenly places in the wonders of God. Explain these things in such a way that the hearer, receiving the words of his instructor, may expound them in those words, according to that will, vision, and instruction. Thus therefore, O human, speak these things that you see and hear. And write them not by yourself or any other human being, but by the will of Him Who knows, sees and disposes all things in the secrets of His mysteries."

And again I heard the voice from Heaven saying to me, "Speak therefore of these wonders, and, being so taught, write them and speak."

It happened that, in the eleven hundred and forty-first year of the Incarnation of the Son of God, Jesus Christ, when I was forty-two years and seven months old; Heaven was opened and a fiery light of exceeding brilliance came and permeated my whole brain, and inflamed my whole heart and my whole breast, not like a burning but like a warming flame, as the sun warms anything its rays touch. And immediately I knew the meaning of the exposition of the Scriptures, namely the Psalter, the Gospel and the other catholic volumes of both the Old and the New Testaments, though I did not have the interpretation of the words of their texts or the division of the syllables or the knowledge of cases or tenses. But I had sensed in myself wonderfully the power and mystery of secret and admirable visions from my childhood—that is, from the age of five—up to that time, as I do now. This, however, I showed to no one except a few religious persons who were living in the same manner as I; but meanwhile, until the time when God by His grace wished it to be manifested, I concealed it in quiet silence. But the visions I saw I did not perceive in dreams, or sleep, or delirium, or by the eyes of the body, or by the ears of the outer self, or in hidden places; but I received them while awake and seeing with a pure mind and the eyes and ears of the inner self, in open places, as God willed it. How this might be is hard for mortal flesh to understand.

But when I had passed out of childhood and had reached the age of full maturity mentioned above, I heard a voice from Heaven saying, "I am the Living Light, Who il-luminates the darkness. The person [Hildegard] whom I have chosen and whom I have miraculously stricken as I willed, I have placed among great wonders, beyond the measure of the ancient people who saw in Me many secrets; but I have laid her low on the earth, that she might not set herself up in arrogance of mind. The world has had in her no joy or lewdness or use in worldly things, for I have withdrawn her from impudent boldness, and she feels fear and is timid in her works. For she suffers in her inmost being and in the veins of her flesh; she is distressed in mind and sense and endures great pain of body, because no security has dwelt in her, but in all her undertakings she has judged herself guilty. For I have closed up the cracks in her heart that her mind may not exalt itself in pride or vainglory, but may feel fear and grief rather than joy and wantonness. Hence in My love she searched in her mind as to where she could find someone who would run in the path of salvation. And she found such a one and loved him [the monk Volmar of Disibodenberg], knowing that he was a faithful man, working like herself on another part of the work that leads to Me. And, holding fast to him, she worked with him in great zeal so that My hidden miracles might be revealed. And she did not seek to exalt herself above herself but with many sighs bowed to him whom she found in the ascent of humility and the intention of good will.

"O human, who receives these things meant to manifest what is hidden not in the disquiet of deception but in the purity of simplicity, write, therefore, the things you see and hear."

But I, though I saw and heard these things, refused to write for a long time through doubt and bad opinion and the diversity of human words, not with stubbornness but in the exercise of humility, until, laid low by the scourge of God, I fell upon a bed of sickness; then, compelled at last by many illnesses, and by the witness of a certain noble maiden of good conduct [the nun Richardis of Stade] and of that man whom I had secretly sought and found, as mentioned above, I set my hand to the writing. While I was doing it, I sensed, as I mentioned before, the deep profundity of scriptural exposition; and, raising myself from illness by the strength I received, I brought this work to a close—though just barely—in ten years.

These visions took place and these words were written in the days of Henry, Archbishop of Mainz, and of Conrad, King of the Romans, and of Cuno, Abbot of Disibodenberg, under Pope Eugenius.

And I spoke and wrote these things not by the invention of my heart or that of any other person, but as by the secret mysteries of God I heard and received them in the heavenly places.

And again I heard a voice from Heaven saying to me, "Cry out therefore, and write thus!"

Book 1, Vision 2

11 *What Things Are to be Observed and Avoided in Marriage*

Because a mature woman was given not to a little boy but to a mature man, namely Adam, so now a mature woman must be married to a man when he has reached the full age of fertility, just as due cultivation is given to a tree when it begins to put forth flowers. For Eve was formed from a rib by Adam's ingrafted heat and vigor, and therefore now it is by the strength and heat of a man that a woman receives the semen to bring a child into the world. For the man is the sower, but the woman is the recipient of the seed.

Wherefore a wife is under the power of her husband because the strength of the man is to the susceptibility of the woman as the hardness of stone is to the softness of earth.

But the first woman's being formed from man means the joining of wife to husband. And thus it is to be understood: This union must not be vain or done in forgetfulness of God, because He Who brought forth the woman from the man instituted this union honorably and virtuously, forming flesh from flesh. Wherefore, as Adam and Eve were one flesh, so now also a man and woman become one flesh in a union of holy love for the multiplication of the human race. And therefore there should be perfect love in these two as there was in those first two. For Adam could have blamed his wife because by her advice she brought him death, but nonetheless he did not dismiss her as long as he lived in this world, because he knew she had been given to him by divine power. Therefore, because of perfect love, let a man not leave his wife except for the reason the faithful Church allows. And let them never separate, unless both with one mind want to contemplate My Son, and say with burning love for Him: "We want to renounce the world and follow Him Who suffered for our sake!" But if these two disagree as to whether they should renounce the world for one devotion, then let them by no means separate from each other, since, just as the blood cannot be separated from the flesh as long as the spirit remains in the flesh, so the husband and wife cannot be divided from each other but must walk together in one will.

But if either husband or wife breaks the law by fornication, and it is made public either by themselves or by their priests, they shall undergo the just censure of the spiritual magisterium. For the husband shall complain of the wife, or the wife of the husband, about the sin against their union before the Church and its prelates, according to the justice of God; but not so that the husband or wife can seek another marriage; either they shall stay together in righteous union, or they shall both abstain from such unions, as the discipline of church practice shows. And they shall not tear each other to pieces by viperous rending, but they shall love with pure love, since both man and woman could not exist without having been conceived in such a bond, as My friend Paul witnesses when he says:

12 *Words of the Apostle on This Subject*

"As the woman is of the man, so is the man for the woman; but all are from God" (1 Cor. 11:12). Which is to say: Woman was created for the sake of man, and man for the sake of woman. As she is from the man, the man is also from her, lest they dissent from each other in the unity of making their children; for they should work as one in one work, as the air and the wind intermingle in their labor. In what way? The air is moved by the wind, and the wind is mingled with the air, so that in their movement all verdant things are subject to their influence. What does this mean? The wife must cooperate with the husband and the husband with the wife in making children. Therefore the greatest crime and wickedest act is to make by fornication a division in the days of creating children, since the husband and wife cut off their own blood from its rightful place, sending it to an alien place. They will certainly incur the deceit of the Devil and the wrath of God, because they have transgressed that bond God ordained for them. Woe to them, therefore, if their sins are not forgiven! But although, as has been shown, the husband and wife work together in their children, nevertheless the husband and the wife and all other creatures come from the divine disposition and ordination, since God made them according to His will.

Book 1, Vision 4

17 *How the Soul Shows Its Powers According to the Powers of the Body*

The soul now shows its powers according to the powers of the body, so that in a person's infancy it produces simplicity, in his youth strength, and in adulthood, when all the person's veins are full, it shows its strongest powers in wisdom; as the tree in its first shoots is tender and then shows that it can bear fruit, and finally, in its full utility, bears it. But then in human old age, when the marrow and veins start to incline to weakness, the soul's powers are gentler, as if from a weariness at human knowledge; as when winter approaches the sap of the tree diminishes in the branches and the leaves, and the tree in its old age begins to bend.

18 *A Person has Three Paths Within Himself*

But a person has within himself three paths. What are they? The soul, the body and the senses; and all human life is led in these. How? The soul vivifies the body and conveys the breath of life to the senses; the body draws the soul to itself and opens the senses; and the senses touch the soul and draw the body. For the soul gives life to the body as fire gives light to darkness, with two principal powers like two arms, intellect and will; the soul has arms not so as to move itself, but so as to show itself in these powers as the sun shows itself by its brilliance. Therefore, O human, who are not just a bundle of marrow, pay attention to scriptural knowledge!

19 *On the Intellect*

The intellect is joined to the soul like an arm to the body. For as the arm, joined to the hand with its fingers, branches out from the body, so the intellect, working with the other powers of the soul, by which it understands human actions, most certainly proceeds from the soul. For before all the other powers of the soul it understands whatever is in human works, whether good or evil, so that through it, as through a teacher, everything is understood; for it sifts things as wheat is purified of any foreign matter, inquiring whether they are useful or useless, lovable or hateful, pertinent to life or death. Thus, as food without salt is tasteless, the other powers of the soul without intellect are insipid and undiscerning. But the intellect is also to the soul as the shoulder is to the body, the very core of the other powers of the soul; as the bodily shoulder is strong, so it understands the divinity and the humanity in God, which is the joint of the arm, and it has true faith in its work, which is the joint of the hand, with which it chooses among the various works wisely as if with fingers. But it does not work in the same way as the other powers of the soul. What does this mean?

20 On the Will

The will activates the work, and the mind receives it, and the reason produces it. But the intellect understands the work, knowing good and evil, just as the angels, who have intellect, love good and despise evil. And where the heart is in the body, there the intellect is in the soul, exercising its power in that part of the soul as the will does in another part. How? Because the will has great power in the soul. How? The soul stands in a corner of the house, that is, by the prop of the heart, like a man who stands in a corner of his house, so that looking through the whole house he may command all its contents, lifting his right arm to point out what is useful in the house and turning to the East. Thus the soul should do, looking along the streets of the body toward the rising sun. Thus it puts its will, like a right arm, as the support of the veins and marrow and the movement of the whole body; for the will does every work, whether it be good or bad.

21 Analogy of Fire and Bread

For the will is like a fire, baking each deed as if in a furnace. Bread is baked so that people may be nourished by it and be able to live. So too the will is the strength of the whole work, for it starts by kneading it and when it is firm adds the yeast and pounds it severely; and, thus preparing the work in contemplation as if it were bread, it bakes it in perfection by the full action of its ardor, and so makes a greater food for humans in the work they do than in the bread they eat. A person stops eating from time to time, but the work of his will goes on in him till his soul leaves his body. And in whatever differing circumstances the work is performed, whether in infancy, youth, adulthood, or bent old age, it always progresses in the will and in the will comes to perfection.

Book 3, Vision 12

3 The Bodies of the Dead will Rise Again in Their Wholeness and Gender

And when, as you saw, the divine command to rise again resounds, the bones of the dead, wherever they may be, are brought together in one moment and covered with their flesh. They will not be hindered by anything; but if they were consumed by fire or water, or eaten by birds or beasts, they will be speedily restored. And so the earth will yield them up as salt is extracted from water; for My eye knows all things, and nothing can be hidden from Me. And so all people will rise again in the twinkling of an eye, in soul and body, with no deformity or mutilation but intact in body and in gender; and the elect will shine with the brightness of their good works, but the reprobate will bear the blackness of their deeds of misery. Thus their works will not there be concealed, but will appear in them openly.

V. HILDEGARD OF BINGEN'S *BOOK OF DIVINE WORKS*[16]

Vision 4: 15

The crown of the human head indicates the beginning of the soul's action, which orders and plans all human deeds in accord with prudent reason. The soul itself is there like a summit which decides on everything in the human organism required and needed by the body. And the soul achieves this by four stages of ascent and descent—seeing, hearing, smelling, and tasting. Through these senses the soul understands creatures and has contact with them. Through them it keeps its fleshly vessel to a certain degree within creation and causes it to desire, along with the soul, what is proper for the soul. With all growing creatures the soul flies, so to speak, like air into all bodily needs in order to appease them; and in its awareness of the names of all creatures the soul rises up in accord with the body—whether in love or in hatred for those creatures.

This is because the human form has the same length and width, if we extend both our hands and arms out from the chest, just as the firmament is also as tall as it is wide. And thus the fact that we are as tall as we are wide gives us a way of measuring our knowledge of good and evil. For we recognize what is good by its advantage to us just as we recognize what is bad by its disadvantage to us. Through our fondness for flesh and blood the soul is involved in the human organism, just as wild game is caught by the hunter. As a result, the soul has scarcely begun to breathe before the body satisfies its own desires. But afterward the soul often causes the body to long for the soul.

Vision 4: 19

The soul has two capacities by which it controls equally well both the tension and the release of its passionate activity. Through its first capacity, the soul ascends to the heights, where it experiences God. Through the other capacity, it takes possession of the whole body in which it exists, in order to achieve its own work by means of that body. For the soul rejoices at being able to achieve things with the body. That body has been formed by God, and thus the soul is most anxious to perfect the body's work (*opus corporis*).

The soul itself experiences the organic functions of the entire body, and thus the soul can ascend into the brain, the heart, and blood, or marrow. In this connection the soul cannot achieve more than the limits of our bodily element allow. No matter how eager the soul may be to do as much good as possible within the body, the soul cannot go further than divine grace permits it to go. Often the soul does things according to the desires of the flesh. It will continue to do so until the blood dries out more and more in our veins as a result of exhaustion, and until sweat is ejected through our marrow. At this point, the soul will retreat into inactivity until it can again warm up the blood of the flesh and replenish the marrow. In this way, the soul urges the body to be vigilant and revives it to do its proper work. And if at times the body succumbs to the desires of the flesh, disgust will usually ensue. While from this time forward the body renews its powers, it will turn again totally to God's service.

Vision 4: 24

Indeed, the soul sustains the flesh, just as the flesh sustains the soul. For, after all, every deed is accomplished by the soul and the flesh. And, therefore, the soul can achieve with the body good and holy things and be revived as a result. In this connection, it often happens that our flesh may feel bored when it cooperates with the soul. In such a case, therefore, the soul may give in to its fleshy partner and let the flesh take delight in earthly things. Similarly, a mother knows how to get her crying child to laugh again. Thus the soul accomplishes good deeds with the body, even though there may be some evil mixed up with them. The soul lets this happen so as not to overburden the flesh too much. Just as the body lives through the soul, the soul also finds life again by achieving good through the body. For the soul is entrusted with the work of the Lord's hands. And as the sun overcomes the night and then rises up until midday, we humans avoid evil deeds and enter into a state of integrity. But when the sun declines in the afternoon, the soul enters into an agreement with the flesh. Finally, just as the sun rekindles the moon to keep it from disappearing, our flesh is preserved by the powers of the soul lest the flesh fall down into perdition.

Vision 4: 100

When God looked upon the human countenance, God was exceedingly pleased. For had not God created humanity according to the divine image and likeness? Human beings were to announce all God's wondrous works by means of their tongues that were endowed with reason. For humanity is God's complete work. God is known to human beings, and for our sake God created all creatures. God has allowed us to glorify and praise God in the kiss of true love through our spirituality.

But the human species still needed a support that was a match for it. So God gave the first man a helper in the form of woman, who was man's mirror image, and in her the whole human race was present in a latent way. God did this with manifold creative power, just as God had produced in great power the first man. Man and woman are in this way so involved with each other that one of them is the work of the other (*opus alterum per alterum*). Without woman, man could not be called man; without man, woman could not be named woman. Thus woman is the work of man, while man is a sight full of consolation for woman. Neither of them could henceforth live without the other. Man is in this connection an indication of the Godhead while woman is an indication of the humanity of God's Son. And thus the human species sits on the judgment seat of the world. It rules over all creation. Each creature is under our control and in our service. We human beings are of greater value than all other creatures.

Letter 39: Hildegard to Wibert of Gembloux

The words which I speak are not my own nor those of any human being, but what I say comes from the vision which I received from above.

O true servant of God, if it had pleased God to raise not only my soul but my body as well to a prophetic vision, still that could not cause the fear to diminish from my spirit and my heart. For I know that I am a human being, even though I have been cloistered from my childhood. There have been many who were wise and whose lives were so filled with wonders that they proclaimed a great number of mysteries. And yet, from a vain pursuit of glory, they ascribed these things to themselves, and thus came to their downfall.

But those, on the other hand, who in their spiritual advancement derived their wisdom from God and regarded themselves as nothing—they became pillars of heaven. This is what happened in the case of St. Paul who, although he excelled the other apostles in preaching, regarded himself as nothing. The same is true of the evangelist John who was filled with tender humility, and because of this was able to obtain so much from the divine spring.

How would it be understood if a poor creature like myself were not to recognize this gift. God works where God wills, for the honor of the divine name and not for the honor of earth-bound mortals. But I am continuously filled with fear and trembling. For I do not recognize in myself security through any kind of personal ability. And yet I raise my hands aloft to God, that I might be held by God, just like a feather which has no weight from its own strength and lets itself be carried by the wind.

I cannot fully understand the things I see, not as long as I remain in bondage to the body and the invisible soul. For in both cases we human beings suffer from want.

I also saw in my vision that the first book of my visions should be called *Scivias*, because it would proclaim the way of the living light . . . and not derive from any other teaching.

From my childhood days, when my limbs, nerves, and veins were not yet strong, the gift of this vision brought joy to my soul; and this has remained true up to this very time when I am a woman of more than seventy years. And as God wants, my soul climbs in this vision high above, even to the height of the firmament. But I do not see these things with my external eyes nor do I hear them with my external ears. I do not perceive them through the thoughts of my heart or through the mediation of my five senses. I see them much more in my soul alone, with my physical eyes open, in such a way that I never experience the unconsciousness of ecstasy, but I see all of this awake, whether by day or night.

The light which I see is not bound by space. It is much, much more light-filled than a cloud that carries the sun in itself. There is nothing in it to recognize of height, length, or breadth. It was described to me as the "shadow of the living light." And just as the sun, the moon, and the stars are reflected in water, so writings, talks, powers, and certain actions of people are illuminated for me in this light.

I was often severely hindered by sickness and involved with heavy sufferings that threatened to bring me to death's door. And yet God has always made me alive again, even to this day.

I keep for a long time in memory all the things I see and learn in the vision, because as soon as I see or hear it, it enters my memory. I simultaneously see, hear, and understand. In an instant I learn what I know through the vision. But whatever I do not see in the vision, I have no knowledge of, for I am without formal education and was only instructed to read simple letters. And I write what I see and hear in the vision and I don't add any other words. I communicate the plain Latin words just as I hear them in the vision. For I do not become educated in my vision so that I can write like the philosophers. The words in the vision do not sound like words from a human mouth, but they are like flaming lightning and like a cloud moving in the pure ether. I am not able to perceive the shape of this light, just as I cannot look with unprotected eyes at the disk of the sun.

It is in this light that I sometimes see, though not often, another light that I call "the living light." When and how I see this, I cannot say. But as long as I see this "living light" all sadness and anxiety are taken away from me. The result is that I feel like a simple young girl and not like an old lady.

[During these experiences] I do not know myself, either in body or soul. And I consider myself as nothing. I reach out to the living God and turn everything over to the Divine that God, who has neither beginning nor end, can preserve me from evil in every situation. And that is why I ask you to pray for me too, since you have requested this reply from me. And ask all of those to pray for me, too, who, like you, desire to hear these words in good faith. Pray that I may persevere in God's service.

But I want to say something to you, too, O son of God, for you seek God in faith and are filled with desire for the Divine. God wants to save you. Pay attention to the eagle who with his two wings flies toward the clouds. If he lost his wings, he would fall down to the Earth and not be able to raise himself up again, no matter how eagerly he sought to lift himself up in flight. Human beings also fly with two wings; the right wing is the knowledge of good and the left wing is the knowledge of evil. The knowledge of evil serves the good, insofar as the good is sharpened and highlighted through the knowledge of evil; and so through this knowledge human beings become wise in all things.

VI. EXCERPTS FROM *HILDEGARD OF BINGEN: MYSTICAL WRITINGS*[17]

Adam and Eve

When God created Adam, Adam experienced a sense of great love in the sleep that God instilled in him. And God gave a form to that love of the man, and so woman is the man's love. And as soon as woman was formed God gave man the power of creating, that through his love—which is woman—he might procreate children. When Adam gazed at Eve, he was entirely filled with wisdom, for he saw in her the mother of the children to come. And when she gazed at Adam, it was as if she were gazing into heaven, or as the human soul strives upward, longing for heavenly things—for her hope was fixed in him. And so there will be and must be one and the same love in man and woman, and no other.

The man's love, compared with the woman's, is a heat of ardor like a fire on blazing mountains, which can hardly be put out, while hers is a wood fire that is easily quenched; but the woman's love, compared with the man's, is like a sweet warmth proceeding from the sun, which brings forth fruits.

But the great love that was in Adam when Eve came forth from him, and the sweetness of the sleep with which he then slept, were turned in his transgression into a contrary mode of sweetness. And so, because a man still feels this great sweetness in himself, and is like a stag thirsting for the fountain, he races swiftly to the woman and she to him—she like a threshing floor pounded by his many strokes and brought to heat when the grains are threshed inside her.

The Four Temperaments of Woman

(*De sanguinea*) Some women are inclined to plumpness, and have soft and delectable flesh and slender veins, and well-constituted blood free of impurities . . . And these have a clear and light coloring, and in love's embraces are themselves lovable; they are subtle in arts, and show self-restraint in their disposition. At menstruation they suffer only a moderate loss of blood, and their womb is well developed for childbearing, so they are fertile and can take in the man's seed. Yet they do not bear many children, and if they are without husbands, so that they remain childless, they easily have physical pains; but if they have husbands, they are well.

(*De flecmatica*) There are other women whose flesh does not develop as much, because they have thick veins and healthy, whitish blood (though it does contain a little impurity, which is the source of its light color). They have severe features, and are darkish in coloring; they are vigorous and practical, and have a somewhat mannish disposition. At menstruation their menstrual blood flows neither too little nor too abundantly. And because they have thick veins they are very fertile and conceive easily, for their womb and all their inner organs, too, are well developed. They attract men and make men pursue them, and so men love them well. If they want to stay away from men, they can do so without being affected by it badly, though they are slightly affected. However, if they do avoid making love with men they will become difficult and unpleasant in their behavior. But if they go with men and do not wish to avoid men's love making, they will be unbridled and over lascivious, according to men's report. And because they are to some extent mannish on account of vital force [viriditas, lit. "greenness"] within them, a little down sometimes grows on their chin.

(*De colerica*) There are other women who have slender flesh but big bones, moderately sized veins, and dense red blood. They are pallid in coloring, prudent and benevolent, and men show them reverence and are afraid of them. They suffer much loss of blood in menstruation; their womb is well developed and they are fertile. And men like their conduct, yet flee from them and avoid them to some extent, for they can interest men but not make men desire them. If they do get married, they are chaste, they remain loyal wives and live healthily with their husband; and if they are unmarried, they tend to be ailing—as much because they do not know to what man they might pledge their womanly loyalty as because they lack a husband.

(*De melancolica*) But there are other women who have gaunt flesh and thick veins and moderately sized bones; their blood is more lead-colored than sanguine, and their coloring is as it were blended with grey and black. They are changeable and free roaming in their thoughts, and wearisomely wasted away in affliction; they also have little power of resistance, so that at times they are worn out by melancholy. They suffer much loss of blood in menstruation, and they are sterile, because they have a weak and fragile womb. So they cannot lodge or retain or warm a man's seed, and thus they are also healthier, stronger, and happier without husbands than with them—especially because, if they lie with their husbands, they will tend to feel weak afterward. But men turn away from them and shun them, because they do not speak to men affectionately, and love them only a little. If for some hour they experience sexual joy, it quickly passes in them. Yet some such women, if they unite with robust and sanguine husbands, can at times, when they reach a fair age, such as fifty, bear at least one child . . . If their menopause comes before the just age, they will sometimes suffer gout or swellings of the legs, or will incur an insanity which their melancholy arouses, or else backache or a kidney ailment . . . If they are not helped in their illness, so that they are not freed from it either by God's help or by medicine, they will quickly die.

Commentary by *Judith Chelius Stark*, Hildegard of Bingen and Augustine of Hippo: A Conversation Across Centuries

INTRODUCTION

At first it may seem odd to pair two figures in Western thought who are separated in time by over seven hundred years. Augustine of Hippo (354–430 C.E.) lived in the cosmopolitan world of the late Roman Empire as it began its final decline and Hildegard of Bingen (1098–1179) lived in a monastic community in twelfth century Germany. Could these two thinkers of vastly different times and places have much in common? Apart from the fact that both lived as fervent Christians and were dedicated to the church, what more can be said about the leading bishop of the fifth century North African Church in relation to the woman who was called the Sybil of the Rhine?

This commentary answers these questions and makes the case for reading this medieval odd couple together, thereby showing that reading them in tandem brings to light the range and depth of each one's work, while also illuminating their works in new and interesting ways. In *The Great Philosophers*, Karl Jaspers writes about how "eternal contemporaries"—thinkers of different times, places, and cultures—may be fruitfully brought together in conversation and communication.[18] Using this approach, I discuss Augustine and Hildegard as eternal contemporaries whose writings present a philosophy as lived experience and who share themes of philosophical significance: the importance of conversion (Augustine), illumination (Hildegard), and "light"; views about the material world and humans, the nature of body and soul; and whether women and men are created equal.

AUGUSTINE AND HILDEGARD AS ETERNAL CONTEMPORARIES

One hardly need argue for the importance of Augustine's writings and for his influence as a major philosopher in the West. His works continue to spark lively scholarly debates about such philosophical issues as the nature of time, memory, and free will versus determinism. If he had written just one of the great books of his prolific career—the *Confessions*, *The City of God*, or *The Trinity*—his reputation would be well established. But in addition to these three masterpieces, he wrote sixty other books, and hundreds of letters and sermons. Moreover he did this, not from the quiet haven of a secluded school of philosophy or a monastic cloister, but as an active and beleaguered bishop in a busy city of the late Roman Empire.

There is no doubt about Augustine's stature and importance, but what about Hildegard of Bingen? Until about twenty years ago, her works were relatively unknown apart from medieval historians and monastic scholars. Since the explosions of the women's movement, beginning in the 1960s, medieval figures like Hildegard, Mechtild of Magdeburg, and Hrosvitha are receiving the attention they deserve.

Hildegard was prominent in her own time; she concerned herself with many contemporary issues and controversies and she was not reluctant to appeal to the Pope or Emperor on matters of monastic governance (such as when she claimed that Emperor Frederick was wrong to support rivals to the Pope in Rome). Nonetheless, she was still a woman and her gender prevented a wide circulation of her works. For complex historic, social, and political reasons, Hildegard's works languished in relative obscurity until recently. The contemporary women's movement's successful challenge to the conception and teaching of traditional academic disciplines (like philosophy) that had largely excluded the voices and works of women writers has meant, in the case of Hildegard, that her works are frequently taught in courses in philosophy, religious studies, history, and literature.

AUGUSTINE AND HILDEGARD AS PHILOSOPHERS

As one reads the excerpts of these two writers, one may wonder, Is it philosophy? The easy answer is, "no," it is not philosophy as generally understood by many thinkers since the Enlightenment in the West. A more nuanced answer asks whether their positions can be accommodated within an understanding of the nature and practice of philosophy that is broader than traditional Western conceptions, especially since 1600. For example, often in teaching the history of Western philosophy, a yawning chasm opens up between the years 500–1500 C.E., with a nod to Augustine of Hippo at the beginning of medieval philosophy and another to Anselm and Thomas Aquinas toward the middle and end. Their writings are presented as the examples of certain ways of thinking about God with one overriding concern—to demonstrate God's existence.

This view is not without merit. They did write a great deal about God—God's nature, proofs for God's existence, and human relationships to God. But they were also concerned with many issues beyond God's existence, especially in a culture that took religious faith as a given. They focused on God's existence for many reasons, but their works were far more multifaceted and various than such a myopic view reveals.

The case is made here that Augustine believed he was engaging in philosophy, as understood at that time. In fact, the first conversion he experienced at age nineteen, as a result of reading a lost work of Cicero's, was a conversation from a dissolute and unfocused life to the practice of philosophy.

Philosophy as a way of life devoted to the search for truth and wisdom was often practiced in small communities in the ancient world. This practice stretches back to Pythagoras, Plato, Aristotle, and Epicurus. Closer to Augustine's time, the philosopher Plotinus of Alexandria founded a philosophic community in the third century and his ideas greatly influenced the young Augustine's search. Augustine and his friends considered starting such a community. Their plans never were implemented, since in the ancient world such a community could not have included their wives, who were considered unequal to their husbands. These communities were based on friendship that could only exist among peers.

Like his contemporaries, Augustine clearly considered that he was doing philosophy, understood as the pursuit of wisdom. They would have disagreed, however, about how to practice it. These disagreements came both from non-Christian thinkers (like Plotinus and Porphry) who thought that Christianity as a philosophy made wisdom too easily accessible to the many, and also from Christian writers, like Tertullian, who claimed that reason was an obstacle to faith. However, they did not doubt that a great deal of Augustine's work was philosophical.

However, the issue with Hildegard is not so clear-cut. Some distinctions might help sort this out: during this period (roughly 300–1200 C.E.), the separate disciplinary identities between philosophy and theology had not yet been fully established. Although Augustine wrote about the differences between acquiring knowledge by reason or by authority, it was not until the thirteenth century that Thomas Aquinas made an explicit and formal distinction between philosophy and theology. Relying on the work of his teacher Albert the Great, Aquinas argues for a distinction between theology and philosophy in terms of the contents and separate methodologies of these disciplines. In Aquinas's view, philosophy uses reason to argue on the basis of principles that are discovered by the mind, whereas theology accepts its principles on faith or on the authority of divine revelation, then uses reason to analyze and understand them.

An example may serve to illustrate Aquinas's approach. In his famous five demonstrations for God's existence, Aquinas claims that reason alone can argue for God's existence without the aid of divine revelation. These demonstrations continue to be debated today in the field called "philosophy of religion." While Aquinas thinks that reason can demonstrate God's existence, reason alone could never come to the notion of the Trinity (that there are three persons in one God). Divine revelation and faith in that revelation are the only ways to come to that knowledge. Once one accepts the Trinity on faith, human reason can attempt to come to a deeper understanding of the true nature of God. Even though Augustine made the distinction between knowledge from reason and knowledge from authority, he did not carry it through the body of his writings in the explicit and formal way that Aquinas would do much later. A challenge in reading Augustine is to understand the context, setting, and purposes of his writings in order to tease out those aspects that are philosophical. And those are legion.

First, Augustine's Christian worldview was not fixed and static. He devoted his life to deepening his understanding of Christianity. His life and writings can be seen as a grand orchestration of the human drama of the person's flight from God (*aversion*) and possible return (*conversio*).[19] So while concerned with God's existence, Augustine also wrote about the nature and meaning of human life, the struggle between good and evil, the nature of knowledge, questions of existence and the material world, and time, memory, and history. These topics continue to engage philosophers to the present day.

Hildegard, unlike Augustine, did not experience dramatic conversion to Christianity as a young adult, since she was raised as a Christian from infancy, already had a Christian worldview in place, and her training in a Benedictine monastery from age eight intensified and deepened it. Nonetheless, her lifelong experience of visions is analogous to Augustine's series of conversions. As with Augustine, Hildegard never took for granted the course and destiny of her journey. Given Hildegard's Christian worldview, what may be properly termed her philosophical concerns?

Hildegard's central preoccupation was with God and human beings' relationship to God. Like Augustine, Christianity was the source and inspiration of her writings. But her interests were far reaching, as spokes of a wheel move out from the hub. Hildegard sought to understand what it is to be human and live an ethical life, the struggle between good and evil, the nature of human knowledge, the status and workings of the material world, and the metaphysical and ethical status of the human body. Although the language she used was often religious, her ideas have clear philosophical dimensions and implications. For example, she emphasized understanding the material world in more dynamic terms (*veriditas*) than other thinkers of her time, who used static concepts like form, essence, and being in their philosophical analyses of their world. Moreover, her commitment to understanding the world on its own terms stands in stark contrast to the much more suspicious, if not downright denigrating, views of the material world and its enticements held by Christian Platonists of her day.

A PHILOSOPHY OF LIVED EXPERIENCE

In one particularly important way, Augustine and Hildegard are linked across the span of centuries: both thought, wrote, and strongly responded to the pressing issues of their times, developing a philosophy of lived experience beginning with their own lives.[20] This can be understood in a twofold sense: first, as grounded in a profound, spiritual relationship with God; second, as responsive to the events and demands of their busy lives and times. Their lives and their reflections on their lives show that philosophy based on lived concrete experience (in contrast to a philosophy based on allegedly objective, abstract, or detached principles) can be genuinely philosophical. Long before the feminist revolutions of the past forty years, Augustine and Hildegard had the genius and confidence to express the personal as the philosophical and to include the particular, living person and the personal voice as subjects of philosophy. Their inclusion of the personal as paradigm for the practice of philosophy stands as revolutionary and prescient of views that would follow.

CONVERSION AND VISION

Augustine's conversion at the age of thirty-two came at the culmination of a series of dramatic turnings that began when he was nineteen. Through these events, Augustine saw God calling him back to Augustine's true self and toward a friendship with God. But, by his own recounting, for many years Augustine turned away from God's call by associating with the Manichaeans, considering skepticism, and studying astrology. Just prior to his conversion to Christianity, Augustine read the texts of the Neoplatonists and the intellectual insights that he gained prepared him to come to a more philosophically sophisticated understanding of Christianity—especially with regard to the spiritual nature of God and the source of evil doing in the human will. His experience of conversion in 386 set Augustine on a course to become one of the most important thinkers in the West. This emphasis on the experiential level is crucial in understanding Augustine and his writings.

Like Augustine, Hildegard's visions are also profoundly experiential. Many contemporary scholars have attempted to get to the root of her visions, often preceded by illness, by suggesting migraine headaches as their cause.[21] Whatever their causes, they clearly had powerful significance and deep spiritual, philosophical, and psychological meanings for her. Hildegard understood them as sources of inspiration for her books and commentaries. Whatever we might make of her visions, Hildegard took them to be directly inspired by God.

Although Augustine did not experience visions as Hildegard did, it is possible to identify three features common to his conversion and her visions. First, both were certain that God initiated these spiritual experiences to which they were free to respond or not. Yet when either of them resisted these divine invitations, serious and dramatic consequences followed. Augustine felt confusion and a deep dissatisfaction with his life and Hildegard experienced inertia, depression, and bodily paralysis. Once they responded as they thought God intended, their lives became clearer, healthier, and more whole—psychologically and spiritually. Both describe God as "physician" and "healer" who restores them to spiritual and moral health (and, at times, physical health for Hildegard).

Second, both Hildegard and Augustine considered these conversion-illumination experiences to be deeply personal in two senses: both knew that they had been deeply transformed by a direct experience with a personal God. These were not instances of do-it-yourself mysticism along the lines of, for example, the Neoplatonists who were convinced that once their intellectual and moral regimen was followed, difficult and arduous as it may be, one would eventually catch a glimpse of the "One." Also, both believed that their experiences were not self-induced, self-contained, heightened states of consciousness, but were truly transformative events through which they believed they had direct contact with a living, personal God.

Third, Augustine and Hildegard realized that their God-given knowledge involved imperatives for them. Augustine redirected his life and rejected his success in the Roman world, a success he had striven for throughout his life. After his conversion, Augustine embarked on an entirely new life in North Africa as a celibate Christian. Hildegard's visions continued to impel her to write and circulate her writings. Earlier in her life, she considered herself just "a poor little figure of a woman."[22] As an uneducated woman removed from the world, she dared not speak about exalted matters, such as God, the scriptures, the cosmos, and the corrupt conditions of church and empire of her day. It was when she received God's gift that she had the courage to challenge the male leadership of her day. In her world of class divisions and female subservience—an age that she described as effeminate—God gave a woman a "virile" voice to challenge and chastise her contemporaries.

Both adhered to the ethical imperatives from God. For Augustine, these included conflicts with the enemies of the church in North Africa, even when this endangered Augustine's life, and for Hildegard, it included rebuking emperors when it was hardly customary for women in convents to speak at all publicly and certainly not to challenge the Emperor about his policies toward the Church.

LIGHT

Since Jesus called himself the "light of the world," the metaphor of light has been powerful and persistent in the Christian tradition, especially with the introduction of Platonism into Christianity.[23] The Platonic tradition is replete with uses of the term "light" as the metaphor for illumination: for example, physical light makes objects in the world visible, intellectual light renders concepts intelligible, and divine light is the way God infuses knowledge into the mind.

Both Augustine and Hildegard use light primarily as a description of God—God is light. This description is formulated in the Gospels and is amplified in the Epistles, particularly in John's First Epistle: "God is light; in him there is no darkness at all" (1 John 1:5). Hildegard's writings add an important dimension by calling God the "Living Light."[24] Augustine and Hildegard agree that this light is not material; it does not occupy either space or time (*Confessions* 7:10, 16). Augustine begins an account of an experience of "unchangeable light" that quickly becomes identified and named as the personal God with whom Augustine longs to have a relationship. Hildegard wrote about her visions as light in a famous letter toward the end of her life:

> The light that I see thus is not spatial, but it is far, far brighter than a cloud that carries the sun. I can measure neither height, nor length, nor breadth in it; and I call it "the reflection of the living Light." And as the sun, moon, and the stars appear in water, so writings, sermons, virtues, and certain human actions take form for me and gleam within it.[25]

Hildegard understands this experience as the living, personal God manifested to her as "Living Light." Both use the notion of light as the cause of whatever true knowledge the human mind can apprehend. In this way, epistemological and metaphysical claims are embedded in their analyses of light; divine light is the primary analogue for other types of illumination of which humans are capable. Light is also the primary referent through which all other things reveal the fullness of being. Augustine understands his experience as an ascent of his mind resulting in a direct encounter with the divine; Hildegard understands her vision as a direct experience of God and one through which she becomes a mouthpiece for the "Living Light."

Augustine's theory of knowledge as divine illumination is much more philosophically developed than is Hildegard's. For him, any true knowledge results from the fact that God is truth as well as light, so that human knowledge can only be affected by an illumination coming directly from God.[26] In this theory of knowledge as illumination, Augustine augments the philosophical tradition begun in Plato's epistemology, which considers knowledge of eternal and necessary ideas as the culmination of the human quest for knowledge and truth. Augustine echoes Plato's and Plotinus's theories of knowledge, but he places the eternal and immutable ideas of the intelligible world into the mind of God.

One aspect of Hildegard's use of light and fire is very different from Augustine's thought and stands apart from other medieval thinkers. Hildegard uses the concept *viriditas*, translated as "life," "greenness," or "fruitfulness" to describe the workings of nature, but she also uses it to describe the nature of God as the source of creation.[27] As Constant Mews shows, Hildegard's use of this dynamic and organic way of understanding God is highly unusual, if not unique, among medieval thinkers.[28] In multiple layers of meaning, the Word of God who is Light becomes incarnate through the power and viriditas of the Spirit and then this "warmth in viridity" is infused into human beings the "way a mother gives milk to her children."[29] By using viriditas to describe God's power, Hildegard ties God as the source of creation to the world he has created in ways that are more unifying and dynamic than the static concepts prevalent among medieval thinkers. Hildegard is not unique among medieval thinkers in using maternal imagery for God, but her model of the universe stresses the infusion of God's power in viriditas more completely and holistically than other medieval thinkers.

HUMAN PERSON: BODY AND SOUL, WOMAN AND MAN

Hildegard and Augustine concur on the following points: God is the source and creator of all human life; human life on earth is the journey of every human person; every person struggles with evil in this life; and the ultimate human destination is happiness with God in the next life. These convictions are grounded in the coming of Christ and in his death and resurrection. While this is the bedrock of their understanding of the human person, they also reveal the distinctly philosophical significance of human life. Three are considered here: the status of the material world; human beings as composed of body and soul; and the question of woman and man and their relationship.

THE MATERIAL WORLD

As the main architect for combining Platonism and Christianity, Augustine is faced with a daunting task. From the biblical tradition, he inherits the view that all creation is good, having been created by a God who is good. However, from the Platonists, he inherits a suspicion. Furthermore, Augustine was tainted with the Manichaean belief that the material world is the evil force in the cosmos and that evil is attempting to overcome good by entrapping it in matter. Augustine struggles with these contradictory perspectives and, although he insists that the material world is good in the metaphysical sense, he never seems to escape entirely from the Platonic suspicion of matter, including the human body.

Hildegard also inherits both the biblical and Christian Platonist views. However, her books on the material world, for example, *Natural History, Causes and Cures*, and *The Book of Divine Works*, are remarkably free of these suspicions. Although these works are set in theological contexts of God's creation of the world and human beings—including Adam and Eve's sin that brought sickness and death into the world—Hildegard presents the workings of nature and the human body on their own terms and not solely as created by God. In doing so, she shows her familiarity with the current medical topics of her day combined with keen observations of and knowledge about humans, plants, animals, and the elements. The fact that she was a woman and a member of a religious order writing these treatises, containing frank and detailed discussions of women's anatomy and sexuality, is nothing short of astonishing. Her treatment of these topics again flies in the face of the dominant Christian Platonism of her time that would have considered the human body primarily as the site of temptation and entrapment of the soul and not worthy of philosophical examination. Hildegard oversteps this paradigm and, through her careful and detailed analyses of the structure and function of the human body, she challenges the superiority-inferiority dualism of the prevailing views that made the soul superior to the body, man superior to woman, and spirituality superior to sexuality.

Although many medieval women had extensive knowledge about herbs and their healing properties, "women's voices are surprisingly underrepresented in the history of medical enterprise, both as practitioners and as medical writers."[30] Hildegard is one of the very rare exceptions to this rule. She far surpasses Augustine in her curiosity and interest in understanding the material world. In striking contrast to Hildegard, late in his career as a prominent bishop, Augustine berates himself for being allured by the sight of a dog chasing a rabbit across the open field.[31] It is difficult to imagine Hildegard upbraiding herself for watching something that catches her interest and keen powers of observation.

BODY AND SOUL

In the philosophical view that he inherits from Platonism (the dualism of soul and body, the hierarchical ordering of entities, and valuing the spiritual over the material world), Augustine considers the human being as two distinct and different substances—body and soul. He accepts the Platonic view that spiritual entities are not only different in kind, but also are superior to physical entities. Nonetheless, he still takes great pains to maintain the essential goodness of creation while retaining a deep suspicion about the material world, especially its capacity to lure humans away from God. It is in this context that Augustine's view of the human being as a "soul using a body" needs to be understood.[32] The soul is clearly superior to and better than the body being used.

In another text, he defines the human soul as "a rational substance designed to rule the body."[33] As his thought matures, he is not as interested in the role and functioning of the body (except in so far as it is the site of temptation), nor in specifying the ways that the soul and body interact. In later works, especially *The Trinity*, Augustine is much more concerned to explore and analyze the spiritual and intellectual powers of the soul—reason, will, and memory—than to give an account of the ways in which the body provides data for the mind's operations.

Hildegard is not so critical of the body as Augustine, although she, too, warns about the moral dangers lurking in the world and with the physical body, especially since the sin of Adam and Eve. However, Hildegard clearly does not share Augustine's deep suspicion of the human body. She devoted an entire work to detail the ills that affect the human body and to recommend treatments. She is far more interested in the actual workings of the human body, with a natural curiosity and feeling for the value of the body and the goodness of the physical world. If anything, we see Augustine struggling to maintain the "goodness of all creation" as an abstract principle while his writings are brimming with warnings about the body and the enticements of the world. Hildegard has a much more balanced approach that presents a view of body and soul in a relationship of reciprocity and mutuality.[34] Surprisingly, she also has a developmental approach to the ways in which the soul's powers are expressed through the powers of the body depending on a person's age.[35]

WOMAN AND MAN

The question about whether women, like men, were made in God's image had been debated since early Christianity. Augustine and Hildegard dealt with it very differently, arriving at divergent conclusions. In a convoluted text in *The Trinity*, Augustine addresses the issue, stating that man alone is the image of God and that it is only when woman is taken together with her husband as "one substance" that she is considered the image of God.[36] Hildegard's approach to the question is very different. As Barbara Newman points out, Hildegard stresses the "incarnational" aspects of the image of God in the sense that woman's role through Mary in the Incarnation of Christ gives all women a unique and important status as image of God. Following an old analogy, Hildegard asserted, "man is like the soul and woman like the body," and by extension "man signifies the divinity and woman the humanity of the Son of God." Herein lies the clue to Hildegard's surprisingly radical anthropology, which would exalt not the male but the female as the representative human being. Adam symbolizes, but does not share, the divine nature. In contrast, Eve both symbolizes and bestows the divine humanity, insofar as she prefigures Mary. It is not by her appearance but by her gift that the woman represents Christ's human nature and bears the stamp of his image.[37]

Again Hildegard emphasizes the value and importance of the body—particularly the woman's body—as created by God. She also considers woman's body to be the vehicle through which a new understanding of women as the image of God is achieved—by revealing "the hidden God by giving him birth" and, in so doing, giving "birth to his image in every child she bears."[38]

Conception and birth lead to the issue of sexuality—one that is very complex for both writers and can only be touched on briefly here. Both use the iconic figures of Eve and Mary as reference points. As with their views of the human body, Augustine is much more negative and wary of human sexuality than Hildegard. In fact, her writings on women's sexuality, menstruation, childbirth, and menopause are remarkable for their openness, candor, and great sympathy. Interestingly, these were the very roles that Hildegard and her nuns were able to avoid by a life of consecrated virginity in the monastery. While Hildegard was able to avoid the travails of these traditional roles, although not rejecting them for women, she casts them in a more positive light than do male thinkers of the Christian tradition.

Both Augustine and Hildegard support the Christian teaching that sexual activity must be limited to marriage for its primary purpose, reproduction. Premarital sex (fornication) and extramarital sex (adultery) are forbidden and seriously sinful. They extol virginity (in particular consecrated virginity in religious life) above marriage, although Hildegard expresses more sympathy than Augustine for the difficulties women face as wives and mothers. As with image of God debates, Hildegard stresses women's contributions in sexuality and has a more nuanced understanding of the complementary roles for women and men beyond mere female passivity and male activity. The man may be "prior" in the sense that Adam was created before Eve and that without his seed, no child may be conceived, but such priority or difference in function does not lead Hildegard to believe in a God-given superiority of men over women.

Hildegard's descriptions of sexual activity are matter of fact, given with an analogy to other natural forces (air and wind) that emphasized sex as completely natural. In this view, Hildegard is light years ahead of Augustine—and most other male writers for centuries to come. She shows an understanding of the sexual aspects of human life and the value of sexual pleasure that Augustine completely rejected. He is, after all, the writer who considered even lawful sexual intercourse between husband and wife beyond the need for reproduction to be sinful (although not seriously sinful).[39]

Conclusion

Despite the separations of time, place, and gender, there are many substantive points of contact between these two thinkers. Christian revelation was the fountain of both their lives, not as abstract doctrines, but as a living encounter with the living God—described by Augustine as "Beauty ever ancient, ever new," lamenting "Late have I loved you,"[40] and by Hildegard as "Living Light." Although faith provided the deep direction of their lives, it did not preclude questions, uncertainties, and efforts to come to greater understanding of Christianity. Both were intensely passionate in their quest for God, not as an object to be apprehended by the mind, but a personal God whose call invited responses from their entire beings. Given the ardor with which they pursued this quest, it is no wonder that images of light and fire figure so prominently.

This dual reading of Augustine and Hildegard reveals points of contact between them. Undoubtedly Augustine's works continue to have monumental importance. Hildegard is shown to be an imaginative thinker in her own right who wrestles with many of the same questions as Augustine, as well as ones he did not address. We have seen their similarities and differences, including those areas that Augustine neglected and the ways his emphasis on human sinfulness led him to certain distortions and blind spots. Augustine had a tremendous passion for life; once he redirected that passion to a life of celibate Christianity, he renders the world, the body, and the entire material universe highly suspect and dangerous. In contrast to Augustine, Hildegard, who was placed in a convent at a very young age, displays a wonder about the world and the human body evidenced by her acute observations and analyses.

Augustine missed much by casting the world in such a suspicious light. Perhaps, since as a young man, he was so caught up in the world's beauties and enticements, he feared he would be caught once more. In contrast, since Hildegard's life was so directed by monastic rule from such a young age, perhaps she did not fear such entrapments. Even beautiful singing in church was a temptation for Augustine:

> Thus I waver between the danger of sensual pleasure and wholesome experience. I am inclined rather to approve the practice of singing in church, . . . so that through the pleasure afforded the ears, the weaker mind may rise to feelings of devotion. However, when it so happens that I am moved more by the singing than by what is sung, I confess that I have sinned, in such wise as to deserve punishment, and at such times I should prefer not to listen to a singer.[41]

How ironic that the woman who spent virtually her entire life in the restricted monastery is the one whose voice sounds so clearly and publicly about the goodness of creation. Hildegard maintained this conviction, not as an abstract principle, but with a vibrancy of images, metaphors, and analogies, as well as art and music, that showed her deep appreciation for the beauty of creation as an expression of divine beauty. Not only was she not suspicious of sacred songs, she herself wrote some of the most beautiful songs of the medieval period in a text called, fittingly, *Symphony of the Harmony of Celestial Revelations*. Let us give Hildegard the last word by quoting one of her songs praising the Holy Spirit:

> The Holy Spirit is the life that gives life.
> Moving all things.

It is the root in every creature
And purifies all things,
Wiping away sins, anointing wounds.
The spirit is radiant life, worthy of praise,
Awakening and enlivening
All things.[42]

Questions for Reflection

Hildegard and Augustine shared many of the same views on Christianity as a religion and
a source of philosophy. In what ways is their thinking different and why are these
differences important? Do you think that either or both Augustine's and Hildegard's
religious views were philosophical? Defend your answer.

Many of their ideas emerged from their experiences and involvement in the major events
of their times. What were some of these experiences that spurred them to develop
specific ideas about God, the world, the human being's nature and place in the
world, and the status of men and women?

In what ways did their gender and experiences influence Hildegard's and Augustine's views
on men and women, the body, and sexuality? Regarding Hildegard in particular, in
terms of life and a conception of philosophy as either felt, lived experiences or as based
on them, how do you think what Hildegard did with her life (what she wrote, the
topics of her writings, and the way she lived her life) influence her thinking?

Notes

1. Frederick Copleston, SJ, *A History of Philosophy*, vol.1, *Greece and Ross, From the Pre-Socratics to Plotinus* (New York: Doubleday, 1995), 484.

2. Sister Prudence Allen, RSM, *The Concept of Woman: The Aristotelian Revolution, 750 B.C.–C.E. 1250* (Grand Rapids, MI: William B. Freedman Publishing Co., 1985), 310.

3. Allen, *Concept*, 3.

4. Allen, *Concept*, 292.

5. Ethel M. Kersey, *Women Philosophers: A Bio-Critical Source Book* (New York: Greenwood Press, 1989), 131.

6. Margaret Alic, *Hypatia's Heritage: A History of Women in Science from Antiquity Through the Nineteenth Century* (Boston: Beacon Press, 1986), 74.

7. Allen, *Concept*, 292.

8. Helen J. John, SND, "Hildegard of Bingen: A New Medieval Philosopher?" in *Presenting Women Philosophers*, eds. Cecile T. Tougas and Sara Ebenreck (Philadelphia, PA: Temple University Press, 2000), 34–35.

9. John, "Hildegard of Bingen," 35, 36, and 37.

10. John, "Hildegard of Binger," 38.

11. Elisabeth Gossman, "Hildegard of Bingen," in *A History of Women Philosophers*, vol. 2, *Medieval, Renaissance and Enlightenment Women Philosophers 500–1600 AD*, ed. Mary Ellen Waithe (Dordrecht, The Netherlands: Kluwer Academic Publisher, 1989), 27 (both quotes).

12. Excerpt's from Augustine's *Confessions*, Book 1, trans. Henry Chadwick (New York: Oxford University Press, 1992), Bk. I, i, 1–ii, 2; VII, x, 16; xi, 17; xii, 18; xiii, 19; xvii, 23; VIII,vii, 16–18; viii, 19; xii, 28–30; IX, x, 23–24; X, xvii, 26; xxvii, 38. Published by permission of Oxford University Press. The parenthetical references in the texts are to the various books, chapters, and verses of the Bible. Please refer to any standard edition of the Bible (including both the Hebrew and Christian scriptures) for the texts that are cited here.

Augustine himself did not include the citations in his manuscript of the *Confessions*. They have been added by subsequent editors. The frequency and variety of Augustine's use of biblical references indicates the extent to which the Bible had come to inform his thinking by the time he wrote the *Confessions* (397–401 C.E.).

13. Augustine, *Literal Commentary on Genesis*, in *The Essential Augustine*, ed. Vernon Bourke (New York: Mentor Books, New American Library, 1964). Excerpts included here are from sections 30, 58; 31, 59. Published with permission from Paulist Press.

14. Augustine, *The Trinity, Book Ten*, in *The Fathers of the Church*, vol. 45, trans. Stephen McKenna, CSSR (Washington, DC: Catholic University Press, 1963). Excerpts included here are from sections Book 10, chapter 5, 7; and Book 12, chapter 7, 9, 10. Published with permission of The Catholic University of America Press.

15. Hildegard of Bingen, *Scivias*, trans. Mother Columba Hart and Jane Bishop (New York: Paulist Press, 1990). Excerpts here are from Declaration, Book 1, Vision 2: 11–12 and Vision 4: 17–21; Book 3, Vision 12: 3. © 1990 by the Abbey of Regina Lauris: Benedictine Congregation Regina Laudis of the Strict Observance, Inc., New York/Wahwah, NJ. Used with permission. www.paulistpress.com.

16. Hildegard of Bingen, *Book of Divine Works*, ed. with intro. by Matthew Fox (Santa Fe, NM: Bear & Co., 1987). Excerpts here are from Vision 4: 15, 19, 24, 100; Letter 39: Hildegard to Wibert of Gembloux. © 1987 Bear & Company, Inc. www.InnerTraditions.com.

17. *Hildegard of Bingen: Mystical Writings*, eds. Fiona Bowie and Oliver Davies (New York: Crossroad, 1992): Excerpts here are from Hildegard's *Causes and Cures*, "Adam and Eve" and "The Four Temperaments" of Woman." Reprinted with permission by Crossroad Publishing Company.

18. Karl Jaspers, *The Great Philosophers*, vol. 1, trans. Ralph Manheim (New York: Harcourt, Brace & World, 1962), xi, xiv.

19. Augustine, *The Trinity*, 15, 2, 2.

20. Jaspers calls Augustine's thinking a "metaphysics of inner experience." "Augustine," in *The Great Philosophers*, 180.

21. Barbara Newman, "Hildegard's Life and Times," in *Voice of the Living Light*, ed. Barbara Newman (Berkeley: University of California Press, 1998), 10.

22. Barbara Newman, *Sister of Wisdom: Hildegard's Theology of the Feminine* (Berkeley: University of California Press, 1987), 2.

23. John 8:12, 9:5, 12:35–36, 46; 1 John 1:5.

24. Newman, *Sister of Wisdom*, 6–7.

25. Newman, *Sister of Wisdom*, 6–7.

26. Augustine, *The Trinity*, 12, 15, 24.

27. Hildegard of Bingen, *Scivias*, 2:1, 2–3.

28. Constant Mews, "Religious Thinker: 'A Frail Human Being' on Fiery Life," in *Voice of the Living Light*, 56.

29. *Scivias*, 2:1, 7.

30. Florence Eliza Glaze, "Medical Writer: 'Behold the Human Creature,'" in *Voice of the Living Light*, 133.

31. *Confessions*, 10:35, 57.

32. Augustine, *On the Morals of the Catholic Church*, 1:27, 52.

33. Augustine, *On the Magnitude of the Soul*, 13, 22.

34. Hildegard, *Book of Divine Works*, 4, 24.

35. Hildegard, *Scivias*, 1:4, 17

36. Augustine, *The Trinity*, 12, 7, 9.

37. Newman, *Sister of Wisdom*, 93, quoting Hildegard, *Book of Divine Works* 2:5, 43.

38. Newman, *Sister of Wisdom*, 93.

39. Augustine, *The Good of Marriage*, 6, 6.

40. Augustine, *Confessions*, 10:27, 38.

41. *Confessions*, 10:33, 50.

42. Hildegard, "Antiphon for the Holy Spirit I," in *Hildegard of Bingen: Mystical Writings*, eds. Fiona Bowie and Oliver Davies (New York: Crossroad, Spiritual Classics, 1992), 118.

CHAPTER 4

Abelard and Heloise

Introduction by *Karen J. Warren*

This chapter introduction has a unique feature: it begins with an edited version of an e-mail interview I initiated with Mary Ellen Waithe, this chapter's commentator. Why include an interview in this chapter when I do not in others? In addition to her status as an Abelard–Heloise scholar, Mary Ellen Waithe is the one who, more than any other single person, created the area of scholarly research called "the recovery project"; her research ultimately resulted in her editing the ground-breaking, four-volume set *A History of Women Philosophers*, from the sixth century B.C.E. to the present. What led Mary Ellen Waithe to understand, appreciate, and do something so major as play a leading role in the recovery project and the four-volume set that she produced as a result?

My edited interview answers this two-part question. It begins with an abbreviated description of Waithe's own account of how she became interested in the recovery project then shifts to her explanation of why there has been a shift in her views about the "tragic affair" that is invariably part of any discussion of Abelard and Heloise. By starting this chapter introduction with an abridged version of that interview, an amazing story about the recovery project that deserves to be told is told, and the telling of it places the reader at the center of a scholarly debate about this chapter's philosophical pair. Inclusion of the "living biographical history" was an opportunity too good to pass up.

AN EDITED VERSION OF MY INTERVIEW WITH MARY ELLEN WAITHE

KJW: What originally prompted you to ask who the neglected women philosophers were?

MEW: It began with a chance encounter with a reference work I came across in 1980. I was sitting in a university basement library before I was scheduled to make a presentation. Casually looking at the bookcase that faced me, I saw a book *Bibliography of Philosophy*. Curious, I took it from the shelf and was thumbing through it when I glimpsed a title

Historia Mulierum Philosopharum. It caught my attention. Although I have never studied Latin, I thought "Mulierum" meant "women" in Latin. At my first opportunity I asked my husband, who once taught Latin, if *Historia Mulierum Philosopharum* meant what I thought it meant. He confirmed my suspicions. To my amazement, the reference was to a book written by Gilles Ménage in the 1600s about women philosophers! Tracking down a microfilm of the book, I read and then photocopied it. That was when and how the recovery project began for me.

Over time I looked up all the names of the women in the book, gathered information about each and determined which women in Ménage's book were what we would call philosophers today. I then began to create a bibliography of women philosophers based on this research. During 1980 and 1981 I located copies of the books they had written, all the same editions cited by Ménage.

KJW: What did you do next?

MEW: Since I had no English translations, just fragments and letters in Greek and Latin, I asked Vicki Harper (commentator, chapter 2) to translate the Greek works I had copied by Pythagorean women and tell me whether the works were philosophy. She agreed to do so; her translations confirmed that these fragments discussed virtue, justice, reason, and other philosophical topics—the same topics as their male counterparts Pythagoras and Plato. Her conclusion was that the fragments were, indeed, philosophy texts.

KJW: How did the rediscovery of the names and texts of these women change you?

MEW: In all my education and training, I had never once heard about any woman philosopher who lived before the twentieth century. So, at first I was angry that neither my teachers nor other women philosophers in our field knew the history of our discipline. But that anger motivated me to find out who these neglected women philosophers were. I focused on following all leads by looking up the women in encyclopedias and history books. I also went through *every single book* on every single shelf at the University of Minnesota library, including the storage stacks, looking for names of females or feminine names associated with texts that might be considered philosophical and the names in Ménage's book Then I made a tentative decision about whether the works fit what I understood philosophy to be.

KJW: At the time, what impact did you think these rediscoveries of women philosophers would have on the discipline of philosophy?

MEW: The inclusion of these women required that one ask, "What is philosophy? Who is a philosopher?" I saw how its definition changed over the millennia. I expected that the inclusion of women philosophers would challenge current conceptions of philosophy and certainly would impact philosophy curricula. In some areas it has to be done. Both mainstream accounts of the history of Western philosophy continue to be highly resistant to the inclusion of these very real, neglected women philosophers.

KJW: I want to switch gears now and ask you about Abelard and Heloise. In an early essay on their tragic love affair you said Heloise was raped. Is that still your view? And does it matter how one describes or assesses this philosophical pair's positions on love and ethics to whether or not Abelard raped Heloise?

MEW: I remain unsettled on this issue, though I have softened the position I took earlier [in *A History of Women Philosophers*, volume 2]. Based on the texts available at the time by Abelard and Heloise, I described the affair as coerced, forcible sex—or rape. That was prior to the discovery of "the unsigned letters" and the attribution of them to Heloise and Abelard (excerpts of which are included in this chapter). That was also when the existing scholarship provided evidence that the relationship between Abelard and Heloise was appropriately described as "one of the greatest love stories ever told." I still think it is. But that traditional view ignores the fact that Abelard himself publicly writes that he often beat Heloise into submission. Furthermore, when the more recent, unsigned or "lost letters" were published, and Abelard and Heloise were identified as their authors, a different perspective emerged. These lost letters show a very flirtatious, seductive Heloise sending her servants back and forth from one side of her house to the other (where Abelard stayed for a time) with very sensual love letters. The letters reveal a mutual sexual attraction. However, since they lived in a society that condemned premarital sex and disallowed marriage for philosophers, Heloise was concerned that Abelard's career as a philosopher would end if he married her.

The new information from these lost letters challenges the traditional description of their relationship. It shifted my view insofar as I now think Heloise loved Abelard so much as a man and as a philosopher that she absolutely refused to marry him, even when he proposed to her. But as a woman, she was sexually attracted to him. So how do I resolve the "rape or love question" now? With the new letters, I would argue that while Heloise was in a dilemma: despite her strong feeling toward him, Heloise did not consent to either sex or marriage. She opposed marriage to Abelard—what he wanted—because she wanted his career as a philosopher to flourish, and she accepted the cultural view that a woman who had premarital sex was not a woman of virtue. As Abelard writes in one letter, he "forced" her consent. Only if she submitted to his sexual advances would she be "committed to him," since she would then be ineligible for other suitors.

Was her submission rape? Technically, yes, because he forced her. But morally speaking, under the circumstances of the time and in light of her sexual advances toward him, was what happened rape? Only Heloise can answer that.

KJW: Thank you Mary Ellen. Your recovery story is one of incredible determination and persistence. This book would not be possible without both your scholarly efforts and those of the book's recovery and inclusion scholars, many of whom are included as expert commentators in your four-volume *A History of Women Philosophers*.

ABELARD

While in his teens Abelard (ca. 1101–1164) moved to Paris to pursue an academic life. There he earned a reputation as an excellent teacher and master of argument in rhetoric, dialectic, theology, and philosophy—a reputation that drew large crowds—some say thousands of students—from many countries.[1]

Abelard's philosophy is known for its scholastic manner, aimed at providing a rational defense and interpretation of ecclesiastical doctrine and for elevating the philosophical positions of Aristotle. Abelard's main writings are his autobiography, *Historia Calamitatum*, and his letters to Heloise. His special area of philosophical expertise is ethics, focusing on the relationship of intention to moral character, moral responsibility, and the moral value of human action, described in the section on Heloise. While he is considered a philosopher in the tradition of medieval philosophy, he was also an accomplished poet and composer and is remembered for the "tragic love affair" with Heloise.

HELOISE

At age sixteen or seventeen, Heloise (1130–1164), whose reputation for learning was well known, became the pupil of Abelard, at the time the foremost philosopher of France.[2] According to Abelard, Heloise knew Latin, Hebrew, and Greek, and she read classical works of philosophy, theology, history, literature, and rhetoric (the art of persuasion through logical argument grammatically and aesthetically composed).[3] The only writings by Heloise that remain are her letters to Abelard.

In those letters, Heloise addresses the philosophy of love and friendship and the nature of moral responsibility. She accepted Cicero's view on love, arguing that "love is disinterested in anything but the giving of love itself. All the true friend or true lover wants is the experience of giving love to the beloved."[4] Her views on moral responsibility echoed Abelard's views: the moral value of an act depends on its intention. Accordingly, one can commit a morally wrong act but not be morally blameworthy or guilty, if the act is done from the right intentions.

Discussion of "the tragic love affair" typically overshadows considerations of Heloise as a philosopher. Abelard writes of this incident: "When you [Heloise] objected to it yourself and resisted with all your might and tried to dissuade me from it, I frequently forced your consent . . . by threats and blows."[5] Heloise became pregnant and ultimately "obeyed Abelard's command to marry her," even though she always regretted the decision. She claimed that marrying was "inconsistent with loving him disinterestedly (i.e., for who he was, rather than for satisfaction of her own desires) and would allow passion to dominate reason."[6] When her uncle Fulbert broke his promise to keep the marriage secret, Abelard and Heloise publicly denied their marriage and Heloise returned to the cloister Argenteuil. Furious about their deception, Fulbert had Abelard castrated.

Interestingly, it is Heloise who *really* believes that philosophy must be practiced in word and deed. She regards Abelard as a hypocrite for not practicing what he preached about love and intentions. She criticizes his proclaimed love for her, since it did not consist of desiring that she attain her highest good, and his marrying her, since his intentions were not honorable. She acknowledged that she wronged Abelard (e.g., by marrying him) but that she was not responsible or guilty, since she did so with the best of intentions. If a decision about whether Heloise was a philosopher is based solely on her correspondence with Abelard, then the reader must decide whether Heloise is appropriately called a philosopher largely on her views about the role of intentions in ethics (see Anscombe, chapter fourteen), her conception of love and friendship, and her conception of the applied nature of philosophy.

WAITHE'S COMMENTARY

In her commentary, Waithe provides detailed biographical, historical, and philosophical information relevant to an understanding of Abelard and Heloise. She focuses on two topics already mentioned—the morality of intent and views on love—to unveil the similarities and differences between the two. When one combines Waithe's commentary with my email interview with her, one appreciates not only the challenges of differentiating the philosophical positions of Abelard and Heloise, but also ways recovering new writings or information can challenge one's own philosophical views (for example, about the relevance of personal lives to an understanding and assessment of a person's philosophical views, to one's conception of philosophy, and to the nature of philosophical methodologies). Abelard is an acknowledged canonical philosopher, taught often in medieval philosophy courses. Although his "love affair" with Heloise is well known—an indelible mark on Abelard's biography, Heloise is rarely included in the canon as a philosopher worthy of study. So one important way to approach this philosophical pair is to ask: Given the views expressed by Heloise on love, friendship, philosophy, and the morality of intentions, and given the similarities and differences between the acknowledged philosophers Abelard and Heloise, as expressed in the primary texts, should Heloise be recognized as a philosopher as well?

Excerpts of Writings by Abelard and Heloise

I. EXCERPTS FROM HELOISE'S *LETTERS TO ABELARD* (AS THEY APPEAR IN THE ORIGINAL TEXT)[7]

Heloise's Unsigned[8] Letter 25 to Abelard

Woman:[9] To her incomparable treasure, more delightful than all the pleasures of the world: blessedness without end and well-being without weakening. I too have been considering with innate reflection what love [*amor*] is or what it can be by analogy with our behavior and concerns, that which above all forms friendships [*amicitia*], and, once considered, leads to repaying you with the exchange of love [*amor*] and obeying you in everything . . . If our love [*amor*] deserted us with so slight a force, then it was not true love [*amor*] but only feigned love. For love [*amor*] does not easily forsake those whom it has once stung. You know, my heart's love [*amor*], that the services of true love [*amor*] are properly fulfilled only when they are continually owed, in such a way that we act for a friend [*amicitia*] according to our strength and not stop wishing to go beyond our strength.

This debt of true love [*dilectio*], therefore, I shall endeavor to fulfill, but alas I am unable to do so in full. However, if the duty of greeting you according to my meager talents is not enough, at least my never-ending desire to do so may be of some merit in your estimation. For know this, my beloved [*dilectio*], and know it truly, that ever since your love [*dilectio*] claimed for itself the guest chamber—or rather the hovel—of my heart, it has always remained welcome and day after day more delightful, without, as often happens, constant presence leading to familiarity, familiarity to trust, trust to negligence, and negligence to contempt. Indeed, you began to desire me with much interest at the very beginning of our friendship [*amicitia*], but with greater longing you strove to make our love grow and last. And so our spirit fluctuates according to how your affairs turn out, so that your joy I count as my gain and your misfortune my most bitter loss. But your fulfilling what you have begun does not seem the same to me as your increasing what you have completed, because in one case what is lacking is added, in the other what is completed is added on. And even if we show perfect kindness to everyone, we still do not love [*caritas*] everyone equally; and what is general for everyone is made particular for certain people. It is one thing to sit at the table of a prince, another to be there in order to advise him, and a greater thing to be drawn out of love, rather than just to be invited to a gathering. So I owe you fewer thanks for not spurning me than for receiving me with open arms. Let me speak plainly to your resplendent mind and heart so pure. It is not a great thing if I love [*diligo*] you, but rather a wicked thing if ever I shall forget you. Therefore, my dear, do not make yourself so scarce to your faithful friend. So far I have somehow been able to bear it, but now, deprived of your presence and stirred by the songs of birds and the freshness of the woods, I languish for your love [*amor*]. Surely I would have rejoiced in all these things if I had been able to enjoy your conversation and presence according to my will. May God do for me such as I desire for you. Farewell.[10]

Heloise's "Unsigned" Letter 49 to Abelard

Woman:[11] To the rose that does not wither, blooming with the flower of blessedness, she who loves [*diligo*] you above all men: may you grow as you flourish and flourish as you grow.

You know, greatest part of my soul, that many people love [*diligo*] each other for many reasons, but no friendship [*amicitia*] of theirs will be as constant as that which stems from integrity and virtue, and from deep love [*diligo*]. For I do not consider the friendship [*amicitia*] of those who seem to love [*diligo*] each other for riches and pleasures to be durable at all, since the very things on which they base their love [*diligo*] seem to have no durability. Consequently, when their riches or pleasure runs out, so too at the same time love [*diligo*] may fail, since they loved [*diligo*] these things not because of each other but each other because of these things.

But my love [*diligo*] is united with you by a completely different pact. And the useless burdens of wealth, more conducive to wrongdoing than anything when the thirst for possession begins to glow, did not compel me to love [*diligo*] you—only the highest virtue, in which lies the root of all honors and every success. Indeed, it is this virtue which is self-sufficient and in need of nothing else, which restrains passion, keeps desires in check, moderates joys, and eradicates sorrows; which provides everything proper, everything pleasing, everything delightful; and than which nothing better can be found. Surely I have discovered in you—and thus I love [*diligo*] you—undoubtedly the greatest and most outstanding good of all. Since it is established that this is eternal, it is for me the proof beyond doubt that you will remain my love [*diligo*] for eternity. Therefore believe me, desirable one, that neither wealth, distinctions, nor all the things that devotees of this world lust after, will be able to sever me from love [*diligo*] for you. Truly there will never be a day in which I would be able to think of myself and let it pass without thinking of you. Know that I am not concerned by any doubt that I may hope the same thing from you.

It is very rash of me to send studied phrases to you, because even someone learned right down to his fingertips, who has transformed every artistic arrangement into habit through long-established practice, would not be capable of painting a portrait of eloquence florid enough to justly deserve being seen by so great a teacher (a teacher so great, I declare, a teacher of virtue, a teacher of character, to whom French pigheadedness rightly yields and for whom at the same time the haughtiness of the whole world rises in respect, that anyone who considers himself even slightly learned would be rendered completely speechless and mute by his own judgment), much less myself, who hardly seem adept at trifles "which neither taste of nibbled nails nor bang the desk."

And so may your generosity trust me: unless I knew the unfailing friendship [*amicitia*] of true love [*dilectio*] to be implanted in you, I would not presume to send you inelegant letters of such unrefined style. But because the spur of tireless care [*caritas*] and sweetness has driven me into a passion [*dilectio*] for loving [*amor*] you, although it might be unpleasing for you (heaven forbid), the ardent feeling of my love [*dilectio*] for you finds that complete devotion can never be hindered by any intervening difficulty. Therefore, if my will could have been fulfilled, certainly that letter and more would have been sent to you, so that I would write to you only if my situation demanded, nor would I care to give my pen a single day's holiday, even though it might annoy you to write to me.

At the beginning, you certainly aroused my hunger for your letters, and you have not yet fully satisfied it. For when, as is usual, I pine deep inside with longing for my friends, you could have relieved much sorrow if you had delivered a longer speech. Nevertheless I accept this tiny abridgment of a caring greeting as if it were an angel, reading and rereading it every single hour. Sometimes even kissing it in place of you, I apply myself to satisfying my intense longing. For you might think that there is nothing in this life more delightful to me than to speak or write to you or to hear you speak—indeed, that honey-like sweetness of your writing clings to my heart and, whenever I think about it, leads me from sorrow to joy and even from grief to cheerfulness. God knows, nothing can be considered more true. Perhaps you scarcely believe it, but I believe the day will come—if it pleases God—when you will admit that you have never heard anything more true. But let my declaration come to an end, for I have given an account of how our love [*dilectio*] should be maintained.

Abelard's Unsigned Letter 50 to Heloise

Man:[12] To the only disciple of philosophy among all the young women of our age, the only one on whom fortune has completely bestowed all the gifts of the manifold virtues, the only attractive one, the only gracious one, he who through your gift is nourished by the upper air, he who lives only when he is sure of your favor: may you advance even further—if she who has reached the summit can advance any further. . . . I admire your talent, you who discuss the rules of friendship so subtly that you seem not to have read Tully[13] but to have given those precepts to Tully himself! Therefore, so that I may come to the reply, if it can rightly be called a reply when nothing equal is given back, I shall reply in my own manner. What you say is true, sweetest of all women, that truly such a love [*dilectio*] does not bind us as often binds those who seek only their own interests, who make friendship [*amicitia*] a source of profit, whose loyalty stands firm or collapses with their fortunes, who do not consider virtue to be of value for its own sake, who call friendship to account, those who with busy fingers keep count of what they ought to get back, for whom indeed nothing is sweet without profit.

Truly we have been joined—I would not say by fortune but rather by God—under a different agreement. I chose you among many thousands because of your countless virtues: truthfully for no other benefit than that I might rest in you, or that you might lighten all my troubles, or that of all the good things in the world only your charm might restore me and make me forget all sorrows. You are my fill when hungry, my refreshment when thirsty, my rest when weary, my warmth when cold, my shade when hot, indeed in every storm you are my most wholesome and true calm.

Perhaps because of some good report you heard about me, you also thought fit to invite to make your acquaintance. I am inferior to you in many ways, or to speak more truthfully, I am inferior in every way, because you surpass me even where I seemed to surpass you. Your talent, your command of language, beyond your years and sex, is now beginning to extend itself into manly strength. What humility, what affability you accord to everyone! What admirable moderation with such dignity! Do not people esteem you more than everybody else, do they not set you up on high, so that from there you can shine forth like a lamp and be observed by all?

I believe and confidently assert that there is no mortal, no relative, no friend whom you would prefer to me, or to speak more boldly, whom you would compare with me. For I am not leaden, I am not a blockhead, I am not so hard-nosed that I cannot scent acutely where true love [amor] exists and who loves [diligo] me from the heart. Farewell, you who make me fare well, and in whatever way I stand in your favor, make me certain, for your favor is my only enjoyment.

Abelard's Unsigned Letter 59 to Heloise

Man: To his most beloved, to be loved more than everything that is or can be: continuous well-being and abundant success in everything good.

An unavoidable matter has intervened and put its left foot against my desire. I am guilty, I who compelled you to sin.

Heloise's Unsigned Letter 60 to Abelard

Woman: To one till now faithfully adored, hereafter not to be loved with the chain of an ailing passion: the firm guarantee nonetheless of love and faith.

I had revealed myself to you with a great pledge of loving care [caritatis] while your true love was founded on a firm root; for I had placed all my hope in you, as though you were an invincible tower. You also know, if you will only grant this, that I have never been deceitful toward you, nor do I wish to be. Now consider and reflect on these and other similar matters. I have truly always borne for you a great many things fully enough and completely, and can never express how strongly, how intensely I began to love you. If it was necessary for the bond that we had established to be broken, even though this might contain much bitterness, at least now it will not be broken again. Take your complaints away from me, I will not hear your words any more. For where I expected many good things to be of benefit to me, there emerged instead tearful sighs of the heart.

May almighty God, who wants no one to perish and who loves sinners with more than paternal love, illuminate your heart with the splendor of His grace and bring you back to the road to salvation, so that you may understand that His will is favorable and perfect. Farewell; your wisdom and knowledge have deceived me, and therefore from now on may all our writing cease.

Abelard's Unsigned Letter 72 to Heloise

Man: To one angered but not forsaking compassion in her anger, he who is restored to favor: may you live happily until such time as I might wish to be without your favor. In this way will our love [*amor*] be immortal: if each of us strives to outdo the other in a friendly and loving contest and if neither of us agreed to be outdone by the other. Indeed, it happens that a friend may grow weary of love [*amor*] if he sees himself loved by a friend less than he deserves. Therefore I would never want to say that I love [*amor*] you more than I feel loved [*amor*], because such a statement is foolish and invites derision. On the contrary, I hold this assertion to be much better: that in a mutual love, I do not want to be the lesser, and which of us surpasses the other I do not know. . . . Someone once said on seeing a thorn sprouting very beautiful flowers from itself: "Such is my lady: no thorn is sharper when she is angry, no flower more delightful or beautiful when she is pleased." Farewell, and make sure that you compare no mortal with me, for I will tenaciously persist with the same intention toward you. Greetings, my most beloved [*dilectio*], and keep me in your memory as forever yours.

Heloise's Unsigned Letter 79 to Abelard

Woman: To one deserving to be embraced with the longing of a special love, a fire of longing for you: may you gather as many greetings as flowers give perfume in the season of delight. If through reflection a person's inner intention [*intencio*] conceives anything great, it is often not brought to fruition without a certain external force. For either it is confounded by despair of ever being completed or it is severely crushed by too much effort before it is completed. As a result, in either case the effort or endeavor itself seems very often to fail when the desired goal cannot be reached.

Heloise's Unsigned Letter 84 to Abelard

Woman: A lover to a lover: joy with well-being for one desiring that saving joy, I declare, never ending and never to be taken away from you. Ever since we first met and spoke to each other, only you have pleased me above all God's creatures and only you have I loved. Through loving you, I searched for you; searching for you, I found you; finding you, I desired you; desiring you, I chose you; choosing you, I placed you before everyone else in my heart, and picked you alone out of thousands, in order to make a pledge with you. With that pledge fulfilled and having tasted the honey of your sweetness, I hoped to put an end to future cares. . . . I love you with a steadfast and whole mind. Thus far you have remained with me, you have manfully fought the good fight with me, but you have not yet received the prize. If the faith falters of the one in whom I had placed—and still keep—all my hope and trust, and if the chain of his love should not firmly hold fast, I have no idea at all in whom else I can subsequently believe.

Like it or not, you are mine and always shall be. Never shall my desire for you be altered, nor will I ever take back my whole spirit from you. In you I have what I searched for, I hold what I chose, I embrace what I desired; only your qualities will do.

Abelard's Unsigned Letter 101 to Heloise

Man: To his starry eye: may it always see what is pleasing and never perceive what is displeasing. I am the person I have been. Nothing has changed in me concerning my ardor for you, except that every day the flame of love for you rises even more. I admit this change alone, this alone do I rightly concede, that it grows in love for you within me in every season. If you care to note, I am now speaking to you more cautiously, and approaching you more cautiously; shame tempers love, modesty checks love, lest it rush out in its immensity. This way we can fulfill our sweet desires and gradually stifle the rumor that has arisen about us. Farewell.

Abelard's Unsigned Letter 103 to Heloise

Man: To one more shiny than silver, more brilliant than any precious stone, and surpassing all spices in aroma and taste, he who is always restored by your new gifts and joys: may you always delight in lovely newness.

Love [*amor*] cannot remain idle. It always rises for a friend, always strives for new ways to be of service, never sleeps, never falls into laziness. These maxims are clearly confirmed in you, my spirit; firmly persisting in the course of the love that has begun, you always indicate to your friend with new signs how you feel about him. How much I value your gifts and how important they are to me, I shall reveal to you privately.

Abelard's Unsigned Letter 106 to Heloise

Man: There is nothing worse than a foolish man blessed by fortune. Now for the first time I realize the good fortune I previously enjoyed, now I have the opportunity to look back on happy times, for hope is fading—I do not know whether ever to be recovered. I am paying the price for stupidity, because I am losing that good thing of which I have been completely unworthy, that good thing which I have not known how to keep as I ought. It is flying elsewhere, forsaking me, because it realizes that I am not worthy of having it. Farewell.

II. EXCERPTS FROM ABELARD'S *HISTORIA CALAMITATUM* (THE STORY OF MY MISFORTUNES)[14]

Abelard Writes Love Letters to Heloise

There was in Paris at the time a young girl named Heloise, the niece of Fulbert, one of the canons, and so much loved by him that he had done everything in his power to advance her education in letters. In looks she did not rank lowest, while in the extent of her learning she stood supreme. A gift for letters is so rare in women that it added greatly to her charm and had won her renown throughout the realm. I considered all the usual attractions for a lover and decided she was the one to bring to my bed, confident that I should have an easy success; for at that time I had youth and exceptional good looks as well as my great reputation to recommend me, and feared no rebuff from any woman I might choose to honor with my love. Knowing the girl's knowledge and love of letters I thought she would be all the more ready to consent, and that even when separated we could enjoy each other's presence by exchange of written messages in which we could speak more openly than in person, and so need never lack the pleasures of conversation.

All on fire with desire for this girl I sought an opportunity of getting to know her through private daily meetings and so more easily winning her over; and with this end in view I came to an arrangement with her uncle, with the help of some of his friends, whereby he should take me into his house, which was very near my school, for whatever sum he liked to ask. As a pretext I said that my household cares were hindering my studies and the expense was more than I could afford. Fulbert dearly loved money, and was moreover always ambitious to further his niece's education in letters, two weaknesses which made it easy for me to gain his consent and obtain my desire: he was all eagerness for my money and confident that his niece would profit from my teaching. This led him to make an urgent request which furthered my love and fell in with my wishes more than I had dared to hope; he gave me complete charge over the girl, so that I could devote all the leisure time left me by my school to teaching her by day and night, and if I found her idle I was to punish her severely. I was amazed by his simplicity—if he had entrusted a tender lamb to a ravening wolf it would not have surprised me more. In handing her over to me to punish as well as to teach, what else was he doing but giving me complete freedom to realize my desires, and providing an opportunity, even if I did not make use of it, for me to bend her to my will by threats and blows if persuasion failed? But there were two special reasons for his freedom from base suspicion: his love for his niece and my previous reputation for continence.

Need I say more? We were united, first under one roof, then in heart; and so with our lessons as a pretext we abandoned ourselves entirely to love. Her studies allowed us to withdraw in private, as love desired, and then with our books open before us, more words of love than of our reading passed between us, and more kissing than teaching. My hands strayed oftener to her bosom than to the pages; love drew our eyes to look on each other more than reading kept them on our texts. To avert suspicion I sometimes struck her, but these blows were prompted by love and tender feeling rather than anger and irritation, and were sweeter than any balm could be. In short, our desires left no stage of love-making untried, and if love could devise something new, we welcomed it. We entered on each joy the more eagerly for our previous inexperience, and were the less easily sated.

Now the more I was taken up with these pleasures, the less time I could give to philosophy and the less attention I payed [sic] to my school. It was utterly boring for me to have to go to the school, and equally wearisome to remain there and to spend my days on study when my nights were sleepless with love-making. As my interest and concentration flagged, my lectures lacked all inspiration and were merely repetitive; I could do no more than repeat what had been said long ago, and when inspiration did come to me, it was for writing love-songs, not the secrets of philosophy. A lot of these songs, as you know, are still popular and sung in many places, particularly by those who enjoy the kind of life I led. But the grief and sorrow and laments of my students when they realized my preoccupation, or rather distraction of mind are hard to realize. Few could have failed to notice something so obvious, in fact to no one, I fancy, except the man whose honor was most involved—Heloise's uncle. Several people tried on more than one occasion to draw his attention to it, but he would not believe them; because, as I said, of his boundless love for his niece and my well-known reputation for chastity in my previous life. We do not easily think ill of those whom we love most, and the taint of suspicion cannot exist along with warm affection.

But what is last to be learned is somehow learned eventually, and common knowledge cannot easily be hidden from one individual. Several months passed and then this happened in our case. Imagine the uncle's grief at the discovery, and the lovers' grief too at being separated! How I blushed with shame and contrition for the girl's plight, and what sorrow she suffered at the thought of my disgrace! All our laments were for one another's troubles, and our distress was for each other, not for ourselves. Separation drew our hearts still closer while frustration inflamed our passion even more; then we became more abandoned as we lost all sense of shame and indeed, shame diminished as we found more opportunities for love-making. And so we were caught in the act as the poet says happened to Mars and Venus.

Soon afterward the girl found that she was pregnant, and immediately wrote me a letter full of rejoicing to ask what I thought she should do. One night then, when her uncle was away from home, I sent her [disguised as a nun—as Abelard later states in signed letter 4] straight to my own country. There she stayed with my sister until she gave birth to a boy, whom she called Astralabe.

On his return her uncle went almost out of his mind. . . . What action could he take against me? . . . In the end I took pity on his boundless misery and went to him, accusing myself of the deceit love had made me commit as if it were the basest treachery. I begged his forgiveness and promised to make any amends he might think fit. I protested that I had done nothing unusual in the eyes of anyone who had known the power of love, and recalled how since the beginning of the human race women had brought the noblest men to ruin. Moreover, to conciliate him further I offered him satisfaction in a form he could never have hoped for: I would marry the girl I had wronged. All I stipulated was that the marriage should be kept secret so as not to damage my reputation. He agreed, pledged his word and that of his supporters, and sealed the reconciliation I desired with a kiss. But his intention was to make it easier to betray me.

I set off at once for Brittany and brought back my mistress to make her my wife. But she was strongly opposed to the risk involved and the disgrace to myself. She swore that no satisfaction could ever appease her uncle, as we subsequently found out. What honor could she win, she protested, from a marriage which would dishonor me and humiliate us both? The world would justly exact punishment from her if she removed such a light from its midst. Think of the curses, the loss to the Church and grief of philosophers that would greet such a marriage! Nature had created me for all mankind—it would be a sorry scandal if I should bind myself to a single woman and submit to such base servitude. She absolutely rejected this marriage; it would be nothing but a disgrace and a burden to me. Along with the loss to my reputation she put before me the difficulties of marriage.

But apart from the hindrances to such philosophic study, consider, she said, the true conditions for a dignified way of life. What harmony can there be between pupils and nursemaids, desks and cradles. . . . Who can concentrate on thoughts of Scripture or philosophy and be able to endure babies crying?

Heloise then went on to the risks I should run in bringing her back, and argued that the name of mistress instead of wife would be dearer to her and more honorable for me—only love freely given should keep me for her not the constriction of a marriage tie, and if we had to be parted for a time, we should find the joy of being together all the sweeter the rarer our meetings were. But at last she saw that her attempts to persuade or dissuade me were making no impression on my foolish obstinacy, and she could not bear to offend me; so amidst deep sighs and tears she ended in these words "We shall both be destroyed. All that is left us is suffering as great as our love has been." In this, as the whole world knows, she showed herself a true prophet.[15]

And so when our baby son was born we entrusted him to my sister's care and returned secretly to Paris. A few days later, after a night's private vigil of prayer in a certain church, at dawn we were joined in matrimony in the presence of Fulbert and some of his, and our, friends. Afterward we parted secretly and went our ways unobserved. Subsequently our meetings were few and furtive, in order to conceal as far as possible what we had done. But Fulbert and his servants, seeking satisfaction for the dishonor done to him, began to spread the news of the marriage and break the promise of secrecy they had given me. Heloise cursed them and swore that there was no truth in this, and in his exasperation Fulbert heaped abuse on her on several occasions. As soon as I discovered this I removed her to a convent of nuns in the town near Paris called Argenteuil, where she had been brought up and educated as a small girl, and I also made for her a religious habit of the type worn by novices, with the exception of the veil, and made her put it on.

At this news her uncle and his friends and relatives imagined that I had tricked them, and had found an easy way of ridding myself of Heloise by making her a nun. Wild with indignation they . . . bribed one of my servants . . . and there took cruel vengeance on me of such appalling barbarity as to shock the whole world; they cut off the parts of my body whereby I had committed the wrong of which they complained.

III. EXCERPTS FROM ABELARD'S *ETHICAL WRITINGS*[16]

That a deed is good by means of a good intention. Indeed we call an intention good (that is, right) in itself. We don't however say that a "doing" takes on any good in itself, but that it proceeds from a good intention. Hence even if the same thing is done by the same person at different times, nevertheless because of the diversity of the intention, his doing is called now good, now bad. So it appears to shift between good and bad, just as the proposition "Socrates is sitting" (or the understanding of it) shifts between true and false according as Socrates is now sitting, now standing. Aristotle says this alteration, the shift between true and false, occurs in these cases not in such a way that the things that shift between true and false take on anything in their changing, but rather that the subject thing, namely, Socrates, is in himself moved from sitting to standing or conversely.

On what basis should an intention be called good? Now there are people who suppose an intention is good or right whenever someone believes that he is acting well and that what he is doing pleases God. For instance, even those who persecuted the martyrs, about whom Truth says in the Gospel, "The hour is coming when everyone who slays you will suppose he is offering obedience to God." In fact, the Apostle pities such people's ignorance when he says, "I testify for them that they have an ardor for God, but not one in accordance with knowledge." That is, they have a great fervor and desire to do what they believe pleases God. But because they are deceived in this zeal or eagerness of the mind, their intention is mistaken and their heart's eye is not simple in such a way that it could see clearly—that is, keep itself from error.

So when the Lord distinguished deeds according to whether their intention is right or not right, he was careful to call the mind's eye (that is, its intention) "simple" and so to speak pure of dirt so it can see clearly, or conversely "cloudy." He said, "If your eye is simple, your whole body will be shining." That is, if the intention is right, the whole mass of deeds arising from it—which, like corporeal things, can be seen—will be worthy of light, that is, will be good. So too the other way around.

Thus an intention isn't to be called good because it appears good, but more than that, because it is such as it is considered to be—that is, when if one believes that what he is aiming at is pleasing to God, he is in addition not deceived in his evaluation. Otherwise the infidels themselves would also have good deeds, just as we do, since they too believe no less than we do that through their deeds they are saved or are pleasing to God.

How many ways is something called a "sin"? Sometimes the deeds of sin themselves, or whatever we don't do or will correctly, we also call "sins." For what is it for someone to have committed a sin except to have carried out the performance of the sin? No wonder we speak this way, since conversely we also call the sins themselves "actions," in accordance with Athanasius' statement: "And they will give an account of their own actions. And those who have done good things will go into eternal life, while those who have done evil things will go into eternal fire." Now what is the meaning of "of their own actions"? Is it as if judgment will be made only about what they have carried out in deed, so that he who will do more in deed will receive more in reward, or he who was lacking in the performance of what he intended is exempt from damnation—for example the Devil himself, who didn't achieve in practice what he anticipated in desire? Hardly! And so Athanasius says "of their own actions" with reference to the consent to what they decided to accomplish.

IV. HELOISE'S SIGNED LETTER 2 TO ABELARD[17]

Your superior wisdom knows better than our humble learning of the many serious treatises which the holy Fathers compiled for the instruction or exhortation or even the consolation of holy women, and of the care with which these were composed. And so in the precarious early days of our conversion long ago I was not a little surprised and troubled by your forgetfulness, when neither reverence for God nor our mutual love nor the example of the holy Fathers made you think of trying to comfort me, wavering and exhausted as I was by prolonged grief, either by word when I was with you or by letter when we had parted. Yet you must know that you are bound to me by an obligation which is all the greater for the further close tie of the marriage sacrament uniting us, and are the deeper in my debt because of the love I have always borne you, as everyone knows, a love which is beyond all bounds.

You know, beloved, as the whole world knows, how much I have lost in you, how at one wretched stroke of fortune that supreme act of flagrant treachery robbed me of my very self in robbing me of you; and how my sorrow for my loss is nothing compared with what I feel for the manner in which I lost you. Surely the greater the cause for grief the greater the need for the help of consolation, and this no one can bring but you; you are the sole cause of my sorrow, and you alone can grant me the grace of consolation. You alone have the power to make me sad, to bring me happiness or comfort, you alone have so great a debt to repay me, particularly now when I have carried out all your orders so implicitly that when I was powerless to oppose you in anything, I found strength at your command to destroy myself. I did more, strange to say—my love rose to such heights of madness that it robbed itself of what it most desired beyond hope of recovery, when immediately at your bidding I changed my clothing along with my mind, in order to prove you the sole possessor of my body and my will alike. God knows I never sought anything in you except yourself; I wanted simply you, nothing of yours. I looked for no marriage-bond, no marriage portion, and it was not my own pleasures and wishes I sought to gratify, as you well know, but yours. The name of wife may seem more sacred or more binding, but sweeter for me will always be the word mistress, or, if you will permit me, that of concubine or whore. I believed that the more I humbled myself on your account, the more gratitude I should win from you and also the less damage I should do to the brightness of your reputation.

You yourself on your own account did not altogether forget this . . . you thought fit to set out some of the reasons I gave in trying to dissuade you from binding us together in an ill-starred marriage. But you kept silent about most of my arguments for preferring love to wedlock and freedom to chains. God is my witness that if Augustus, Emperor of the whole world, thought fit to honor me with marriage and conferred all the earth on me to possess for ever, it would be dearer and more honorable to me to be called not his Empress but your whore.

For a man's worth does not rest on his wealth or power; these depend on fortune, but worth on his merits. And a woman should realize that if she marries a rich man more readily than a poor one, and desires her husband more for his possessions than for himself, she is offering herself for sale. Certainly any woman who comes to marry through desires of this kind deserves wages, not gratitude, for clearly her mind is on the man's property, not himself, and she would be ready to prostitute herself to a richer man, if she could.

It is a holy error and a blessed delusion between man and wife, when perfect love can keep the ties of marriage unbroken not so much through bodily continence as chastity of spirit. But what error permitted other women, plain truth permitted me, and what they thought of their husbands, the world in general believed, or rather, knew to be true of yourself; so that my love for you was the more genuine for being further removed from error. What king or philosopher could match your fame? . . . You had besides, I admit, two special gifts whereby to win at once the heart of any woman—your gifts for composing verse and song. . . . And as most of these songs told of our love, they soon made me widely known and roused the envy of many women against me. For your manhood was adorned by every grace of mind and body, and among the women who envied me then, could there be one now who does not feel compelled by my misfortune to sympathize with my loss of such joys? Who is there who was once my enemy, whether man or woman, who is not moved now by the compassion which is my due? Wholly guilty though I am, I am also, as you know, wholly innocent. It is not the deed but the intention of the doer which makes the crime, and justice should weigh not what was done but the spirit in which it is done. What my intention toward you has always been, you alone who have known it can judge. I submit all to your scrutiny, yield to your testimony in all things.

Tell me one thing, if you can. Why, after our entry into religion, which was your decision alone, have I been so neglected and forgotten by you that I have neither a word from you when you are here to give me strength nor the consolation of a letter in absence? Tell me, I say, if you can—or I will tell you what I think and indeed the world suspects. It was desire, not affection which bound you to me, the flame of lust rather than love. So when the end came to what you desired, any show of feeling you used to make went with it. This is not merely my own opinion, beloved, it is everyone's. There is nothing personal or private about it; it is the general view which is widely held. I only wish that it were mine alone, and that the love you professed could find someone to defend it and so comfort me in my grief for a while. I wish I could think of some explanation which would excuse you and somehow cover up the way you hold me cheap.

Up to now I had thought I deserved much of you, seeing that I carried out everything for your sake and continue up to the present moment in complete obedience to you. It was not any sense of vocation which brought me as a young girl to accept the austerities of the cloister, but your bidding alone, and if I deserve no gratitude from you, you may judge for yourself how my labors are in vain. I can expect no reward for this from God, for it is certain that I have done nothing as yet for love of him. When you hurried toward God I followed you, indeed I went first to take the veil—perhaps you were thinking how Lot's wife turned back when you made me put on the religious habit and take my vows before you gave yourself to God. Your lack of trust in me over this one thing, I confess, overwhelmed me with grief and shame. I would have had no hesitation, God knows, in following you or going ahead at your bidding to the flames of Hell. My heart was not in me but with you, and now, even more, if it is not with you it is nowhere; truly without you it cannot exist.

While I enjoyed with you the pleasures of the flesh, many were uncertain whether I was prompted by love or lust; but now the end is proof of the beginning. I have finally denied myself every pleasure in obedience to your will, kept nothing for myself except to prove that now, even more, I am yours. Consider then your injustice, if when I deserve more you give me less, or rather, nothing at all, especially when it is a small thing I ask of you and one you could so easily grant. And so, in the name of God to whom you have dedicated yourself, I beg you to restore your presence to me in the way you can—by writing me some word of comfort, so that in this at least I may find increased strength and readiness to serve God. When in the past you sought me out for sinful pleasures your letters came to me thick and fast, and your many songs put your Heloise on everyone's lips, so that every street and house echoed with my name. Is it not far better now to summon me to God than it was then to satisfy our lust? I beg you, think what you owe me, give ear to my pleas, and I will finish a long letter with a brief ending: farewell, my only love.

V. ABELARD'S SIGNED LETTER 4 TO HELOISE: TO THE BRIDE OF CHRIST, CHRIST'S SERVANT[18]

I come at last to what I have called your old perpetual complaint,[19] in which you presume to blame God for the manner of our entry into religion instead of wishing to glorify him as you justly should. I had thought that this bitterness of heart at what was so clear an act of divine mercy had long since disappeared. The more dangerous such bitterness is to you is wearing out body and soul alike, the more pitiful it is and distressing to me. If you are anxious to please me in everything, as you claim, and in this at least would end my torment, or even give me the greatest pleasure, you must rid yourself of it. If it persists you can neither please me nor attain bliss with me. Can you bear me to come to this without you—I whom you declare yourself ready to follow to the very fires of hell? Seek piety in this at least, lest you cut yourself off from me who am hastening, you believe, toward God; be the readier to do so because the goal we must come to will be blessed, and our companionship the more welcome for being happier. Remember what you have said, recall what you have written, namely that in the manner of our conversion, when God seems to have been more my adversary, he has clearly shown himself kinder. For this reason at least you must accept his will, that it is most salutary for me, and for you too, if your transports of grief will see reason. You should not grieve because you are the cause of so great a good, for which you must not doubt you were specially created by God. Nor should you weep because I have to bear this. . . . If it had befallen me justly, would you find it easier to bear? Would it distress you less? In fact if it had been so, the result would have been greater disgrace for me and more credit to my enemies, since justice would have won them approval while my guilt would have brought me into contempt. And no one would be stirred by pity for me to condemn what was done.

However, it may relieve the bitterness of your grief if I prove that this came upon us justly, as well as to our advantage, and that God's punishment was more properly directed against us when we were married than when we were living in sin. After our marriage, when you were living in the cloister with the nuns at Argenteuil and I came one day to visit you privately, you know what my uncontrollable desire did with you there, actually in a corner of the refectory, since we had nowhere else to go. I repeat, you know how shamelessly we behaved on that occasion in so hallowed a place, dedicated to the most holy Virgin. Even if our other shameful behavior was ended, this alone would deserve far heavier punishment. Need I recall our previous fornication and the wanton impurities which preceded our marriage, or my supreme act of betrayal, when I deceived your uncle about you so disgracefully, at a time when I was continuously living with him in his own house? Who would not judge me justly betrayed by the man whom I had first shamelessly betrayed? Do you think that the momentary pain of that wound is sufficient punishment for such crimes? Or rather, that so great an advantage was fitting for such great wickedness? What wound to you suppose would satisfy God's justice for the profanation such as I described of a place so sacred to his own Mother? Surely, unless I am much mistaken, not that wound which was wholly beneficial was intended as a punishment for this, but rather the daily unending torment I now endure.

You know too how when you were pregnant and I took you to my own country you disguised yourself in the sacred habit of a nun, a pretence which was an irreverent mockery of the religion you now profess. Consider, then, how fittingly divine justice, or rather, divine grace brought you against your will to the religion which you did not hesitate to mock, so that you should willingly expiate your profanation in the same habit, and the truth of reality should remedy the lie of your pretence and correct your falsity. And if you would allow consideration of our advantage to be an element in divine justice, you would be able to call what God did to us then an act not of justice, but of grace.

See then, my beloved, see how with the dragnets of his mercy the Lord has fished us up from the depth of this dangerous sea. . . . Think and think again of the great perils in which we were and from which the Lord rescued us; tell always with the deepest gratitude how much the Lord has done for our souls. Comfort by our example any unrighteous who despair of God's goodness, so that all may know what may be done for those who ask with prayer, when such benefits are granted sinners even against their will. Consider the magnanimous design of God's mercy for us, the compassion with which the Lord directed his judgement [sic] toward our chastisement, the wisdom whereby he made use of evil itself and mercifully set aside our impiety, so that by a wholly justified wound in a single part of my body he might heal two souls.

You know the depths of shame to which my unbridled lust had consigned our bodies, until no reverence for decency or for God . . . could keep me from wallowing in this mire. Even when you were unwilling, resisted to the utmost of your power and tried to dissuade me, as yours was the weaker nature I often forced you to consent with threats and blows. So intense were the fires of lust which bound me to you that I set those wretched, obscene pleasures, which we blush even to name, above God as above myself; nor would it seem that divine mercy could have taken action except by forbidding me these pleasures altogether, without future hope. And so it was wholly just and merciful, although by means of the supreme treachery of your uncle, for me to be reduced in that part of my body which was the seat of lust and sole reason for those desires, so that I could increase in many ways; in order that this member should justly be punished for all its wrongdoing in us, expiate in suffering the sins committed for its amusement, and cut me off from the slough of filth in which I had become wholly immersed in mind as in body. Only thus could I become more fit to approach the holy altars, now that no contagion of carnal impurity would ever again call me from them.

Come too, my inseparable companion, and join me in thanksgiving, you who were made my partner both in guilt and in grace. For the Lord is not unmindful also of your own salvation, indeed, he has you much in mind, for by a kind of holy presage of his name he marked you out to be especially his when he named you Heloise, after his own name, Elohim. In his mercy, I say, he intended to provide for two people in one, the two whom the devil sought to destroy in one; since a short while before this happening he had bound us together by the indissoluble bond of the marriage sacrament. At the time I desired to keep you whom I loved beyond measure for myself alone, but he was already planning to use this opportunity for our joint conversion to himself. Had you not been previously joined to me in wedlock, you might easily have clung to the world when I withdrew from it, either at the suggestion of your relatives or in enjoyment of carnal delights. See then, how greatly the Lord was concerned for us, as if he were reserving us for some great ends, and was indignant or grieved because our knowledge of letters, the talents which he had entrusted to us, were not being used to glorify his name; or as if he feared for his humble and incontinent servant.

It was [God] who truly loved you, not I. My love, which brought us both to sin, should be called lust, not love. I took my fill of my wretched pleasures in you, and this was the sum total of my love. You say I suffered for you, and perhaps that is true, but it was really through you, and even this, unwillingly; not for love of you but under compulsion, and to bring you not salvation but sorrow. . . . He wounds the body, and heals the soul; he makes to live what he should have destroyed, cuts out impurity to leave what is pure. He punishes once so that he need not punish forever. One suffers the wound so that two may be spared death; two were guilty, one pays the penalty. That, too, was granted by divine mercy to your weaker nature and, in a way, with justice, for you were naturally weaker in sex and stronger in continence, and so the less deserving of punishment.

VI. HELOISE'S SIGNED LETTER 3 TO ABELARD: TO HER ONLY ONE AFTER CHRIST, [FROM] SHE WHO IS HIS ALONE IN CHRIST[20]

I am surprised, my only love, that contrary to custom in letter-writing and, indeed, to the natural order, you have thought fit to put my name before yours in the greeting which heads your letter, so that we have woman before man, wife before husband, handmaid before master, nun before monk, deaconess before priest and abbess before abbot. Surely the right and proper order is for those who write to their superiors or equals to put their names before their own, but in letters to inferiors, precedence in order of address follows precedence in rank.

We were also greatly surprised when instead of bringing us the healing balm of comfort you increased our desolation and made the tears to flow which you should have dried. For which of us could remain dry-eyed on hearing the words you wrote toward the end of your letter: "But if the Lord shall deliver me into the hands of my enemies so that they overcome and kill me" . . . ? My dearest, how could you think such a thought? How could you give voice to it? Never may God be so forgetful of his humble handmaids as to let them outlive you; never may he grant us a life which would be harder to bear than any form of death. The proper course would be for you to perform our funeral rites, for you to commend our souls to God, and to send ahead of you those whom you assembled for God's service—so that you need no longer be troubled by worries for us, and follow after us the more gladly because freed from concern for our salvation. Spare us, I implore you, master, spare us words such as these which can only intensify our existing unhappiness; do not deny us, before death, the one thing by which we live. "Each day has trouble enough of its own," and that day, shrouded in bitterness, will bring with it distress enough to all it comes upon. "Why is it necessary," says Seneca, "to summon evil" and to destroy life before death comes?

But if I lose you, what is left for me to hope for? What reason for continuing on life's pilgrimage, for which I have no support but you, and none in you save the knowledge that you are alive, now that I am forbidden all other pleasures in you and denied even the joy of your presence which from time to time could restore me to myself? O God—if I dare say it—cruel to me in everything! O merciless mercy! O Fortune who is only ill-fortune, who has already sped on me so many of the shafts she uses in her battle against mankind that she has none left with which to vent her anger on others. She has emptied a full quiver on me, so that henceforth no one else need fear her onslaughts, and if she still had a single arrow she could find no place in me to take a wound. Her only dread is that through my many wounds death may end my sufferings; and though she does not cease to destroy me, she still fears the destruction which she hurries on.

Of all wretched women I am the most wretched, and among the unhappy I am the unhappiest. The higher I was exalted when you preferred me to all other women, the greater my suffering over my own fall and yours, when I was flung down; for the higher the ascent, the heavier the fall. Has Fortune ever set any great or noble woman above me or made her my equal, only to be similarly cast down and crushed with grief? What glory she gave me in you, what ruin she brought upon me through you! Violent in either extreme, she showed no moderation in good or evil. To make me the saddest of all women she first made me blessed above all, so that when I thought how much I had lost, my consuming grief would match my crushing loss, and my sorrow for what was taken from me would be the greater for the fuller joy of possession which had gone before; and so that the happiness of supreme ecstasy would end in the supreme bitterness of sorrow.

Moreover, to add to my indignation at the outrage you suffered, all the laws of equity in our case were reversed. For while we enjoyed the pleasures of an uneasy love and abandoned ourselves to fornication (if I may use an ugly but expressive word) we were spared God's severity. But when we amended our unlawful conduct by what was lawful, and atoned for the shame of fornication by an honorable marriage, then the Lord in his anger laid his hand heavily upon us, and would not permit a chaste union though he had long tolerated one which was unchaste. The punishment you suffered would have been proper vengeance for men caught in open adultery. But what others deserve for adultery came upon you through a marriage which you believed had made amends for all previous wrong doing; what adulterous women have brought upon their lovers, your own wife brought upon you. Nor was this at the time when we abandoned ourselves to our former delights, but when we had already parted and were leading chaste lives, you presiding over the school in Paris and I at your command living with the nuns at Argenteuil. Thus we were separated, to give you more time to devote yourself to your pupils, and me more freedom for prayer and meditation on the Scriptures, both of us leading a life which was holy as well as chaste. It was then that you alone paid the penalty in your body for a sin we had both committed. You alone were punished though we were both to blame, and you paid all, though you had deserved less, for you had made more than necessary reparation by humbling yourself on my account and had raised me and all my kind to your own level—so much less then, in the eyes of God and of your betrayers, should you have been thought deserving of such punishment.

What misery for me—born as I was to be the cause of such a crime! Is it the general lot of women to bring total ruin on great men? Hence the warning about women in Proverbs: "But now, my son, listen to me, attend to what I say: do not let your heart entice you into her ways, do not stray down her paths; she has wounded and laid low so many, and the strongest have all been her victims. Her house is the way to hell, and leads down to the halls of death." And in Ecclesiastes: "I put all to the test . . . I find woman more bitter than death; she is a snare, her heart a net, her arms are chains. He who is pleasing to God eludes her, but the sinner is her captive."

It was the first woman in the beginning who lured man from Paradise, and she who had been created by the Lord as his helpmate became the instrument of his total downfall.

At least I can thank God for this: the tempter did not prevail on me to do wrong of my own consent, like the women I have mentioned, though in the outcome he made me the instrument of his malice. But even if my conscience is clear through innocence, and no consent of mine makes me guilty of this crime, too many earlier sins were committed to allow me to be wholly free from guilt. I yielded long before to the pleasures of carnal desires, and merited then what I weep for now. The sequel is fitting punishment for my former sins, and an evil beginning must be expected to come to a bad end. For this offence, above all, may I have strength to do proper penance, so that at least by long contrition I can take your pain from the wound inflicted on you; and what you suffered in the body for a time, I may suffer, as is right throughout my life in contrition of mind, and thus make reparation to you at least, if not to God.

How can it be called repentance for sins, however great the mortification of the flesh, if the mind still retains the will to sin and is on fire with its old desires? It is easy enough for anyone to confess his sins, to accuse himself, or even to mortify his body in outward show of penance, but it is very difficult to tear the heart away from hankering after its dearest pleasures.

In my case, the pleasures of lovers which we shared have been too sweet—they can never displease me, and can scarcely be banished from my thoughts. Wherever I turn they are always there before my eyes, bringing with them awakened longings and fantasies which will not even let me sleep. Even during the celebration of the Mass, when our prayers should be purer, lewd visions of those pleasures take such a hold upon my unhappy soul that my thoughts are on their wantonness instead of on my prayers. I should be groaning over the sins I have committed, but I can only sigh for what I have lost. Everything we did and also the times and places are stamped on my heart along with your image, so that I live through it all again with you. Even in sleep I know no respite. Sometimes my thoughts are betrayed in a movement of my body, or they break out in an unguarded word. In my utter wretchedness, that cry from a suffering soul could well be mine: "Miserable creature that I am, who is there to rescue me out of the body doomed to this death?" . . . This grace, my dearest, came upon you unsought—a single wound of the body by freeing you from these torments has healed many wounds in your soul. Where God may seem to you an adversary he has in fact proved himself kind: like an honest doctor who does not shrink from giving pain if it will bring about a cure. But for me, youth and passion and experience of pleasures which were so delightful intensify the torments of the flesh and longings of desire, and the assault is the more overwhelming as the nature they attack is the weaker.

Men call me chaste; they do not know the hypocrite I am. They consider purity of the flesh a virtue, though virtue belongs not to the body but to the soul. I can win praise in the eyes of men but deserve none before God, who searches in the hearts and loins and sees in our darkness. I am judged religious at a time when there is little in religion which is not hypocrisy, when whoever does not offend the opinions of men receives the highest praise. And perhaps there is some merit and it is somehow acceptable to God, if a person whatever his intention gives no offense to the Church in his outward behavior, does not blaspheme the name of the Lord in the hearing of unbelievers nor disgrace the Order of his profession among the worldly. And this too is a fight of God's grace and comes through his bounty—not only to do good but to abstain from evil—though the latter is vain if the former does not follow from it, as it is written: "Turn from evil and do good." Both are vain if not done for love of God.

Commentary by *Mary Ellen Waithe,* Heloise and Abelard: Love, Sex, and Morality

INTRODUCTION

Our pair of philosophers, Heloise and Abelard, really was a pair. They were first student and teacher, then lovers and spouses, and finally nun and religious superior. Perhaps more than any other philosophers, their philosophical views were reflected in how they lived (or wanted to live) their lives. For that reason, and because Heloise left no traditional philosophical writings, I am presenting them largely through letters they wrote to each other, although I am also including a few brief experts from Abelard's published work. Considered together, these writings give us a glimpse of the personal lives of this pair, especially in relation to each other, and a glimpse of views they had on sex and love. As I will show from these letters, sex and love were philosophically significant topics for Heloise and Abelard.

It is important to acknowledge at the outset that love and sex are legitimate philosophical topics. Not too many write about it, but in the texts that follow, Abelard and Heloise thought about it from the perspective of both philosophy and lived experience. I cannot recall a single other philosopher or philosophical pair in the entire history of philosophy (other than Pythagoras) for whom it is the case that their life tells us as much about their philosophical views as do their teachings or writings. Clearly, one cannot understand Abelard and Heloise's views on love, and on friendship as a special kind of love, without understanding their love life as they tell us about it.

This chapter is arranged a little differently than other chapters in this book for a very good reason: much of what was written by Heloise and by Abelard was written to each other in letters. These letters will make the most sense if read in the order presented here—the order in which scholars think they were written—rather than reading all of Abelard's work followed by all of Heloise's work. And although you are reading philosophy, remember that these were two real people who had a real, albeit strange, relationship. They are not a model of a professor–student relationship!

BIOGRAPHICAL INFORMATION

Peter Abelard was born in Bretagne, or Brittany, in northwestern France. He became a well-educated man at a time in which the nature of higher education was undergoing tremendous changes. The tradition for education had been through the monasteries, studying the seven liberal arts. The curriculum was broken up into the trivium (three subjects) followed by the quadrivium (four subjects). The trivium consisted of the study of classical Latin language and literature (grammar and rhetoric) and classical Aristotelian logic, also called dialectic. These studies were followed by the quadrivium, which included arithmetic, music, geometry, and astronomy. The study of theology, canon law, and medicine presupposed this rigorous course of study.

Abelard moved around France in search of his education. The Catholic Church ran the monasteries, and different monastic orders, living under vastly different rules, accepted students. The old monastic tradition was gradually becoming supplemented with what was known as Cathedral schools, attached to such famous big-city cathedrals as Notre Dame in Paris. Students paid teachers, and all teachers were clerics of one sort or another. In the twelfth century, becoming a cleric did not necessarily mean becoming a priest; any male who held any church job including that of acolyte and porter was a cleric. In order to become a priest one needed to move up through the clerical ranks over a period of many years of hands-on learning, as well as formal education, and the closer one got to becoming a priest, the more worldly things one gave up. Clerical work, including becoming a priest, was popular for men who were widowed, as well as for young men. Most lived with their families or were housed by church members in their homes. Not all church jobs paid, and since those that did pay did not pay very well, so many clerics had other employment.

In about 1100, Abelard began teaching at the Cloister School of Notre Dame. After years of fighting his way up the ranks of teachers (known as regular canons) in the school, being supported directly by the tuition his students paid him, Abelard finally politically out-maneuvered his competitors by setting up his own school at Mont Ste. Geneviève and attracting other canons' students to it. Abelard's school would become the first in a hot new experiment in higher education: the first university. Later on it would be called the University of Paris, nicknamed "La Sorbonne" (old French for "the very best"). Abelard eventually was named canon of the Paris schools, that is, of all of the schools attached to or affiliated with Notre Dame. Experts still disagree as to what exactly this entailed, but two things were certain: it was a very respectable and highly visible job, and any academic advancement in the Church beyond this would be cinched if Abelard proceeded through the preparatory clerical ranks and became a priest. Canons, especially a canon of the most important institution of higher education, were not permitted to marry.

By this time Abelard is approximately thirty years old. He wanted time away from his clerical and administrative duties in order to have uninterrupted time for writing and study. Always the innovator, he was quite probably the only canon in Paris willing to experiment with teaching a woman. Of course, it had to be the right young woman, one whose intellectual gifts had already been well proven. The niece of Fulbert, one of the ordinary canons, already had quite a reputation as one of the most gifted writers in all of France. Abelard offered to take her as a student. Her name was Heloise.

Born in 1100 or 1101 and educated at the Benedictine convent of Argenteuil in France, Heloise went to Paris to live with her maternal uncle Fulbert. Although we do not have any of her earlier writings, we do know that by the time she was sixteen and Abelard agreed to become her private tutor, she already had a reputation as being one of the most gifted women writers in all of France. He lusted after this beautiful, brilliant young woman. Mistaking his lust for love, she very quickly fell in love with him. Approximately a year after becoming Abelard's student, her uncle Fulbert agreed to provide Abelard with rooms in his home, apparently as a way of reducing Abelard's fees for teaching Heloise. Not only was this cost-effective for both men, but it extended the opportunities for Heloise and Abelard to work together. Although Heloise came to love him, she refused to have sex with him—a refusal that was consistent with the ideal of a virtuous woman of her day. She composed rhetorically beautiful Latin poems about him and her love for him. In return she was the subject of numerous bawdy songs composed about her by Abelard and sung on every Paris street corner. (I used to think that Heloise didn't know about those songs, but the Signed Letters suggest she probably did, and she probably was offended by them.) According to Abelard's own writing, he threatened her and beat her (as her teacher, it was part of his job to discipline his student using corporal punishment) until, as he says, he "forced" her "consent."

Being sexually intimate with someone outside of marriage was considered a sin. With her virginity lost, even a woman as famous as Heloise had her reputation impugned and became less marriageable. Under pressure from the man she loved, admired, was attracted to, and obligated as student to obey, Heloise willingly engaged in a full-fledged affair with

Abelard. Soon pregnant, she went with Abelard to his home province of Brittany, staying with his sister for the duration of her pregnancy and giving birth to a son she named Astralabe (after a scientific instrument used in astronomy).

Uncle Fulbert was not amused. As his niece's guardian, and as a canon himself, he had become the butt of gossip as the songs attributed to Abelard made the rounds of the close-knit Paris ecclesiastical society. It had been possible for Fulbert to deny that the rumors were true, at least until his pregnant niece eloped to Brittany. When the couple returned—the baby remained behind to be raised by his aunt—Fulbert insisted that the two marry. We see in her Signed Letters why Heloise had always been against marrying Abelard. From her point of view, the demands of married life were incompatible with the needs of a great philosopher-theologian for peace, quiet, and an academic environment. Moreover, the political realities of Abelard's position as head of the Paris schools could well be jeopardized since marriage precluded Abelard from continuing any preparation for the priesthood. Lay theologians did not teach. But in order to placate a wronged and angry uncle Fulbert, Abelard agreed to marry Heloise, so long as the marriage was kept secret. Heloise continued to refuse to marry him, and Fulbert became physically abusive toward her. She eventually went along with the idea so long as the marriage was kept secret. Immediately after the private ceremony, she returned to live in her uncle's home, and Abelard returned to Notre Dame. In order to save his reputation, Fulbert bragged that Heloise was now married. Much to his displeasure, both she and Abelard denied it. Furious, Fulbert again started beating Heloise.

Under the moral and religious authority of being Heloise's husband, Abelard removed her from Fulbert's house, disguised her as a nun, and moved her back into the same convent where she received her early education, Argenteuil. Having once again been made a fool of by Heloise and Abelard, Uncle Fulbert hired some low-life bullies, bribed Abelard's servant to let them into the secret room where Abelard slept, and had Abelard castrated. Away in Argenteuil, Heloise knew nothing about it. But with sexual access to his student-wife-religious subordinate now forever precluded, Abelard joined a monastery. For decades the two had no contact.

WRITINGS

Of the two, Abelard was the more prolific, but since he was a professional philosopher and Heloise held no such academic appointment—no woman in France did—we would expect him to have written more philosophy.[21] Abelard wrote a four-volume work on logic (the Aristotelian "syllogistic" logic had only recently been rediscovered and translated into Latin from Greek) called *Dialectica*. He wrote a book that academics would now consider to be about rhetoric, *Liber Divisionum et Definitionum* (the book on divisions and definitions [of concepts]). He also wrote what are called "glosses" or "readings interpreting" the philosopher Porphyry and Aristotle's *Categories*, and a brief essay on Genus and Species. These works are all basically about the logic of language. But Abelard's most famous works were *Scito Te Ipsum*, known as Ethics—a book that is usually considered a work of logic, but is a set of pro/con arguments about a group of theological issues, known as *Sic et Non* (Yes and No). It would be a mistake to consider his theological works as nonphilosophical. So any complete account of Abelard's writings would include his *Tractatus de Unitate et Trinitate Divina* (Treatise on the Unity of the Holy Trinity) and a revised second edition of it called *Introductio in Theologia*{m} (I've inserted the curly brackets to indicate that there is a letter there that doesn't belong—it's kind of odd that a great rhetorician of the Latin language made an elementary error in the title of his book). But the title of the book translates as *Introductory Theology.*

To me, one of Abelard's more interesting works is *Dialogus inter Philosophum, Judaeum, et Christianum* (*Dialogue Among a Philosopher, a Jew, and a Christian*) in which the Christian wins the debate about faith and truth. There are also some hymns that have survived, in addition to the letters between him and Heloise, a new group of which has recently been authenticated by Constant Mews. Some of those unsigned, early (before their marriage) letters here were included in the preceding section.

For our purposes, what's most important about Abelard's works (since we are limiting ourselves to considering them alongside Heloise's) is the emphasis he placed on clear, methodical reasoning that analyzed all concepts and brought reason and logic to bear upon theological questions. Most philosophers and theologians of his time focused on discussing the benefits of prayer and personal religious experiences, especially mystical experiences. But Abelard wanted to show that reasoning philosophically about religious questions can actually strengthen someone's faith and even cause nonbelievers and infidels (non-Catholics) to believe in the tenets of the Catholic faith. (Catholicism was generally called "Christianity" until the time of Martin Luther and other "Protestants" objected to the abuses of Catholic clergy.) His most self-serving work is his autobiographical *Historia Calamitatum* (*The Story of My Calamities*) and it is from it that we learn much about his relationship with Heloise. Its primary philosophical interest is in how his description of his actions and attitudes contrast markedly with everything else he wrote and taught about how people ought to act.

Heloise wrote a lot, but little survives. She was known as a poet when she was in her early teens, but none of that work seems to have survived. What we do have is her *Epistolae* ([Signed] *Letters*) that were mostly written to Abelard, and her *Problemata* (*Problems*). A large group of letters that were not included in *Patrologia Latine* has recently been attributed to Heloise and Abelard by Constant Mews, who has translated them into English. I refer to these as the Unsigned Letters. They are unsigned probably because they were written when Abelard was Heloise's tutor, both prior to and during the time that he was living at her uncle's house, where she also lived. It is most likely that a servant carried these unsigned letters back and forth between the two. The *Problemata*, which is also addressed to Abelard, concerns theological issues of the nature of faith and the certainty of revealed (biblical) knowledge. What (to me) is most interesting about Heloise's writings are the discussions of the morality of intent and the analysis of the nature of love and what love requires morally of the person who loves another.

MORALITY OF INTENT

Although Abelard was a philosopher and theologian, his checkered career after Uncle Fulbert had him castrated was one in which he was constantly challenging prevailing theological positions. This led to him having to move around quite a lot because he would annoy the heads of monasteries at which he stayed. Sometimes he fled for his life. So, when Abelard challenged the prevailing view that there were some acts that were good and some that were sinful (morally wrong) and that there was no clear, objective way to determine what acts were good and what were evil or sinful, his views were not well received. This seriously challenged the authority of the Church that had declared some acts, for example killing, to be morally wrong. Not so, Abelard said. It is neither the act of killing itself that is morally wrong, nor the fact that killing offends God that makes it morally wrong or sinful. What makes it wrong (or right) is that the killer (in this example) intends to offend God by intending to commit a wrongful act. Such wrongful intent shows contempt for God and for God's moral law.

This is essentially what he taught Heloise and later published in his *Ethics*. She accepted his doctrine of the morality of intent. One can sin or do wrong by merely intending to do wrong (one is as guilty if one intends to commit murder but fails, as one would be if one had succeeded). This makes a certain amount of sense and is a concept that is reflected, for example, in laws that excuse someone from legal responsibility for killing someone if they did not formulate the intent. Or, to give a different example, a toddler who causes the death of her infant brother by stuffing cookies down the infant's throat is not morally or legally guilty of murder even though her act caused the baby's death. Similarly, someone who is profoundly mentally ill and kills his philosophy professor because he thinks she is a lemon he is slicing in order to make lemonade will be found not guilty by reason of insanity. The way Heloise stated the position, in a wicked deed, rectitude of action depends not on the effect of the thing but on the affections of the agent, not on what is done but with what dispositions it is done.[22]

VIEWS ON LOVE

The recent discovery of a large number of letters between an unnamed man and woman believed to be Abelard and Heloise adds considerably to our understanding of their philosophical views, especially Heloise's views on love. We assume that Heloise's views on love came about as a result of her discussions with Abelard, when she was still his student, of Cicero's *De Amicitia*. We know what Cicero (Tully) said, and we know what Heloise said about love by what she says in *Unsigned Letters*, but we know little of Abelard's actual views. According to Cicero, the fruit of true love is the love itself. When one person loves another they are interested in nothing other than loving the beloved. The lover wants nothing for him/herself. The lover is disinterested in anything but the giving of love. The true friend or true lover wants nothing other than the experience of loving the beloved. The lover loves disinterestedly, completely unselfishly, wanting nothing other than the true happiness of the beloved.

In Heloise's *Signed Letters* she summarizes the argument that she had made decades earlier against marrying Abelard. At that time, his true good, from her perspective, was to become a philosopher. That could not have happened if he lost his position at Notre Dame, because he would then lose the position at (what would later become) the Sorbonne. To become a full-time philosopher who could devote all his time to research and teaching he needed to advance in the clerical ranks. And he could not advance to full priesthood if he was been married. As his student who loved him, Heloise preferred being his mistress to being his wife. She loved him disinterestedly. She wanted nothing for herself, no wedding ring, no title, no social status, no married life, because such a life would not have been compatible with Abelard remaining a philosopher. The distractions of domestic life, and the need to support his family, would take time and energy away from concentrating on his writing.

The *Unsigned Letters* clearly indicate that Heloise was sexually attracted to Abelard. As I said in the interview in the introduction to this chapter, this is something I did not know back when I first wrote about her in my essay, "Heloise," in *A History of Women Philosophers*, volume 2 (1989). At that time the *Unsigned Letters* had not been published yet. Abelard was older, he was her teacher, and now I see that she was quite smitten with him. But as attracted to him as she was, the *Unsigned Letters* also show us that she did not and would not consent to having sex with him. She cared nothing for her reputation (she says), but his would be ruined. (Even though he was writing bawdy songs about her that were being sung by every drunk in Paris, she did not know about that until much later.) Her virginity was the prize he would not have. But then he eventually forced Heloise to have sex with him "by threats and blows" as he himself writes. Contemporary morality would call that rape. And even though she had been attracted to him, she still said "no" and that is still rape. But even if Abelard did not rape her, their sexual relationship was not what we would find acceptable between a teacher and a student.

However, once her virginity was lost to him, Heloise was delighted to continue the sexual relationship: it kept Abelard happy and productive; she loved him; and she loved him for himself. So she was happy to indulge his passion. From that point onward, the relationship appears to have been consensual. But then she got pregnant and the story of what happened after that unfolds. Reluctantly, Heloise gave in, even though she considered the marriage to be a sin against Abelard. Why? Because Heloise was the only person who benefited from their marriage. Abelard would, she predicted, lose his job and with it the opportunity to live the life of a philosopher. In order to forestall this happening, they both denied they had gotten married.

Their sexual relationship, in Heloise's view, represented her innocent role in his downfall. Why was she innocent? Because he initially coerced her to have sex. She may have loved their love life, but she was not going to take responsibility for its consequences because she had never formulated the intention to lose her virginity, get pregnant, or get married. She was coerced, she says—coerced first by Abelard (into sex and pregnancy) and then by him and Fulbert (into marriage). Still, at the point when she was still resisting getting married, she argues that her pregnancy was no reason to let Abelard's temporary triumph of passion over reason turn into a permanent abandonment of his pursuit of the philosophical life.

THE SELECTED READINGS

Constant J. Mews argues that what I am labeling the *Unsigned Letters* "seem to have been exchanged by Heloise and Abelard over a period of at least a year, perhaps between late 1115 and sometime in 1117. Many of the letters may have been exchanged before Abelard obtained lodging in Fulbert's house." Presumably—if one believes Abelard's *Historia Calamitatum*—the pair became sexually active only after he moved into her house. Unsigned Letter 59 in which Abelard apologizes for forcing Heloise to sin appears to have been written shortly after what today would be considered his rape of Heloise.

Abelard's book *Historia Calamitatum* appeared in 1132 and was read by Heloise within a few years of its distribution. Remember that this was prior to the invention of the printing press; books were hand-copied and distributed individually. She initiated correspondence that I labeled the Signed Letters. Indeed, it is only recently because of the translation of a group of anonymous letters between "Man" and "Woman" and the establishment of their authorship as that of Abelard and Heloise that we have any contemporaneous knowledge of these thinkers-lovers' views during the period prior to their marriage.

The excerpts from their correspondence raise many questions about their philosophical perspectives on love, marriage, friendship, and the morality of intent. The questions below are designed to assist one in reflecting on these excerpts, especially in determining what these views are and whether or not they are plausible.

Questions for Reflection

In Unsigned Letter 25, Heloise says that she is unable to fully fulfill the debt of true love to Abelard. What do you think she means by this? What is she not willing to do? Do you agree with her position? Why or why not? In the same letter, Heloise also says that Abelard's joy is her joy and his gain is her gain. This is an example of her acceptance of Cicero's (Tully's) view on love. In that view, the lover wants for the beloved that which is best for the beloved. Where else in the readings do you find evidence that Heloise held that view? Do you find evidence that Abelard shared the view (he taught it to her when he taught her Cicero's writings)? If so, where?

In Unsigned Letter 50, Abelard draws our attention to the fact that Heloise is familiar with Cicero's (Tully's) views on friendship. What does Abelard say in this and other letters to indicate that he does or does not share those views on friendship? Does he apply the same Ciceronian principles to his views on romantic, sexual love?

Taking the entire set of readings as a whole, what clues do you find on each philosopher's views of the morality of intent? Does each maintain a consistent view, or does the philosophical position not seem to apply to the way either or both thinkers approach their views of the morality of their actual, personal behavior?

Notes

1. Peter Abelard, from Wikipedia, the online encyclopedia at http://en.wikipedia.org/wiki/Abelard%2C_Peter

2. Ethel M. Kersey, *Women Philosophers: A Bio-Critical Source Book* (New York: Greenwood Press, 1989), 129.

3. Mary Ellen Waithe, "Heloise," *A History of Women Philosophers*, vol. 2, *Medieval, Renaissance, and Enlightenment Women Philosophers AD 500–1600* (Dordrecht, The Netherlands: Kluwer Academic Publisher, 1989), 68–69.

4. Mary Ellen Waithe, "Heloise and Abelard," in *Presenting Women Philosophers*, eds. Cecile T. Tougas and Sara Ebenreck (Philadelphia, PA: Temple University Press, 2000), 73.

5. Quotation cited in Waithe, "Heloise and Abelard," in *Presenting Women Philosophers*, 117. The quotation is provided by Étienne Gilson, *Héloïse and Abélard*, trans. L. K. Shook (Chicago: Henry Regnery Co., 1951), 48.

6. Waithe, "Heloise," in *A History of Women Philosophers*, vol. 2, 73.

7. Constant J. Mews. *The Lost Love Letters of Heloise and Abelard: Perceptions of Dialogue in Twelfth-Century France* (New York: Palgrave, 2001). Hereafter as Mews, *Lost Letters*. Written circa 1115–1117. Note: Latin terms for core concepts are indicated in [square] brackets. The number following each piece of correspondence is that given by Mews. Reprinted with permission of Palgrave Macmillan.

8. The unsigned letters were written during the period when Abelard was Heloise's tutor; she was his student. He boarded at the home of her uncle, with whom Heloise lived. She soon became pregnant. They married, then lived apart when he sent her to the convent. The writings of Heloise and Abelard are presented here in the order in which they were written, even though scholars do not know the exact dates of either their correspondence or Abelard's later published works.

9. The letters were identified by the medieval monk who found them as having been written by a "man" or by a "woman" based on the handwriting.

10. In *Lost Letters*, Mews's translations into English appear on the odd-numbered or right-hand pages, usually referred to as recto. The even-numbered pages or verso contain the original Latin letters as "established" or deciphered by Mews.

11. The word "Woman" appears in angle brackets to indicate that the translator, Mews, has assumed that this letter is from the party identified as "Man" by the monk who originally found and sorted the letters, but who neglected to mark this one. The monk did, however, include this letter with others he identified as having been written by the woman. The angle brackets are a European style; American style generally uses square brackets for this purpose.

12. (Compare with note 9.) The word "Man" appears in angle brackets to indicate that the translator, Mews, has assumed that this letter is from the party identified as "Man" by the monk who originally found and sorted the letters but did not mark this one, although he included it in with others identified as by the man.

13. Tully is another name for the Roman philosopher Cicero.

14. Peter Abelard, *Historia Calamitatum* in *The Letters of Abelard and Heloise*, trans. Betty Radice (New York: Penguin Books, 1974), 66–75. Hereafter as Radice, *Letters*. Although *Historia Calamitatum* is written in epistolary form as a letter to a friend, it was published as a book. It was written circa 1132. © Betty Radice, 1974.

15. In Signed Letter 4, Abelard tells Heloise that he married her because "At the time I desired to keep you . . . for myself alone. . . . Had you not previously joined me in wedlock, you might easily have clung to the world when I withdrew from it, either at the suggestion of your relatives or in enjoyment of carnal delights." Radice, *Letters*, 149.

16. Peter Abelard, *Ethical Writings and Dialogue Between a Philosopher, a Jew and a Christian*, trans. Paul V. Spade (Indianapolis, IN: Hackett Publishing Co., 1995), 23–25.

17. Radice, *Letters*. The letters translated by Radice were written decades after the letters translated by Mews. These signed letters have been well known to philosophers for centuries. However, the unsigned letters translated by Mews have only recently been attributed to Heloise and Abelard. There are no dates on the letters, so each translator has numbered them in the order that the translator believes they were written.

18. Abelard's letter begins on page 137 in Radice, *Letters*. Although I do not begin our readings until much later in the letter, I thought readers would be interested to see how Abelard addresses Heloise now that their relationship is "official" and semi-public years after their marriage. The term "bride of Christ" refers to a nun. He is addressing Heloise as her religious superior, not as her husband.

19. Abelard's mention of Heloise's "perpetual complaint" is a tacit acknowledgement that she has written him twice about their personal relationship, but his response to her first letter only addressed the spiritual guidance for the nuns in Heloise's convent.

20. Read Heloise's greeting very carefully. She is saying that Christ comes first in her life and Abelard second, but she is also reminding Abelard that through the sacrament of matrimony, she was given by Christ to Abelard to be his faithful wife.

21. To look at the original Latin writings by both of our pair, see the multivolume *Patrologia Latine* by Migne. Their work is under Petrus Abelardus in volume 178. This massive collection contains works of most of the greats who wrote in Latin. For those who wrote in Greek check out Migne's *Patrologia Graeca*, also more than a hundred volumes. These are the sources that scholars use.

22. Heloise, *Signed Letter 2*.

CHAPTER 5

Descartes and Elisabeth

Introduction by *Karen J. Warren*

In her commentary, Andrea Nye uses the philosophical correspondence between Descartes and Elisabeth to describe a wide range of philosophical themes and differences in perspectives characteristic of this philosophical pair. In order to not duplicate the terrain that Nye covers, this introduction provides a brief, canonical account of key metaphysical and epistemological elements of Descartes's philosophy, followed by comments on Elisabeth that complement Nye's commentary.

DESCARTES

Descartes is often named the "father of modern philosophy" for four interrelated reasons. First, Descartes is among the earliest but most famous philosophers to embrace "the new science" (the scientific revolution) and adopt its "rational method" and experimental approach as the model for philosophy. Second, Descartes's philosophy represents an "epistemological turn" away from religious and theological orientations of medieval philosophy to a focus on both the nature and objects of knowledge and the nature of the knower. Third, Descartes offers a new dualist—mind versus body—metaphysics as the foundation for both explanations in the sciences and epistemologically certain truths in philosophy. Last, Descartes's epistemological and metaphysical positions set the basic agenda of philosophical inquiry for modern philosophy through Kant (roughly 300 years).

The basics of Descartes's metaphysics and epistemology are stated in his two books, *Discourse on Method* (1637) and *Meditations* (1642). (I discuss only the latter.) *Meditations* begins with Descartes's statement of his decision to systematically doubt everything capable of being doubted in order to determine whether there is some *epistemologically* (not psychologically) certain, indubitable claim—one that cannot be denied without self-contradiction—that would function as a foundational, axiomatic claim in philosophy. If there is such a claim, its axiomatic status, like an axiom in mathematics, would be the irrefutable starting point from which Descartes would deductively derive the truths of philosophy. Because the foundation and truths of philosophy would be established by the methods of the new science, philosophy's central historical place as "queen of the sciences" would be preserved and the conclusions of philosophy would be both compatible with and as reliable as the conclusions and methodology of the new science.

Descartes's "method of systematic doubt" applies to three sources of information and two hypotheses. He doubts all information arrived at through sense perception, conclusions arrived at through logical reasoning, and anything he "knows" based on his memory. In addition, he presumes the hypotheses that he might be asleep and that there might be an "evil genius" who is spending all his energy deceiving Descartes into believing as true claims that are false (and vice versa). Even with this method of systematic doubt in place, Descartes claimed that there was one truth that survived as epistemologically certain. What is that axiomatic truth?

In *Discourse on Method*, Descartes stated the truth as his famous *Cogito; ergo, sum*: "I think; therefore, I am." (Here, "I am" seems to be the conclusion of an argument.) Five years later, in *Meditations*, Descartes states the axiomatic truth differently (and not as the conclusion of an argument, since conclusions arrived at through reasoning are among those categories of things that are systematically doubted: "The proposition 'I am' or 'I exist' is necessarily true each time I pronounce it or conceive it mentally." To leapfrog a host of scholarly issues about Descartes's method and the meaning and implications of his asserting "I am," we will presume that, for Descartes "I am" or "I exist," as given in the *Meditations*,[1] is the axiomatic foundation of philosophy.

Having established that "I [Descartes] exist," Descartes asks, what is the nature of the "I" who exists? Descartes's answer is that he is a mind, a "thinking thing." Descartes's position presupposes his (Cartesian) dualistic metaphysics: there are two kinds of substances, minds and bodies. Minds are nonextended, noncorporeal, immaterial substances, *res cogitans*; bodies are extended, corporeal, material substances, *res extensa*. Descartes claims that the I in "I am" refers to a mind—Descartes's mind—the essential nature of which is to be wholly a "thinking thing," not a thinking thing that has a body.

Having established as indubitable his existence as a thinking thing, Descartes proceeds to assert or establish four important claims: First, he asserts the principle that "whatever I clearly and distinctly perceive is true" (or, as Nye states in her commentary, Descartes's cardinal rule is to never accept anything as true that one does not clearly and distinctly understand or perceive). Second, he defends causal, representative realism—the position that the sense impressions one has about an object are caused by actual objects that have just those sensory qualities one perceives them to have.

Third, Descartes defends two different arguments for the existence of God, a causal argument and an ontological argument. Stated in the briefest forms, the causal argument assumes that the idea of a perfect being must be caused by something that contains in itself more reality than the idea itself or the idea of a less perfect being. Since Descartes has the idea of a perfect being, Descartes's idea of a perfect being must be caused by a perfect being. But since the only perfect being is God, God must exist. The ontological argument assumes that whatever belongs to the idea or essence of a thing belongs to that thing. This argument then proceeds as follows: Since existence belongs to the idea (essence) of God, existence belongs to God. But if existence belongs to God, then God exists.

Last, Descartes claims that there are innate ("primitive") ideas that are known through "the natural light of reason." These four claims, taken together, are the essentials Descartes needs to argue that: there are "other minds" (a denial of solipsism—here, a denial of the view that only Descartes and his ideas exist); there is an external world that exists independent of Descartes's existence and perceptions; and there are corporeal bodies that causally interact with noncorporeal minds.

Notice two basic features of Descartes's philosophy as summarized above. First, Descartes's claim that the I in "I [Descartes] am" refers to a mind ("a thinking thing") presupposes "Cartesian dualist metaphysics" (the position that there are two distinct, mutually exclusive kinds of substances, minds and bodies). The "two substances" metaphysics is the foundation of Descartes's philosophy. Second, in his (alleged) derivation of the truths of philosophy from the (axiomatic) claim "I am," Descartes proposes solutions to many of the historically well-entrenched problems of philosophy that are internal features of The House (see Lead Essay): the problem of the existential predicament (or, the problem of solipsism), the other minds problem, the problem of the external world, the problem of appearance versus reality, the mind-body problem, and the problem of proving the existence of God (see Glossary).

Although this account of Descartes's metaphysics and epistemology barely skims the surface in describing Descartes's philosophy, it provides background information for Nye's commentary and for understanding the significance of Descartes's philosophy to the philosophical preoccupations of modern philosophy.

ELISABETH

Elisabeth, Princess Palatine and Abbess of Herford (1618–1680), was one of thirteen children. She was raised by her grandmother and aunt until, at age nine, she joined her parents in Holland, where they had been exiled after being deposed as the King and Queen of Bohemia. Elisabeth was carefully educated in music, dancing, art, Latin, Greek (her family nicknamed her "La Greque" for her fondness for Greek), some natural sciences, and philosophy. She became a friend of Anna Maria van Schurman who, due to religious persecution, was forced to take refuge in Elisabeth's convent.

When she was twenty-four Elisabeth initiated a philosophical correspondence with Descartes—a correspondence that lasted until Descartes's death in 1650. Descartes acknowledged Elisabeth's intellect and unique understanding of his views when he offered a dedication to her in his The Principles of Philosophy (1644). Descartes wrote,

> I have met no one who has such a thorough and comprehensive understanding of my writings as yourself. . . . The only mind, as far as my experience goes, to whom both alike [mathematics and philosophy] are easy, is yours; and I am therefore compelled to regard it as incomparable.[2]

Kersey writes that this dedication is a "rare tribute to anyone and especially a woman."[3]

Elisabeth's reputation as a philosopher rests almost exclusively on her correspondence with Descartes. The part of their correspondence for which she is best known is when she challenges Descartes's dualist mind-body metaphysics by asking a simple but devastating question—devastating because it both challenges the heart of Descartes's metaphysics and is, I think, a question he never adequately answers: If the mind is a purely immaterial substance, how is it able to move a body? Nye elaborates on this in her commentary, claiming that Elisabeth says it is clear how bodies causally interact by impact or pressure with other bodies, but presses Descartes on how a nonspatial mind or soul can do the same. Elisabeth never accepted Descartes's subsequent explanations.

Elisabeth also expresses concerns about the moral implications of Descartes's dualistic metaphysics. Descartes's claims that philosophy and science must be grounded in dispassionate reason, with ethics—which Descartes understood as a "provisional ethics" of prudence—surfacing only after science has determined what is best.[4] Elisabeth's response is, basically, that Descartes has his priorities in the wrong order. Elisabeth puts ethics first, and then, as part of her challenge to the alleged independence of mind (reason) from body (emotion), poses the following dilemma to Descartes: if mind and body are really separate, reason could not move the body (or embodied emotions) to behave ethically, to do what is best; if they are not really separate, then mind (reason) cannot provide a foundation for philosophy.[5]

Elisabeth's worries about the ethical implications of Descartes's dualist metaphysics are relevant today. Many contemporary feminist (and other) philosophers critique Cartesian mind-body dualism on similar grounds: (1) it is a false gender-valued dualism—one that historically associates inferior bodies and emotions with stereotypical female-identified traits, while historically associating superior mind and reason with stereotypical male-identified traits; (2) it fails to recognize that, without a resolution of the issue of the causal interaction of mind and body, Descartes has no defensible basis for claiming that reason can and should control emotions; (3) it fails to recognize the centrality of "moral emotions" (e.g., being angry at an injustice) and moral values and activities (e.g., care, empathy, ethical sensibility to the plight of others, "emotional intelligence") to ethics and ethical decision making; (4) it perpetuates the mistaken views that reason alone is the proper basis for ethics and that emotion compromises objectivity in ethics; and (5) it does not fit the facts (as Nye claims in her commentary): perfect, certain knowledge based on reason alone simply is not possible or desirable.

To illustrate the real-life significance of these objections consider Descartes's response to Elisabeth's descriptions of several deeply troubling events in her life (e.g., her brother's attitude toward Protestantism, a brother's killing of another in a street brawl, the beheading of her uncle, King Charles I of England). Descartes told her to separate her mind from her body, so that she could use reason to overcome her grief. It was a sort of "change your mind (cognitions) and get over it" response. Elisabeth thought Descartes's response was bad advice for three related reasons: she did not want to become unaffected by real-life events that deserved a moral and emotional response; his response was bad morality since it assumed that a complete separation of mind and body, and an ethics based on reason alone, was both possible and desirable for behaving ethically and making ethical decisions; and it rested on bad metaphysics, since it was based on a flawed, dualist separation of mind and body.

Nye states elsewhere that "inherent in the disagreement between Elisabeth and Descartes are differing views on the function and purpose of philosophy."[6] Descartes never abandons his dualist metaphysics as the foundations of his philosophy and Elisabeth never accepts it. The details of their differences and similarities are described in Nye's commentary.

NYE'S COMMENTARY

Andrea Nye's commentary is a beautifully nuanced description of the biographical, historical, political, familial, and personal factors that shaped the philosophical perspectives of Descartes and Elisabeth. It begins with a description of a controversy that arose in the middle of the seventeenth century in Europe. It was initially between the scholastic Aristotelianism espoused by most Christian denominations and proponents of the rational and experimental approaches of the new science promoted by Galileo, Descartes, and other reformers. As certain historical events (described by Nye) unfolded, the debate centered on "the controversial dualist metaphysics proposed by Descartes as the rational foundation for mathematical science."

Princess Elisabeth's intellectual interest in these debates, particularly Descartes's claim that minds causally interact with bodies, is revisited by Nye in different contexts (e.g., historical, political, biographical), in different ways (e.g., through examples, quotations, interpretations of texts, and descriptions of basic philosophical positions), and on different topics (e.g., morality, the problem of evil, the nature of philosophy). Nye also provides the reader with something special—a portrayal of Descartes and Elisabeth as individuals with different personalities, bound by a shared commitment to an on-going and intellectually stimulating philosophical friendship—something lacking in most canonical accounts of Descartes's philosophy. Nye's commentary is an informative, insightful, and engaging philosophical story about this unique pair.

Excerpts of Writings from the Correspondence of Descartes and Elisabeth[7]

I. EXCERPTS FROM ELISABETH'S FIRST EXCHANGE OF LETTERS WITH DESCARTES

The twenty-four-year-old Palatine Princess Elisabeth, living in The Hague with her family under the protection of the House of Orange, took a lively interest in science and philosophy. Intrigued by controversy at the University of Utrecht over René Descartes's claim that soul and body are separate substances, she made inquiries. News of her interest reached Descartes. Eager for royal patronage in his battle with the Dutch theologians, Descartes promptly called on Elisabeth at her mother's house, but did not find her at home. Elisabeth, finding that she missed his visit, writes a letter, raising questions about metaphysical dualism.

The Hague, 16 May 1643
Monsieur Descartes:

I learned of the desire you had to see me a few days ago with much joy and much regret, touching on first your charity in being willing to communicate with such an ignorant and intractable person as myself and then the misfortune which prevented me from enjoying a conversation that would have been so profitable. M. Palloti [Pollot] has much strengthened this last regret by repeating to me the answers that you have given him to the objections [to your work] contained in the Physics of M. Rhegius, answers about which I would have been better instructed out of your own mouth. I also proposed a question to that same professor when he was in this town, with the result that he referred me to you for the required satisfaction. Shame in showing to you a writing style so disordered has prevented me from asking this favor of you by letter up to now.

But today M. Palloti has given me so many assurances of your kindness for everyone and especially for me that I have chased all other considerations aside other than to profit from that kindness in asking you to answer this question: How can the soul of a man determine the spirits of his body so as to produce voluntary actions if the soul is only a thinking substance? For it seems that all determination of movement is made by the pushing of a thing moved, either that it is pushed by the thing which moves it or that it is affected by the quality or shape of the surface of that thing. For the first two conditions, touching is necessary; for the third extension. For touching, you exclude entirely the notion that you have of the soul, and extension seems to me incompatible with an immaterial thing. This is why I ask you to give a definition of the soul more specific than the one you gave in your *Metaphysics*, that is to say of its substance as distinct from its thinking action. For even if we suppose the two to be inseparable (which anyway is difficult to prove in the womb of the mother and in fainting spells), like the attributes of God we can, considering them separately, acquire a more perfect idea of them.

It is because you know the best medicine that I expose to you so liberally the errors in these speculations and hope that, observing the oath of Hippocrates, you will bring to them remedies without publicity, which I ask you to do just as you suffer the importunities of

Your affectionate friend at your service.
Elisabeth

Egmond du Hoef, 21 May 1643
Madame,

The favor with which your Highness has honored me in allowing me to receive your commandments by letter is far greater than I could ever have dared hope. And it makes my defects easier to bear than the one event I would have fervently wished for, to have received them from your own mouth if I had the honor of paying you my respects and offering you my very humble services when I was last in The Hague. There I would have had so many marvels to admire all at once, seeing a discourse more than human come from a body so like those painters give to angels. I would have been in the same rapture it seems must be those who, coming from earth, enter for the first time into heaven. All of which would have made me even less able to respond to your Highness, who without doubt has already remarked this defect in me when I had the honor to speak to you before.[8] Your clemency in leaving me the traces of your thoughts in writing make me hope that, reading them several times, and getting used to considering them, I will be, in truth, less overcome. But in fact I only have that much more admiration, remarking that your thoughts not only seem ingenious at first reading, but even more judicious and solid the more I examine them.

And I can say, with truth, that the question that your Highness proposes appears to be one that I could very reasonably be asked, considering the writings I have published. There I wrote of two things in the human soul on which depends all the knowledge we can have of nature. One is that the soul thinks. The other is that, being united with a body, the soul can act and suffer with the body. But I said almost nothing about the latter of these, and only worked to make the first better understood. This was because my principal design was to prove the distinction between the soul and the body, for which the first was useful and the other would have been harmful. But as your Highness sees matters so clearly that one cannot get anything by her, I will try here to explain the way in which I conceive the union of the soul and the body, and how the soul can have the power to move the body.

First, I consider that there are in us certain primitive ideas, which are like originals, on the model of which we form all our knowledge. There are very few of these ideas. After the most general of them—being, number, duration, etc., which have to do with all that we can conceive—we have for the body specifically only the idea of extension from which follows the ideas of figure and movement, and for the soul only the idea of thought, in which are included perceptions of the understanding and inclinations of will. Finally for the soul and the body together, we have only the idea of their union. On this idea depends the idea of the power the soul has to move the body and the power the body has to act on the soul in causing the feelings and the passions.

I believe that up to now we have confused the idea of the power with which the soul acts in the body with the power by which one body acts in another body. And that we have attributed both the one and the other, not to the soul, for we do not understand that yet, but to various qualities of bodies, such as heaviness, heat, and others, which we have imagined to be real, that is, we have imagined them to have an existence distinct from that of the body, and by consequence to be substances, even though we have named them qualities. And we use these ideas, just as we use ideas that are in us to understand bodies and ideas that are in us to understand the soul, according to whether we take them to be material or immaterial. For example, in supposing that heaviness is a real quality—of which we have no other acquaintance than that it has the power to move the body it is in toward the center of the earth—we avoid the trouble of understanding how it moves the body, or how it is joined to it, and we think only that it is done by a real touching of one surface against another, for we look in ourselves to see if we have a particular idea to conceive of that. I believe that we use that idea badly if we apply it to heaviness, which is not really anything distinct from the body—as I hope to show in my Physics—but that this idea has been given to us to conceive the way in which the soul moves the body. . . .

The very humble and obedient servant of Your Highness
Descartes

The Hague, 20 June 1643

Monsieur Descartes,

Your kindness is apparent, not only in pointing out to me and correcting the faults in my reasoning, as I have understood them, but also in trying to make their recognition less upsetting by attempting to console me with false praise to the prejudice of your own judgment. This might have been necessary to encourage me to work on the remedy for my faults, if it were not for my upbringing. In an environment where the ordinary fashion of conversing has accustomed me to listening to people incapable of telling the truth, I presume to be always sure of the contrary of their discourses, which makes the consideration of my imperfections so familiar to me that they give me no more emotion than is necessary for the desire to undo them.

This makes me confess, without shame, to have found in myself all the causes of error that you have remarked in my letter, and to not be able to banish them completely. The life I am forced to lead does not leave me the disposition of enough leisure time to acquire a habit of meditation according to your rules. So many interests of my family that I must not neglect, so many interviews and civilities that I cannot avoid batter my weak spirit with such anger and boredom that it is rendered for a long time afterward useless for anything else. All of which will excuse my stupidity, I hope, in not having been able to understand the idea by which we must judge how the soul (not extended and immaterial) can move the body by an idea we have in another regard of heaviness, nor why a power which we have falsely attributed to things under the name of a quality (of carrying a body toward the center of the earth) must persuade us that a body could be pushed by something immaterial, especially when the demonstration of a contrary truth (which you promised in your Physics) confirms us in thinking it impossible. This idea of a separate independent quality of heaviness—since we are not able to pretend to the perfection and objective reality of God—could be made up out of ignorance of that which truly propels bodies toward the center of the earth. Because no material cause represents itself to the senses, one attributes heaviness to matter's contrary, the immaterial, which, nevertheless, I would never be able to conceive but as a negation of matter, and that could have no communication with matter.

I confess that it is easier for me to concede the materiality and the extension of the soul than to concede that an immaterial being has the capacity to move a body and to be moved by it. For if the former is done by giving information, it is necessary that the animal spirits that perform the movement be intelligent, which you do not accord to anything corporal. And although, in your Meditations, you show the possibility of the soul being moved by the body, it is nevertheless very difficult to comprehend how a soul, as you have described it, after having had the faculty and habit of good reasoning, would lose all that by some sort of vapors, or that being able to subsist without the body and having nothing in common with it, it would allow itself to be so ruled by the body.

But since you have undertaken my instruction, I do not entertain these sentiments except as friends, which I do not count on keeping, assuring myself that you will explain the nature of an immaterial substance and the movements of its actions and passions in the body, as you have all the other things that you have wished to teach. I pray you also to believe that you could not perform this charity for anyone more sensible of the obligation she owes you than,

Your very affectionate friend,
Elisabeth

Egmond du Hoef, 28 June 1643
Madame,

I am under a great obligation to your Highness in that, after having explained things so badly in response to your question in my previous letter, you have the patience to listen to me again and give me the chance to say more about what I left out. It seems to me the principal question is this: after having distinguished three kinds of primitive ideas or notions, each known in their own way and not by comparison one with the other, what then is the idea we have of the soul, of the body, and of the union between soul and body? I need to explain the difference between these three powerful ideas and the difference between the ways each is made familiar and easy for us. Then, I need to explain why I used the comparison with weight to show how, even though one might want to think of the soul as material (which is actually to think of its union with the body), one cannot fail to see, a bit later, that it is separable from what is material. These are, I believe, all the matters your Highness wrote to me about.

First then, I note a great difference between these three powerful ideas. The soul does not conceive itself except by pure understanding. The body (that is to say extension, figure, movements) can be understood by the understanding alone but much better by understanding aided by imagination. Things that pertain to the union of soul and body are conceived only obscurely by understanding alone or by understanding aided by imagination, but are very clearly conceived by the senses, which is why those who never philosophize, and who use only their senses, are in no doubt that the soul moves the body and that the body acts on the soul. But they think of the two as one thing, that is to say, they conceive their union because to conceive the union between two things is to conceive them as one.

Metaphysics, which exercises pure understanding, makes the notion of the soul familiar. The study of mathematics, which exercises principally the imagination in considering figures and movements, accustoms us to form the very different idea of body. Finally, in the living of life, in ordinary intercourse and abstaining from reflection and the study of things that exercise the imagination, one learns how to conceive the union of soul and body.

I am almost afraid that your Highness will think I am not speaking seriously, which would be contrary to the respect that I owe her and would never fail to render to her. But I can say with truth that the principal rule which I have always observed in my studies and the rule I have used most in acquiring any knowledge at all has been to devote only a very few hours a day to thoughts which use imagination, and only a few hours a year for thinking which uses pure understanding. I have given all the rest of my time to the relaxation of the senses and repose for the spirit. I include in exercises of the imagination even all serious conversation and anything that requires close attention. This is why I retired to the country. Even though in the busiest city in the world I could still have as much time to myself for study as I have now, I could not use it as well because my spirit would be tired out by the attention which the traffic of life requires. I take the liberty to write this to your Highness to witness to her that I truly admire that amid the affairs and concerns which are never lacking with people of noble spirit and high birth, she has been able to find time for the reflection required to grasp the distinction between the soul and the body.

But I also think that it was that reflection, rather than thoughts that require less attention, that made her find obscurity in the idea we have of their union. This is because it does not seem to me that the human mind is capable of conceiving very clearly and at the same time both the distinction between the soul and the body and their union. For that it would be necessary to conceive soul and body as one thing and then at the same time to think of them as two things, which is contradictory. In this I am supposing that your Highness still has the arguments that prove the distinction between soul and body forcefully present in her mind and that she doesn't wish to make that distinction go away in order to represent to herself the idea of their union, a union that every person all the time experiences in himself without any help from philosophers and experiences just because he is a single person who has together both body and thought which are such that thought can move the body and feel the things that happen to it. This is why I used the comparison of weight and other qualities that we commonly imagine to be one with some body, just as thought is one with our body. I did not concern myself that this comparison was defective in that these causalities are not real the way we imagine them because I believed that your Highness was already completely persuaded that the soul is a substance distinct from the body.

But since your Highness remarked that is easier to attribute matter and extension to the soul than it is to attribute to it the capacity to move a body or be moved by it without being material, I say this. Go ahead, attribute matter to the soul, because that is nothing more than to conceive it united with the body. And after having clearly conceived that union, and experiencing it in herself, it will be easy to consider that the matter she attributes to this thinking is not the thinking itself and that the extension of matter is of another nature than the extension of thinking. The first is located at a certain place from which is excluded any other extended body, but this is not true of the soul. And so your Highness will not fail to arrive easily at understanding the distinction between the soul and the body, notwithstanding that she has conceived their union. Finally, since I believe that it is very necessary to have understood well, at some time in one's life, the principles of Metaphysics—because these give us knowledge of God and our soul—I believe also that it is dangerous to too often occupy one's understanding in reflecting on them because this makes it impossible to attend to the faculties of imagination and sense. The best is to be content to keep in one's memory, and on account so to speak, conclusions once drawn, then to use the rest of the time one has for study for the thinking in which understanding acts along with imagination and sense. . . .

The very humble and obedient servant of your Highness,
Descartes

II. DOCTOR PHILOSOPHER

Throughout her life Elisabeth suffered from a variety of ailments. In the exchange that follows, Descartes seizes an opportunity to put the new philosophy into practice. For Descartes, the benefits of science based on mathematics and physical law are not only theoretical. Modern science, he hoped, would usher in a new era in medicine, replacing the old bleeding and purging with a sound knowledge of bodily function.

Egmond, 18 May 1645
Madame,

I have been extremely surprised to learn, by letter from Palloti, that Y. H. has been sick for a long time, and I blame my solitude for making it so that I did not know this sooner. Even though it is true that I have been so retired from the world that I know nothing of what is happening, still the zeal that I have in the service of your Highness should not have allowed me to go so long without knowing the state of her health. I would have gone to The Hague expressly to enquire about her if Monsieur Palloti, writing to me in haste about two months ago, had not promised to write again by the next mail. And since he never omits to tell me how your Highness is doing, and since I did not receive any letters, I had supposed that you were the same. But I have learned in his last letter that your Highness has had for three or four weeks a slow fever, accompanied by a dry cough, and that after being delirious for five or six days, the illness returned and that, anyway, at the time that he wrote his letter (which was close to fifteen days in transit) your Highness began again to do better. With this I detected the signs of serious illness, and even though it is one from which your Highness will certainly recover, I cannot omit sending her my regards. For though I am not a medical doctor, the honor which your Highness gave me last summer, of wanting to know my opinion on another indisposition that she then suffered makes me hope that such a liberty will not be disagreeable to her.

The usual cause of a slow fever is sadness. The perseverance of Fortune in the persecution of your house continually brings on you irritation so public and so striking that it is not possible to use much conjecture or to be very much involved in these matters to judge that this is the principal cause of your indisposition. And it is probable that you would be completely cured if only, by the power of your virtue, you would make your soul content in spite of the disgraces of Fortune. I know that it would be imprudent to want to persuade a person to feel joy when every day sends her new subjects for displeasure, and I am not one of those cruel Philosophers who wish their sages to be without feeling. I also know that your Highness is not so affected by what regards her in particular as she is by what regards the interests of her House and the persons she cares about. This I esteem as the most likable of virtues.

However, it seems to me that the difference between great souls and base vulgar souls consists principally in that vulgar souls give themselves up to their passions and are only happy or unhappy insofar as the things that happen to them are agreeable or displeasing. On the other hand, noble souls have arguments so strong and so powerful that, even when they too suffer from passion—and even from passions more violent than the usual ones—nevertheless, for them reason remains the master and even makes afflictions serve it and contribute to the perfect felicity that noble souls enjoy thereafter in this life. For on the one side considering themselves immortal and capable of receiving very great contentment, and on the other side considering that they are joined with a mortal and fragile body subject to many infirmities which cannot not help but perish in a few years, they do everything they can to make Fortune favorable in this life, but at the same time they value it so little in regard to Eternity that they almost think of events only as acted-out dramas. Just as the sad and lamentable Histories which we see represented in the theater often give us as much entertainment as happy Histories even as they bring tears to our eyes, so the greatest souls, of which I am speaking, get an interior satisfaction in themselves from all the things which happen to them, even the most infuriating and unbearable. Feeling grief in their heart, they work to bear it patiently, and the proof that they have of their own power is agreeable to them. Seeing their friends in great affliction, they sympathize with their trouble, and do all that is possible to help them and do not fear even death in this endeavor if necessary. Meanwhile, however, the witness their conscience gives them that they are doing their duty and are performing actions that are lovable and virtuous make them more happy than all the sadness that compassion inflicts on them can make them sad. And, in the end, just as the greatest good Fortune does not go to their head or make them more insolent, so the greatest adversities cannot strike them down or make them so sad that the body to which they are joined falls ill.

I fear that this advice would be ridiculous if I wrote it to anyone else. Because I believe that your Highness is the noblest and more elevated soul in my acquaintance, I believe that she must also be the happiest, and that she will be happy in fact, provided that she cast her eyes on what is before her and compares the value of the goods she possesses—which can never be taken away—both with what Fate has deprived her of and with the disgrace with which Fortune persecutes her in the person of some of those near to her. Then she will see the great reason she has to be content with her own advantages. The extreme regard I have for her is the reason that I have allowed myself this prescription that I entreat her humbly to follow, as coming from a person who is

The very humble and obedient servant of Your Highness
Descartes

The Hague, 24 May 1645
Monsieur Descartes,

I see that the charms of the solitary life have not robbed you of the virtues required in society. The generous kindness you have for your friends and for me is witnessed in the concern you have for my health. I am angry that they would have involved you in making a trip all the way here given that M. Palloti told me that you have judged that repose is necessary to your health. And I assure you that the doctors, who see me every day and look at all the symptoms of my illness, have not found the cause, nor have they ordered remedies as salutary as those you have ordered from a distance. If they had been sufficiently wise to suspect the part my spirit plays in disordering my body, I would not have had the frankness to confess it to them. But to you, Monsieur, I confess it without scruple, assuring myself that such a naive recitation of my defects would not lose me the part I have in your friendship but would confirm it all the more, since you will see how necessary it is to me.

Know then that I have a body imbued with a great part of the weakness of my sex, know that it registers very easily afflictions of the soul and does not have the strength to be quit of them, being of a temperament subject to obstructions and having to remain in a climate that contributes to these obstructions. For persons who cannot do much exercise like myself, a long oppression of the heart from sadness is not necessary to disrupt the spleen and infect the rest of the body with vapors. I think that the slow fever and dry cough which is still there even with the heat of the season and the walks which I take to rally my forces come from this lack of exercise. It is this which makes me consent to the advice of the doctors, that I should drink in a month's time Spa waters (which will be brought here without letting them spoil), having found, by experience, that they dispel obstructions. But I will not take them before I know your opinion, since you have the kindness to wish me to cure my body along with the mind.

I continue to confess to you that although I do not rest my happiness only on things which depend on fortune or on the will of men, or think myself absolutely unfortunate, when I see that my House will never be reinstated or my dear ones far from misery, I cannot consider the sad accidents that befall them as other than evil. Nor can I see the actions I take to serve them useless without much inquietude, which, as soon as it is calmed by reason, is aroused by yet another disaster. If my life was completely known to you, you would find it strange that I have managed to survive so long with a sensitive spirit like mine and a weak body, given that I have only the counsel of my own reason and the consolation of my conscience—that very conscience which you make the cause of my present illness . . . I would never be stronger and more constant than in being, all my life,

Your very affectionate friend at your service,
Elisabeth

Egmond, May or June 1645
Madame,

I was not able to read the letter that your Highness gave me the honor of writing without great emotion, seeing that virtue so rare and accomplished is not accompanied by health or with the prosperity that it merits. I easily can conceive the many annoyances that constantly present themselves, ones so difficult to overcome and often of such a nature, that reason itself would not rule that one should oppose them directly or try to drive them away. With enemies at home among people with whom one must have dealings, one must be constantly on guard to keep from harm. I have found only one remedy for this: divert the imagination and senses as much as possible, and use understanding alone in considering the source of annoyance, and that only when one is obliged by prudence.

One can easily note here, it seems to me, the difference between understanding on the one hand and imagination or sense on the other. Take a person who otherwise has all the reason in the world to be content, but who sees continually played out before her Tragedies in which all the action is sad. She is thus only occupied in considering objects that are sad and pitiful. Even though they are made-up and fabulous, the sad scenes never stop from bringing tears to her eyes, affecting her imagination without touching her understanding. I believe that this alone would be enough to condition such a person's heart to contract and force sighs, and as a result the circulation of blood would be held back and slowed down. Larger particles of blood would attach one to another, and could easily burden the spleen, backing up and stopping up its pores. The more subtle particles of blood, retaining their movement, would have an effect on her lungs and cause a cough, which in the long term would be cause for alarm.

On the other hand, take a person who had in reality an infinity of true reasons for unhappiness, but who worked with great care to divert her imagination, never thinking of her troubles, except when the necessity of events makes it obligatory, and who used all the rest of her time to consider only objects which can bring her contentment and joy. Not only would that attitude be very useful for that person in that she could judge with more sanity the things which have to do with her because she looked at them without passion, but in addition I do not doubt that this would be enough to restore her health in that the reason her spleen and her lungs were working poorly was because of the bad state of the blood caused by depression. In principle, if she also used medical remedies to thin that part of the blood which caused the obstructions, I would think Spa water very appropriate for this purpose, if, when taking it, your Highness observes what doctors usually recommend: she must completely free the spirit from any kind of sad thought, and even from any kind of serious meditation having to do with the sciences. She should occupy herself only in imitating those who, looking at the greenery of the woods, the colors of a flower, the flight of a bird, and such things that require no concentration, make themselves think of nothing at all. This is not wasting time, but using time well, because one can in the process take satisfaction in thinking that in this way one is recovering perfect health, the foundation of all the other goods that are possible in this life.

I know that I am not writing here anything that your Highness does not know better than myself, and that it is not so much the theory as the practice that is difficult in matters like this. But the extreme favor that she has witnessed for me, in indicating that it is not disagreeable for her to hear what I think, makes me take the liberty to write my thoughts to her, such as they are. And it gives me in addition the liberty to add that I myself have experienced in my own case proof that a similar illness and one even more dangerous can be cured by the remedy that I have just described. Being born from a mother who died a few days after my birth of a lung disease caused by a certain unhappiness, I inherited from her a dry cough and a pallor that I kept up to the age of more than twenty and that made all the doctors who examined me before that time, condemn me to early death. But I believe that the tendency I always have had to look at anything that happens from a bias which makes it seem most favorable to myself, and to make it so that my main happiness depends only on myself, caused this indisposition, which was part of my very nature, little by little to pass away . . . As there is nothing in the world that I desire with so much passion then to be able to render service to your Highness, there is nothing that would make me happier than to have the honor of receiving her commandments, I am

The very humble and obedient servant of Your Highness,
Descartes

22 June 1645
Monsieur Descartes:

Your letters always serve as an antidote for melancholy, even when they do not instruct me—by turning my spirit away from the disagreeable things which are furnished to
it every day—how to make my spirit contemplate the happiness which I possess in having
the friendship of a person of your merit to whose counsel I can commit the conduct of
my life. If I could follow your last advice, I do not doubt that I would cure myself right
away of the maladies of my body and weaknesses of my spirit. But I confess that I have
trouble separating sense and imagination from things that are continually represented in
discussion and letters. The reason for this is I do not know how to do so without sinning
against my duty.

I understand well that in taking away from an idea of an affair everything that makes
me angry (which I believe is only represented by the imagination), I would judge more
sanely and would soon find a remedy for the emotion I bring to it. But I have never
known how to practice this except after passion has played its role. There is something
surprising about misfortune, which, even when it is foreseen, I can master only after a
period of time. And emotion disorders my body so strongly that I need several months to
put it aside, months that never pass without the arrival of some new subject of trouble.
Even though I make myself govern my spirit with care and give it agreeable objects to
contemplate, the least weakness makes it dwell again on subjects that affect it adversely.
I know that even if I do not govern myself at all while I am taking the waters, it will not
make me more melancholy. Even if I could profit, as you do, from all that is presented
to the senses, I would divert myself but without ridding myself of melancholy . . . This
is when I feel the inconvenience of being a little rational. Because, if I were not at all
rational, I would find pleasures in common with those with whom I must live, and take
that medicine with profit. And if I were as rational as you are, I would cure myself as you
have done.

In this, the malediction of my sex prevents the contentment I would get from a trip
to Egmond, so I could understand at first hand the truths that you draw from your new
garden. Nevertheless, I console myself with the liberty you give me to ask from time to
time for news, in the quality of

Your very affectionate friend, at your service
Elisabeth

III. THE HAPPY LIFE

Elisabeth continued to suffer from poor health. To distract her from rigorous study, Descartes proposed that they undertake together some light reading. His choice is Seneca the
Younger's *On the Happy Life*, but it is a choice he immediately regrets.

Egmond, 4 August 1645
Madame,

When I chose the book by Seneca, *De Vita Beata* to propose to your Highness as an agreeable undertaking, I had in mind the reputation of the author and the dignity of the subject. I did not think of the way in which he treated the subject, which now that I look at it, I do not find exact enough . . . What is it to "vivre beata?" I would say in French, "vivre heureusement," if there were not a difference between fortune and beatitude. Being fortunate depends solely on things outside us, from which it comes that those who have it are judged more fortunate than wise when some good comes to them not procured by their own efforts. Beatitude, on the other hand, it seems to me, consists rather in a perfect contentment of spirit and an interior satisfaction that those who are the most favored by fortune may not have, and that wise men can achieve without being fortunate at all. Thus, "*vivre beata*" is nothing other than to have a spirit perfectly content and satisfied.

Considering, after that, what are the things that give us supreme contentment, I note that there are two kinds: those that depend on us like virtue and wisdom, and those that do not depend on us like honors, riches, and health. It may be certain that a well-born man who is not sick, who lacks nothing, and who is also as wise and virtuous as another man who is poor, sick, and crippled can enjoy a more perfect contentment than the poor man. Nevertheless, just as a little vessel can be as full as a bigger one even though it contains less liquid, taking each person's contentment as the fulfillment of desire regulated according to reason, I do not doubt that those who are the most poor and disgraced by fortune or nature could still be as completely content and satisfied as anyone else, even though they do not enjoy so many advantages. And this is the only sort of contentment there is. Since no other is in our power, the pursuit of any other would be superfluous.

It seems to me that anyone can make himself content and satisfied without waiting for anything from outside, provided only that he does three things, namely follow the three moral rules that I put in my *Discourse on Method*.

The first is try always to use, as much as you can, your own mind to know what you ought to do or not do in all the events of life.

The second is be firm and resolute in executing all that reason tells you to do, without letting either passions or appetites distract you. It is the firmness of this resolution that I believe should be taken as virtue. (I don't know if anyone has ever explained it in this way. Instead virtue is usually divided into different kinds, to which different names are given depending on the different objects to which they refer.)

The third is keep in mind, while you are conducting yourself in this way according to reason, that all the goods that you do not possess are entirely out of your power one and all so that by this means you accustom yourself not to desire them. Nothing but desire and regret or repentance can keep us from being content. And if we always do all that our reason dictates, we will never have any reason to repent, even if events make us see afterward that we were mistaken, because it was not by any fault of our own. . . .

For the rest, not all sorts of desires are incompatible with this sort of happiness, but only those that are accompanied by impatience and sadness. It is not necessary that our reason not be mistaken; it is enough that our conscience tells us that we have lacked neither resolution nor virtue in executing all the things that we have judged to be the best. Virtue alone is enough to make us content in this life.

What Seneca should have talked about are all the principal truths which understanding requires in order to facilitate the practice of virtue, to regulate our desires and passions, and to enjoy a natural beatitude. This would have made his book the best and most useful book a pagan philosopher could have written. Of course, this is only my opinion, which I submit to the judgment of your Highness, and if she will give me the favor of giving me notice of what my judgment lacks I will be under a great obligation if she will correct me. Being,

The very humble and obedient servant of Your Highness
Descartes

The Hague, 16 August 1645
Monsieur Descartes,

I do not know how to get rid of the doubt that one could arrive at the happiness of which you speak without the assistance of what does not depend entirely on one's own will. There are illnesses that prevent people from reasoning at all and consequently prevent any rational satisfaction, and other illnesses which diminish the power of reason and keep us from following the maxims that good sense has forged and that make man more moderate, illnesses which make a man subject to being carried away by emotion and less capable of disentangling himself from accidents of fortune which require prompt resolution.

When Epicurus tells a lie at his deathbed, assuring his friends he feels well instead of crying out like an ordinary man, he lives the life of a philosopher, not a Prince, Captain, or courtier. He knows that nothing outside himself can make him forget his role and prevent him from acting according to the rules of his philosophy. But on these occasions, it seems to me repentance is inevitable. One cannot defend oneself with the knowledge that failure is as natural to a man as being sick, and one cannot know if we may be exonerated for each particular fault. But I assure myself that you will clarify these difficulties and many others of which I am not aware at this moment, when you teach me the truths that must be known to facilitate the use of virtue. Do not abandon, I beg you, your project of obliging me by your precepts and believe that I esteem them as much as they merit.

It has been eight days since the bad humor of a sick brother has prevented me from making this request in that I was kept always at his bedside to try to make him either submit to the regime of the doctors because of the liking he has for me, or to recount to him my own regime to try to divert him because he thinks I am capable of it. I wish to assure you I will be, all my life,

Your very affectionate friend at your service,
Elisabeth

Egmond, 1 September 1645
Madame,

When I spoke of a happiness that depends entirely on our own free will and that all men can have without any assistance from outside, you remarked that there are illnesses which take away the power of reason and so also take away also the power to enjoy the satisfactions of a rational spirit. And that reminds me that what I have said of the general run of men should not be understood as true of those who have the free use of their reason and who know the methods one must use to arrive at interior happiness. There is no one who does not want to be happy, but few know the means to it, and indeed often a bodily indisposition can prevent the will from being free . . . For indispositions, however, that do not affect sensation, but which change only mood and cause an inclination to sadness, anger, or some other passion, these no doubt give pain, but they can be surmounted and even offer a means for the soul to achieve a satisfaction as much greater as these dispositions are difficult to conquer. And I believe that all of the distractions from outside which ordinarily keep one from playing the role of philosopher—such as intrigues at court, adversity of fortune, and also great wealth—are only a disadvantage. When you have everything to wish for, you forget to think of yourself. When, afterward, fortune changes, you find yourself surprised to the same degree you trusted to that fortune.

The true use of reason for the conduct of life consists only in examining and considering without passion the value of all the perfections—of body as much as of spirit—that can be acquired through our own conduct, so that, being usually obliged to deprive ourselves of some in order to have others, we always choose the best. And since perfections of the body are the least, one can say generally that, without them, there is still a way to be happy. Nevertheless, I am not of the opinion that one must entirely despise these perfections, or that one must exclude passion altogether. It is enough to render passions subject to reason. Once tamed, they are sometimes more useful than when they tended to excess. I myself would wish to have no passion more excessive that that which inclines me to the respect and the veneration that I owe to you and that make me

The very humble and obedient servant of Your Highness,
Descartes

꙳

The Hague, 13 September 1645
Monsieur Descartes,

If my conscience were as satisfied with the excuses you give for my ignorance as I am with the remedies you give for that ignorance, I would be very obliged. And I would be exempt from repentance for having so badly used the time I do have for the use of my reason, which for me is longer than for others of my age. Birth and fortune force me to use my judgment promptly in order to lead a life sufficiently difficult and free of prosperity to prevent me from thinking of myself, just as if I were forced to trust to the rule of a stern governess.

I believe it is not always prosperity or the flattery that accompanies it that can decisively keep fortitude of spirit from well-born people and prevent them from bearing changes of fortune philosophically. I am persuaded that the accidents that surprise people governing the public, who are without the time to find the most expedient means, carry them (no matter what virtue they have) into actions that afterward cause the repentance that you say is one of the principal obstacles to happiness. It is true that having a habit of valuing goods according to how they contribute to contentment, and measuring that contentment according to perfections which cause pleasure, and judging without passion those perfections and pleasures, can protect from many faults. But to evaluate goods, it is necessary to be completely acquainted with them, and to be acquainted with all those among which we must choose in an active life would require an infinite science. You say that one must be content when one's conscience witnesses that one has used all possible precautions. But this never happens, because one does not simply find one's story; there always remain things to consider and revise. To measure contentment according to the perfection that causes it, it is necessary to see clearly the value of each thing, to see whether those that only serve ourselves or those that make us more useful to others are preferable. The latter seem to be valued more by persons in whom there is an excess of spirit that torments itself for others, the former by persons in whom there is an excess of spirit that only lives for itself. And both inclinations can be supported with reasons strong enough to make the tendency continue all one's life.

It is the same with other perfections of the body and the spirit. Unspoken sentiment makes reason approve, sentiment that you ought not to call passion but rather approval by something innate. Tell me then, if you please, to what point we should follow such a sentiment—it being a gift of nature—and how do we correct it?

Your very affectionate friend at your service,
Elisabeth

15 September 1645
Madame,
There are only, it seems to me, two things that are required to be always disposed to judge well. One is to understand the truth, and the other is to remember and accept that truth whenever the occasion requires it. Since only God knows perfectly all things, we must be content to know the truths that are of most use to us.

Among these the first and principal truth is that there is one God, on which everything is dependent . . . The second is the nature of the soul—in that it exists in the body, is more noble than the body, and is capable of enjoying an infinity of contentments not found in this life. This is what keeps us from fearing death. This is what detaches our affections from the things of this world, so that whatever is in the power of Fortune we look on with scorn . . . If we imagine that this earth is our principal dwelling place and this life our best life, then in place of understanding perfections that are truly in us, we attribute to other creatures imperfections that they do not have. We put ourselves above them, and so entertain an impertinent presumption: we wish to be of the council of God, and to take on with God the charge of running the world, which causes an infinity of vain iniquities and falsehoods.

After one understands the goodness of God and the immortality of our souls and the grandeur of the universe, there is one more truth that it seems to me is very useful. Even though each of us is a person separate from others and a person whose interests are to some degree distinct from the interests of others, one must nevertheless think that we could not subsist alone and we are, in effect, part of this earth, part of this nation, this society, and this family. To these one is connected by residence, by allegiance, and by birth. Therefore, it is necessary to give the interests of the whole of which one is a part preference over the interests of oneself alone, understood that it is always within measure and with discretion. One would be wrong to expose oneself to a great danger to procure only a small good for family and country. If a man is worth more in himself alone than all the rest of his city, it makes no sense for him to want to destroy himself to save the city. But if he thinks only of himself, he would not fear doing great harm to other men as long as he thinks of receiving some small accommodation, and one would have no true friend, no loyalty, nor any virtue. On the other hand, when one considers oneself part of the public, one takes pleasure in doing good to everyone, and even does not fear risking one's own life in service to others if the occasion presents itself—indeed some would even lose their soul if they could to save others. This consideration is the source and the origin of all the most heroic actions that men do. Those who risk death by vanity, or because they hope to be paid, or out of stupidity because they do not understand the danger, these are more to complain of than to praise.

When someone risks himself because he thinks it is his duty, or when he suffers some other harm so that he can do some good for another—even if he does not consciously think that he does it more for what he owes to the public of which he is a part than for what he owes as an individual—it is always in virtue of this consideration, which is there in his thoughts in a confused way. And it is natural to think this when one knows and loves God as one should. In abandoning oneself completely to God's will, a person leaves aside his own interests and has no other passion than to do what he believes is agreeable to God. As a result he has satisfactions of spirit and contentment incomparably more valuable than all the little passing joys that depend on sense.

I have said before that other than understanding the truth, habit is required in order to be always disposed to judge well. For since we cannot be continually attentive to the same thing, no matter how clear and evident the reasons by which we were persuaded before of some truth, we can, afterward, be turned from believing it by false appearances, Only by long and frequent meditation, can we sufficiently imprint the truth on our spirit so the spirit will turn to it habitually. In this, it was right in the schools to say that virtues are habits, because actually, one does not so much lack in theory the understanding of what one must do as to lack the practice of it, that is to say a firm habit of believing it. And so that, while I am here examining these truths, I increase also in me the habitude of them, I have a particular obligation to your Highness in that she allows me to lay them out, and there is no where I think my loyalty better placed than in witnessing that I am

The very humble and obedient servant of your Highness
Descartes

Riswyck, 30 September 1645
Monsieur Descartes,

The consideration that we are a part of a whole, whose advantage we ought to seek may be the force behind all generous actions, but I find much difficulty in the conditions that you prescribe. How can one measure the evils one gives oneself for the public against the good that will come of it, without those evils appearing greater, inasmuch as their idea is more distinct? And what rule would we have for the comparison of things that are not equally known to us, such as our own merit against the merit of those with whom we live? A natural arrogance would always make us tip the balance our own way; a natural modesty would esteem itself at less than its true value.

To profit from the particular truths of which you speak, it would be necessary to know exactly all the passions and all the predispositions, the majority of which are insensible. Also, in observing the customs of the countries in which we live we find much irrational that is nevertheless necessary to observe to avoid even greater inconvenience.

Since I have been here, I have very angering proof of this. I hoped to profit from a stay in the country by having more time for study, and I find here, beyond comparison, less leisure than at The Hague because of being distracted by those who do not know what to do with themselves. Although it is for me very hard to have to deprive myself of real goods to give these people goods that are imaginary, I am constrained to cede to pressing and established laws of civility so as not to make enemies. Since I have been writing here, I have been interrupted more than seven times by inconvenient visits. It is excessive kindness which protects your letters from a similar predicament on your end, and which obliges you to wish to add to your usual labors, by communicating them to such an indocile person as

Your very affectionate, at your service,
Elisabeth

Commentary by *Andrea Nye*, Princess Elisabeth and Descartes: A Philosophical Correspondence

INTRODUCTION

It was the middle of the seventeenth century in Europe. Philosophers were arguing for new rational and experimental approaches in natural science. Aristotelians in institutions of higher learning were retaliating, protective of principles and methods that had established their academic reputations. Descartes, a supporter of the new science, settled in relatively tolerant Holland, determined to avoid the fray and pursue scientific studies in peace. Although he kept quiet and published little, his presence soon became known in the Dutch universities. One of his early supporters there was a doctor of medicine, Henri de Roy, otherwise known as Regius. He read and approved Descartes's work in physics and anatomy. Drawing on Cartesian principles, he published *Treatise on Physiology*, which won him a professorship at the University of Utrecht. Unfortunately also at Utrecht, the acting rector was the conservative Protestant theologian Voetius.

At Utrecht Regius quickly won adherents for the claim that final causes and essences cannot serve as explanations in the physical sciences, but he managed to avoid the controversial dualist metaphysics proposed by Descartes as the rational foundation for mathematical science. In his classes Regius liberally mixed traditional medicine and physics with Descartes's studies in anatomy or optics, but saw no need to prove Descartes's thesis that mind and body are different substances. Then one day in Regius's class a Cartesian thesis was proposed for disputation: "that the union of soul and body produces not a unity, which is an entity on its own account, but one that is accidental." The thesis touched off a scandal. Voetius called for Regius's dismissal, claiming the proposal was grounds for heresy. An outraged Descartes became involved in the dispute. An acrimonious legal battle resulted that went on for years, making Descartes's sojourn in Holland increasingly uncomfortable.

The controversy surrounding this seemingly innocuous academic hypothesis has deep roots in the ongoing struggle between the scholastic Aristotelianism espoused by most Christian denominations as the basis for teaching in the universities, and the new science promoted by Galileo, Descartes, and other reformers. Theologians like Voetius argued that if the Cartesian thesis were correct—if there is no essential unity between mind and body, if their junction is only accidental—then physical phenomena can be explained as mechanisms governed solely by natural law. Although Descartes protested that he had also proved decisively in his *Meditations* that nonmaterial substances like God and the soul exist, theologians insisted that to posit two different kinds of substance—immaterial, nonextended substances or minds and material, extended substance or bodies—opened the door to atheism. It would only be a matter of time before God and the soul dropped out, leaving only godless materialism.

The young precocious Palatine princess Elisabeth followed the controversy with interest. Known for learning and well connected in university circles, she had her own question about the now infamous Cartesian thesis—a question that she proposed to her acquaintance, Professor Regius: if the mind is a purely immaterial substance, how is it able to move the body? Regius referred her to Descartes, who was living in the countryside near The Hague. Through the good offices of a mutual friend, Elisabeth invited the philosopher to call at her family's town house to discuss philosophy. Descartes, flattered and eager for any support he might win from those in high places, immediately obliged but found the princess not at home. Regretting that she missed him, Elisabeth wrote Descartes a letter. It would be the first overture in a philosophical correspondence that continued with only occasional interruptions until Descartes's death seven years later in 1650.

DIFFERENCES

The philosophical friendship between Elisabeth and Descartes was an unlikely one in many respects. Descartes's interests were in science and mathematics. Reflecting on his education in his *Discourse on Method*, he made clear how irrelevant he found literature, history, and classics. Truth is truth, he argued, whereas literature is made-up stories, history is doubtful accounts of past mistakes, and classical authors are influenced by myth and legend. Elisabeth's interests were wider. Fascinated by science and mathematics, she also found value in nonscientific thinkers such as Seneca, Epicurus, and Machiavelli.

Both were professed Christians, but here too there were differences. Elisabeth was devoutly religious, devoted to the Protestant cause, and unwilling to give up the idea of a personal God. Descartes, a Catholic, saw God as the remote author of the universe, not an object for personal piety or appeal. His proofs for the existence of God and his use of God in proofs for the truth of mathematics and the existence of the external world were a matter of logic and deduction, not religious faith or sentiment.

Descartes and Elisabeth were very different in material circumstance. Descartes was estranged from his family and lived alone with only servants. He had little interest in the complex geopolitical and religious conflicts that continued to destroy the economy and decimate the population of Europe, except as those conflicts prevented him getting support for and recognition for rational science. Avoiding politics of any kind, shunning the frivolous distractions of city life that had seduced him in his youth as well as intellectual disputes that might put him in danger from the authorities, he enjoyed, as Elisabeth put it in one of her letters, "the charms of the solitary life." In contrast, Elisabeth was deeply and painfully embroiled in European affairs, constantly bombarded with crisis after crisis that not only endangered her family but also compromised the chances for economic and social reconstruction in her homeland, the Rhineland.

Given these differences in commitment and circumstance, Descartes and Elisabeth came to the question of the nature of mind and body with different concerns. Descartes was intently focused on proving the value of rational method in the sciences and subordinated all other issues to that end. As he saw it, the proper use of metaphysics is to provide the basis and justification for mechanical explanations in the sciences that he believed would lead to advances in knowledge and technology. Elisabeth shared his belief in the efficacy and importance of science but looked also to the specific application of rational method in practical life. Is the mind, in practice as well as theory, separate from the body? If so how can thought or thinking direct action? Is it possible or even desirable for the mind of a person—a person like herself responsible for the well-being of others in insecure and dangerous times—to separate reason from bodily and emotional response? Elisabeth shared Descartes's modernist impatience with medieval medicine and Aristotelian physics. She shared his conviction that careful experimentation and analytic principles would lead to advances in the sciences, but she refused to lay aside, in the name of that conviction, problems she found in Cartesian metaphysics: the apparent impossibility of causal interaction between separate substances of mind and body, the practical difficulty of mental detachment in times of stress, the moral danger in a purely rational approach to moral responsibility.

THE RELATION BETWEEN MIND AND BODY

The question in Elisabeth's first letter to Descartes has to do with the relation between mind and body. Elisabeth was not alone in wondering how it is possible that a separate and immaterial soul could move a material extended body. A body moves another body by impact or pressure, she pointed out, and it is hard to see how a nonphysical soul could have the same effect. Certainly in Elisabeth's experience, "pure reason" and "rational understanding"—the hallmarks of soul in Descartes's philosophy—often seemed to have little power over impulsive bodies.

Elisabeth's resistance to Descartes's dualism was not the same as that of theologians like Voetius who barred the advance of science on religious and sectarian grounds. She saw the opposition of the clerics as much less threatening than did Descartes, and she often tried to assure him that, in a relatively democratic Protestant country like Holland, if he would refrain from outraged counterattack, controversy would soon die down. It was not academic wrangling over the nature and extent of "essence" or "form" that motivated her questions, but a more practical worry. How can those in power be made to act rationally, to stop killing each other, to attend to the health of the people, to build instead of destroy? For Elisabeth the "definition" of soul was not only the first premise in an argument for the truth of "clear and distinct" ideas in the mathematical sciences, as expressed in Descartes's *Meditations*; it was also an important and necessary description that one must get right in order to find the truth, live at peace, act morally, and avoid illness.

Descartes's first letter gives little credence to her concern that metaphysical dualism may not be consistent with human experience. At loggerheads with the powerful Voetius and headed for trouble both with the University of Utrecht and with the Utrecht City Council, Descartes no doubt saw advantage in further contact with Elisabeth and her relatives in the ruling House of Orange. He would not, however, have hoped for much in the way of philosophical discussion from a member of the aristocracy. Prejudice as to the intellectual capability of "les grandes" may go some way toward explaining how little effort he took at first to give adequate answers to Elisabeth's questions. He is disarmingly frank, if not flippant, about the reasons why he has not said much in print about the interaction between mind and body. To talk about the separation between mind and body advanced his cause, he said; to have dwelt on their union would be harmful to that cause. He flatters Elisabeth. Of course she is sharp enough not to let him get away with this, so he will offer her a more sophisticated way to put her mind at rest. We falsely imagine that heaviness or heat is a separate body within a body that moves that body. Although this is a mistake, why not assume that the "idea has been given us to conceive the way in which the soul moves the body?" We have the idea of something that is not a certain body but that moves that body, which we falsely associate with certain physical qualities. Why not use that same idea to represent the action of the soul on the body?

In her reply, Elisabeth deftly deflates both Descartes's compliments and his less than credible solution to her problem. "False praise" is unnecessary, she tells him. It can only "prejudice his judgment." Unlike other royals she is not dependent on a diet of insincere flattery. Yes, given family and diplomatic responsibilities, she is unable to devote as much time to philosophy and science as he is. Even so, she says gently, she is not satisfied by his answer. Mistaken ideas are not necessarily reusable; they may have been "made up out of ignorance." In short, she is not content to simply find a convenient way to think about how the mind can move the body and then leave the problem of interaction unsolved.

For Elisabeth, the issue of the soul is not one of abstract definition or logic, but has practical experiential import. In what way can material actions be made intelligent? In what way can the mind protect itself from passions that cloud judgment? In what way can one be sure that bias due to circumstance or temperament has not distorted logic? The tone of Descartes's second letter is different. Gone is obligatory flattery and comparisons with angelic beings. Without preamble, he now undertakes a more serious explanation of the interaction of mind and body.

THE USES OF METAPHYSICS

In his second letter, Descartes begins to mark out real differences between him and Elisabeth not only on mind and body, but on the uses of philosophy. For Descartes, metaphysics is not the wide-ranging and ongoing inquiry into profound questions of meaning that it is for Elisabeth. The purpose of metaphysics, he implies, is to establish intellectual bedrock. That bedrock, once it is established as the support for rational method in the science, is not to be disturbed. Science requires that extended material substance have nothing in it of spirit. Occult forces, magic, ethereal substances, if they exist at all, must be kept separate from the material substance that is the object of science. Once this is understood scientists can proceed to discover and manipulate the mechanisms that govern physical substance, including the human body. Descartes, with a flattery more sincere than his first letter's extravagant compliments, now seems willing to accept Elisabeth as a fellow philosopher. He was certain, he says, that as a philosopher she was convinced of the separation of mind and body. It was that certainty that made him propose the comparison with heaviness. Since she was a philosopher, he assumed that she would not be shaken in her conviction that mind and body are different substances.

Descartes is often named as the first modern philosopher, but his advice to Elisabeth, if it is to be taken seriously, warns against too steady a diet of philosophy. A few hours a year suffices, he tells her. Satisfy yourself as to basic truths such as the separation of mind from body and the existence of God; then leave philosophy alone. Even theoretical science should be pursued for only a few hours a day, he advises, so as not to tax the mind. The rest of one's time should be spent in relaxation, experimentation, and ordinary sensuous activity in which the mind and body are united. At the end of his letter Descartes proposes a new device to put Elisabeth's doubts to rest. In her letter, Elisabeth suggested that it was easier for her to imagine that there was material substance to the soul than to imagine that something immaterial could move the body. Go ahead, says Descartes, think that the soul is material. Do that and then look at the consequences. If the soul is material it should be locatable, but it is not. By elementary logic, the soul cannot be material; if a thesis leads to a contradiction the thesis must be false. Accept the logic and get on with inquiries that mix pure reason with mathematical imagination and sensory experience and that discover truths in nature.

There is some practical sense to Descartes's advice. He understands that worry and stress are taking a great toll on the princess's mind and body. He worries that philosophy can become obsessive, a symptom of irrational anxiety with the same unanswerable questions asked over and over. Descartes himself was more than impatient with the never-ending deductive tangles that occupied professional philosophers and logicians in the medieval universities and impeded advances in knowledge. But as the friendship deepened between him and Elisabeth it became clear that her refusal to leave metaphysics alone was not scholastic addiction to logical puzzles. Her concern was not to protect an academic discipline or institutional privilege but with ethical, existential, and practical implications of science as envisioned by Descartes. Against Descartes she used his own weapons. In his *Meditations* and *Discourse on Method*, Descartes laid down a cardinal rule: never accept anything as true that you do not clearly and distinctly understand or perceive. If the philosophical basis of science is not clearly understood, if the nature of the soul and the body and their interaction is not clearly understood, then the truth of science might be in peril. If the rational mind is not separate from the body, if the body is not a mechanical system running on hydraulic principles, if understanding can never be pure and untainted by bias, then any physics based on that assumption will also be in doubt.

ETHICS

In the winter of 1644–1645 Elisabeth fell ill with a recurring fever that caused fears for her life. Returning to Holland after a wearisome and disappointing trip to France in the spring of 1645, Descartes learned about her illness. Convinced that science's new understanding of the body could be used to heal, and sure that stress and worry were the root cause of her distress, Descartes now took on the role of philosopher-physician. A rational mind separate from the body, he wrote, can refrain from disturbing the healthy workings of the body. Even if demands made on that body make health impossible, the rational mind can learn to view illness and grief from a comfortable distance. Here was his dualist metaphysics pressed into action, not an empty possibly counterfactual assumption that justifies mechanical principles, but a real acting out of the Cartesian thesis. The union of mind and body is not essential; it is accidental. Realize this, Descartes told the suffering Elisabeth; separate your mind from your body, and you will be cured of your malady. Furthermore, you will be a better person and better able to make decisions for the common good.

Now Descartes touched on themes close to Elisabeth's own concerns. Anguished by the bad judgment of her family, horrified by the death and destruction of the Thirty Years War, moral responsibility was at the heart of her questions about dualism. How is it possible to find mental peace in the midst of physical turmoil? How, in difficult and confusing circumstances, can one bring about the greatest possible good, or the least possible harm? How can one be a moral person?

Morality was not a subject on which Descartes had expended much energy up to this point. In *Discourse on Method*, in answer to critics who argued that radical doubt would lead to irresolution, Descartes proposed a "provisional ethics," a temporary "shelter" while the house of knowledge was rebuilt on rational principles. While everything is still in doubt, while the foundations of the sciences that will insure human welfare are not yet established, one should obey the customs and laws of one's country and hold fast to the tenets of traditional religion, namely Catholicism. Be firm and decisive in one's behavior. Do not let doubt interfere with resolute action. Do not waste time complaining about bad fortune, but revise one's own goals and expectations instead. Last, and most important, choose the best of occupations, the pursuit of reason.

It was an ethics opposed to all of Elisabeth's moral instincts. Deeply involved in the Protestant struggle against authoritarian Catholicism, there were many laws in many countries that Elisabeth would have felt no duty to obey and much in Catholicism she abhorred. Decisive but misguided actions had been the downfall of too many members of her family for her to endorse acting without hesitation and painful questioning of alternatives and consequences. More often she had found herself advising caution and circumspection. Certainly she was not ready to resign herself to whatever fate had in store for her family and Europe. In opposition to Descartes's assumption of a fixed natural law that determines the course of events according to God's plan, Elisabeth saw the future as open. The Palatine and the German territories could be reconstructed. Religious freedom could become the rule rather than the exception. The ambition of princes could give way to concern for their subjects. Given these commitments, Descartes's last proviso, the choice of profession, was impossible. Much as Elisabeth might have liked to become a full-time scientist or researcher, family and civic responsibilities barred her way as they would the way of many aspiring women scholars in centuries to come.

Descartes's medical-moral advice to the ailing Elisabeth retained the flavor of his provisional ethics along with important insights into the physiological and moral effects of stress and anxiety. Worry and stress can bring on physical illness, he pointed out in graphic physiological detail. It can interrupt the proper functioning of heart, lungs, and spleen. The remedy he proposes is a version of the ethics described as provisional in the *Discourse*, buttressed by physiology. She will recover her physical health and find peace of mind, if only she can separate the mechanisms of her body from her mind. The vulgar, ordinary man may never manage to separate mind from body, said Descartes. He may be content to live a sensuous life that recognizes no distinction between the two. As a result not only will he make no discoveries in theoretical physics, he will suffer along with the body whatever pleasures or pains fate has in store for him. This man can fall ill from worry and not recover.

For Elisabeth, Descartes recommended the more "noble" attitude of metaphysical dualism. If she can separate her rational soul from emotions thrown up by her body, if she can contemplate material misery around her—scandal, ruin, war—as "acted-out drama," the negative passions disturbing her health will subside. She will find a way to derive contentment from tragedy. She will appreciate the grief of those around her and do her best by them only when she can do so without harm to herself. If tragedy occurs, she will take pleasure in her power to rise above it. For Elisabeth, driven almost mad by the folly of those close to her, it was not advice she could accept for reasons she would patiently attempt to explain to Descartes.

First, she is a woman. Descartes himself was on record that in intellectual matters all humans are equal. Everyone has a mind, Descartes argued, although not everyone is willing to use it. Never did Descartes suggest what so many of his contemporaries assumed: that women have inferior minds. Elisabeth attributes to her sex not a weakened power of mind, but a heightened degree of interaction between mind and body. Are men and women different in this regard? Do men have a capacity to separate themselves from their feelings that women do not? "Know then that I have a body imbued with a great part of the weakness of my sex, know that it registers very easily afflictions of the soul." Elisabeth, in perhaps ironic deference to common prejudice, uses the word "weakness" but in subsequent letters she would suggest that her feminine sensitivity may allow understanding of events that, painful though it may be, leads to better judgment.

Also important, in her view, is physical circumstance. As a woman, she does not have the opportunity Descartes has to withdraw from society and lead a solitary life. As a woman and an aristocrat she has very restricted opportunities for exercise, a restraint, she thinks, that may have much to do with her physical problems. He has not understood the kind of life she lives as a woman bound by propriety and involved in family and politics. He has not understood that she must take responsibility for improving the situation of those around her and trying to make the world a better place.

Descartes's response testifies to the genuine affection and respect he has come to have for Elisabeth, and his concern for her health. If only she could bring herself to see things his way, her suffering would be less. A person in the best of circumstances, who, if only in imagination, dwells on unhappy events, will make herself ill, he tells her. Alternately, someone embroiled in trouble as she is, but who keeps herself from thinking about those troubles except when absolutely necessary, can regain health and judge more sanely what is best. Especially, said Descartes in advice prophetic of nineteenth-century cures for hysteria, she should rest, look at flowers, undertake no serious reading or meditation, do no philosophy. Elisabeth's response shows how much, surrounded as she is by misunderstanding and enmity, she has come to rely on Descartes's friendship. She is grateful to him, if not for "instructions" that she cannot follow without "sinning against her duty," for a concern about her health and desire to help not always forthcoming from her own family. Nevertheless his advice, she continues to insist, cannot be followed. It takes no account of how misfortune can surprise and how pain and disappointment can persist well beyond an actual event. It takes no account of the responsibility she feels for the well-being of others.

These differences became acute and threatened to destroy their friendship in a later exchange over a family scandal. When Elisabeth's brother married a Catholic and converted to Catholicism, not out of conviction but out of convenience, Elizabeth was prostrate with grief and anger. His action trivialized the Protestant cause. The family was ridiculed and reviled in the Dutch press. The protection of The House of Orange on which they depended was compromised, along with their standing at the peace negotiations in Utrecht that would determine the fate of the Rhineland. When she expressed her unhappiness to Descartes, he bristled, offended at what he took as a slight to Catholicism. First, he wrote, Catholics like himself, who made up the majority in Europe and were in power in most locales, would clearly approve her brother's action even if he did it for the wrong reasons. Furthermore, if someone does the right thing, even for the wrong reasons, it must be God's plan that good will result. Elisabeth did not respond for some time. What was there to say? The distance between them at that moment must have seemed unbridgeable. Descartes had trivialized religious conviction. Faith, he implied, was not a matter of conscience but of how one is brought up or of what alliances chance to come one's way. He seemed to say that since one can assume God organized things for the best it does not much matter what one professes.

References by Descartes to the sad plight of her family only made matters worse:

> As for what constitutes the prudence of the times, what is true is that those who have fortune with them have some reason to keep to themselves and to close ranks to keep it from escaping, but those members of a house from which fortune has fled are not wrong, it seems to me, to agree to follow different roads, so that, if they do not all find fortune, there will be at least one who will encounter it.[9]

It is not hard to see how Elisabeth would cringe at sentiments so counter to everything she stood for. If the Catholics were going to win at the bargaining table at Utrecht, she should join them? She should profit from a friend in the winning camp? For Elisabeth, deeply committed to the Protestant cause and convinced that liberalism and freethinking would never flourish in Catholic countries, such an attitude was treason.

The correspondence continued for five more years. Events in Elisabeth's family went from bad to worse. Her brother stabbed a man to death in the street; she was banished from her mother's house in The Hague, her uncle (the king of England) was beheaded and with him went most of the family fortune. Descartes and she expanded their discussion to the good life, the proper rule of princes, the nature of the passions. Through it all the basic terms of their philosophical friendship remained, on both sides genuine and appreciative interest and concern with the other's ideas, but also deep and challenging disagreement—on the nature of reason in science, on medical applications of Cartesianism, and on the nature of ethics.

Emerging Themes

In their exchanges there emerged themes that continue to be at the heart of philosophical concern in the modern period and postmodern periods.

1. First, the status of reason in science. For Descartes, science is pure understanding, a deduction from the God-given logical and mathematical ideas that provide the theoretical framework for sensory observation and geometric and algebraic imaging. Emotion or passion, which might compromise objectivity, has no place in science. Descartes takes for granted that a purely rational science will facilitate labor and repair bodily dysfunction. If God gave man the means to understand the mechanisms of nature, he also gave man the ability to adapt those mechanisms for his own use. In her letters Elisabeth does not directly address the question of perspective or bias in science, but her comments about the unintelligibility of metaphysical dualism set the stage for later controversies in philosophy of science. Is it intelligible that a mind, even a rational scientific mind, can completely separate itself from a body? Or is thinking always permeated by and colored with emotion, interest, and passion? Are there pristine God-given ideas that can be counted on as necessarily reflective of reality? Or do all ideas come from human experience and so are necessarily from particular embodied and therefore limited perspectives? In the seventeenth century, with science a beleaguered specialty, the practical import of these questions was not immediately evident. In the twentieth-first century, with mathematical science ascendant and many of its products of dubious value, the questions become more urgent. Do paradigms or "images" borrowed from social structures shape scientific thought in particular times and places? Might such images impede the discovery of truth? Is knowledge always from a certain standpoint as some feminist modernist theorists have argued? Might science from perspectives other than that of Western professional men be of equal or more use?

   Two alternative visions emerge in the correspondence between Elisabeth and Descartes. Descartes knew that science could not advance without many researchers and the institutional support that would fund their work. His dream was a scientific establishment supported by the state, working according to fixed methods to produce results that increase human happiness. Given the rationalist deductive nature of Cartesian science, it was inevitable that science would become an exclusive club of official practitioners. Elisabeth's doubts about the independence of reason might lead to a different future for science. If there are many perspectives—if the search for knowledge is not carried on by rational immaterial minds but by intelligent bodies and material souls—then a more open science might result where foundational principles can be called into question. The virtue of such a science would not be the sameness of its practitioners and methods, but their diversity. Intuitive styles of research, approaches that emphasize interacting functions rather than linear causation and fixed mechanisms, concepts based on changing metaphors, might lead to new insights into nature.

2. The question of truth in science had practical application for Elisabeth and Descartes in medicine. Descartes was critical of medical practice based on questionable customary procedures like bloodletting and purging. He was contemptuous of fanciful theories of humors and vital spirits. Instead, medicine should be based on a sound understanding of anatomy and physiology. His letters to Elisabeth about the state of her health and the workings of bodily organs are examples of that understanding. While Elisabeth does not quarrel with the idea of mechanical malfunction, she does question Descartes on both the cause of the malfunction and its treatment. Yes, grief and worry can cause some of the physical symptoms that he describes, but for her, the body is never an isolated mechanical system but a body responsive to its environment. She cites the physical restrictions placed on a woman's body in dress and behavior. She cites lack of exercise and lack of freedom. She cites the quality of the air and the lack of proper hygiene. Even as her health troubles mount, she never accepts Descartes's cure of rest and positive thinking. Involved with people and affairs, events will always surprise and disturb her equanimity. More important, even if she could follow his advice and example, even if she could manage to observe what is going on around her as if it were acted-out drama, she would not because it might keep her from acting effectively. On this view medicine might require not only drugs or surgery, but also public health initiatives and holistic approaches to disease.

3. The issue that dominates the later letters is neither the independence of reason nor the best medicine for stress-related illnesses, but the nature of ethics and the moral life. Stimulated by Elisabeth's questioning, Descartes eventually moved beyond his cursory treatment of a provisional ethics in the *Discourse* to give a full-fledged description of his version of the good life in *The Passions of the Soul*. It was a subject he probably would not have bothered to spend time on without Elisabeth's prodding and it drove Descartes into territory he might otherwise have avoided. Elisabeth never stopped questioning his rejection of repentance and the implications of determinism for effective action. For Descartes repentance, or a sense one has acted badly or unwisely, was unnecessary and destructive of happiness. For Elisabeth, on the other hand, repentance played a role in moral progress. Morality for Descartes is a matter of a properly separate and schooled reason that tells the physical body what to do. For Elisabeth goodness is more complex. Given the limits of reason, given that reason can never know everything that might occur, moral deliberation must combine thinking with instinct and feeling and here painful repentance plays an important role.

Descartes never strays from the philosophical foundations of his Cartesian system: The soul or mind is separate from the body and immortal. God exists and has ordered the world. The "grandeur of the heavens" indicates that what happens is according to natural law and God's plan and is therefore good. It follows, for Descartes, that reforming zeal—a drive to change the world for the better—is always misguided. Seeing evil in events or persons and wanting to change them is by Cartesian principles "impertinent."

In place of understanding the perfections which are truly in us, [man] attributes to other creatures imperfections which they do not have and puts himself above them, and so enters on an impertinent presumption: he wishes to be of the council of God, and to take on with God the charge of running the world, which causes an infinity of vain iniquities and falsehoods.[10]

But this was exactly how Elisabeth understood the moral mission. As a responsible family member, as advisor to her brother as he tried to restore the Palatine, as abbess of the imperial convent at Herford, her job was to detect evil in people and events and attempt to mitigate that evil. Although natural law might dictate events like floods and earthquakes, she could not think that God had determined, in advance, human will. Moral responsibility for Elisabeth depends on an open future, on the freedom of men and women to do harm or good, on the power of persuasion and good advice.

Reconciling freedom of will with the mechanisms that supposedly govern all of nature was a problem that forced Descartes to some fancy metaphysical footwork borrowed from his old mentors the Jesuits. At one point he tells Elisabeth, suppose a king has forbidden duels, but he orders affairs so that two men, so angry at each other that he knows they will fight if they see each other, find themselves face to face. He knows that they will attack each other but "they are still responsible for their action and the King can still punish them."[11] Theologians understand this, he told Elisabeth, with some condescension, even if she cannot. Furthermore there is no need to think that in a deterministic universe altruistic deeds will not be undertaken. The world is providentially arranged so that self-interest is often served by helping others.

This was very far from Elisabeth's understanding of the moral life. For Elisabeth responsible action meant painful grappling with how far one should give up one's own interests and happiness for others, with the balancing of self-interest and altruism. These were problems for which Cartesian metaphysics provided convenient answers. God, Descartes insisted, providently arranged things in His wisdom so that self-interest and public interest coincide. A man cannot subsist alone. He needs others. Therefore prudence dictates that since a man is part of the public he must work, to some extent, for public good. If you do a favor for someone, they will do one in turn for you. In this apparent endorsement of patronage and influence mongering, Descartes seemed to praise the very insincerity and pomp Elisabeth always condemned.

In the exchange of ideas between these two thinkers, many themes that occupy philosophers in the twentieth and twenty-first centuries were introduced. What is the relation between reason and emotion or mind and body? Are women incapable of the separation of mind from body? Does such separation indicate masculine pathology? Does feeling play a role in knowledge? If natural law governs events, how is moral action possible? Most striking, however, in the correspondence is a style of philosophizing. Philosophy often takes the form of adversarial debate, a contest to see who will make the best arguments or frame the most unassailable definitions. This was not the case with Elisabeth and Descartes. Disagreement and hurt feelings after her brother's marriage, and again when Descartes clumsily attempted to get her to see a bright side to her uncle's beheading, made both of them miserable. Either of them might have claimed to have won an argument, but both knew they had failed at philosophy as practiced between friends. Between friends, attempting to grapple together with deep intellectual and existential worries, impasse is not an opportunity to declare a winner but regrettable inability to come to terms with a shared human problem.

Questions for Reflection

In what ways might gender affect a philosopher's metaphysics? In particular, do you think it affected the metaphysics of either Elisabeth or Descartes? Defend your answer.

What do you think Elisabeth does or might mean when she suggests that reliance on reason alone in moral matters can lead to "sins against duty"? Do you think her view is plausible? Why or why not?

Elisabeth gives several examples to illustrate the inseparability of mind and body. What are they? Do you think Elisabeth's examples make a compelling case for the inseparability of mind and body? (If not, can you think of any other examples—ones you think do provide a compelling case?)

Notes

1. I make no attempt here, or in any of the chapter introductions, to introduce or engage in contemporary scholarly discussions about the proper interpretation or criticisms of a philosopher's positions; they are simply beyond the scope and objectives of the book

2. Kuno Fischer, *History of Modern Philosophy: Descartes and His School* (New York: Charles Scribner's Sons, 1886), 219, cited in Ethel M. Kersey, *Women Philosophers: A Bio-Critical Source Book* (New York: Greenwood Press, 1989), 95–96.

3. Kersey, *Women Philosophers*, 95.

4. Andrea Nye, "Elisabeth, Princess Palatine: Letters to René Descartes," "in *Presenting Women Philosophers*, eds. Cecile T. Tougas and Sara Ebenreck (Philadelphia, PA: Temple University Press, 2000), 129–30. See also Andrea Nye, *The Princess and the Philosopher: Letters of Elisabeth of the Palatine to René Descartes* (Lanham, MD: Rowman & Littlefield, 1999), especially 9–10.

5. Nye, "Elisabeth, Princess Palatine," 130.

6. Nye, "Elisabeth, Princess Palatine," 136.

7. Elisabeth's letters and parts of Descartes's letters are taken from Andrea Nye, *The Princess and the Philosopher*. The letters reprinted in this chapter comprise only the early part of the correspondence. Readers are encouraged to consult *The Princess and the Philosopher* for all of the letters and for more on the philosophical differences between Elisabeth and Descartes.

8. Descartes was a guest on one previous occasion at the house of Elisabeth's mother. At that time, he had no particular conversation with Elisabeth, nor was he aware of her interest in science and philosophy.

9. Nye, *The Princess and the Philosopher*, 85.

10. Nye, *The Princess and the Philosopher*, 61.

11. Nye, *The Princess and the Philosopher*, 86.

CHAPTER 6

Hobbes and Macaulay

Introduction by *Karen J. Warren*

Thomas Hobbes (1588–1679) and Catharine Macaulay (1731–1791) lived nearly one hundred years apart, but pairing them enables one to have a historically informed conversation about a topic of interest to both: moral and political philosophy, especially the nature and relevance of the human condition to the role, obligations, and rights of governments and citizens within democratic structures. Because this topic has engaged (male) philosophers throughout the history of philosophy, a conversation could take place *without* the inclusion of women philosophers—*as if* their inclusion would not alter how the debate was framed. So, with the inclusion of Macaulay in that discussion—a woman philosopher who wrote explicitly on Hobbes's political philosophy—it is worth asking: "Does her inclusion with Hobbes on topics of mutual interest change how one understands their views, particularly Hobbes's views, or how one conceptualizes philosophy and philosophical methodology?" If so, the inclusion of women philosophers does more than simply satisfy considerations of equity; it may alter how one approaches and engages in philosophical inquiry,

HOBBES

The seventeenth-century English philosopher Thomas Hobbes was born in Wiltshire, England, and lived with his uncle until he went to a private school and then, around 1603, to Hertford College at Oxford. There he learned scholastic philosophy and studied classic Greek and Latin authors. He became a tutor to William Cavendish's son, William, and continued a life-long relationship with him and the family.

Hobbes is best known as a political philosopher whose masterwork, *Leviathan* (published in English in 1651, with a Latin revision in 1668), set the standard for political philosophy and social contract theorists to the present.[1] The main question of political philosophy historically has been, "When, and on what grounds, does a government (or political authority) have the right to rule and citizens have the obligation to obey?" Hobbes's infamous, perhaps counterintuitive, answer is that an authority or sovereign—a "leviathan"—has the right to rule (is morally legitimate) when free persons in a "state of nature" (a precivil society) voluntarily consent to turn over their unlimited freedoms in a state of nature to an artificially created sovereign with absolute power *on one condition*: the sovereign agrees (contracts) to protect the lives of its subjects or citizens. This condition is necessary to motivate people to agree to the social contract in a state of nature, where individuals have unlimited rights, the one right they cannot be guaranteed to secure for themselves is the most important of all rights—the right to self-preservation.

Some, including John Locke (chapter 7) in his *Second Treatise of Government*, have challenged Hobbes's argument in favor of forming a sovereign (government), claiming that the state of nature is preferable to subjection to the arbitrary power of an absolute sovereign. Others have challenged the assumption which arises in many social contract theories based on a negative view of humans in a state of nature, that it is part of the human condition for humans to always act out of self-interest (a doctrine known as psychological egoism) or to act only in accordance with their own individual judgments. These theorists claim that, in many societies and cases, humans act in ways that do, and are intended to, enhance communal life, serve altruistic ends, or be for the good of a larger (perhaps intentional) community or kinship clan. Still others have argued that since not every citizen or group of citizens (e.g., humans brought to the United States as slaves) has consented, overtly or covertly (tacitly), to any social contract, either they are not bound by any such contract or the existence of such a tacit (or implied) contract is insufficient to establish the grounds of any obedience they may be said to owe a government.

But Hobbes stood his ground, describing in specific detail the dreadful conditions of a precivil state of nature as "a condition of war" of all against all, where "the life of man [is] solitary, poor, nasty, brutish, and short." The social contract is essential since it supplies the moral justification for the legitimacy of the government (sovereign, leviathan) formed by freely consenting humans. It also offers a psychologically powerful motivation for agreeing to join a civil society, since it promises citizens a society governed by laws that make possible all of the basic securities upon which comfortable, sociable, civilized life depends, which could not occur in a state of nature.

Hobbes seemed to assume that the state of nature was not merely a hypothetical construct. He also pointed to various groups of individuals whom he thought at the time were existing in such a state. But even if there never were such a state, "the state of nature" is a useful, hypothetical, heuristic device for imagining what life without law or civilization might be like. As such, it has an important philosophical role to play in attempts to describe which precivil conditions might be sufficient for humans to freely choose the principles by which they would choose to be governed were they to choose to leave a state of nature.

Hobbes's moral philosophy is far less clear. He has been described variously as subscribing to ethical positions that are mutually incompatible—for example, as a relativist, subjectivist, psychological egoist, ethical egoist, divine command theorist, virtue ethicist, natural law and natural rights theorist. The long-standing interpretation of Hobbes as a psychological egoist—that is, one who holds that humans cannot act in ways other than those that do, or are assumed to, bring about their self-interest—is no longer widely held.

But no alternative theory of Hobbes's moral psychology has been offered that Hobbes scholars generally accept. In contrast, Hobbes's political philosophy, especially his social contract theory, influenced not only his contemporaries (e.g., Locke, Rousseau, and Hume); it continues to be studied for its continued importance as a moral justification for the legitimacy of governments.[2] But he had dissenters from the start. One of them was Catharine Macaulay.

MACAULAY

Catharine Sawbridge Macaulay was born near Canterbury, England. Little is known about her early years, including whether she ever had a formal education. But her writings reveal expertise in Latin, English literature, history, and philosophy. Macaulay married physician George Macaulay in 1761, with whom she had one daughter. George Macaulay died five years later. In 1778, she scandalously married twenty-one-year-old William Graham.

Macaulay wrote extensively. During her lifetime, she was best known as a foremost historian, author of *The History of England*—the hugely influential eight-volume scholarly history of England, published over a twenty-year period, during the English Civil War and the Restoration. But Macaulay also wrote two distinctly philosophical works that deserve attention, a pamphlet titled *Loose Remarks on Certain Positions to be found in Mr. Hobbes's Philosophical Rudiments of Government and Society* and a 400-page document, *Letters on Education* (1790).

Macaulay's writings address a range of topics. The most philosophical ones provide a theory of individual rights, arguments for women's equality, a political philosophy that defends a contractarian theory of government—one opposed to the pro-monarchical view of Hobbes and Rousseau—a philosophy of education, and arguments against free will. They also include a range of topics in moral philosophy—such as her defense of the views that there is only one moral rule of right conduct, one set of virtues, and one notion of moral excellence that applies equally to men and women.

In her book *Rediscovering Women Philosophers: Philosophical Genre and the Boundaries of Philosophy*, commentator Catherine Villaneuva Gardner defends the view that the epistolary form of much of Macaulay's writings is a primary reason that her work has not received the philosophical attention it deserves.[3] For example, Gardner claims that scholars too often dismiss, undervalue, or fail to recognize the moral philosophy presented in Macaulay's *Letters on Education* (1790) because of their epistolary form. The (mistaken) assumption is that when the letters are written "in the form of personal advice or instructional letters to a female friend (a genre typically associated with women authors), it cannot contain any systematized philosophical thought."[4] This concern surfaces in many places in this book, for example in chapter 2, regarding the letters of the Late Pythagorean women.

Defending the epistolary form as a legitimate philosophical methodology, Gardner describes the importance of Macaulay's arguments for the equality of women in *Letters on Education*:

> Macaulay's work is important, not simply because of the way that she offers
> a sustained, self-contained argument for the equality of women based on her
> ethicoreligious system, but also because this argument predates [by two years]

Mary Wollstonecraft's polemical argument for female equality in *A Vindication of the Rights of Women*.[5]

In *Letters* Macaulay argues that women's apparent deficiencies are due to their inferior education, not to any genetic or innate differences from men. According to Mary Ellen Waithe, Macaulay argues against a theory of sex complementarity that held that

> men and women are biological, intellectual, and moral opposites whose funda-
> mental differences complement/complete each other's nature. Together male and
> female form a whole. The halves of this whole were physical, intellectual, and
> moral opposites: men were superior, women inferior to them. This natural infe-
> riority provided the moral justification for the subjugation of women by men.[6]

(This interpretation of a "theory of sex complementarity" is quite like the theory by that name described by Sister Prudence Allen in chapter 3.) Macaulay's rejection of the theory of sex complementarity was the basis of her rejection of the logic of Rousseau's complementarian argument concerning the morally relevant differences between men and women. It also was the basis of Macaulay's argument that women and men should receive the same kind of education and training and that moral principles, values, and virtues applied to men and women equally. She even defends chastity and celibacy, rather than sexual freedom, as possible forms of empowerment for women, a brave position to advocate, especially in her times.

Whether one describes Macaulay as basically a historian with philosophical views or a philosopher with historical views, there is no doubt that her writing, especially her *Letters on Education*, addresses philosophical topics and critiques the philosophical positions of many well-known male philosophers. In fact, the importance of studying Macaulay's views in a historical and gendered context in which Macaulay is "conversing" with men philosophers is an underlying theme of the structure and content of Gardner's commentary.

GARDNER'S COMMENTARY

Gardner's commentary shows ways Hobbes and Macaulay are connected philosophi-cally, not only by the politics of seventeenth-century England. They are particularly interested in two areas of philosophy: moral and political philosophy. Gardner first pro-vides Hobbes's views on the human condition and the need for a sovereign, followed by Macaulay's different views on the human condition. Gardner also explores Macaulay's equation of happiness with rectitude. She ends with an evaluation of three criticisms Macaulay offers of Hobbes's philosophy.

One of the most significant features of Gardner's commentary is not about the philosophical views of Hobbes and Macaulay per se; it is about how to read and discuss Hobbes and Macaulay, something she demonstrates by how she writes about them. She shows that, when "read together as part of a debate taking place in the seventeenth and eighteenth centuries," one begins to appreciate that the framework of canonical philoso-phy (what I have called The House in the Lead Essay) is not what it says it is: it is actu-ally a historically situated, socially constructed, gendered framework. As such, Gardner's commentary *also* should be read for the challenge to canonical accounts of philosophy that it offers.

Excerpts of Writings by Hobbes and Macaulay

I. EXCERPTS FROM HOBBES'S *LEVIATHAN*[7]

Chapter 13: Of the Natural Condition of Mankind, As Concerning Their Felicity, and Misery

[1] Nature hath made men so equal in the faculties of body and mind as that, though there be found one man sometimes manifestly stronger in body or of quicker mind than another, yet when all is reckoned together the difference between man and man is not so considerable as that one man can thereupon claim to himself any benefit to which another may not pretend as well as he. For as to the strength of body, the weakest has strength enough to kill the strongest, either by secret machination, or by confederacy with others that are in the same danger with himself.

[2] And as to the faculties of the mind—setting aside the arts grounded upon words, and especially that skill of proceeding upon general and infallible rules called science (which very few have, and but in few things), as being not a native faculty (born with us), nor attained (as prudence) while we look after somewhat else—I find yet a greater equality among men than that of strength. For prudence is but experience, which equal time equally bestows on all men in those things they equally apply themselves unto. That which may perhaps make such equality incredible is but a vain conceit of one's own wisdom, which almost all men think they have in a greater degree than the vulgar, that is, than all men but themselves and a few others whom, by fame or for concurring with themselves, they approve. For such is the nature of men that howsoever they may acknowledge many others to be more witty, or more eloquent, or more learned, yet they will hardly believe there be many so wise as themselves. For they see their own wit at hand, and other men's at a distance. But this proveth rather that men are in that point equal, than unequal. For there is not ordinarily a greater sign of the equal distribution of anything than that every man is contented with his share.

[3] From this equality of ability ariseth equality of hope in the attaining of our ends. And therefore, if any two men desire the same thing, which nevertheless they cannot both enjoy, they become enemies; and in the way to their end, which is principally their own conservation, and sometimes their delectation only, endeavor to destroy or subdue one another. And from hence it comes to pass that, where an invader hath no more to fear than another man's single power, if one plant, sow, build, or possess a convenient seat, others may probably be expected to come prepared with forces united, to dispossess and deprive him, not only of the fruit of his labor, but also of his life or liberty. And the invader again is in the like danger of another.

[4] And from this diffidence of one another, there is no way for any man to secure himself so reasonable as anticipation, that is, by force or wiles to master the persons of all men he can, so long till he see no other power great enough to endanger him. And this is no more than his own conservation requireth, and is generally allowed. Also, because there be some that taking pleasure in contemplating their own power in the acts of

conquest, which they pursue farther than their security requires, if others (that otherwise would be glad to be at ease within modest bounds) should not by invasion increase their power, they would not be able, long time, by standing only on their defense, to subsist. And by consequence, such augmentation of dominion over men being necessary to a man's conservation, it ought to be allowed him.

[5] Again, men have no pleasure, but on the contrary a great deal of grief, in keeping company where there is no power able to overawe them all. For every man looketh that his companion should value him at the same rate he sets upon himself, and upon all signs of contempt, or undervaluing, naturally endeavors, as far as he dares (which among them that have no common power to keep them in quiet, is far enough to make them destroy each other), to extort a greater value from his condemners, by damage, and from others, by the example.

[6] So that in the nature of man we find three principal causes of quarrel: first, competition; secondly, diffidence; thirdly, glory.

[7] The first maketh men invade for gain; the second, for safety; and the third, for reputation. The first use violence to make themselves masters of other men's persons, wives, children, and cattle; the second, to defend them; the third, for trifles, as a word, a smile, a different opinion, and any other sign of undervalue, either direct in their persons, or by reflection in their kindred, their friends, their nation, their profession, or their name.

[8] Hereby it is manifest that during the time men live without a common power to keep them all in awe, they are in that condition which is called war, and such a war as is of every man against every man. For WAR consisteth not in battle only, or the act of fighting, but in a tract of time wherein the will to contend by battle is sufficiently known. And therefore, the notion of *time* is to be considered in the nature of war, as it is in the nature of weather. For as the nature of foul weather lieth not in a shower or two of rain, but in an inclination thereto of many days together, so the nature of war consisteth not in actual fighting, but in the known disposition thereto during all the time there is no assurance to the contrary. All other time is PEACE.

[9] Whatsoever therefore is consequent to a time of war, where every man is enemy to every man, the same is consequent to the time wherein men live without other security than what their own strength and their own invention shall furnish them withal. In such condition there is no place for industry, because the fruit thereof is uncertain, and consequently, no culture of the earth, no navigation, nor use of the commodities that may be imported by sea, no commodious building, no instruments of moving and removing such things as require much force, no knowledge of the face of the earth, no account of time, no arts, no letters, no society, and which is worst of all, continual fear and danger of violent death, and the life of man, solitary, poor, nasty, brutish, and short.

[10] It may seem strange, to some man that has not well weighed these things, that nature should thus dissociate, and render men apt to invade and destroy one another. And he may, therefore, not trusting to this inference made from the passions, desire perhaps to have the same confirmed by experience. Let him therefore consider with himself—when taking a journey, he arms himself, and seeks to go well accompanied; when going to sleep, he locks his doors; when even in his house, he locks his chests; and this when he knows there be laws, and public officers, armed, to revenge all injuries shall be done him—what opinion he has of his fellow subjects when he rides armed; of his fellow citizens, when

he locks his doors; and of his children and servants, when he locks his chests. Does he not there as much accuse mankind by his actions, as I do by my words? But neither of us accuse man's nature in it. The desires and other passions of man are in themselves no sin. No more are the actions that proceed from those passions, till they know a law that forbids them—which till laws be made they cannot know. Nor can any law be made, till they have agreed upon the person that shall make it.

[11] It may peradventure be thought, there was never such a time nor condition of war as this; and I believe it was never generally so, over all the world. But there are many places where they live so now. For the savage people in many places of *America* (except the government of small families, the concord whereof dependeth on natural lust) have no government at all, and live at this day in that brutish manner as I said before. Howsoever, it may be perceived what manner of life there would be where there were no common power to fear, by the manner of life which men that have formerly lived under a peaceful government use to degenerate into, in a civil war.

[12] But though there had never been any time wherein particular men were in a condition of war one against another, yet in all times kings and persons of sovereign authority, because of their independency, are in continual jealousies and in the state and posture of gladiators, having their weapons pointing and their eyes fixed on one another, that is, their forts, garrisons, and guns upon the frontiers of their kingdoms, and continual spies upon their neighbors, which is a posture of war. But because they uphold thereby the industry of their subjects, there does not follow from it that misery which accompanies the liberty of particular men.

[13] To this war of every man against every man, this also is consequent: that nothing can be unjust. The notions of right and wrong, justice and injustice, have there no place. Where there is no common power, there is no law; where no law, no injustice. Force and fraud are in war the two cardinal virtues. Justice and injustice are none of the faculties neither of the body, nor mind. If they were, they might be in a man that were alone in the world, as well as his senses and passions. They are qualities that relate to men in society, not in solitude. It is consequent also to the same condition that there be no propriety, no dominion, no *mine* and *thine* distinct, but only that to be every man's that he can get, and for so long as he can keep it. And thus much for the ill condition which man by mere nature is actually placed in, though with a possibility to come out of it, consisting partly in the passions, partly in his reason.

[14] The passions that incline men to peace are fear of death, desire of such things as are necessary to commodious living, and a hope by their industry to obtain them. And reason suggesteth convenient articles of peace, upon which men may be drawn to agreement. These articles are they which otherwise are called the Laws of Nature, whereof I shall speak more particularly in the two following chapters.

Chapter 14: Of the First and Second Natural Laws and of Contracts

[1] The RIGHT of NATURE, which writers commonly call *jus naturale*, is the liberty each man hath to use his own power, as he will himself, for the preservation of his own nature, that is to say, of his own life, and consequently of doing anything which, in his own judgment and reason, he shall conceive to be the aptest means thereunto.

[2] By LIBERTY is understood, according to the proper signification of the word, the absence of external impediments, which impediments may oft take away part of a man's power left him, according as his judgment and reason shall dictate to him.

[3] A LAW OF NATURE (*lex naturalis*) is a precept or general rule, found out by reason, by which a man is forbidden to do that which is destructive of his life or taketh away the means of preserving the same, and to omit that by which he thinketh it may be best preserved. For though they that speak of this subject use to confound *jus* and *lex* (*right* and *law*), yet they ought to be distinguished, because RIGHT consisteth in liberty to do or to forbear, whereas LAW determineth and bindeth to one of them; so that law and right differ as much as obligation and liberty, which in one and the same matter are inconsistent.

[4] And because the condition of man (as hath been declared in the precedent chapter) is a condition of war of everyone against everyone (in which case everyone is governed by his own reason and there is nothing he can make use of that may not be a help unto him in preserving his life against his enemies), it followeth that in such a condition every man has a right to everything, even to one another's body. And therefore, as long as this natural right of every man to everything endureth, there can be no security to any man (how strong or wise soever he be) of living out the time which nature ordinarily alloweth men to live. And consequently it is a precept, or general rule, of reason *that every man ought to endeavor peace, as far as he has hope of obtaining it, and when he cannot obtain it, that he may seek and use all helps and advantages of war.* The first branch of which rule containeth the first and fundamental law of nature, which is *to seek peace, and follow it.* The second, the sum of the right of nature, which is *by all means we can, to defend ourselves.*

[5] From this fundamental law of nature, by which men are commanded to endeavor peace, is derived this second law: that a man be willing, when others are so too, as far-forth as for peace and defense of himself he shall think it necessary, to lay down this right to all things, and be contented with so much liberty against other men, as he would allow other men against himself. For as long as every man holdeth this right of doing anything he liketh, so long are all men in the condition of war. But if other men will not lay down their right as well as he, then there is no reason for anyone to divest himself of his; for that were to expose himself to prey (which no man is bound to), rather than to dispose himself to peace. This is that law of the Gospel: "whatsoever you require that others should do to you, that do ye to them." And that law of all men: *quod tibi fieri non vis, alteri ne feceris.*

[6] To *lay down* a man's *right* to anything is to *divest* himself of the *liberty* of hindering another of the benefit of his own right to the same. For he that renounceth or passeth away his right giveth not to any other man a right which he had not before (because there is nothing to which every man had not right by nature), but only standeth out of his way, that he may enjoy his own original right without hindrance from him, not without hindrance from another. So that the effect which redoundeth to one man by another man's defect of right is but so much diminution of impediments to the use of his own right original.

[7] Right is laid aside either by simply renouncing it or by transferring it to another. By *simply* RENOUNCING, when he cares not to whom the benefit thereof redoundeth. By TRANSFERRING, when he intendeth the benefit thereof to some certain person or persons. And when a man hath in either manner abandoned or granted away his right, then is he said to be OBLIGED or BOUND not to hinder those to whom such right is granted or

abandoned from the benefit of it; and [it is said] that he *ought*, and it is his DUTY, not to make void that voluntary act of his own, and that such hindrance is INJUSTICE, and INJURY, as being *sine jure* [without right], the right being before renounced or transferred. So that *injury* or *injustice*, in the controversies of the world, is somewhat like to that which in the disputations of scholars is called absurdity. For as it is there called an *absurdity* to contradict what one maintained in the beginning, so in the world it is called injustice and injury voluntarily to undo that which from the beginning he had voluntarily done.

The way by which a man either simply renounceth or transferreth his right is a declaration, or signification by some voluntary and sufficient sign or signs, that he doth so renounce or transfer, or hath so renounced or transferred the same, to him that accepteth it. And these signs are either words only, or actions only, or (as it happeneth most often) both words and actions. And the same are the BONDS by which men are bound and obliged, bonds that have their strength, not from their own nature (for nothing is more easily broken than a man's word) but from fear of some evil consequence upon the rupture.

[8] Whensoever a man transferreth his right or renounceth it, it is either in consideration of some right reciprocally transferred to himself or for some other good he hopeth for thereby. For it is a voluntary act, and of the voluntary acts of every man the object is some *good to himself*. And therefore there be some rights which no man can be understood by any words or other signs to have abandoned or transferred. As, first, a man cannot lay down the right of resisting them that assault him by force, to take away his life, because he cannot be understood to aim thereby at any good to himself. [Second], the same may be said of wounds, and chains, and imprisonment, both because there is no benefit consequent to such patience (as there is to the patience of suffering another to be wounded or imprisoned), as also because a man cannot tell, when he seeth men proceed against him by violence, whether they intend his death or not. [Third] and lastly, the motive and end for which this renouncing and transferring of right is introduced, is nothing else but the security of a man's person, in his life and in the means of so preserving life as not to be weary of it. And therefore if a man by words or other signs seem to despoil himself of the end for which those signs were intended, he is not to be understood as if he meant it, or that it was his will, but that he was ignorant of how such words and actions were to be interpreted.

[9] The mutual transferring of right is that which men call CONTRACT.

[10] There is difference between transferring of right to the thing and transferring (or tradition, that is, delivery) of the thing itself. For the thing may be delivered together with the translation of the right (as in buying and selling with ready money, or exchange of goods or lands); and it may be delivered some time after.

[11] Again, one of the contractors may deliver the thing contracted for on his part, and leave the other to perform his part at some determinate time after (and in the meantime be trusted); and then the contract on his part is called PACT, or COVENANT; or both parts may contract now, to perform hereafter, in which cases he that is to perform in time to come, being trusted, his performance is called *keeping of promise*, or *faith*, and the failing of performance (if it be voluntary) *violation of faith*.

Chapter 15: Of Other Laws of Nature

[1] From that law of nature by which we are obliged to transfer to another such rights as, being retained, hinder the peace of mankind, there followeth a third, which is this *that men*

perform their covenants made, without which covenants are in vain, and but empty words, and the right of all men to all things remaining, we are still in the condition of war.

[2] And in this law of nature consisteth the foundation and original of JUSTICE. For where no covenant hath preceded, there hath no right been transferred, and every man has right to everything; and consequently, no action can be unjust. But when a covenant is made, then to break it is *unjust*; and the definition of INJUSTICE is no other than *the not performance of covenant*. And whatsoever is not unjust, is *just*.

[3] But because covenants of mutual trust where there is a fear of not performance on either part (as hath been said in the former chapter [xiv: 18–20]) are invalid, though the original of justice be the making of covenants, yet injustice actually there can be none till the cause of such fear be taken away, which, while men are in the natural condition of war, cannot be done. Therefore, before the names of just and unjust can have place, there must be some coercive power to compel men equally to the performance of their covenants, by the terror of some punishment greater than the benefit they expect by the breach of their covenant, and to make good that propriety which by mutual contract men acquire, in recompense of the universal right they abandon; and such power there is none before the erection of a commonwealth. And this is also to be gathered out of the ordinary definition of justice in the Schools; for they say that *justice is the constant will of giving to every man his own*. And therefore where there is no *own*, that is, no propriety, there is no injustice; and where there is no coercive power erected, that is, where there is no commonwealth, there is no propriety, all men having right to all things; therefore where there is no commonwealth, there nothing is unjust. So that the nature of justice consisteth in keeping of valid covenants; but the validity of covenants begins not but with the constitution of a civil power sufficient to compel men to keep them; and then it is also that propriety begins.

Chapter 17: Of the Causes, Generation, and Definition of a Commonwealth

[1] The final cause, end, or design of men (who naturally love liberty and dominion over others) in the introduction of that restraint upon themselves in which we see them live in commonwealths is the foresight of their own preservation, and of a more contented life thereby; that is to say, of getting themselves out from that miserable condition of war, which is necessarily consequent (as hath been shown [chapter xiii] to the natural passions of men, when there is no visible power to keep them in awe, and tie them by fear of punishment to the performance of their covenants and observation of those laws of nature set down in the fourteenth and fifteenth chapters.

[2] For the laws of nature (as *justice, equity, modesty, mercy*, and (in sum) *doing to others as we would be done to*) of themselves, without the terror of some power to cause them to be observed, are contrary to our natural passions, that carry us to partiality, pride, revenge, and the like. And covenants without the sword are but words, and of no strength to secure a man at all. Therefore notwithstanding the laws of nature (which every one hath then kept, when he has the will to keep them, when he can do it safely), if there be no power erected, or not great enough for our security, every man will, and may lawfully rely on his strength and art, for caution against all other men. And in all places where men have lived by small families, to rob and spoil one another has been a trade, and so far from being reputed against the law of nature that the greater spoils they gained, the greater was their honor; and men observed no other laws therein but the laws of honor,

that is, to abstain from cruelty, leaving to men their lives and instruments of husbandry. And as small families did then, so now do cities and kingdoms (which are but greater families) for their own security enlarge their dominions upon all pretences of danger and fear of invasion or assistance that may be given to invaders, [and] endeavor as much as they can to subdue or weaken their neighbors, by open force and secret arts for want of other caution, justly (and are remembered for it in after ages with honor).

[3] Nor is it the joining together of a small number of men that gives them this security; because in small numbers, small additions on the one side or the other make the advantage of strength so great as is sufficient to carry the victory; and therefore gives encouragement to an invasion. The multitude sufficient to confide in for our security is not determined by any certain number, but by comparison with the enemy we fear, and is then sufficient, when the odds of the enemy is not of so visible and conspicuous moment, to determine the event of war, as to move him to attempt.

[4] And be there never so great a multitude, yet if their actions be directed according to their particular judgments and particular appetites, they can expect thereby no defense, nor protection, neither against a common enemy, nor against the injuries of one another. For being distracted in opinions concerning the best use and application of their strength, they do not help, but hinder one another, and reduce their strength by mutual opposition to nothing; whereby they are easily, not only subdued by a very few that agree together, but also when there is no common enemy, they make war upon each other, for their particular interests. For if we could suppose a great multitude of men to consent in the observation of justice and other laws of nature without a common power to keep them all in awe, we might as well suppose all mankind to do the same; and then there neither would be, nor need to be, any civil government or commonwealth at all, because there would be peace without subjection.

[5] Nor is it enough for the security, which men desire should last all the time of their life, that they be governed and directed by one judgment for a limited time, as in one battle or one war. For though they obtain a victory by their unanimous endeavor against a foreign enemy, yet afterwards, when either they have no common enemy, or he that by one part is held for an enemy is by another part held for a friend, they must needs by the difference of their interests dissolve, and fall again into a war among themselves.

[6] It is true that certain living creatures (as bees and ants) live sociably one with another (which are therefore by *Aristotle* numbered among political creatures), and yet have no other direction than their particular judgments and appetites, nor speech whereby one of them can signify to another what he thinks expedient for the common benefit; and therefore some man may perhaps desire to know why mankind cannot do the same. To which I answer,

[7] First, that men are continually in competition for honor and dignity, which these creatures are not; and consequently, among men there ariseth, on that ground, envy and hatred, and finally war; but among these not so.

[8] Secondly, that among these creatures the common good differeth not from the private; and being by nature inclined to their private, they procure thereby the common benefit. But man, who joy consisteth in comparing himself with other men, can relish nothing but what is eminent.

[9] Thirdly, that these creatures (having not, as man, the use of reason) do not see, nor think they see, any fault in the administration of their common business; whereas

among men there are very many that think themselves wiser, and abler to govern the public, better than the rest; and these strive to reform and innovate, one this way, another that way; and thereby bring it into distraction and civil war.

[10] Fourthly, that these creatures, though they have some use of voice (in making known to one another their desires and other affections), yet they want that art of words by which some men can represent to others that which is good in the likeness of evil, and evil in the likeness of good, and augment or diminish the apparent greatness of good and evil, discontenting men, and troubling their peace at their pleasure.

[11] Fifthly, irrational creatures cannot distinguish between *injury* and *damage*; and therefore, as long as they be at ease, they are not offended with their fellows, whereas man is then most troublesome, when he is most at ease; for then it is that he loves to shew his wisdom, and control the actions of them that govern the commonwealth.

[12] Lastly, the agreement of these creatures is natural; that of men is by covenant only, which is artificial; and therefore, it is no wonder if there be somewhat else required (besides covenant) to make their agreement constant and lasting, which is a common power to keep them in awe, and to direct their actions to the common benefit.

[13] The only way to erect such a common power as may be able to defend them from the invasion of foreigners and the injuries of one another, and thereby to secure them in such sort as that by their own industry, and by the fruits of the earth, they may nourish themselves and live contentedly, is to confer all their power and strength upon one man, or upon one assembly of men, that may reduce all their wills, by plurality of voices, unto one will, which is as much as to say, to appoint one man or assembly of men to bear their person, and every one to own and acknowledge himself to be author of whatsoever he that so beareth their person shall act, or cause to be acted, in those things which concern the common peace and safety, and therein to submit their wills, every one to his will, and their judgments, to his judgment. This is more than consent, or concord; it is a real unity of them all, in one and the same person, made by covenant of every man with every man, in such manner as if every man should say to every man *I authorize and give up my right of governing myself to this man, or to this assembly of men, on this condition, that thou give up thy right to him, and authorize all his actions in like manner.* This done, the multitude so united in one person is called a COMMONWEALTH, in Latin CIVITAS. This is the generation of that great LEVIATHAN, or rather (to speak more reverently) of that *Mortal God* to which we owe, under the *Immortal God,* our peace and defense. For by this authority, given him by every particular man in the commonwealth, he hath the use of so much power and strength conferred on him that by terror thereof he is enabled to conform the wills of them all to peace at home and mutual aid against their enemies abroad. And in him consisteth the essence of the commonwealth, which (to define it) is *one person, of whose acts a great multitude, by mutual covenants one with another, have made themselves every one the author, to the end he may use the strength and means of them all, as he shall think expedient, for their peace and common defense.*

[14] And he that carrieth this person is called SOVEREIGN, and said to have *Sovereign Power;* and every one besides, his SUBJECT.

[15] The attaining to this sovereign power is by two ways. One, by natural force, as when a man maketh his children to submit themselves and their children to his government, as being able to destroy them if they refuse or by war subdueth his enemies to his will, giving them their lives on that condition. The other is when men agree among

themselves to submit to some man, or assembly of men, voluntarily, on confidence to be by him against all others. This latter may be called a political wealth, or commonwealth by *institution*, and the former, a commonwealth by *acquisition*.

Chapter 24: Of Crimes, Excuses, and Extenuations

[4] The source of every crime is some defect of the understanding, or some error in reasoning, or some sudden force of the passions. Defect in the understanding is *ignorance*; in reasoning, *erroneous opinion*. Again, ignorance is of three sorts: of the *law*, and of the *sovereign*, and of the *penalty*. Ignorance of the law of nature excuseth no man, because every man that hath attained to the use of reason is supposed to know, he ought not to do to another what he would not have done to himself. Therefore, into what place soever a man shall come, if he do anything contrary to that law, it is a crime. If a man come from the *Indies* hither, and persuade men here to receive a new religion, or teach them anything that tendeth to disobedience of the laws of this country, though he be never so well persuaded of the truth of what he teacheth, he commits a crime, and may be justly punished for the same, not only because his doctrine is false, but also because he does that which he would not approve in another, namely, that coming from hence, he should endeavor to alter the religion there. But ignorance of the civil law shall excuse a man in a strange country, till it be declared to him, because till then no civil law is binding.

[5] In the like manner, if the civil law of man's own country be not so sufficiently declared as he may know it if he will, nor the action against the law of nature, the ignorance is a good excuse; in other cases ignorance of the civil law excuseth not.

[6] Ignorance of the sovereign power in the place of a man's ordinary residence excuseth him not; because he ought to take notice of the power by which he hath been protected there.

[7] Ignorance of the penalty, where the law is declared, excuseth no man; for in breaking the law, which without a fear of penalty to follow were not a law, but vain words, he undergoeth the penalty, though he know not what it is; because whosoever voluntarily doth any action accepteth all the known consequences of it; but punishment is a known consequence of the violation of the laws in every commonwealth; which punishment, if it be determined already by the law, he is subject to that; if not, then is he subject to arbitrary punishment. For it is reason that he which does injury, without other limitation than that of his own will, should suffer punishment without other limitation than that of his will whose law is thereby violated.

Chapter 28: Of Punishments and Rewards

[1] A PUNISHMENT is an evil inflicted by public authority on him that hath done or omitted that which is judged by the same authority to be a transgression of the law, to the end that the will of men may thereby the better be disposed to obedience.

[2] Before I infer anything from this definition, there is a question to be answered of much importance, which is: by what door the right or authority of punishing in any case came in? For by that which has been said before, no man is supposed bound by covenant not to resist violence; and consequently, it cannot be intended that he gave any right to another to lay violent hands upon his person. In the making of a commonwealth, every

man giveth away the right of defending another, but not of defending himself. Also, he obligeth himself to assist him that hath the sovereignty in the punishing of another, but of himself not. But to covenant to assist the sovereign in doing hurt to another, unless he that so covenanteth have a right to do it himself, is not to give him a right to punish. It is manifest therefore that the right which the commonwealth (that is, he or they that represent it) hath to punish is not grounded on any concession or gift of the subjects.

But I have also showed formerly [xiv, 4] that before the institution of commonwealth, every man had a right to everything, and to do whatsoever he thought necessary to his own preservation, subduing, hurting, or killing any man in order thereunto. And this is the foundation of that right of punishing which is exercised in every commonwealth. For the subjects did not give the sovereign that right, but only (in laying down theirs) strengthened him to use his own as he should think fit, for the preservation of them all; so that it was not given, but left to him, and to him only, and (excepting the limits set him by natural law) as entire as in the condition of mere nature, and of war of every one against his neighbor.

[3] From the definition of punishment, I infer, first, that neither private revenges nor injuries of private men can properly be styled punishments, because they proceed not from public authority.

[4] Secondly, that to be neglected and unpreferred by the public favor is not a punishment, because no new evil is thereby on any man inflicted; he is only left in the estate he was in before.

[5] Thirdly, that the evil inflicted by public authority without precedent public condemnation is not to be styled by the name of punishment, but of a hostile act, because the fact for which a man is punished ought first to be judged by public authority to be a transgression of the law.

[6] Fourthly, that the evil inflicted by usurped power, and judges without authority from the sovereign, is not punishment, but an act of hostility, because the acts of power usurped have not for author the person condemned, and therefore are not acts of public authority.

[7] Fifthly, that all evil which is inflicted without intention or possibility of disposing the delinquent (or, by his example, other men) to obey the laws is not punishment, but an act of hostility; because without such an end, no hurt done is contained under that name.

[8] Sixthly, whereas to certain actions there be annexed by nature divers hurtful consequences (as when a man, in assaulting another, is himself slain or wounded, or when he falleth into sickness by the doing of some unlawful act), such hurt, though in respect of God, who is the author of nature, it may be said to be inflicted, and therefore a punishment divine, yet it is not contained in the name of punishment in respect of men, because it is not inflicted by the authority of man.

[9] Seventhly, if the harm inflicted be less than the benefit or contentment that naturally followeth the crime committed, that harm is not within the definition, and is rather the price, or redemption, than the punishment of a crime, because it is of the nature of punishment to have for end the disposing of men to obey the law; which end (if it be less than the benefit of the transgression) it attaineth not, but worketh a contrary effect.

[10] Eighthly, if punishment be determined and prescribed in the law itself, and after the crime committed there be a greater punishment inflicted, the excess is not punish-

ment, but an act of hostility. For seeing them aim of punishment is not a revenge, but terror, and the terror of a great punishment unknown is taken away by the declaration of a less, the unexpected addition is no part of the punishment.

But where there is no punishment at all determined by the law, there whatsoever is inflicted hath the nature of punishment. For he that goes about the violation of a law wherein no penalty is determined expecteth an indeterminant, that is to say, an arbitrary punishment.

[11] Ninthly, harm inflicted for a fact done before there was a law that forbade it is not punishment, but an act of hostility; for before the law there is not transgression of the law; but punishment supposeth a fact judged to have been a transgression of the law; therefore, harm inflicted before the law made is not punishment, but an act of hostility.

[12] Tenthly, hurt inflicted on the representative of the commonwealth is not punishment, but an act of hostility, because it is of the nature of punishment to be inflicted by public authority, which is the authority only of the representative itself.

[13] Lastly, harm inflicted upon one that is a declared enemy falls not under the name of punishment, because seeing they were either never subject to the law, and therefore cannot transgress it, or having been subject to it and professing to be no longer so, by consequence deny they can transgress it, all the harms that can be done them must be taken as acts of hostility. But in declared hostility all infliction of evil is lawful. From whence it followeth, that if a subject shall, by fact or word, wittingly and deliberately deny the authority of the representative of the commonwealth, (whatsoever penalty hath been formerly ordained for treason) he may lawfully be made to suffer whatsoever the representative will. For in denying subjection he denies such punishment as by the law hath been ordained, and therefore suffers as an enemy of the commonwealth, that is, according to the will of the representative. For the punishments set down in the law are to subjects, not to enemies; such as are they, that having been by their own act subjects, deliberately revolting, deny the sovereign power.

II. EXCERPTS FROM MACAULAY'S *LETTERS ON EDUCATION: WITH OBSERVATIONS ON RELIGIOUS AND METAPHYSICAL SUBJECTS*[8]

Part 1: Introductory Letter

It must be acknowledged then, that the gift of reason and the powers of imagination have indeed made a fatal havoc on human happiness. But these gifts are absolutely necessary to support man's state of preeminence on this globe, and to fit him for an exalted station in a future life. It is true, that from the creation, men have generally exercised their powers in such a manner as to occasion much misery in the world to the far greater number of the species, and to cloud their hopes in futurity; but this phenomenon does not prove that reason and the enlarged powers of imagination will finally and absolutely produce more misery than good to any being who has possessed them. It is far from a necessary consequence, that these gifts should ever produce evil; and when misery attends them, it always proceeds from incidental causes. The human faculties rise, by practice and education, from mere capacity to an excellence and an energy which enables man to become the carver of his own happiness. It is the capital and distinguishing characteristic of our species, says lord Monboddo, [that] we can make ourselves as it were over again, so that the original nature is so little obvious, that it is with great difficulty we can distinguish it from the acquired.

The attention I have given to my own character, Hortencia, and to the means by which it has been formed, obliges me to subscribe, without reserve, to this opinion of the Scottish sage, viz. that man, in a state of society, is as artificial a being as his representation on the canvas of the painter. Nature indeed supplies the raw materials, and the capacity of the workman; but the effect is the mere production of art. I have often smiled, when I have heard persons talk of their natural propensities; for I am convinced, that these have undergone so great a change by domestic education, and the converse of the world, that their primitive modes are not in many beings even discernable. No; there is not a virtue or a vice that belongs to humanity, which we do not make ourselves; and if their qualities should be hostile to our happiness, we may ascribe their malignancy to human agency. There is not a wretch who ends his miserable being on a wheel, as the forfeit of his offences against society, who may not throw the whole blame of his misdemeanors on his education; who may not look up to the very government, by whose severe laws he is made to suffer, as the author of his misfortunes; and who may not with justice utter the hardest imprecations on those to whom the charge of his youth was entrusted, and to those with whom he associated in the early periods of his life. The very maniac, who languished out his miserable existence in the phrenzy of distraction, and that more unfortunate madman, who retains a sufficient semblance of reason to color his misfortune with the deformity of turpitude, might have found a cure, or a softening remedy to their maladies, from the sources of philosophy, had its balsam been administered before the passions had taken root in the mind.

To abate the pride of the lofty minded, let it be remembered, that our talents, our accomplishments, and our virtues, are chiefly owing to the care and the wisdom of others; for when they are gained by the price of our own exertions, it is almost always at the expense of our innocence and our peace.

If this is the case, and that it certainly is so, the history of man sufficiently proves, why, though the magistrate should neglect his charge, dies the parent consign to misery, the wretched offspring of whose fate he is entirely the master? Why does he not rear the moral plant, committed to his care, to a vigorous maturity? And thus, by the powers of sympathy, partake of the good he bestows, and lay up a treasure in filial piety and virtue for the necessary wants of age.

It is a barbarous ignorance which has hitherto defrauded man of the means which he enjoys from his reasoning powers, to secure his happiness in the present and future slate.

The ancients, to their honor be it spoken, had a much more anxious care for the morals of their offspring, than the moderns, and were consequently more elaborate in their plan of education. I have often read with pleasure, in the letter of the great men of Rome, at the time when the republic had almost touched the height of its depravity, the strongest sentiments of parental tenderness, and the most anxious care for the educational improvement of their children. In the dialogues of Plato, we may find, that no expense was spared by the Athenians to bestow the benefits of learning on their sons; and even the Europeans, after the revival of letters, made the education of their children the object of their most important concern. The slow progress of philosophical knowledge, retarded by foreign and domestic broils, by the continual wars which nation waged against nation, and family against family, the errors of paganism, and the superstitions which in general fastened on Christianity, rendered it impossible that education in those times should be sufficiently correct to effect its best purposes.

But in these enlightened days, when we have gained some useful insights into the wondrous fabrick of the human mind, much might be done in the way of education toward the happiness of nations and individuals; but, good God! What use are we making of our advances in knowledge? A senseless course of dissipation, and an unwearied exertion to procure the means of luxury, diverts our attention from the objects of our true felicity, and renders us callous to the woes of others. We are always looking over the point within our reach, and attempting to lay hold of good, where it is impossible to be found. Generation still continues to impel generation to those abysses of misery which error prepares for her votaries.

Oh magistrates! Oh legislators! Admit of some variation in your views of interest; consider, that in attempting to teach others, you may gain truths of the utmost importance to yourselves. Consider what will be the solid satisfaction, which a benign temper must feel, in becoming the instrument of the present and future welfare of numberless beings. And you, parents, remember, that the misery or bliss of your posterity, in a great measure depends upon yourselves, and that an inattention to your duty, may draw on your head the guilt of many generations.

Part 2: Letter 7, Duty of Governments toward Producing a General Civilization

Before we enter into the examination of such means, Hortensia, as shall appear to us the most likely to conduce to the highest degree, and the most universal extent of possible good, we must enquire into the nature of those high and important obligations which, in the reason of things, must be annexed to the office of government.

What may be the nature and extent of those duties of government which, on a principle of equity, subjects have a right to demand for all the splendid gifts they bestow on their governors, is a question which so nearly concerns the interests of man, that it becomes a matter of wonder the accuracy of their reasoning should not, in this point, have produced a uniformity of opinion. But important as is this subject, there is no speculation on which a greater variety of opinions have been formed, on which the prejudices of the species have been more at war with their interests, or on which the feebleness or the inactivity of the reasoning powers have been more exposed, or which more proves man to be the slave of custom and of precept.

It is well known, that a great part of the ancient, and even of the modern world, have made a deity of their government, in whose high prerogatives they have buried all their natural rights. The monstrous faith of millions made for one; has been at different times adopted by the greater part of civilized societies; and even those enlightened nations who have been the most famed for asserting and defending their liberties, ran into another species of idolatry, which is almost as much as war with the happiness of individuals. Instead of making a deity of the government, they made a deity of the society in its aggregate capacity; and to the real or imagined interests of this idol, they sacrificed the dearest interests of those individuals who formed the aggregate. Thus they reversed a very plain and reasonable proposition. Society with them was not formed for the happiness of its citizens, but the life and happiness of every citizen was to be devoted to the glory and welfare of the society.

When the happiness of an individual is properly considered, his interest will be found so intimately connected with the interests of the society of which he is a member, that he cannot act in conformity to the one, without having a proper consideration for the other. But reason will revolt against a service for which it finds no adequate return; and when we admire the virtue of the ancients, we admire only that inflexible conduct which carried them to sacrifice every personal interest to principle.

The moderns are grown so lax in their devotions to the shrine of patriotism, as to bury in the ruins of public virtue all good faith and common honesty; a depravity in manners, which too plainly manifests that the change of conduct proceeds from the total want of principle, rather than from the having formed just ones. We have duties of government, or on the duties of a good citizen; and individuals, from the prevalent power of custom and precepts, are content with privations which have no foundation in the common good.

Man is ever apt to run into extremes; no sooner do we discard one gross error, than we deviate into another of an opposite nature. It is said, that truth is always to be found in the mean; if so, those must differ widely from her, who, to avoid the evil of such a power as is claimed by despots, of interfering with all private as well as public concerns, assert, that the true and only office of government, is to act the part of a good constable in preserving the public peace.

Thus, according to the opinion of the most liberal of the moderns, governors have little else to do but to eat and drink, and to enjoy all the various emoluments annexed to the diadem and the purple, without disturbing their repose by fulfilling any of those parental duties which subjects, in their political connexion, have a much greater right to expect from their sovereign, than children have to expect from their natural parent; for where much is given, much may with justice be required.

The marquis of Beccario, in his excellent treatise on crimes and punishments asserts, that government has no right to punish delinquency in its subjects, without having previously taken care to instruct them in the knowledge of the laws, and of those duties in public and private life which are agreeable to the dictates of moral rectitude. This observation coincides with that strain of benevolence which runs through the whole of this excellent treatise. For not to dwell on the high injustice of assuming the power of punishment, without fulfilling the duties of instruction, it must be obvious to enlightened reason, that the sublime office of government consists in limiting as far as the nature of things will allow, the bounds of evil, and extending the bounds of good. And thus much may be said, that whatever be the sanguine expectations formed from some useful discoveries made in the science of physics, the conveniences and the happiness enjoyed by the generality of the world, will continue to be very moderate, unless the united force of society is steadily used to carry on the glorious work of improvement.

The education of the people, in the most extensive sense of this word, may be said to comprehend the most important duties of government. For as the education of individuals is for ever going on, and consists of all the impressions received through the organs of sense, from the hour of birth to the hour of death; public education, if well adapted to the improvement of man, must comprehend good laws, good examples, good customs, a proper use of the arts, and wise instructions conveyed to the mind, by the means of language, in the way of speech and writing.

Letter 8: Sympathy—Equity

If we trace, Hortensia, the origin of those virtues in man, which render him fit for the benign offices of life, we shall find that they all center in sympathy. For had the mind of man been totally divested of this affection, it would not in all probability have ever attained any ideas of equity. Yes, it was the movements of sympathy which first inclined man to a forbearance of his own gratifications, in respect to the feelings of his fellow creatures; and his reason soon approved the dictates of his inclination. A strict adherence to the principles of equity, may be said to include the perfection of moral rectitude. This being granted, all human virtue will be found to proceed from equity; consequently, if the principle of equity itself owes its source in the human mind to the feelings of sympathy, all human virtue must derive its source from this useful affection.

When this benign affection holds a superiority in the mind to other affections, inclination will lead to the performance of the duties of humanity. But in those insensible minds where this affection is originally weak, or where it is extinguished by the excess of hostile passions, equity, unsupported by benevolence, has either no place in the mind, or through the cold precept of tuition, bears a feeble sway.

We have reason to believe that all the passions which belong to humanity lie latent in every mind; but we find by experience that they continue inactive till put in motion by the influence of some corresponding impression; and that their growth and prevalence in a great measure depends on the repetition of those impressions which are in their nature adapted to affect them. Thus it will appear, that where we have power to direct the course of impression, we have power to command the slate of the passions; and as laws, example, precept, and custom, are the prime sources of all our impressions, it must be greatly in the power of government to effect, by a proper rule of these sources, that improvement on which true civilization depends.

It is known, that the power of custom over the mind arises from such a repetition of the same impression, as act to the weakening or destroying the force of every impression of a contrary tendency. Could we therefore, by the spirit of our laws, exclude from society the operation of every impression which partook of the smallest tincture of cruelty, and did we encourage the operation of every impression which had a benevolent tendency, it appears probable, that we should exalt the sympathizing feeling to a degree which might act more forcibly than the coercion of rigorous laws—to the restraining all acts of violence, and consequently all acts which militate against the public peace.

For example, were government to act on so liberal a sentiment of benevolence, as to take under the protection of law the happiness of the brute species, so far as to punish in offenders that rigorous, that barbarous treatment they meets with in the course of their useful services, would it not tend to increase sympathy? Would it not highly enlarge our notions of equity, by pointing out to public observation this moral truth, that tenderness is due to those creatures, without whose daily labor society would be bereaved of every enjoyment which renders existence comfortable?

When a large and gentle bullock, says Mandeville, after having resisted a ten times greater force of blows than would have killed his murderer, falls stunned at last, and his armed head is fastened to the ground with cords, as soon as the wide wound is made, and the jugulars are cut asunder, what mortal can, without compassion, hear the painful bellowings intercepted by his blood, the bitter sighs that speak the sharpness of his anguish, and the deep founding groans with loud anxiety fetched from the bottom of his strong and palpitating heart; or see the trembling and violent convulsions of his limbs, the seeking gore streaming from his wounds, and his struggling gasps, and last efforts for life, the certain signs of his approaching fate.

Mandeville is mistaken; so forcible is the power of habit that these dreadful fights are daily seen without exciting horror, or one soft tear or sigh of sympathy; and consequently, habits such as these, must tend to weaken and even to destroy this heavenly quality. Oh! then let all slaughter houses be treated as nuisances; let them be sequestered from the haunts of men; let premiums be given to those who can find out the least painful manner of taking away the lives of those animals which are necessary for sustenance; let every other manner of depriving them of life be forbidden, under severe penalties; let the privation of life, by way of sport and amusement, be discouraged by example and precept; and it is more than probably, that such a spirit of benevolence will be diffused over the minds of the public, as may tend to the general practice of those virtues which reason approves, and which Christianity ordains.

It has been a question lately much agitated, whether any such necessity exists, as is pretended, of depriving those delinquents of their lives, who act against the public peace by treasonable offenses, and by injuring a fellow citizen's life or property. Those who take the benevolent side of the question, maintain, that the depriving a citizen of his life, is a breach of one of the fundamental obligations of government, and that there may be found a variety of punishments more fully adequate to the preservation of the public peace, than acts of violence which shock the sensibility of the feeling mind, and harden to a state of barbarism the unfeeling one. Those who take the adverse side of the question, oppose these positions with many plausible arguments; but whether the necessity contended for really exists in the nature of things, or whether it exists only in the indolence of government, and their inattention to the happiness of the community in their individual capacity, certain it is, that the interests of humanity and the dictates of good policy, require that the examples of taking away life should be as few as the nature of things will admit. That all the ceremonies which attend this melancholy act, should be made as awful as possible; and that to prevent the public from receiving any impression which may shock the compassionate part of the society, or contribute to steal the hearts of the more insensible, all executions should be performed in private.

The English, from the number of their charitable donations, from the heavy taxes they lay on themselves to maintain their poor, and above all, for that general diffusion of sentiment, which in a late attempt on the life of his Majesty, deterred the most servile courtier of the train to compliment their prince at the expense of justice and humanity, have proved themselves to be in a comparative sense, a benevolent people. Yet the long lift of wretches who, on particular seasons of the year, are led out to execution without exciting a sufficient sympathy in the public to stop for an instant the career of trifling dissipation, proves too strongly that the English, like their neighbors, are yet in a state of barbarism. A moments attention to the melancholy situation into which a fellow creature is reduced, for errors from which we are preserved by a more happy destiny, is sufficient to spread the gloom of sorrow over a reflecting mind; and as every indulgence of sentiment tends to strengthen its force, such solemnities should be used at executions, as might serve to augment the compassion of the sympathizing, and raise terror in the gay and thoughtless.

Civilized Rome never saw scaffolds stained with the blood of her citizens; and she granted civic crowns to those who preserved their lives. The moderns have too widely departed from this line of policy, and in so doing have relaxed the ties of social life. Would it not be graceful, would it not be setting a due estimation on the life of a citizen, the supreme magistrate, in the tender character of a political parent, with the judge who is necessitated by the duties of his office to pass the fatal sentence, to put on black, and to continue this garb of mourning till after the execution of the criminal? Would it not be raising useful impressions in the minds of the public, were the following solemnities to be used at the execution? The prisoner to be conducted to the place of punishment with a long train of the officers of justice and their proper attendants, in mourning. The train to be led up by an officer of state, with the sword of justice elevated in his hand. The officer of state to be immediately followed by the officers of justice, and they by the executioner, with the instruments of his office; the executioner to be immediately followed by the criminal; the criminal to be followed by persons dressed in black, bearing his coffin; the procession to be closed by the inferior officers of justice and their affiliates, and all the bells in the city to be made to toll during the passing of the procession.

To give strength to the impressions which these solemnities are calculated to make, the fear of execution, in the form of a large square, fenced in with high walls, should be placed at the further end of the city; the sword of justice, and other emblematical pieces of sculpture, may ornament its gates, and over them may be written in large capitals, "*These are the gates which lead to death.*" At the entrance of this tremendous square the multitude ought to be dismissed, and none but the officers of justice with their attendants, the executioner, and the criminal with his relations or friends, be permitted to enter. After the execution, the body ought to be interred in a burying ground adjoining to the square, and kept sacred for that purpose. The procession should return with the same solemnities with which it set out; and all public amusements or meetings, of a dissipated kind, should be prohibited on this day.

Letter I: Influence of Domestic and National Education

The modes of domestic education, Hortencia, as practiced by the moderns, are not calculated to instill that wisdom into youth which is necessary to guard against the dangers that surround it. In a total ignorance of the nature of those things which contribute the happiness and the misery of the species, young persons are commonly initiated into the circles of conversation and the dissipated amusements of the age, at that period of life when the affections of childhood are by repeated impressions strengthened into passions, and when the passions of adults spring up in the mind.

It is now, as Helvetius observes, that the youth finds himself attacked by a greater number of sensations; all that surrounds strikes him, and strikes him forcibly. The imagination easily fascinated, both from its natural warmth, and the novelty of untried pleasures stamp on the ductile mind those various propensities which form its character through life. At this important period of existence, a public education, if it uniformly tends to instill the principles of equity and benevolence; if it uniformly tends to refine the mind and increase its sympathy, will undoubtedly correct the intemperance of the gross and the malevolent affections. But though the education of the world will necessarily give a turn to the passions, yet it cannot teach the way to moderate the subdue them. It cannot teach us to be content with those limitations within which God has thought proper to confine human happiness; nor can it teach us to govern the imagination with such judgment as shall convert it from a source of perpetual evil, into a fountain of inexhaustible good.

It is indeed sufficient for the bulk of the people, if they are civilized in such a manner as to be innoxious in their conduct as citizens. That industry, which is necessary to their subsistence, will tame the turbulence of the imagination, and prevent it from being the source of mischief to themselves or others. But this is not the case with the higher class of citizens whose circumstances and situation give them leisure, and opportunity, to indulge all the caprices of fancy. That wisdom which accompanies knowledge, is necessary to the great and opulent to prevent them from falling into those follies which blast in their bud the fairest fruits of fortune, and cloud the brightest prospects of human felicity.

If the higher classes of the people have not wisdom, who will be the framers of those laws which enlighten the understandings of the citizens in the essentials of right and wrong? Where shall we find those examples which are to direct the steps of the ignorant in the paths which lead to righteousness? Where that public instruction, which teaches to the multitude the relative duties of life? And where those decent and well regulated customs, which form the difference between civilized and uncivilized nations?

As the senses, Hortencia, are the only inlets to human knowledge, consequently human knowledge can only be gained by experience and observation. Men as they gained ideas of good and evil, by experience, communicated their observations to their offspring. Domestic education therefore, must have began with the beginning of the life of man; and when the species formed themselves into societies, their ideas were necessarily extended from the variety of impressions and instructions which they received in such associations.

With the increase of the stock of his ideas, man increased his power of making comparisons, and consequently enlarged his knowledge of the relation of things. Some modes of conduct generally adopted, some rules and exercises fitted to a state of offence and defense, necessarily belong to all associations. Education then, in a state of the rudest society, must necessarily be more complex and more methodical than education in the natural, or more solitary state of man; who as he rises from this rude state of society, through all the degrees which form the difference between the savage and the civilized nations, must receive impressions more numerous; his motives for action must grow more complex; his duties and his obligations must enlarge; the rules for his conduct must become more nice and various; his actions be more critically observed; his offenses more certain punished; and consequently his good or ill fate must depend in a more particular manner on his education, than when in a state of nature, or in a state savage society. But when the manners of society refine, when standards of taste are established, when arts are practiced, when sciences are studies, and when laws are numerous; it is then that the education of citizens, and more especially of the better fort, becomes a matter of the highest importance and difficulty.

Commentary by *Catherine Villanueva Gardner*, Macaulay and Hobbes: Citizens and Subjects

INTRODUCTION

At first glance, Thomas Hobbes and Catharine Macaulay may seem to share little in common. Hobbes paints a bleak picture of the human condition without government; we can only be saved from ourselves by a sovereign with absolute power. Macaulay, on the other hand, sees that humans are ultimately destined for moral perfection, and that good (i.e., for her, a republican) government is a necessary part of our progress. Yet despite these differences, and the fact that more than a hundred years separates the actual lives of Thomas Hobbes and Catharine Macaulay, they are connected philosophically by the politics of seventeenth-century England.

Hobbes's *Leviathan* can be taken as a discussion of the timeless questions of political philosophy. Yet, as Johann Sommerville has argued, "it should also be seen as a dialogue with his contemporaries, in particular those whose political thought Hobbes saw with disapproval as having led to the English civil war."[9] Indeed, he began work on *Leviathan* during the years that King Charles I had become a prisoner of Parliament after a royalist defeat in the civil war. Given Hobbes's royalist sympathies and connections, it comes as no surprise to find him describing in his verse autobiography the parliament established after the execution of Charles I as "Blood-thirsty leeches, hating all that's good/Glutted with innocent and noble blood."[10]

A century later these disputes of the seventeenth century had not been forgotten; instead they fed into and framed the radical politics of the eighteenth century. In her political history of the seventeenth century, Macaulay claimed that the period of the commonwealth was "the brightest age that ever adorned the page of history," and criticized Charles I for his "passion for power" and "idolatry" of "royal prerogatives."[11]

Although our interest here in Macaulay is as a philosopher, her career as a historian should not be underplayed, as it provides an important key to understanding her moral and political philosophy. Macaulay believed in the doctrine of "postmillennialism": there is a divine plan for a gradual improvement in human nature and society leading to a time of perfection on earth signaling the Second Coming.[12] Her *History of England* thus serves to chart the progress of humankind and to show how this progress is produced both through governments and key individuals. Her political and moral work—*Letters on Education*—then provides an examination of how humans can contribute—both individually and collectively—to this divine plan.

HOBBES: THE HUMAN CONDITION

Beginning with Hobbes's account of the human condition, we see that he offers a striking picture of humans in a dismal "pre-social" state: a state of "war." By war he does not mean that they are in a constant state of actual battle, but rather that pre-social human life is a life of insecurity or uncertainty. As such, this life leaves no place for the possibility of industry or civilization.

Hobbes is not necessarily making a historical claim here about human society; rather he is describing life without government.[13] Moreover he does not hold that humans arrive at this state of war because of some kind of innate or overriding selfishness or aggressiveness, but rather because of the situation in which they are placed. For, Hobbes holds, we are by nature equal both physically and intellectually.[14] From this equality of ability, he says, comes an equality of hope in attaining the fulfillment of our desires. Thus the problem is not so much with human nature itself, but with the presence of other similar humans.

What is important to notice at this stage is that Hobbes holds that people have a natural right to do things that will allow them to avoid harm and to best preserve their life. Essentially then, this means that people have a natural right to everything and anything.[15] Furthermore it is also clear that there can be no property and no law, and thus justice and injustice do not exist in the state of nature.

Yet just as the problem is in part a product of human passions or desires, so there is a sense in which the solution comes from our other passions and desires. People fear death and desire to live well and thus in this way are drawn toward a peaceful coexistence. Moreover, according to Hobbes, humans are also governed by a law of nature that forbids them to act in a way that would be self-harming. While the right of nature grants us liberty in action, there is a law of nature that places a rational restraint on that action: if and when it is possible to obtain peace, people are bound by their rationality to aim for this peace.

THE SOVEREIGN

Hobbes holds that, given the alternative, people will agree on the need for a sovereign. The sovereign need not necessarily be an individual human being, rather it is an entity defined by its authorization to act on behalf of its subjects. This sovereign may come into power through conquest, or through voluntary agreement, although, obviously, the latter is of more interest both for Hobbes and for us.

Given the initial equality in the state of nature, even if the sovereign body was a group of individuals, it would not have enough power to govern effectively. How then does the sovereign obtain sufficient power to enforce its commands and laws? According to Hobbes, the natural right of the subjects to self-defense is voluntarily transferred or given up to the sovereign who will then have supreme power over the subjects; this amount of power is necessary in order to ensure that the subjects do not break their voluntary agreement to have (and obey) a sovereign. In addition, the sovereign is to use this power to ensure a peaceful society and to protect it from foreign invasion.

Protection by, and absolute obedience to, this sovereign power is then the only chance of escape from the state of nature, and the only hope of achieving sufficient liberty to pursue a life of well-being and to benefit from the fruits of one's labor.

MACAULAY: THE HUMAN CONDITION AND SYMPATHY

Even though Hobbes does not reject the possibility that humans can act from benevolent motives, he does not think it is common enough to be of importance for political theorizing. In contrast, Macaulay holds that *all* humans, with varying degrees, do have a natural feeling of what she terms "sympathy": a consideration for others and a willingness to sacrifice some of our own pleasures for them.

Macaulay explicitly holds that, without this feeling of sympathy, our reason could not have produced the idea or principle of equity. As she believes that all human virtues come from this idea of equity; this feeling of sympathy is ultimately the foundation stone of all human virtue. While reason clearly plays the *pivotal* role in the development of virtue, she believes that an understanding or an education in moral principles alone cannot hold our mind; the feeling of sympathy is necessary. Yet this feeling does not come fully formed. While all humans have a potential to feel sympathy, it must be stimulated to come alive and to grow.

But how does Macaulay believe that this can be accomplished? Macaulay acknowledges that her understanding of the human mind finds its basis in Locke's notion of the mind as a *tabula rasa*. She then claims that human mental development, specifically human moral development, is purely the product of education and environment.

This development is not haphazard or arbitrary, nor is it a development grounded on feeling rather than reason. Macaulay holds that errors and inconsistencies in our moral judgment spring from our undisciplined passions or desires. She argues for an education based on rational moral principles that will produce moral excellence in the Lockean mind.[16] Without a proper knowledge of what she calls the "immutable principles" of morality, which she states are grounded in reason, even the most intelligent of us is prone to make errors in our moral judgments, or to be inconsistent in our moral evaluations of acts and characters. If we wish to know what these immutable principles are, Macaulay's answer is simple: the standard for our behavior is the divinely authored invariable rule of right.

HAPPINESS EQUATED WITH RECTITUDE

Once Macaulay's view of the human mind and its moral development is placed within the context of her religious views, specifically her belief in postmillennialism, its philosophical significance can be appreciated. Humans do not have a passive role in the divine plan; they must also contribute actively toward future perfection. Our sympathy for others is the motivating force for our contributions, but we must both act on and understand the immutable principles if we are to follow the path of perfection.

Given this monumental task, it is clear that the perfection of the human race cannot be achieved by individual parents or even family groups. Macaulay holds that society has been formed for the purpose of this perfection—and thus the happiness—of its human citizens. Indeed, Macaulay explicitly equates human happiness with what she calls rectitude (right thinking). She holds that true happiness is incompatible with ignorance: the untrained mind. What is interesting here is that she does not see happiness purely in terms of the individual; society itself will benefit by an overall increase in wisdom.

Human happiness, for Macaulay, does not just stop at the level of this earth. Macaulay holds that our happiness in the next world will be dependent on our rectitude, and thus our education: "To enter into the kingdom of heaven we must follow the principles of morality; to follow these principles we must be properly educated." A provocative implication of this equation of happiness and rectitude is that it allowed Macaulay to argue for the equal education of men and women. Not only was this a controversial claim for her era, but it predates the better-known arguments of Mary Wollstonecraft.

Macaulay offers three brief arguments in *Letters on Education* for the equality of education. The first is based on the acknowledged consistency of moral principles. What is right or virtuous behavior for one sex must be the same for the other. Thus the education of the two sexes must be the same. The second argument essentially states that not giving women equal education is to ignore our own interest in a morally excellent society. If society will benefit by an overall increase in the wisdom of its citizens, then keeping half of them in ignorance will do nothing to move society further toward happiness. Moreover, ignorance in women themselves will ensure their own unhappiness. The third argument states that inequality of education may prevent the possibility of women's happiness in the next world. Without proper education—education equal to that of men—in the principles of morality, women will stand little chance of leading the kind of life in this world that will ensure entrance into the next.

Thus, while Hobbes's view of the human condition leads him to endorse government by a supreme sovereign as a way of delivering us from ourselves, Macaulay argues that the structure of the human mind and the divine plan for humans require effective government in order to deliver us into the kingdom of heaven. Both philosophers agree that it is through our reason that we recognize the prudence of this deliverance, and that our passions—whether fear of death or sympathy—add a motivating force. But, having said this, there is little doubt that Hobbes and Macaulay hold very different notions of the "civilization" humans can achieve, something which can best be brought out by a discussion of their notions of the role of government.

DIFFERENCES ON THE ROLE OF GOVERNMENT

Given Hobbes's account of the state of nature, namely that it is "solitary, poor, nasty, brutish and short," it is clear that the primary role of government is to provide security for its subjects—both from each other and from outside attack. The sovereign is granted the right to make laws and ensure that they are kept. This entity, or its appointed representative, decides whether these laws have been followed or not, and punishes those who have failed to follow them. Hobbes holds that this security can only be guaranteed by giving an absolute power to the sovereign—absolute *except* in the sole case where the sovereign fails in its one duty on which its legitimacy or "right to rule" is based: when humans decided to leave the state of nature to form a civil society, they did so to ensure their self-preservation (something they could not secure in the state of nature). They formed a leviathan or sovereign and turned over all their "rights" from the state of nature on the condition that the sovereign has the duty to protect its citizens' lives (or, their rights to self-preservation). So, if a sovereign fails to perform its duty, its citizens have a right to overthrow it (a basis for a defense of anarchy).

Unlike Hobbes, Macaulay holds that the role of government is *not* just focused on limiting actual or potential harm; it also must work actively toward producing good, which is understood as "human progress." Given Macaulay's view of human nature and its destiny, the primary role of government is the education of its citizens—both women and men. She held that the more sophisticated a society becomes, the more its citizens—especially those who will form the governing or ruling classes—will need what she calls national education as well as a parental education. Without a proper education, she asks, how will these classes be able to frame laws that will teach ordinary citizens right from wrong?

Since Macaulay holds that we gain knowledge through our senses, and thus we can only learn through experience and observation, government must pay careful attention to the sensations to which its subjects—especially the young and impressionable—are exposed. It must offer suitable impressions to their senses through such things as good laws, good examples, and the use of the arts—all aimed at producing sympathy and teaching what she calls (but never defines) the "principles of equity" and "benevolence." Government is then an essential part of the improvement of mankind, as it has the power over the laws, customs, and so forth that affect the mind.

The laws made and upheld by government are not human laws *per se*. Macaulay does not believe that human laws are sufficient to produce a well-ordered society—the morally excellent society. Instead, laws must be based on Christian principles. She argues that laws without the backing of religion cannot always influence the agency of humans, which laws must be able to do. Furthermore, even the most virtuous of minds may fall into indifference or despair at the thought of a universe that is not ordered.[17] All the more reason for laws.

Finally, and perhaps most important, Macaulay held that the *type* of government will affect the development of individual humans. Government based on power, like the type she believed Hobbes espoused, would not produce the appropriate environment for the moral improvement of the human mind. A republican government, on the other hand, would produce the necessary intellectual liberty for such improvement.[18]

DIFFERENCES ON PUNISHMENT

Their differing views of the roles of government imply not only that Hobbes and Macaulay hold differing views of the purpose of punishment for disobeying the laws, but also that their approach to the discussion of the subject differs as well. For Hobbes the definition of punishment is simple: it is an evil or harm done to a transgressor of the law by an authority.[19] The purpose of punishment is equally simple: to produce obedience in the subjects. When punishment is meted out to a disobedient citizen, it is not in revenge (or retribution) for the breaking of the law; it is to produce sufficient terror in both the guilty party and other subjects to produce future obedience (or deterrence). While he allows that there are some people who may not fit into this mold, he holds that *most* of us are only held back from breaking a law by fear when it would seem to profit us in some way to do otherwise.

Where Hobbes believes that the issue of punishment becomes more complex is not in defining it or outlining its purpose, but in offering the justification for its use by the authority against the transgressor. In the original covenant (or agreement made while in the state of nature to create a sovereign with certain rights and duties), there was no agreement by the subjects to give the sovereign the right to violent treatment against them. This would have been an irrational thing to include in the covenant since the moral legitimacy of the covenant is based in the voluntary consent of the people to transfer all their rights to the sovereign *except* the right to self-preservation, in exchange for the duty or obligation of the sovereign to protect or ensure the continuation of their lives. As such, the sovereign is never "given" this right. Instead, Hobbes holds that the sovereign's right to punish his subjects comes from the original right of nature that allows us to do anything necessary for our self-preservation. The covenanters laid down this right, but the sovereign kept it and is now empowered to legitimately use his right to protect his subjects.

Clearly, however, people do sometimes break the law and Hobbes identifies the three causes of this: ignorance, defective reasoning, or a spontaneous outburst of the passions (and he sees pride as the most frequent passion behind crime). Once identified as *causes*, it then seems obvious why Hobbes will not allow these factors or explanations—as the modern reader might—to count as *excuses* or *justifications* for breaking the law. He does, however, allow for some circumstances in which the crime may be excused or, at least, extenuated. Examples he gives are the excuse of someone who completely lacks the means to know the law (such as a child), or the extenuation of law breaking that comes out of attending to a faulty interpretation of the law from a teacher or public authority.

In contrast, not only does Macaulay place far greater limitations on the ability of government to punish, she places far more responsibility on government, and correspondingly less on citizens, to ensure that laws are followed. Given its educative function, she claims that government cannot punish if it has not first taught its citizens properly about the law and public and private morality. Moreover, punishment is to be used in part to fulfill this educative function. To explain how this works, Macaulay spends considerable time discussing how to perform an execution so that it produces the appropriate impressions of combined sympathy and terror.

Unlike the terror produced by Hobbesian-style punishment, Macaulay intends that this feeling of terror will lead to ideas about the value of human life and the wrongness of unjustified killing. Moreover, and again unlike Hobbes, Macaulay does not see punishment as a necessary part of the role of government. She believes it is possible that—with appropriately designed legislation and education—humans could become sympathetic enough that they would automatically restrain themselves from violent acts. In this way there would no need for coercive laws and their accompanying punishments.

CITIZENS AND SUBJECTS

Hobbes sets out clearly a subject's obligation of obedience to the instituted sovereign. Once the sovereign is instituted, the subjects cannot change allegiance to another sovereign or return to the state of nature.[20] Nor can the sovereign be said to have forfeited his power because of a breach of the covenant, as the covenant is between the subjects not between sovereign and subjects.[21] The reason for this is clear: if a group of subjects have a right to do this, then this group would be the true sovereign.[22] It may seem that Hobbesian subjects have no liberty at all under this authoritarian rule. However, it is important to notice that in the dedicatory letter to *Leviathan*, Hobbes describes himself as passing between the extremes of liberty and the extremes of authority.[23]

In chapter xxi of *Leviathan,* on the liberty of subjects, Hobbes argues that their obligation is conditional on the power by which he is able to protect them. Simply because the sovereign commands something of a subject need not mean that s/he must obey. The subject can disobey if it is something that he could not rationally consent to, such as killing or hurting himself. The reason a subject could not rationally consent to this is because consenting would contradict the one inviolable right to self-preservation that the subject has. Moreover a subject can refuse any command that would place him/her in personal danger if that refusal does not go against the sovereign's goal of protection. Hobbes allows then for the possibility that, for example, one can justly refuse a command to go to war if one has substituted a soldier in one's place. Finally, outside of these direct commands and the laws made by the sovereign, the individual subject is at liberty to act as s/he pleases.

On the other hand, while Macaulay offers a detailed account of the obligations of government to citizens, she says little about the corresponding obligations of citizens to government. One of the few comments she makes is when she criticizes societies that have made a deity of the government and have thus given up their natural rights. Based on her postmillennialist view and her politics, it would be safe to assume that she held that obedience of citizens to an instituted government was only required as long as the government worked for the development, and thus the happiness, of its citizens.

Despite Macaulay's claims that appropriate government—a democratic republic—offers the liberty necessary for a happy and virtuous society, she remains somewhat silent on the actual liberties she believes this will offer citizens. Her focus instead is on the *lack* of liberty she equates with any system not of this kind, for she holds that a lack of liberty will affect the virtue of citizens. She claims that such "slavish dependence" hurts our inherent virtues, for its aim to please and adore ultimately affects "the innate generous principles of the soul."[24] Yet while these political liberties allow citizens to develop morally, they also bring with them the troubling question of the overall freedom Macaulay allows us. If the increased perfection of humankind is part of the divine plan, then it may appear that humans do not have free will once they understand good, they must choose the path to perfection. This is something that Macaulay herself explicitly recognizes but is happy to accept.

A further issue to consider is that her belief in the central value of *liberty* is not equivalent to or connected with a claim for *equality*. Macaulay was not a democrat; indeed she held that God created socioeconomic inequality. As such, we must understand this inequality as a good. Since Macaulay held that power ultimately stemmed from property, she was concerned with how this divinely sanctioned inequality could be preserved without allowing an accumulation of property that would place power in the hands of a small aristocratic class.[25]

There is a sense, therefore, in which Macaulay's government, while obviously not an authoritarian one, plays a quite invasive role in the day-to-day lives of its citizens, albeit for their own good. Not only will government ensure the proper education of its citizens, but it will endeavor to provide them with suitable impressions through its laws and customs. While Macaulay believes that this form of government will offer liberty, she does not intend that it lead to equality. In this respect, it contrasts with a notion of an authoritarian Hobbesian government, which, perhaps paradoxically, plays a far more minimal role in the lives of its subjects: meaning it is outside obeying the laws and commands of the sovereign, and the subject is at liberty to do what s/he pleases. So, while

Hobbes holds that humans are equal in the state of nature, he accepts that social inequalities are produced by civil law. Needless to say, both Hobbes's and Macaulay's accounts find their justification for particular forms and powers of government in their initial views of the human condition.

MACAULAY'S CRITICISM OF HOBBES

Bringing out similarities and differences between Hobbes and Macaulay may only take us so far in our understanding of their work. We may also want to ask how they would have understood and critiqued the work of the other. What makes any comparison of their work so fascinating is that Macaulay clearly saw Hobbes as a central opponent to her views. Indeed, she went so far as to write a critical commentary on one of his earlier works of political philosophy, *De Cive*. Furthermore throughout *Letters on Education*, the occasional references to Hobbes make it clear that her work is directed, at least in part, toward a refutation of his thought. Thus she saw herself as taking part in an ongoing intellectual debate.

It is important to point out that Macaulay's *Loose Remarks on Certain Positions* to be found *in Mr. Hobbes's Philosophical Rudiments of Government and Society* is directed at Hobbes's earlier work *De Cive*, rather than at *Leviathan*. There are, however, strong parallels between Hobbes's two works, and thus, even though Macaulay's criticisms of the former cannot be applied wholesale to the latter, it is possible to isolate some central criticisms that apply to both works.[26]

The *first* of the central criticisms offered by Macaulay is that the absolute power Hobbes claims for the sovereign is in fact limited power. For this entity can only apply fixed penalties to those who transgress given laws. This is then an executive power, as the offender is punished under the law, not by what she calls the will of the punisher. It is only an absolute power when the sovereign has regal privileges and is bound by no laws: there is no greater law that can override the power and privileges of the sovereign.[27]

It may seem, initially, that Macaulay has misunderstood Hobbes on this point. If Hobbes is simply discussing the question of the generation and role of government, then these objections do not appear to be particularly strong. On the other hand, if Macaulay is reading Hobbes as offering some kind of practical proposal for the strength of government by a monarchy, then her critique would seem more pertinent.

Macaulay's *second* major criticism is directed at an issue that has puzzled other scholars. She asks how a contract between the people and the sovereign can be initially made without a spoken or assumed obligation to maintain it.[28] She claims that without this assumed contractual obligation to obey the sovereign, no one would willingly give up their natural rights. It is not clear how to take this criticism. Is Macaulay questioning, as other scholars have done, how we are to understand the nature of the initial agreement and the subsequent obligation to keep that agreement? Or, is she asking whether real humans would, even in the state of nature—that most miserable of circumstances—willingly sacrifice the only thing they have, namely unlimited freedoms or liberties without the certainty of a return? Macaulay never definitively offers how to interpret her claim.

Her *third* criticism seems to echo the latter interpretation. Here she is concerned about giving up our rights and our power to another, especially when power can so easily corrupt. In this way she questions whether it is more likely that the ruler would offer the security he is supposed to provide, or be a greater threat himself.

Looking at Macaulay's antimonarchy comments later on in *Loose Remarks* (that are not included in the excerpted texts here), it is clear that her criticisms of the monarchy as a institution find a lot of their basis in the actual failures of European monarchs, rather than with the potential sole theoretical problems of this form of government. It would seem that this is Macaulay the historian speaking here, not Macaulay the philosopher. The reason that she takes this approach is clear. As we have seen, for Macaulay, rule by a monarch or an aristocratic class leads *automatically* to a morally inferior society and vice among both the rulers and citizens. Hence, she believes that all she need offer are illustrative examples of this phenomenon to make this argument.

EVALUATION OF MACAULAY'S CRITICISM OF HOBBES

What are we to make of Macaulay's criticisms of Hobbes? I suggest that part of our judgment of their strength comes from how Macaulay interpreted Hobbes. While the modern reader may see Hobbes as offering a discussion of the timeless questions of political philosophy, Hobbes may have been read differently by Macaulay. It is plausible, and indeed rather likely, that she read Hobbes's philosophy for its practical potential rather than its theoretical sustainability. Her criticisms seem, ultimately, to be focused on whether he can respond to what she saw as the political and moral needs and problems of the European society of her time.

It is certainly clear from *Letters on Education* that Macaulay saw her own political philosophy as having just such direct practical applications. What is even more telling is that her criticisms of Hobbes are accompanied by (and were published with) a letter to Signor Paoli, the leader of the fight for Corsican freedom, setting out what she saw as the proper form of a democratic republic. In this way, Hobbes provides the platform for an attack on the type of government she wished to reject, while her instructions to Signor Paoli offer her an opportunity to offer a positive argument for what she saw as the proper form of government.

Conclusion

Despite their chronological and political differences, Hobbes and Macaulay make a well-matched pair. Initially, contrasting and comparing their particular political philosophies allows us a fuller picture of these philosophies and an insight into their relative strengths and weaknesses. Also, they work well when read together as part of several debates taking place in the seventeenth and eighteenth centuries, such as debates about the best forms of government, the concept of a social contract, and the nature and legitimacy of assumed contractual obligation to obey a sovereign. They raise an important question about a standard assumption that operates within the history of philosophy. This assumption holds that philosophers work within a framework of timeless, historically neutral problems that make philosophy intellectually independent of culture and context.

While Hobbes's work can be read in this way, it is far harder to read Macaulay's work within this neutral framework. This may then serve to explain, at least in part, Macaulay's disappearance from our histories of philosophy. The damage that has been done by this point of view—in particular, the way it has contributed to the disappearance of some women philosophers—is starting to surface. By connecting work by men and women philosophers, this anthology is thus, in part, a testament to this damage as well as an attempt to heal it.

Questions for Reflection

What role does the notion of sympathy play for Macaulay's account of human nature? Do you find her claims about the existence of sympathy in human nature to be convincing? Why or why not?

Macaulay and Hobbes offer two types of government. What are they—a Hobbesian and a Macaulay republican form of government, and which do you think offers the most liberties to its citizens? Which one do you think is the more appealing for someone living in your country in the present day? Provide reasons for your answers,

On what grounds would Macaulay reject a Hobbesian form of government and, conversely, on what grounds would Hobbes reject Macaulay's type of republican government? In your view, does either offer cogent criticisms of the other's views? Are there any elements of the Hobbesian form of government Macalay would accept? Defend your answers.

Notes

1. Although Hobbes is best remembered for his work on political philosophy, he wrote extensively on ethics, political science, history, theology, philosophical anthropology, and geometry.

2. Contemporary philosopher John Rawls, for example, defends a version of the social contract theory that utilizes the notion of "a state of nature" that is testimony to the enduring significance of Hobbes's political philosophy, John Rawls, *A Theory of Justice* (Boston: Harvard University Press, 1971).

3. Catherine Villanueva Gardner, "Macaulay as Philosopher," in her book *Rediscovering Women Philosophers: Philosophical Genre and the Boundaries of Philosophy* (Boulder, CO: Westview, 2000), 17–46.

4. Gardner, "Macaulay as Philosopher," 17.

5. Gardner, "Macauley as Philosopher," 17–18.

6. Mary Ellen Waithe, "Macaulay as Philosopher," in *A History of Women Philosophers*, vol. 3, *Modern Women Philosophers 1600–1900*, ed. Mary Ellen Waithe (Dordrecht, The Netherlands: Kluwer Academic Publisher, 1991), 219.

7. Thomas Hobbes, *Leviathan*, ed. Edwin Curley (Indianapolis, IN: Hackett, 1994), lix, 74–82, 89, 106–10, 191–92, 203–6. Reprinted by permission of Penguin Group Ltd.

8. Catharine Macaulay, *Letters on Education with Observations on Religious and Metaphysical Subjects 1790* (New York: Woodstock Books, 1994), Part 1, 9–14, Part 2, 235–39, 275–82. Excerpts are published with gratitude to Woodstock Books.

9. Johann P. Sommerville, *Thomas Hobbes* (New York: St. Martin's Press, 1992), 1.

10. Catharine Macaulay, *The History of England from the Accession of James I to that of the Brunswick Line*, vol. 5 (London: J. Nourse, 1771), 382; Macaulay, *The History of England from the Accession of James I to that of the Brunswick Line*, vol. 4 (London: J. Nourse, 1768), 418–19.

11. Thomas Hobbes, *Leviathan*, edited with introduction by Edwin Curley (Indianapolis, IN: Hackett, 1994), Introduction, lix.

12. See Lynne E. Withey, "Catharine Macaulay and the Uses of History: Ancient Rights, Perfectionism, and Propaganda," in *The Journal of British Studies* 16 (1976): 59–83.

13. Curley, xxi.

14. Hobbes, *Leviathan*, chapter xiii: 1.

15. Hobbes, *Leviathan*, chapter xiv: 4.

16. Macaulay is Lockean in denying the existence of innate moral principles and an interest in replacing them with an educated morality founded on reason. Macaulay is certainly drawing on Locke when she sees that moral principles are not universally applied, yet, unlike Locke, her focus is on asking why this is the case.

17. Macaulay, *Letters on Education*, part 2, letter xiii.

18. Withey, "Uses of History," 5.

19. Hobbes, *Leviathan*, xxviii:1.

20. Hobbes, *Leviathan*, xxviii:3.

21. Hobbes, *Leviathan*, xxviii:4.

22. Curley, xxxvii.

23. Curley, xxxvii.

24. *Loose Remarks on Certain Positions* to be found in Mr. Hobbes's "Philosophical Rudiments of Government and Society," with a Short Sketch of a Democratical Form of Government, In a Letter to Signor Paoli (London, 1767), 30.

25. See Bridget Hill, *The Republican Virago* (Oxford: Clarendon Press, 1992), 175–76.

26. Macaulay cites particular passages from *De Cive*. Where relevant, parallel passages from *Leviathan* will be footnoted.

27. See Hobbes, *Leviathan*, xviii:14, 16, 18; xx:14.

28. See Hobbes, *Leviathan*, chapter xvii.

CHAPTER 7

Locke and Masham

Introduction by *Karen J. Warren*

This chapter's philosophical pair, John Locke (1632–1704) and Damaris Cudworth Masham (1659–1708), address the topic of the relationship between reason and faith. While this topic is not one most frequently identified with Locke, it provides an opportunity to discuss a different aspect of Locke's philosophy than usual, and one that fits pairing Locke with Masham.

This introduction provides two different contexts for understanding Locke's and Masham's positions on the relation between reason and faith (and religion, revelation, morality, and education). One context is the rationalism versus empiricism debate, which framed epistemological debates during the modern period of philosophy (roughly, from Descartes to Kant); the other context is the Divine Command Theory (DCT) that raises very different concerns and provides an alternative context for understanding the views of Locke, Masham, and ultimately Lois Frankel's commentary.

LOCKE

John Locke was born in Somerset, England, to puritan parents. In 1646, at age fourteen, he enrolled at Westminster School, where his introduction to philosophy focused on Descartes. As a junior he transferred to Christ Church, Oxford in 1652, where he had a home for more than thirty years. He graduated in 1656 and obtained a master's degree in 1658. Although he never earned the degree of doctor of medicine, he received a bachelor of medicine in 1674 and served as a private physician for many years. After a self-imposed exile in Holland, he returned to England in 1688. His arrival back in England marks the beginning of the publication of his most well-known works: *Essay Concerning Human Understanding* (henceforth, *Essay*) (1690), the *Two Treatises of Civil Government* (1690), and *A Letter Concerning Toleration* (1689). Locke's political philosophy, defense of liberalism, social contract theory, and advocacy of the right to private property profoundly influenced the framing of the U.S. Constitution and Declaration of Independence.

Locke met Damaris Cudworth in 1682, became friends with Isaac Newton and Robert Boyle, and joined the Royal Society. After Damaris Cudworth married Sir Francis Masham, she invited him to join her at the family's country house in Essex, where he remained until he died.

MASHAM

Little is known about the early life and education of Damaris Masham, the daughter of the Cambridge Platonist Ralph Cudworth, Master of Christ's College, Cambridge. Her family had a considerable library and she learned French and taught herself Latin later in life, using the method recommended in Locke's *Some Thoughts Concerning Education*. (No women of her time were permitted access to higher educational institutions.) By the time she met Locke at age twenty-three in 1682, she was already interested in philosophy. In 1685, she married widower Sir Francis Masham who had nine children; they had one son.

Soon after Masham met Locke, they were involved in a romantic relationship, revealed through their earliest letters, written under the *noms de plume* Philoclea and Philander. But before long it was their intellectual friendship that carried their relationship.

Masham's two books, *A Discourse Concerning the Love of God* (1696) and *Occasional Thoughts in Reference to a Virtuous or Christian Life* (1705), were printed anonymously. Both books expressed sufficiently Lockean views that some attributed their authorship to him.[1] Her works also included her correspondence with Locke, about forty letters, and the first published biography on Locke. Locke wrote of Masham:

> The lady herself is so well versed in theological and philosophical studies and of such an original mind, that you will not find many men to whom she is not superior in wealth of knowledge and ability to profit by it. Her judgment is excellent, and I know few who can bring such clearness of thought to bear upon the most abstruse subjects, or such capacity for searching through and solving the difficult questions beyond the range, I do not say of most women, but even of most learned men. From reading, to which she once devoted herself with much assiduity, she is not to a great extent debarred by the weakness of her eyes, but this defect is abundantly supplied by the keenness of her intellect.[2]

THE FIRST CONTEXT: THE RATIONALISM VERSUS EMPIRICISM CONTROVERSY

The first context for understanding Locke's and Masham's views on the relationship between reason and faith (religion) is in terms of the rationalism versus empiricism debate concerning the sources and kinds of knowledge. One way to define the debate is to appeal to terminology introduced later, at the end of the modern period, by Kant (see chapter 10). Regarding (1) *what* is known (knowable), Kant distinguished between "synthetic" claims about the sensory world and "analytic" claims about mathematics, logic, and definitions. Regarding (2) *how* something is known (knowable), Kant distinguished between "*a poste-*

riori" claims based on sense perception and *"a priori"* claims based on "reason alone." Both *a priori* and *a posteriori* claims require that one have experience of the sensory world, but *a priori* claims are justified (proven, verified) by appeal to reason, not sensory information.

These Kantian distinctions generate four possible types of knowledge claims, given in diagram 7.1.

Rationalists and empiricists agree that there are analytic *a priori* and synthetic *a posteriori* truths, represented by the two boxes demarcated "Yes." And both agree that there are no analytic *a posteriori* truths, represented by the "No" box. What they disagree about is whether there any synthetic *a priori* truths. Rationalists (Descartes, Spinoza. Leibniz) answer yes, while empiricists (Locke, Berkeley, Hume) answer no. Their disagreement is represented by the box with the question mark. So Kant's question "Is there any synthetic *a priori* knowledge?" provides a useful way to distinguish rationalism from empiricism, while pinpointing the central issue that divides them.

Given Locke's reputation as a leading empiricist of the modern period, one could appeal to Lockean empiricism in order to try to understand both Locke's and Masham's views about the relationship between reason and faith.[3] They both claimed: (1) It is rational to be religious and religion should be rational; (2) Reason and faith together are necessary for knowledge of moral principles; (3) Any expressions of faith that fly in the face of reason are examples of religious fanaticism; (4) Religious belief must conform to the requirements of rationality; (5) The proper use of reason should support religious faith; (6) Revelation may provide rational grounds for belief, but no revelation can be contrary to reason; (7) The role of reason in religious matters includes the relationship between religion and morality; and (8) It is part of one's religious duty to make good use of and be governed by reason.

What do these claims mean? Is Lockean empiricism a helpful context for understanding these claims? That question is not easy to answer. Consider why.

In his *Essay* Locke advances the empiricist principle that all knowledge is founded in and derived from experience. Experience is the source of all ideas—which are either sensations or reflections—and of all knowledge. Locke's famous claim is that the mind is a *tabula rasa* (a blank slate); there are no innate ideas. However, in *Essay*, Locke also makes other claims about the relationship between reason, religion, and morality that seem to conflict with both his empiricism and claims (1)–(8). For example, Locke also claimed that: (9) Morality is capable of demonstration in the same way that mathematics is; (10) We can demonstrate God's existence from our intuitive knowledge of our own

Diagram 7.1. Claims about What Is Known or Knowable.

(Claims about *what* is known or knowable)

↓

	Analytic	Synthetic
A priori	YES	?
A posteriori	NO	YES

A priori
↑
A posteriori
↑

**(Claims about *how* something
is known or knowable)**

existence (from self-reflection); (11) Natural law can be shown to be true by reason alone (a view Masham denied in *Occasional Thoughts*); and (12) We have intuitive knowledge of our own existence (a view similar to Descartes's). Yet claims (9)–(12) seem to be ones a rationalist—not an empiricist like Locke—would make. So how does one reconcile the apparent inconsistency between a rationalist slant to claims (9)–(12), with an empiricist interpretation of claims (1)–(8)?

Appeal to Locke's definitions of reason and faith are not much help. In *Essay*, Locke defines reason as "the discovery of certainty or probability of such propositions or truth, which the mind arrives at by deduction made from such ideas which it has got by the use of its natural faculties, namely, by sensation or reflection" (IV.xviii.2). He claims this (13) reason cannot discern whether a revelation is true or false, but (14) revelation cannot be accepted if it conflicts with evidence provided by reason. Locke defines faith as the acceptance of revelation; so (15) faith cannot be accepted without evidentiary support of reason. These three additional claims suggest that reason can discover with certainty claims deduced only from experience—the sort of claim a rationalist makes and an empiricist denies—that reflect a commitment to the existence of synthetic *a priori* truths. Is Locke, the empiricist, offering such "certain claims" as examples of synthetic *a priori* truths? James Clapp claims: "An effort can be made to reconcile Locke's empiricism and his rationalism, his grounding of all ideas and knowledge in experience and his going beyond experience to the existence of things."[4] Minimally Clapp's claim is striking for its historically anomalous construal of Locke as both an empiricist and a rationalist. Yet it appears from Locke's commitment to claims (1)–(12) that he does straddle (if not just inconsistently hold) the two historically opposed positions when it comes to describing the relation between reason and faith (religion, morality). It is worth considering whether there is a different way to understand Locke's (and Masham's) views on reason, religion, and morality than through the lens of empiricism and rationalism.

THE SECOND CONTEXT: THE DIVINE COMMAND THEORY

In Plato's *Euthyphro*, Socrates asks, "What is piety?" The character Euthyphro proposes several answers, one of which involves an early statement of the Divine Command Theory (DCT) of ethics. Euthyphro says: "Piety is what all the gods love, and impiety is what all the gods hate." Socrates then asks Euthyphro, "Do the gods love piety because it is pious, or it is pious because they love it?" A modernized version of Socrates's question might be stated this way: "Does God command right acts because they are right, or are right acts right because God commands them?" In her commentary, Frankel states Socrates's question this way: "Are God's commands good for us simply because God commands it and will enforce those commands, or does God command it because, in God's omniscience, God knows better than we what is good for us?"

Socrates's basic question permits three different types of answers. The first is (1) God commands something, X, and therefore X is right (or good for us). The second is (2) X is right (or good for us) and therefore God commands X. The third combines the two claims: (3) God commands something, X, if and only if, X is right (or good for us).[5]

The main difference among the three is this: (1) asserts that ultimately it is God's commanding something that makes it right (or good for us); (2) asserts that what is right (or good for us), exists first, so to speak, and God, being all-knowing and all-good, picks out those acts that are right and commands them. (3) is the conjunction of (1) and (2) taken together. If one assumes that one ought to do what God commands, then all three answers imply that one ought to do X. But only (1) makes God's commanding X—a claim in the realm of religion—the basic ground (basis, reason, justification) for X as right (or good for us)—a claim in the realm of philosophy.

Which answer constitutes a statement of DCT? The weaker but common version of DCT is (1); the stronger version is (3). Only (2) is not, by itself, a statement of DCT, since (2) locates God's knowledge of what is right (or good for us) in some external standard of rightness for goodness, perhaps some universal ethic, rule, or principle, that is logically prior to God's nature. By contrast, in (1) God is the source of right acts (or goodness).

Notice several things about DCT, construed—for our purposes—as (1). The first is that DCT asserts that the relationship between morality (ethics) and religion is necessary (i.e., not merely accidental or contingent); ultimately it locates (philosophical) ethics or morality in religion. The second is that, if one is obligated to do whatever God commands, then one presumably would assume that God is rational (not evil or capricious or indifferent). Otherwise, one would not have good reason (rational justification) to do whatever God wills. The third is that many religious believers reject DCT, but accept claim (2). A Christian, for example, may have faith in the will of an existent God and faith that one should do what God commands, yet claim that such faith must be based in (justified by, inseparable from) reason—and that the ultimate reason is given by humans figuring out for themselves what makes right acts right (or what makes what is good for us good). Furthermore, the religious believer who accepts (2) but rejects DCT may believe that humans have free will, which we must exercise by *choosing* to do what God commands on the basis of *reason* (or, for *good reasons*)—not blindly, unthinkingly, habitually, or from mere obedience, faith, or revelation that is not supported by reason. So a religious believer might believe it rational to follow God's commands only when or after one uses reason to ascertain what makes things right, good for us, virtuous, or conducive to human happiness—answer (2).

Is the Divine Command Theory a more fruitful context than the rationalism-empiricism context, for understanding Locke's and Masham's claims that reason and faith are intimately connected? Consider the reasons it may well be. First, they are Christian philosophers whose response to Socrates's question seems clearly to be answer; (2) second, the DCT context does not in any obvious way generate the worry about the internal inconsistency of claims (1)–(15) that Lockean empiricism did; third, using Lockean empiricism to understand claims (1)–(15) strongly suggested some inconsistencies with the attribution of empiricism to Locke—inconsistencies that arose from Locke's apparently empiricist bent on some issues and rationalist bent on others; finally, discussion of the Divine Command Theory, especially why religious believers (like Locke and Masham) might reject the DCT but accept (2), offers a context that sets up and supports Frankel's commentary in a way the rationalism versus empiricism context does not.

FRANKEL'S COMMENTARY

Frankel's commentary addresses four topics: Locke's and Masham's approach to the relationship between faith and reason; Masham's argument for the improvement of educational opportunities for women and girls; Locke and Masham's shared view that reason, religion, and education are important in motivating people to be virtuous (and happy); and those aspects of Masham's writing that suggest she was a feminist. Consider now the difference it could make to one's understanding of the primary texts, as well as Frankel's commentary, whether one reads this pair in the context of the rationalism versus empiricism debate or the Divine Command Theory.

Excerpts of Writings by Locke and Masham

I. EXCERPTS FROM MASHAM'S *OCCASIONAL THOUGHTS IN REFERENCE TO A VIRTUOUS CHRISTIAN LIFE*[6]

Nor is any thing more obvious to observe than the power of education . . .

. . . and even the most solicitous about it, have usually employed their care here-in but by halves with respect to the Principal Part in so great a concernment; for the information and improvement of the Understanding be useful Knowledge, (a thing highly necessary to the right regulation of the Manners) is commonly very little thought of in reference to one whole Sex . . . But to this omission in respect of one Sex, it is manifestly very much to be attributed, that that pains which is often bestowed upon the other, does so frequently, as it does, prove ineffectual: Since the actual assistance of Mothers, will (generally speaking) be found necessary to the right forming of the Minds of their Children of both sexes.

Those Notions, or Ideas of Virtue, and consequent Rules of Action, which are usually given to such young Persons, do rarely carry along with them an entire conviction of their Truth and Reasonableness: Whence if these Instructions at any time happen strongly to cross the Inclinations of those to whom they are given, it will appear rational to question their solidity: And when Principles that thwart People's passions or interests, come once to be doubted of by them, it is great odds, that they will sooner be slighted, than better examined.

Now, this want of apparent Truth and Reasonableness, is not only where the Notions and Precepts given, are in themselves such as either in Whole, or in Part, are not True or Rational; but also (oftentimes) where they are altogether conformable to right Reason. In these cases, the want of apparent Reasonableness, proceeds from a defect of such antecedent knowledge in those who are designed to be instructed, as is necessary to the seeing their Reasonableness of the Instructions given them. That is to say, to their discerning the conformity with, or evident deduction of such instructions from some Truths which are unquestioned by them: the which should be the Principles of True Religion, so clearly made out to them as to be by them acknowledged for Verities. Religion being (as I shall take it at present for granted) the only sufficient ground or solid support of Virtue. For the belief of a Superior, Omnipotent Being, inspecting our Actions, and who will Reward or Punish us accordingly, is in all Men's Apprehensions the strangest, and in

Truth the only stable and irresistible Argument for submitting our Desires to a constant Regulation, wherein it is that Virtue does consist.

How far Natural Religion alone is sufficient for this, is very fit to be considered. But I conclude that among us, there are few who pretend to recommend Virtue, but who do so either with no respect at all to Religion and upon principles purely Humane, or else with reference to the Christian Religion. The first of these, it is already said, will be ineffectual; and it is no less certain that the Christian Religion cannot be a solid Foundation for Virtue, where Virtue being inculcated upon the Declarations of the Gospel, those who are thus instructed, are not convinced of the Authority and Evidence of that Revelation; which but too commonly is the Case. Instructors, instead of Teaching this necessary previous knowledge of Religion, generally, supposing it to be already in them whom they instruct, who in reality neither have it, or have ever been so before-hand taught, as to make it a Reasonable presumption that they should have it. Whence all the endeavors of making them Virtuous in consequence of their Christianity, are but attempting to raise a real superstructure upon an only imaginary foundation. For Truths received upon any other Ground than their own evidence, though they may, perhaps, find entertainment, yet will never gain to themselves a sure hold upon the mind. And so soon as they become troublesome, are in great danger of being questioned, whereby whatever is built upon them, must be likewise liable to be suspected for fallacious. And however empty Declamations do oftentimes make livelier impressions upon young people than substantial Reasoning. Yet these impressions are, for the most part, easily effaced, and especially are so out of their Minds who naturally are the most capable of the right Reason. As among other instances appears in this, that profane Wits do often even rally Women of the Best Parts (Religiously Bred as they call it) out of their Duty. These not seeing (as they should have been early taught to do) that what they have learned to be their Duty is not grounded upon the uncertain and variable Opinion of Men, but the unchangeable Nature of things; and has an indissolvable connection with their Happiness or Misery.

It is yet true that many who have Learned, and who well remember long Catechisms, with all their pretended Proofs, are so far from having that knowledge which Rational Creatures ought to have of a Religion they profess to Believe that they can only be saved by, as that they are not able to say, either what this Religion does consist in, or why it is they Believe it; and are so little instructed by their catechisms, as that, oftentimes, they understand not so much as the very terms they have Learned in them. And more often find the Propositions there in contained, so short in the Information of their ignorance; or so unintelligible to their Apprehensions; or so plainly contradictory of the most obvious Dictates of common sense; that Religion (for the which they never think of looking beyond these systems) appears to them indeed a thing not Built upon, or defensible by Reason. In consequence of which opinion, the weakest attacks made against it, must needs render such persons (at the least) wavering in their Belief of it. Whence those Precepts of Virtue, which they have received as bottomed thereon, are, in a time wherein Skepticism and Vice, pass for wit and Gallantry, necessarily brought under the suspicion of having no solid Foundation; and the recommenders thereof, are Guilty either of Ignorance, or Artifice.

But the not making Young People understand their Religion, is a fault not peculiar in regard to the instruction of one Sex alone, and any otherwise than as considered in its consequences; whereby (ordinarily speaking) Women do the most inevitably suffer; as not having the advantage (at least early enough) of Correcting Ignorance, or Errors of their childhood that Men have.

The other thing which I imagine faulty, does more peculiarly concern the Sex, but is it chiefly practiced in regard of Those of it who are of Quality, and that is, the insinuating into them such Notion of Honor as if the praise of Men ought to be the supreme object of their desires, and the great Motive with them to Virtue: A term which when applied to women is rarely designed, by some people, to signify any thing but the single Virtue of Chastity.

It is indeed only Rational Fear of God, and desire to approve our selves to him, that will teach us in all things, uniformly to live as becomes out Reasonable Nature; to enable us to do which must needs be the greatest business and end of a Religion which comes from God.

But how differently from this has the Christian Religion been represented by those who place it in useless Speculations, Empty Forms, or Superstitious Performances? The Natural Tendency of which things being to persuade Men that they may please God at a cheaper Rate than by the Denial of their Appetites, and the Mortifying of their Irregular Affections, these Misrepresentations of a pretended divine Revelation have been highly prejudicial to Morality: and thereby, been also a great occasion of Skepticism; for the obligation to virtue being loosened, Men easily become Vicious; which when once they are, the Remorse of their consciences bringing them to desire that there should be no future reckoning for their actions; and even that there should be no God to take any cognizance of them; they often come (in some degree at least) to be persuaded both of the one, and the other of these. And thus, many times, there are but a few steps between a zealous Bigot, and an infidel to all Religion.

Skepticism, or rather Infidelity, is the proper Disease of our Age, and has proceeded from diverse causes: But be the remoter of original ones what they will, it could never have prevailed as it has done, had not Parents very generally contributed thereto, either by negligence of their children's instruction; or Instructing them very ill in respect to Religion.

But it being sufficiently obvious that want of Instruction concerning Religion does in a Skeptical age dispose Men to Skepticism and Infidelity, which often terminates in downright Atheism; let us see whether, or no, Ill, by which I mean all irrational Instruction in regard of Religion, has not the same Tendency.

Reason ought to be Rational Creatures the Guide of Men's Belief. That is to say, that their Assent to any thing, ought to be governed by that proof of its Truth, whereof Reason is the Judge; be it either Argument, or Authority, for in both cases Reason must determine our Assent according to the validity of the Ground it finds it Built on. By Reason being here understood that Faculty in us which discovers, by the intervention of intermediate Ideas, what connection those in the Proposition have one with another. Whether certain; probable; or none at all; according whereunto, we ought to regulate our Assent.

Authority yet is not hereby so subjected to Reason, as that a Proposition which we see not the Truth of, may not nevertheless be Rationally assented to by us. For though Reason cannot from the Evidence of the thing itself induce out assent to any proposition, where we cannot perceive the connection of the ideas therein contained; yet if it appears that such a proposition was truly revealed by God, nothing can be more rational than to

Believe it. Since we know that God can neither deceive, nor be deceived: That there are Truths above our conception, and that God may (if he so pleases) communicate these to us by supreme revelation.

The part of Reason then, in regard of such a proposition as this, is, only to examine whether it be indeed a Divine Revelation: which should Reason not attest to the Truth of; it is then evidently Irrational to give or require assent to it as being so.

And as plainly Irrational must it be to give or require assent to anything as a Divine Revelation which is evidently contrary to Reason; no less being, herein implied than that God has made us so as to see clearly that to be a Truth, which is yet a Falsehood; the which, were it so, would make the Testimony of our Reason useless to us; and thereby destroy also the Credit of all revelation; for no stronger proof can be had of the Truth of any revelation that the evidence of our Reason that it is a revelation.

Now if the Christian Religion be very often represented as teaching Doctrines clearly contrary to Reason; or as exacting belief of what we can neither perceive the Truth of, nor do find to be revealed by Christ, or his Apostles: And, (what is still more) that this pretended Divine Religion does even conflict in such a Belief as this, so that a Man cannot be a Christian without believing what he neither from Arguments or Authority has any Ground for Believing; what must the Natural Consequence of this be upon all who ever so little consult their Reason, when in riper years they come to reflect hereupon, but to make them recall, and suspend, at least, their assent to the Truth of a Religion that appears to them thus irrational? Since an irrational Religion can never Rationally be conceived to come from God.

And if Men once come to call into question such Doctrines as (though but upon slender grounds for it) they had received for unquestionable Truths of Religion, they are ordinarily more likely to continue Skeptics or to proceed to an entire disbelief of this Religion, than to take occasion from hence to make a just search after its Verity.

Irrational Instruction concerning Religion, as well as want of Instruction, disposes to Skepticism. And this being so, what wonder can it be that Skepticism having once become fashionable, should continue so? the un-instructed, and the ill-instructed, making by so great odds, the Majority.

Instead of having their Reasonable Inquiries satisfied, and encouraged, Children are ordinarily rebuked for making any. From whence, not daring in a short time to question anything that is taught them in reference to Religion, they . . . are brought to say, that they do Believe whatever their teachers tell them they must Believe; whilst in Truth they remain in an ignorant unbelief, which exposes them to be seduced by the most pitiful arguments of the Atheistical, or of such as are disbelievers of revealed Religion.

The Foundation of all Religion is the belief of a God; or of a Maker and a Governor of the World; the evidence of which, being visible in everything; and the general Profession having usually stamped it with awe upon Children's minds, they ought perhaps most commonly be supposed to Believe this, rather than have doubts raised in them by going about to prove it to them: because those who are incapable of long deductions of Reason, or attending to a train of Arguments, not finding the force thereof when offered to prove what they had always taken for a clear, and obvious verity, would be rather taught thereby to suspect that a Truth which they had hitherto looked on as unquestionable, might rationally be doubted of, than be any ways confirmed in the belief of it. But if any doubts concerning the Existence of God, do arise in their minds, when they own this, or that. This can be discovered by discoursing with them: such doubts should always be endeavored to be removed by the most solid Arguments of which children are capable. Nor should they ever be rebuked for having those doubts; since not giving leave to look into the grounds of asserting any Truth, whatever it may be, can never be the way to establish that Truth in any rational mind; but, on the contrary, must be very likely to raise a suspicion that it is not well grounded.

The belief of a Deity being entertained; what should be first taught us should be what we are in the first place concerned to know. Now it is certain that what we are in the first place concerned to know is that which is necessary to our Salvation; and it is as certain that whatever God has made necessary to our Salvation, we are at the same time capable of knowing. All Instruction therefore which obtrudes upon any one as necessary to their salvation, what there cannot understand of see the evidence of, is to that person, wrong instruction; and when any such unintelligible, or unevident propositions are delivered to children as if they were so visible Truths that a Reason, or proof of them was not to be demanded by them, what effect can this produce in their minds but to teach them betimes to silence and suppress their Reason; from whence they have afterwards no Principle of virtue left; and their practices as well as opinions, must needs (as is the usual consequence hereof) become exposed to the conduct of their own, or other Men's fancies?

The existence of God being acknowledged as a Truth so early received by us, and so evident to our Reason, that it looks like Natural Inscription; the Authority of that revelation by which God has made known his Will to men, is to be firmly established in People's minds upon its clearest, and most rational evidence; and consequently they are then to be referred to the Scriptures themselves, to see therein what it is that God requires of them to Believe and to do; the great obligation they are to under diligently to study these divine oracles being duly represented to them. But to exhort any one to search the Scriptures to the end of seeing therein what God requires of him, before he is satisfied that the Scriptures are a revelation form God, cannot be rational: since any ones saying that the Scriptures are God's Word, cannot satisfy a rational and inquisitive Mind that they are so.

These two things, viz. a rational assurance of the Divine Authority of the Scriptures, and a liberty of fairly examining them, are absolutely necessary to the satisfaction of any rational person, concerning the certainty of the Christian Religion, and what it is that this Religion does consist in.

How dangerous a thing then is such instruction in Religion, as it teaches nothing unless it be to stifle the suggestions of our natural light? But that such instruction as this is all that the far greatest number of people have, there is too much ground to conclude, from the visible Ignorance even of the most of Those who are Zealous in some Profession of Christian Faith, and Worship.

It is a good question in the same Catechism; how doth it appear the Scriptures are the word of God? But who would imagine that for the information of anyone who wanted to be informed herein, it should be answered, That the Scriptures manifest themselves to be the Word of God by their Majesty and Purity: by the consent of all the Parts, and by the scope of the whole; which is to give all Glory to God: by their Light and Power to convince, and convert Sinners; to comfort and build up Believers to Salvation: but the Spirit of God bearing witness by and with the Scriptures, in the Heart of Man is alone able fully to persuade that they are the very word of God. One would almost be tempted to suspect that men who talked thus, were not themselves thoroughly persuaded that the Scriptures were indeed the word of God; for how is it possible not only for a Young boy, or Girl, but even for an Indian Man, or woman, to be by this answer more convinced than they were before, of the Scriptures being what they are pretended to be?

The Instruction then of most young peoples younger years being such as we have seen in regard of Religion: and Virtue, viz. The right regulation of you passions and Appetites, having (as has been above said) no other sufficient enforcement than the Truths of Religion; can it Reasonably be thought strange, that there is so little Virtue in the World as we find there is or that correspondently to their principles, peoples actions generally are (at best) unaccountable to their Reason? For time, and more years, if they give strength to our judgments whereby we may be thought able to inform our selves, and correct the errors and defects of our education, give also strength to our passions; which grow strong, do furnish and suggest principles suited to the purposes and ends that they propose; besides, that Ill Habits once settled are hardly changed by the force of any principles of which Reason may come to convince men at their riper age: A Truth very little weighed; though nothing ought more to be so with respect to a virtuous Education; since rational Religion, so soon as they are capable of knowing any other reason for what they are taught to do, than that it is the will of those who have a just power over them that they should do so. For as without a Knowledge of the Truths of Religion, we should want very often sufficient motives, and encouragements to submit our Passions and Appetites to the government of Reason; so without early Habits established of denying our Appetites, and restraining our inclinations, and the Truths of Religion will operate but upon a very few, so far as they ought to do.

By Religion I understand still revealed Religion. For though without the help of revelation, the commands of Jesus Christ (two positive Institutions only excepted) are as dictates likewise of Nature, discoverable by the light of Reason; and are no less the law of God to rational Creatures than the injunctions of revelation are; yet few would actually discern this Law of Nature in its full extent, merely by the light of Nature; or if they did would find the enforcement thereof a sufficient balance to that natural love of present pleasure which often opposes our compliance therewith; since before we come to such a ripeness of understanding as to be capable by unassisted Reason to discover from the Nature of things the just measures of our actions, together with the obligations we are under to comply therewithal; an evil indulgence of our inclinations has commonly established habits in us too strong to be overruled by the force of arguments; especially were they are not of very obvious deduction. Whence it may justly be inferred that the Christian Religion is the alone universally adapted means of making men truly virtuous; the law of Reason or the eternal rule of rectitude being in the word of God only, to those of all capacities, plainly, and authoritatively delivered as the Law of God, duly enforced by Rewards and Punishments.

Yet in that Conformity with, and necessary support which our Religion brings to the law of Reason, or Nature, that is to say, to those dictates which are the result of the determinate and unchangeable constitution of things (and which as being discoverable to us by our rational faculties, are therefore sometimes called the law of Reason, as well as the law of Nature) Christianity does most conspicuously and evidently appear to be a divine Religion; viz. to be from the author of Nature; however incongruous some men may fancy it to be for God supernaturally to reveal to men what is naturally discoverable to them by those faculties he has given them: The which conceit together with not considering, or rightly weighing the enforcements which natural Religion needs, and receives from revelation, has very much disposed many to reject revealed Religion. Whereunto such notions of Christianity as agree not to the Attributes of an Infinitely wise and good being which Reason teaches the first cause of all things to be, have also not a little contributed; for from hence many Men, zealous for the honor of God and lovers of Mankind, have been prejudiced against the Truth of the Christian Religion: In consequence whereof they have Reasonably concluded that there was no such thing as revealed Religion; and from thence have again inferred that men had no need thereof to the ends of natural Religion.

Those yet who think revelation to be needless in this regard, how well so ever they may, possibly, intend to Natural Religion, do herein entertain an Opinion that would undermine it: Experience showing us that natural light, unassisted by revelation, is insufficient to the ends of Natural Religion . . . But how far revelation is needful to assist natural light, will be the best seen in reflecting a little upon what we receive from each of these guides that God has given us.

And if it shall appear . . . that natural Religion has need of revelation to support it; and that the revelation which we have by Jesus Christ is exquisitely adapted to the end of enforcing Natural Religion; this will both be the highest confirmation possible, that to enforce Natural Religion or Morality, was the design of Christianity.

To see what light we receive from Nature to direct our actions, and how far we are Naturally able to obey that light; Men must be considered purely as in the state of Nature, viz. as having no intrinsic Law to direct them, but endued only with a faculty of comparing their distant ideas by intermediate ones, and thence of deducing, of inferring one thing from another; whereby our knowledge immediately received from sense, or reflection, is enlarged to a view of Truths remote, or future, in an application of which Faculty of the mind to a consideration of our own existence and Nature, together with the beauty and order of the universe, so far as it falls under our view, we may come to the knowledge of a First Cause; and that this must be an Intelligent Being, Wise and Powerful, beyond what we are able to conceive. And as we delight in our selves, and receive pleasure from the objects which surround us, sufficient to endear to us the possession and enjoyment of Life, we cannot from thence but infer, that this Wise and Powerful Being is also most Good, since he has made us out of nothing to give us a Being wherein we find such happiness, as makes us very unwilling to pat therewith.

We being thus endued, as we are, with a capacity of perceiving and distinguishing these differences of Things; and also with a liberty of acting, of not, suitably and agreeably hereunto; whence we can according to the preference of our own minds, act either in conformity to, or disconformity with, the Will of the Creator (manifested in his Works no less than the will of any humane architect is in his) it follows, that to act answerably to the Nature of such beings as we are requires that we attentively examine, and consider the several Natures of things, so far as they have any relation to our own actions.

Which attentive consideration of the Works of God objected to our views, implies an exercise thereupon of that Faculty in us by which we deduce, or infer, one thing from another: Whence (as has been said) our knowledge immediately derived to us from sensation, or reflection, is enlarged by the perception of remote, or distant Truths. The more obviously eminent advantages accruing to us from which faculty of Reason, plainly make known the Superiority of its Nature; and that its suggestions, ought to be hearkened to by us preferably to those of sense; where these (as it too often happens) do not concur. For did we know nothing by Inference and Deduction, both our knowledge and enjoyment would be very short of what they now are; many considerable pleasures depending almost entirely upon Reason; and there being none of the greatest enjoyments of sense which would not lose their best relish, separated from those concomitant satisfactions which accompany them only as we are rational creatures. Neither is it our greatest happiness alone which is manifestly provided for in our being induced with this faculty; but our much greater safety, and preservation likewise; since these require a capacity in us of foreseeing distant events, and directing many to an End, oftentimes through a long train of actions; which is what we can only do by that in us, whereby the relations, dependencies and consequences of things are discoverable to us.

But as Reason is that which either in kind of degree, differences Men from Brutes ... it is by common consent acknowledged that Reason is in respect of all other, a preferable endowment. And if Beasts, only inferior to Men in the advantages of the Faculty, appear hereby intended to be subjected to Men, it cannot be less evident that that part in men which they have in common with beasts, was likewise designed by their maker to be subjected to their Reason also. From all which it undeniably follows that we do not act answerably to the will, or pleasure of God, in making us such creatures as we are, if we either neglect the search of those Measures of our actions prescribed to us by the discernable Natures of things; of, if seeing these, we yet conform not ourselves thereunto.

Now for any Creature knowingly to oppose the will of its creator, is not only disingenuity in regard of what is owing from it to its sovereign benefactor, and folly in respect of that dependence which it has on him for its being, as it is commonly represented to us to be; but is also in the Nature of things (simply considered) so repugnant to right Reason, that were such a creature consistent with it self herein, and could act pursuantly to that will, it would operate to its own destruction; since its existence evidently depends upon that of its maker ... So that sin, or disobedience to our maker is manifestly the greatest Nonsense, folly and contradiction conceivable. With regard purely to the immutable perfection of the divine Nature, and to the Natural constitution of things, independently upon any positive command of God to us, or his irresistible power over us.

But as without a capacity in the Creature to act contrary to the will of the creator there could be no desert, or self-excellency in any created being; contrariety to the will of God is therefore permitted in the universe as a necessary result of Creaturely imperfection, under the greatest endowment that a created Being is capable of having, viz. That of Freedom or Liberty of Action: And as the constitution of such a creature, as this, implies that what is best in reference to the design of the creator, and of its own happiness, should not be always necessarily present to the mind as best; such a creature may oppose the will of his maker with various degrees of guilt in so doing; or (possibly) with none at all; for no agent can offend farther than he willfully abuses the freedom he has to act.

But God having made men so as that they find in themselves, very often, a liberty of acting according to the preferences of their own minds, it is incumbent upon them to study the will of their maker; in an application of the faculty of Reason which he has given them, to the consideration of the different respects, consequences, and dependencies of things, so as to discern from thence the just measures of their actions. . . . And these manifestations of God's will, thus discoverable to us, ought to be regarded by us, as his commands.

Yet however certain it is, that the dictates of Reason, or Nature, discernable by our natural faculties, are the commands of God to us, as rational creatures; it is equally true that the love of happiness (which consists in pleasure) is the earliest, and strongest principle of Human Nature; and therefore whatever measures Reason does, or might, prescribe, when particular occasions occur, the sentiment of what men find pleasing or displeasing to them, however contrary to those dictates of right Reason, is very apt to determine their choice. God yet who is the author of order, and not of confusion, has framed all things with consistency and harmony; and however, in Fact, it too often happens that we are misled by that strong desire of happiness implanted in us, yet does this no way necessarily interfere with our acting in an entire conformity to the prescriptions of the Law of Reason; but the contrary: for from hence it is that this law has its sanction, viz. that, duly considering it, we shall evidently find our happiness, and misery, are annexed to the observance, or neglect, of that unalterable rule of Rectitude, discoverable to us by the Nature of things; so that this rule of rectitude, or eternal will of God, has also the force of a law given to it by that inseparable accord that there is betwixt our happiness or misery, with our obedience, or disobedience, hereunto. Thus our duty and happiness, can never be divided, but when we prefer a less happiness to a greater; and therein act not conformably to the dictates of our natural desire of happiness, or pleasure; which two terms differ only in this, that we apply the term Pleasure to any agreeable sentiment, or sensation, how small, or short so ever in its duration; but that of Happiness, only to such degrees of pleasure, as do, in some considerable degree, out-balance our evils.

The gratification of our present desires and appetites, does sometimes for a short, or small pleasure, procure to us a greater, and more durable pain; and that on the contrary, the denial, or restraint of our present desires, and appetites, does sometimes for a short, or small pain, procure to us a greater, or more durable pleasure.

However true yet it is that happiness, or chief Good, does consist in pleasure; it is not less true that the irregular love of pleasure is a perpetual source to us of Folly, and misery. That we are liable to the which irregularity, is but a necessary result of our Creaturely imperfection: for we cannot love pleasure, and not love present pleasure: and the love of present pleasure it is which misleads our narrow, and inattentive Minds from a just comparison of the present, with what is future.

Religion has, I think, been rightly defined to be the knowledge how to please God, and thus taken, does necessarily include virtue, that is to say, Moral Rectitude; but as men have usually applied these terms Virtue and Religion, they stand for things very different and distinct, one from another. For by a virtuous man, in all countries of the world, or less societies of men, is commonly meant, by those who so call any one, such a man as steadily adheres to that Rule of his actions which is established for a rule in his country tribe, or society, be that what it will. Hence it has been that Virtue has in different time and places changed face; and sometimes so far, as that what has been esteemed virtuous in one Age, and in one country, has been looked upon as quite the contrary in others.

And how few parents are there of quality, even among such as are esteemed the most virtuous, who do not permit their daughters to pass the best part of their youth in that Ridiculous Circle of Diversions, which is pretty generally thought the proper business of young ladies; and which so engrosses them that they can find no spare hours, wherein to make any such improvements of their understanding, and the leisure which they have for it exacts from them as rational Creatures; or as is requisite of useful to the discharging well their present of future duties?

The improvements of Reason, however requisite to ladies for their accomplishment, as rational creatures; and however needful to them for the well educating of their children, and to their being useful in their families, yet re rarely any recommendation of them to men; who foolishly thinking, that money will answer to all things, so, for the most part, regard nothing else in the Woman they would marry: and not often finding what they do not look for, it would be no wonder if their offspring should inherit no more sense than themselves. But be Nature ever so kind to them in this respect, yet through want of cultivating the Talents she bestows upon those of the female sex, her bounty is usually lost upon them; and Girls, betwixt silly fathers and ignorant Mothers, are generally so brought up, that traditionary opinions are to them, all their lives long, instead of Reason. They are, perhaps, sometimes told in regard of what Religion exacts, that they must Believe and Do such and such things, because the word of God requires it; but they are not put upon searching the Scriptures for themselves, to see whatever, or no, these things are so; and they so little know why thy should look upon Scriptures to be the word of God, that but too often they are easily persuaded out of the reverence due to them as being so: and (if they happen to meet with such bad examples) are not seldom brought from thence, even to scoff at the Documents of their Education; and in consequence thereof, to have no Religion at all. Whilst others (naturally more disposed to be Religious) are either (as divers in the Apostles Days were) carried away with every wind of Doctrine, ever learning and never coming to the knowledge of the Truth; Weak, Superstitious, Useless Creatures; or else if more tenacious in their Natures, blindly and conceitedly wedded to the Principles and opinions of their Spiritual Guides. . . . But what is here said implying what ladies should so well understand their Religion, as to be able to answer both to such who oppose, and to such who misrepresent it; this may seem, perhaps, to require that they should have the Science of Doctors, and be well skilled in Theological Disputes and Controversies; than the Study of which I suppose there could scarce be found for them a more useless Employment. But whether such patrons of ignorance as know nothing themselves which they ought to know, will call it Learning, or not, to understand the Christian Religion, and the grounds of receiving it; it is evident that they who think so much knowledge, as that, to be needless for a woman, must either not be persuaded of the Truth of Christianity; or else must Believe that Women are not concerned to be Christians. For if Christianity be Religion from God, and women have Souls to be saved as well as men; to know what this Religion consists in, and to understand the grounds on which it is to be received, can be no more than necessary knowledge to a woman, as well as to a man: which necessary knowledge is sufficient to enable any one so far to answer to the opposers or corrupters of Christianity, as to secure them from the danger of being imposed upon by such Men's Argumentations; which is all that I have thought requisite for a lady; and not that she should be prepared to challenge every Adversary to Truth.

II. EXCERPTS FROM LOCKE'S
ESSAY CONCERNING HUMAN UNDERSTANDING[7]

Book 4, Chapter 18: Of Faith and Reason, and Their Distinct Provinces

It has been above shown, (1) That we are of necessity ignorant, and want knowledge of all sorts, where we want ideas. (2) That we are ignorant, and want rational knowledge where we want proofs. (3) That we want certain knowledge and certainty, as far as we want clear and determined specific ideas. (4) That we want probability to direct our assent in matters where we have neither knowledge of our own, nor testimony of other men, to bottom our reason upon.

From these things thus premised, I think we may come to lay down the measures and boundaries between faith and reason; the want whereof may possibly have been the cause, if not of great disorders, yet at least of great disputes, and perhaps mistakes in the world. For till it be resolved, how far we are to be guided by reason, and how far by faith, we shall in vain dispute, and endeavor to convince one another in matters of religion.

2. I find every sect, as far as reason will help them, make use of it gladly: And where it fails them, they cry out, it is matter of faith, and above reason. And I do not see how they can argue, with any one, or ever convince a gainsayer who makes use of the same plea, without setting down strict boundaries between faith and reason; which ought to be the first point established in all questions, where faith has any thing to do.

Reason therefore here, as contradistinguished to faith, I take to be the discovery of the certainty or probability of such propositions or truths, which the mind arrives at by deduction made from such ideas, which it has got by the use of its natural faculties; viz. by sensation or reflection.

Faith, on the other side, is the assent to any proposition, not thus made out by the deductions of reason; but upon the credit of the proposer, as coming from God, in some extraordinary way of communication. This way of discovering truths to men we call revelation.

3. First, then I say, that no man inspired by God can by any revelation communicate to others any new simple ideas, which they had not before from sensation or reflection. For whatsoever impressions he himself may have from the immediate hand of God, this revelation, if it be of new simple ideas, cannot be conveyed to another, either by words, or any other signs. . . . For words seen or heard, recall to our thoughts those ideas only, which to us they have been wont to be signs of; but cannot introduce any perfectly new, and formerly unknown simple ideas. . . . For our simple ideas then, which are the foundation and sole matter of all our notions and knowledge, we must depend wholly on our reason, I mean our natural faculties; and can by no means receive them, or any of them, from traditional revelation; I say, traditional revelation, in distinction to original revelation. By the one, I mean that first impression, which is made immediately by God, on the mind of any man, to which we cannot set any bounds; and by the other, those impressions delivered over to others in words, and the ordinary ways of conveying our conceptions one to another.

4. Secondly, I say, that the same truths may be discovered, and conveyed down from revelation, which are discoverable to us by reason, and by those ideas we naturally may have. So God might, by revelation, discover the truth of any proposition in Euclid; as well as men, by the natural use of their faculties, come to make the discovery themselves. In all things of this kind, there is little need or use of revelation, God having furnished us with natural and surer means to arrive at the knowledge of them. For whatsoever truth we come to the clear discovery of, from the knowledge and contemplation of our own ideas, will always be certainer to us than those which are conveyed to us by traditional revelation. For the knowledge we have, that this revelation came at first from God, can never be so sure, as the knowledge we have from the clear and distinct perception of the agree-

ment or disagreement of our own ideas; e.g. if it were revealed some ages since, that the three angles of a triangle were equal to two right ones, I might assent to the truth of that proposition, upon the credit of the tradition, that it was revealed; but that would never amount to so great a certainty as the knowledge of it, upon the comparing and measuring my own ideas of two right angles, and the three angles of a triangle. The like holds in matter of fact, knowable by our senses; e.g., the history of the deluge is conveyed to us by writings, which had their original from revelation: And yet nobody, I think, will say he has as certain and clear a knowledge of the flood, as Noah that saw it; or that he himself would have had, had he then been alive and seen it. For he has no greater an assurance than that of his senses, that it is writ in the book supposed writ by Moses inspired: But he has not so great an assurance that Moses writ that book, as if he had seen Moses write it. So that the assurance of its being a revelation is less still than the assurance of his senses.

5. In propositions, then, whose certainty is built upon the clear perception of the agreement or disagreement of our ideas, attained either by immediate intuition, as in self-evident propositions, or by evident deductions of reason in demonstrations, we need not the assistance of revelation, as necessary to gain our assent, and introduce them into our minds. Because the natural ways of knowledge could settle them there, or had done it already; which is the greatest assurance we can possibly have of any thing, unless where God immediately reveals it to us: And there too our assurance can be no greater than our knowledge is, that it is a revelation from God. But yet nothing, I think, can, under that title, shake or over-rule plain knowledge; or rationally prevail with any man to admit it for true, in a direct contradiction to the clear evidence of his own understanding. For since no evidence of our faculties, by which we receive such revelations, can exceed, if equal, the certainty of our intuitive knowledge, we can never receive for a truth any thing that is directly contrary to our clear and distinct knowledge: E.g., the ideas of one body and one place, do so clearly agree, and the mind has so evident a perception of their agreement, that we can never assent to a proposition, that affirms the same body to be in two distant places at once, however it should pretend to the authority of a divine revelation: Since the evidence, first, that we deceive not ourselves, in ascribing it to God; secondly, that we understand it right; can never be so great, as the evidence of our own intuitive knowledge, whereby we discern it impossible for the same body to be in two places at once. . . . In propositions therefore contrary to the clear perception of the agreement or disagreement of any of our ideas, it will be in vain to urge them as matters of faith. They cannot move our assent, under that or any other title whatsoever. For faith can never convince us of any thing that contradicts our knowledge. Because though faith be founded on the testimony of God (who cannot lye) revealing any proposition to us; yet we cannot have an assurance of the truth of its being a divine revelation, greater than our own knowledge: . . . For if the mind of man can never have a clearer (and perhaps not so clear) evidence of any thing to be a divine revelation, as it has of the principles of its own reason, it can never have a ground to quit the clear evidence of its reason, to give a place to a proposition, whose revelation has not a greater evidence than those principles have.

6. Thus far a man has use of reason, and ought to hearken to it, even in immediate and original revelation, where it is supposed to be made to himself: But to all those who pretend not to immediate revelation, but are required to pay obedience, and to receive the truths revealed to others, which by the tradition of writings, or word of mouth, are conveyed down to them; reason has a great deal more to do, and is that only which can

induce us to receive them. . . . Faith, as we use the word, (called commonly divine faith) has to do with no propositions, but those which are supposed to be divinely revealed. So that I do not see how those, who make revelation alone the sole object of faith, can say, that it is a matter of faith, and not of reason, to believe that such or such a proposition, to be found in such or such a book, is of divine inspiration; unless it be revealed, that that proposition, or all in that book, was communicated by divine inspiration. Without such a revelation, the believing, or not believing that proposition or book to be of divine authority, can never be matter of faith, but matter of reason; and such as I must come to an assent to, only by the use of my reason, which can never require or enable me to believe that which is contrary to itself: It being impossible for reason ever to procure any assent to that, which to itself appears unreasonable.

7. But, thirdly, there being many things, wherein we have very imperfect notions, or none at all; and other things, of whose past, present, or future existence, by the natural use of our faculties, we can have no knowledge at all; these, as being beyond the discovery of our natural faculties, and above reason, are, when revealed, the proper matter of faith. Thus, that part of the angels rebelled against God, and thereby lost their first happy state; and that the dead shall rise, and live again; these and the like, being beyond the discovery of reason, are purely matters of faith; with which reason has directly nothing to do.

8. But since God in giving us the light of reason has not thereby tied up his own hands from affording us, when he thinks fit, the light of revelation in any of those matters, wherein our natural faculties are able to give a probable determination; revelation, where God has been pleased to give it, must carry it against the probable conjectures of reason. Because the mind not being certain of the truth of that it does not evidently know, but only yielding to the probability that appears in it, is bound to give up its assent to such a testimony; which, it is satisfied, comes from one who cannot err, and will not deceive. But yet it still belongs to reason to judge of the truth of its being a revelation, and of the signification of the words wherein it is delivered. Indeed, if any thing shall be thought revelation, which is contrary to the plain principles of reason, and the evident knowledge the mind has of its own clear and distinct ideas; there reason must be hearkened to, as to a matter within its province: Since a man can never have so certain a knowledge, that a proposition which contradicts the clear principles and evidence of his own knowledge, was divinely revealed, or that he understands the words rightly wherein it is delivered; as he has, that the contrary is true: And so is bound to consider and judge of it as a matter of reason, and not swallow it, without examination, as a matter of faith.

9. First, whatever proposition is revealed, of whose truth our mind, by its natural faculties and notions, cannot judge; that is purely matter of faith, and above reason. Secondly, all propositions whereof the mind, by the use of its natural faculties, can come to determine and judge from naturally acquired ideas, are matter of reason; with this difference still, that in those concerning which it has but an uncertain evidence, and so is persuaded of their truth only upon probable grounds, which still admit a possibility of the contrary to be true, without doing violence to the certain evidence of its own knowledge, and overturning the principles of all reason; in such probable propositions, I say, an evident revelation ought to determine our assent even against probability. For where the principles of reason have not evidenced a proposition to be certainly true or false, there clear revelation, as another principle of truth, and ground of assent, may determine; and so it may be matter of faith, and be also above reason. Because reason, in that particular

matter, being able to reach no higher than probability, faith gave the determination where reason came short; and revelation discovered on which side the truth lay.

10. Thus far the dominion of faith reaches, and that without any violence or hindrance to reason; which is not injured or disturbed, but assisted and improved, by new discoveries of truth coming from the eternal fountain of all knowledge. Whatever God hath revealed is certainly true; no doubt can be made of it. This is the proper object of faith: But whether it be a divine revelation or no, reason must judge; which can never permit the mind to reject a greater evidence to embrace what is less evident, nor allow it to entertain probability in opposition to knowledge and certainty. There can be no evidence, that any traditional revelation is of divine original, in the words we receive it, and in the sense we understand it, so clear and so certain, as that of the principles of reason; and therefore nothing that is contrary to, and inconsistent with, the clear and self-evident dictates of reason, has a right to be urged or assented to as a matter of faith, wherein reason hath nothing to do. Whatsoever is divine revelation, ought to over-rule all our opinions, prejudices, and interest, and hath a right to be received with full assent. Such a submission as this, of our reason to faith, takes not away the land-marks of knowledge: This shakes not the foundations of reason, but leaves us that use of our faculties for which they were given us.

11. If the provinces of faith and reason are not kept distinct by these boundaries, there will, in matters of religion, be no room for reason at all; and those extravagant opinions and ceremonies that are to be found in the several religions of the world, will not deserve to be blamed. For, to this crying up of faith, in opposition to reason, we may, I think, in good measure ascribe those absurdities that fill almost all the religions which possess and divide mankind.

Book 4, Chapter 19: Of Enthusiasm

1. The evidence that any proposition is true (except such as are self-evident) lying only in the proofs a man has of it, whatsoever degrees of assent he affords it beyond the degrees of that evidence, it is plain that all the surplusage of assurance is owing to some other affection, and not to the love of truth. . . . In any truth that gets not possession of our minds by the irresistible light of self-evidence, or by the force of demonstration, the arguments that gain it assent are the vouchers and gage of its probability to us; and we can receive it for no other, than such as they deliver it to our understandings. Whatsoever credit or authority we give to any proposition, more than it receives from the principles and proofs it supports itself upon, is owing to our inclinations that way, and is so far a derogation from the love of truth as such: Which, as it can receive no evidence from our passions or interests, so it should receive no tincture from them.

3. Upon this occasion I shall take the liberty to consider a third ground of assent, which with some men has the same authority, and is as confidently relied on as either faith or reason; I mean enthusiasm: Which laying by reason, would set up revelation without it. Whereby in effect it takes away both reason and revelation, and substitutes in the room of it the ungrounded fancies of a man's own brain, and assumes them for a foundation both of opinion and conduct.

4. Reason is natural revelation, whereby the eternal father of light, and fountain of all knowledge, communicates to mankind that portion of truth which he has laid within

the reach of their natural faculties: Revelation is natural reason enlarged by a new set of discoveries communicated by God immediately, which reason vouches the truth of, by the testimony and proofs it gives, that they come from God. So that he that takes away reason, to make way for revelation, puts out the light of both, and does much-what the same, as if he would persuade a man to put out his eyes, the better to receive the remote light of an invisible star by a telescope.

5. Immediate revelation being a much easier way for men to establish their opinions and regulate their conduct, than the tedious and not always successful labor of strict reasoning, it is no wonder that some have been very apt to pretend to revelation, and to persuade themselves that they are under the peculiar guidance of heaven in their actions and opinions, especially in those of them which they cannot account for by the ordinary methods of knowledge and principles of reason. Hence we see that in all ages, men . . . have often flattered themselves with a persuasion of an immediate intercourse with the Deity, and frequent communications from the Divine Spirit.

6. Their minds being thus prepared, whatever groundless opinion comes to settle itself strongly upon their fancies, is an illumination from the spirit of God, and presently of divine authority: And whatsoever odd action they find in themselves a strong inclination to do, that impulse is concluded to be a call or direction from heaven, and must be obeyed; it is a commission from above, and they cannot err in executing it.

7. This I take to be properly enthusiasm, which, though founded neither on reason nor divine revelation, but rising from the conceits of a warmed or over-weening brain, works yet, where it once gets footing, more powerfully on the persuasions and actions of men, than either of those two, or both together: Men being most forwardly obedient to the impulses they receive from themselves; and the whole man is sure to act more vigorously, where the whole man is carried by a natural motion. For strong conceit, like a new principle, carries all easily with it, when got above common sense, and freed from all restraint of reason, and check of reflection, it is heightened into a divine authority, in concurrence with our own temper and inclination.

8. Though the odd opinions and extravagant actions enthusiasm has run men into, were enough to warn them against this wrong principle, so apt to misguide them both in their belief and conduct; yet the love of something extraordinary, the ease and glory it is to be inspired, and be above the common and natural ways of knowledge, so flatters many men's laziness, ignorance, and vanity, that when once they are got into this way of immediate revelation, of illumination without search, and of certainty without proof, and without examination, it is a hard matter to get them out of it. Reason is lost upon them, they are above it: They see the light infused into their understandings, and cannot be mistaken; it is clear and visible there, like the light of bright sunshine; shows itself, and needs no other proof but its own evidence: They feel the hand of God moving them within, and the impulses of the spirit, and cannot be mistaken in what they feel.

9. This is the way of talking of these men: They are sure, because they are sure: And their persuasions are right, because they are strong in them. For, when what they say is stripped of the metaphor of seeing and feeling, this is all it amounts to: And yet these similes so impose on them, that they serve them for certainty in themselves, and demonstration to others.

10. But to examine a little soberly this internal light, and this feeling on which they build so much. These men have, they say, clear light, and they see; they have awakened

sense, and they feel; this cannot, they are sure, be disputed them. For when a man says he sees or feels, nobody can deny it him, that he does so. But here let me ask: This seeing, is it the perception of the truth of the proposition, or of this, that it is a revelation from God? This feeling, is it a perception of an inclination or fancy to do something, or of the spirit of God moving that inclination? These are two very different perceptions, and must be carefully distinguished . . . So that the knowledge of any proposition coming into my mind, I know not how, is not a perception that it is from God. Much less is a strong persuasion, that it is true, a perception that it is from God, or so much as true. But however it be called light and seeing, I suppose it is at most but belief and assurance: And the proposition taken for a revelation, is not such as they know to be true, but take to be true. For where a proposition is known to be true, revelation is needless: And it is hard to conceive how there can be a revelation to any one of what he knows already. If therefore it be a proposition which they are persuaded, but do not know, to be true, whatever they may call it, it is not seeing, but believing. For these are two ways, whereby truth comes into the mind, wholly distinct, so that one is not the other. What I see I know to be so by the evidence of the thing itself: What I believe I take to be so upon the testimony of another: But this testimony I must know to be given, or else what ground have I of believing? I must see that it is God that reveals this to me, or else I see nothing. The question then here is, how do I know that God is the revealer of this to me; that this impression is made upon my mind by his Holy Spirit, and that therefore I ought to obey it? If I know not this, how great so ever the assurance is that I am possessed with, it is groundless; whatever light I pretend to, it is but enthusiasm. . . . For if I mistake not, these men receive it for true, because they presume God revealed it. Does it not then stand them upon, to examine upon what grounds they presume it to be a revelation from God? or else all their confidence is mere presumption: And this light, they are so dazzled with, is nothing but an ignis fatuus that leads them constantly round in this circle; it is a revelation, because they firmly believe it, and they believe it, because it is a revelation.

11. In all that is of divine revelation, there is need of no other proof but that it is an inspiration from God: For he can neither deceive nor be deceived. But how shall it be known that any proposition in our minds is a truth infused by God; a truth that is revealed to us by him, which he declares to us, and therefore we ought to believe? Here it is that enthusiasm fails of the evidence it pretends to. . . . If they say they know it to be true because it is a revelation from God, the reason is good: But then it will be demanded how they know it to be a revelation from God. If they say, by the light it brings with it, which shines bright in their minds, and they cannot resist: I beseech them to consider whether this be any more than what we have taken notice of already, viz. that it is a revelation, because they strongly believe it to be true. For all the light they speak of is but a strong, though ungrounded persuasion of their own minds, that it is a truth. . . . For if the light, which every one thinks he has in his mind, which in this case is nothing but the strength of his own persuasion, be an evidence that it is from God, contrary opinions have the same title to be inspirations; and God will be not only the father of lights, but of opposite and contradictory lights, leading men contrary ways; and contradictory propositions will be divine truths, if an ungrounded strength of assurance be an evidence, that any proposition is a divine revelation.

13. Light, true light, in the mind is, or can be nothing else but the evidence of the truth of any proposition; and if it be not a self-evident proposition, all the light it has,

or can have, is from the clearness and validity of those proofs, upon which it is received. To talk of any other light in the understanding is to put ourselves in the dark, or in the power of the Prince of darkness, and by our own consent to give ourselves up to delusion to believe a lie. For if strength of persuasion be the light, which must guide us; I ask how shall any one distinguish between the delusions of Satan, and the inspirations of the Holy Ghost?

14. God, when he makes the prophet, does not unmake the man. He leaves all his faculties in the natural state, to enable him to judge of his inspirations, whether they be of divine original or no. When he illuminates the mind with supernatural light, he does not extinguish that which is natural. If he would have us assent to the truth of any proposition, he either evidences that truth by the usual methods of natural reason, or else makes it known to be a truth which he would have us assent to, by his authority; and convinces us that it is from him, by some marks which reason cannot be mistaken in. Reason must be our last judge and guide in every thing. I do not mean that we must consult reason, and examine whether a proposition revealed from God can be made out by natural principles, and if it cannot, that then we may reject it: But consult it we must, and by it examine, whether it be a revelation from God or no. And if reason finds it to be revealed from God, reason then declares for it, as much as for any other truth, and makes it one of her dictates. Every conceit that thoroughly warms our fancies must pass for an inspiration, if there be nothing but the strength of our persuasions, whereby to judge of our persuasions: If reason must not examine their truth by something extrinsical to the persuasions themselves, inspirations and delusions, truth and falsehood, will have the same measure, and will not be possible to be distinguished.

15. If this internal light, or any proposition which under that title we take for inspired, be conformable to the principles of reason, or to the word of God, which is attested revelation, reason warrants it, and we may safely receive it for true, and be guided by it in our belief and actions; if it receive no testimony nor evidence from either of these rules, we cannot take it for a revelation, or so much as for true, till we have some other mark that it is a revelation, besides our believing that it is so. Thus we see the holy men of old, who had revelations from God, had something else besides that internal light of assurance in their own minds, to testify to them that it was from God. They were not left to their own persuasions alone, that those persuasions were from God; but had outward signs to convince them of the author of those revelations. And when they were to convince others, they had a power given them to justify the truth of their commission from heaven, and by visible signs to assert the divine authority of a message they were sent with. Moses saw the bush burn without being consumed, and heard a voice out of it. This was something besides finding an impulse upon his mind to go to Pharaoh, that he might bring his brethren out of Egypt: And yet he thought not this enough to authorize him to go with that message, till God, by another miracle of his rod turned into a serpent, had assured him of a power to testify his mission, by the same miracle repeated before them, whom he was sent to.

16. In what I have said I am far from denying that God can, or doth sometimes enlighten men's minds in the apprehending of certain truths, or excite them to good actions by the immediate influence and assistance of the holy spirit, without any extraordinary signs accompanying it. But in such cases too we have reason and scripture, unerring rules to know whether it be from God or no. Where the truth embraced is

consonant to the revelation in the written word of God, or the action conformable to the dictates of right reason or holy writ, we may be assured that we run no risk in entertaining it as such; because though perhaps it be not an immediate revelation from God, extraordinarily operating on our minds, yet we are sure it is warranted by that revelation which he has given us of truth. But it is not the strength of our private persuasion within ourselves that can warrant it to be a light or motion from heaven; nothing can do that but the written word of God without us, or that standard of reason which is common to us with all men.

Commentary by *Lois Frankel*, Masham and Locke: Reason, Religion, and Education

INTRODUCTION

Damaris Cudworth Masham (1659–1708) and John Locke (1632–1704) shared not only a close friendship but also many philosophical views. This essay will discuss their approach to the relationship between faith—particularly the Christian faith—and reason, and the connections Masham finds between that relationship and the need to improve educational opportunities for women and girls. We will see that both philosophers link faith closely with reason, holding that it is rational to be religious and that religion should be rational. In addition, both believe that reason, religion, and education are important to inducing people to be virtuous, and that virtue is important for happiness. I will also suggest that Masham's views on these subjects are somewhat more consistent than Locke's, and that there are threads in Masham's thought that are arguably feminist. The primary sources for my discussion of Locke and Masham's views, excerpted here, are from Locke's major work, *An Essay Concerning Human Understanding* (1689) and one of Masham's two central works, *Occasional Thoughts in Reference to a Virtuous and Christian Life* (1705).

LOCKE AND MASHAM ON REASON AND RELIGION

The relationship between reason and faith is one of perpetual interest to Western philosophers, many of whom view "faith" as equivalent to the Christian religion. Locke and Masham are committed to giving each what is, in their estimation, its due, without (again, in their estimation—some of their critics disagreed) subordinating one to the other. For them, both faith and reason are closely connected with each other and with the ultimate good of individuals and society. The proper use of reason, they argue, should support religious faith, and it is part of one's religious duty to make good use of and be governed by reason.

In his chapter "Of Reason," after describing several ways in which the term "reason" is commonly used, Locke states that he will use it to refer to the human faculty that distinguishes humans from other animals and that establishes humans' superiority. It is the faculty of reason (or rationality) that allows us to see either immediate connections between ideas, as in the movement from one step to the next in a formal demonstration (such as a "proof" in logic), or mediated connections, such as those between the premise and the conclusion of a completed multistep proof.[8] Masham adopts essentially the same view of reason, as comprising immediate and mediated connections, describing reason as "that faculty in us which discovers, by the intervention of intermediate ideas, what connections those in the proposition have one with another."[9]

Regarding religion, Masham writes that the best definition of religion is "the knowledge how to please God, and thus taken, does necessarily include virtue, that is to say Moral Rectitude."[10] Pleasing God is important because doing so will result in our eternal happiness, which is our ultimate good. Locke makes a similar claim about religion in his *Letter Concerning Toleration* (1689), where he declares that the eternal happiness of our soul depends on our obtaining God's favor through our beliefs and actions.[11]

But what does pleasing God have to do with moral rectitude? Both Locke and Masham consider religion in general, and the Christian religion in particular, to be closely connected with, even essential for, moral rectitude and for human happiness, both in life and in an afterlife. Masham draws a distinction between true happiness and pleasure, observing with dismay that we tend to equate the two. She argues that indulging too much in present pleasure will subject us to later pain. Accordingly, virtuous behavior, which, she believes, requires us to keep our appetites (desire for short-term pleasure through self-indulgence) in check, will actually be conducive to our greater happiness.[12] The unregulated gratification of our desires and appetites, Masham argues, risks a greater and longer-lasting pain than the "short, or small pleasure" that we would obtain; likewise, a "short, or small pain" may yield us a greater longer-lasting pleasure in the end.[13]

Of course, Masham's view here is, in large part, mere common sense: overindulgence or neglect of sometimes-unpleasant preventive measures can yield undesirable short- and long-term results. It might be argued that many of these undesirable results may harm only ourselves, and, as such, should be labeled merely imprudent, not immoral. Masham does not offer support for the connection she assumes between prudence and virtue, nonetheless she states that there is "an inseparable connection, or relation of moral good and evil, with our natural good, and evil."[14]

Although Masham's support for this position is minimal, consisting primarily of an assertion that the dictates of reason (in this case, meaning concerns for long-term goals over short-term ones) coincide with the requirements of virtue, which she equates with the requirements of the Christian religion, the position does have precedent in the works of Aristotle (see chapter 2). Although she does not say so explicitly, perhaps Masham assumes that the support offered by Aristotle for connecting prudence with virtue is sufficient. Aristotle holds that happiness, as that which is desired for its own sake (as intrinsically good), is the highest good for individuals. Aristotle makes virtue, as intrinsically good, a necessary though not sufficient condition of individual happiness, stating that "an activity of soul in accordance with perfect virtue" is an essential part of human happiness, but is not in itself sufficient for human happiness.[15] Aristotle further understands virtue as, in general, a disposition to choose the mean between extremes—that is, to behave with moderation (although for some things, such as harmful or evil acts, he does not consider moderation to be virtuous). Thus, Masham's statement that virtue consists in "submitting our desires to a constant regulation" is in keeping with the Aristotelian position. In "Some Thoughts Concerning Education" (1693), Locke expresses a similar view: "the principle of all virtue and excellency lies in a power of denying ourselves the satisfaction of our own desires, where reason does not authorize them."[16]

We have seen that both Masham and Locke take the Aristotelian position that virtue is necessary to human happiness. They extend the notion to coincide with the Christian doctrine of eternal happiness as a divine reward for virtuous behavior. In doing so, they provide for external enforcement. We will see shortly that Masham, the daughter of Cambridge Platonist Ralph Cudworth, also incorporates elements of Cambridge Platonist thought in her idea of virtue. In doing so, I will argue, she grounds the connection between moral good and evil with natural good and evil more securely than would one who sees the connection as merely one of divine fiat. I will suggest that there are at least hints that Locke may have that latter view in mind.

REASON, FAITH, AND KNOWING THE GOOD

For Locke, moral principles are deduced from prior principles.[17] In practice, people may derive these principles from requirements of the public good, or from human nature, without knowing or acknowledging what Locke thinks is their true origin: God.[18] That is, the prior principles from which moral principles are properly deduced are, in Locke's view, religious ones, and so there is a logical connection (but one put there deliberately by God) between religion and morality: "the true ground of morality . . . can only be the will and law of a God . . . God having, by an inseparable connexion, joined virtue and public happiness together, and made the practice thereof necessary to the preservation of society, and visibly beneficial to all, with whom the virtuous man has to do."[19]

Locke claims that the notion that humans are dependent for their existence on a supreme and perfect being forms a foundation from which principles of "our Duty and Rules of Action" can be deduced with the same degree of necessity as a mathematical demonstration.[20] Thus for Locke, reason—both as the source of the premise of God's existence and the process of deducing our duty from that premise—and faith together are necessary for our knowledge of moral principles.

Masham, while agreeing with Locke that religion is important for virtue, appears to differ somewhat with him as to the origin of our knowledge of morality. She writes that many rules of morality are, at least in theory, available to us through the "light of reason" because they are based on the nature of things. That suggests that, unlike Locke, who denies the possibility of innate ideas, Masham may consider moral rules independent of any prior principles, including the dictates of God. Masham's view is consistent with her claim that our natural good coincides with our moral good. Her view is likely related to the Cambridge Platonists's interpretation of the notion of the world's (and thus humanity's) being created in the "image of God" as implying that the moral law is in the nature of things themselves. According to another Cambridge Platonist, John Smith, the law of nature is based on God's love as expressed in the human soul, and it is our human frailty that can make it hard for us to find and follow that law within us and see the good for ourselves. Because of that, external sanctions and motivations are needed.[21]

However (and here Masham's views are more in agreement with Locke's), "few would actually discern the law of nature in its full extent merely by the light of nature; or if they did, would find the enforcement thereof a sufficient balance to that natural love of present pleasure which often opposes our compliance therewith."[22] That is, for most people the light of reason provides us at best with the basic notion that we should conform our actions to God's will. To know the details of that will (and, thus, of the moral laws dictated by nature itself), it is in practice necessary for most people to consult scripture, which is based on revelation[23] with "experience showing us that natural light, unassisted by revelation, is insufficient to the ends of natural religion."[24] Thus, the general need to regulate our appetites and to plan for and choose our long-term happiness over short-term pleasures may be knowable through reason alone, but reason alone does not always allow us to discern what will truly make us happy in the long run. For that, we must turn to revelation.[25]

Both philosophers hold that even should we discover, through reason or revelation, which actions will conduce to our long-term happiness, we often lack the will to take those actions and avoid others that will result in long-term unhappiness. According to Masham, only fear of punishment—a "rational fear of God"[26]—can provide sufficient motivation for most people to avoid being overwhelmed by their passions and appetites, which make it difficult for us to comply with the divine laws that ought to govern behavior.[27] In this sense, Masham provides both a psychological explanation of what motivates humans to seek the good, to seek long-term human happiness, and a rational explanation based on the role of religion and revelation in ethics. Locke takes a similar line, stating that "good, the greater good, though apprehended and acknowledged to be so, does not determine the will, until our desire, raised proportionably to it, makes us uneasy in the want of it."[28] He goes on to argue that it is very difficult to move people to sacrifice present pleasures for the sake of some future greater happiness—even eternal happiness.[29] It is necessary, in his view, for people to realize somehow that virtue and religion are necessary for happiness, to see "God the righteous judge, ready to render to every man according to his deeds."[30] He emphasizes the risk of eternal misery brought about by divine punishment for those who fail to act virtuously.

How, then, do Locke and Masham characterize God's role in securing human happiness or misery? Do they see it as that of an all-knowing guide who issues rules to us for our own good, or as that of an autocratic commander, whose rule is good for us and ought to be followed primarily because God will punish us if we fail to do so? In other words, to adapt Socrates's question in the *Euthyphro*—a question that continues to prompt serious philosophical debate about the so-called Divine Command Theory of ethics: Is what God commands good for us simply because God commands it and will enforce those commands, or does God command it because, in God's omniscience, God knows better than we what is good for us? Even if God is assumed (as Masham and Locke do assume) to be completely good, it can still be asked whether God's goodness is based on some external standard of goodness, whether God's goodness is based in some universal ethics that is logically prior to God's nature—or whether God itself is the source of the definition of goodness—thereby making God and religion logically prior to and the source of ethics.

Leibniz, one of Masham's correspondents, addresses this issue in his essay, "Reflections on the Common Concept of Justice" (ca. 1702):

> It is generally agreed that whatever God wills is good and just. But there remains the question whether it is good and just because God wills it or whether God wills it because it is good and just. . . . And to say, Stat pro ratione voluntas—"Let my will stand for the reason"—is definitely the motto of a tyrant. Moreover, this opinion [that it is good and just because God wills it] would hardly distinguish God from the devil. . . . This [opinion] does violence to those attributes which make God love-worthy and destroys our love for God, leaving only fear.[31]

Although Locke does not address this issue at the heart of debates over the Divine Command Theory directly, the following passage illustrates how he appeals both to God's right of command and also to God's goodness to establish the source and nature of what is right), and seems comfortable with attributing both characteristics to the deity:

> The Laws that Men generally refer their Actions to, to judge of their Rectitude, or Obliquity, seem to me to be . . . [f]irst, the divine law, whereby I mean that law which God has set to the actions of men, whether promulgated to them by the light of nature, or the voice of revelation. That God has given a rule whereby men should govern themselves, I think there is nobody so brutish as to deny. He has a right to do it, we are his creatures: He has goodness and wisdom to direct our actions to that which is best; and he has power to enforce it by rewards and punishments, of infinite weight and duration in another life: . . . This is the only true touchstone of moral rectitude.[32]

Locke adds that obedience to God is good for humanity in general, not just for individuals. Since Locke thinks obedience to God is beneficial to society as a whole, he indirectly provides an answer to the question of how regulating our appetites is not only good for our own well-being, but also good in some larger, more morally relevant sense: "There being nothing that so directly and visibly secures and advances the general good of mankind in this world, as obedience to the laws he has set them, and nothing that breeds such mischiefs and confusion, as the neglect of them."[33]

Locke's discussion of morality is distinctive (and consistent with his political philosophy, which emphasizes social interaction) in that he emphasizes social and political relationships—not individuals—in his conception of ethics. In contrast, Masham focuses on the individual. She seems less comfortable with the notion of God-the-commander and instead writes in her other major work, *A Discourse Concerning the Love of God* (1696), about why, in her view, God should be loved. She argues that the reason we should love God is not that God is our creator and has power over us, but that God is good and the ultimate source of our happiness. The mere act of creation itself provides no reason to love our creator, because mere existence does not guarantee happiness: Why love a creator if it is the source of misery? But to the extent that God is good and responsible for our happiness—for example, by creating other people and things that make us happy, as well as by more spiritual means—God is deserving of our love and devotion. That is, God is to be loved because God uses God's great power for our benefit, and not just because God has great power over us.[34] This view also has roots in the Cambridge Platonism of Masham's father, Ralph Cudworth, who held that a person's relationship with God should be one of love, not fear.

But, Masham notes, God must be obeyed as well as loved: Just as God can be the source of our eternal happiness, God can also be the source of our eternal misery if God chooses to punish us for disobedience. But our obedience must be based on reason or understanding, not mere rule following. True virtue is behavior in accordance with "right reason," which, Masham claims, is "one and the same" with the Gospel.[35] But although Masham considers obedience important, she has much more to say about the importance of loving God. Those who consider an emphasis on a loving God over a punishing one to be indicative of a less patriarchal, and thus more feminist, mode of thinking may accordingly find grounds for attributing some elements of feminism to Masham. In addition, some feminist philosophers argue that the "female experience" and the "male experience" shape women's and men's views, respectively, of morality and even their approaches to epistemology. I discuss these issues, and their applicability to Masham's thought, elsewhere.[36] We will see in Masham's arguments in favor of greater educational opportunities for women more overt and incontestable grounds for considering her a feminist.

RELIGION AND REASON

Because of Masham's and Locke's view that religion is necessary or nearly so, in a practical sense, for morality, both writers denounce atheism as something that renders morality difficult to nearly impossible. Masham thinks atheists have more difficulty behaving virtuously because they lack the fear of God that would help reinforce virtuous habits. Locke goes further, claiming that atheism is incompatible with morality because it undermines the social contract—the tacit agreement that, according to Locke, citizens make to give up some of their natural rights in return for the protection afforded by living in a rule-governed society—which Locke considers essential to social and political life. Because this contract is based on the keeping of agreements (the contract), those who cannot or will not keep their agreements constitute a danger to society. Locke argues in the ironically titled *A Letter Concerning Toleration* (1689), that although the state ought to tolerate a variety of (but not all) forms of religion, it should not tolerate atheism at all, because atheists have, he claims, no incentive to keep their agreements. "Those are not at all to be tolerated who deny the being of a God. Promises, covenants, and oaths, which are the bonds of human society, can have no hold upon an atheist."[37] Of course, Locke's view is undermined by the likelihood that relatively immediate social and legal sanctions for oath-breaking are as good or better incentives for keeping one's promises, covenants, and oaths as any eventual divine punishments that might be inflicted in an afterlife were such a thing to exist.

Similarly Masham, though not advocating political sanctions against atheists, holds them in contempt, accusing them of a "certain sottish disbelief of whatsoever they cannot either see or feel."[38] She blames this "sottish" (foolish) atheism on a failure to make proper use of one's ability to reason, for, she believes, anyone who does make use of reason would assent to the precepts of Christianity. She offers a version of the Cosmological Argument for the existence of God:

And thus, by a consideration of the attributes of God, visible in the works of the creation, we come to a knowledge of his existence, who is an invisible being: For since Power, Wisdom and Goodness, which we manifestly discern in the production and conservation of our selves and the universe, could not subsist independently on some substance for them to inhere in, we are assured that there is a substance whereunto they do belong, or of which they are the attributes.[39]

Locke's argument for God's existence also follows these lines, though at greater length.[40] According to Masham, just as reason should lead one to religion, so should religion be reasonable. This view is in accord with Masham's Cambridge Platonist associations. Cambridge Platonists held that part of God's essential nature is to be rational and that, accordingly, true Christians should emulate that rationality by basing their religious belief on rational grounds. Furthermore, Masham argues that rational Christians must count nothing as a revelation that conflicts with reason,[41] even though she (like Locke) considers revelation to be a valid source of religious knowledge. Without certainty that one has, in fact, received a revelation, one has no warrant for believing what was supposedly revealed. For both Masham and Locke, the certainty required must go beyond what Locke calls the "ungrounded persuasion" of our own minds.[42] That is, it is not enough merely to feel that one has been the recipient of a revelation. It is helpful, Locke adds, to have some additional evidence, such as a miracle, of having received a revelation.[43] Miracles, in turn, are evidenced primarily by the appropriateness of their results and their divergence from the ordinary course of things. Locke writes, "For where such supernatural events are suitable to ends aimed at by him, who has the power to change the course of nature, there, under such circumstances, they may be the fitter to procure belief, by how much the more they are beyond, or contrary to ordinary observation."[44] He adds that multiple miracles provide even more evidence for the divine origin of a supposed revelation.[45] Reason and revelation are really not all that different, according to Locke: reason is just "natural revelation" and revelation is "natural reason enlarged by a new set of discoveries communicated by God immediately."[46] Similarly, Masham, as we have noted above, claims that "right reason" is identical in the Gospel, suggesting that reason and revelation are virtually the same. She argues further that, because of the close connection between reason and religion, which is based on a close connection between God's intellect and God's will, it is unreasonable to act contrary to the will of God:

[God's] will, as revealed to us, being but a different consideration of his attributes, the knowledge whereof is all the knowledge we have of God, cannot be so much as conceived by us separable from the being of God, unless the God, which we conceive, be a fiction of our own imagination, and not the creator of all things; who is an invisible being only knowable to us in, and by, the exemplifications of his attributes: the infinite perfection and the inseparable correspondence, and harmony of which (discernible in the frame and government of the universe) plainly tells us, that the divine will cannot be (like ours) successive determinations without dependence, or connection one upon another; much less inconsistent, contradictory, and mutable; but only steady, uniform, unchangeable result of infinite wisdom and benevolence, extending to, and including all his works. So that sin, or disobedience to our maker is manifestly the greatest nonsense, folly and contradiction conceivable, with regard purely to the immutable perfection of the divine nature.[47]

With this need to keep religion rational in mind, Locke and Masham deride any expressions of faith that fly in the face of reason as "enthusiasm" (religious fanaticism) which, according to Locke, "takes away both reason and revelation, and substitutes for them the ungrounded fancies of a man's own brain, and assumes them for a foundation both of opinion and conduct."[48] This refusal to admit religious claims that conflict with reason prompted some critics to accuse Locke of subordinating faith to reason and encouraged Masham to write in Locke's defense. According to Masham, not only does uncritical acceptance of an experience as a revelation conflict with God's very nature; it is also poor strategy for a supporter of Christianity. To give any evidentiary weight to alleged revelations that are contrary to reason is to open up Christianity to the charge of being unreasonable, leaving only two alternatives: enthusiasm, characterized by rejection of reason in favor of faith, or skepticism about religion, characterized by rejection of faith in favor of reason. Enthusiasm in some encourages skepticism about religion in others by making religion appear foolish. Given the connection she sees between religion and morality, anything that promotes skepticism will also, she believes, promote immorality. One example she offers of expressions of religion that make it appear irrational is the suggestion that religion is opposed to pleasure of any kind:

> Such declamations as are sometimes made against pleasure absolutely (not the irregular pursuit of it), as if pleasure was in its own nature, a false, and deceitful, not a real and solid good, have produced this ill effect. Many from the absurdity hereof are confirmed in an evil indulgence of their appetites, as if to gratify these was indeed the truest wisdom of a rational creature.[49]

In summary, to defend Christianity against skepticism, the "proper disease of our age,"[50] it is important to ensure that religious belief conform to the requirements of rationality. To that end, Masham argues, religious training must emphasize understanding, not mere rote learning,[51] and it must provide solid evidence for religious beliefs. If a person doesn't understand her religion sufficiently to defend it against detractors, Masham argues, she is likely to be easily swayed toward religious skepticism, enthusiasm, or some religion other than Christianity. In other words, a faith that can withstand questioning is a more secure faith than one with no rational underpinnings. Education, then, plays an essential role in promoting both religion and virtue.

EDUCATION

Knowing what we should do and wishing to do what we ought is not always enough to ensure that we will in fact behave virtuously. In order to become and continue to be virtuous, both Locke and Masham hold that one needs early instruction in religion both to establish habits of virtue and to develop the rational acceptance and understanding of religion that serves to reinforce those habits. Because Masham perceives such instruction and rational acceptance as rare, she asks rhetorically whether it can "reasonably be thought strange, that there is so little virtue in the world as we find there is?"[52] It is, she thinks, not strange at all, but she hopes that if education is changed as she recommends, then virtue will be more prevalent.

Locke also stresses the importance of early education:

> He that is not us'd to submit his will to the reason of others when he is young, will scarce hearken to submit to his own reason when he is of an age to make use of it.[53]
>
> Children should be us'd to submit their desires, and go without their longings, even from their very cradles. The first thing they should learn to know, should be, that they were not to have anything because it pleas'd them, but because it was thought fit for them.[54]

Locke's and Masham's views begin to diverge, however, with regard to the relative merits of obedience versus independence of thought. Locke places a very great stress on teaching children to be obedient and not to question their religious instruction. In fact, he counsels adults and children alike to avoid asking too many religious questions that may be difficult to answer, for fear of encouraging skepticism. Despite his condemnation of enthusiasm—religious beliefs that conflict with or even oppose reason—he seems to think that the reasoning faculty in most people is inadequate to apply itself to matters concerning religion.

> As the foundation of this, there ought very early to be imprinted on his mind a true notion of God, as of the independent Supreme Being, Author and Maker of all things, from Whom we receive all our good, Who loves us, and gives us all things. And consequent to this, instill into him a love and reverence of this Supreme Being. This is enough to begin with, without going to explain this matter any farther; . . . And I think it would be better if men generally rested in such an idea of God, without being too curious in their notions about a Being which all must acknowledge incomprehensible; whereby many, who have not strength and clearness of thought to distinguish between what they can, and what they cannot know, run themselves in superstitions or atheism, making God like themselves, or (because they cannot comprehend any thing else) none at all.[55]

Comparing Locke's attitude with Masham's, we see that both emphasize obedience, with Masham even adopting some language similar to Locke's. However, Masham holds that it is as important to reason with children as it is to enforce desired behaviors. This is consistent with her view that beliefs or actions not supported by reason are in danger of being abandoned. It also shows Masham's views to be more consistent than Locke's regarding their shared view of the importance of reason: Masham is willing for everyone, even children, to subject religious claims to rational examination, while Locke prefers for "men generally" to limit their questioning of religious matters. For Masham, subjecting religion to rational examination strengthens it, while for Locke, it potentially weakens it. Masham writes,

> The care of [children] should begin with the first years . . . in curbing at the earliest appearance thereof, every their least evil inclination; and accustoming them to an absolute, constant, and universal submission and obedience to the will of those who have the disposal of them: Since they will hardly ever after (especially in a great fortune) be governed by their own reason, who are not made supple to

that of others, before they are able to judge of fit and unfit, by any other measure
than as it is the will, or not, of such whom they believe to have a just power
over them,[56] doubts [about religion, on the part of children] should always be
endeavored to be removed by the most solid arguments of which children are
capable. Nor should they ever be rebuked for having those doubts.[57]

Locke's program of education is intended particularly for young gentlemen—
upper-class boys and young men—though he thinks its principles are applicable as well
to other young men. Nonetheless, he regards the education of young gentlemen as most
important because they are the ones who will, if well-educated, "quickly bring all the rest
into order."[58] Masham's indirect reference to counterrational and self-indulgent tendencies of the upper classes in the passage quoted above suggests that she might disagree
with Locke's claim that young gentlemen are likely to "bring all the rest into order." Or
perhaps she might think their positions of influence all the more reason to educate them
to overcome those tendencies. Locke notes that some (unspecified) modifications would
be necessary for girls and young women,[59] but he has little else to say on the subject of
girls' education. It is, thus, unclear whether he would approve of expanded educational
opportunities for women, but if he did approve of such opportunities, it was obviously
not a priority for him. Masham finds women's education more worthy of discussion. She
notes that the neglect of women's education, which might compensate for the "ignorance
or errors of their childhood,"[60] renders them in particular danger of becoming skeptical
about religion:

> For if Christianity be a religion from God, and women have souls to be saved
> as well as men; to know what this religion consists in, and to understand the
> grounds on which it is to be received, can be no more than necessary knowledge
> to a woman, as well as to a man: Which necessary knowledge is sufficient to en-
> able any one so far to answer to the opposers or corrupters of Christianity.[61]

If concern for women's religious status alone fails to move her readers to accept the
importance of education to girls and women, Masham adds a second reason: women are
responsible for the upbringing of their children. So, if women are not sufficiently educated to understand and, thus, to defend their religion against skepticism, how can they
be capable of conveying such understanding to their children (including their male children, whom Locke stresses should have such education)? Masham is not naïve here. She
clearly recognizes that men are reluctant to open educational opportunities to women and
so offers arguments that go beyond considerations of fairness. Masham complains that a
woman with even such a minimal level of understanding is in danger of being ridiculed
and, for that reason, is discouraged from study:

> A lady who is able but to give an account of her faith . . . that is capable of
> instructing her children in the reasonableness of the Christian religion; and of
> laying in them the foundations of a solid virtue; that a lady (I say) no more
> knowing than this does demand, can hardly escape being called learned by the
> men of our days; and in consequence thereof, becoming a subject of ridicule
> to one part of them, and of aversion to the other; with but a few exceptions of
> some virtuous and rational persons. And is not the incurring of general dislike,
> one of the strongest discouragements that we can have to any thing?[62]

Masham complains that upper-class young women are discouraged from intellectual activity and kept busy with social activities instead.[63] (Like Locke, Masham has little to say about the experiences of women of other classes, but they had even less access to education than did those of the wealthier classes.) She blames this discouragement on the fact that most men of the time were not themselves very interested in scholarly activity and were thus threatened by learned women.[64] While Masham herself was fortunate in being encouraged by Locke, Leibniz, and her father to pursue her studies, her writing suggests that she still experienced the limitations enforced by her society, complaining that the difficulty of obtaining education in religion is minor compared to the difficulty of obtaining education in other subjects, which men, in their ignorance, consider "improper" for women.[65]

Conclusion

We have seen that for Masham and Locke the good for individuals and society depends on virtuous behavior, primarily understood as the moderation of our appetites through the influence of reason and religion. Reason and religion are so closely entwined that for both Masham and Locke they are to some extent equated. In particular, both join reason with the Christian religion. Like other philosophers of their time writing within a Christian tradition, they offer arguments for the existence of a deity, but they accept uncritically the notion that the deity in question is best described by the Christian religion. In order for both reason and religion to be developed properly, both philosophers recommend education: Locke discussing in detail that of young gentlemen, and Masham adding a plea that young ladies likewise be educated well. Neither, however, has much to say of the education of young people outside the leisure class. The consistency of Masham's views on reason, religion, and education benefits (where that of Locke's does not) from the strong Cambridge Platonist elements that inform her thought. These elements create a metaphysical link between God's intellect, will, and the nature of the universe—and thus of humanity. The absence of such a link in Locke's work leaves his attempts to link reason, religion, and education less well grounded. Of course, the greater consistency of Masham's views does not guarantee their soundness. After all, Masham, like Locke—indeed, like most philosophers—takes many of her fundamental starting points for granted.

Questions For Reflection

Both Locke and Masham associate prudence (or the natural good) with virtue (or the moral good), and both provide limited or no justification for doing so. Have you found more satisfying justifications of such a connection in other philosophical works, or do you think that there is any such justification? (You might consider whether you agree with Locke's or Masham's notions of what, in fact, constitutes prudence and virtue.)

Some philosophers have argued that divine command theories of ethics are a variation of moral relativism, given the variety of views that exist with regard to the existence of deities, their natures, and what, if anything, they might command. What is meant by the Divine Command Theory of Ethics and ethical (or moral) relativism? Given your understanding, do you think the Divine Command Theory is a form of ethical relativism? If so, is that a devastating criticism of it or merely an observation? If not, how would you differentiate the Divine Command Theory from moral relativism?

Masham and Locke argue that religion ought to be rational, and that so-called revelations can be shown to be legitimate by being shown to be rationally acceptable. What do you understand them to mean when they make such a claim, and how do they defend it? Do you agree with their view that revelations are or may be "rationally acceptable," and what is the philosophical significance of the issue? Be sure to defend your answer.

Notes

1. Sarah Hutton, "Lady Damaris Masham," *Stanford Encyclopedia of Philosophy*, 2007, http://plato.stanford.edu/entries/lady-masham/ Jan. 2007.

2. The quotation is in Lois Frankel's essay, "Damaris Cudworth Masham," in *A History of Women Philosophers*, vol. 3: *Modern Women Philosophers 1600–1900*, ed. Mary Ellen Waithe (Dordrecht, The Netherlands: Kluwer Academic Publishers, 1991), 74.

3. Margaret Atherton claims that Masham generally accepted Lockean empiricism with regard to epistemology (though not ethics). "Damaris Cudworth, Lady Masham," *Women Philosophers of the Early Modern Period*, ed. Margaret Atherton (Indianapolis, IN: Hackett Publishing Co., 1994), 77.

4. James Gordon Clapp, "John Locke," *Encyclopedia of Philosophy*, vol. 4 (New York: Macmillan Publishing Co., & The Free Press, 1967), 496.

5. I do not discuss a fourth meta-ethical version of the Divine Command Theory (IV) "Right" or "good for humans" means "whatever God commands."

6. Damaris Masham, *Occasional Thoughts in Reference to a Virtuous or Christian Life*. Printed in London in 1705 for A. and J. Churchil at the Black-Swan in Paternoster-Row.

7. John Locke, *An Essay Concerning Human Understanding*, ed. Peter H. Nidditch. (New York: Oxford University Press, 1975, orig, pub. 1689), 7–8, 13–17, 19–22, 27–29, 32–56, 59–62, 65–73, 75, 82–86, 151, 161–66.

8. Locke, *Essay*, IV.xvii.2.

9. Masham, *Occasional Thoughts*, 33. For additional background on Locke's views on reason, see *Essay*, IV.i–ii.

10. Masham, *Occasional Thoughts*, 84.

11. "A Letter Concerning Toleration," in John Locke, *On Politics and Education* (Roslyn, NY: Walter J. Black, 1947), 53.

12. See also Locke, *Essay*, II.xxi.70.

13. Masham, *Occasional Thoughts*, 75.

14. Masham, *Occasional Thoughts*, 77–78.

15. Aristotle, *Nicomachean Ethics*, 1:13.

16. John Locke, "Some Thoughts Concerning Education" (1693), sec. 38; see also sec. 36.

17. Locke. *Essay*, I.iii.4.

18. Locke, *Essay*, I.iii.6.

19. Locke, *Essay*, I.iii.6.

20. Locke, *Essay* IV.iii.18, see also *Essay*, IV.iii.20 and x.7.

21. For a general discussion of Cambridge Platonism see Sarah Hutton, "The Cambridge Platonists," in *The Stanford Encyclopedia of Philosophy*, ed. Edward N. Zalta (Winter 2001), http://plato.stanford.edu/archives/win2001/entries/cambridge-platonists/.

22. Masham, *Occasional Thoughts*, 52–53.

23. Masham, *Occasional Thoughts*, 43.

24. Masham, *Occasional Thoughts*, 55–56.

25. Masham, *Occasional Thoughts*, 103.

26. Masham, *Occasional Thoughts*, 27; see also 14–15 and Locke, *Essay*, II.xxviii.5.

27. Masham, *Occasional Thoughts*, 52–3.

28. Locke, *Essay*, II.21.35.

29. Locke, *Essay*, II.xxi.44.

30. Locke, *Essay*, II.xxi.60, quoting the Bible: Rom. 2:6–9; see also Locke, *Essay*, II.xxi.70.

31. Leibniz, "Reflections on the Common Concept of Justice," in *Leibniz: Philosophical Papers and Letters*, 2nd ed., ed. Leroy E. Loemker (Dordrecht, The Netherlands: D. Reidel, 1969, orig. pub. 1702), 561.

32. Locke, *Essay*, II.xxviii.7–8.

33. Locke, *Essay*, 11.

34. Damaris Masham, *A Discourse Concerning the Love of God*. Printed in London in 1696 for A. and J. Churchil at the Black-Swan in Paternoster-Row, 64–5.

35. Masham, *Occasional Thoughts*, 97–98.

36. Lois Frankel, "Damaris Cudworth Masham," in *A History of Women Philosophers*, vol. 3, 80–83.

37. "A Letter Concerning Toleration," in John Locke, *On Politics and Education* (New York: Walter J. Black, The Classics Club, 1947), 58.

38. Masham, *Occasional Thoughts*, 31.

39. Masham, *Occasional Thoughts*, 62.

40. For Locke's discussion of the demonstrability of God's existence, see Locke, *Essay* IV.10.

41. Masham, *Occasional Thoughts*, 34–5.

42. Locke, *Essay*, IV.xix.11.

43. Locke, *Essay*, IV.14.

44. Locke, *Essay*, IV.xvi.13.

45. Locke, *Essay*, IV.15.

46. Locke, *Essay*, IV.xix.4.

47. Masham, *Occasional Thoughts*, 68–69.

48. Locke, *Essay*, VI.xix.3.

49. Masham, *Occasional Thoughts*, 79.

50. Masham, *Occasional Thoughts*, 28.

51. Masham, *Occasional Thoughts*, 20.

52. Masham, *Occasional Thoughts*, 50–51.

53. Locke, "Some Thoughts Concerning Education," Sec. 36.

54. Locke, "Some Thoughts Concerning Education," Sec. 38.

55. Locke, "Some Thoughts Concerning Education," Sec. 136.

56. Masham, *Occasional Thoughts*, 181–82.

57. Masham, *Occasional Thoughts*, 41.

58. Locke, "Some Thoughts Concerning Education," Dedication.

59. Locke, "Some Thoughts Concerning Education," Sec. 6.

60. Masham, *Occasional Thoughts*, 21.

61. Masham, *Occasional Thoughts*, 166.

62. Masham, *Occasional Thoughts*, 175; see also 162.

63. Masham, *Occasional Thoughts*, 151.

64. Masham, *Occasional Thoughts*, 174.

65. Masham, *Occasional Thoughts*, 169.

CHAPTER 8

Leibniz and Conway

Introduction by *Karen J. Warren*

The common topic of this chapter is the metaphysical positions of Gottfried Wilhelm Leibniz (1646–1716) and Anne Conway (Viscountess Anne Finch Conway, 1631–1679). Since their views are complicated and not easily accessible for a newcomer, this introductory "metaphysical first run" is designed to help the reader navigate through some technical terminology in preparation for reading and discussing both the primary texts and Duran's commentary. I begin with some biographical background.

LEIBNIZ

Leibniz was born in Leipzig, Germany. When he was six years old, his father, a professor of moral philosophy at the University of Leipzig, died. He left a personal library to which Leibniz was granted free access from age seven. By age twelve Leibniz had taught himself Latin and began learning Greek. He entered the University of Leipzig at fourteen and mastered courses in logic, scholastic philosophy, and the classics. In 1666, at twenty years old, he completed his studies and published his first book in philosophy, *On the Art of Combinations*. The University of Leipzig declined to offer him a law teaching position, so Leibniz submitted his thesis to the University of Altdorf instead and obtained his doctorate in law five months later. He declined an academic appointment at Altdorf and spent most of the rest of his life in the service of two noble German families.

Leibniz's diplomatic efforts were often unscrupulous (e.g., backdating and altering manuscripts). Never married, he died in Hanover in 1716, much out of favor with his many associates. Only his personal secretary attended his funeral. Neither George I (who was near Hanover) nor the Royal Society and the Berlin Academy of Sciences, organizations to which he belonged, acknowledged his death. For more than fifty years, Leibniz's grave was unmarked. Leibniz's reputation remained in disrepair a long time. It was not until Bertrand

Russell published a study of Leibniz's metaphysics in 1900 that twentieth-century scholars, particularly analytical and linguistic philosophers, began paying attention to his work.

Leibniz wrote in three languages: mostly in scholastic Latin and French, with less than one-fourth of his writings in German. During his lifetime, he published many pamphlets and scholarly articles, but only three philosophical books, the *Combinatorial Art* (1666), the *Theodicy* (1710), and *Monadology* (1714).

Leibniz is often associated with several metaphysical principles featured in *Monadology*. For example, Leibniz appeals to the Principle of the Best of All Possible Worlds (sometimes known as the Principle of Optimism) to explain God's choice to actualize this world from all the possible worlds. This actual universe is the best God could have made. Part of what makes it the best is explained by a second principle, the Principle of Preestablished Harmony. According to it, what happens to one substance corresponds to what happens to all others, without substances acting upon one another directly or causally. The connection between these two principles is that this world is "the best of all possible worlds," in part, because it exhibits this preestablished harmony among substances. A third principle, the Principle of Sufficient Reason, states that there must be a sufficient reason, often known only to God, for anything to exist, for there to be something rather than nothing, for any event to occur, for any truth to be obtained. Stated simply, all things happen for (according to) some reason.

Leibniz's metaphysics uses these principles to articulate his theory of "monads." Monads are the ultimate substances; they have the properties of being eternal, unchangeable, individual, subject to their own laws, immaterial, and noninteractive causally. Everything (individual monads) that exists does so for a reason (the principle of sufficient reason). Each monad is programmed with a set of instructions peculiar to it (what contemporary scholars call a "complete individual concept" or CIC) about how to act in accordance with the "pre-established harmony"; this CIC assures that "this is the best of possible worlds."

The ontological essence of a monad is its irreducible simplicity: monads possess no material or spatial properties though monads individually "mirror" the entire universe. God is the ultimate monad (or substance) who wills the preestablished harmony. There is no longer a Cartesian dualistic metaphysics (i.e. two kinds of substances, mind and matter) since monads—the only substances—are immaterial. The apparent imperfections of the world are explained away by the principle of optimism: they fit together in a way that creates the best of all possible worlds.

Leibniz was preoccupied with the "problem of evil" because it challenged his metaphysics. Scholars disagree about the proper statement of the problem. Consider the following: (1) If God were all-powerful, all-knowing, and all-good, then this world would be the best possible world. (2) But surely this world is not the best possible world (given the existence of evil). (3) Thus, God is either not all-powerful, not all-knowing, or not all-good. Since Leibniz rejects as obviously false the conclusion (3), and he is committed to the truth of the description of God's nature (1), Leibniz does (and must) argue that (2) is false. How does he defend this position?

Begin by asking why someone might think (2) is true. The answer seems obvious: given all the human-created immorality in the world, combined with all the natural disasters (e.g., monsoons and tornados) that harm humans, nonhuman animals and the environment, we can easily conceive of worlds that are better than this actual world insofar as neither kind of evil exists. So (2) is true.

Leibniz disagrees. He provides two different responses. First, we cannot know that eliminating particular evils in the world will, collectively, create a better world, since we cannot know what the connections are between the particular evils and other collective events. Second, the best world produces the greatest variety (richness) of phenomena—a reflection of God's perfection and goodness. Leibniz would claim that simple, indivisible, changeless monads mirror all the phenomena of the world in a way preestablished by the principle of harmony. So, Leibniz holds that either (2) is false or there is insufficient reason (using the Principle of Sufficient Reason) for assuming (2) is true.

The breadth of Leibniz's other interests and writings is remarkable. He believed much of human reasoning could be reduced to calculations. He developed principles of logic and made mathematical discoveries, including, with Newton, the infinitesimal calculus. He distinguished between different theories of causation. He articulated an intimate connection between the form and content of language and the operations of the mind, leading some scholars to see Leibniz's view as an early version of artificial intelligence. He wrote on physics and technology, advanced the geological view that the earth has a molten core, and articulated a roughly stated distinction between conscious and unconscious states in psychology. His experience with affairs of state was extensive, and in 1677 he called for a European confederation (a precursor to today's European Union) to be governed by a council or senate, whose members would represent entire nations and would be free to vote their conscience. He had a keen interest in Chinese civilization (especially Confucianism), deliberately cultivated through correspondence with Christian missionaries in China. These are just some of Leibniz' unique contributions as an intellectual and philosopher.

CONWAY

In 1631, one week after her father died, Anne Conway was born in London to a wealthy, aristocratic family. Like so many women of her time, she had no formal education. Her brother John gave her books and engaged her in philosophical conversations. She avidly studied French, Greek, Hebrew, Latin, mathematics, and philosophy. John introduced her to the Cambridge Platonist Henry More when John was More's pupil at Christ's College, University of Cambridge. More agreed to instruct Conway in philosophy. Since, as a woman, she was barred from attending the university, he instructed her by letter. Thereafter, Conway and More remained friends for the remainder of her life. She had a permanent link to intellectual life beyond the confines of her domestic situation.

In 1643, at the age of twelve, Conway became ill with a fever. Although she recovered, she was plagued with debilitating headaches (migraines?) for the remainder of her life. It was in pursuit of a cure for her headaches that Conway met the second most important influence in her life, Francis Mercury van Helmont, whose father was persuaded to come to her estate to try to cure Conway's headaches.[1]

In 1650, at age nineteen, a marriage was arranged between Anne and Viscount Edward Conway. They had one child, a son, who died in infancy of smallpox. Conway refused to leave her ill son and became desperately ill with smallpox herself. Her family feared that she, too, would die. Slowly she began to recuperate although her headaches continued unabated.

The Conway family possessed one of the finest private libraries of the period. Her husband was also interested in philosophy and had himself been tutored by Henry More. He encouraged his wife's intellectual pursuits, as well as her close relationship to More. In 1652, More produced his first important prose work, *An Antidote Against Atheism*, and dedicated it to Anne as:

> one whose Genius I know to be so speculative, and Wit so penetrant, that in the knowledge of all things as well Natural as Divine, you have not only outgone all of your own Sex, but even of that other also, whose ages have not given them over-much the start of you.[2]

After her marriage, her salon was a darkened bedroom "where, too weak to raise her head, she held captive such notables as Jeremy Taylor, George Rust, Isaac Pennington, and . . . Henry More. He, at such times, would fondly refer to her as "my heroine pupil."[3]

Conway's only extant work is *The Principles of the Most Ancient and Modern Philosophy*. This work was written somewhat illegibly in a notebook and left unfinished and unrevised at Conway's death. It was published posthumously, though not in its entirety, in Latin some twelve years later. Conway's name was omitted, referring to her only as "a certain English Countess." Scholars seem to agree *The Principles* is an original philosophical document.

During the last decade of her life, the younger Van Helmont lived in her household. It was through van Helmont that Conway was introduced to kabalistic thought and to Quakerism. She converted to Quakerism shortly before she died in 1679 at her country estate, Ragley Hall, where she had lived the last twenty years of her life.

Conway's *Principles* is on metaphysics, particularly the nature of substances. Unlike Descartes's dualistic metaphysics of mind and body, Conway argues for a monistic unity of spirit and matter. She disagreed with the claims of "the new science" that nature is inert, mechanistic substance; rather, it is a vitalistic, organic unity. Some claim Conway held that there are exactly three kinds of substances: God, wholly immutable; Christ, both mutable and immutable; and everything else that exists called individual substances.[4]

Mary Warnock claims that Conway's theories oppose three philosophical systems: (1) the materialism of Thomas Hobbes (who held that matter or substance be divided only according to the arbitrary categories which language imposes on it); (2) the dualism of Descartes (who held that there were two, and only two, kinds of substance—thinking substance, and material or extended substance—and that humans were essentially thinking beings); and (3) the pantheism of Spinoza (according to whom the whole of nature is identical with God but seen under a different aspect).[5]

There is evidence that Leibniz was greatly influenced by Conway's philosophy. He probably learned of it around 1696, when van Helmont gave him a copy of Conway's *Principles*. Leibniz acknowledged her work in his correspondence and, according to Carolyn Merchant, Leibniz credits Conway for the term "monad" and other important philosophical ideas.[6]

DURAN'S COMMENTARY

In her commentary, Duran compares Leibniz's and Conway's metaphysical and ontological views concerning nature, hierarchical order, and causal interaction between individual substances. She provides a helpful historical context for understanding differences between Leibniz's and Conway's philosophical goals and emphases. She then offers a brief description of similarities between the pair. That Conway could just as easily be paired with Descartes or Spinoza suggests that her significance as a philosopher transcends any limitations she experienced by her gender.

Excerpts of Writings by Leibniz and Conway

I. EXCERPTS FROM CONWAY'S *PRINCIPLES OF THE MOST ANCIENT AND MODERN PHILOSOPHY*[7]

Chapter 6: Overview of Section Topics

S.1. That all creatures are mutable in respect to their natures. S.2. To what point this mutability extends, whether to the essential nature of things or only to their attributes and modes of being? S.3. That only the modes of being are mutable but not the essences. S.4. That there are only three kinds of being essentially distinct from each other, namely, God, who is supreme, Christ, the mediator, and creatures, who are lowest. S.5. That these distinctions are very necessary and protect us from falling into either of the extreme positions which are available to us—one of which is Ranterism, the other crass ignorance, both of which obscure the glory of the divine attributes. S.6. An example of this is given. S.7. That the justice of God gloriously appears in the transmutation of things from one species to another. S.8. That when the human spirit changes itself through impiety into the qualities and conditions of animals, it is according to God's justice that the animal-like spirit enters the body of the animal and is punished there for some length of time. S.9. How many erroneous ideas there are about God and how men conceive of God erroneously. S.10. Why the world was first destroyed by water and must finally be destroyed by fire; and that all these punishments are medicinal. S.11. That every creature is made of body and spirit, and in what way every creature, just as it has many bodies within itself, also has many spirits under one predominant general spirit, which rules all the others.

Chapter 6: Each Section (S.1–S.11) Discussed

S.1. Since all creatures are mutable in respect to their natures, the difference between God and creature, rightly considered, is clearly demonstrated by daily experience. Now, if any creature is mutable in respect to its nature, it is mutable inasmuch as it is a creature. Consequently, all creatures are mutable according to the same law, namely, that whenever one thing is like another insofar as it belongs to one or another species, it is like everything contained in that species. In fact, since mutability is appropriate for a creature insofar as it is a creature (this is the most general name of the species which includes all creatures), it appears that there is no other distinction between God and creatures. For if any creature were by its nature immutable, it would be God since immutability is one of his incommunicable attributes.

S.2. Now let us consider the extent of this mutability. First, can one individual be changed into another, either of the same or of a different species? I say that this is impossible, for then the essential nature of things would change, which would cause great confusion not only for creatures but also for the wisdom of God, which made everything. For example, if one man could change into another, namely Paul into Judas or Judas into Paul, then he who sinned would not be punished for that sin but another in his stead who was innocent and virtuous. Thus a righteous man would not receive the reward of his virtue but another steeped in vice. But if we suppose that one righteous man is changed into another, as Paul into Peter and Peter into Paul, then Paul would surely not receive his proper reward but that of Peter, nor would Peter receive his but that of Paul. This confusion would not suit the wisdom of God. Besides, if the essential nature of individuals could change one into another, it would follow that creatures would not have a true being inasmuch as we could not be certain of anything nor could we have true knowledge or understanding of anything. Therefore all the innate ideas and precepts of truth, which all men find in themselves, would be false and, consequently, so would the conclusions drawn from them. For all true science or certainty of knowledge depends on the truth of objects, which we commonly call objective truths. If these objective truths were interchangeable, then the truth of any statement made about the object would also change. Therefore no statement could be invariably true, not even the clearest and most obvious, for example, the following: that the whole is greater than its parts and that two halves make a whole.

S.3. Furthermore, we must consider whether one species can change into another. But first we must distinguish as carefully as possible how one species differs from another. For there are many species which are commonly said to differ, but nevertheless are not distinct from each other in substance or essence, but only in certain modes or attributes. And when these modes or attributes change, the thing itself is said to have changed its species. But indeed, it is not the essence or entity itself but only its mode of being which thus changes. For example, water does not change but stays the same, although when cold it freezes, where it was fluid before. When water turns to stone, there is no reason to suppose that a greater change of substance has occurred than in the earlier example when it changed from water to ice. And when a stone changes back into softer and more pliant earth, this too is no change of substance. Thus, in all other changes which can be observed the substance or essence always remains the same. There is merely a change of form inasmuch as the substance relinquishes one form and takes on another. These arguments prove that in terms of its substance or essence one species cannot change from one into another and equally that one individual cannot change into another. For species are nothing but individual entities subsumed under one general and common idea of the mind or one common term, as, for instance, man is a species including all individual men and horse is a species including all individual horses. If one man cannot change into another, much less can that man change into an individual of another species. Thus, if Alexander cannot change into Darius, he also cannot change into his own horse, Bucephalus.

S.4. Since we know to what extent things are able to change, we must now determine how many species of things there are which are distinguished from each other in terms of their substance or essence. If we look closely into this, we will discover there are only three, which, as was said above, are God, Christ, and creatures; and that these three species are really distinct in terms of their essence has already been proved. No argument can prove that there is a fourth species distinct from the other three. Indeed, a fourth species seems altogether superfluous. Since all phenomena in the entire universe can be reduced to these three aforementioned species as if into their original and peculiar causes, nothing compels us to recognize a further species according to this rule: whatever is correctly understood is most true and certain. Entities should not be multiplied without need. Furthermore, because the three aforementioned species exhaust all the specific differences in substances which can possibly be conceived by our minds, then that vast infinity of possible things is fulfilled in these three species. How could a place or space be found for a fourth, fifth, sixth, or seventh species? It has already been shown that these three species have this capacity. Certainly insofar as something can be called an entity, it is either altogether immutable like God, the supreme being, or altogether mutable, that is for good or bad, like a creature, which is the lowest order of being, or partly mutable in respect to good, like Christ, the son of God, the mediator between God and creatures. In what category then could we place some fourth, fifth, sixth, or seventh, etc. species which is nor clearly immutable or clearly mutable, nor partly mutable nor partly immutable. Besides, whoever posits some fourth species distinct from the previously mentioned three in terms of essence or substance destroys, in fact, the most excellent order which we find in the universe, since there would be not only one mediator between God and creatures but two, three, four, five, six, or however many can be imagined between the first and the last. Furthermore, since it agrees with sound reason and with the order of things that just as God is one and does not have two or three or more distinct substances in himself, and just as Christ is one simple Christ without further distinct substances in himself (insofar as he is the celestial man or Adam, the first of all creatures), so likewise all creatures, or the whole of creation, are also a single species in substance or essence, although it includes many individuals gathered into subordinate species and distinguished from each other modally but not substantially or essentially. Thus, what Paul says about human beings can also be understood about all creatures (which in their primitive and original state were a certain species of human being designated according to their virtues, as will be shown), namely, that God made all tribes and troops of creatures from one blood. Surely this is the explanation of the following two things: that God made all tribes of human beings from one blood so that they would love one another and would be bound by the same sympathy and would help one another. Thus God has implanted a certain universal sympathy and mutual love into his creatures so that they are all members of one body and all, so to speak, brothers, for whom there is one common Father, namely, God in Christ or the word incarnate. There is also one mother, that unique substance or entity from which all things have come forth, and of which they are the real parts and members. And although sin has weakened this love and sympathy in creatures to an astonishing degree, nevertheless it has not altogether destroyed it.

S.5. Having acknowledged the three previously mentioned types of being, and these three alone, which are completely noninterchangeable among each other, we will proceed securely in the middle way of truth concerning the nature of substance, leaving the greatest errors and confusion to the right and left. First, there are those who maintain that all things are one substance, of which they are the real and proper parts. These confuse God and his creatures, as if these two notions were only one essential thing, so that sin and the devils would be nothing but parts or the slightest modification of this divine being. From this come dangerous consequences. Although I would not want this to be taken badly by all those who have fallen into this opinion by mistake, I should warn my readers where such principles lead so that they might consider them better and avoid their absurdity. Second, there are others who maintain that there are two kinds of substance, God, that supreme and utterly immutable being, and creatures, the lowest and altogether mutable beings. These, moreover, do not sufficiently consider that excellent order, described above, which appears in all things. Since they might perhaps have observed elsewhere that in addition to the two extremes there is also a certain mediator which partakes of both, and this is Jesus Christ, whom the wiser among the Jews recognize, no less than some among the so-called Gentiles, maintaining that there is such a mediator, which they call by different names such as Logos, Son of God, first-born Son of God, Mind, Wisdom, the Celestial Adam, etc. And, thus, they also call him the eternal mediator.

If these matters are correctly considered, they will contribute greatly to the propagation of the true faith and Christian religion among Jews and Turks and other infidel nations; if, namely, it is agreed that there are equally strong reasons by which we can prove that there is a mediator between God and human beings, indeed, between God and all creatures, as there are for proving that there is a God and a creation. Therefore, those who acknowledge such a mediator and believe in him can be said truly to believe in Jesus Christ, even though they do not yet know it and are not convinced that he has already come in the flesh. But if they first grant that there is a mediator, they will indubitably come to acknowledge also, even if they are unwilling, that Christ is that mediator.

There are others, moreover, who multiply specific entities into their own distinct essences and attributes almost to infinity. This altogether upsets that exceptional order of things and quite obscures the glory of the divine attributes so that it cannot shine with its due splendor in creatures. For if a creature were entirely limited by its own individuality and totally constrained and confined within the very narrow boundaries of its own species to the point that there was no mediator through which one creature could change into another, then no creature could attain further perfection and greater participation in divine goodness, nor could creatures act and react upon each other in different ways.

S.6. We shall illustrate these things with one or two examples. Let us first imagine a horse, a creature endowed by its creator with different degrees of perfection, such as not only bodily strength but also certain notions, so to speak, of how to serve his master. In addition, a horse exhibits anger, fear, love, memory, and various other qualities which are in human beings and which we can also observe in dogs and many other animals. Therefore, since the divine power, goodness, and wisdom has created good creatures so that they may continually and infinitely move toward the good through their own mutability, the glory of their attributes shines more and more. And this is the nature of all creatures, namely that they be in continual motion or operation, which most certainly strives for their further good (just as for the reward and fruit of their own labor), unless they resist that good by a willful transgression and abuse of the impartial will created in them by God. Now, I ask, to what further perfection or degree of goodness of being or essence does or can a horse attain after he has performed good services for his master and has done what was and is appropriate for such a creature? Is a horse a mere machine or dead matter, or does it indeed have some kind of spirit which possesses thought, sense, love, and various other properties which are appropriate to its spirit? If it has such a spirit—something which must clearly be conceded—what happens to this spirit when the horse dies? If it is said that it returns to life and obtains the body of another horse, so that it becomes a horse as it was before but stronger and more beautiful and with a better spirit than before, excellent! If it dies a second, third, or fourth time, does it always remain a horse, even though it becomes continuously better and more excellent, and how often does its spirit return? Now, I ask, whether the species of horse possesses such infinite perfection that a horse can always become better and better to infinity, yet always remain a horse? To be sure, it is almost common knowledge that this visible earth will not always remain in its present state, which can be proven by the best arguments. Therefore it necessarily follows that the continual generation of animals in their crass bodies will also cease. For, if the earth assumes another form and produces no more vegetation, then horses and similar animals will cease to be as they were before. Since they would not have their proper nourishment, they could not remain the same species. Nevertheless, they will not be annihilated, as it is easy to conclude, for how can anything be annihilated since the goodness of God toward his creatures always remains the same and since the preservation or continuation of his creatures is a constant act of creation? It is generally agreed, as has been demonstrated above, that God is a perpetual creator acting with as much freedom as necessity. Yet, if one replies that the earth will change, as suggested above, then horses and other animals would change their configurations along with the earth, and the earth would produce nourishment for them according to their new configurations because of their changed condition. I then ask whether the creatures remain the same species during such a change, or whether there is not indeed some future difference between this and that state, such as, for example, that between a horse and a cow, which is commonly recognized as a different species. Furthermore, I ask whether some species of creatures so excel others to infinity that a certain individual of one species always increases in perfection and comes closer to some other species, yet is never able to reach that species? For example, a horse approaches the species of human being in many ways more than many other creatures. Is human nature therefore infinitely different from the nature of a horse or only finitely? If this distance is finite, the horse will surely change eventually into a human being—to be sure, in respect to its spirit, for in respect to its body, the matter is obvious. If this distance is infinite, then a certain actual infinite excellence will be attributed to a human being of the lowest and meanest understanding, an excellence such as only accords with God and Christ but to no creature. For the highest excellence of a creature is to be infinite only in potentiality, not in actuality. That is, it is always able to become more perfect and more excellent to infinity, although it never reaches this infinity. For however far a certain finite being may progress, it is nevertheless always finite, although there are no limits to its progress. For instance, if we could ever attain the least minute of eternity or a similar part of an infinite duration, this would not be infinite but finite.

In saying this, we do not contradict what was said in chapter 3 about the infinity of creatures, for that does not concern their infinite goodness and excellence but only their number and size, neither of which may be numbered or measured by any understanding of a created intellect. Nevertheless, individual creatures are only finitely good and finitely distant in terms of species. However, they are also potentially infinite, that is, they are always capable of greater perfection without end. Thus if someone places a stairs which is infinitely long and has an infinite number of steps, nevertheless the steps are not infinitely distant from each other, for otherwise there would be no possibility of ascent or descent. Moreover, the steps in this example signify species which cannot be infinitely distant from each other, or from those which are closest to them. In fact, daily experience reaches us that various species change into each other: earth changes into water, water into air, air into fire or ether and, vice versa, fire into air, air into water, etc., and these are nevertheless distinct species. Similarly, stones change into metals and one metal into another. However, let no one say that these are only bare bodies and have no spirit. We observe the same thing not only in plants but in animals. Just as wheat and barley can change into each other and in fact often do so, which is well known to farmers in many countries, especially in Hungary where, if barley is sown, wheat grows. In other more barren places, and especially in rocky places such as are found in Germany, if wheat is sown, barley grows instead, and in other places barley becomes plain grass. Among animals, moreover, worms change into flies, and beasts and fish that feed on beasts and fish of another species change into their nature and species. And does not rotting matter, or body of earth and water, produce animals without any previous seed of those animals? And in the creation of this world did not the waters produce fish and birds at God's command? Did the earth not also at the same command bring forth reptiles and beasts, which were, on this account, real parts of earth and water? And just as they have their bodies from the earth, so they have their spirits, or souls, from the earth. For the earth produced living souls, as the Hebrew text says, and not simply material bodies lacking life and spirit. For this reason the difference between human beings and beasts is exceedingly striking. For it is said about human beings that God made them in his image and breathed into them the breath of life and they became living souls, so that they received his life, the principal part that makes them human beings, which is really distinct from the divine soul or spirit which God breathed into them.

Moreover, since the human body was made from earth, which, as has been proved, contained various spirits and gave those spirits to all the animals, without doubt the earth gave human beings the best and most excellent spirits which it contained. But all these spirits were far inferior to the spirit of human beings, which they received from above and not from the earth. The human spirit ought to have dominion over these spirits, which are only terrestrial, so that it might rule over them and raise them to a higher level and, indeed, to its own proper nature; and this would have been its true increase and multiplication. For their sake, it allowed the earthly spirits existing in it to have dominion over it, so that it would be like them. For this reason it is said, "You are of the earth and you shall return to earth," which has a spiritual as well as a literal meaning.

S.7. We already see how the justice of God shines so gloriously in this transmutation of one species into another. For it is most certain that a kind of justice operates not only in human beings and angels but also in all creatures. Whoever does not see this must be called completely blind. This justice appears as much in the ascent of creatures as in their descent, that is, when they change for better or worse. When they become better, this justice bestows a reward and prize for their good deeds. When they become worse, the same justice punishes them with fitting penalties according to the nature and degree of their transgression. The same justice imposes a law for all creatures and inscribes it in their very natures. Whatever creature breaks this law is punished accordingly. But any creature who observes this law receives the reward of becoming better.

Thus under the law which God gave to the Jews, if a beast has killed a man, the beast had to be killed. A human life, it is said, is to be sought at the hand of every beast (Gen. 9:5). If anyone has sexual dealings with a beast, not only the man but the beast must be killed. Thus, not only the wife and her husband (Adam and Eve) received a sentence and punishment from God after their transgression but also the serpent, which was the brute part in man that he took from the earth. God endowed man with the same instinct for justice toward beasts and the trees of the field. For any man who is just and good loves the brute creatures which serve him, and he takes care of them so that they have food and rest and the other things they need. He does not do this only for his own good but out of a principle of true justice; and if he is so cruel toward them that he requires work from them and nevertheless does not provide the necessary food, then he has surely broken the law which God inscribed in his heart. And if he kills any of his beasts only to satisfy his own pleasure, then he acts unjustly, and the same measure will be measured out to him. Thus, a man who has a tree in his orchard that is fruitful and grows well fertilizes and prunes it so that it becomes better and better. But if it is barren and a burden to the earth, he fells it with an ax and burns it. Therefore, there is a certain justice in all these things, so that in the very transmutation from one species to another, either by ascending from a lower to a higher or by descending in the opposite way, the same justice appears. For example, is it not just that if a man lives a pure and holy life on this earth, like the heavenly angels, that he is elevated to the rank of angels after he dies and becomes like them, since the angels also rejoice over him? However, a man who lives such an impious and perverse life that he is more like the devil raised from hell than like any other creature, then, if he dies in such a state without repenting, does not the same justice hurl him down to hell, and does he not justly become like the devils, just as those who live an angelic life become equal to angels? But if someone lives neither an angelic nor a diabolical life but rather a brutish or animal life, so that his spirit is more like the spirit of beasts than any other creature, does the same justice not act most justly, so that just as he became a brute in spirit and allowed his brutal part and spirits to have dominion over his most excellent part, he also (at least as regard his external shape) changes his corporeal shape into that species of beast to which he is most similar in terms of the qualities and conditions of his mind? And since that brute spirit is now superior and predominant and holds the other spirit captive, is it not likely that when such a man dies, his brute spirit always has dominion over him and takes away his human spirit and compels it to serve the animal spirit in every possible way? And when that brute spirit returns again into some other body, it rules over that body and has the ability and freedom to shape the body according to its own ideas and inclinations (which it did not previously have in the human body). It necessarily follows that this body, which the vital spirit forms, will be that of a brute and not a human, for the brute spirit cannot produce or form any other shape because its formative power is governed by its imagination, which imagines and conceives as strongly as possible its own image, according to which the external body must take shape.

S.8. In this way the justice of God shines forth wonderfully, since it assigns the due and appropriate punishment for each kind and degree of wrongdoing nor does it demand hellfire and damnation for every single wicked sin and transgression. For Christ taught the opposite in that parable where he shows that only the third degree of punishment is to be sent down to Gehenna, as when one rashly says to his brother, "You fool!" (Matt. 5:22).

What objection can be made to the justice of God? If it is said that the dignity and nobility of human nature is diminished and sullied when it is decreed that the body and soul is to be turned into the nature of a brute, one may reply according to the common axiom, "the worst corruption is that of the beast." For when a human being has so greatly degraded himself by his own willful wrongdoing and has brought his nature, which had been so noble, to a lower state, and when that nature has demeaned itself in spirit to the level of a most foul brute or animal so that it is wholly ruled by lust and earthly desires and becomes like any beast, indeed, worse than any beast, what injustice is this if God compels him to bear the same image in his body as in that spirit into which he has internally transformed himself? Or which degeneration do you think is worse, to have the image of a beast in one's spirit or body? Certainly it must be said that to be like a brute in spirit is the greatest possible degeneration. There is hardly anyone with any genuine nobility of soul who does not admit that to be a brute internally is worse than to be a brute externally. For it is far worse to be a brute in spirit than to be a brute in outward form and shape. However, if someone says that it is too mild a punishment or those who have a brutal life throughout all their days merely to return after death in the condition and state of a beast, let them know that the most just creator and maker of all things is wiser than they and knows better what punishment is appropriate for each sin. God has arranged all things as justly and wisely as possible so that no one living carnally like a beast can enter the kingdom of heaven. Furthermore, Christ expressly teaches us that not every sin must be punished with the penalty of hell and that "where the treasure is, there also is the heart and spirit of man" (Matt. 6:21). Also, if a man is united and joined with something, he then becomes one with that thing. He who unites himself to God is one with him in spirit, and he who unites himself to a prostitute is one in flesh with her. Shouldn't someone who is united to a beast become one with that beast for the same reason and similarly in every other case? For, according to Scripture, anyone who obeys another is his servant inasmuch as he obeys him. Besides, it is said that, "by whatsoever measure you shall measure, you shall be measured by the same" (Luke 6:38). That is to say, that all degrees and kinds of sin have their appropriate punishments, and all these punishments tend toward the good of creatures, so that the grace of God will prevail over judgment and judgment turn into victory for the salvation and restoration of creatures. Since the grace of God stretches over all his work, why do we think that God is more severe and more rigorous a punisher of his creatures than he truly is? This obscures and darkens the glory of God's attributes in an astonishing way and does not foster love for God and admiration for his goodness and justice in the hearts of men as it should, but does precisely the opposite.

S.9. For the common notion of God's justice, namely, that whatever the sin, it is punished by hellfire and without end, has generated a horrible idea of God in men, as if he were a cruel tyrant rather than an benign father toward all his creatures. If, however, an image of a lovable God was more widely known, such as he truly is and shows himself in all his dealings with his creatures, and if our souls could inwardly feel and taste him, as he is charity and kindness itself and as he reveals his intrinsic self through the light and spirit of our Lord Jesus Christ in the hearts of men, then, and only then, will men finally love God above everything and acknowledge him as the most loving, just, merciful God, fit to be worshipped before everything, and as one who cannot inflict the same punishment on all sinners.

S.10. Then, why did he destroy the original world with water and decide to destroy this world with fire, such as happened with Sodom? Surely, to show that he uses different kinds of punishments for different kinds of sins. The first world was bad, and this one, which had to be destroyed by fire, would have been worse. For this reason it was to have a greater punishment. But the different nature of this transgression, for which different punishments have been devised, seems to consist in this, that the sins of the old world were more carnal and brutal, as the word of God reveals when he said, "My spirit will not always strive in man because he was made flesh" (Gen. 6:3); that is, he was made completely brutal or bestial by obeying the desires of the flesh. Consequently, if that generation had not been wiped out, the whole human race (with the exception of Noah and his family) would have been bestial in the following generations, which evil God wished to avert by drowning them in water so that by this punishment they might revert from the nature of beasts to that of men. But the sins of this world, like those of Sodom, which had to be destroyed by fire, appear to be more like the sins of the devil than anything else because of their hostility, malice, cruelty, fraud, and cunning. Therefore their appropriate punishment is fire, which is the original essence of those so noble, yet degenerate, spirits, and by this same fire they must be degraded and restored.

For what is fire, but a certain kind of ethereal and imperfect substance enclosed in combustible bodies, which we always see ascend and immediately vanish because of its remarkable tenuousness? In regard to their spirits, angels as well as men originate from this ethereal substance, just as brutes originate from water. Just as all the punishments inflicted by God on his creatures are in proportion to their sins, so they tend, even the worst, to their good and to their restoration and they are so medicinal as to cure these sickly creatures and restore them to a better condition than they previously enjoyed.

S.11. Now, let us consider briefly how creatures are composed and how the parts of this composition can change into one another because they originally had one and the same essence and being. In every visible creature there is body and spirit, or a more active and a more passive principle, which are appropriately called male and female because they are analogous to husband and wife. For just as the normal generation of human beings commonly requires the conjunction and cooperation of male and female, so too does every generation and production, whatever it may be, require the union and simultaneous operation of those two principles, namely spirit and body. Moreover, spirit is light or the eye looking at its own proper image, and the body is the darkness which receives this image. And when the spirit beholds it, it is as if someone sees himself in a mirror. But he cannot see himself reflected in the same way in clear air or in any diaphanous body, since the reflection of an image requires a certain opacity, which we call body. Nevertheless, it is not an essential property of anything to be a body, just as it is not a property of anything to be dark. For nothing is so dark that it cannot become bright. Indeed, darkness itself can become light. In the same way, light which is created can turn to darkness, as the words of Christ plainly show when he says, "If the light within you is darkness," etc., by which he means the eye or spirit which is in the body and which sees the image of something. Just as every spirit needs a body to receive and reflect its image, it also needs a body to retain the image. For every body has this retentive nature in itself to a greater or a lesser degree, and the more perfect a body is—that is, the more perfectly mixed it is—the more retentive it is. Thus water is more retentive than air, and earth is more retentive of certain things than water. The semen of a female creature, on account of its so perfect mixture, because it is the purest extract of the whole body, has a remarkable power of retention. In this semen, as in the body, the masculine semen, which is the spirit and image of the male, is received and retained together with the other spirits which are in the woman. And whatever spirit is strongest and has the strongest image or idea in the woman, whether male or female, or any other spirit received from outside of one or the other of them, that spirit predominates in the semen and forms a body as similar as possible to its image. And thus every creature receives its external shape.

In the same way, the internal productions of the mind (namely the thoughts which are true creatures according to their kind and which have a true substance appropriate to themselves) are generated. These are our inner children, and all are masculine and feminine; that is, they have a body and spirit. For, if they did not have a body, they could not be retained nor could we reflect on our own thoughts. For all reflection takes place because of a certain darkness, and this is the body. Thus memory requires a body in order to retain the spirit of the thing conceived of; otherwise it vanishes, just as an image in a mirror immediately vanishes when the object is removed. Thus when we remember something, we see within ourselves its image, which is the spirit that proceeded from it, while we looked at it from the outside. This image, or spirit, is retained in some body, which is the semen of our brain. Thus a certain spiritual generation occurs in us. Consequently, every spirit has its own body and every body its own spirit. Just as a body, whether of a man or brute, is nothing but a countless multitude of bodies collected into one and arranged in a certain order, so the spirit of man or brute is also a countless multitude of spirits united in this body, and they have their order and government, such that one is the principal ruler, another has second place, and a third commands others below itself, and so on for the whole, just as in an army. For this reason, creatures are called armies and God the leader of these armies. Just as the devil, who assaulted the man, was called Legion because there were many of them. Thus every human being, indeed, every creature whatsoever, contains many spirits and bodies. (The many spirits which exist in men are called by the Jews Nizzuzuth, or sparks.) Truly, every body is a spirit and nothing else, and it differs from a spirit only insofar as it is darker. Therefore the crasser it becomes, the more it is removed from the condition of spirit. Consequently, the distinction between spirit and body is only modal and incremental, not essential and substantial.

II. EXCERPTS FROM LEIBNIZ'S *MONADOLOGY*[8]

The monad which we shall discuss here is nothing other than a simple substance that enters into composites. Simple means without parts.

And there must be simple substances, since there are composites; for the composite is nothing but an accumulation or aggregate of simples.

However, where there are no parts at all, no extension or figure or divisibility is possible. And these monads are the true atoms of nature, and, in a word, the elements of things.

There is also no dissolution to fear in them and there is no way conceivable in which a simple substance can perish naturally.

For the same reason, there is no way in which a simple substance could begin naturally, since it cannot be formed by composition.

So one can say that monads can neither come into being nor end save all at once; that is, they can begin only by creation and end only by annihilation. By contract, that which is composite begins and ends part by part.

There is, furthermore, no way to explain how a monad could be altered or changed in its inner make-up by some other created being. For one can transpose nothing in it, nor conceive in it any internal motion that could be excited, directed, increased, or diminished within it, as can happen in composites, where there is change among the parts. Monads just have no windows through which something can enter into or depart from them. Accidents cannot be detached, nor wander about outside of substances, as the sensible species of the Scholastics formerly did. And so, neither substance nor accident can enter a monad from without.

However, monads must have some qualities, otherwise they would not even be beings. And if simple substances did not differ by their qualities at all, there would be no way at all of perceiving any change in things, since that which is present in the composite can only come from its simple constituents. And then monads, being without qualities, would be indistinguishable from one another, since they do not differ quantitatively at all. In consequence, a plenum being supposed, each place would always receive in any motion only the equivalent of what it already had, and one state of things would be indistinguishable from another.

It is even necessary that every monad be different from every other. For there are never in nature two beings that are perfectly alike and in which it would not be possible to find a difference that is internal or founded on an intrinsic denomination.

I also take it for granted that every created being is subject to change, and in consequence the created monad also, and even that this change is continuous in each one.

It follows from what has just been said that the natural changes of the monads proceed from an internal principle. For an external cause cannot influence their inner make-up.

But beyond the principle of change, there must also be an internal complexity (detail) of that which changes, which would produce, so to speak, the specification and the variety of simple substances.

This internal complexity (detail) must enfold a multiplicity in unity or in the simple. For as every natural change happens by degrees, something always changes and something remains. Consequently, there must be a plurality of properties and relations within a simple substance, even though it has none of parts.

The transitory state which enfolds and represents a multiplicity in a unity, or in the simple substance, is exactly what one calls perception. One must distinguish this from apperception and from consciousness, as will become clear below. This is where the Cartesians went badly wrong in taking no account of perceptions that are not apperceived. This led them to think that "spirits" alone are monads, and that there are no souls of beasts nor other entelechies. And it led them to confuse, as ordinary people do, a prolonged stupor with death in the strict sense, which again misled them into the Scholastic prejudice that there are wholly separated souls and even confirmed misguided minds in a belief in the mortality of souls.

The action of the internal principle which brings about the change or the passage from one perception to another may be called appetition. It is true that appetite cannot always attain altogether the whole perception to which it tends, but it always obtains some part of it, and so attains new perceptions.

We ourselves experience multiplicity in a simple substance when we find that the slightest thought of which we are conscious in ourselves enfolds a variety in its object.

Accordingly, all who recognize that the soul is a simple substance must also recognize this multiplicity within the monad, and Monsieur Bayle ought nowise to have found difficulty in this, as he did in his Dictionary article "Rorarius."

Furthermore, one is obliged to admit that perception and what depends upon it is inexplicable on mechanical principles, that is, by figures and motions. In imagining that there is a machine whose construction would enable it to think, to sense, and to have perception, one could conceive it enlarged while retaining the same proportions, so that one could enter into it, just like into a windmill. Supposing this, one should, when visiting within it, find only parts pushing one another, and never anything by which to explain a perception. Thus it is in the simple substance, and not in the composite or in the machine that one must look for perception. Moreover, there is nothing besides this—besides perceptions and their changes—that one could possible find in a simple substance. It is also in this alone that all the internal actions of simple substances can consist.

One could give the name entelechies to all simple substance or created monads. For they all have in them a certain perfection (echousi to enteles); there is a certain self-sufficiency (*autarkeia*) that makes them sources of their own internal actions and, so to speak, incorporeal automata.

If we are willing to call soul anything that has perceptions and appetites in the general sense I have just explained, then all simple substances or created monads could be called souls. But as sentience is something more than a mere perception, I hold that the generic name of monads or entelechies suffices for simple substances which have nothing but this, and that one should call souls only those whose perception is more distinct and accompanied by memory.

For we experience in ourselves a state where we remember nothing and have no distinct perception, as when we fall into a swoon or when we are overcome by a deep and altogether dreamless sleep. In this state the soul does not differ noticeably from a simple monad. But as this state is not at all durable, and the soul emerges from it, the soul is something more.

But it by no means follows from this that a simple substance is now wholly without perception. This is even impossible for the aforementioned reasons. For a substance cannot perish, nor can it subsist without some affection, which is nothing other than its perception. But when there is a large multiplicity of minute perceptions where there is nothing distinct, one is stupefied, as when we turn continually in the same direction several times in succession, whence arises a dizziness which can make us faint and which lets us distinguish nothing. Death can give this state for a time to animals.

And as every present state of a simple substance is a natural consequence of its preceding state, so is its present pregnant with the future.

Therefore, since when reawakened from unconsciousness one apperceives one's perceptions, it must be that one had some of them immediately before, although one was not at all aware of them. For a perception can come naturally only from another perception, just as one motion can come naturally only from another motion.

One sees from this that if we had in our perceptions nothing distinct and, so to speak, heightened and of an enhanced flavor, we should always remain in unconsciousness. And this is the state of the totally bare monads.

We see too that nature has given heightened perceptions to animals by the care she has taken to furnish them with organs which collect many rays of light or many vibrations of air to make them more effective through their unification. There is something similar in smell, taste, and touch, and perhaps in many other senses that are unknown to us. And I shall explain presently how what happens in the soul represents what happens in the organs.

Memory provides a kind of connectedness (consecution) to souls which resembles reason but must be distinguished from it. For we see that animals which have a perception of something that strikes them and of which they have previously had a similar perception expect, from the representation in their memory, that which has been conjoined in that previous perception, and are thus led to sensations similar to those they have had before. For example, when one shows a stick to dogs, they recall the pain that it has caused them and whine and run off.

The potent imaging that strikes and moves them comes either from the size or from the number of the preceding perceptions. For often a strong impression has at one blow the effect of a long-formed habit, or that of a great many repeated perceptions of modest size.

Men function like beasts insofar as the connections among their perceptions come about only through the agency of memory, resembling empirical physicians who have mere practice without theory. We are all mere empirics in three-quarters of our actions. For example, when one expects a sunrise tomorrow, one acts as an empiric, seeing that this has always been so heretofore. Only the astronomer judges this by reason.

But the knowledge of necessary and eternal truths is what distinguishes us from mere animals and provides us with reason and the sciences, elevating us to a knowledge of ourselves and of God. And it is this within us that is called the rational soul or spirit.

It is also through the knowledge of necessary truths and through their abstraction that we are raised to Reflexive Acts, which enable us to think of what is called I and to consider that this or that lies within ourselves. And, it is thus that in thinking of ourselves we think of being, of substance, of the simple and compound, of the immaterial, and of God himself, by conceiving that what is limited in us is unlimited in him. And these reflexive acts furnish the principal objects of our reasonings.

Our reasonings are founded on two great principles: that of Contradiction, in virtue of which we judge to be false that which contains contradiction, and to be true that which is opposed or contradictory to the false.

And that of Sufficient Reason, in virtue of which we consider that no fact can be real or actual, and no proposition true, without there being a sufficient reason for its being so and not otherwise, although most often these reasons just cannot be known by us.

There are two kinds of truths, those of reasoning and those of fact. Truths of reasoning are necessary and their opposite is impossible, while those of fact are contingent and their opposite is possible. When a truth is necessary one can find its reason through analysis, resolving it into ever more simple ideas and truths until one reaches primitives.

This is how, among mathematicians, theoretical theorems and practical rules are reduced by analysis to definitions, axioms, and postulates.

There are, ultimately, simple ideas of which no definition can be given. And there are also axioms and postulates, or, in work primitive principles, which cannot be proved and have no need of it, either. And these are the identical propositions, whose opposite contains an explicit contradiction.

But a sufficient reason must also be present in contingent truths or truths of fact; that is to say, in the sequence of things dispersed through the universe of created beings. Here the resolution into particular reasons can go on into endless detail, because of the immense variety of things in nature and the ad infinitum division of bodies. There is an infinity of shapes and motions, present and past, that enter into the efficient cause of my present writing, and there is an infinity of minute inclinations and dispositions of my soul, present and past, that enter into its final cause.

And as all this detail only contains other prior, or yet more detailed contingents each of which also requires a similar analysis to provide its reason, one is no further ahead. The sufficient or final reason must lie outside of the sequence of series of this detail of contingencies, however infinite it may be.

And so the ultimate reason of things must be in a necessary substance in which the detail of the changes is present only eminently, as in its source. It is this that we call God.

Now as this substance is a sufficient reason of all this detail, which is also interconnected throughout, there is only one God and this God is all sufficient.

One can also conclude that this Supreme Substance, which is unique, universal, and necessary—having nothing outside it that is independent of it, and being a direct consequence of merely being possible—must be incapable of limits and must contain as much reality as is possible.

From this it follows that God is absolutely perfect, perfection being nothing but the amount of positive reality taken separately, putting aside the limits or bound in the things that have them. And where there are no bounds at all, namely in God, perfection is absolutely infinite.

It follows also that created beings owe their perfections to the influence of God, but owe their imperfections to their own nature, which is incapable of being without limits. For it is in this that they differ from God.

It is true also that in God lies not only the source of existences, but also that of essences, insofar as they are real.

For it must be that, if there is a reality in essences or possibilities, or indeed in eternal truths, this reality be founded in something existent and actual, and consequently in the existence of the Necessary Being, in whom essence includes existence, or in whom being possible suffices for being actual.

Thus only God, or the Necessary Being, has this privilege, that he must exist if he is possible. And since nothing can prevent the possibility of that which contains no limits and no negation, and consequently no contradiction, this by itself suffices to establish the existence of God a priori. And we have also proved this through the reality of the eternal truths.

However, we must not imagine, as some do, that the eternal truths, being dependent on God, are arbitrary and depend upon his will, as Descartes seems to have held, and Monsieur Poiret after him. That is true only of contingent truths, whose principle is fitness or the choice of the best. Instead, the necessary truths depend solely on God's understanding, and are its internal object.

Commentary by *Jane Duran*, Conway and Leibniz: The Ideal and The Real

INTRODUCTION

Although much has been made of the comparison between Anne Conway and Gottfried Wilhelm von Leibniz, a great deal of the extant commentary on Conway fails to elucidate the intersection between the two thinkers, or glosses over it. Part of the reason may well be simply that Leibniz's work is notoriously difficult—of the major rationalist thinkers, there is probably the smallest amount of clear commentary on Leibniz available in English.[9] Another reason may have to do with the simple fact that, in a sense, comparison between Conway and Descartes, or even Conway and Spinoza, is easier to establish. Because their work was available to a greater number, at an earlier Conway-Leibniz juxtaposition the two thinkers do converge on at least one or two major points having to do with metaphysics and ontology. Perhaps more important, more discussion of each thinker's views, especially vis-à-vis the other's views, is badly needed. Instead of simply noting that each of them employs concepts that seem to buttress a strongly idealist metaphysics, more careful consideration to a number of facets of their work is due. As we will see, Anne Conway stands out, even among the now more generally recognized group of women thinkers whom we categorize as seventeenth-century women philosophers. We will see precisely where it is that Anne Conway begins to take issue with Leibnizian metaphysics. What follows provides a brief overview and summary of the comparison of Leibniz's and Conway's views.

Because students are more likely to have encountered Leibniz's name than Conway's, it is perhaps best to start off with this preeminent male rationalist thinker. Rescher calls Leibniz a philosopher "on a par with the very greatest"; whether the extant commentary has done justice to this philosopher is open to dispute.[10] In any case, Leibniz's *Metaphysics* is famous for its tersely set out ontology (or description of things that are real), with the universe composed of an infinite number of "simples." Simples are without extension or standard secondary predicates, and are termed "monads" by Leibniz. Monads are probably best thought of as the seventeenth-century analogue of today's smallest units of matter—the relevant components of contemporary atomic theory. But one major difference from those who practice what we call "the scientific method" and Leibniz's methodology is that Leibniz employed the standard practice of rationalists, reasoning by definition, deduction, and careful construction. Once defined, the monads are portrayed by Leibniz in such a way as to make his system maximally coherent and maximally explanatory, at least by his own lights.[11]

One major difficulty with Leibniz's theory of monads, however, is that they are defined by Leibniz at the outset as substances that are not capable of interacting (causally) with other monads. Although seemingly a minor point, this sets up a number of problems for Leibniz that, by contrast, are not ones that beset Conway's theory of individual substances even though, as we shall see, she employs a somewhat similar concept as Leibniz's monads.

Here is what Leibniz says about the nature of the monad: "The monad which we shall discuss here is nothing other than a simple substance that enters into composites. Simple means without parts."[12] Although Leibniz makes ninety such statements in his work *Monadology*, each of a seemingly greater degree of complexity (insofar as the hapless reader is concerned), it is the opening statements that do the most work; they provide a springboard for comparison with the work of the Cambridge Platonists in general and Anne Conway in particular.

THREE KEY AREAS OF DIFFERENCE BETWEEN CONWAY AND LEIBNIZ

Although some find a great deal of similarity between Conway and Leibniz, they differ enormously in three key areas: (1) the complexity and ultimate composition of individual substances; (2) the hierarchy of such substances; and (3) the question of the possible interaction of substances. For the moment we will concentrate on the first of these areas, the composition of the substances that Leibniz calls monads and their relation to each other.

Area 1: Individual Substances

Rescher's helpful commentary on the *Monadology* eschews the use of the term "monist" for Leibniz, since Rescher reminds us that these monads, or points (they have no material admixture or dimension), are infinite in number. That is, although nonmaterial, they compose an infinity of substances.[13] The obvious question then is: how it is that nonmaterial monads form larger, visible entities (substances) in the material world? Leibniz's position here—his answer—is one of the least explicated parts of Leibniz's doctrine, and one of the parts that employs the vaguest terminology. Nonetheless, Leibniz claims that by attunement, so to speak, and by prespecified internal principles that he names and discusses elsewhere in the *Monadology*, the monads compose the material universe that we know.[14]

Although Leibniz's stance as a rationalist and as a trained mathematician allows him to argue in the form of a broadly deductive argument that the foregoing claims about monads, composites, and the material nature of the universe must be the case—in order that things should appear to us phenomenally (as they are). Leibniz's claim that monads are, in principle, preestablished to function in a certain manner cannot help but leave one with a vague sense of dissatisfaction with Leibniz's position and defense of it.

In contrast, Conway scarcely uses the term "monad," although the term is used to some extent by her close friend and collaborator, Henry More.[15] What is more important than the term itself is the general concept it is meant to capture. It is in an analysis of the conceptual problems associated with what are called "monads" that the most exciting work is to be done.

Conway is a monistic vitalist who sees the universe as composed of an intriguing mixture of spirit and matter, differing in the proportions of each with respect to various individuals. As such, when she writes of monads, or the barest units, she is already making a crucial departure from Leibniz's concept of monads as simple, nonmaterial substances.[16] For Conway, there is no unit of matter that is not itself (save God, of course) "enspirited," or a complex mingling of both matter and spirit. We might hypothesize that the notion of matter is more important for Conway and the Cambridge circle in general than for Leibniz because, living in Great Britain, they had much more exposure to the work of Newton and the newer work in the sciences.

But whatever the explanation, the underlying philosophical rationale behind the two systems is different from the outset: like his rationalist predecessors Descartes and Spinoza, Leibniz wants to achieve a deductive system that generates the truths of philosophy from axiomatic principles, as they perceive the new sciences do. In contrast, while Conway's treatise is closely argued, she is more concerned (as is More) to answer the charges of the scientific thinkers that matter can, on its own, be accountable for all that is seen in the realm of the visible (making "the spirit" unnecessary), than to make her account compatible with theirs. Given such differences, a comparison of the two systems—Leibniz's and Conway's—can reveal important conceptual and philosophical differences between them and between rationalism, on the one hand, and empiricism and vitalism, on the other.[17]

Before proceeding to a discussion of their differences, one might argue that there is a great deal of resemblance between Conway and Leibniz on the notion of substance, given that they both use the term "monad" and employ a concept that is at least somewhat atomistic. But this (alleged) similarity does not go very far in describing and comparing their views. As Popkin and others argue, a great deal of what philosophically motivates Anne Conway is the desire to expose the falsity of the bare, mechanistic account of the universe, of emerging scientific views of nature as inert, dead substance, with which she (and others who were aware and literate at the time) was becoming increasingly familiar.[18] The argument (presumed to be one Anne Conway would endorse) is that, since it would be impossible for "dead matter" to give rise to motion, it is necessary to hypothesize that from the beginning of the material world, gradations of spirit were already found in all existent things.

In addition, one might argue that not only do Conway and Leibniz disagree on the vitalist versus materialist account; they also disagree about how to tell the story of the divine creation of substances. (We will shortly revisit this second key area of contrast between Conway and Leibniz.) Conway held an explicitly graded hierarchy of being—which included God, an intermediate figure, "Adam Kadmon" (whom she identified with Christ), and all the rest of created matter. In contrast, throughout the *Monadology,* Leibniz stoutly maintained his original definition of a monad as "nothing other than a simple substance," one "without parts," while also—to the perplexity of many—devoting a great deal of time to defending the nature of certain preexistent principles of the contingent world that gave a necessity to and sufficient reason for why things are one way rather than another.[19] For our purposes, although Conway indicates that all that has been created has been present for all time, she does not go into anything like the detail with respect to the origins of the material world as Leibniz does.[20]

To summarize what has been said so far, a preliminary analysis of parts of the works of Anne Conway and Gottfried Leibniz indicates that there is a striking difference in their metaphysics—their views about what is real or the nature of reality—that may not be immediately apparent from the citations in the literature to the effect that Leibniz received or took the term "monad" from Conway's work.[21] But an analysis that features Conway's vitalism is only a beginning one, since there are at least two other areas of traditional importance to philosophers that call out for examination when comparing and contrasting the views of Leibniz and Conway: the issue of the hierarchy of such substances and the question of the possible interaction of substances.

Area 2: Hierarchy of Substances

Conway's more precise delineation of her hierarchy of being is directly related both to her personal Christianity and to her concept of what it means to be human. As such, to understand Conway's view it is necessary to become clear on the meaning and significance of the gradations. Because of the way in which he has defined "monad," Leibniz has left little room for maneuvering with respect to the notion of individual substance except for his account of God. But Conway's less formal definition leaves room for other avenues or areas of development, and these become crucially important in any examination of her philosophy.

Much has been made of Conway's study of the Kabbalah and of the general influence of this work on the circle of Platonists.[22] Although it might be naively thought that most of what is represented by Conway's interest in this work has to do with some of the more recondite aspects of her relationship to More, or of her notion of substance, much that can be attributed to her study of the Kabbalah has to do with a specific issue in her gradations of being.

We have already discussed the differences between Conway and Leibniz insofar as the mere notion of the monad is concerned—area 1—and the fact that Leibniz has, to be fair, a much more fully fleshed-out notion, and takes it to a mathematical precision, so to speak. But Conway also has a strong difference from Leibniz in terms of her ability to manipulate levels of being, at least argumentatively, and this difference is spelled out in her notion of Adam Kadmon.

If it is the case for both Conway and Leibniz that the deity has a status for them different from that of any other monad—and this is an accurate statement—then a crucial difference that Conway articulates, as a believing Christian, is the status of Christ. For Conway, the gradations of being encompass the entire plant and animal kingdoms, human beings—all of creation,—but Christ is on an ontological level by himself, halfway between God and the rest of created being.

Scholars attribute this notion of Conway's directly to the Kabbalah. As Conway herself says, Christ is called "the First Begotten of all Creatures, wherein is signified the relation he hath to Creation."[23] It is not only a crucial notion insofar as an adumbration of Conway's Christianity is concerned; it also sets the stage for the rest of Conway's hierarchy. For clearly, if Christ came to earth as a sort of human, then it is at least possible for creatures to be transmogrified, and at least some change or interpenetration is possible. This will become a crucial difference between Conway and Leibniz (as we will see shortly). If, as Popkin and others argue, part of Conway's response to the materialists is to attempt to work with the notion of the developing sciences, the concept of Adam Kadmon is critical.

Leibniz has no such notion of an individualized monad—one that by its status between the deity and humans could be singled out. Leibniz sometimes refers to monads as "entelechies" in *Monadology*—Rescher glosses this term as an encompassing one, designed to allow for the inclusiveness (or "different sorts") of possible monads.[24] Although Leibniz distinguishes between the apperceptive monads of humans, sometimes called "spirits," and the minimally apperceptive, but still more than bare, monads of at least some animals, there is no equivalent of Adam Kadmon in Leibniz's *Metaphysics*.[25] In two sections of *Monadology*, Leibniz comes as close as possible to addressing some of the issues, such as that of gradation, that is created by Conway's insistence on Adam Kadmon. He writes, in sections 40 and 47:

> Sec. 40: One can also conclude that this Supreme Substance, which is unique, universal and necessary—having nothing outside it that is independent of it, and being a direct consequence of merely being possible—must be incapable of limits and must contain as much reality as is possible.[26] Sec. 47: Accordingly, God alone is the primary unity or the original simple substance, of which all the created or derivative monads are products. They originate, so to speak, through continual fulgurations of the divinity from moment to moment, limited by the receptivity of the created being, to which it is essential to be limited.[27]

The key phrase in section 47, insofar as Adam Kadmon is concerned, is "of which all the created or derivative monads are products." In Leibniz's ontology, the rest of being stands much more on a par with itself, taken in total, and without gradations than is the case for Conway. Insofar as Jesus was born in a human body, on Leibniz's account he has the highest type of monadic existence within the confines of "spirit" or "mind," but this is no more than the type of existence, ontologically, that every other human being would have, seen from the standpoint of monads or monadology.

Additionally, it is clear that for Leibniz, God is not only a creator essentially and by definition, but in a much more complex alembication, as the possessor, at least on the level of explanation, of all the other monads. As Rescher points out, we may be able to distinguish these substances according to formal reality, or definitionally, but God is the ontological basis of them all. As Rescher says, "In this sense (and in this sense only) is Leibniz a pantheist who sees God as omnipresent in that his power is everywhere."[28]

Conway never gives us a description of the relationship of God to the rest of creation in terms of some sort of necessity that is as fully fleshed out as that provided by Leibniz. So, although both seem to agree that necessity inheres in what has been created, Leibniz is willing to go so far as to endorse what he calls the Principle of Sufficient Reason, meaning that all things exist rationally insofar as they are part of the deity's creation, and argue that things could not have been otherwise, given the perfect nature of God.[29] Conway's argument, in a shortened version, amounts to an assertion that created entities have existed either eminently or in some other form for an eternity, but this is far from being as strong a claim as the set of claims that Leibniz makes—Conway's system allows for change and variation.

To do justice to Conway's approach to the difficulty posed for clear ontological gradation by the intermediate status of Adam Kadmon, it must be remarked again that for the Cambridge Platonists, addressing issues having to do with Christianity and its intersection with the emerging new sciences was of crucial importance. As such, Conway no doubt felt much more constrained, as a devout believing Christian, to at least inquire into the problems posed by the Christian ontology when addressed within the overarching framework of her notion of vitalistic monads. In a sense, Conway's account is a great deal more consistent with a biblical conception of Christianity. But it is in her work on the interpenetrability of substances (the third key area) that the most profound differences between Conway and Leibniz can be seen.

Area 3: Interaction of Substances

Conway's work is most original when she addresses the notion of mutability of creatures. Conway's account of the interaction of substances is an intriguing, non-Leibnizian, way that allows for interaction, or interpenetration, between substances. Since Leibniz's doctrine allows for the monads to "reflect" each other, causal interaction as such is not addressed directly as an issue. In other words, Leibniz uses somewhat unusual terminology to get around the difficulty of how the independent substances affect each other, although it still might be concluded that he does not sufficiently address the issue. But Anne Conway's writings precede, in an unusual sort of way, some of the work of the nineteenth century in the biological sciences, while still retaining the flavor of the Cambridge Platonist circle.

Since her atomistic parts—or "monads"—are themselves composed of gradations of spirit and matter, they themselves are interpenetrable, and hence their general motion allows for change in creatures and in matter over a long period of time; the interpenetrability principle in and of itself allows for causal interaction, and hence alteration. With our contemporary eye, we may be somewhat puzzled about what it is that these changes amount to, but it appears that Conway is thinking in terms of at least two great sorts of alterations. One, intriguingly enough, has to do with changes in creatures due to changes in the earth over a period of time; in other words, Anne Conway appears to allow for a sort of change that is almost evolutionary, and she seems to be aware, at least minimally, that changes in rock formation, water configuration, and so forth have taken place throughout the earth's history.[30] In addition, Conway appears to have some beliefs that are consistent with reincarnation or, as it is sometimes called, metempsychosis. We may think of the two as being roughly synonymous.

The first of these interpretations of the general notion of change, that which might be deemed to be evolutionary, is probably the most philosophically interesting, and it is directly opposed to most of Leibniz's thoughts on matters related to this issue. With respect to gradual change over time, Conway writes:

> For, if the earth assumes another form and produces no more vegetation, then horses and similar animals will cease to be as they were before. Since they would not have their proper nourishment, they could not remain the same species. Nevertheless, they will not be annihilated, as it is easy to conclude.[31]

When we remind ourselves that Conway also held that "every creature whatsoever, contains many spirits and bodies,"[32] and that "the distinction between spirit and body is only modal and incremental,"[33] we can see that one of the ways that alteration, or species change in creatures, might take place over time, is that the "subtler intermediating parts" of creatures might come between them and act upon one another.[34]

Although Conway does not provide further details about how this might occur, it is, in its own way, a doctrine oddly consonant with at least some of what we know about molecular structure in that, for example, accidental changes in DNA sequencing can lead to changes in species over time. In addition, it is directly opposed to Leibniz's position that there is no direct interaction between monads.

To address briefly Conway's second take on alteration, namely the doctrine that is often referred to in writings on the Cambridge Platonists as "metempsychosis," most of us have contemporary qualms about doctrines that smack of reincarnation. However, at least from the standpoint of Conway's articulated philosophy, this sort of change—rebirth of spirit in another body—would be somewhat easier to explain. The reincarnation of someone's pet horse as a Belmont Stakes winner could be hypothesized on the basis of movements of spirit from one being to another of the same species; Conway herself uses horses as an example. Intriguingly enough, Conway apparently had enough interest in the world of animals around her that she more or less addresses this issue:

> If it is said that it [a spirited horse] returns to life and obtains the body of another horse, so that it becomes a horse as it was before but stronger and more beautiful and with a better spirit than before, excellent! If it dies a second, third or fourth time, does it always remain a horse . . . and how often does its spirit return?[35]

It is difficult to know what to make of this passage unless we can claim that it supports a notion similar to reincarnation, rather than that of gradual, evolutionary change as indicated in other passages.

In any case, there is nothing in Leibniz that supports such notions—notions of either evolutionary or reincarnational change—nor ought there to be, given Leibniz's original definition of the monad as a simple substance that does not change. C. D. Broad, for one, is a clear articulator of parts of this doctrine, and although Conway is not cited in his text, one cannot help but wonder if Broad did not originally address these issues with the care that he did at least partly because of the interest in the problems of change and alteration over vitalist substance posed by the Cambridge Platonists. With respect to the "dynamical properties of bodies," Broad writes,

> We want to find an extensible quality which, like extension, is common to all bodies under all conditions, e.g., whether they are solid, liquid or gaseous. Leibniz suggests that this characteristic is impenetrability. In so far as a body is considered as an extended object it is conceived as characterized by impenetrability diffused throughout a certain volume or over a certain closed surface. . . . [This property] may be defined as the fact that two bodies may not at the same time continuously occupy the same region.[36]

Here we get to the heart of the matter, at least as far as Conway's important doctrine of interpenetrability is concerned. Her "subtler parts" would have to, at some point, occupy the same region in order for the alleged or purported change to occur.

To be sure, Conway gives us no hint as to how this might take place; but then, to try to adjudicate the dispute, Conway does not begin with a definition of a monad that is as stringent as the one employed by Leibniz throughout the *Monadology*. The conceptual situation for Conway's account has the virtues of its defects and the defects of its virtues: Since Conway works from a less formal set of standards she can leave several areas open— such as change and alteration—and at least partially unexplained. (This phenomenon is not unknown among philosophers.)

In contrast, Leibniz's greater attempt at formal consistency means that there is no way in which he can accept a doctrine other than impenetrability; on Leibniz's account, change must be accounted for as "appetition" and "perception," using his own formal definitions of these terms which are, of course, fairly far from common usage. The terms appear to be interchangeable, and "perception" has to do with the Leibnizian notion of change. To be brief, the change inherent in a creature must already have been mapped into the creature, so to speak, and would be accounted for by the Principle of Sufficient Reason. The oddity of Leibniz's ontology is that, ultimately, all consists of monads—and monads are defined in such a way as to be immaterial. Thus, what we—and the new science of the time at Cambridge (a materialist science, to be sure)—call matter is ultimately something other than "dead matter." Conway gives us a world in which matter and spirit intermix, and spirit accounts for much that would otherwise remain inexplicable, such as mind-body interaction, with respect to "dead matter."

Neither of these systems is without its flaws. But if we think of Conway as one who was ultimately perhaps more concerned to reply to Descartes—especially with respect to mind-body interaction—than she was to any other thinker, we can see why she was driven to conceptualize substance in the way that she did. Both systems avoid Cartesian dualism. Leibniz, however, must ask us to accept the Principle of Sufficient Reason, that philosophical rarity that ultimately became the subject of Voltaire's satire, *Candide*, insofar as his use of the phrase "best of all possible worlds" is concerned. Conway tries to account for change as matter animated by spirit, but she is, of course, less than precise about how this could occur. To be generous, we may hypothesize that, with the mixture of empirically based knowledge and religious belief available in her time, no more precise account could be given.

SUMMARY OF THREE AREAS OF DISSIMILARITY BETWEEN CONWAY AND LEIBNIZ

I have been arguing that, although there are a number of bases for comparison between Conway and Leibniz, accounts of their similarities are somewhat exaggerated. That they both conceive of an ontology, the primary component of which is an infinite number of small points, or entities, is beyond dispute. Conway and Leibniz agree on the ultimate composition of all as having to do with the points or entities that Leibniz frequently refers to as monads.[37] As we have said, however, the primary impetus or driving force behind Conway's philosophizing is Descartes.

Once one moves beyond this established area, one finds, however, that the areas of commonality are few and the realms of disagreement many. First, for Leibniz, these points (monads) cannot themselves be composed of matter. As Philip Wiener says, "They are spiritual rather than physical points, but aggregations of them make up dynamic bodies in space."[38] For Conway, on the other hand, these atomlike entities are a mixture of matter and spirit, at various levels and combinations. Furthermore, for Conway, they themselves compose greater individuals, and these individuals constitute a metaphysical or ontological hierarchy of graded beings, from the most spiritual to the most material. However, for Leibniz, although he will admit to different sorts of monads, the notion of a hierarchy is not as important, and he is much more concerned about the establishment of definitional standards that will allow him (as he does in *Monadology*) to be specific about the workings of the monads according to a preestablished plan, and the Principle of Sufficient Reason.

The third contrast between Conway and Leibniz is that for Conway, as a believing Christian determined to promulgate Christian doctrine during the era of the new Newtonian science arising from Cambridge, it is important to pay special attention to the status of "Adam Kadmon." No small portion of her *Principles* is devoted to the delineation of Christ as an entity within an ontological framework and of the relationship of that entity to the divine and to other creatures. Leibniz admits of no special status for the Son of God, although portions of his works do discuss such issues as divine foreknowledge of Jesus' betrayal and so forth.

Finally, Conway admits of change insofar as individual creatures are concerned, and she asserts that this change is due, in general, to interpenetrations between her monadic entities. For Leibniz, no such interpenetration is possible: as Wiener says, "Leibniz's doctrine of internal relations compelled him logically to deny any external causal interactions among monads."[39]

AREAS OF SIMILARITY BETWEEN CONWAY AND LEIBNIZ

Anne Conway and Gottfried Leibniz do have, however, some areas of commonality that may never have received enough attention. First, both were philosophers living and working in European countries during the latter part of the seventeenth century, when the combination of religious wars, new work in science, and the general spirit of the Reformation made for very stimulating times. Second, both were concerned primarily about metaphysics: we do not see in their philosophies, for example, the overwhelming concern with epistemology that drove some other thinkers of the seventeenth and eighteenth centuries. As a third point, both thinkers, if we must employ the rather unhelpful empiricist/rationalist distinction—sometimes thought to be cast in terms far too grossly generalist—were rationalists. They believed that reason alone could be used to give an account of the ultimate nature of reality that would be consistent, and that would shed light on what appeared to be the empirically driven discoveries of others.

But differences arise again on a more personal level. Anne Conway was virtually an invalid; Leibniz traveled extensively. Conway had few discussants other than Henry More. Leibniz had not only a great many discussants, but numerous correspondents. Perhaps most important, Conway was a woman; Leibniz was a male thinker in a tradition of the many male thinkers who preceded him. He could not have known the difficulties involved in attempting to philosophize from the standpoint of female embodiment. Nevertheless, in part because of what is now called "the recovery project" (see Preface) their names are frequently linked now, and it is clear that, thanks to Henry More and others, their names were linked at least occasionally during their lifetimes.

Conclusion

An account of their individual ontologies, that is, an account of the entities Conway and Leibniz took to be real, and the impetus that drove each of them to philosophize coherently within the Christian tradition, is exciting; perhaps it helps illuminate some of the disputes, philosophical and otherwise, of our own time. We might be inclined to think that ours is the only time in which fiery disputes have arisen between believers in religious doctrines and those who might label themselves "scientists," but a perusal of the seventeenth century should prove reassuring. In their time, as in ours, women and men philosophized and struggled publicly and privately with the nature and interconnections (even if only conceptual) between the substances, hierarchies of substances, scientific data and methodology, and religious issues.

Questions for Reflection

How might one describe, in a brief way, the differences between Conway and Leibniz on the use of the term "monad"? Provide and defend such a description.

Conway wrote that the earth might "assume another form and produce no more vegetation." Does Conway's notion of change, particularly evolutionary and vast ecological change, have any relevance to contemporary environmental (and related) concerns? If so, what are they and why are they relevant? If not, why not?

What can we make of Conway's notion that a horse "might return to life and obtain the body of another horse"? Is there anything in our observed behavior of animals that might lead us to hypothesize why Conway chose this example? Identify candidate behaviors and take a stand on whether they might lead you to hypothesize about reincarnational change, as Conway did.

Notes

1. Margaret Atherton, "Anne Viscountess Conway," in *Women Philosophers of the Early Modern Period*, ed. Margaret Atherton (Indianapolis, IN: Hackett Publishing Co., 1994), 46.

2. Source http://oregonstate.edu/instruct/phl302/philosophers/conway.html (n.d.).

3. Ethel M. Kersey, *Women Philosophers: A Bio-Critical Source Book* (New York: Greenwood Press, 1989), 83.

4. Atherton, "Anne Viscountess Conway," 47.

5. Mary Warnock, "Anne Conway (1631–79)," in *Women Philosophers*, ed. Mary Warnock (London: Orion Publishing Group, 1997), 4.

6. Carolyn Merchant, "The Vitalism of Anne Conway: Its Impact of Leibniz's Concept of the Monad," in *Journal of the History of Philosophy*, vol. XVII no. 3 (1979): 256.

7. Anne Conway, *The Principles of the Most Ancient and Modern Philosophy*. eds. Allison P. Coudert and Taylor Corse (Cambridge, UK: Cambridge University Press, 1996), 28–40. Unless otherwise specified, all references to *Principles* are to this edition. Excerpts reprinted by permission of Cambridge University Press.

8. G. W. Leibniz, *Monadology: An Edition for Students*, ed. Nicholas Rescher (Pittsburgh, PA: University of Pittsburgh Press, 1990). Unless specified otherwise, all references to *Monadology* are to this edition. Excerpts reprinted by permission of the University of Pittsburgh Press.

9. A comment on the back cover of the *Monadology* notes that the book has been "sorely needed," since "Leibniz's major work has never before been readily accessible for students."

10. Rescher notes that Leibniz never wrote all of the major philosophical works that he had intended to set down on paper. The citation and the comparison to Plato, Aristotle, and others are in Rescher's Introduction to *Monadology*, p. 7.

11. There is available ample commentary, some of it by Rescher himself, on whether the system is as coherent as Leibniz thought.

12. Leibniz, *Monadology*, 17.

13. Leibniz, *Monadology*, 52.

14. Leibniz, *Monadology*, 90.

15. For a superb collection of essays on Leibniz, Conway, More, and others, see Henry More, *Tercentenary Studies*, ed. Sarah Hutton (Dordrecht, The Netherlands: Kluwer Academic Publishers, 1990). The essays by Stuart Brown and Richard H. Popkin are particularly helpful.

16. The 1996 edition (Coudert and Taylor) of Conway's *Principles* shows only one usage of the term "monad" (p. 20). It is now standard to mention that both Conway and Leibniz used the term "monad." There is great disagreement on who originated the term. This issue and the different conclusions that are advanced are beyond the scope of this essay, which focuses on the points of both convergence and divergence of Leibniz and Conway.

17. Like all the Cambridge Platonists, she was influenced by recent translations of the Kabbalah. For valuable commentary, see Hutton, *Tercentenary Studies*.

18. See Popkin, *Tercentenary Studies*.

19. There is much sophisticated and recondite philosophical commentary on this aspect of Leibniz's thought, employing complex logical tools (such as modal logic), but it is not necessary to discuss that literature here.

20. Leibniz, *Monadology*, 122–23.

21. Popkin also addresses this issue in *Tercentenary Studies* (see endnote 16). It is unclear, partly due to chronology, who borrowed what and from whom, but it is a matter of historical record that Leibniz was aware of Conway's work. He may have heard of her from Francis Mercury van Helmont or from Henry More himself. Popkin writes of Leibniz's "high regard" for her (p. 111).

22. See Popkin, *Tercentenary Studies*.

23. Conway, *Principles of the Most Ancient and Modern Philosophy*, ed. Peter Loptson (The Hague, The Netherlands: Martinus Nijhoff, 1982), 149.

24. Leibniz, *Monadology*, 90.

25. Rescher has an excellent tripartite distinction among these terms in his commentary on section 19. Leibniz, *Monadology*, 92.

26. Leibniz, *Monadology*, 22.

27. Leibniz, *Monadology*, 22–23.

28. Leibniz, *Monadology*, 142.

29. In his commentary on *Monadology*, section 33 (p. 123), Rescher develops his own modal logic to address the issues presented by the account Leibniz provides of types of necessity.

30. Conway, *Principles*, 32–34 and 38–40. This is a recurring theme throughout this work, but it is addressed most straightforwardly in chapter 6.

31. Conway, *Principles*, 33.

32. Conway, *Principles*, 39.

33. Conway, *Principles*, 40.

34. Conway, *Principles*, 20.

35. Conway, *Principles*, 32.

36. C. D. Broad, *Leibniz: An Introduction* (Cambridge, UK: Cambridge University Press, 1975), 61.

37. Those who have been swayed by what they take to be the use of similar terminology—"monad"—have not noticed, for example, that Anne Conway is more concerned about Descartes and the Cartesian philosophy in general than she is with any other thinker.

38. Philip P. Wiener, *Leibniz: Selections* (New York: Charles Scribner's Sons, 1951), xxxviii.

39. Wiener, *Leibniz*, xlii.

CHAPTER 9

Rousseau and Wollstonecraft

Introduction by *Karen J. Warren*

This chapter's philosophical pair, Jean-Jacques Rousseau (1712–1778) and Mary Woll-stonecraft (1759–1797), share an interest in social and political philosophy, in particular the issue whether women are naturally inferior to men. This introduction provides biographical information on the pair, followed by a description of Rousseau's political philosophy—and some on his view of education—and a suggestion on philosophically significant issues to consider when reading and assessing Wollstonecraft's writing on women.

ROUSSEAU

Rousseau was born in Geneva (then an independent republic, today part of Switzerland). His mother died of complications from childbirth nine days after his birth.

The most life-shaping events in Rousseau's life occurred during his childhood, particularly the realities of his lack of childhood supervision and his access to his mother's library. His father taught him to read when he was six; he read primarily the Romance books from the library from night until dawn. Later he read the library's French history and literary books; they affected Rousseau's somewhat old-fashioned but quaint literary writing style.

In order to avoid imprisonment for wounding a Polish army officer in a brawl, Rousseau's father abandoned Rousseau in 1722. Rousseau's uncle put him in the care of a pastor near Geneva. In *Confessions*, Rousseau described this period as the most serene part of growing up; he spent much unsupervised time in public gardens and fields, reading and playacting the heroes from the books he read.

One theme that runs through Rousseau's writings is his criticism of religion and the arts. In need of money, Rousseau decided to submit an essay in a contest. He took an unpopular position, thinking it might enhance his chances at winning, arguing that the sciences and arts are the cause of corruption of virtue and morality in society. The essay won first place and resulted in the publication of his first book, *A Discourse on the Sciences and Arts* (1750). In his second book, *The Discourse on the Origin of Inequality* (1755), Rousseau argued that religion and the arts contributed to the corruption of otherwise good humans. His work on the philosophy of education, *Émile* (1762), and his major work, *The Social Contract* (1762), also criticized religion. Both books were banned in France and Geneva. Rousseau fled to Switzerland, where he and his writing continued to attract controversy and conflict. By the end of Rousseau's life, he was preoccupied with justifying his life and work—a theme laced throughout *The Confessions* (1772) and *Rousseau: Judge of Jean-Jacques* (1776).

Rousseau's lifetime was crisscrossed with different jobs and controversial experiences. In 1728, when in France, Rousseau had no money, no real skills, and was vulnerable to arrest for a previous infraction. A French Catholic baroness, Françoise-Louise de Warens, thirteen years his elder, took him in and supported him; he became her lover. She provided Rousseau with an education that included studying Aristotle and training in Latin and the dramatic arts.

Rousseau had hopes of a political appointment. He moved to Paris in 1742 and was secretary to the French ambassador in Venice from 1743 to 1744 but his jobs were a series of disappointments. Later, in 1745, he lived with Thérèse Le Vasseur, a semi-literate seamstress, with whom he had at least five children (all of whom probably died in a foundling hospital where he placed them after their births). As a theorist of education, Rousseau's abandonment of his five children was both a source of embarrassment and information his enemies, including Voltaire, used against him. While in Paris, he became friends with French philosopher Diderot and wrote some articles on music in 1749. His interest in music remained throughout his life; his opera Le Devin du Village was performed for King Louis XV in 1752.

Rousseau returned to Geneva in 1754, where he continued to alienate people through his work. The stoning of his house in 1765 led him to take refuge with the philosopher David Hume in Great Britain. There Rousseau suffered a serious decline in his mental health and began to experience paranoid fantasies about plots against him involving Hume and others. He fled back to France in 1767, three years before he was officially permitted; he then violated the restriction of his return that he was not allowed to publish any books by giving private readings of *Confessions* in 1771. Violating a police order to stop, *Confessions*, like all his subsequent works, was published posthumously in 1782, four years after Rousseau's death.

Rousseau's political philosophy influenced the French Revolution, the development of socialist theory, and the growth of nationalism. In addition to his political philosophy, Rousseau made important contributions to literature (e.g., with his novel: *Julie, ou la nouvelle Héloïse*, 1761), autobiography as a literary genre (with *Confessions*), the development of romanticism and music.

But Rousseau is best known for his political philosophy, particularly his social contract theory. Rousseau's version of the social contract is based in a fundamental belief in man's natural goodness and the distinction between human nature—man's goodness in a precivil state—and man's corruption in a civil society. Rousseau's belief in man's natural goodness does not mean or imply that humans in the state of nature act morally. But, according to Rousseau, by joining together and abandoning their individual claims of natural rights individuals can, paradoxically, both preserve themselves (their lives, important freedoms) through the social contract and remain free. This is because, by each man's freely choosing to submit to (obey) the authority of the collective "general will," each man is, in effect, choosing to be bound by laws they have authored. Paradoxically, humans preserve their freedom by submitting to the common will. Much of the controversy about Rousseau's social contract theory turns on just this claim that citizens who obey the general will, including constraints it imposes on individuals, are thereby rendered free.

Rousseau's social contract theory distinguishes between the "sovereign" and the "government." Sovereignty remains directly in the hands of the people; humans make laws directly (not through representatives). The government is not the people; it is a separate institution charged with implementing and enforcing the general will. Rousseau was bitterly opposed to the idea that the people should exercise sovereignty via a representative assembly.

Rousseau also is known for his views on education, especially as advanced in *Émile*. *Émile* is a story about the growth of a young boy, Émile, under the guidance of Rousseau. Émile is the unsocialized boy who reincarnates Rousseau's youth, spent in the free and happy play world of gardens and fields. The philosophical position advocated in the story is that the goal of education is to learn how to live, and the best way to learn this is through a guardian who helps the youth understand the nature and way to healthy living. This involves learning how to protect one's natural goodness from the vices of society, private property, and urban living. Rousseau was one of the first modern writers to seriously attack the institution of private property as injurious to personal growth, individual freedom, and the goal of education.

Rousseau's view of education is not gender-neutral. The education of Sophie (women) is to be governed by Émile (men, husbands), while Émile is educated to be self-governing. Utilizing an age-old, canonical distinction between "the public" and "the private" spheres as the philosophical basis of the work, Rousseau argues that "good or healthy living" in the private sphere depends on the "natural" subordination of women.

WOLLSTONECRAFT

Mary Wollstonecraft often has been called the first feminist or the mother of feminism. Wollstonecraft's first best-selling book was *Vindication of the Rights of Men* (1790), in which she defended the democratic rights of men against those who would restrict those rights to landed gentry or inherited titles. But she objected to talk of the "rights of man" that excluded the rights of women. That motivated Wollstonecraft to write *A Vindication of the Rights of Woman* (1792), described as a classic of feminist thought. In this book she argues that women are not naturally inferior to men, but appear to be only because they lack education.

Wollstonecraft was born in 1759 in London, into a family fraught with financial and other difficulties. Her primary role within the family was as caregiver for both her mother and siblings. Her mother was submissive to her husband and, after receiving his inheritance, her father "led the family down the social scale through a series of failed farming ventures. He drank a great deal and became increasingly violent and brutal at home."[1]

When she was fifteen, the family moved to a suburb of London. Here Wollstonecraft met Fanny Blood, who became her closest friend. When she was twenty-one, her mother died, her sister Elizabeth ("Eliza") married, and Wollstonecraft moved in with her friend Fanny and her family, helping to support the family through her needlework. When her sister gave birth the following year, Wollstonecraft again returned to help her sister Eliza. Convinced that Eliza's husband was abusive, Wollstonecraft helped her sister leave her husband. Under the laws of the time, Eliza had to leave her young son with his father; the son died before his first birthday.

Wollstonecraft needed to find employment. At Newington Green she met clergyman Richard Price and many of England's leading liberal intellectuals, "the Dissenters." The dissenter community nourished her intellectually, provided the context in which Wollstonecraft developed her political and philosophical views, enabled her economic independence, financed the establishment of a school that she headed, and helped hide her and Eliza, since leaving one's husband was a criminal act. Without the dissenter community, Wollstonecraft's writings may never have materialized or reached the levels of recognition they did.

During her time at Newington Green, her friend Fanny decided to marry, and, pregnant soon after the marriage, called Wollstonecraft to be with her for the birth. Sadly, Fanny and her baby died soon after the premature birth. After a short time as a governess, Wollstonecraft again needed work. John Hewett, of the dissenter community, encouraged Wollstonecraft to write; Hewett's publisher, Joseph Johnson, paid to publish her first book, *Thoughts on the Education of Daughters* (1787). Within a year she had joined Johnson's publishing firm as a writer and reviewer. Wollstonecraft also published a book about a trip she took to Sweden (1796), but it was rejected by critics for her emotional descriptions of another culture. In the same year Wollstonecraft renewed an old acquaintance with the philosopher William Godwin, whom she eventually married. They had one daughter, Mary Shelley, author of *Frankenstein*. Tragically, Wollstonecraft died at the age of thirty-eight, within two weeks of the baby's birth of "childbed fever" or septicemia—a complication of childbirth. Godwin published his *Memoirs of the Author of a Vindication of the Rights of Woman* of Wollstonecraft not long after her death. Godwin's disclosures of Wollstonecraft's troubled love relationships, financial struggles, unorthodox lifestyle, and suicide attempts were material used by conservative critics to denigrate all women's rights. It also had the unfortunate effect of destroying Wollstonecraft's reputation and undermining the significance of her scholarly position on women's rights for about a century. The biographical material and primary texts by Wollstonecraft, as with other women philosophers in this book, illustrate the philosophical position that reflection on one's own and other's felt, lived experience—the concrete features of their actual lives—is important to the conception of philosophy/a philosopher and the nature of philosophical theorizing/methodology.

Wollstonecraft's writings illustrate four ways this occurs. (1) Although Wollstonecraft accepts the canonical belief that women's sphere is the home, she, like so many contemporary feminists, rejects the "public versus private" dualism of canonical philosophy, refusing to separate the home from public life. Wollstonecraft's rejection of this dualism can be found in Wollstonecraft's support of the need for equal rights for women in both the domestic sphere of the family, marriage, and child-rearing and the public arena of education, employment, politics, and law. (2) Even though most of Wollstonecraft's writings were best sellers at the time, the systematic exclusion of women philosophers, including Wollstonecraft, in canonical accounts of the history of Western philosophy maintained and reinforced the assumption that women are naturally inferior to men. This assumption has been historically defended by claiming that women (Wollstonecraft) lack sufficient rationality for equal moral, political, and educational status and rights with men. As long as this assumption remains in place—and the public versus private, culture versus nature dualisms presupposed by it—any proposed counterexamples (e.g., Wollstonecraft's writings) will be rejected outright (without argumentation) as false. (3) Wollstonecraft's personal observations about the multiple ways "rights of man" did not include "rights of women" led her to claim that reform of basic societal institutions was necessary for woman to have equal rights with men. (4) The omission of Wollstonecraft's writings and arguments from the philosophical canon illustrates that, when overlooked, excluded, or neglected, writings by women, no matter how popular or acclaimed as philosophy/philosophical in their own time, reinforced male-biased assumptions about women and the inability of women to do philosophy. Even when men philosophers such as Rousseau write about women, it is *other texts* by these men, typically ones not concerned with issues about women or gender, that are studied. This sort of exclusion of women—by studying only those texts by male philosophers that do not focus on women or gender as the subject matter—is a different form of male bias that needs to be corrected. Study of this philosophical pair helps to do that.

LINDEMANN'S COMMENTARY

Kate Lindemann's commentary puts the issue of woman's natural inferiority to men center stage for both Rousseau and Wollstonecraft. Rousseau held what Wollstonecraft denied: that women and men, by nature, have differences in characters—a female's is to be passive and weak, a male's is to be active, assertive, and physically strong—that necessitate different educations and justify as "natural" women's duty to submit in an agreeable manner to men as their masters. For Wollstonecraft, women may be passive and weak, but the socialization of women and the failures of educational systems, not natural or inherent differences, are the explanation. Careful to point out important, often subtle, similarities and differences between their views, Lindemann's commentary ends with a question relevant today: Is there a single human nature or are there separate constitutions for men and women? How one answers this question, and the philosophical (not merely empirical or psychological) support one provides for one's answer, will put the reader in the middle of a controversy that is, literally, as old as Western philosophy itself.

Excerpts of Writings by Rousseau and Wollstonecraft

I. EXCERPTS FROM ROUSSEAU'S *ÉMILE*[2]

The Final Stage of Youth

We have reached the last act in the drama of youth but the denouement has still to come. It is not good for man to be alone. Émile is now a man. We must give him the mate we have promised him. The mate is Sophie. Once we know what kind of a person she is we will know better where to find her and we will be able to complete our task.

The Education of Women

1. The Differences between the Sexes

Sophie should be as typically woman as Émile is man. She must possess all the characteristics of humanity and of womanhood which she needs for playing her part in the physical and the moral order. Let us begin by considering in what respects her sex and ours agree and differ.

In everything that does not relate to sex the woman is as the man: they are alike in organs, needs, and capacities. In whatever way we look at them the difference is only one of less or more. In everything that relates to sex there are correspondences and differences. The difficulty is to determine what in their constitution is due to sex and what is not. All we know with certainty is that the common features are due to the species and the differences to sex. From this twofold point of view we find so many likenesses and so many contrasts that we cannot but marvel that nature has been able to create two beings so much alike with constitutions so different.

The sameness and the difference cannot but have an effect on mentality. This is borne out by experience and shows the futility of discussions about sex superiorities and inequalities. A perfect man and a perfect woman should no more resemble each other in mind than in countenance: and perfection does not admit of degrees.

In the mating of the sexes each contributes in equal measure to the common end but not in the same way. From this diversity comes the first difference which has to be noted in their personal relations. It is the part of the one to be active and strong, and of the other to be passive and weak. Accept this principle and it follows in the second place that woman is intended to please man. If the man requires to please the woman in turn the necessity is less direct. Masterfulness is his special attribute. He pleases by the very fact that he is strong. This is not the law of love, I admit. But it is the law of nature, which is more ancient than love.

If woman is made to please and to be dominated, she ought to make herself agreeable to man and avoid provocation. Her strength is in her charms and through them she should constrain him to discover his powers and make use of them. The surest way of bringing these powers into active operation is to make it necessary by her resistance. In this way self-esteem is added to desire and the man triumphs in the victory which the woman has compelled him to achieve. Out of this relation comes attack and defense, boldness on the one side and timidity on the other, and in the end the modesty and sense of shame with which nature has armed the weak for the subjugation of the strong.

Hence as a third consequence of the different constitution of the sexes, the stronger may appear to be master, and yet actually be dependent on the weaker: not because of a superficial practice of gallantry or the prideful generosity of the protective sex, but by reason of an enduring law of nature. By giving woman the capacity to stimulate desires greater than can be satisfied, nature has made man dependent on woman's good will and constrained him to seek to please her as a condition of her submission. Always there remains for man in his mastered weakness, or there has been a willing subjection; and the woman has usually the guile to leave the doubt unresolved.

Men and women are unequally affected by sex. The male is only a male at times; the female is a female all her life and can never forget her sex.

Plato in his *Republic* gives women the same physical training as men. That is what might be expected. Having made an end of private families in his state and not knowing what to do with the women, he found himself compelled to make men of them. That wonderful genius provided for everything in his plans, and went out of his way to meet an objection that nobody was likely to make, while missing the real objection. I am not speaking about the so-called community of wives, so often charged against him by people who have not read him. What I refer to is the social promiscuity which ignored the differences of sex by giving men and women the same occupations, and sacrificed the sweetest sentiments of nature to the artificial sentiment of loyalty which could not exist without them. He did not realize that the bonds of convention always develop from some natural attachment: that the love one has for his neighbors is the basis of his devotion to the state; that the heart is linked with the great fatherland through the little fatherland of the home; that it is the good son, the good husband, the good father, that makes the good citizen.

2. Differences in Education

Once it has been shown that men and women are essentially different in character and temperament, it follows that they ought not to have the same education. In accordance with the direction of nature they ought to co-operate in action, but not to do the same things. To complete the attempt we have been making to form the man of nature, we must now go on to consider how the fitting mate for him is to be formed.

If you want right guidance, always follow the leadings of nature. Everything that characterizes sex should be respected as established by nature.

II. EXCERPTS FROM ROUSSEAU'S *THE SOCIAL CONTRACT OR PRINCIPLES OF POLITICAL RIGHT* [3]

Subject of the First Book

Man is born free; and everywhere he is in chains. One thinks himself the master of others, and still remains a greater slave than they: how did this change come about? I do not know. What can make it legitimate? That question I think I can answer.

If I took into account only force, and the effects derived from it, I should say: "As long as a people is compelled to obey, and obeys, it does well; as soon as it can shake off the yoke, and shakes it off, it does still better; for, regaining its liberty by the same right as took it away, either it is justified in resuming it, or there was no justification for those who took it away." But the social order is a sacred right which is the basis of all other rights. Nevertheless, this right does not come from nature, and must therefore be founded on conventions. Before coming to that, I have to prove what I have just asserted.

The First Societies

The most ancient of all societies, and the only one that is natural, is the family: and even so the children remain attached to the father only so long as they need him for their preservation. As soon as this need ceases, the natural bond is dissolved. The children, released from the obedience they owed to the father, and the father, released from the care he owed his children, return equally to independence. If they remain united, they continue so no longer naturally, but voluntarily; and the family itself is then maintained only by convention.

This common liberty results from the nature of man. His first law is to provide for his own preservation, his first cares are those which he owes to himself; and, as soon as he reaches years of discretion, he is the sole judge of the proper means of preserving himself, and consequently becomes his own master.

The family then may be called the first model of political societies: the ruler corresponds to the father, and the people to the children and all, being born free and equal, alienate their liberty only for their own advantage.

The Right of the Strongest

The strongest is never strong enough to be always the master, unless he transforms strength into right, and obedience into duty. Hence the right of the strongest, which, though to all seeming meant ironically, is really laid down as a fundamental principle. But are we never to have an explanation of this phrase? Force is a physical power, and I fail to see what moral effect it can have. To yield to force is an act of necessity, not of will—at the most, an act of prudence. In what sense can it be a duty?

Suppose for a moment that this so-called "right" exists. I maintain that the sole result is a mass of inexplicable nonsense. For, if force creates right, the effect changes with the cause: every force that is greater than the first succeeds to its right. As soon as it is possible to disobey with impunity, disobedience is legitimate; and, the strongest being always in the right, the only thing that matters is to act so as to become the strongest. But what kind of right is that which perishes when force fails? If we must obey perforce, there is no need to obey because we ought; and if we are not forced to obey, we are under no obligation to do so. Clearly, the word "right" adds nothing to force: in this connection, it means absolutely nothing.

Slavery

Since no man has a natural authority over his fellow, and force creates no right, we must conclude that conventions form the basis of all legitimate authority among men.

To say that a man gives himself gratuitously, is to say what is absurd and inconceivable; such an act is null and illegitimate, from the mere fact that he who does it is out of his mind. To say the same of a whole people is to suppose a people of madmen; and madness creates no right.

Even if each man could alienate himself, he could not alienate his children: they are born men and free; their liberty belongs to them, and no one but they has the right to dispose of it. Before they come to years of discretion, the father can, in their name, lay down conditions for their preservation and well-being, but he cannot give them irrevocably and without conditions: such a gift is contrary to the ends of nature, and exceeds the rights of paternity. It would therefore be necessary, in order to legitimize an arbitrary government, that in every generation the people should be in a position to accept or reject it; but, were this so, the government would be no longer arbitrary.

To renounce liberty is to renounce being a man, to surrender the rights of humanity and even its duties. For him who renounces everything no indemnity is possible. Such a renunciation is incompatible with man's nature; to remove all liberty from his will is to remove all morality from his acts. Finally, it is an empty and contradictory convention that sets up, on the one side, absolute authority, and, on the other, unlimited obedience. Is it not clear that we can be under no obligation to a person from whom we have the right to exact everything? Does not this condition alone, in the absence of equivalence or exchange, in itself involve the nullity of the act? For what right can my slave have against me, when all that he has belongs to me, and, his right being mine, this right of mine against myself is a phrase devoid of meaning?

The Social Compact

I suppose men to have reached the point at which the obstacles in the way of their preservation in the state of nature show their power of resistance to be greater than the resources at the disposal of each individual for his maintenance in that state. That primitive condition can then subsist no longer; and the human race would perish unless it changed its manner of existence.

But, as men cannot engender new forces, but only unite and direct existing ones, they have no other means of preserving themselves than the formation, by aggregation, of a sum of forces great enough to overcome the resistance. These they have to bring into play by means of a single motive power, and cause to act in concert.

This sum of forces can arise only where several persons come together: but, as the force and liberty of each man are the chief instruments of his self-preservation, how can he pledge them without harming his own interests, and neglecting the care he owes to himself? This difficulty, in its bearing on my present subject, may be stated in the following terms:

"The problem is to find a form of association which will defend and protect with the whole common force the person and goods of each associate, and in which each, while uniting himself with all, may still obey himself alone, and remain as free as before." This is the fundamental problem of which the *Social Contract* provides the solution.

The clauses of this contract are so determined by the nature of the act that the slightest modification would make them vain and ineffective; so that, although they have perhaps never been formally set forth, they are everywhere the same and everywhere tacitly admitted and recognized, until, on the violation of the social compact, each regains his original rights and resumes his natural liberty, while losing the conventional liberty in favor of which he renounced it.

These clauses, properly understood, may be reduced to one—the total alienation of each associate, together with all his rights, to the whole community; for, in the first place, as each gives himself absolutely, the conditions are the same for all; and, this being so, no one has any interest in making them burdensome to others.

Moreover, the alienation being without reserve, the union is as perfect as it can be, and no associate has anything more to demand: for, if the individuals retained certain rights, as there would be no common superior to decide between them and the public, each, being on one point his own judge, would ask to be so on all; the state of nature would thus continue, and the association would necessarily become inoperative or tyrannical.

Finally, each man, in giving himself to all, gives himself to nobody; and as there is no associate over whom he does not acquire the same right as he yields others over himself, he gains an equivalent for everything he loses, and an increase of force for the preservation of what he has.

If then we discard from the social compact what is not of its essence, we shall find that it reduces itself to the following terms:

"Each of us puts his person and all his power in common under the supreme direction of the general will, and, in our corporate capacity, we receive each member as an indivisible part of the whole."

At once, in place of the individual personality of each contracting party, this act of association creates a moral and collective body, composed of as many members as the assembly contains votes, and receiving from this act its unity, its common identity, its life and its will. This public person, so formed by the union of all other persons formerly took the name of city, and now takes that of Republic or body politic; it is called by its members State when passive, Sovereign when active, and Power when compared with others like itself. Those who are associated in it take collectively the name of people, and severally are called citizens, as sharing in the sovereign power, and subjects, as being under the laws of the State. But these terms are often confused and taken one for another: it is enough to know how to distinguish them when they are being used with precision.

The Sovereign

This formula shows us that the act of association comprises a mutual undertaking between the public and the individuals, and that each individual, in making a contract, as we may say, with himself, is bound in a double capacity; as a member of the Sovereign he is bound to the individuals, and as a member of the State to the Sovereign. But the maxim of civil right, that no one is bound by undertakings made to himself, does not apply in this case; for there is a great difference between incurring an obligation to yourself and incurring one to a whole of which you form a part.

Attention must further be called to the fact that public deliberation, while competent to bind all the subjects to the Sovereign, because of the two different capacities in which each of them may be regarded, cannot, for the opposite reason, bind the Sovereign to itself; and that it is consequently against the nature of the body politic for the Sovereign to impose on itself a law which it cannot infringe. Being able to regard itself in only one capacity, it is in the position of an individual who makes a contract with himself; and this makes it clear that there neither is nor can be any kind of fundamental law binding on the body of the people—not even the social contract itself. This does not mean that the body politic cannot enter into undertakings with others, provided the contract is not infringed by them; for in relation to what is external to it, it becomes a simple being, an individual.

But the body politic or the Sovereign, drawing its being wholly from the sanctity of the contract, can never bind itself, even to an outsider, to do anything derogatory to the original act, for instance, to alienate any part of itself, or to submit to another Sovereign.

Violation of the act by which it exists would be self-annihilation; and that which is itself nothing can create nothing.

As soon as this multitude is so united in one body, it is impossible to offend against one of the members without attacking the body, and still more to offend against the body without the members resenting it. Duty and interest therefore equally oblige the two contracting parties to give each other help; and the same men should seek to combine, in their double capacity, all the advantages dependent upon that capacity.

Again, the Sovereign, being formed wholly of the individuals who compose it, neither has nor can have any interest contrary to theirs; and consequently the sovereign power need give no guarantee to its subjects, because it is impossible for the body to wish to hurt all its members. We shall also see later on that it cannot hurt any in particular. The Sovereign, merely by virtue of what it is, is always what it should be.

This, however, is not the case with the reaction of the subjects to the Sovereign, which, despite the common interest, would have no security that they would fulfill their undertakings, unless it found means to assure itself of their fidelity.

In fact, each individual, as a man, may have particular will contrary or dissimilar to the general will which he has a citizen. His particular interest may speak to him quite differently from the common interest: his absolute and naturally independent existence may make him look upon what he owes to the common cause as a gratuitous contribution, the loss of which will do less harm to others than the payment of it is burdensome to himself; and, regarding the moral person which constitutes the State as a persona ficta, because not a man, he may wish to enjoy the rights of citizenship without being ready to fulfill the duties of a subject. The continuance of such an injustice could not but prove the undoing of the body politic.

In order then that the social compact may not be an empty formula, it tacitly includes the undertaking, which alone can give force to the rest, that whoever refuses to obey the general will shall be compelled to do so by the whole body. This means nothing less than that he will be forced to be free; for this is the condition which, by giving each citizen to his country, secures him against all personal dependence. In this lies the key to the working of the political machine; this alone legitimizes civil undertakings, which, without it, would be absurd, tyrannical, and liable to the most frightful abuses.

The Civil State

The passage from the state of nature to the civil state produces a very remarkable change in man, by substituting justice for instinct in his conduct, and giving his actions the morality they had formerly lacked. Then only, when the voice of duty takes the place of physical impulses and right of appetite, does man, who so far had considered only himself, find that he is forced to act on different principles, and to consult his reason before listening to his inclinations. Although, in this state, he deprives himself of some advantages which he got from nature, he gains in return others so great, his faculties are so stimulated and developed, his ideas so extended, his feelings so ennobled, and his whole soul so uplifted, that, did not the abuses of this new condition often degrade him below that which he left, he would be bound to bless continually the happy moment which took him from it for ever, and, instead of a stupid and unimaginative animal, made him an intelligent being and a man.

Let us draw up the whole account in terms easily commensurable. What man loses by the social contract is his natural liberty and an unlimited right to everything he tries to get and succeeds in getting; what he gains is civil liberty and the proprietorship of all he possesses. If we are to avoid mistake in weighing one against the other, we must clearly distinguish natural liberty, which is bounded only by the strength of the individual, from civil liberty, which is limited by the general will; and possession, which is merely the effect of force or the right of the first occupier, from property, which can be founded only on a positive title.

We might, over and above all this, add, to what man acquires in the civil state, moral liberty, which alone makes him truly master of himself; for the mere impulse of appetite is slavery, while obedience to a law which we prescribe to ourselves is liberty. But I have already said too much on this head, and the philosophical meaning of the word liberty does not now concern us.

Real Property

Each member of the community gives himself to it, at the moment of its foundation, just as he is, with all the resources at his command, including the goods he possesses. This act does not make possession, in changing hands, change its nature, and become property in the hands of the Sovereign; but, as the forces of the city are incomparably greater than those of an individual, public possession is also, in fact, stronger and more irrevocable, without being any more legitimate, at any rate from the point of view of foreigners. For the State, in relation to its members, is master of all their goods by the social contract, which, within the State, is the basis of all rights; but, in relation to other powers, it is so only by the right of the first occupier, which it holds from its members.

The right of the first occupier, though more real than the right of the strongest, becomes a real right only when the right of property has already been established. Every man has naturally a right to everything he needs; but the positive act which makes him proprietor of one thing excludes him from everything else.

III. EXCERPTS FROM WOLLSTONECRAFT'S *A VINDICATION OF THE RIGHTS OF WOMAN*[4]

In the present state of society it appears necessary to go back to first principles in search of the most simple truths, and to dispute with some prevailing prejudice every inch of ground. To clear my way, I must be allowed to ask some plain questions, and the answers will probably appear as unequivocal as the axioms on which reasoning is built; thought, when entangled with various motives of action, they are formally contradicted, either by words or conduct of men.

In what does man's pre-eminence over the brute creation consist? The answer is as clear as that a half is less than the whole, in Reason.

What acquirement exalts one being above another? Virtue, we spontaneously reply.

For what purpose were the passions implanted? That man by struggling with them might attain a degree of knowledge denied to the brutes, whispers Experience.

Consequently the perfection of our nature and capability of happiness must be estimated by the degree of reason, virtue, and knowledge, that distinguish the individual, and direct the laws which bind society: and that from the exercise of reason, knowledge, and virtue naturally flow, is equally undeniable, if mankind be viewed collectively.

The rights and duties of man thus simplified, it seems almost impertinent to attempt to illustrate truths that appear so incontrovertible; yet such deeply rooted prejudices have clouded reason, and such spurious qualities have assumed the name of virtues, that it is necessary to pursue the course of reason as it has been perplexed and involved in error, by various adventitious circumstances, comparing the simple axiom with casual deviations.

Men, in general, seem to employ their reason to justify prejudices, which they have imbibed, they can scarcely trace how, rather than to root them out. The mind must be strong that resolutely forms its own principles; for a kind of intellectual cowardice prevails which makes many men shrink from the task, or only do it by halves. Yet the imperfect conclusions thus drawn, are frequently very plausible, because they are built on partial experience, on just, though narrow, views.

That the society is formed in the wisest manner, whose constitution is founded on the nature of man, strikes, in the abstract, every thinking being so forcibly, that it looks like presumption to endeavor to bring forward proofs; though proof must be brought, or the strong hold of prescription will never be forced by reason; yet to urge prescription as an argument to justify the depriving men (or women) of their natural rights, is one of the absurd sophisms which daily insult common sense.

The civilization of the bulk of the people of Europe is very partial; nay, it may be made a question, whether they have acquired any virtues in exchange for innocence, equivalent to the misery produced by the vices that have been plastered over unsightly ignorance, and the freedom which has been bartered for splendid slavery. The desire of dazzling by riches, the most certain pre-eminence that man can obtain, the pleasure of commanding flattering sycophants, and many other complicated low calculations of doting self-love, have all contributed to overwhelm the mass of mankind, and make liberty a convenient handle for mock patriotism. For whilst rank and titles are held of the utmost importance, before which Genius "must hide its diminished head," it is, with a few exceptions, very unfortunate for a nation when a man of abilities, without rank or property, pushes himself forward to notice. Alas! What unheard-of misery have thousands suffered to purchase a cardinal's hat for an intriguing obscure adventurer, who longed to be ranked with princes, or lord it over them by seizing the triple crown!

Such, indeed, has been the wretchedness that has flowed from hereditary honors, riches, and monarchy, that men of lively sensibility have almost uttered blasphemy in order to justify the dispensations of Providence. Man has been held out as independent of His power who made him, or as a lawless planet darting from its orbit to steal the celestial fire of reason; and the vengeance of Heaven, lurking in the subtile [sic] flame, like Pandora's pent-up mischiefs, sufficiently punished his temerity, by introducing evil into the world.

Impressed by this view of the misery and disorder which pervaded society, and fatigued with jostling against artificial fools, Rousseau became enamored of solitude, and, being at the same time an optimist, he labors with uncommon eloquence to prove that man was naturally a solitary animal. Misled by his respect for the goodness of God, who

certainly—for what man of sense and feeling can doubt it!—gave life only to communicate happiness, he considers evil as positive, and the work of man; not aware that he was
exalting one attribute at the expense of another, equally necessary to divine perfection.

Reared on a false hypothesis, his arguments in favor of a state of nature are plausible,
but unsound. I say unsound; for to assert that a state of nature is preferable to civilization, in all its possible perfection, is, in other words, to arraign supreme wisdom; and
the paradoxical exclamation, that God had made all things right, and that error has been
introduced by the creature, whom He formed, knowing what He formed, is as unphilo-
sophical as impious.

When that wise Being who created us and placed us here, saw the fair idea, He willed,
by allowing it to be so, that the passions should unfold our reason, because He could see
that present evil would produce future good. Could the helpless creature whom He called
from nothing break loose from his providence, and boldly learn to know good by practicing evil, without His permission? No. How could that energetic advocate for immortality
argue so inconsistently? Had mankind remained for ever in the brutal state of nature,
which even his magic pen cannot paint as a state in which a single virtue took root, it
would have been clear, though not to the sensitive unreflecting wanderer, that man was
born to run the circle of life and death, and adorn God's garden for some purpose which
could not easily be reconciled with His attributes.

But if, to crown the whole, there were to be rational creatures produced, allowed
to rise in excellence by the exercise of powers implanted for that purpose; if benignity
itself thought fit to call into existence a creature above the brutes, who could think and
improve himself, why should that inestimable gift, for a gift it was, if man was so created,
as to have a capacity to rise above the state in which sensation produced brutal ease, be
called, in direct terms, a curse? . . . His wisdom and goodness excites, if these feelings
were not set in motion to improve our nature, of which they make a part, and render
us capable of enjoying a more godlike portion of happiness? Firmly persuaded that no
evil exists in the world that God did not design to take place, I build my belief on the
perfection of God.

Rousseau exerts himself to prove that all *was* right originally: a crowd of authors that
all *is* now right: and I, that all will *be* right.

But, true to his first position, next to a state of nature, Rousseau celebrates barbarism,
and apostrophizing the shade of Fabricius, he forgets that, in conquering the world, the
Romans never dreamed of establishing their own liberty on a firm basis, or of extending
the reign of virtue. Eager to support his system, he stigmatizes, as vicious, every effort of genius; and, uttering the apotheosis of savage virtues, he exalts those to demi-gods, who were
scarcely human—the brutal Spartans who, in defiance of justice and gratitude, sacrificed,
in cold blood, the slaves who had shown themselves heroes to rescue their oppressors.

Disgusted with artificial manners and virtues, the citizen of Geneva, instead of properly sifting the subject, threw away the wheat with the chaff, without waiting to inquire
whether the evils which his ardent soul turned from indignantly, were the consequences
of civilization or the vestiges of barbarism. He saw vice trampling on virtue, and the semblance of goodness taking the place of the reality; he saw talents bent by power to sinister
purposes, and never thought of tracing the gigantic mischief up to arbitrary power, up to
the hereditary distinctions that clash with the mental superiority that naturally raises a man

above his fellows. He did not perceive that regal power, in a few generations, introduces idiotism into the noble stem, and holds out baits to render thousands idle and vicious.

Nothing can set the regal character in a more contemptible point of view, than the various crimes that have elevated men to the supreme dignity. Vile intrigues, unnatural crimes, and every vice that degrades our nature, have been the steps to this distinguished eminence; yet millions of men have supinely allowed the nerveless limbs of the posterity of such rapacious prowlers to rest quietly on their ensanguined thrones.

What but a pestilential vapor can hover over society when its chief director is only instructed in the invention of crimes, or the stupid routine of childish ceremonies? Will men never be wise?—will they never cease to expect corn from tares, and gifts from thistles?

It is impossible for any man, when the most favorable circumstances concur, to acquire sufficient knowledge and strength of mind to discharge the duties of a king, entrusted with the uncontrolled power; how then must they be violated when his very elevation is an insuperable bar to the attainment of either wisdom or virtue, when all the feelings of a man are stifled by flattery, and reflection shut out by pleasure! Sure it is madness to make the fate of thousands depend on the caprice of a weak fellow-creature, whose very station sinks him *necessarily* below the meanest of his subjects! But one power should not be thrown down to exalt another—for all power inebriates weak man; and its abuse proves that the more equality there is established among men, the more virtue and happiness will reign in society. But this and any similar maxim deduced from simple reason, raises an outcry—the Church or the State is in danger, if faith in the wisdom of antiquity is not implicit; and they who, roused by the sigh of human calamity, dare to attack human authority, are reviled as despisers of God, and enemies of man. These are bitter calumnies, yet they reached one of the best of men, whose ashes still preach peace, and whose memory demands a respectful pause, when subjects are discussed that lay so near his heart.

After attacking the sacred majesty of kings, I shall scarcely excite surprise by adding my firm persuasion that every profession, in which great subordination of rank constitutes its power, is highly injurious to morality.

A standing army, for instance, is incompatible with freedom; because subordination and rigor are the very sinews of military discipline; and despotism is necessary to give vigor to enterprises that one will directs. A spirit inspired by romantic notions of honor, a kind of morality founded on the fashion of the age, can only be felt by a few officers, whilst the main body must be moved by command, like the waves of the sea; for the strong wind of authority pushes the crowd of subalterns forward, they scarcely know or care why, with headlong fury.

Besides, nothing can be so prejudicial to the morals of the inhabitants of country towns as the occasional residence of a set of idle superficial young men, whose only occupation is gallantry, and whose polished manners render vice more dangerous, by concealing its deformity under gay ornamental drapery. An air of fashion, which is but a badge of slavery, and proves that the soul has not a strong individual character, awes simple county people into an imitation of the vices, when they cannot catch the slippery graces, of politeness. Every corps is a chain of despots, who, submitting and tyrannizing without exercising their reason, become deadweights of vice and folly on the community. A man of rank or fortune, sure of rising by interest, has nothing to do but to pursue some extravagant freak; whilst the needy *gentleman*, who is to rise, as the phrase turns, by his merit, becomes a servile parasite or vile pander.

Sailors, the naval gentlemen, come under the same description, only their vices assume a different and a grosser cast. They are more positively indolent, when not discharging the ceremonials of their station; whilst the insignificant of soldiers may be termed active idleness. More confined to the society of men, the former acquire a fondness for humor and mischievous tricks; whilst the latter, mixing frequently with well-bred women, catch a sentimental cant. But mind is equally out of the question, whether they indulge the horse-laugh, or polite simper.

May I be allowed to extend the comparison to a profession where more mind is certainly to be found—for the clergy have superior opportunities of improvement, though subordination almost equally cramps their faculties? The blind submission imposed at college to forms of belief serves as a novitiate to the curate, who must obsequiously respect the opinion of his rector or patron, if he means to rise in his profession. Perhaps there cannot be a more forcible contrast than between the servile dependent gait of a poor curate and the courtly mien of a bishop. And the respect and contempt they inspire render the discharge of their separate functions equally useless.

It is of great importance to observe that the character of every man is, in some degree, formed by his profession. A man of sense may only have a cast of countenance that wears off as you trace his individuality, whilst the weak, common man has scarcely ever any character, but what belongs to the body; at least, all his opinions have been so steeped in the vat consecrated by authority, that the faint spirit which the grape of his own vine yields, cannot be distinguished.

Society, therefore, as it becomes more enlightened, should be very careful not to establish bodies of men who must necessarily be made foolish or vicious by the very constitution of their profession.

In the infancy of society, when men were just emerging out of barbarism, chiefs and priests, touching the most powerful springs of savage conduct, hope, and fear, must have had unbounded sway. An aristocracy, of course, is naturally the first form of government. But, clashing interests soon losing their equipoise, a monarchy and hierarchy break out of the confusion of ambitious struggles, and the foundation of both is secured by feudal tenures. This appears to be the origin of monarchical and priestly powers, and the dawn of civilization. But such combustible materials cannot long be pent up; and, getting vent in foreign wars and intestine insurrections, the people acquire some power in the tumult, which obliges their rulers to gloss over their oppression with a show of right. Thus, as wars, agriculture, commerce, and literature, expand the mind, despots are compelled to make covert corruption hold fast the power that was formerly snatched by open force. And this baneful lurking gangrene is most quickly spread by luxury and superstition, the sure dregs of ambition. The indolent puppet of a court first becomes a luxurious monster, or fastidious sensualist, and then makes the contagion which his unnatural state spread, the instrument of tyranny.

It is the pestiferous purple that renders the progress of civilization a curse, and warps the understanding, till men of sensibility doubt whether the expansion of intellect produces a greater portion of happiness or misery. But the nature of the poison points out the antidote; and had Rousseau mounted one step higher in his investigation, or could his eye have pierced through the foggy atmosphere, which he almost disdained to breathe, his active mind would have darted forward to contemplate the perfection of man in the establishment of true civilization, instead of taking his ferocious flight back to the night of sensual ignorance.

Commentary by *Kate Lindemann*, Wollstonecraft and Rousseau: Philosophers of Controversy

INTRODUCTION

It is difficult to find two philosophers who have stirred more controversy than Jean-Jacques Rousseau and Mary Wollstonecraft. Rousseau often engaged in controversy in his lifetime, arguing with friends and benefactors. Since his death scholars have offered controversial interpretations of his work. Some have called him a great Romantic; others a writer of classical reasoned argument. He has been called a champion of individualism and freedom and a proponent of despotism. There is disagreement about the meaning of some of his key concepts and many claim his later work contradicts his early theories, despite Rousseau's own claim that his work is a continuous piece.

Mary Wollstonecraft also engaged in controversy in her lifetime. She was an outspoken writer who did not shirk from criticizing popular authors or ideas. Her two philosophical works, *A Vindication of the Rights of Men* and *A Vindication of the Rights of Woman*, were written as critical responses to publications by others. She also provoked controversy by her lifestyle. Wollstonecraft lived the philosophy she believed in and was known to disregard some social mores of eighteenth-century England. Unlike Rousseau, however, there is little controversy about the meaning of her works. Both of her philosophical works may have been written at great speed, but her concepts and arguments are stated plainly and few readers find ambiguity in her texts.

Both philosophers share a common interest in social and political philosophy as well as philosophy of education. Their philosophies of education were, of course, based on their views about human nature and both saw education-socialization as central to creating the sort of society they believed to be right and wholesome. Both prized human freedom and believed that all classes should exercise that freedom.

However, there are several fundamental differences between them. One major point of contention concerns the nature and status of men and women. Rousseau believed that men and women have been given different constitutions, while Wollstonecraft believes that there is one human nature that both men and women share. A second is in the way these two philosophers practiced their craft. Rousseau developed his philosophy over a lifetime through a series of essays, while Wollstonecraft's philosophical ideas are expressed in two popular works written within a few years of each other. Rousseau's entire work is founded on a hypothesized history of the human race while Wollstonecraft uses empirical observations as the foundation for her arguments. A related third difference is that Rousseau's writing style has much of the calm and clarity of seventeenth-century French thought, while Wollstonecraft writes with the passion of a polemicist denouncing errant thinkers.

In this essay, I describe some of the theories of Rousseau and Wollstonecraft, explain Wollstonecraft's major criticism of Rousseau's work, and note other differences between them. I do not attempt to resolve all the ambiguities and problems in their texts. My hope is that this essay will provoke readers to return to the primary sources and to consult some secondary source materials to help formulate their own views about the texts. It is this personal study of texts that is one of the main skills to be obtained from reading original works in the history of philosophy. The mere listing of philosophical tenets and theories is more the work of an encyclopedia than a philosophical work.

ROUSSEAU

It has been said that all theory is but autobiography writ large. There is no philosopher of whom this is more true than Jean-Jacques Rousseau. Peter Gay states in the introduction to Ernest Cassiers's definitive study of Rousseau that it is not possible to understand Rousseau's work "unless we trace that work back to its point of departure in Rousseau's life and to its roots in his personality."[5] Rousseau's life is key to understanding his philosophy and its development. Gay holds that this study makes it possible to understand Rousseau's own claim that his work forms a single, noncontradictory piece.[6]

It should be clear from the biographical section that Rousseau's life appears directionless. The death of his mother after his birth affected him deeply: "I cost my mother her life and my birth was the first of my misfortunes."[7] Of the abandonment by his father who left Geneva and his son rather than accept a sentence for wounding a man during a brawl, Rousseau says little. His early life was marked by imaginative reverie and play, free wandering in the countryside, a lack of any sort of discipline coupled with penetrating political discourse with his father. Some thinkers believe that his early existence is idealized in his concepts of natural man and the state of nature.

Rousseau set out on his own as a teen and through his life meandered from place to place and occupation to occupation. After his unfettered youth, he was appalled by the mannered society of the French court.[8] His lack of socialization and discipline made it difficult for him to enter into any social strata with enduring success. He wanted to make his mark in society but seemed unable to do so. His inability to secure permanent employment meant that he also knew poverty. His philosophy emphasizes the value of every man, both the commoners and the members of the upper class and he brings nature (and precivil society) back into social consciousness. His philosophy struggles with the issue of personal freedom in light of the importance of society and state governance.

Just as his first independent venture into the world ended in his seeking charity, Rousseau often relied on others to rescue him from the indigence brought on by failed ventures. He appears to have found co-equal relationships difficult to maintain. His arguments with friends and associates were significant and his relationships with women, especially his long-term relationship with Thérèse Le Vasseur, were never based on equality. In fact, in Wollstonecraft's criticism of Rousseau's views about women she says that his choice to live with an illiterate and apparently uneducable woman (Le Vasseur) is an example of Rousseau's need to bring all women down to that level.[9]

ROUSSEAU'S PHILOSOPHICAL THEORIES

Rousseau is best known in literature for his *Confessions*. His *Social Contract* is often studied in political philosophy and *Émile* remains a classic in philosophy of education. What many people do not realize is that his first two philosophical works, *Discourse on the Origin of Inequality* and *Discourse on Political Economy*, provide the foundations without which his later work cannot be properly understood.

Rousseau's *Discourse on the Origin of Inequality* was composed in hopes of winning prize money offered by the academy of Dijon for a work on the subject Has the Progress of the Arts and Sciences Contributed more to the Corruption or the Purification of Morals? Rousseau decided to take the negative. Some say he did so for the tactical reason that it would have less competition from other submissions; others say he did so out of deeply felt experience about the unfairness of contemporary society.[10] In any case, this *Discourse on the Origin of Inequality* is foundational for understanding any of Rousseau's later work.

In his opening paragraphs Rousseau makes a distinction between natural inequality and moral or political inequality. The first inequality, of height, strength, etc., is given at birth but the latter is established by men as they leave the natural state and transform themselves later into members (citizens) of artificial states of society.[11] It states that contemporary society is unnatural; it is the sixth form of society that evolved away from an original natural state.

Rousseau hypothesized an original state of nature when man had no need for reason or morality. He says there are "two principles, prior to reason, one of them deeply interesting us in our own welfare and the other exciting a natural repugnance at seeing any sensible being, and particularly any of our own species, suffer pain or death."[12]

Rousseau notes that many philosophers speak of a state of nature but that none of them really understands it. He, Rousseau, does. In original nature, man's life is solitary. He is dispersed among the plants and animals. He is more adroit than animals and more adaptable to eating different foods. In this original state he needs no possessions and so owns nothing. Like the animals, he sleeps once his needs are met. He has an ability to choose (free will) among different courses of action and he is not bought by nature (determined). Man has no moral qualities because none are needed. He may see another human being only a few times in his lifetime. He may find a woman with whom to copulate but there is no real relationship. She may nurse the child who might come from this meeting but there is no real relationship between mother and child. At this first stage, the state of original nature or state of nature, man has no morality; only natural actions for survival or the feeling of pity mentioned above.[13]

From this first state, Rousseau hypothesizes, man begins to evolve. Rousseau believes that the first person who made a claim of property and who got others to accept that claim was the real founder of civil society.[14] The act establishing property was transformative of nature and Rousseau holds that all war, all crime, murders and human horrors stem from this one action. Civil society is founded on the concept of property.[15] After accepting the concept of property, man, according to Rousseau, goes though a number of social evolutionary stages. As he increases in number and comes into more frequent contact with other men, he needs to communicate and language develops.[16]

Next man begins to recognize that mutual assistance can benefit his self-interest and so the first cooperation evolves. Family develops and with it comes a moral expansion of the human heart to include conjugal love and paternal affection. Gender difference is established in work. Soon man develops a more settled existence; the roving, wandering state is abandoned. Rousseau says that,

> At this state equality might have been sustained, had the talents of individuals been equal, and had, for example, the use of iron and the consumption of commodities always exactly balanced each other; but, as there was nothing to preserve this balance, it was soon disturbed; the strongest did the most work; the most skillful turned his labor to best account; the most ingenious devised methods of diminishing his labor etc.[17]

Slowly natural inequality begins to generate inequalities among groups of men and political inequality comes into existence.

At this stage, Rousseau claims, a great burst toward artificial civilization takes place. Language advances, other arts are invented, the use and abuse of excess riches, memory, and imagination come into full play. Reasoning develops, egoism comes into existence since one now needs to either possess or affect qualities needed in this society. Man, for the first time, needs to appear to be what he is not and so pomp, cheating, and deceit develop. This leads to a need for morality and for the state.[18] Without a civil state, there is no government to make and enforce laws that protect the lives and liberties of its subjects (citizens)—something subjects in a state of nature could not guarantee for themselves. In the *Social Contract* Rousseau is most concerned with this late state of civilized society and its state.

A central problem for the *Social Contract* is the reconciliation of man's inherent natural freedom with the need for and participation in a state with its entire governing apparatus. Here there are differing interpretations of Rousseau's thought. Clearly he approves of state and government. He states that the individual must obey. How does one reconcile this with his view of individual freedom as the mark of man's nature? Some claim that Rousseau weakens his earlier views about freedom as definitive for man. However, Rousseau said that all his work was a single piece. If we are to take him seriously, we need to examine this issue.

It could be that Rousseau is making an intellectual move akin to Augustine's when the latter said, "Love God and do what you will." This, too, appears to be a contradictory claim for someone, like Augustine, who believes that we should live by God's law. However, Augustine's insight is that we become like that which we love. If one truly loves God, one will become like God and will want (will) that which God would will. Thus, if you love God, you will want the same as God and so you can do what you want without violating divine precepts. If Rousseau is making a similar philosophical move, then his claim that all his work is a single piece can stand. He would be claiming that when one is so free that one can freely will the same things as willed by all free men [the common will], then there is no contradiction between one's exercise of one's freedom and being bound by the common will.

Rousseau viewed *Émile* as the crowning piece of his work and if that is true, then *Émile* makes it clear that when Rousseau speaks of man or men, he means male persons. He does not see men and women as both having the same constitution or character. There is a character of man and a separate character of woman. Man is the doer, the actor in the world. Woman is weak and passive and her aim is to please man. Since nature has given them such different constitutions, their roles in the world should be different and thus the education of males and females needs to be different.

> In everything that does not relate to sex the woman is as man; they are alike in organs, needs and capacities. . . . In everything that relates to sex there are correspondences and differences. The difficulty is to determine what in their constitution is due to sex and what is not. . . . The perfect man and perfect woman should no more resemble each other in mind than in countenance. . . . It is the part of one to be active and strong, and that of the other to be passive and weak . . . woman is intended to please man of the constitution of the sexes, the stronger may appear to be master, and yet actually be dependent on the weaker. . . . By giving woman the capacity to stimulate desires greater than can be satisfied, nature has made man dependent on woman's good will and constrained him to seek to please her as a condition of her submission. . . . Men and women are unequally affected by sex. The male is only male at times; the female is female all her life and can not forget her sex.[19]

This view of the two different characters for men and women undergirds Rousseau's philosophy of education. Young Émile is to be educated by means that will allow him to remain aware of and in touch with his natural man and the qualities of original state of nature. Rousseau believes that every man is aware, at least vaguely, of the original state of natural man, "a state which no longer exists, perhaps never did exist, and probably never will exist."[20] His prescription for allowing Émile freedom to follow his orientation in learning flows from Rousseau's notion that there is in each man some sense of original nature and its freedom and that this original nature is better than "civilized man."

Since it is the character of females to be passive, weak, and wanting to please men, girls by the very constitution given them by nature require a different form of education from boys. It is this claim and the educational practices that flow from it that impelled Mary Wollstonecraft to criticize Rousseau in her chapter "Animadversions on Some of the Writers who have Rendered Women Objects of Pity, Bordering on Contempt" in *A Vindication of the Rights of Woman*.

First, it is important to be clear that Wollstonecraft agrees with much of Rousseau's description of women. She believes that many women are weak, passive, and wanting to please. The chapter in which she criticizes Rousseau and several other thinkers comes after her own observations about "The State of Degradation to which Woman is Reduced." She opens the next chapter, "Animadversions on Some of the Writers who have Rendered Women Objects of Pity, Bordering on Contempt" by saying that she will examine a "number of publications on the female character and education:"[21]

> I shall begin with Rousseau, and give a sketch of his character of woman in his own words, interspersing comments and reflections . . . Sophia, says Rousseau, should be as perfect a woman, as Emilius is a man, and to render her so it is necessary to examine the character which nature has given to the sex.

He then proceeds to prove that woman ought to be weak and passive, because she has less bodily strength than man; and hence infers that she was formed to please and to be subject to him, and that it is her duty to render herself *agreeable* to her master—this being the grand end of her existence. Still, however, to give a little mock dignity to lust, he insists that man should not exert his strength, but depend on the will of the woman when he seeks for pleasure with her.[22]

In this section of her text, Wollstonecraft quotes Rousseau extensively and after each quotation gives her critical response. She often agrees with the philosopher when he claims that women are weak, disordered, or adept at pleasing, but in each instance she claims that these qualities are the result of the socialization-education of girls and women and not the result of their nature. For example, Wollstonecraft disagrees with Rousseau when she writes:

Woman and man were made for each other, but their mutual dependence is not the same. The men depend on the women only on account of their desires; the women on the men both on account of their desires and their necessities. We could subsist better without them than they without us.

Girls are from their earliest infancy fond of dress. Not content with being pretty, they are desirous of begin thought so. We see by all their little airs that this thought engages their attention; and they are hardly capable of understanding what it said to them, before they are to be governed by talking to them of what people will think of their behavior. The same motive, however, indiscreetly made us of with boys, has not the same effect.[23]

The first main claim to make about Wollstonecraft's disagreement with Rousseau is that she agrees that girls exhibit these characteristics, but she claims that this is a result of the way they are trained from their earliest years, rather than their natural character. In support of her position, she calls upon her own experiential knowledge of French culture and its centralization of pleasing, of regulation of manners and social coquetry, of its teaching subservience to men through religious confession [to men], and the expected practice of girls establishing themselves in society through marriage as the real source of the characteristics Rousseau describes.

She offers similar criticisms about each of Rousseau's prescriptions for keeping girls and women subject to authority and oriented towards needing and pleasing men. Wollstonecraft does not disagree that girls and women show the characteristics that Rousseau states. What she disagrees with is the source of these characteristics. She blames nurture and says that if girls and women were treated in accord with the same free and intelligent nature as boys and men, girls and women also would be independent beings.[24] In other words, Wollstonecraft claims that it is nurture and not nature that makes women as they are and that if nurture is changed, then women will behave differently. Rousseau claimed that it is nature and not nurture that is the cause.

It is interesting to note that Rousseau is not the only author she critiques. She believes that erroneous claims about the nature of girls and women are common. She critiques other popular writers who agree with Rousseau's position: Dr. Fordyce, Dr. Gregory, and Madam Genlis. She believes that these authors and their works of advice about childraising are the sources for the inappropriate socialization of women. She holds that their theories are pernicious to the welfare of women and society as a whole. After roundly criticizing these authors, she suggests some writers who do advocate treating women as full, coequal human beings. She mentions Mrs. Chaparone and the philosopher, educator Catharine Macaulay.[25]

The second criticism discussed here is about what Wollstonecraft makes of Rousseau's view of society and the original state of nature. She states this criticism in chapter 1 of *A Vindication of the Rights of Woman* and this section speaks for itself:

> Impressed by this view of the misery and disorder which pervaded society, and fatigued with the jostling against artificial fools, Rousseau became enamored of solitude, and, being at the same time an optimist, he labors with uncommon eloquence to prove that man was naturally a solitary animal. Misled by his respect for the goodness of God, who certainly—for what man of sense and feeling can doubt it!—gave life only to communicate happiness, he considers evil as positive, and the work of man; not aware he was exalting one attribute at the expense of another, equally necessary to divine perfection.
>
> Reared on a false hypothesis; his arguments in favor of a state of nature are plausible, but unsound. I say unsound, for to assert that a state of nature is preferable to civilization, in all its possible perfection, is, in other words, to arraign supreme wisdom; and the paradoxical exclamation, that God had made all things right, and that error has been introduced by the creature, whom He formed, knowing what He formed, is as unphilosophical as impious.
>
> When that wise Being who created us and placed us here. . . . He willed, by allowing it to be so, that the passions should unfold our reason, because He could see that present evil would produce future good. Could the helpless creature whom He called from nothing break loose from his providence, and boldly learn to know good by practicing evil, without his permission? No. How could that energetic advocate for immortality argue so inconsistently? Had mankind remained forever in the brutal state of nature, which even his magic pen cannot paint as a state in which a single virtue took root, it would have been clear, though not to the sensitive unreflecting wanderer, that man was born to run the circle of life and death, and adorn God's garden for some purpose which could not be reconciled with His attributes. [She ends with] Rousseau exerts himself to prove that all was right originally: a crowd of authors that all is now right: and I, that all will be right.[26]

WOLLSTONECRAFT

Mary Wollstonecraft was the second child and eldest daughter in what today might be called a dysfunctional family. Her father belonged to the lower gentry but his drinking and gambling reduced the family through the social ranks. Her mother was compliant to her husband and demanding of Mary who took on the role of family caretaker. Mary not only cared for her brothers and sisters but also protected her mother by lying across her parent's bedroom threshold to head off her father when he came home drunk and was likely to beat his wife.[27]

Mary's life was filled with people and their needs. Like many resilient children in difficult circumstances, she sought positive relationships outside her family and found adults who nourished her intellectual capacities and encouraged her reading. She sought independence at an early age and, as the biographical section notes, went through a series of occupations. She became acquainted with a number of the English dissenters and remained associated with that movement. It was the publisher Joseph Johnson who affected her life significantly as a writer. Under his tutoring she honed her writing skills. Some of her books were best sellers and she reveled in her success amidst the community of political radicals that surrounded Johnson. Among these, William Blake immortalized her in a poem and William Godwin later became her spouse.

Wollstonecraft had no idealized childhood, and nothing in her writings idealizes childhood. She is aware of the burdens of childcare. An astute observer of life, she learned much about British society through her variety of occupations. In *A Vindication of the Rights of Woman* she describes and criticizes the deplorable state of women in her day—many of whom she believes unfit for raising moral, healthy children because they themselves have been kept from developing their reasoning.[28] She also criticized idleness as a source of vice and she castigates the landed gentry and upper classes as parasites on society because they do no real work.[29]

WOLLSTONECRAFT'S PHILOSOPHICAL WORK

Although Wollstonecraft's philosophy is embedded in her letters and in her novel, *Maria or the Wrongs of Women*, it is most clearly expressed in the two *Vindications* that were written within a few years of each other. The first, *A Vindication of the Rights of Men*, was published within a month of Edmund Burke's attack on the French Revolution, *Reflections on the Revolution in France. A Vindication of the Rights of Men* became an overnight best seller. Other authors, including the American Thomas Paine, would follow with new responses to Burke, but hers was the first to defend all humanity in light of Burke's lament for the losses both of the French aristocratic tradition and of property as the basis for society. Wollstonecraft and her book were praised by the French and it established her place among the English political radicals.[30]

In 1792, Wollstonecraft again took up the pen. Despite the revolutionary changes that had swept America and Europe, women were not faring well among these changes. For example, they were not allowed to vote under either constitution.[31] She wrote *A Vindication of the Rights of Woman* and dedicated it to Talleyrand, a French diplomat and statesman who had written a report on French education. In this second *Vindication*, Wollstonecraft argues that men and women share the same common humanity and that socialization and education systems that fail to address this common human nature are the causes of the sad state of women's minds and behavior. She offers suggestions for educational reform that she believes will remedy many social ills.

One characteristic of Wollstonecraft's two main philosophical works is that they are written with a force and passion common to much nineteenth-century political writing. It is not just polemics, however, that influences her style. As the opening chapter of *A Vindication of the Rights of Woman* states, passions are basic to human nature. These passions need to be shaped and dominated by reason but they are a given and should be used. Readers of her work will recognize the force of Wollstonecraft's logic and the organization of her arguments but they will also sense the current of passion that underlies her sentences.

A second characteristic of Wollstonecraft's philosophical work is its grounding in empirical observations. She accepts society as a given. She does not feel the need to justify its existence. She uses insights and observations gathered from her exposure to a variety of classes and occupations. It is these observations that form the content for her arguments. Noteworthy is an argument in which she demonstrates that it is a difference in socialization and not a difference in nature that makes women's behavior so different from that of men. She uses observations of military men as her evidence. She notes that they exhibit many of the same moral characteristics of attention to fashion and an inability to make reasoned decisions as found in women. She shows that military men, like women, are taught to obey and are not allowed to act as independent decision makers concerning any matters of significance. She concludes that since some men exhibit the same qualities as many women, it is socialization and not nature that makes them so.[32]

Third, one may characterize (or summarize) Wollstonecraft's fundamental principles as a series of questions and answers that are stated in the first chapter of *A Vindication of the Rights of Woman*:

> In what does man's pre-eminence over the brute in creation consist? The answer is as clear as that a half is less than the whole, in Reason. What acquirement exalts one being above the other? Virtue, we spontaneously reply. For what purpose were the passions implanted?
>
> That man by struggling with them might attain a degree of knowledge denied to the brutes, whispers Experience.
>
> Consequently the perfection of our nature and capability of happiness must be estimated by the degree of reason, virtue and knowledge, that distinguish the individual, and direct the laws which bind society; and that from the exercise of reason, knowledge and virtue naturally flow, is equally undeniable, if mankind be viewed collectively.[33]

If we add to these claims her strong belief in the necessity of contributing to society through honest work, we have a summary of the foundation of Wollstonecraft's philosophy. All else follows from these principles.

ROUSSEAU AND WOLLSTONECRAFT COMPARED

It should be obvious to the reader that Rousseau and Wollstonecraft both treasured freedom and both were democrats; they believed the suffrage based on economic class was mistaken. They both propose philosophies to undergird social reform and they both recognize education-socialization as the most potent force for social change.

What is different is that Rousseau believes that man was originally solitary and that his original, natural, premoral state was better than his later civilized state. Wollstonecraft believes that human beings are naturally in relationship and that civilization is better than any original premoral state. Also, Rousseau holds that there are two different human constitutions based on sex and that woman's character made her incapable of the kind of moral and rational development as men. Women, according to Rousseau, if they are true to the character given them by nature, have their own orientations, tasks, and moral virtues. Thus women should serve and please men and leave the governance to men who by nature are able to reason. Education should, of course, reinforce this. Wollstonecraft believes that there is a single human nature and thus one human development and one set of virtues. If courage is a virtue, it should be a virtue for both men and women and both sexes should strive to develop it. The notion that there are two separate natures for women and for men is mistaken and girls should receive the same basic education as boys.

Other differences between them appear to be grounded in what Aristotle would call their formal orientations. Rousseau hypothesizes an early premoral, more perfect existence state for the human race. He says that this state may, in fact, have never existed. Still, his whole philosophy idealizes it and he wants its characteristics to be emphasized in man's orientation in life. Rousseau blames the development of civilization for the ills experienced by men. It is society, the abandonment of the solitary life that led to social ills. Rousseau's solution is a new society where all free men are in perfect conformity to the common will of other free men. Of course, he includes practicalities such as the power of the state to govern and punish but his goal is perfect freedom in conformity to the common will.

Wollstonecraft does not hypothesize anything. She begins her analysis with current, existing society. She argues that its ills are the result of bad theory and explanation about the true nature of human beings that is being used to socialize and educate human beings. She argues that if that theory is discarded and all citizens are educated to take their places as moral beings and contributors to society, then an entire society can be changed and present ills can be removed. Nature, either in the real or the ideal, does not predominate in her thought. Hers is a philosophy centered on human beings in relation to one another; a society where contributing to society through work is considered central and where a solitary life is not championed.

Conclusion

Ludwig Wittgenstein claimed that the real power of a theory is its ability to charm us. Both Rousseau and Wollstonecraft have created powerful theories. Certainly Rousseau's theories have shown a power to charm whole groups of people, whether members of the French court who began going to the country and dressing as simple farm folk or moderns who embrace rural life and a return to a nature. Wollstonecraft's theories also charmed. Her works were an impetus for many middle-class women of her day to educate themselves through reading and her view of universal suffrage became a reality in much of the world of Europe and the Americas.

One central issue that divided the pair still continues to be debated today. Is there a single human nature or are there separate constitutions for men and women? This is a serious philosophical question, and if Wittgenstein is to be believed, the answer we choose is the one that "captures or charms us." As you read these two philosophers, it might be useful to examine which of their theories attracts you and why you find it so attractive. Your answer may tell you a great deal about yourself.

Questions for Reflection

As you read the selections from each philosopher, did you find that their writing style affected how you thought or felt about their ideas? How important is a philosopher's writing style to describing and evaluating her or his claims as philosophical claims?

Consider Rousseau's claim that contemporary society is unnatural. What do you think he meant by that and do you think Wollstonecraft would agree? Why or why not?

Both Rousseau and Wollstonecraft are concerned with what contemporary theorists call the nature versus nurture question: Do all humans (men and women) have the same (human) nature whereby differences between them are the result of socialization (nurture) or are men and women naturally (biologically) different? What do you understand to be their answers? What role do you think socialization plays in how men and women act, feel, or develop? Be sure to defend your answers.

Notes

1. Kate Lindemann, "Mary Wollstonecraft," in *A History of Women Philosophers*, vol. 3, *Modern Women Philosophers 1600–1900*, ed. Mary Ellen Waithe (Dordrecht, The Netherlands: Kluwer Academic Publishers, 1991), 153.

2. Jean-Jacques Rousseau, *The Émile of Jean-Jacques Rousseau*, trans. William Boyd (New York: Teachers College Columbia University, 1963), 130–32. © 1963 Teachers College, Columbia University. All rights reserved.

3. Jean-Jacques Rousseau, "The Social Contract," *Rousseau* in Great Books of the Western World, vol. 38, ed. Mortimer J. Adler, Clifton Fadiman, and Philip W. Goetz (Chicago: Encyclopedia Britannica, 1952). © 1952, 1990 Encyclopedia Britannica, Inc.

4. Mary Wollstonecraft, *A Vindication of the Rights of Woman: With Strictures on Political and Moral Subjects* (London: J. Johnson, 1792), 1:15–31.

5. Peter Gay, "Introduction" in *The Question of Jean-Jacques Rousseau*, ed. Ernst Cassirer (Bloomington: Indiana University Press, 1975), 3.

6. Gay, *The Question*, 3.

7. Jean-Jacques Rousseau, *The Confessions of Jean-Jacques Rousseau* (New York: Modern Library, 1945), 5.

8. Ernst Cassirer claims that it was not until Rousseau entered Paris that he acquired any real intellectual self-awareness. See *The Question*, 40–41.

9. Mary Wollstonecraft, *A Vindication of the Rights of Woman: An Authoritative Text, Backgrounds, the Wollstonecraft Debate, Criticism*, 2nd ed., ed. Carol H. Poston (New York: W. W. Norton & Co, 1988), 71. Excerpts are published with permission of Random House.

10. Cassirer, *The Question*, 46–47.

11. Jean-Jacques Rousseau, "A Dissertation on the Origin and Foundation of the Inequality of Mankind," in *Montesquieu and Rousseau*, Great Books of the Western World, vol. 38, ed. Robert Maynard Hutchins (Chicago: Encyclopedia Britannica, 1954), 333.

12. Rousseau, *Origin and Foundation*, 330–31.

13. Rousseau notes his differences from other philosophers. On pages 343–44 in *Origin and Foundation*, for example, he notes the things overlooked by Hobbes in his characterization of original man.

14. Rousseau, *Origin and Foundation*, 348.

15. Rousseau, *Origin and Foundation*, 348.

16. Rousseau, *Origin and Foundation*, 350.

17. Rousseau, *Origin and Foundation*, 353.

18. Rousseau, *Origin and Foundation*, 353.

19. Rousseau, *Émile*, 130–32.

20. Rousseau, "A Dissertation on the Origin and Foundation of the Inequality of Mankind," 329.

21. Mary Wollstonecraft. "Animadersions on Some of the Writers who have Rendered Women Objects of Pity, Bordering on Contempt," in *A Vindication of the Rights of Woman*. (New York: Modern Library, 2001), 74.

22. Wollstonecraft, "Animadersions," 74.

23. Wollstonecraft, "Animadersions," 76.

24. Wollstonecraft, "Animadersions," 78.

25. Wollstonecraft, "Animadersions," 90–103.

26. Wollstonecraft, "Animadersions," 5–6.

27. See Lindemann, "Mary Wollstonecraft," 153–54.

28. Wollstonecraft, *Rights of Woman*, 153–54.

29. Wollstonecraft, *Rights of Woman*, 142–45.

30. Barbara Taylor, "Introduction," *A Vindication of the Rights of Woman* (New York: Alfred Knopf, 1992), xi.

31. Taylor, "Introduction," *Vindication*, xi.

32. Wollstonecraft, *Rights of Woman*, 8–9; 16–17; 3 respectively.

33. Wollstonecraft, *Vindication*, 15.

CHAPTER 10

Kant and van Schurman

Introduction by *Karen J. Warren*

In addition to some brief biographical comments about this chapter's philosophical pair, I describe the basic epistemology and ethics of Immanuel Kant (1724–1804) and the significance of the argument by Anna Maria van Schurman (1607–1679) that "a maid may be a scholar." My comments about van Schurman use the sort of syllogistic reasoning she uses to generate conclusions that confirm or complement van Schurman's while suggesting implications of her views. These remarks are intended to provide helpful background material for understanding both the primary texts and the commentary in this chapter.

KANT

Immanuel Kant was a German philosopher from Königsberg in East Prussia (now Kaliningrad, Russia), a town he lived in and never traveled far from throughout his life. Kant was raised in a pietistic household, where he received a strict, punitive, stern education, mostly in Latin and religious instruction. He attended the University of Königsberg (1740), where he studied Leibniz, British philosophers, and Newtonian metaphysics.

By the age of forty-six, Kant was an established scholar and an increasingly influential philosopher. But he stopped publishing work in philosophy for eleven years—time spent in solitude, attempting to understand and defend the relation between our sensible and intellectual faculties. Only in 1781, with the completion of his eight-hundred-page *Critique of Pure Reason*, did Kant leave his isolation.

Although recognized now as one of the greatest works in the history of philosophy, *Critique of Pure Reason* was largely ignored upon publication. Kant decided to write a shorter summary of his views from the *Critique* and, in 1783, published his *Prolegomena to any Future Metaphysics*. From then his reputation rose until, at the time of his death, he was recognized as one of Europe's greatest philosophers.

Kant's Epistemology

The beginning of modern philosophy, a period in which epistemological issues reigned supreme, is identified with Descartes and its ending with Kant. Descartes's use of the rational method to find indubitable philosophical truths set in motion the rationalism versus empiricism debate (see chapter 5), which lasted through Kant.

In the *Critique of Pure Reason* Kant provided an alternative to how that debate was framed. Recall (chapter 5) the question Kant raised—one that persists in canonical philosophy today: Is there synthetic *a priori* knowledge? Rationalists answered yes; empiricists answered no. Kant's view, known as "transcendental idealism," is different. Kant, like Descartes, was interested in saving the certainty of philosophy and science, but through a critical method (critique) that went to the roots of the controversy by providing an account of pure knowledge (pure reason, pure judgment), which was not about what humans know through reason, but about the nature of "pure reason itself" and "pure meaning ideas"—*a priori* concepts. Kant's view is that knowledge is the interaction between intuition (primitive sense data unmediated by reason) and categories of understanding (*a priori* concepts). Kant answered his own question; here is synthetic *a priori* knowledge

To illustrate Kant's account of pure reason, consider the distinction between objects and events. One is free to perceive an object, such as a table, from multiple directions and in different order—from the top to the bottom, from one leg at a time, from underneath or on top of it. In contrast, Kant argued that how one perceives events or experiences that occur in space and over time is restricted by categories of reason. When watching a ship move downstream, one is *not* free to see first its launch, then its docking at the end of its journey, followed by it midcourse, and then just after it set sail. The perception of the ship moving downstream presupposes certain categories of understanding—for example, concepts (or categories) of causation, temporal succession, and spatial location—that are, in effect, hardwired in our minds. Experience of the ship's movement downstream occurs in the spatiotemporal world but is known through, and dependent on, categories of reason.

This is the dyadic interrelationship between our sensible and intellectual faculties that Kant defended in *Critique of Pure Reason*. Pure knowledge is of "things-in-themselves"— what Kant called *noumena*—that are inaccessible through perception of the sensory world of "things-as-they appear," what Kant called *phenomena*.

Kant's Ethics

Kant's ethic is a deontological (nonconsequentialist) ethics of duty based on what Kant called "the categorical imperative" as the supreme, principle of morality. Kant's categorial imperative is based on three assumptions about humans and three assumptions about ethics that Kant thinks any ordinary person would grant (see diagram 10.1). The three assumptions or insights about humans are: (1) Humans are rational beings— beings capable of entertaining abstract principles, of making moral judgments, and exercising a will. (2) Humans are "ends-in-themselves." Humans have intrinsic—not merely extrinsic or instrumental—value (value just for the kind of beings we are) and

Diagram 10.1.

3 Insights About Humans	3 Assumptions About Ethics	3 Informal Versions of the C.I.	Kant's Statements of the C.I.
(1) Humans are rational being—beings capable of entertaining abstract principles, of making moral judgments, and exercising a will.	(4) There is something objectionable about a person who acts in a way that person would not want others to act	(1) & (4): One should act in a way one would want others to act. (The maxim underlying one's action is *universalizable*)	"Act only on that maxim that you can at the same time will to be a universal law." (The Imperative Duty)
(2) Humans are "ends in themselves." Humans have intrinsic value and dignity; humans do not have a market price.	(5) Human actions must respect the intrinsic worth of human life; any act that *merely* uses humans as a means to an end is wrong.	(2) & (5): One ought never treat oneself or another human merely a means to an end (but always as an end).	"Act in such a way that you always treat humanity, whether in your own person or in the person of any other, never simply as a means, but always at the same time as an end." (The Practical Imperative)
(3) Humans are autonomous (self-legislating). Insofar as reason dictates the laws to which humans submit, human freedom is preserved by submission to moral law.	(6) A person cannot be compelled to be moral; persons must accept the demands of morality as binding on themselves.	(3) & (6): One ought always act autonomously (not heteronomously)	"Every rational being as an end in himself must be able to regard himself as also the maker of universal law in respect of any law whatever to which he may be subjected." (The Formula of the Autonomy of the Will)

dignity (meaning that there is no substitute or equivalent for humans; humans do not have a market price). (3) Humans are autonomous (self-legislating). That is, reason legislates the laws to which humans submit. As rational beings (rather than as individual, particular beings located in specific, historical contexts) humans may regard themselves as the authors of the moral law. Paradoxically, reason preserves its freedom by submission to moral law.

Kant's three basic assumptions about ethics are: (4) There is something objectionable about a person who acts in a way that person would not want others to act; (5) Human actions must respect the intrinsic worth of human life; any act that merely or simply uses humans as a means to an end is wrong; and, (6) A person cannot be compelled to be moral; each person must accept the demands of morality as binding on herself/himself.

Kant combines (1)–(6) in ways that result in three formulations of his categorical imperative. Combining (1) and (4), Kant generates the first formulation of the categorical imperative, what Kant calls the Imperative of Duty: "Act only on that maxim that you can at the same time will to be a universal law." This is the formulation scholars generally refer to as Kant's primary or basic statement of the Categorical Imperative. Combining (2) and (5), Kant generates the second formulation of the categorical imperative, the Practical Imperative: "Act in such a way that you always treat humanity, whether in your own person or in the person of any other, never simply as a means, but always at the same time as an end." Combining (3) and (6), Kant generates the third formulation, the Formula of the Autonomy of the Will: "Every rational being as an end in himself must be able to regard himself as also the maker of universal law in respect of any law whatever to which he may be subjected." That is, one ought never perform an act that is motivated purely by desire or inclination—a "heteronomous" act; one ought always act from the motive of duty and in accordance with the dictates of reason—act "autonomously."

This description of how these assumptions about humans, (1)–(3), and about ethics, (4)–(6), combine to generate Kant's three formations of the categorical imperative (CI #1–CI#3) is summarized by diagram 10.1.

The categorical imperative is a categorical (not hypothetical) command (imperative) of the form, "One ought to do X;" it requires that one act from a motive of duty in order for one's act to have moral worth. To determine what one ought to do in a particular case, ask: "Is the maxim (or principle) underlying my action universalizable? Does acting in accordance with it result in the statement of a universal principle that all human beings, *as* human beings, are obligated to obey?" If the answer is yes, then it is right to do the act or kind of act; otherwise, it is not.

VAN SCHURMAN

Anna Maria van Schurman was educated at home and is claimed to have "learned seven or eight different languages, including (allegedly) Ethiopian, for which she composed a grammar."[1] She became knowledgeable in mathematics, calculus, astronomy, rhetoric, dialectics, philosophy, and poetry.[2] She was a renowned scholar of the seventeenth century.

The Learned Maid uses deductive syllogistic reasoning to prove "a maid may be a scholar"—that women are capable of rational thinking and, so, could be scholars (and philosophers). Van Schurman wrote *The Learned Maid* "to encourage and excite young women to be educated, and parents to educate their children."

Van Schurman's proof in *The Learned Maid* challenges the philosophical canon in five distinct ways. First, by her deliberate choice to use the method of syllogistic reasoning with herself as the subject (in subject-predicate statements), she shows that women are capable of reason (rationality) and, therefore, of doing philosophy. Second, insofar as the concept of reason has historically been inextricably connected to the reason versus emotion dualism, whereby women are identified with inferior emotion, van Schurman's use and display of reason to establish her conclusion shows that she is fully capable of entertaining abstract principles or considering maxims underlying actions; as a consequence, the reason versus emotion dualism has functioned historically as a male gender-biased dualism. This constitutes an important criticism of a foundation-level distinction of The House. Third, van Schurman's argument shows that neither the words "man" or "men," nor the *concept* of reason, have functioned historically as gender-neutral concepts. If the concepts "man," "men," and "reason" were conceptually generic, then one should be able to *preserve* the canonical meanings of (1) the man of reason, (2) the man of practical wisdom, and (3) men as rational beings when the terms "woman" and "women" are "substituted for the allegedly gender-neutral terms "man" and "men" in (1), (2), and (3). But that is not the case (as I will soon show). The historical meanings of (1), (2), and (3) are not preserved in any of the following: (1a) the woman of reason, (2a) the woman of practical wisdom, and (3a) women as rational beings. This relates to a fourth feature of van Schurman's arguments: establishing the *conceptual* (and not merely *distributive*) male-biased notion of "men" and "reason" in canonical philosophy has serious implications concerning textbook examples of valid and sound syllogisms. Consider Arguments 1 and 2:

Argument 1
1. All men are rational.
2. Socrates is a man.
3. Hence, Socrates is rational.

Argument 2
1. All rational beings are mortal.
2. Socrates is a rational being.
3. Hence, Socrates is mortal.

Van Schurman's arguments about a woman's ("a learned maid's") rational and scholarly capacities show that, *on historical, canonical accounts,* the soundness of Arguments 1 and 2 is not preserved when a woman's name or the term "women" is "substituted in" the appropriate places (producing Arguments 1a and 2a).

Argument 1a
1. All men are rational.
2. Van Schurman is a man.
3. Hence, van Schurman is rational.

Argument 2a
1. All rational beings are mortal.
2. Van Schurman is a rational being.
3. Hence women are mortal.

On the canonical view, the second premises of Arguments 1a and 2a are false: Van Schurman is neither a male nor (according to canonical views about women through at least the eighteenth century) rational. In fact, the time-honored *validity* of Arguments 1 and 2 is also challenged by Van Schurman's "proof" when the male-gendered notions of "men" and "reason" (rationality) are revealed, as they are in Arguments 3 and 4:

Argument 3
1. All males are rational.
2. Van Schurman is not a male.
3. Hence, ?

Argument 4
1. All rational beings are mortal.
2. Women are not rational beings.
3. Hence, ?

Both arguments 3 and 4 are formally fallacious (invalid). The only way to make Arguments 3 and 4 valid requires, once again, false second premises, thereby making the resulting arguments, Arguments 3a and 4a, unsound:

Argument 3a
  1. All males are rational.
  2. Van Schurman is a male.
  3. Hence, Van Schurman is rational.

Argument 4a
  1. All rational beings are mortal.
  2. Women are rational beings.
  3. Hence, women are mortal.

To summarize, the eight arguments given above mirror the kind of syllogistic arguments Van Schurman gives for the conclusion that "women may be scholars" (rational). But they do more than that. As a fifth and final point, the eight arguments above also reveal implications that are supported by Van Schurman's arguments: women may be philosophers; the historical "reason versus emotion" dualism is male gender-biased; historically, the terms "man" and "reason" are both distributively and conceptually male-gender biased; and concerns about gender-biased language are logically relevant to the validity and the soundness of arguments, whether in syllogistic or symbolic logic. These are five stunning points to make in a rigorously logical style of reasoning. Van Schurman's syllogistic arguments use traditionally favored philosophical methodology to derive claims that are incompatible with traditionally favored philosophical views about "men," "women," and "reason" (or "rationality"). It is no wonder Ethel Kersey describes van Schurman's *The Learned Maid* as "a feminist treatise on the advisability of educating women"[3] or that Margaret Alic describes her as "one of the first feminists to speak out for women's scientific education."[4] As Dykeman claims elsewhere, "what van Schurman adds to the canon in the very least is a feminist epistemology that emphasizes logic and science and is proven with scholastic reason."[5]

DYKEMAN'S COMMENTARY

Dykeman's commentary provides a necessarily brief but detailed account of the epistemological and the religious and ethical views of van Schurman and Kant. Dykeman's commentary provides basic justification for viewing van Schurman as a philosopher and for understanding the significance of Kantian epistemology, especially, for moving epistemology beyond the "rationalism versus empiricism" debate to a critique of reason itself. Dykeman shows that the honorific inclusion of one, and unjustified exclusion of the other, from the history of Western philosophy are examples of unjustifiable male bias in the canon.

Excerpts of Writings by Kant and van Schurman

I. EXCERPTS FROM IMMANUEL KANT'S INTRODUCTION TO *THE CRITIQUE OF PURE REASON*[6]

I. The Distinction between Pure and Empirical Knowledge

There can be no doubt that all our knowledge begins with experience. For how should our faculty of knowledge be awakened into action did not objects affecting our senses partly of themselves produce representations, partly arouse the activity of our understanding to compare these representations, and, by combining or separating them, work up the raw material of the sensible impressions into that knowledge of objects which is entitled experience? In the order of time, therefore, we have no knowledge antecedent to experience, and with experience all our knowledge begins.

But though all our knowledge begins with experience, it does not follow that it all arises out of experience. For it may well be that even our empirical knowledge is made up of what we receive through impressions and of what our own faculty of knowledge (sensible impressions serving merely as the occasion) supplies from itself. If our faculty of knowledge makes any such addition, it may be that we are not in a position to distinguish it from the raw material, until with long practice of attention we have become skilled in separating it.

This, then, is a question which at least calls for closer examination, and does not allow of any off-hand answer:—whether there is any knowledge that is thus independent of experience and even of all impressions of the senses. Such knowledge is entitled *a priori*a and distinguished from the *empirical*, which has its sources *a posteriori*, that is, in experience.

The expression "*a priori*" does not, however, indicate with sufficient precision the full meaning of our question. For it has been customary to say, even of much knowledge that is derived from empirical sources, that we have it or are capable of having it *a priori*, meaning thereby that we do not derive it immediately from experience, but from a universal rule—a rule which is itself, however, borrowed by us from experience. Thus we would say of a man who undermined the foundations of his house, that he might have known *a priori* that it would fall, that is, that he need not have waited for the experience of its actual falling. But still he could not know this completely *a priori*. For he had first to learn through experience that bodies are heavy, and therefore fall when their supports are withdrawn.

In what follows, therefore, we shall understand by *a priori* knowledge, not knowledge independent of this or that experience, but knowledge absolutely independent of all experience. Opposed to it is empirical knowledge, which is knowledge possible only *a posteriori*, that is, through experience. *A priori* modes of knowledge are entitled pure when there is no admixture of anything empirical. Thus, for instance, the proposition, "every altercation has its cause," while an *a priori* proposition, is not a pure proposition, because altercation is a concept which can be derived only from experience.

II. We Are in Possession of Certain Modes of A Priori *Knowledge, and Even the Common Understanding Is Never Without Them*

What we here require is a criterion by which to distinguish with certainty between pure and empirical knowledge. Experience teaches us that a thing is so and so, but not that it cannot be otherwise. First, then, if we have a proposition which in being thought is thought as *necessary*, it is *a priori* judgment; and if, besides, it is not derived from any proposition except one which also has the validity of a necessary judgment, it is an absolutely *a priori* judgment. Secondly, experience never confers on its judgments true or strict, but only assumed and comparative *universality*, through induction. We can properly only say, therefore, that, so far as we have hitherto observed, there is no exception to this or that rule. If, then, a judgment is thought with strict universality, that is, in such manner that no exception is allowed as possible, it is not derived from experience, but is valid absolutely *a priori*. Empirical universality is only an arbitrary extension of a validity holding in most cases to one which holds in all, for instance, in the proposition, "all bodies are heavy." When, on the other hand, strict universality is essential to a judgment, this indicates a special source of knowledge, namely, a faculty of *a priori* knowledge. Necessity and strict universality are thus sure criteria of *a priori* knowledge, and are inseparable from one another. But since in the employment of these criteria the contingency of judgments is sometimes more easily shown than their empirical limitation, or, as sometimes also happens, their unlimited universality can be more convincingly proved than their necessity, it is advisable to use the two criteria separately, each by itself being infallible.

Now it is easy to show that there actually are in human knowledge judgments which are necessary and in the strictest sense universal, and which are therefore pure *a priori* judgments. If an example from the sciences be desired, we have only to look to any of the propositions of mathematics; if we seek an example from the understanding in its quite ordinary employment, the proposition "every alteration must have a cause" will serve our purpose. In the latter case, indeed, the very concept of a cause so manifestly contains the concept of a necessity of connection with an effect and of the strict universality of the rule, that the concept would be altogether lost if we attempted to derive it, as Hume has done, from repeated association of that which happens with that which precedes, and from a custom of connecting representations, a custom originating in this repeated association, and constituting therefore a merely subjective necessity. Even without appealing to such examples, it is possible to show that pure *a priori* principles are indispensable for the possibility of experience, and so to prove their existence *a priori*. For whence could experience derive its certainty, if all the rules, according to which it proceeds, were always themselves empirical, and therefore contingent? Such rules could hardly be regarded as first principles. At present, however, we may be content to have established the fact that our faculty of knowledge does have pure employment, and to have shown what are the criteria of such an employment.

Such *a priori* origin is manifest in certain concepts, no less than in judgments. If we remove from our empirical concept of a body, one by one, every feature in it which is [merely] empirical, the color, the hardness or softness, the weight, even the impenetrability, there still remains the space which the body (now entirely vanished) occupied, and this cannot be removed. Again, if we remove from our empirical concept of any object, corporeal or incorporeal, all properties which experience has taught us, we yet cannot take away that property through which the object is thought as substance or as inhering in a substance (although this concept of substance is more determinate than that of an object in general). Owing, therefore, to the necessity with which this concept of substance forces itself upon us, we have no option save to admit that it has its seat in our faculty of *a priori* knowledge.

III. Philosophy Stands in Need of a Science Which Shall Determine the Possibility, the Principles, and the Extent of all A Priori Knowledge

But what is still more extraordinary than all the preceding is this, that certain modes of knowledge leave the field of all possible experiences and have the appearance of extending the scope of our judgments beyond all limits of experience, and this by means of concepts to which no corresponding object can ever be given in experience.

It is precisely by means of the latter modes of knowledge, in a realm beyond the world of the senses, where experience can yield neither guidance nor correction, that our reason carries on those enquiries which owing to their importance we consider to be far more excellent, and in their purpose far more lofty, than all that the understanding can learn in the field of appearances. Indeed we prefer to run every risk of error rather than desist from such urgent enquiries, on the ground of their dubious character, or from disdain and indifference. These unavoidable problems set by pure reason itself are *God, freedom,* and *immortality.* The science which, with all its preparations, is in its final intention directed solely to their solution is metaphysics; and its procedure is at first dogmatic, that is, it confidently set itself to this task without any previous examination of the capacity or incapacity of reason for so great an undertaking.

Now it does indeed seem natural that, as soon as we have left the ground of experience, we should, through careful enquiries, assure ourselves as to the foundations of any building that we propose to erect, not making use of any knowledge that we possess without first determining whence it has come, and not trusting to principles without knowing their origin. It is natural, that is to say, that the question should first be considered, how the understanding can arrive at all this knowledge *a priori,* and what extent, validity, and worth it may have. Nothing, indeed, could be more natural, if by the term "natural" we signify what fittingly and reasonably ought to happen. But if we mean by "natural" what ordinarily happens, then on the contrary nothing is more natural and more intelligible than the fact that this enquiry has been so long neglected. For one part of this knowledge, the mathematical, has long been of established reliability, and so gives rise to a favorable presumption as regards the other part, which may yet be of quite different nature. Besides, once we are outside the circle of experience, we can be sure of not being *contradicted* by experience. The charm of extending our knowledge is so great that nothing short of encountering a direct contradiction can suffice to arrest us in our course; and this can be avoided, if we are careful in our fabrications—which none the less will remain fabrications. Mathematics gives us a shining example of how far, independently of experience, we can progress in *a priori* knowledge. It does, indeed, occupy itself with objects and with knowledge solely in so far as they allow of being exhibited in intuition. But this circumstance is easily overlooked, since this intuition can itself be given *a priori,* and is therefore hardly to be distinguished from a bare and pure concept. Misled by such a proof of the power of reason, the demand for the extension of knowledge recognizes no limits. The light dove, cleaving the air in her free flight, and feeling its resistance, might imagine that its flight would be still easier in empty space. It was thus that Plato left the world of the senses, as setting too narrow limits to the understanding, and ventured out beyond it on the wings of the ideas, in the empty space of all pure understanding. He did not observe that with all his efforts he made no advance—meeting no resistance that might, as it were, serve as a support upon which he could take a stand, to which he could apply his powers, and so set his understanding in motion. It is, indeed, the common fate of human reason to complete its speculative structures as speedily as may be, and only afterward to enquire whether the foundations are reliable. All sorts of excuses will then be appealed to, in order to reassure us of their solidity, or rather indeed to enable us to dispense altogether with so late and so dangerous an enquiry. But what keeps us, during the actual building, free from all apprehension and suspicion, and flatters us with a seeming thoroughness, in this other circumstance, namely, that a great, perhaps the greatest, part of the business of our reason consists in analysis of the concepts which we already have of objects. This analysis supplies us with a considerable body of knowledge, which, while nothing but explanation or eluci-dation of what has already been thought in our concepts, though in a confused manner, is yet prized as being, at least as regards its form, new insight. But so far as the matter or content is concerned, there has been no extension of our previously possessed concepts, but only an analysis of them. Since this procedure yields real knowledge *a priori*, which progresses in an assured and useful fashion, reason is so far misled as surreptitiously to introduce, without itself being aware of so doing, assertions of an entirely different order, in which it attaches to given concepts others completely foreign to them, and moreover attaches them *a priori*. And yet it is not known how reason can be in position to do this. Such a question is never so much as thought of. I shall therefore at once proceed to deal with the difference between these two kinds of knowledge.

IV. The Distinction between Analytic and Synthetic Judgments

In all judgments in which the relation of a subject to the predicate is thought (I take into consideration affirmative judgments only, the subsequent application to negative judgments being easily made), this relation is possible in two different ways. Either the predicate B belongs to the subject A, as something which is (covertly) contained in this concept A; or B lies outside the concept A, although it does indeed stand in connection with it. In the one case I entitle the judgment analytic, in the other synthetic. Analytic judgments (affirmative) are therefore those in which the connection of the predicate with the subject is thought through identity; those in which this connection is thought without identity should be entitled synthetic. The former, as adding nothing through the predicate to the concept of the subject, but merely breaking it up into those constituent concepts that have all along been thought in it, although confusedly, can also be entitled explicative. The latter, on the other hand, add to the concept of the subject a predicate which has not been in any wise thought in it, and which no analysis could possibly extract from it; and they may therefore be entitled ampliative. If I say, for instance, "All bodies are extended," this is an analytic judgment. For I do not require to go beyond the concept which I connect with "body" in order to find extension as bound up with it. To meet with this predicate, I have merely to analyze the concept, that is, to become conscious to myself of the manifold which I always think in that concept. The judgment is therefore analytic. But when I say, "All bodies are heavy," the predicate is something quite different from anything that I think in the mere concept of body in general; and the addition of such a predicate therefore yields a synthetic judgment.

Judgments of experience, as such, are one and all synthetic. For it would be absurd to found an analytic judgment on experience. Since, in framing the judgment, I must not go outside my concept, there is no need to appeal to the testimony of experience in its support. That a body is extended is a proposition that holds *a priori* and is not empirical. For, before appealing to experience, I have already in the concept of body all the conditions required for my judgment. I have only to extract from it, in accordance with the principle of contradiction, the required predicate, and in so doing can at the same time become conscious of the necessity of the judgment—and that is what experience could never have taught me. On the other hand, though I do not include in the concept of a body in general the predicate "weight," none the less this concept indicates an object of experience through one of its parts, and I can add to that part other parts of this same experience, as in this way belonging together with the concept. From the start I can apprehend the concept of body analytically through the characters of extension, impenetrability, figure, etc., all of which are thought in the concept. Now, however, looking back on the experience from which I have derived this concept of body, and finding weight to be invariably connected with the above characters, I attach it as a predicate to the concept; and in doing so I attach it synthetically, and am therefore extending my knowledge. The possibility of the synthesis of the predicate "weight" with the concept of "body" thus rests upon experience. While the one concept is not contained in the other, they yet belong to one another, though only contingently, as parts of a whole, namely, of an experience which is itself a synthetic combination of intuitions.

But in *a priori* synthetic judgments this help is entirely lacking: [I do not here have the advantage of looking around in the field of experience.] Upon what, then, am I to rely, when I seek to go beyond the concept A, and to know that another concept B is connected with it? Through what is the synthesis made possible? Let us take the proposition, "Every thing which happens has its cause." In the concept of "something which happens," I do indeed think an existence which is preceded by a time, etc., and from this concept analytic judgments may be obtained. But the concept of a "cause" lies entirely outside the other concept, and signifies something different from "that which happens," and is not therefore in any way contained in this latter representation. How come I then to predicate of that which happens something quite different, and to apprehend that the concept of cause, though not contained in it, yet belongs, and indeed necessarily belongs, to it? What is here the unknown = X which gives support to the understanding when it believes that it can discover outside the concept A a predicate B foreign to this concept, which it yet at the same time considers to be connected with it? It cannot be experience, because the suggested principle has connected the second representation with the first, not only with greater universality, but also with the character of necessity, and therefore completely *a priori* and on the basis of mere concepts. Upon such synthetic, that is, ampliative principles, all our *a priori* speculative knowledge must ultimately rest; analytic judgments are very important, and indeed necessary, but only for obtaining that clearness in the concepts which is requisite for such a sure and wide synthesis as will lead to a genuinely new addition to all previous knowledge.

V. In all Theoretical Sciences of Reason Synthetic A Priori Judgments Are Contained as Principles

1. *All mathematical judgments, without exception, are synthetic.* This fact, though incontestably certain and in its consequences very important, has hitherto escaped the notice of those who are engaged in the analysis of human reason, and is, indeed, directly opposed to all their conjectures. For as it was found that all mathematical inferences proceed it accordance with the principle of contradiction (which the nature of all apodictic certainly requires), it was supposed that the fundamental propositions of the science can themselves be known to be true through that principle. This is an erroneous view. For though a synthetic proposition can indeed be discerned in accordance with the principles of contradiction, this can only be if another synthetic proposition is presupposed, and if it can then be apprehended as following from this other proposition; it can never be so discerned in and by itself.

First of all, it has to be noted that mathematical propositions, strictly so called, are always judgments a priori, not empirical; because they carry with them necessity, which cannot be derived from experience. If this be demurred to, I am willing to limit my statement to *pure* mathematics, the very concept of which implies that it des not contain empirical, but only pure *a priori* knowledge.

We might, indeed, at first suppose that the proposition $7 + 5 = 12$ is a merely analytic proposition, and follows by the principle of contradiction from the concept of a sum of 7 and 5. But if we look more closely we find that the concept of the sum of 7 and 5 contains nothing save the union of the two numbers into one, and in this no thought is being taken as to what that single number may be which combines both. The concept of 12 is by no means already thought in merely thinking this union of 7 and 5; and I may analyze my concept of such a possible sum as long as I please, still I shall never find the 12 in it. We have to go outside these concepts, and call in the aid of the intuition which corresponds to one of them, our five fingers, for instance, or, as Segner does in his *Arithmetic*, five points, adding to the concept of 7, unit by unit, the five given in intuition. For starting with the number 7, and for the concept of 5 calling in the aid of the fingers of my hand as intuition, I now add one by one to the number 7 the units which I previously took together to form the number 5, and with the aid of that figure [the hand] see the number 12 come into being. That 5 should be added to 7, I have indeed already thought in the concept of a sum $= 7 + 5$, but not that this sum is equivalent to the number 12. Arithmetical propositions are therefore always synthetic. This is still more evident if we take larger numbers. For it is then obvious that, however we might turn and twist our concepts, we could never, by the mere analysis of them, and without the aid of intuition, discover what [the number is that] is the sum.

Just as little is any fundamental proposition of pure geometry analytic. That the straight line between two points is the shortest is a synthetic proposition. For my concept of *straight* contains nothing of quantity, but only of quality. The concept of the shortest is wholly an addition, and cannot be derived, through any process of analysis, from the concept of the straight line. Intuition, therefore, must here be called in; only by its aid is the synthesis possible. What here causes us commonly to believe that the predicate of such apodictic judgments is already contained in our concept, and that the judgment is therefore analytic, is merely the ambiguous character of the terms used. We are required to join in thought a certain predicate to a given concept, and this necessity is inherent in the concepts themselves. But the question is not what we *ought* to join in thought to the given concept, but what we *actually* think in it, even if only obscurely; and it is then manifest that, while the predicate is indeed attached necessarily to the concept, it is so in virtue of an intuition which must be added to the concept, not as thought in the concept itself.

Some few fundamental propositions, presupposed by the geometrician, are, indeed, really analytic, and rest on the principle of contradiction. But, as identical propositions, they serve only as links in the chain of method and not as principles; for instance, a = a; the whole is equal to itself; or (a + b) > a, that is, the whole is greater than its part. And even these propositions, though they are valid according to pure concepts, are only admitted in mathematics because they can be exhibited in intuition.

2. *Natural science (physics) contains a priori synthetic judgments as principles.* I need cite only two such judgments: that in all changes of the material world the quantity of matter remains unchanged; and that in all communication of motion, action and reaction must always be equal. Both propositions, it is evident, are not only necessary, and therefore in their origin *a priori*; but also synthetic. For in the concept of matter I do not think its permanence, but only its presence in the space which it occupies. I go outside and beyond the concept of matter, joining to it *a priori* in thought something which I have not thought *in* it. The proposition is not, therefore, analytic, but synthetic, and yet is thought *a priori*; and so likewise are the other propositions of the pure part of natural science.

3. *Metaphysics,* even if we look upon it as having hitherto failed in all its endeavors, is yet, owing to the nature of human reason, a quite indispensable science, and *ought to contain a priori synthetic knowledge.* For its business is not merely to analyze concepts which we make for ourselves *a priori* of things, and thereby to clarify them analytically, but to extend our *a priori* knowledge. And for this purpose we must employ principles which add to the given concept something that was not contained in it, and through an *a priori* synthetic judgments venture out so far that experience is quite unable to follow us, as, for instance, in the proposition, that the world must have a first beginning, and such like. Thus metaphysics consists, at least *in intention*, entirely of *a priori* synthetic propositions.

VI. The General Problem of Pure Reason

Much is already gained if we can bring a number of investigations under the formula of a single problem. For we not only lighten our own task, by defining it accurately, but make it easier for others, who would test our results, to judge whether or not we have succeeded in what we see out to do. Now the proper problem of pure reason is contained in the question: How are *a priori* synthetic judgments possible?

That metaphysics has hitherto remained in so vacillating a state of uncertainty and contradiction, is entirely due to the fact that this problem, and perhaps even the distinction between analytic and synthetic judgments, has never previously been considered. Upon the solution of this problem, or upon a sufficient proof that the possibility which it desires to have explained does in fact not exist at all, depends the success or failure of metaphysics. Among philosophers, David Hume came nearest to envisaging this problem, but still was very far from conceiving it with sufficient definiteness and universality. He occupied himself exclusively with the synthetic proposition regarding the connection of an effect with its cause (*principium causalitatis*), and he believed himself to have shown that such an *a priori* proposition is entirely impossible. If we accept his conclusions, then all that we call metaphysics is a mere delusion whereby we fancy ourselves to have rational insight into what, in actual fact, is borrowed solely from experience, and under the influence of custom has taken the illusory semblance of necessity. If he had envisaged our problem in all its universality, he would never have been guilty of this statement, so destructive of all pure philosophy. For he would then have recognized that, according to his own argument, pure mathematics, as certainly containing *a priori* synthetic propositions, would also not be possible; and from such an assertion his good sense would have saved him.

In the solution of the above problem, we are at the same time deciding as to the possibility of the employment of pure reason in establishing and developing all those sciences which contain a theoretical *a priori* knowledge of objects, and have therefore to answer the questions:

> How is pure mathematics possible?
> How is pure science of nature possible?

Since these sciences actually exist, it is quite proper to ask *how* they are possible; for that they must be possible is proved by the fact that they exist. But the poor progress which has hitherto been made in metaphysics, and the fact that no system yet propounded can, in view of the essential purpose of metaphysics, be said to really exist, leaves everyone sufficient ground for doubting as to its possibility.

Yet, in a certain sense, this *kind of knowledge* is to be looked upon as given; that is to say, metaphysics actually exists, if not as a science, yet still as natural disposition (*metaphysica naturalis*). For human reason, without being moved merely by the idle desire for extent and variety of knowledge, proceeds impetuously, driven on by an inward need, to question such as cannot be answered by any empirical employment of reason, or by principles thence derived. Thus in all men, as soon as their reason has become ripe for speculation, there has always existed and will always continue to exist some kind of metaphysics. And so we have the question:

> How is metaphysics, as natural disposition, possible?

That is, how from the nature of universal human reason do those questions arise which pure reason propounds to itself, and which it is impelled by its own need to answer as best it can?

But since all attempts which have hitherto been made to answer these natural questions—for instance, whether the world has a beginning or is from eternity—have always met with unavoidable contradictions, we cannot rest satisfied with the mere natural disposition to metaphysics, that is, with the pure faculty of reason itself, from which, indeed, some sort of metaphysics (be it what it may) always arises. It must be possible for reason to attain to certainty whether we know or do not know the objects of metaphysics, that is, to come to a decision either in regard to the objects of its enquiries or in regard to the capacity or incapacity of reason to pass any judgment upon them, so that we may either with confidence extend our pure reason or set to it sure and determinate limits. This last question, which arises out of the previous general problem, may, rightly stated, take the form:

> How is metaphysics, as science, possible?

Thus the critique of reason, in the end, necessarily leads to scientific knowledge; while its dogmatic employment, on the other hand, lands us in dogmatic assertions to which other assertions, equally specious, can always be opposed—that is, in *scepticism*.

This science cannot be of any very formidable prolixity, since it has to deal not with the objects of reason, the variety of which is inexhaustible, but only with itself and the problems which arise entirely from within itself, and which are imposed upon it by its own nature, not by the nature of things which are distinct from it. When once reason has learnt completely to understand its own power in respect of objects which can be presented to it in experience, it should easily be able to determine, with completeness and certainty, the extent and the limits of its attempted employment beyond the bounds of all experience.

We may, then, and indeed we must, regard as abortive all attempts, hitherto made, to establish a metaphysic *dogmatically*. For the analytic part in any such attempted system, namely, the mere analysis of the concepts that inhere in our reason *a priori*, is by no means the aim of, but only a preparation for, metaphysics proper, that is, the extension of its *a priori* synthetic knowledge. For such a purpose, the analysis of concepts is useless, since it merely shows what is contained in these concepts, not how we arrive at them *a priori*. A solution of this latter problem is required, that we may be able to determine the valid employment of such concepts in regard to the objects of all knowledge in general. Nor is much self-denial needed to give up these claims, seeing that the undeniable, and in the dogmatic procedure of reason also unavoidable, contradictions of reason within itself have long since undermined the authority of every metaphysical system yet propounded. Greater firmness will be required if we are not to be deterred by inward difficulties and outward opposition from endeavoring, through application of a method entirely different from any hitherto employed, at last to bring to a prosperous and fruitful growth a science indispensable to human reason—a science whose every branch may be cut away but whose root cannot be destroyed.

VII. The Idea and Division of a Special Science, Under the Title "Critique of Pure Reason"

In view of all these considerations, we arrive at the idea of a special science which can be entitled the Critique of Pure Reason. For reason the faculty which supplies the principles of *a priori* knowledge. Pure reason is, therefore, that which contains the principles whereby we know anything absolutely *a priori*. An organon of pure reason would be the sum-total of those principles according to which all modes of pure *a priori* knowledge can be acquired and actually brought into being. The exhaustive application of such an organon would give rise to a system of pure reason. But as this would be asking rather much, and as it is still doubtful whether, and in what cases, any extension of our knowledge be here possible, we can regard a science of the mere examination of pure reason, of its sources and limits, as the *propaedeutic* to the system of pure reason. As such, it should be called a critique, not a doctrine, of pure reason. Its utility, in speculation, ought properly to be only negative, not to extend, but only to clarify our reason, and keep it free from errors—which is already a very great gain. I entitle *transcendental* all knowledge which is occupied not so much with objects as with the mode of our knowledge of objects in so far as this mode of knowledge is to be possible *a priori*. A system of such concepts might be entitled transcendental philosophy. But that is still, at this stage, too large an undertaking. For since such a science must contain, with completeness, both kinds of *a priori* knowledge, the analytic no less than the synthetic, it is, so far as our present purpose is concerned, much too comprehensive. We have to carry the analysis so far only as is indispensably necessary in order to comprehend, in their whole extent, the principles of *a priori* synthesis, with which alone we are called upon to deal. It is upon this enquiry, which should be entitled not a doctrine, but only a transcendental critique, that we are now engaged. Its purpose is not to extend knowledge, but only to correct it, and to supply a touchstone of the value, or lack of value, of all *a priori* knowledge. Such a critique is therefore a preparation, so far as may be possible, for an organon; and should this turn out not to be possible, then at least for a canon, according to which, in due course, the complete system of the philosophy of pure reason—be it in extension or merely in limitation of its knowledge—may be carried into execution, analytically as well as synthetically. That such a system is possible, and indeed that it may not be of such great extent as to cut us off from the hope of entirely completing it, may already be gathered from the fact that what here constitutes our subject-matter is not the nature of things, which is inexhaustible, but the understanding which passes judgment upon the nature of things; and this understanding, again, only in respect of its *a priori* knowledge. These *a priori* possessions of the understanding, since they have not to be sought for without, cannot remain hidden from us, and in all probability are sufficiently small in extent to allow of our apprehending them in their completeness, of judging as to their value or lack of value, and so of rightly appraising them. Still less may the reader here expect a critique of books and systems of pure reason; we are concerned only with the critique of the faculty of pure reason itself. Only in so far as we build upon this foundation do we have a reliable touchstone for estimating the philosophical value of old and new works in this field. Otherwise the unqualified historian or critic is passing judgments upon the groundless assertions of others by means of his own, which are equally groundless.

Transcendental philosophy is only the idea of a science, for which the critique of pure reason has to lay down the complete architectonic plan. That is to say, it has to guarantee, as following from principles, the completeness and certainty of the structure in all its parts. It is the system of all principles of pure reason. And if this critique is not itself to be entitled a transcendental philosophy, it is solely because, to be a complete system, it would also have to contain an exhaustive analysis of the whole of *a priori* human knowledge. Our critique must, indeed, supply a complete enumeration of all the fundamental concepts that go to constitute such pure knowledge. But it is not required to give an exhaustive analysis of these concepts, nor a complete review of those that can be derived from them. Such a demand would be unreasonable, partly because this analysis would not be appropriate to our main purpose, inasmuch as there is no such uncertainty in regard to analysis as we encounter in the case of synthesis, for the sake of which alone our whole critique is undertaken; and partly because it would be inconsistent with the unity of our plan to assume responsibility for the completeness of such an analysis and derivation, when in view of our purpose we cart be excused from doing so. The analysis of these *a priori* concepts, which later we shall have to enumerate, and the derivation of other concepts from them, can easily, however, be made complete when once they have established as exhausting the principles of synthesis, and if in this essential respect nothing be lacking in them.

The critique of pure reason therefore will contain all that is essential in transcendental philosophy. While it is the complete idea of transcendental philosophy, it is not equivalent to that latter science; for it carries the analysis only so far as is requisite for the complete examination of knowledge which is *a priori* and synthetic.

What has chiefly to be kept in view in the division of such a science, is that no concepts be allowed to enter which contain in themselves anything empirical, or, in other words, that it consist in knowledge wholly *a priori*. Accordingly, although the highest principles and fundamental concepts of morality are *a priori* knowledge, they have no place in transcendental philosophy, because, although they do not lay at the foundation of their precepts the concepts of pleasure and pain, of the desires and inclinations, etc., all of which are of empirical origin, yet in the construction of a system of pure morality these empirical concepts must necessarily be brought into the concept of duty, as representing either a hindrance, which we have to overcome, or an allurement, which must not be made into a motive. Transcendental philosophy is therefore a philosophy of pure and merely speculative reason. All that is practical, so far as it contains motives, relates to feelings, and these belong to the empirical sources of knowledge.

If we are to make a systematic division of the science which we are engaged in presenting, it must have first a *doctrine of the elements*, and secondly, a *doctrine of the method of pure reason*. Each of these chief divisions will have its subdivisions, but the grounds of these we are not yet in a position to explain. By way of introduction or anticipation we need only say that there are two stems of human knowledge, namely, *sensibility* and *understanding*, which perhaps spring from a common, but to us unknown, root. Through the former, objects are given to us; through the latter, they are thought. Now in so far as sensibility may be found to contain *a priori* representations constituting the condition under which objects are given to us, it will belong to transcendental philosophy. And since the conditions under which alone the objects of human knowledge are given must precede those under which they are thought, the transcendental doctrine of sensibility will constitute the first part of the science of the elements.

II. EXCERPTS FROM ANNA MARIA VAN SCHURMAN'S *THE LEARNED MAID*[7]

A Logical Exercise Upon This Question: Whether a Maid May be a Scholar?

We hold the *affirmative* and will endeavor to make it good.

These *praecognita* [presuppositions] we permit: First on the part of the *subject*, and then of the *predicate*.

By a *maid or woman*, I understand her that is a Christian, and that not in profession only, but in fact.

By a *scholar*, I mean one that is given to the study of *letters*, that is, the knowledge of *tongues* and *histories*, all kinds of learning, both superior entitled *faculties*; and inferior, called *philosophy*. We except only *scriptural theology* properly so named, as that which without controversy belongs to all Christians.

When we inquire, *whether she may be*, we mean whether it be suitable, that is, expedient, fit, decent.

The *words* being thus distinguished, the *things* are to be distinguished also.

For some *maids* are *ingenious*, others *not so*: some are rich, some poor: some engaged in domestic cares, others at liberty. The studies of a *scholar* are either *universal*, when we give our selves to all sorts of learning: or *particular*, when we learn some one language or science, or one distinct faculty.

Wherefore we make use of these limitations:

First of the *subject*; and first, that our *maid* be endowed at least with an indifferent good ability, and not inapt for learning. Secondly, that she be provided of necessaries and not oppressed with want: which exception I therefore put in, because few are so happy to have parents to bread them up in studies, and teachers are chargeable.

Thirdly, that the condition of the times, and her quality be such, that she may have spare hours from her general and special calling, that is, from the exercises of piety and household affairs. To which end will conduce, partly her immunity from cares and employments in her younger years, partly her immunity from cares and employments in her younger years, partly in her elder age either celibate, or the ministry of handmaids, which are wont to free the richer sort of matrons also from domestic troubles.

Fourthly, let her end be, not vain glory and ostentation, or unprofitable curiosity: but beside the general end, God's glory and the salvation of her own soul; that both herself may be the more virtuous and the more happy, and that she may (if that charge lie upon her) instruct and direct her family, and also be useful, as much as may be to her whole sex.

Next, *limitations* of the *predicate, scholarship*, or the study of *letters* I so limit, that I clearly affirm all honest discipline, or the whole the circle and crown of liberal arts and sciences (as the proper and universal good and ornament of mankind) to be suitable for the *head* of our *Christian maid:* yet so, that according to the dignity and nature of every art or science, and according to the capacity and condition of the maid herself, all in their order, place and time succeed each other in the learning of them, or be commodiously conjoined. But especially let regard be had unto those arts which have nearest alliance to *theology* and the *moral virtues*, and are principally subservient to them. In which number we reckon *grammar; logic, rhetoric*; especially *logic*, fitly called *the key of all sciences*; and then, *physics, metaphysics, history* etc. and also the knowledge of languages, chiefly of the *Hebrew* and *Greek*. All of which may advance to the more facile and full understanding of *Holy Scripture*: to say nothing of other books. The rest, i.e. *mathematics* (to which is also referred *music*) *poetry, painting*, and the like, not illiberal arts, may obtain the place of pretty ornaments and ingenious recreations.

Lastly, those studies which pertain to the practice of the law, military discipline, oratory in the church, court, university, as less proper and less necessary, we do not very much urge. And yet we in no wise yield that our *maid* should be excluded from the Scholastic knowledge or theory of those, especially, not from understanding the most noble doctrine of the politics or civil government.

And when we say a maid may be a scholar, it is plain we do not affirm learning to be a property, or a thing requisite, and precisely needful to eternal salvation: no; nor as such a good thing which makes for the very *essence* of happiness in this life: but as a mean and very useful, conferring much to the integrity and perfection thereof: and as that, which by the contemplation of excellent things will promote us to a higher degree in the love of God, and everlasting felicity.

Therefore let our thesis or proposition be: A maid may be a scholar.

For the confirmation whereof we bring these *arguments*:

On the part of the *subject*;
On the part of the *predicate*.

I. *Argument, from the Property of the Subject.*

Whosoever is naturally endowed with the *principles,* or powers of the principles of all arts and sciences, may be a student in all arts and sciences:

But maids are naturally endowed with the *principles,* etc.

Therefore, maids may be a student in all arts and sciences.

The proposition is thus proved.

They that may have the knowledge of *conclusions* deduced from *principles,* they may be students, etc.

But they that are naturally endowed with the *principles* and have the knowledge of *conclusions* deduced from those *principles.*

Therefore, etc.

The assertion may be proved both from the property of the *form* of this subject, or the rational soul: and from the very acts and effects themselves. For it is manifest that maids do *in actuality* learn arts and sciences. Now, no *acts* can be without their *principles.*

II. *Argument, Again from the Property of the Subject.*

Whosoever hath naturally a desire of arts and sciences, may study the arts and sciences.

But a maid hath naturally a desire of arts and sciences.

Therefore, a maid may study the arts and sciences.

The reason of the *major* premise is manifest: because nature doth nothing in vain.

The minor premise is thus confirmed.

That which is in the whole *species* or kind, is in every *individual* or particular person; in maids also.

But all mankind have in them by nature a desire of knowledge.

Therefore, etc.

III. *Argument, from the External Property, or Adjunct.*

Whosoever is by God created with a *sublime countenance,* and erected toward heaven, may (and ought) give himself to the contemplation and knowledge of sublime and heavenly things. [in image of God, made transcendent]

But God hath created woman also with a sublime and erected countenance: *Os homini sublime,* etc. Therefore, etc.

IV. *Argument.*

Whosoever is in most *need of* solid and continual employment, may suitably give himself to learning:

But woman is in most *need* of solid and continual employment:

Therefore, etc.

The *major* is good, because nothing doth more exercise and intend all the nerves and powers of the mind; and as the great Erasmus says, nothing takes so full possession of the fair temple of a virgin's breast, as learning and study, whither, on all occasions she may fly for refuge.

The minor is proved by these two reasons.

1. Whosoever through imbecility and inconstancy of disposition or temper, and the innumerable snares of the world, is in most danger of *vanity*, is in most need of solid and perpetual employment.

But woman, through the imbecility and inconstancy, etc.

Therefore.

The *major* in this syllogism is true; because contraries are best cured by contraries: and nothing more effectually opposes vanity, than serious and constant occupation.

The *minor* we take to be without controversy: for hardly any, though heroical virtue can safely pass by the sirens of the world and of youth unless it be busied about serious and solid things.

2. The second reason to prove the assumption of minor of Argument VI is this:

They that abound with *leisure* have most need of solid and continual employment:

But women of higher rank, most part abound with leisure.

Therefore.

The major of this syllogism is good, because leisure (or idleness) is of itself tedious, yea, burdensome, so that divine [St. Gregory] *Nazianzen* justly said, *Tis the greatest pain to be out of action*. And because idleness is the mother of wickedness: *Homines nihil agende male agere discunt*. Men by doing nothing learn to do ill.

V. Argument.

They that have the happiness of a more quiet and free course of life, may with most convenience follow their studies:

But maids for the most part, have the happiness of a more quiet and free course of life: Therefore.

The reason of the *major* is evident; for nothing is so great a friend to studies as tranquility and liberty.

The minor is proved thus:

They, which for the most part have their time to bestow *upon themselves*, and are exempt from public cares and employments, have the happiness of a more quiet and free course of life:

But maids (especially during their celibate, or single life) [for the] most part have their time to bestow on themselves, etc.

Therefore.

VI. Argument.

To whom is agreeable the study of the *principal sciences*, to the same is also agreeable the study of sciences instrumental and subservient:

But, to a Christian woman agrees the study of the principal sciences.

Therefore:

The *major* is firm for this reason:

To whom the *end* agrees, to the same is suitable also the lawful *means*, whereby we are most easily brought unto that end:

But the instrumental or subservient sciences are the lawful means, etc.

Therefore.

The *minor* is true, because to a Christian woman agrees the study, or assiduous and serious meditation of God's word, the knowledge of God, and contemplation of his most beautiful works, as being of most concernment to all Christians whatsoever.

VII. Argument.

The study of letters is suitable to them, for whom it is more decent to find themselves both business and recreation *at home* and in private, than abroad among others.

But it is more decent for a Christian maid to find herself both work and recreation *at home* than abroad:

Therefore etc.

The *major* is most true: because studies have this prerogative, to give us delightful exercise, and to recreate as when we have no other company, whence in the Greek proverb, *A wise man is self-sufficient*.

The *minor* is no less: because the Apostle requires women to be. And moreover, experience testifies; whose tongues, ears, eyes often travail abroad, hunting after pleasures; their faith, diligence, and modesty too, is generally called into question.

VIII. Argument, from the Genus of the Predicate, or, of Learning.

Arts and sciences are suitable for those, to whom *all virtue* in general is suitable:

But all virtue in general is suitable for a maid.

Therefore:

The *major* is evident from the division of virtue into intellectual and moral: under the former whereof, the philosopher comprehends arts and sciences.

The *minor* hath no need of proof for virtue, as *Seneca* said, choose her servants, neither by their state nor sex.

IX. Argument, from the End of Sciences.

Whatsoever *perfects* and *adorns* the intellect of man, that is fit and decent for a Christian woman:

But arts and sciences do perfect and adorn the intellect.

Therefore:

The reason of the *major* is, because all creatures tend unto their last and highest perfections as that which is most suitable for them.

The *minor* is plain, because arts and sciences are *habits*, and by these habits are the natural *powers* and faculties of the soul proved and perfected.

X. Argument.

The things that by their nature conduce to the greater *love of God* and the exciting of his greater reverence in us, are suitable and fit for a Christian woman:

But arts and sciences by their nature conduce to the greater *love of God* and the exciting of his greater reverence in us.

Therefore:

The verity of the *major* is clearer than the light. For the most perfect love and reverence of God becomes all mankind; so that none can here offend in the excess.

The *minor* is thus confirmed:

That which exhibits and proposes God and his works to be seen and known by us in a more eminent degree, naturally conduces to the stirring up in us the greater love of God and reverence:

But arts and sciences exhibit and propose God and his works to be seen and known by us in a more eminent degree.

Therefore.

The *major* in this last syllogism is proved by this reason:

Whatsoever is indeed most beautiful, most excellent and most perfect that, the more it is known, the more it is loved, and accounted more worthy of reverence or celebration:

But God and his works are indeed most beautiful, most excellent and most perfect.

Therefore.

The *minor* likewise may be proved from the end or effects of sciences, which do all confer somewhat to the more facile and more distinct knowledge of God and his works.

XI. Argument.

That which arms us against *heresies*, and detects their fraud, is suitable for a Christian woman:

But sciences arm us against *heresies*, and detect their fraud.

Therefore.

The reason of the *major* is evident because no Christians in this common danger, ought to neglect their duty.

The *minor* is proved, because sound philosophy is as a hedge and fence (to use the words of *Clemens Alexandrinus*) of the Lord's vineyard, or of our savior's doctrine: or, being compared with the gospel, it is (in Saint Basil's similitude) like the *leaves* which are an *ornament* and *muniment* to fruit. Indeed by right reason, that corrupt and false reason, upon which heresies mainly depend, may most easily be refuted.

XII. Argument.

What teaches *prudence* without any detriment of fame or modesty is suitable for a Christian woman:

But the studies of good learning teach prudence without any detriment of fame or modesty.

Therefore.

The *major* is confessed: for no man is ignorant, that the honor of the female sex is most tender and needs nothing more than prudence: and how hard a thing it is and full of hazard, to draw prudence from use and experience.

The *minor* is proved, because the writings of learned men do offer us not only excellent *precepts*, but notable *examples*, and do lead us as it were by the hand to virtue.

XIII. Argument.

That which makes to true *magnanimity*, is suitable for a Christian woman:

But the study of letters makes to true magnanimity.

Therefore.

I prove the *major*; because, the more any one is by nature prone to the vice of pusillanimity, so much the more need there is of aid from the opposite virtue. But a woman is by nature prone to the vice of pusillanimity.

Therefore.

The *minor* is proved, because learning erects the mind and puts courage into the heart, and takes off the visor from those things, which are feared by the vulgar, or impotently affected.

XIV. Argument.

That which affects and replenishes the mind with honest and ingenuous *delight*, is suitable for a Christian woman:

But learning doth so.

Therefore.

The reason of the *major* is because nothing is more agreeable to human nature, than honest and ingenuous delight, which represents in man a certain similitude of divine gladness. Which *Aristotle* also highly extols. *Pleasure* is by nature a *Divine thing* implanted in the hearts of men.

The *minor* is proved then: Because there is no delight or pleasure (except that of Christians which is supernatural) either more worthy of an ingenuous soul, or greater than this, which arises from the study of letters: as by examples and various reasons might easily be evinced.

XV. Argument, from the Opposite.

Where *ignorance* and want of knowledge is not convenient suitable, there the study of knowledge is suitable:

But ignorance and want of knowledge is not suitable for a Christian woman.

Therefore.

The *minor* is confirmed thus:

That which is of self, nor only the cause of error in the understanding, but of vice in the will or action not suitable for a Christian woman:

But ignorance and want of knowledge is of itself the cause of error, etc.

Therefore.

The *major* of this syllogism is demonstrated; First, in respect of error in the understanding; because ignorance in the understanding (which is called the *eye* of the soul) is nothing else but blindness, and darkness which is the cause of all error. Secondly, in respect of vice in the will or action: because, whatsoever makes men proud, fierce, etc. that is the cause of vice in the will or action. But ignorance and want of knowledge makes men proud, etc.

Therefore.

The *major* is evident, the *minor* is proved hence; because, the less a man knows himself, the more will he please himself and contemn others: and he who knows not how much he is ignorant of, will be wise in his own conceit. And then (as to fierceness) nothing is more intractable than ignorance, as *Erasmus* upon much experience testifies: And that I may relate a Sentence of Divine Plato, *Man well bred and instructed becomes the mildest and gentlest of creatures, but being ill brought up is the wildest of all the beasts of the earth.* Add quod ingenuas etc. *Learning mollifies and sweetens a man and takes away roughness of manners and rusticity.* Lastly, the danger of ignorance, in respect of vice, may be shown from the nature of vice and virtue. For whereas to every virtuous action is required such *exactness*, that it must be conformable on every part to the rule of right reason; to the nature of vice even the least *inordination*, which follows ignorance, may be sufficient.

Testimonies and examples I do here omit for brevity sake.

A REFUTATION OF THE ADVERSARIES

These praecognita are to be permitted.

First, there are some of the *adversaries*, who being as it were blinded by I know not what prejudices, do not limit our *subject*; but think it follows from our *thesis*, that there is no *choice* neither of wits, nor of conditions, to make the *predicate* agree unto it.

Others there are, who seem to acknowledge no other *end* of studies, than either gain or vainglory: which is the *prime error*, and shameful enough: as if it were supervacaneous to philosophize *for the avoidance of ignorance.* And some there are lastly who deny not altogether that studies are suitable for a maid, but only an *eminent degree* of knowledge. Who are perhaps vexed with emulation, or certainly with fear, lest that should at any time, come to pass.

Many scholars excel their masters: and that other saying of a very ancient poet. Those men are spirited like women, that virgin like a man.

The Thesis of the Adversaries

A Christian maid or woman except she be perhaps divinely excited to it by some peculiar motion or instinct, may not suitably give herself to the study of letters.

I. *Argument, on the Part of the Subject.*

Whosoever hath a *weak wit* may not give herself to the study of letters:
But women are of weak wits.
Therefore.

They will prove the *major*; because, to the study of letters is required a wit firm and strong: unless we will labor in vain, or fall into the danger of disease of the intellect.

The *minor*, they think, needs no proof.

We *answer* to the *major*: that by our limitation such are exempted which by imbecility of their wit are altogether inapt for studies; when we state it, that at least *indifferent good wits* are here required. Then, we say, not always *heroical wits* are precisely necessary to studies: for the number even of learned men, we see, is made up in good part, of those that are of the *middle* sort.

To the *minor* we answer: it is not *absolutely* true, but *comparatively* only in respect of the male sex. For though women cannot be equaled for their wit with those more excellent men, who are *Eagles in the Clouds:* yet, the matter itself speaks thus much; not a few are found of so good wit, that they may be admitted to studies, not without fruit.

But *on the contrary we infer* they that are less able by dexterity of *wit*, may most suitably addict themselves to studies:

But women are less able by dexterity of wit.

Therefore.

We prove the *major*, because studies do supply us with aids and helps for our weakness:

Therefore.

II. *Objection.*

Whose mind is not *inclined* to studies, they are not fit to study;

But the minds of women are not inclined to studies.

They prove the *major*, because nothing is to be done *invita Minerva*, as we say, *against the hair.*

The *minor* they will prove from use and custom; because very seldom do women apply their mind to study.

We *answer* to the *major*. It should be thus: *whose mind, after all means duly tried, is not inclined to studies*: otherwise it is denied.

To the *minor* we say, no man can rightly judge of our inclination to studies, before he hath encouraged us by the best reasons and means to set upon them: and altogether have given us some *taste* of their sweetness, although in the meantime we do not want examples to evidence the contrary to be true.

III. *Objection.*

The studies of learning are not suitable for those that are destitute of *means* necessary to their studies.

But women are destitute of means, etc.

Therefore.

The *major* is without controversy.

They endeavor to prove the *minor*, because there be no academies and colleges, wherein they may exercise themselves.

But we deny this consequence; for it suffice, that under the conduct of their *parents*, or of some private teacher, teacher, they may exercise themselves at home.

IV. *Objection.*

Studies are not fit for them whose labor misses of its proper *end*.

But the labor of women misses of its proper *end*.

Therefore.

The *major* may be proved, because the *end* is that for which all things are done.

They prove the *minor* by this, that women are seldom or never preferred to public offices, political, ecclesiastical, or academical.

We *answer* to the *major*: women, in speculative sciences are never frustrated of their *end*: and in the *practical* (now spoken of) though they attain not the *primary*, or that public *end*; yet do they attain a *secondary end*, as I may say, and more private.

V. *Objection.*

To whom, for their vocation, it is sufficient to know a *little*, to them is not convenient [suitable] the *encyclopedia*, or a more sublime degree of knowledge.

But it is sufficient to women, etc.

Therefore.

They prove the *major*, because it is not suitable for any one to study things superfluous and impertinent to his calling.

The *minor* they will prove; because forsooth the vocation of a maid, or woman, is included in very narrow limits, the terms of a private or economical life.

Let the *major* pass, we *answer* to the *minor*. There is an ambiguity in the words; first, *vocation* of a private life, opposed to public offices, we say by the same reason the *encyclopedia* or a more sublime degree of knowledge is denied all *men* too, that lead private life: when yet, that most grave sentence of *Plutarch* is pronounced of all men of what rank forever without exception; *It becomes a perfect man, to know what is to be known, and to do what is to be done.*

But if they understand a *special vocation*, in order to a family and economical cares; we say that the *universal* calling which pertains chiefly to us all, either as Christians, or at least as men, is in no wise excluded by it. Yea, I may be bold to affirm, that a virgin both may and ought especially to attend upon this *universal* calling, as being usually more free from the impediments of the former. *She that is unmarried care for the things of the Lord.* Again, there is ambiguity in the words, *it is sufficient*, which is sufficiently taken away by what is above said in the *limitation* of the convenience and necessity of studies.

Wherefore our *thesis* stands firm.

A Christian maid, or woman, may suitably give herself to learning.

Whence we draw this consectary (consequence).

That *maids* may and ought to be excited and encouraged by the best and strongest *reasons*, by the *testimonies* of wise men: and lastly, by the *examples of illustrious women*, to the embracing of this kind of life especially *those* who are above others provided of *leisure*, and other *means* and *aides* for their *studies*. And, because it is *best*, that the mind be seasoned with *learning* from the very *infancy*: therefore the *parents* themselves are *chiefly* to be stirred up, as we suppose, and to be admonished of their duty.

Commentary by *Therese Boos Dykeman,* van Schurman and Kant: Logic in *The Learned Maid;* Thinking in *Critique of Pure Reason*

INTRODUCTION

> Hence it is that to one reading the history often of very long expanses of time the monuments of our name seem no greater than the traces of a ship passing in the sea.
>
> —Van Schurman, Letter to André Rivet, 1637[8]

Two things fill the mind with ever new and increasing admiration
and awe, the more oftener and more steadily we reflect upon them:
the starry heavens above me and the moral law within me.

—Kant, *Critique of Practical Reason*, 1788[9]

The Learned Maid, published in Holland in 1641 by Anna Maria van Schurman, exists
today as a rare manifesto for female philosophers. *The Critique of Pure Reason* by Immanuel Kant, published in Germany in 1781, exists today as a well-established text in the
philosophical canon of the Western tradition as a great innovation in philosophical thinking.[10] Yet, reading these two works together offers a better sense of a two-gendered universe than does each alone. Both works have epistemological aims. Van Schurman's is to
convince the world with compelling logic that women be allowed to study all knowledge.
The world *The Learned Maid* responds to has defined women as less than rational and
therefore incapable of learning or writing philosophy.[11] Kant's aim is to critique men's
philosophical writings on knowledge. While Kant critiques the subject matter of thinking, van Schurman demonstrates in a logical exercise a thinking process by a woman. The
methods of these two thinkers diverge. Van Schurman's Scholastic method arose when
translations of Aristotle's *Categories* became available. Medieval universities adopted the
mode for formal debate in the form of posing a proposition or question (*quaestio*) and
submitting it to proof or refutation with deductive arguments. It was retained as the
accepted form for university dissertations in seventeenth-century Holland, even as the
humanistic method began to repudiate it. This method, however, had not before been
adapted to this particular subject matter. Kant's method lies in the humanistic tradition
as well as the rationalistic, for it brings together two foundations of knowledge, experience
and reason. Because this comprehensive method seeks to establish the proper limits and
use of reason, it is also a critical method.

THE LEARNED MAID: A HUMANISTIC LESSON IN SCHOLASTIC LOGIC

The Learned Maid was published in Dutch, English, and Latin. It did not change the
status of women in education, yet it served to inspire individual women to become scholars, even to write philosophy. In *The Learned Maid*, van Schurman asserts a one-sentence
proposition—that "a maid may be a scholar," that she then proves with a syllogistic or
deductive method of reasoning. By using this method, she aimed not only for logical
certainty but for serious academic approval.

The simplicity of the style van Schurman chose, however, belies the great advance
she made in the historical argument, "a maid may be a scholar," an argument negated by
mainstream philosophy's insistence on defining woman as less than fully human or, worse,
evil. It is clear that van Schurman consciously chose this method of argument, for in her
letters to the professor of theology, André Rivet, answering his objections to the tenets of
The Learned Maid, for example, she chose a different style of argument. The compelling
eloquence in her letters to Rivet written to oppose negative views on women; it contrasts
with the bold, arid dissertation style of *The Learned Maid* in which she foregoes that kind

of rhetoric. To strengthen her logical proofs with authority, van Schurman references Plato, Aristotle, the Bible, Plutarch, Seneca, and Erasmus. Perhaps, to confirm her own credentials, she adjoins letters by contemporary scholars—Pierre Gassendi, philosopher and scientist; Johan Beverwyck, physician and feminist; Dorothy Moore, scholar of languages; and Frederick Spanheim, Calvinist theologian.

Van Schurman believed in the importance of logic. Beneath the title, *The Learned Maid or Whether "A Maid May Be a Scholar?"* in the 1659 English translation is the added designation, *A Logical Exercise.* Van Schurman's aim to convince readers logically of the soundness of the proposition and to convince parents to educate daughters as well as sons is made clear. To this end, Anna van Schurman claims to have developed the "best and strongest reasons." Logic, she affirms, is "fitly called the key of all sciences" in the study of liberal arts and sciences. By "key" she means that without logic, there would be no science, for it is logic that opens the possibility for the reasoning required in the disciplines of science.[12]

The Learned Maid argues in dissertation style not only because it appealed to the university-educated reader, but, more important, because van Schurman believes in its power. In correspondence with Elizabeth of Bohemia, van Schurman wrote, "I have high regard for the Scholastic Doctors" because they have both clarified ideas and conjured objections and also because they have been "led by those two great stars of the divine and human sciences, St. Augustine and Aristotle."[13] This scholastic logic, retaining Aristotelian syllogisms as well as the medieval proposition, rests on assent to the terms as defined and on the inferences arrived at from the premises. A syllogism is defined as a three-part deduction; propositions are declarative statements to be affirmed or denied by deductive argument. So, as much as logic is capable of certitude, this treatise aims to prove with certainty the proposition: "a maid may become a scholar."

Having considered van Schurman's logical method as important to the aim of *The Maid,* and having explained the general meaning of the logical method, I now turn to its particulars. First, so that the proposition is clearly understood, van Schurman defines its terms. She begins by defining the grammatical terms of the proposition "a maid may be a scholar" as words. The grammatical subject of the proposition is the subject. That subject of the argument is the word "maid" defined first as "Christian," indicating that nothing more is meant by "maid" other than Christian woman. The grammatical object of the proposition is the object of the proposition. Here, the word "scholar" is object of the proposition and defined as one given to study. What a "Christian" woman scholar means is that she necessarily studies scriptural theology in addition to all other disciplines. Finally, the predicate or verb of the proposition, the words "may be convenient," mean suitable, as used here as a more readily understood synonym.

Note that throughout the treatise, van Schurman continues to differentiate the terms of the proposition grammatically when she designates that she will submit the argument to the subject first before she submits to the predicate of each premise for each argument. Once van Schurman has clarified the meaning of the words as parts of the sentence, she next defines the terms as things rather than words (i.e., "maid" being an actual maid who is more or less bright, and "scholar" being an actual scholar or student of particular and universal studies).

Last, van Schurman defines the terms of the proposition not as words or things but as meaning. She does this by setting the limits of their meaning—meaning she designates.

The meaning of "Maid" is limited to one possessing natural ability, financial capability, time and freedom, and viability of aims, four limitations not unlike those that today's subject of study must possess. Once the subject's limitations are clarified, then the predicate's limitations follow. Limiting particular studies suitable for a Christian maid, van Schurman lists by order those closest to theology and moral virtues with the most important discipline being logic, and she then lists those studies necessary for particular occupations (e.g., church, court, military).

Before she proceeds to the proof itself, van Schurman adds an important explanation; that is, that learning is not a thing necessary to salvation or happiness but rather a means, a way to human perfection, which is the end of learning. The end of learning is not outside the human being or "maid," such as a job or a place in heaven would be, but rather inside, within the maid. This notion agrees with what Immanuel Kant proposed in his groundbreaking ethics, *Fundamental Principles of the Metaphysics of Morals* (also titled *Groundwork of the Metaphysics of Morals*). Here Kant claimed that the end of all ethical action is not in the effect outside a person but is already present within the person who acts. For as a person makes choices to act in this or that way, that person becomes the result of his or her choices, good or bad. Most ethical theories considered the end of an ethical act to be particular goods, such as charity aspires to provide, or a final good, such as the contemplation of God. But for Kant the rational nature of human beings discloses them as ends in themselves; consequently, as a moral action, studying promotes the worth of an individual, or as van Schurman maintains, "perfection" of an individual as an end.

Now to the proof of the proposition: "A maid may be a scholar." Again van Schurman begins with the subject of the proposition. The method of proof is a syllogistic method, meaning that the proof follows the deductive form in the three parts of a syllogism:

> Major premise (includes all): All women who have a desire to learn may be scholars.
> Minor premise (a particular case of all): This woman has a desire to learn.
> Conclusion (predicate fitting particular subject): Therefore, this woman may be a scholar.

So when van Schurman refers to "the major" and "the minor," she means these two parts of the syllogism. The inference or logical step moves the premises to proof in the conclusion. Briefly, the logical form means this: if the logical sequence is correct, the syllogism is valid; if the major premise is true and the sequence is valid, then the conclusion or proof must also be true. Once the reader assents to the premises, the reader must assent to the conclusion or proof.

Inaugurating the proof, Anna van Schurman states the thesis or proposition as "A maid may be a scholar," and then proceeds to make seven syllogistic arguments from the subject and eight from the predicate. The proofs result from inferences made from the definitions. The first two arguments define the subject as to the properties (or what can be predicated) of the species or the essence of maid; the next four from properties adjoined to those properties:

> A maid is defined first as "naturally endowed with the principles" or "powers of the principles" meaning "knowledge of conclusions deduced from principles"

i.e. endowed with the ability to make inferences or to reason. What is deduced from "the property of the form of the subject" is that a maid has a "rational soul," and thus to act from that "form" is to reason or learn. In this van Schurman submits to Aristotle, who had claimed that what can be said of a species, such as the human species can be said of an individual of the species, and that no action can occur without there having been a power or principle for action.

Second, if a maid is rational, then logically it follows that she will desire to learn—rationality being ever in want of correct reason and naturally it follows because "nature does nothing in vain," that is, from the law of physics, a natural capacity or in Aristotelian terms, potentiality, naturally seeks fulfillment. Desire is the passion or curiosity, the feeling or will for learning that engages reason with the physical world.

Third, if a rational nature is a nature made in God's image, then a maid, being one who has a rational nature, must be made in God's image and thus given to transcendent motivation, for as the philosopher Boëthius had argued, the aim or motivation of a rational nature is to return to God, and is thus transcendent.[14]

Fourth, if rational, one is created for contemplation and thus is destined to engage in exercising that which is necessary for contemplation, reasoning or learning and studying. The dangers of an idle mind of which women were accused of having, would be mitigated if the mind were directed toward the lofty contemplation that study makes possible.

Fifthly, a certain amount of time and freedom is necessary for study, and maids have that time.

Sixthly, those to whom all the principle studies of theology and ethics are amenable, so too are the subservient studies of liberal arts and sciences listed in the limitations of the term "scholarship."

The seventh and last conjoining "property," concerns where study, reason, and reflection can be carried on in both work and recreation. While van Schurman finds that for all scholars the best place to study is at home and in private, it is even more so for a Christian maid—not intrinsically so or from rational principle—but based on authority and experience. One benefit of scholarly exercise is self-sufficiency, which Aristotle's *Nichomachean Ethics* claims is a mark of happiness. Hence, for van Schurman, one who is self-sufficient is happy in solitude as well as in the company of others. Further, scripture advises maids to remain in the home; experience, too, demonstrates that public space is particularly dangerous to maids' morals. Moral virtue, a principal inquiry of those studies in which a maid may engage, is not an argument of necessity but rather one of "decency." In this logical exercise, authority and experience, although credible, are but additional arguments to those made from principle.

These seven arguments express that within the confines of the proposition, the term "maid" is defined as being suitable for studying God and all God's universe. Made in the image of God, a maid's suitability is assured, that is, as one with a "countenance" that has the capacity for lofty contemplation, looking to God and transcendence rather than only to the world. Van Schurman derives the next seven arguments from the predicate of the proposition (i.e., "learning," which is the class or "genus" of the predicate). The eighth argument of the predicate (i.e., the fifteenth argument and last of the whole) takes the argument to the opposite of knowing, "ignorance."

To summarize, the arguments proceed in this way: Learning, not as end but as means to "contemplation of excellent things," is valuable because it perfects the natural powers of the soul or intellect. Learning leads to love of God through observation of God's works. It also arms one against heresies and fraud. Because the liberal arts teach prudence (i.e., worldly wisdom and personal wisdom, as well as magnanimity or nobility of mind) they are suitable for women who especially need strength in these virtues, despite the fact that these particular virtues have traditionally belonged to men engaged in public activity, earning for them praise for being noble and worldly wise. Last, the study of arts and science ameliorates ignorance, which is not suitable for women's understanding and will; the term "scholar" means one studying all the intellectual subjects and moral virtues for the purpose of gaining perfection, a pursuit, which is suitable to one who loves God.

Adhering to the scholastic method, the final portion of the treatise addresses the "thesis of the adversaries" and disproves their definitions and inferences. The five objections take into account the nature and conditions of the subject and both the end and extent of learning in regard to the subject. The full claim admits to a backward *Cogito*, Descartes' "I think, therefore I am"—I am a maid; therefore, I think, and so have the capacity to reason, and thus to learn to perfect my reason or thinking capacity.

In her later work *Eukleria*, van Schurman voiced concern that the Scholastic method was capable of bringing harm as well as good depending on whether there is the "inward teacher" or "true wisdom."[15] In the *Maid*, the Scholastic proposition is not about a legality, but about whosoever by nature has those properties of the human species, already granted to the male of the species. As a legality it would have been merely "a logical exercise." But it is more than "a logical exercise" in that it confronts that half of the human species denied the means for perfection, the means for more fully attaining Godliness, love of God, and appreciation for God's works. Since Aristotle defined man as representative "rational animal," that same fullness had been denied woman up to and including the seventeenth century.[16] Note that while van Schurman's friend de Gournay had argued that human nature demanded activity, public as well as private, van Schurman limits cultivation of activity to learning itself, narrowing the feminist claim only to what is inferred from the proposition.

The epistemological theory of the *Maid* advocates all medieval liberal arts disciplines with the additions of science and scripture.[17] Interested in the scientific revolution burgeoning in Europe and acquainted with women scientists, van Schurman is often cited as being the first to recommend the study of science for women.

The ethical theory, advising against vanity, idleness, and ignorance, promotes prudence, magnanimity, and courage to deal with and improve the world. In short, both intellectual and moral virtues attained by habit and study perfect the "faculties of the soul." The foundational claim that a capacity seeks its perfection is presented as universal law. Maid, whose defining capacity is reason, is delineated consistently in relation to the object, hence in grammatical terms as subject, and in ethical terms as agent, agent in relationship to world and God, as in the Greek proverb, "Self-choice is also self-experience,"[18] and in epistemological terms, one capable of inference. Thus, within the confines of the proposition, woman is in these senses subject and not object. And so in this treatise van Schurman disentangles one proposition from many, dissecting it with the scalpel of the Scholastic method. While philosophically the proposition of whether "a maid may be a scholar" is enmeshed with natural science, ethics, and political considerations, here, the question is answered only within the confines of propositional logic.

CRITIQUE OF PURE REASON: THE LIGHT OF REASON
AT THE TORCH OF EXPERIENCE

In the *Critique of Pure Reason* Kant took up the problem of two opposing theories of knowledge and solved it in a unique way, revolutionizing philosophy by bringing the "light of reason to the torch of experience."[19] Unlike Descartes, who found certitude in the mind, the English empiricists, in particular David Hume, argued that all knowledge must be derived from sensory experience of what exists outside the mind. Immanuel Kant made this disagreement a subject of investigation. If reality were explained only by mechanical science, the question that remains is what would account for metaphysical notions of freedom, morality, and God? Could there be a third possibility that knowledge comes from both the reasoning mind and the experiencing senses in primary ways? Hume's claim that science could never rise above probability—that science never would be more than or better than the best opinions of logicians and scientists—that philosophers could never transcend experience, pushed Kant into an epistemological revolution.

In *The Treatise on Human Nature* (1737) Hume demonstrated that if human knowledge comes from experience and ends in experience, then there is no finality or certainty in knowing in our conclusions. For the fullness of experience is neither before us, present to us, nor inclusive of what is after us (the future), and until it is, we have only a partial sum of what has been and or is now; now never including the full truth of all human experience. Furthermore, according to Hume, since all experience is made up of our personal impressions and ideas, no one has genuine access to the impressions and ideas of another. Hence, in this pure empiricism, all knowledge is only personal human opinion.

It is this epistemological position advanced by Hume that Kant claims awoke him from his "dogmatic slumber."[20] To save the finality and certainty of philosophy and science, Kant initiated the critical evaluation of the foundations of pure and certain knowledge—a critical examination of rationality in itself, as the proper first inquiry into the possibilities and necessities of all philosophy and all science. This he calls "a second Copernican revolution."[21] Philosophy now, for Kant, will not revolve only around an experiential "reality" as such, but around the nature of true knowledge and epistemology, independent of man's experience, independent of human nature, namely, the examination of pure reason, pure practical reason, and pure judgment and their object, "pure" meaning ideas prompted by experience but produced by reason alone. Kant did this in the *Critique of Pure Reason* (1781–1783), in the *Critique of Practical Reason* (1788) and in the *Critique of Judgment* (1790).

Kant called his new method "critique," giving it the meaning of analysis of the powers of human reason to discover, apart from experience, what reason can know. Having been the cause of a revolution in philosophy, his works are significant for their divorce from experiential and probabilistic logics and sciences as means and sources of foundational knowledge.

Before examining the text of the *Critique of Pure Reason*, it is necessary to note that the text offers the reader a labeling of "A" and "B" to the side of the text. The explanation is that there are two versions of the *Critique of Pure Reason*, the first edition in 1781 labeled "A" and the second edition in 1783, labeled "B."

It should also be noted that in the *Critique*, Kant is not speaking about what we as human beings can and do with our minds, but what pure reason in itself, abstractly and logically, must be. Without these abstract and logical characteristics, reason in itself could not possibly and necessarily be understood according to the requirements of reason itself. Kant prefaces his inquiry in the second edition of the *Critique of Pure Reason* by distinguishing logic from the faculty of reason. He claims that, "from the earliest times logic has already proceeded upon the sure path of science, evidenced by the fact that since Aristotle it has not had to retrace a single step."[22] And even more remarkably "logic has not been able to advance a single step."[23] This is because logic's sphere is so systematically limited. "It's sole concern is to give an exhaustive exposition and a strict proof of the formal rules of all thought, whether it be *a priori* or empirical," whether it deals with the pure objects of reason or with the impressions or ideas of experience.[24] "*A priori*" means independent of experience. Logic is a "propaedeutic," or a presupposition in any critical examination of science; it is, therefore, "only the vestibule of the sciences."[25] Kant wants to lay out a second propaedeutic or presupposition to the sciences, one that is "much more difficult since it has to deal not with itself alone [Pure Reason] but also with objects."[26] Reason deals with that which is known *a priori* either as theory "determining it [in a science] and its concepts," or as a practical knowledge "making it actual"—thus the *Critique of Pure Reason* and the *Critique of Practical Reason*.[27]

In section I of the introduction to the first *Critique*, Kant distinguished pure knowledge from empirical knowledge. "In the order of time," there is no doubt experience is the beginning of all our knowledge, but "it does not follow that it all arises out of experience."[28] Knowledge of strict universality, true necessity, absolute simplicity, to which reason is so dedicated, cannot come from experience, these must have as their source a faculty of *a priori* knowledge. In section II of the same introduction, Kant turns to the first examination of a criterion, the criterion of necessity and strict universality, which establishes the distinction between "pure and empirical knowledge." He examines propositions that cannot be thought to be otherwise than they are—necessarily certain propositions. Kant points out that "pure *a priori* principles are indispensable for the possibility of experience," that is, without the organizing unity provided by *a priori* concepts contained in propositions, the manifold of sensual impression could not be linked in common understanding.[29] How else would those disparate impressions, thick, lettered, bound, be known as a thing or a "book?" Only with *a priori* concepts could there be foundations of knowing at all, and what is known when all the empirical concepts of a book are removed is the remaining *a priori* concept of space.

In section III of the introduction, Kant proposes that this critique provides the opportunity for philosophy to extend "the scope of our judgments beyond the limits of experience and this by means of concepts to which no corresponding object can ever be given in experience."[30] Ideas that lead us beyond our experience are called transcendental. This is the reason why Kant called this philosophy "transcendental," and why Ralph Waldo Emerson and Margaret Fuller designated the American idealism of 1840 "transcendentalism." According to Kant, after examination the epistemology of the critical philosophy finds "things in themselves," "God," "freedom," and "immortality," outside of its realm. (American transcendentalism found in these same concepts the true subject matters of its realm.) We cannot know God or we would be God, cannot know freedom or we would be free from impediments, and cannot know immortality or we would be immortal. In saying, "The unavoidable problems set by pure reason itself are God, freedom, and immortality,"[31] Kant means that the critical philosophy, or the analysis of the powers of reason itself, must analyze the nature and the character of such concepts as God and immortality and the possibilities or impossibilities of particular sciences dealing with such objects of knowledge. For Kant "this process [of critical philosophy or analysis of reason] yields real knowledge *a priori*."[32] It brings Kant to section IV, "The Distinction Between Analytic and Synthetic Judgments":

> Analytic judgments (affirmative) are therefore those in which the connection of the predicate with the subject is thought through identity, those in which this connection is thought without identity should be entitled synthetic. Thus it is evident: 1. that through analytic judgments our knowledge is not in any way extended, and that the concept which I already have is merely set forth and made intelligible to me; 2. that in synthetic judgments I must have besides the concept of the subject something else (X) upon which the understanding may rely, if it is to know that a predicate, not contained in this concept, nevertheless belongs to it.[33]

In analytic propositions the predicate is contained in the subject. In the usual illustration, "All bachelors are unmarried," the predicate is said to be known because it is identical with or contained in its subject, "All bachelors are unmarried" unlike "The bachelor has red hair." The latter cannot be known by reference to the proposition alone; it needs a synthesis with or understanding of something outside, or in addition to, the proposition itself. Of course, Kant is not interested in empirical illustrations but in the fundamental *a priori* concepts and principles—those that are not knowable in or provable by appeal to experience but are, nonetheless, necessary for true, necessary, and universal knowledge in philosophy and science. For Kant analytic judgments provide only explication and clearness, since, for them the concept and knowledge of the predicate is already contained in the concept and knowledge of the subject. As such, genuinely new scientific knowledge is based on the "ampliative principles" of synthetic judgments and upon them "all of our *a priori* speculative knowledge must ultimately rest."[34]

In section V of the introduction, Kant shows how specific theoretical sciences of reason, for example, mathematics, natural science, and metaphysics, are based on "synthetic *a priori* judgments." Kant looks at the theory of mathematics, the theory of physics, and metaphysics. In the first, mathematics, he claims, "All mathematical judgments, without exception, are synthetic."[35] In the proposition $7 + 5 = 12$, 7 does not contain 12 nor does it combined with 5 present an analytical judgment. It demands something more than can be found in the concept or number 12. Stated differently, one must go outside the proposition $7 + 5 = 12$ to determine or find the truth of the proposition. Yet, for Kant, mathematics is not an experimental science either: its claims are not proven or shown true simply by appeal to experience. For Kant, its foundations must lie in *a priori* knowledge. Kant uses plane geometry as a further illustration. "That the straight line between two points is the shortest is a synthetic proposition."[36] The truth of this proposition, like the truth of $7 + 5 = 12$, is not based on human experience alone, or on empirical beliefs. (In fact, most contemporary physicists maintain that in actuality the shortest distance is curved.) So, once again according to Kant, the truth of the proposition in plane geometry must rely on something outside of itself. For Kant, "straight line" is not a matter of quantity but of quality alone, quality meaning a characteristic of the concept not arrived at by analysis of the concept. Therefore, the proposition must rest upon a foundation outside of it and outside of human experience, hence on an *a priori* foundation.

Like mathematics, for Kant, the notions and the fundamental proposition of theoretical physics are also beyond experience (empirical confirmation) and are not merely analytical (or logically true or verifiable). Kant uses the example of matter and the concepts of space, time, motion, and cause, and their interrelations. All are beyond human experience and hence, *a priori* concepts. They are concepts whose very meaning is established through reason alone, although they are about experience or the spatio-temporal world.

One can now see the link between Kant's views on mathematics and physics and his view on metaphysics. Metaphysics is the science of ultimate causes and ultimate reality; because it studies what lies beyond nature, it studies what comes before human experience. Since, for Kant, the origins of reality, the knowledge of absolute truth, and goodness itself are all beyond human experience, their foundations must be *a priori* propositions; otherwise, they are unknowable. Thus, in all three of these theoretical sciences, reason and knowledge are based on foundational synthetic *a priori* judgments (or propositions).

In section VI of the introduction, Kant sets forth the general problem of the whole *Critique of Pure Reason*, citing David Hume as the philosopher who came closest to envisaging the problem. The problem concerns the foundations of all scientific reason. It can be stated in a general question: how is a science of the knowledge of reason possible? The particular questions are how are *a priori* synthetic judgments possible? And how is metaphysics, as a natural disposition or as a science, possible? These questions require a special science or critique of pure reason. In the last section, section VII, Kant outlines how a first step, the examination of pure reason rather than the formation of a whole system of pure reason, is "only negative, not to extend, but only to clarify our reason and keep it free from errors."[37] He calls the inquiry in section VII "a critique" and specifies its subject matter as "transcendental"; it concerns "all knowledge which is occupied not so much with objects as with the mode of our knowledge of objects insofar as this mode of knowledge is possible *a priori*."[38] This critique, if successful, will lay down an architectonic plan—a scheme specifying "a complete enumeration of all the fundamental principles that go to constitute such pure knowledge."[39] He finishes the introduction by laying out what the divisions of this book, the *Critique of Pure Reason*, will be.

SIMILARITIES AND DIFFERENCES BETWEEN VAN SCHURMAN AND KANT

The *Critique* is a great and powerful work that continues to be one of the most influential of all books in philosophy. Nevertheless, some find in it the problem that it separates philosophy from everyday experience. While Kant wrote on political, social, legal, historical, and everyday problems of his time, his dogmatic disciples have generally denied philosophical importance to such works. A conception of philosophy that denies philosophical importance to Kant's less theoretical, more applied writings, is just the sort of biased view of philosophy that helps keep the work of many women philosophers out of the academy, the canon, and university curricula.

Bias is often directed to the issues of gender that Anna van Schurman's philosophy addresses: (1) in topics and arguments given for the rationality, equality, and education of women, countering arguments of male contemporaries and cultural contexts; (2) as part of the explanation of why women have not figured in the canon of Western philosophy; (3) in the insistence on intellectual and moral virtues as being nongendered; (4) in the practical aim for the admittance of women into the world of ideas; and most important (5) in the defense of defining women as fully rational and transcendental.

The Learned Maid and the *Critique* are complementary. Demonstrating the thinking process in a logical exercise, *The Learned Maid* illustrates philosophical method applied to a practical question of metaphysical import. The thinking process Kant critiques in his *Critique of Pure Reason* and his *Fundamental Principles of the Metaphysics of Morals* asks and gives answer to the question: How does this "capacity" of the mind work?

In their understanding of the knower or what René Descartes called the "thinking thing," both van Schurman and Kant are surprisingly similar. The epistemological questions—whether women should know in *The Learned Maid*, and what it means to know in the *Critique*, differ partly in reaction to their historical and philosophical milieu. Van Schurman's argument responds to an actual existing situation as well as to a theoretical position; Kant's responds to a theoretical situation when new theories of knowledge were challenging old theories.

Although Kant had yet to formulate in the *Metaphysics of Morals* that "duty" is established by moral principles, *The Learned Maid* might possibly be stated in Kantian terms: if "a maid may be a scholar," then a maid has a "duty" to learn; to choose not to fulfill that duty constitutes immoral action. The duty, derived from the metaphysical definition of woman as possessing a rational capacity, is in this case to perfect that capacity. It is the subject herself whose perfection is realized when she chooses and participates in the activity of learning.[40] Kant's instruction, "Have courage to use your own reason," is a moral imperative similar to van Schurman's: Fulfill thyself with moral and intellectual virtue.[41]

Reading Anna van Schurman's proof together with Kant's theory recalls for us the absence of women in the academic world over their two centuries. Yet both were attempting to counteract "chaotic muddles of errors" in thinking—about women in the first instance and about thinking itself in the second.[42] The great irony is this: that the rational idealist Kant continued the tradition of confining "a maid" in such a way that she "may *not* be a scholar," by distinguishing the virtue of women as being beautiful and of men as being noble in section 3 of his *Observations on the Feeling of the Beautiful and Sublime*, and claiming, "A woman, therefore, will learn no geometry" nor "the principle of sufficient reason" . . . for:

> Laborious learning or painful pondering, even if a woman should greatly succeed in it, destroy the merits that are proper to her sex . . . A woman who has a head full of Greek . . . or carries on fundamental controversies about mechanics . . . might as well even have a beard [!] . . . Her philosophy is not to reason, but to sense.[43]

These words offer the most compelling reason why *The Learned Maid* should be studied with *Critique of Pure Reason*.

Questions for Reflection

Explain what van Schurman means by the term "principles" and what its importance is to her thesis.

Explain what Kant means by an "*a priori* synthetic judgment" and how it is distinguished from other kinds of judgment.

"Experience" is an explicit concept in Kant's understanding of the nature of knowledge. What is it? Do you think it is an implicit concept in van Schurman as well? If so, compare and contrast Kant's and van Schurman's notions of "experience" as it pertains to their arguments.

Notes

1. Ethel M. Kersey, *Women Philosophers: A Bio-Critical Source Book* (New York: Greenwood Press, 1989), 188.

2. Therese Boos Dykeman, ed., *The Neglected Canon: Nine Women Philosophers* (Boston: Kluwer Academic Publishers, 1999), 119.

3. Kersey, *Women Philosophers*, 188.

4. Margaret Alic, *Hypatia's Heritage: A History of Women in Science* (Boston: Beacon, 1987), 78.

5. Dykeman, *The Neglected Canon*, 119.

6. Immanuel Kant, *The Critique of Pure Reason*, trans. Norman Kemp Smith (New York: St. Martin's Press, 1965), 41–62. Excerpts reproduced with permission of Palgrave Macmillan.

7. Anna Maria van Schurman, *The Learned Maid* or *Whether a Maid May be a Scholar?: A Logic Exercise*. Written in Latin and Dutch by Anna Maria van Schurman of Utrecht. Based on John Redmayne's London publication (1641) 1659, with some modernizations, 124–38. All references to *The Learned Maid* are to this edition.

8. Anna Maria Van Schurman, "Letter to André Rivet," in *Anna Maria van Schurman: Whether a Christian Woman Should Be Educated and Other Writings from Her Intellectual Circle*, ed. Joyce L. Irwin (Chicago: University of Chicago Press: 1998), 6–7.

9. Immanuel Kant, *Critique of Practical Reason*, trans. Lewis White Beck (New York: Liberal Arts Press, 1956), 166.

10. My acknowledgement to King J. Dykeman for sharing his insights on Kant.

11. Erasmus' early sixteenth-century colloquy, "The Abbot and the Learned Woman," is an exception—"The maid reasons that learning allows a woman to know God and His works, and the abbot responds that women would not be kept in subjection if they were allowed learning." *Twenty Select Colloquies of Erasmus*, trans. Sir Roger L'Estrange (London: Chapman & Dodd, 1923), 208–14.

12. Van Schurman's insistence on the importance of logic was reiterated by her admirer, English educator Bathsua Makin, who said "logic is key—those that have this in their heads may unlock other sciences . . ." As quoted from the "Third Letter, Defending Women's Education," in Makin's *An Essay to Revive the Antient Education of Gentlewomen* (Los Angeles: William Andrews Clark Memorial Library, University of California, 1980; orig. pub. 1673), Publication 202. Makin, in praising van Schurman in that same letter, quotes Spanhemius who called van Schurman "nature's master-piece among women."

13. Joyce L. Irwin, ed. "Learned Women of Utrecht," Letter dated January 26, 1644, in *Anna Maria van Schurman, Whether A Christian Woman Should Be Educated and Other Writings from Her Intellectual Circle* (Chicago: University of Chicago Press, 1998), 66–67. In this book, Irwin provides translations of letters between van Schurman and André Rivet and Elizabeth of Bohemia, Dorothy Moore, Anne de Rohan, Bathsua Makin, and Marie de Gournay from van Schurman's 1647 *Opuscula*, as well as the first two chapters of her 1673 *Eukleria* and the three chapters of *Voetius' 1663–1676 Concerning Women* in this book.

14. The Roman Anicius Manlius Severinus Boëthius (ca. 475–525), accused of treason, wrote the highly regarded *The Consolation of Philosophy* from his prison cell when he was awaiting death.

15. Van Schurman, *Eukleria* in Irwin, *Anna Maria van Schurman*, 92.

16. Gisbertus Voetius included a treatise, "Concerning Women," in his *Politicia Ecclesiastica* (Amsterdam, 1663–1676) giving great space to "Whether a woman is human . . . a mistake of nature?" in Irwin, *Anna Maria van Schurman*, 97–137.

17. See "Medieval Liberal Arts" in the glossary.

18. Joyce L. Irwin has translated the Greek proverb that reads here as, "a wise man is self-sufficient" in *Anna Maria van Schurman*, 30.

19. Eighteenth century American philosopher Judith Sargent Murray's (1751–1820) admired Newton as one occupied with "lighting the torch of reason at the flame of experience" in *The Gleaner: A Miscellaneous Production in Three Volumes* (Boston: I. Thomas and E. T. Andrews, 1798) Vol. 1, Essay 27, 269.

20. Kant makes this statement in the preface to the 1783 *Prolegomena to Any Future Metaphysics* and means here the empiricism of Locke, Reid, and Beattie. Kant thought John Locke's empiricism had put an end to the dogmatism of metaphysics and Descartes, and Hume had put an end to the dogmatism of empiricism.

21. Nicolaus Copernicus (1473–1543) determined a heliocentric or sun-centered theory of the universe displacing the earth-centered theory; Johannes Kepler (1571–1630) and Galileo Galilei (1564–1642) provided supporting theories with telescope and mathematics, making possible the work of Isaac Newton (1642–1727). A "second Copernican Revolution" means Kant's revolutionary theory that the mind brings something to its objects as *The Critique of Pure Reason* explains.

22. Kant, *Pure Reason*, Bviii.

23. Kant, *Pure Reason*, Bviii.

24. Kant, *Pure Reason*, Bix.

25. Kant, *Pure Reason*, Bix.

26. Kant, *Pure Reason*, Bix.

27. Kant, *Pure Reason*, Bx.

28. Kant, *Pure Reason*, B1.

29. Kant, *Pure Reason*, B5.

30. Kant, *Pure Reason*, A3.

31. Kant, *Pure Reason*, B7.

32. Kant, *Pure Reason*, B10.

33. Kant, *Pure Reason*, A7–8.

34. Kant, *Pure Reason*, B13–14.

35. Kant, *Pure Reason*, B14.

36. Kant, *Pure Reason*, B17.

37. Kant, *Pure Reason*, B25.

38. Kant, *Pure Reason*, A12.

39. Kant, *Pure Reason*, B27.

40. In a 1637 letter to Rivet, van Schurman argues that God would be frustrated in his ends if, having "introduced us into this theater to show forth . . . and celebrate his most beautiful works," we did not inspect nature, being endowed as Aristotle confirmed in the *Metaphysics*, 1.980a22, "with the desire to know." Irwin, *Anna Maria van Schurman*, 45.

41. Mary Astell asserted some years after van Schurman that, while the great aim of learning is Truth, the learner gains "inner beauty," or moral virtue by the activity of choosing intellectual virtue in *A Serious Proposal to the Ladies for the Advancement of their True and Greatest Interest*, first published in London, 1701.

42. Van Schurman's phrase from a letter to Elizabeth of Bohemia dated January 26, 1644. From Joyce L. Irwin, "Learned Women of Utrecht: Anna Maria van Schurman," in *Women Writers of the Seventeenth Century*, eds. K. M. Wilson and F. J. Warnke (Athens: University of Georgia Press, 1989), 164–185; quote from p. 173.

43. Mary Briody Mahowald, *Philosophy of Woman: Classical to Current Concepts* (Indianapolis, IN: Hackett, 1978) presents Kant's text that contains this quotation, 117–18.

CHAPTER 11

Mill and Taylor

Introduction by *Karen J. Warren*

This introduction provides brief biographies of John Stuart Mill (1806–1873) and Harriet Taylor Mill (1807–1858) and descriptions of key positions advocated by each, because of its on-going controversial nature; it also considers Taylor's intellectual influence, collaboration, and coauthorship of writings published by Mill.

MILL

John Stuart Mill was arguably the most influential English-speaking philosopher of the nineteenth century. He was born in a suburb of London, the eldest son of Harriet Barrow and James Mill and godson of Jeremy Bentham. Although his mother seems to have played a minor role in his life, his father and Bentham were actively involved in all aspects of young Mill's upbringing. It is infamous among philosophers that Mill's education was, at best, highly unusual. Mill began to learn Greek at age three, Latin at eight, and by age fourteen he had read most of the Greek and Latin classics, studied history, logic, and mathematics, and mastered the basics of economic theory. At fifteen, Mill studied Bentham's works and at eighteen began editing Bentham's manuscripts. In 1823 he took an entry-level job in the East India Company, where he eventually became chief examiner—a position once held by his father. In 1829 he traveled to France, became fluent in French, and engaged in what became a life-long interest in French philosophy and history.

In 1826 Mill became quite depressed and came to believe that his father's rigorous educational influence on him had developed his intellect but not his capacity for emotions. Although the depression gradually lifted, the impact of what he came to believe about his feelings, his father, and his education, which was designed by his father to prepare Mill to be a leading proponent of utilitarianism, took its toll on young Mill.

Mill's philosophical interests complemented his desire to be a social reformer (not just a critic) of prevailing social and political institutions. His interest in utilitarianism, for example, was to use it as the basis for social change that protected the rights and liberties of individuals.

In 1830 Mill met Harriet Taylor, who, although married, was quite ill and lived apart from her husband. Mill and Taylor became intimate friends, and in his *Autobiography* (1873), Mill gives Taylor significant credit for many of his publications, often referring to them as joint works. They married in 1851 (two years after her husband's death) and she continued to have an enormous impact on his scholarship. When she died at Avignon during a trip they took to France in 1858, Mill was heartbroken. Each year thereafter, Mill spent half a year at a house in Avignon so that he could be near her grave. Although he was elected to what turned out to be one term in the House of Commons in 1865, he left politics to return to his writing for "radical" causes. In 1869 *The Subjection of Women* was published.

Mill was a prolific author. His *System of Logic* (1843) established his scholarly reputation, reinvigorating interest in the study of logic and providing an account of the philosophy of science that set the standard for the day. Mill's *The Principles of Political Economy* (1848), an economics textbook and defense of liberalism, became a mainstay of political thought for the next several decades. The main theme of *Political Economy* is "how to unite the greatest individual liberty of action, with a common ownership in the raw material of the globe, and an equal participation of all in the benefits of combined labour."[1] We see a version of this view later in Mill's *Subjection of Women*—that the liberation of women requires their political and economic independence from men.

Mill's best-known works in moral philosophy are *On Liberty* (1859) and *Utilitarianism* (1861). *On Liberty* remains significant as a defense of classical liberalism. It answered a central question in political philosophy: When, and on what grounds, is a government justified in interfering with or restricting the liberties of individuals? His answer is a defense of "The Harm Principle": restricting the freedoms of individuals is justified only to prevent (greater) harm to others—either other humans or institutions. Restricting individual freedoms for any other reason—to prevent (greater) harm to oneself, for the individual's own good, to enforce morality—is unjustified. With exceptions for such cases as young children or the mentally incompetent, the Harm Principle provides the most liberal (justifies the least amount of coercion) of all liberty-limiting principles.

Unlike many defenders of liberalism, Mill did not view the moral justification of a government's right to rule as based on a theory of natural rights or a social contract. Rather, forms of government are legitimate and justified according to their utility—their capacity to enable each person to develop their capacities for higher forms of human happiness. To ensure such self-development, liberty is and must be the fundamental right; persons and society should be permitted the means to maximize their own well-being through freedom of speech and expression in accordance with the Harm Principle. These positions are part of his argument in *Subjection of Women* for ending the subordination of women.

Evaluating forms of government in terms of utility bridges Mill's political philosophy with his moral philosophy (or ethics). The classic statement of the ethical position "utilitarianism" is given in Mill's book *Utilitarianism*. Utilitarianism is a consequentialist ethical position, one that assesses the moral worth of actions in terms of their consequences, rather than in terms of nonconsequentialist (or deontological) considerations such as motive or duty.[2] Mill provided different formulations of the principle of utilitatianism; probably the most famous formulation is known as the "greatest happiness principle": one must always act to produce the greatest happiness for the greatest number of people.[3]

Two significant ways that Mill's utilitarianism differed from Bentham's turn on the distinctions between short-term and long-term pleasures, and between higher-order pleasures (such as intellectual and moral pleasures) and lower-order pleasures (such as pleasures of physical desire and appetite). Mill's utilitarianism concerned those actions that produced long-term, higher-order pleasures. Despite criticisms of Mill's position, *Utilitarianism* continues to be one of the most important works in moral philosophy, with implications for both political philosophy and economic theory.

Mill's *Subjection of Women* (1869) is a defense of women's rights, women's suffrage, and equal access to education for women. Mill wavered at times between his philosophical convictions and culturally inculcated views about women's roles, as Jacobs's commentary makes clear. Nonetheless, *Subjection of Women* remains an important text authored by a male philosopher.[4]

TAYLOR

Harriet Taylor Mill (Taylor) was born Harriet Hardy. She was raised in a Unitarian household and was largely self-educated. Hardy knew enough French, German, Italian, Greek, and Latin to insert quotes and phrases in these languages into informal notes to herself as well as her published works. She married John Taylor in 1826, when she was eighteen, and he was twenty-nine. The couple had three children together.

Taylor's introduction to Mill in 1830 is claimed to have been arranged by the Reverend W. J. Fox, to whom she had complained about John Taylor's lack of interest in philosophy and the arts. Mill and Taylor were immediately drawn to each other. Mill visited Taylor almost nightly at her home (with John Taylor) until, in 1833, John Taylor insisted that she establish a separate residence. In 1848 John Taylor refused to allow Mill to dedicate *The Principles of Political Economy* to his wife. So Mill inserted the dedication into copies of the book they distributed to friends.

In 1849 John Taylor became ill with cancer. Taylor eventually agreed to move back to the family home, caring for her husband until he died later that year. Two years later, in 1851, Taylor married Mill. Both Taylor and Mill suffered from tuberculosis. They set out for Montpellier, France, in search of medical attention, but Taylor died of a respiratory failure en route, in Avignon, in 1858.

Taylor was a fiercely independent woman who wrote about issues quite unpopular at the time. Taylor's primary interest was on women's subordination and suffrage, domestic violence, the lack of work and occupations for women, and—perhaps her most radical idea—the necessity of women's economic independence from men for women to be free (a view Karl Marx also held).

According to Taylor, Britain's political system was fundamentally unjust to women. British constitutional law is founded on the principle of no taxation without representation. Yet, women pay taxes and are not represented. Taylor also claimed that while no man would be expected to be tried in a court of law by any but his peers, no woman is ever tried by her peers, since the lawyers, jurors, and judges are all male.

Her essay, "The Enfranchisement of Women," was published in *The Westminster Review* in 1851. Taylor argues that to grant women's suffrage and choice of work would promote the interests and improve the characters of both women and men. Taylor's claim that the fundamental injustice to women is women's lack of economic and political power makes a connection between male dominance in the home and male economic and political dominance in the so-called public sphere. She viewed marriage in this context as a way to perpetuate male dominance, through such policies as those which legally prohibited women from divorcing. Taylor's essay was an important precursor to the women's rights movement that took hold as a social movement in the United States and elsewhere during the early 1920s.

THE CONTROVERSY CONCERNING TAYLOR'S CONTRIBUTIONS TO MILL'S WRITINGS

Mill frequently acknowledged Taylor's intellectual contributions to his writings, including identifying her as coauthor of *Principles of Political Economy* and *On Liberty*. In his article "Harriet Taylor Mill," Dale E. Miller quotes many critics who offer explanations of how Mill could have been so misled about Taylor's contributions to his writing and publications: "he fell victim to her 'feminine wiles'"; "she imbibed all his views, and gave them back in her own form, by which he was flattered and pleased"; being accustomed "to the acceptance of ascetic, masculine values he was completely overpowered by her intensely feminine atmosphere"; "Mill . . . had never met a really soft cushion before [a reference to Taylor]"; "after the death of his domineering father James Mill, [Mill] felt a need to invent another parental authority in order that he might submit to." Miller cites Jacobs (this chapter's commentator) as one who is outspoken in denying that [Taylor] lacked influence over Mill and that this influence had any other basis than his appreciation of her superb intellect. She writes that [Mill] "was a big boy and could evaluate her reasoning" . . . and claims that the failure of [Mill's] critics to recognize that she possessed a first-rate mind and that she engaged in genuine collaboration with [Mill] on roughly equal terms is largely due to sexism.[5]

Miller's own conclusion is that "even if [Taylor] bears little responsibility for the specifics of [Mill's] arguments for the social and political institutions and practices that she advocated—arguments on which much of his philosophical reputation rests—she would still be responsible for inspiring him to make those arguments." How one resolves this controversy is critical to one's assessment of both the philosophical contributions of Taylor and her role as coauthor or collaborator with Mill.

JACOB'S COMMENTARY

Jacob's commentary discusses three main differences between Taylor and Mill on (1) the nature versus nurture question regarding women's alleged inferiority to men, (2) the importance of economic independence for women, and (3) the gendered division of labor within the family and marriage. Jacob deftly draws attention to the often nuanced "Yes, but . . ."

nature of Mill's views, in contrast to Taylor's unconditional claims on these topics. Jacobs also provides a bulleted list of similarities between Mill and Taylor, based mostly on *Subjection of Women*. She concludes her commentary by claiming that the Mill-Taylor writings reveal how "questions of gender" are hidden in basic canonical philosophical questions about ethics and political philosophy.

Excerpts of Writings by Mill and Taylor

I. EXCERPTS FROM HARRIET TAYLOR MILL'S "ENFRANCHISEMENT OF WOMEN"[6]

Most of our readers will probably learn from these pages for the first time that there has arisen in the United States, and in the most civilized and enlightened portion of them, an organized agitation on a new question—new, not to thinkers, nor to any one by whom the principles of free and popular government are felt as well as acknowledged, but new, and even unheard of, as a subject for public meetings and practical political action. This question is, the enfranchisement of women; their admission, in law and in fact, to equality in all rights, political, civil, and social, with the male citizens of the community. . . . On the 23rd and 24th of October last, a succession of public meetings was held at Worcester in Massachusetts under the name of a "Women's Rights Convention," of which the president was a woman, and nearly all the chief speakers women; numerously reinforced, however, by men, among whom were some of the most distinguished leaders in the kindred cause of negro emancipation.

The following is a brief summary of the principal demands.

Education in primary and high schools, universities, medical, legal, and theological institutions.
Partnership in the labors and gains, risks and remunerations, of productive industry.
A coequal share in the formation and administration of laws—municipal, state, and national—through legislative assemblies, courts, and executive offices.

While, far from being expedient, we are firmly convinced that the division of mankind into two castes, one born to rule over the other, is in this case, as in all cases, an unqualified mischief; a source of perversion and demoralization, both to the favored class and to those at whose expense they are favored; producing none of the good which it is the custom to ascribe to it, and forming a bar, almost insuperable while it lasts, to any really vital improvement, either in the character or in the social condition of the human race.

These propositions it is now our purpose to maintain. But before entering on them, we would endeavor to dispel the preliminary objections which, in the minds of persons to whom the subject is new, are apt to prevent a real and conscientious examination of it. The chief of these obstacles is that most formidable one, custom. Women never have had equal rights with men. . . . This strongest of prejudices, the prejudice against what is new and unknown, has, indeed, in an age of changes like the present, lost much of its force; if it had not, there would be little hope of prevailing against it. Over three-fourths of the habitable world, even at this day, the answer, "it has always been so," closes all discussion. But it is the boast of modern Europeans, and of their American kindred, that they know and do many things which their forefathers neither knew nor did; and it is perhaps the most unquestionable point of superiority in the present above former ages, that habit is not now the tyrant it formerly was over opinions and modes of action, and that the worship of custom is a declining idolatry. An uncustomary thought, on a subject which touches the greater interests of life, still startles when first presented; but if it can be kept before the mind until the impression of strangeness wears off, it obtains a hearing, and as rational a consideration as the intellect of the hearer is accustomed to bestow on any other subject.

In the present case, the prejudice of custom is doubtless on the unjust side. Great thinkers, indeed, at different times, from Plato to Condorcet, besides some of the most eminent names of the present age, have made emphatic protest in favor of the equality of women. And there have been voluntary societies, religious or secular, of which the Society of Friends is the most known, by whom that principle was recognized. But there has been no political community or nation in which, by laws and usage, women have not been in a state of political and civil inferiority. In the ancient world the same fact was alleged, with equal truth, in behalf of slavery. It might have been alleged in favor of the mitigated form of slavery, serfdom, all through the middle ages. It was urged against freedom of industry, freedom of conscience, freedom of the press; none of these liberties were thought compatible with a well-ordered state, until they had proved their possibility by actually existing as facts. That an institution or a practice is customary is no presumption of its goodness, when any other sufficient cause can be assigned for its existence. There is no difficulty in understanding why the subjection of women has been a custom. No other explanation is needed than physical force.

That those who were physically weaker should have been made legally inferior is quite conformable to the mode in which the world has been governed. Until very lately, the rule of physical strength was the general law of human affairs. Throughout history, the nations, races, classes, which found themselves the strongest, either in muscles, in riches, or in military discipline, have conquered and held in subjection the rest. If, even in the most improved nations, the law of the sword is at last discountenanced as unworthy, it is only since the calumniated eighteenth century. Wars of conquest have only ceased since democratic revolutions began. The world is very young, and has but just begun to cast off injustice. It is only now getting rid of monarchial despotism. It is only now getting rid of hereditary feudal nobility. It is only now getting rid of disabilities on the ground of religion. It is only beginning to treat any men as citizens, except the rich and a favored portion of the middle class. Can we wonder that it has not yet done as much for women? As society was constituted until the last few generations, inequality was its very basis; association grounded on equal rights scarcely existed; to be equals was to be enemies; two persons could hardly cooperate in anything, or meet in any amicable relation, without the law's appointing that one of them should be superior of the other. Mankind have outgrown this state, and all things now tend to substitute, as the general principle of human relations, a just equality, instead of the dominion of the strongest. But of all relations, that between men and women being the nearest and most intimate, and connected with the greatest number of strong emotions, was sure to be the last to throw off the old rule and receive the new: for in proportion to the strength of a feeling, is the tenacity with which it clings to the forms and circumstances with which it has even accidentally become associated.

When a prejudice, which has any hold on the feelings, finds itself reduced to the unpleasant necessity of assigning reasons, it thinks it had done enough when it has re-asserted the very point in dispute, in phrases which appeal to the pre-existing feeling. Thus, many persons think they have sufficiently justified the restrictions on women's field of action, when they have said that the pursuits from which women are excluded are unfeminine, and that the proper sphere of women is not politics or publicity, but private and domestic life.

We deny the right of any portion of the species to decide for another portion, or any individual for another individual, what is and what is not their "proper sphere." The proper sphere for all human beings is the largest and highest which they are able to attain to. What this is, cannot be ascertained, without complete liberty of choice. The speakers at the Convention in America have therefore done wisely and right, in refusing to entertain the question of the peculiar aptitudes either of women or of men, or the limits within this or that occupation may be supposed to be more adapted to the one or to the other. They justly maintain, that these questions can only be more adapted to the one or the other. They justly maintain, that these questions can only be satisfactorily answered by perfect freedom. Let every occupation be open to all, without favor or discouragement to any, and employments will fall into the hands of those men or women who are found by experience to be most capable of worthily exercising them. There need be no fear that women will take out of the hands of men any occupation which men perform better than they. Each individual will prove his or her capacities, in the only way in which capacities can be proved—by trial; and the world will have the benefit of the best faculties of all its inhabitants. But to interfere beforehand by an arbitrary limit, and declare that whatever be the genius, talent, energy, or force of mind of an individual of a certain sex or class, those faculties shall not be exerted, or shall be exerted only in some few of the many modes in which others are permitted to use theirs, is not only an injustice to the individual, and a detriment to society, which loses what it can ill spare, but is also the most effectual mode of providing that, in the sex or class so fettered, the qualities which are not permitted to be exercised shall not exist.

We shall follow the very proper example of the Convention, in not entering into the question of the alleged differences in physical or mental qualities between the sexes; not because we have nothing to say, but because we have too much; to discuss this one point tolerably would need all the space we have to bestow on the entire subject. But if those who assert that the "proper sphere" for women is the domestic, mean by this that they have not shown themselves qualified for any other, the assertion evinces great ignorance of life and of history. Women have shown fitness for the highest social functions, exactly in proportion as they have been admitted to them. By a curious anomaly, though ineligible to even the lowest offices of State, they in some countries admitted to the highest of all, the regal; and if there is any one function for which they have shown a decided vocation, it is that of reigning. . . . [Taylor briefly lists a number of excellent queens both in England and in other parts of the world.]

Concerning the fitness, then, of women for politics, there can be no question: but the dispute is more likely to turn upon the fitness of politics for women. When the reasons alleged for excluding women from active life in all its higher departments are stripped of their garb of declamatory phrases, and reduced to the simple expression of a meaning, they seem to be mainly three: first, the incompatibility of active life with maternity, and with the cares of a household; secondly, its alleged hardening effect on the character; and thirdly, the inexpediency of making an addition to the already excessive pressure of competition in every kind of professional or lucrative employment.

The first, the maternity argument, is usually laid most stress upon: although (it needs hardly be said) this reason, if it be one can apply only to mothers. It is neither necessary nor just to make imperative on women that they shall be either mothers or nothing; or that if they have been mothers once, they shall be nothing else during the whole remainder of their lives. Neither women nor men need any law to exclude them from an occupation, if they have undertaken another which is incompatible with it. No one proposes to exclude the male sex from Parliament because a man may be a soldier or sailor in active service, or a merchant whose business requires all his time and energies. Nine-tenths of the occupations of men exclude the de facto from public life, as effectually as if they were excluded by law; but that is not reason for making laws to exclude even the nine-tenths, much less the remaining tenth. The reason of the case is the same for women as for men. There is no need to make provision by law that a woman shall not carry on the active details of a household, or of the education of children, and at the same time practice a profession, or be elected to parliament. Where incompatibility is real, it will take care of itself: but there is gross injustice in making the incompatibility, pretence for the exclusion of those in whose case it does not exist. And these, if they were free to choose, would be a very large proportion. The maternity argument deserts its supporters in the case of single women, a large and increasing class of the population; a fact which, it is not irrelevant to remark, by tending to diminish the excessive competition of numbers, is calculated to assist greatly the prosperity of all. There is no inherent reason or necessity that all women should voluntarily choose to devote their lives to one animal function and its consequences. Numbers of women are wives and mothers only because there is no other career open to them, no other occupation for their feelings or their activities. Every improvement in their education, and enlargement of their faculties, everything which renders them more qualified for any other mode of life, increases the number of those to whom it is an injury and an oppression to be denied the choice. To say that women must be excluded from active life because maternity disqualifies them for it is, in fact to say, that every other career should be forbidden them in order that maternity may be their only resource.

But secondly, it is urged, that to give the same freedom of occupation to women as to men, would be an injurious addition to the crowd of competitors, by whom the avenues to almost all kinds of employment are choked up, and its remuneration depressed. This argument, it is to be observed, does not reach the political question. It gives no excuse for withholding from women the right of citizenship. The suffrage, the jury-box, admission to the legislature and to office, it does not touch. It bears only on the industrial branch of the subject. Allowing it, then, in an economical point of view, its full force; assuming that to lay open to women the employments now monopolized by men, would tend, like the breaking down of other monopolies, to lower the rate of remuneration in those employments; let us consider what is the amount of the evil consequence, and what the compensation for it. The worst ever asserted, much worse than is at all likely to be realized, is that if women competed with men, a man and a woman could not together earn more than is now earned by the man alone. Let us make this supposition, the most unfavorable supposition possible: the joint income of the two would be the same as before, while the woman would be raised form the position of a servant to that of a partner. Even if every woman, as matters now stand, had a claim on some man for support, how infinitely preferable is it that part of the income should be of the woman's earning, even if the aggregate sum were but little increased by it, rather than that she should be compelled to stand aside in order that men may be the sole earners, and the sole dispensers of what is earned. Even under the present laws respecting the property of women, a woman who contributes materially to the support of the family, cannot be treated in the same contemptuously tyrannical manner as one who, however she may toil as a domestic drudge, is a dependent on the man for subsistence. As the depression of wages by increase of competition, remedies will be found for it in time. Pallatives might be applied immediately; for instance, a more rigid exclusion of children from industrial employment, during the years in which they ought to be working only to strengthen their bodies and minds for after-life. Children are necessarily dependent, and under the power of others; and their labor, being not for themselves but for the gain of the parents, is a proper subject for legislative regulation. With respect to the future, we neither believe that improvident multiplication, and the consequent excessive difficulty of gaining a subsistence, will always continue, nor that the division of mankind into capitalist and hired laborers, and the regulation of the reward of the laborers mainly be demand and supply, will be for ever, or even much longer, the rule of the world. But so long as competition is the general law of human life, it is tyranny to shut out one-half of the competitors. All who have attained the age of self government have an equal claim to be permitted to sell whatever kind of useful labor they are capable of, for the price which it will bring.

The third objection to the admission of women to political or professional life, its alleged hardening tendency, belongs to an age not past, and is scarcely to be comprehended by people of the present time. There are still, however, persons who say that the world and its avocations render men selfish and unfeeling; that the struggles, rivalries, and collisions of business and of politics make them harsh and unamiable; that if half the species must unavoidably be given up to these things, it is the more necessary that the other half should be kept free from them; that to preserve women from the bad influences of the world, is the only chance of preventing men from being wholly given up to them.

There would have been plausibility in this argument when the world was still in the age of violence; when life was full of physical conflict, and every man had to redress his injuries or those of others, by the sword or by the strength of his arm. Women, like priests, by being exempted from such responsibilities, and from some part of the accompanying dangers, may have been enabled to exercise a beneficial influence. But in the present condition of human life, we do not know where those hardening influences are to be found, to which men are subject and from which women are at present exempt. Individuals now-a-days are seldom called upon to fight hand to hand, even with peaceful weapons; personal enmities and rivalries count for little in worldly transactions; the general pressure of circumstances, not the adverse will of individuals, is the obstacle men now have to make head against. That pressure, when excessive, breaks the spirit, and cramps and sours the feelings, but not less of women than of men, since they suffer certainly not less from its evils. There are still quarrels and dislikes, but the sources of them are changed. The feudal chief once found his bitterest enemy in his powerful neighbor, the minister or courtier in his rival for place: but opposition of interest in active life, as a cause of personal animosity, is out of date; the enmities of the present day arise not from great things but small, from what people say of one another, more than from what they do; and if there are hatred, malice, and all uncharitableness, they are to be found among women fully as much as among men. In the present state of civilization, the notion of guarding women from the hardening influences of the world, could only be realized by secluding them from society altogether. The common duties of common life, as at present constituted, are incompatible with any other softness in women than weakness. Surely weak minds in weak bodies must ere long cease to be even supposed to be either attractive or amiable.

But, in truth, none of these arguments and considerations touch the foundations of the subject. The real question is, whether it is right and expedient that one-half of the human race should pass through life in a state of forced subordination to the other half. If the best state of human society is that of being divided into two parts, one consisting of persons with a will and a substantive existence, the other of humble companions to these persons, attached, each of them to one, for the purpose of bringing up his children, and making his home pleasant to him; if this is the place assigned to women, it is but kindness to educate them for this; to make them believe that the greatest good fortune which can befall them, is to be chosen by some man for this purpose; and that every other career which the world deems happy or honorable, is closed to them by the law, not social institutions, but of nature and destiny.

When, however, we ask why the existence of one-half the species should be merely ancillary to that of the other—why each woman should be a mere appendage to a man, allowed to have no interest of her own, that there may be nothing to compete in her mind with his interests and his pleasure; the only reason which can be given is, that men like it. . . . How truly this is said of mankind in general, and how wonderfully the ideas of virtue set afloat by the powerful, are caught and imbibed by those under the dominion, is exemplified by the manner in which the world were once persuaded that the supreme virtue of subjects was loyalty to kings, and are still persuaded that the paramount virtue of womanhood is loyalty to men. Under a nominal recognition of a moral code common to both, in practice self-will and self-assertion form the type of what are designated as manly virtues, while abnegation of self, patience, resignation, and submission to power, unless when resistance is commanded by other interests than their own, have been stamped by general consent as pre-eminently the duties and graces required of women. The meaning being merely, that power makes itself the center of moral obligation, and that a man likes to have his own will, but does not like that his domestic companion should have a will different from his.

We are far from pretending that in modern and civilized times, no reciprocity of obligation is acknowledged on the part of the stronger. Such an assertion would be very wide of the truth. But even this reciprocity, which has disarmed tyranny, at least in the higher and middle classes, of its most revolting features, yet when combined with the original evil of the dependent condition of women, has introduced in its turn serious evils.

In the beginning, and among tribes which are still in a primitive condition, women were and are the slaves of men for purposes of toil. . . . In a state somewhat more advance, as in Asia, women were and are the slaves of men for purposes of sensuality. In Europe there early succeeded a third and milder dominion, secured not by blows, nor by locks and bars, but by sedulous inculcation on the mind; feelings also of kindness, and ideas of duty, such as a superior owes to inferiors under his protection, became more and more involved in the relation of companionship, even between unequals. The lives of the two persons were apart. The wife was part of the furniture of home—of the resting-place to which the man returned from business or pleasure. His occupations were, as they still are, among men; his pleasures and excitements also were, for the most part, among men— among his equals. He was a patriarch and a despot within four walls, and irresponsible power had its effect, greater or less according to is disposition, in rendering him domi- neering, exacting, self-worshipping, when not capriciously or brutally tyrannical. But if the moral part of his nature suffered, it was not necessarily so, in the same degree, with the intellectual or the active portion. He might have as much vigor of mind and energy of character as his nature enabled him, and as the circumstances of his times allowed. He might write the Paradise Lost, or win the battle of Marengo. This was the condition of the Greeks and Romans, and of the moderns until a recent date. Their relations with their domestic subordinates occupied a mere corner, though a cherished one, of their lives. Their education as men, the formation of their character and faculties, depended mainly on a different class of influences.

It is otherwise now. The progress of improvement has imposed on all possessors of power, and of domestic power among the rest, an increased and increasing sense of cor- relative obligation. No man now thinks that this wife has no claim upon his actions but such as he may accord to her. All men of any conscience believe that their duty to their wives is one of the most binding of their obligations. Nor is it supposed to consist solely in protection, which, in the present state of civilization, women have almost ceased to need: it involves care for their happiness and consideration of their wishes, with a not unfrequent sacrifice of their own to them. The power of husbands has reached the stage which the power of kings had arrived at, when opinion did not yet question the rightful- ness of arbitrary power, but in theory, and to a certain extent in practice, condemned the selfish use of it. This improvement in the moral sentiments of mankind, and increased sense of the consideration due by every man to those who have no one but himself to look to, has tended to make home more and more the center of interest, and domestic circumstances and society a larger and larger part of life, and of its pursuits and pleasures. The tendency has been strengthened by the changes of tastes and manners which have so remarkable distinguished the last two of three generations. In days not far distant, men found their excitement and filled up their time in violent bodily exercises, noisy merri- ment, and intemperance. They have now, in all but the very poorest classes, lost their inclination for these things and for the coarser pleasures generally; they have now scarcely any tastes but those which they have in common with women, and, for the first time in the world, men and women are really companions. a most beneficial change, if the com- panionship were between equals; but being between unequals, it produces, what good observers have noticed, though without perceiving its cause, a progressive deterioration among men in what had hitherto been considered the masculine excellences. Those who are so careful that women should not become men, do not see that men are becoming, what they have decided that women should be—are falling into the feebleness which they have so long cultivated in their companions. Those who are associated in their lives, tend to become assimilated in character. In the present closeness of association between the sexes, men cannot retain manliness unless women acquire it.

There is hardly any situation more unfavorable to the maintenance of elevation of character or force of intellect, than to live in the society, and seek by preference the sympathy, of inferiors in mental endowments. Why is it that we constantly see in life so much of intellectual and moral promise followed by such inadequate performance, but because the aspirant has compared himself only with those below himself, and has not sought improvement or stimulus from measuring himself with his equals or superiors. In the present state of social life, this is becoming the general condition of men. They care less and less for any sympathies, and are less and less under any personal influences, but those of the domestic roof. Not to be misunderstood, it is necessary that we should distinctly disclaim the belief, that women are even now inferior in intellect to men. There are women who are the equals in intellect of any men who ever lived; and comparing ordinary women with ordinary men, the varied though petty details which compose the occupation of most women, call forth probably as much of mental ability, as the uniform routine of the pursuits which are the habitual occupation of a large majority of men. It is from nothing in the faculties themselves, but from the petty subjects and interests on which alone they are exercised, that the companionship of women, such as their present circumstances make them, so often exercises a dissolvent influence on high faculties and aspirations in men. If one of the two has no knowledge and no care about the great ideas and purposes which dignify life, or about any of its practical concerns save personal interests and personal vanities, her conscious, and still more her unconscious influence, will, except in rare cases, reduce to a secondary place in his mind, if not entirely extinguish, those interests which she cannot or does not share.

Our argument here brings us into collision with what may be termed the moderate reformers of the education of women; a sort of person who cross the path of improvement on all great questions; those who would maintain the old bad principles, mitigating their consequences. These say, that women should be, not slaves, nor servants, but companions; and educated for that office (they do not say that men should be educated to be the companions of women). But since uncultivated women are not suitable companions for cultivated men, and a man who feels interest in things above and beyond the family circle wishes that his companion should sympathize with him in that interest; they therefore say, let women improve their understanding and taste, acquire general knowledge, cultivate poetry, art, even coquet with science, and some stretch their liberality so far as to say, inform themselves on politics; not as pursuits, but sufficiently to feel an interest in the subjects, and to be capable of holding a conversation on them with the husband, or at least of understanding and imbibing his wisdom. Very agreeable to him, no doubt, but unfortunately the reverse of improving. It is from having intellectual communion only with those to whom they can lay down the law, that so few men continue to advance in wisdom beyond the first stages. The most eminent men cease to improve, if they associate only with disciples. When they have overtopped those who immediately surround them, if they wish for further growth, they must seek for others of their own stature to consort with. The mental companionship which is improving, is communion between active minds, not mere contact between an active mind and a passive. This inestimable advantage is even now enjoyed, when a strong-minded man and a strong-minded woman are, by a rare chance, united: and would be had far oftener, if education took the same pains to form strong-minded women which it takes to prevent them from being formed. The modern, and what are regarded as the improved and enlightened modes of education of women, abjure, as far as words go, an education of mere show, and profess to aim at solid instruction, but mean by that expression, superficial information on solid subjects. Except accomplishments, which are now generally regarded as to be taught well if taught at all, nothing is taught to women thoroughly. Small portions only of what it is attempted to teach thoroughly to boys, are the whole of what it is intended or desired to teach to women. What makes intelligent being is the power of thought: the stimuli which call forth that power are the interest and dignity of thought itself, and a field for its practical application. Both motives are cut off from those who are told from infancy that thought, and all its greater applications, are other people's business, while theirs is to make themselves agreeable to other people. High mental powers in women will be but an exceptional accident, until every career is open to them, and until they, as well as men, are educated for themselves and for the world-not one sex for the other.

In what we have said on the effect of the inferior position of women, combined with the present constitution of married life, we have thus far had in few only the most favorable cases, those in which there is some real approach to that union and blending of characters and of lives, which the theory of the relation contemplates as its ideal standard. But if we look to the great majority of cases, the effect of women's legal inferiority, on the character both of women, and of men, must be painted in far darker colors. We do not speak here of the grosser brutalities, not of the man's power to seize on the woman's earnings, or compel her to live with him against her will. We do not address ourselves to any one who requires to have it proved that these things should be remedied. We suppose average cases, in which there is neither complete union nor complete disunion of feelings and character; and we affirm that in such cases the influence of the dependence on the woman's side, is demoralizing to the character of both.

The common opinion is that whatever may be the case with the intellectual, the moral influence of women over men is almost salutary. It is, we are often told, the great counteractive of selfishness. However the case may be as to personal influence, the influence of the position tends eminently to promote selfishness. The most insignificant of men, the man who can obtain influence or consideration nowhere else, finds one place where he is chief and head. There is one person, often greatly his superior in understanding, who is obliged to consult him, and whom he is not obliged to consult. He is judge, magistrate, ruler, over their joint concerns; arbiter of all differences between them. The justice or conscience to which her appeal must be made, is his justice and conscience: it is his to hold the balance and adjust the scales between his own claims or wishes and those of another. His is now the only tribunal, in civilized life, in which the same person is judge and party. A generous mind, in such a situation, makes the balance incline against his own side, and gives the other not less, but more, than a fair equality; and thus the weaker side may be enabled to turn the very fact of dependence into an instrument of power, and in default of justice, take an ungenerous advantage of generosity; rendering the unjust power, to those who make an unselfish use of it, a torment and a burden. But how is it when average men are invested with this power, without reciprocity and without responsibility? Give such a man the idea that he is first in law and in opinion—that to will is his part, and hers to submit; its is absurd to suppose that this idea merely glides over his mind, without sinking into it, or having any effect on his feelings and practice. The propensity to make himself the first object of consideration, and others at most the second, is not so rare as to be wanting where everything seems purposely arranged for encouraging its indulgence. If there is any self-will in the man, he becomes either the conscious or unconscious despot of is household. The wife, indeed, often succeeds in gaining her objects, but it is by some of the many various forms of indirectness and management.

Thus the position is corrupting equally to both; in the one it produces the vices of power, in the other those of artifice. Women, in their present physical and moral state, having stronger impulses, would naturally be franker and more direct than men; yet all the old saws and traditions represent them as artful and dissembling. Why? Because their only way to their objects is by indirect paths. In all countries where women have strong wishes and active minds, this consequence is inevitable; and if it is less conspicuous in England than in some other places, it is because Englishwomen, saving occasional exceptions, have ceased to have either strong wishes or active minds.

We are not now speaking of cases in which there is anything deserving the name of strong affection on both sides. That, where it exists, is too powerful a principle not to modify greatly the bad influences of the situation; it seldom, however, destroys then entirely. Much oftener the bad influences are too strong for the affection, and destroy it. The highest order of durable and happy attachments would be a hundred times more frequent than they are, if the affection which the two sexes sought from one another were that genuine friendship, which only exists between equals in privileges as in faculties. But with regard to what is commonly called affection in married life—the habitual and almost mechanical feeling of kindliness, and pleasure in each other's society, which generally grows up between persons who constantly live together, unless there is actual dislike there is nothing in this to contradict or qualify the mischievous influence of the unequal relation. Such feelings often exist between a sultan and his favorites, between a master and his servants; they are merely examples of the pliability of human nature, which accommodates itself in some degree even to the worst circumstances, and the commonest natures always the most easily.

With respect to the influence personally exercised by women over men, it, no doubt, renders them less harsh and brutal; in ruder times, it was often the only softening influence to which they were accessible. But the assertion, that the wife's influence renders the man less selfish, contains, as things now are, fully as much error as truth. Selfishness toward the wife herself, and toward those in whom she is interested, the children, though favored by her dependence, the wife's influence, no doubt, tends to counteract. But the general effect on him of her character, so long as her interests are concentrated in the family, tends but to substitute for individual selfishness a family selfishness, wearing an amiable guise, and putting on the mask of duty. How rarely is the wife's influence on the side of public virtue; how rarely does it do otherwise that discourage any effort of principle by which the private interests or worldly vanities of the family can be expected to suffer. Public spirit, sense of duty toward the public good, is of all virtues, as women are now educated and situated, the most rarely to be found among them; they have seldom even, what in men is often a partial substitute for public spirit, a sense of personal honor connected with any public duty. Many a man, whom no money or personal flattery would have bought, has bartered his political opinions against a title or invitations for his wife; and a still greater number are made mere hunters after the puerile vanities of society, because their wives value them. As for opinions: in Catholic countries, the wife's influence is another name for that of the priest; he gives her, in hopes and emotions connected with a future life, a consolation for the sufferings and disappointments which are her ordinary lot in this. Elsewhere, her weight is thrown into the scale either of the most commonplace, or of the most outwardly prosperous opinions: either those by which censure will be escaped, or by which worldly advancement is likeliest to be procured. In England, the wife's influence is usually on the illiberal and anti-popular side: this is generally the gaining side for personal interest and vanity; and what to her is the democracy of liberalism in which she has no part—which leaves her the Pariah it found her? The man himself, when he marries, usually declined into Conservatism; begins to sympathize with the holders of power, more than with its victims, and thinks it his part to be on the side of authority. As to mental progress, except those vulgar attainments by which vanity or ambition are promoted, there is generally an end to it in a man who marries a woman mentally his inferior; unless, indeed, he is unhappy in marriage, or becomes indifferent. From a man of twenty-five or thirty, after his is married, an experienced observer seldom expects any further progress in mind or feelings. It is rare that the progress already made is maintained. Any spark of the mans divinior which might otherwise have spread and become a flame, seldom survives for any length of time unextinguished. For a mind which learns to be satisfied with what is already is—which does not incessantly look forward to a degree of improvement not yet reached—becomes relaxed, self indulgent, and loses the spring and the tension which maintain it even at the point already attained. And there is no fact in human nature to which experience bears more invariable testimony that to this-that all social or sympathetic influences which do not raise up, pull down; if they do not tend to stimulate and exalt the mind, they tend to vulgarize it.

For the interest, therefore, not only of women but of men, and of human improvement in which the modern world often boasts of having effected, and for which credit is sometimes given to civilization, and sometimes to Christianity, cannot stop where it is. If it were either necessary or just that one portion of mankind should remain mentally and spiritually only half developed, the development of the other portion ought to have been made, as far as possible, independent of their influence. Instead of this, they have become the most intimate, and it may now be said, the only intimate associates of those to whom yet they are sedulously kept inferior; and have been raised just high enough to drag the others down to themselves.

We have left behind a host of vulgar objections either as not worthy or an answer, or as answered by the general course of our remarks. A few words, however, must be said on one plea, which in England is made much use of for giving an unselfish air to the upholding of selfish privileges, and which, with unobserving, unreflecting people, passes for much more than it is worth. Women, it is said, do not desire—do not seek, what is called their emancipation. On the contrary, they generally disown such claims when made in their behalf, and fall with *acharnement* upon any one of themselves who identifies herself with their common cause.

Supposing the fact to be true in the fullest extent ever asserted, if it proves that European women ought to remain as they are, it proves exactly the same with respect to Asiatic women; for they too, instead of murmuring at their seclusion, and at the restraint imposed upon them, pride themselves on it, and are astonished at the effrontery of women who receive visits from male acquaintances, and are seen in street unveiled. Habits of submission make men as well as women servile-minded. The vast population of Asia do not desire or value, probably would not accept, political liberty, nor the savage of the forest, civilization; which does not prove that either of those things is undesirable for them, or that they will not, at some future time, enjoy it. Custom hardens human beings to any kind of degradation, by deadening the part of their nature which would resist it. And the case of women is, in this respect, even a peculiar one, for no other inferior caste that we have heard of have been taught to regard degradation as their honor. The argument, however, implies a secret consciousness that the alleged preference of women for their dependent state is merely apparent; and arises from their being allowed no choice; for if the preference be natural, there can be no necessity for enforcing it by law. To make laws compelling people to follow their inclination had not hitherto been thought necessary by any legislator. The plea that women do not desire any change, is the same that has been urged, times out of mind, against the proposal of abolishing any social evil—"there is not complaint"; which is generally not true, and when true, only so because there is not that hope of success, without which complaint seldom makes itself audible to unwilling ears. How does the objector know that women do not desire equality and freedom? He never knew a woman who did not, or would not, desire it for herself individually. It would be very simple to suppose, that if they do desire it they will say so. Their position is like that of the tenants or laborers who vote against their own political interest to please their landlords or employers; with the unique addition, that submission is inculcated on them from childhood, as the peculiar attention and grace of their character. They are taught to think, that to repel actively even an admitted injustice done to themselves, is somewhat unfeminine, and had better be left to some male friend or protector. To be accused of rebelling against anything which admits of being called an ordinance of society, they are taught to regard as an imputation of a serious offence, to say the least, against the proprieties of their sex. It requires unusual moral courage as well as disinterestedness in a woman, to express opinions favorable to women's enfranchisement, until, at least, there is some prospect of obtaining it. The comfort of her individual life, and her social consideration, usually depend on the good-will of those who hold the undue power, and to possessors of power any complaint, however bitter, of the misuse of it, is a less flagrant act of insubordination than to protest against the power itself. The professions of women in this matter remind us of the State offenders of old, who, on the point of execution, used to protest their love and devotion to the sovereign by whose unjust mandate they suffered. . . . Successful literary women are just as unlikely to prefer the cause of women to their own social consideration. They depend on men's opinion for their literary as well as for their feminine successes; and such is their bad opinion of men, that they believe that is not more than one in ten thousand who does not dislike and fear strength, sincerity, or high spirit in a woman. They are therefore anxious to earn pardon and toleration for whatever of these qualities their writings may exhibit on other subjects, by a studied display of submission on this: that they may give no occasion for vulgar men to say (what nothing will prevent vulgar men from saying), that learning makes women unfeminine, and that literary ladies are likely to be bad wives.

The fact which affords the occasion for this notice, makes it impossible any longer to assert the universal acquiescence of women (saving individual exceptions) in their dependent condition. In the United States, at least, there are women, seemingly numerous, and now organized for action on the public mind, who demand equality in the fullest acceptation of the word, and demand it by a straightforward appeal to men's sense of justice, not plead for it with a timid deprecation of their displeasure.

What is wanted for women is equal rights, equal admission to all social privileges; not a position apart, a sort of sentimental priesthood.

II. EXCERPTS FROM JOHN STUART MILL'S "THE SUBJECTION OF WOMEN"[7]

The principle which regulates the existing social relations between the two sexes—the legal subordination of one sex to the other—is wrong in itself, and now one of the chief hindrances to human improvement; and that it ought to be replaced by a principle of perfect equality, admitting no power or privilege on the one side, nor disability on the other.

The least that can be demanded is, that the question should not be considered as prejudged by existing fact and existing opinion, but open to discussion on its merits, as a question of justice and expediency: the decision on this, as on any of the other social arrangements of mankind, depending on what an enlightened estimate of tendencies and consequences may show to be most advantageous to humanity in general, without distinction of sex. And the discussion must be a real discussion, descending to foundations, and not resting satisfied with vague and general assertions. It will not do, for instance, to assert in general terms, that the experience of mankind has pronounced in favor of the existing system. Experience cannot possibly have decided between two courses, so long as there has only been experience of one. If it be said that the doctrine of the equality of the sexes rests only on theory, it must be remembered that the contrary doctrine also has only theory to rest upon. All that is proved in its favor by direct experience, is that mankind have been able to exist under it, and to attain the degree of improvement and prosperity which we now see; but whether that prosperity has been attained sooner, or is now greater, than it would have been under the other system, experience does not say. On the other hand, experience does say, that every step in improvement has been so invariably accompanied by a step made in raising the social position of women, that historians and philosophers have been led to adopt their elevation or debasement as on the whole the surest test and most correct measure of the civilization of a people or an age. Through all the progressive period of human history, the condition of women has been approaching nearer to equality with men. This does not of itself prove that the assimilation must go on to complete equality; but it assuredly affords some presumption that such is the case.

Neither does it avail anything to say that the nature of the two sexes adapts them to their present functions and position, and renders these appropriate to them. Standing on the ground of common sense and the constitution of the human mind, I deny that any one knows, or can know, the nature of the two sexes, as long as they have only been seen in their present relation to one another. If men had ever been found in society without women, or women without men, or if there had been a society of men and women in which the women were not under the control of men, something might have been positively known about the mental and moral differences which may be inherent in the nature of each. What is now called the nature of women is an eminently artificial thing—the result of forced repression in some directions, unnatural stimulation in others. It may be asserted without scruple that no other class of dependents have had their character so entirely distorted from its natural proportions by their relation with their masters.

But how, it will be asked, can any society exist without government? In a family, as in a state, some one person must be the ultimate ruler. Who shall decide when married people differ in opinion? Both cannot have their way, yet a decision one way or the other must be come to.

It is not true that in all voluntary association between two people, one of them must be absolute master: still less that the law must determine which of them it shall be. The most frequent case of voluntary association, next to marriage, is partnership in business: and it is not found or thought necessary to enact that in every partnership, one partner shall have entire control over the concern, and the others shall be bound to obey his orders. No one would enter into partnership on terms which would subject him to the responsibilities of a principal, with only the powers and privileges of a clerk or agent. If the law dealt with other contracts as it does with marriage, it would ordain that one partner should administer the common business as if it were his private concern; that the others should have only delegated powers; and that this one should have only delegated powers; and that this one should be designated by some general presumption of law, for example as being the eldest. The law never does this: nor does experience show it to be necessary that any theoretical inequality of power should exist between the partners, or that the partnership should have any other conditions than what they may themselves appoint by their articles of agreement. Yet it might seem that the exclusive power might be conceded with less danger to the rights and interests of the inferior, in the case of partnership than in that of marriage, since he is free to cancel to power by withdrawing from the connexion. The wife has no such power, and even if she had, it is almost always desirable that she should try all measures before resorting to it.

It is quite true that things which have to be decided every day, and cannot adjust themselves gradually, or wait for a compromise, ought to depend on one will: one person must have their sole control. But it does not follow that this should always be the same person. The natural arrangement is a division of powers between the two; each being absolute in the executive branch of their own department, and any change of system and principle requiring the consent of both. The division neither can nor should be pre-established by the law, since it must depend on individual capacities and suitabilities. If the two persons chose, they might pre-appoint it by the marriage contract, as pecuniary arrangements are now often pre-appointed. There would seldom be any difficulty in deciding such things by mutual consent, unless the marriage was one of those unhappy ones in which all other things as well as this, become subjects of bickering and dispute. The division of rights would naturally follow the division of duties and functions; and that is already made by consent, or at all events not by law, but by general custom, modified and modifiable at the pleasure of the persons concerned.

The real practical decision of affairs, to whichever may be given the legal authority, will greatly depend, as it even now does, upon comparative qualifications. The mere fact that he is usually the eldest, will in most cases give the preponderance to the man; at least until they both attain a time of life at which the difference in their years is of no importance. There will naturally also be a more potential voice on the side, whichever it is, that brings the means of support. Inequality from this source does not depend on the law of marriage, but on the general conditions of human society, as now constituted. The influence of mental superiority, either general or special, and of superior decision of character, will necessarily tell for much. It always does so at present. And this fact shows how little foundation there is for the apprehension that the powers and responsibilities of partners in life (as of partners in business), cannot be satisfactorily apportioned by agreement between themselves. They always are so apportioned, except in cases in which the marriage institution is a failure. Things never come to an issue of downright power on one side, and obedience on the other, except where the connexion altogether has been a mistake, and it would be a blessing to both parties to be relieved from it.

I need not hope that this treatise can make any impression upon those who need anything to convince them that a woman's inheritance or gains ought to be as much her own after marriage as before. The rule is simple: whatever would be the husband's or wife's if they were not married, should be under their exclusive control during marriage; which need not interfere with the power to tie up property by settlement, in order to preserve it for children. Some people are sentimentally shocked at the idea of a separate interest in money matters, as inconsistent with the ideal fusion of two lives into one. For my own part, I am one of the strongest supporters of community of goods, when resulting from an entire unity of feeling in the owners, which makes all things common between them. But I have no relish for a community of goods resting on the doctrine, that what is mine is yours but what is yours is not mine; and I should prefer to decline entering into such a compact with any one, though I were myself the person to profit by it.

This particular injustice and oppression to women, which is, to common apprehensions, more obvious than all the rest, admits of remedy without interfering with any other mischiefs: and there can be little doubt that it will be one of the earliest remedied. Already, in many of the new and several of the old States of the American Confederation, provisions have been inserted even in the written Constitutions, securing to women equality of rights in this respect: and thereby improving materially the positions, in the marriage relations, of those women at least who have property, by leaving them one instrument of power which they have not signed away; and preventing also the scandalous abuse of the marriage institution, which is perpetrated when a man entraps a girl into marrying him without a settlement, for the sole purpose of getting possession of her money. When the support of the family depends, not on property, but on earnings, the common arrangement, by which the man earns the income and the wife superintends the domestic expenditure, seems to me in general the most suitable division of labor between the two persons. If, in addition to the physical suffering of bearing children, and the whole responsibility of their care and education in early years, the wife undertakes the careful and economical application of the husband's earnings to the general comfort of the family; she takes not only her fair share, but usually the larger share, of the bodily and mental exertion required by their joint existence. If she undertakes any additional portion, it seldom relieves her from this, but only prevents her from performing it properly. The care which she is herself disabled from taking of the children and the household, nobody else takes, those of the children who do not die, grow up as they best can, and the management of the household is likely to be so bad, as even in point of economy to be a great drawback from the value of the wife's earnings. In an otherwise just state of things, it is not, therefore, I think a desirable custom that the wife should contribute by her labor to the income of the family. In an unjust state of things, her doing so may be useful to her, by making her of more value in the eyes of the man who is legally her master; but, on the other hand, it enables him still farther to abuse his power, by forcing her to work, and leaving the support of the family to her exertions, while he spends most of his time in drinking and idleness. The *power* of earning is essential to the dignity of a woman, if she has not independent property. But if marriage were an equal contract, not implying the obligation of obedience; if the connexion were no longer enforced to the oppression of those to whom it is purely a mischief, but a separation, on just terms (I do not now speak of a divorce), could be obtained by any woman who was morally entitled to it; and if she would then find an honorable employments as freely open to her as to men; it would not be necessary for her protection, that during marriage she should make this particular use of her faculties. Like a man when he chooses a profession, so, when a woman marries, it may in general be understood that she makes choice of the management of a household, and the bringing up of a family, as the first call upon her exertions, during as many years of her life as may be required for the purpose; and that she renounces, not all other objects and occupations, but all which are not consistent with the requirements of this. The actual exercise, in a habitual or systematic manner, of outdoor occupations, or such as cannot be carried on at home, would by this principle be practically interdicted to the greater number of married women. But the utmost latitude ought to exist for the adaptation of general rules to individual suitabilities; and there ought to be nothing to prevent faculties exceptionally adapted to any other pursuit, from obeying their vocation notwithstanding marriage: due provision being made for supplying otherwise any falling-short which might become inevitable, in her full performance of the ordinary functions of mistress of a family. These things, if once opinion were rightly directed on the subject, might with perfect safety be left to be regulated by opinion, without any interference of law.

I consider it presumption in any one to pretend to decide what women are or are not, can or cannot be, by natural constitution. They have always hitherto been kept, as far as regards spontaneous development, in so unnatural a state, that their nature cannot but have been greatly distorted and disguised; and no one can safely pronounce that if women's nature were left to choose its direction as freely as men's, and if no artificial bent were attempted to be given to it except that required by the conditions of human society, and given to both sexes alike, there would be any material difference, or perhaps any difference at all, in the character and capacities which would unfold themselves. I shall presently show, that even the least contestable of the differences which now exist, are such as may very well have been produced merely by circumstances, without any difference of natural capacity. But, looking at women as they are known in experience, it may be said of them with more truth than belongs to most other generalizations on the subject, that the general bent of their talents is towards the practical. This statement is conformable to all the public history of women, in the present and the past. It is no less borne out by common and daily experience. Let us consider the special nature of the mental capacities most characteristic of a woman of talent. They are all of a kind which fits them for practice, and makes them tend toward it. What is meant by a woman's capacity of intuitive perception? It means a rapid and correct insight into present fact. It has nothing to do with general principles. Nobody ever perceived a scientific law of nature by intuition, nor arrived at a general rule of duty or prudence by it. These are results of slow and careful collection and comparison of experience; and neither the men nor the women of intuition usually shine in this department, unless, indeed, the experience necessary is such as they can acquire by themselves. For what is called their intuitive sagacity makes them peculiarly apt in gathering such general truths as can be collected from their individual means of observation. When, consequently, they chance to be as well provided as men are with the results of other people's experience, by reading and education, (I use the word chance advisedly, for, in respect to the knowledge that tends to fit them for the greater concerns of life, the only educated women are the self-educated) they are better furnished than men in general with the essential requisites of skilful and successful practice. Men who have been much taught, are apt to be deficient in the sense of present fact; they do not see, in the facts which they are called upon to deal with, what is really there, but what they have been taught to expect. This is seldom the case with women of any ability. Their capacity of "intuition" preserves them from it. With equality of experience and of general faculties, a woman usually sees much more than a man of what is immediately before her. Now this sensibility to the present, is the main quality on which the capacity for practice, as distinguished from theory, depends. To discover general principles, belongs to the speculative faculty: to discern and discriminate the particular cases in which they are and are not applicable, constitutes practical talent: and for this women as they now are have a peculiar aptitude. I admit that there can be no good practice without principles, and that the predominant place which quickness of observation hold among a woman's faculties, makes her particularly apt to build over-hasty generalizations upon her own observation; though at the same time no less ready in rectifying those generalizations, as her observation takes a wider range. But the corrective to this defect, is access to the experience of the human race; general knowledge—exactly the thing which education can best supply. A woman's mistakes are specifically those of a clever self-educated man, who often sees what men trained in routine do not see, but falls into errors for want of knowing things which have long been known. Of course he has acquired much of the pre-existing knowledge or he could not have got on at all; but what he knows of it he has picked up in fragments and at random, as women do.

But this gravitation of women's minds to the present, to the real, to actual fact, while in its exclusiveness it is a source of errors, is also a most useful counteractive of the contrary error. The principal and most characteristic aberration of speculative minds as such, consists precisely in the deficiency of this lively perception and ever-present sense of objective fact. For want of this, they often not only overlook the contradiction which outward facts oppose to their theories, but lose sight of the legitimate purpose of speculation altogether, and let their speculative faculties go astray into regions not peopled with real beings, animate or inanimate, even idealized, but with personified shadows created by the illusions of metaphysics or by the mere entanglements of words, and think these shadows the proper objects of the highest, the most transcendent, philosophy. Hardly anything can be of greater value to a man of theory and speculation who employs himself not in collecting materials of knowledge by observation, but in working them up by processes of thought into comprehensive truths of science and laws of conduct, than to carry on his speculations in the companionship, and under the criticism, of a really superior woman. There is nothing comparable to it for keeping his thoughts within the limits of real things, and the actual facts of nature. A woman seldom runs wild after an abstraction. A habitual direction of her mind to dealing with things as individuals rather than in groups, and (what is closely connected with it) her more lively interest in the present feelings of persons, which makes her consider first of all, in anything which claims to be applied to practice, in what manner persons will be affected by it—these two things make her extremely unlikely to put faith in any speculation which loses sight of individuals, and deals with things as if they existed for the benefit of some imaginary entity, some mere creation of the mind, not resolvable into the feelings of living beings. Women's thoughts are thus as useful in giving reality to those of thinking men, as men's thoughts in giving width and largeness to those of women. In depth, as distinguished from breadth, I greatly doubt if even now, women, compared with men, are at any disadvantage.

It will be said, perhaps, that the greater nervous susceptibility of women is a disqualification for practice, in anything but domestic life, by rendering them mobile, changeable, too vehemently under the influence of the moment, incapable of dogged perseverance, unequal and uncertain in the power of using their faculties. I think that these phrases sum up the greater part of the objects commonly made to the fitness of women for the higher class of serious business. Much of all this is the mere overflows of nervous energy run to waste, and would cease when the energy was directed to a definite end. Much is also the result of conscious or unconscious cultivation; as we see by the almost total disappearance of "hysterics" and fainting fits, since they have gone out of fashion. Moreover, when people are brought up, like many women of the higher classes (though less so in our own country than in any other) a kind of hothouse plants, shielded from the wholesome vicissitudes of air and temperature, and untrained in any of the occupations and exercises which give stimulus and development to the circulatory and muscular system, while their nervous system, especially in its emotional department, is kept in unnaturally active play; it is no wonder if those of them who do not die of consumption, grow up with constitutions liable to derangement from slight causes, both internal and external, and without stamina to support any task, physical or mental, requiring continuity of effort. But women brought up to work for their livelihood show none of these morbid characteristics, unless indeed they are chained to an excess of sedentary work in confined and unhealthy rooms. Women who in their early years have shared in the healthful physical education and bodily freedom of their brothers, and who obtain a sufficiency of pure air and exercise in after-life, very rarely have any excessive susceptibility of nerves which can disqualify them for active pursuits. There is indeed a certain proportion of persons, in both sexes, in whom an unusual degree of nervous sensibility is constitutional, and of so marked a character as to be the feature of their organization which exercises the greatest influence over the whole character of the vital phenomena. This constitution, like other physical conformations, is hereditary, and is transmitted to sons as well as daughters; but it is possible, and probably, that the nervous temperature (as it is called) is inherited by a greater number of women than of men. We will assume this as a fact: and let me then ask, are men of nervous temperament found to be unfit for the duties and pursuits usually followed by men? If not, why should women of the same temperament be unfit for them? The peculiarities of the temperament are, no doubt, within certain limits, an obstacle to success in some employments, though an aid to it in others. But when the occupation is suitable to the temperament, and sometimes even when it is unsuitable, the most brilliant examples of success are continually given by the men of high nervous sensibility. They are distinguished in their practical manifestations chiefly by this, that being susceptible of a higher degree of excitement than those of another physical constitution, their powers when excited differ more than in the case of other people, from those shown in their ordinary state: they are raised, as it were, above themselves, and do things with ease which they are wholly incapable of at other times. But this lofty excitement is not, except in weak bodily constitutions, a mere flash, which passes away immediately, leaving no permanent traces, and incompatible with persistent and steady pursuit of an object. It is the character of the nervous temperament to be capable of *sustained* excitement, holding out through long continued efforts. It is what is meant by *spirit*. It is what makes the highbred racehorse run without slackening speed till he drops down dead. It is what has enabled so many delicate women to maintain the most sublime constancy not only at the stake, but through a long preliminary succession of mental and bodily tortures. It is evident that people of this temperament are particularly apt for what may be called the executive department of the leadership of mankind. They are the material of great orators, great preachers, and impressive diffusers of moral influences. Their constitution might be deemed less favorable to the qualities required from a statesman in the cabinet, or from a judge. It would be so; if the consequence necessarily followed that because people are excitable they must always be in a state of excitement. But this is wholly a question of training. Strong feeling is the instrument and element of strong self-control: but it requires to be cultivated in that direction. When it is, it forms not the heroes of impulse only, but those also of self-conquest. History and experience prove that the most passionate characters are the most fanatically rigid in their feelings of duty, when their passion has been trained to act in that direction.

Supposing it, however, to be true that women's minds are by nature more mobile than those of men, less capable of persisting long in the same continuous effort, more fitted for dividing their faculties among many things than for traveling in any one path to the highest point which can be reached by it: this may be true of women as they now are (though not without great and numerous exceptions), and may account for their having remained behind the highest order of men in precisely the things in which this absorption of the whole mind in one set of ideas and occupations may seem to be most requisite. Still, this difference is one which can only affect this kind of excellence, not the excellence itself, or its practical worth: and it remains to be shown whether this exclusive working of a part of the mind, this absorption of the whole thinking faculty in a single subject, and concentration of it on a single work, is the normal and healthful condition of the human faculties, even for speculative uses. I believe that what is gained in special development by this concentration, is lost in the capacity of the mind for the other purposes of life; and even in abstract thought, it is my decided opinion that the mind does more by frequently returning to a difficult problem, than by sticking to it without interruption. For the purposes, at all events, of practice, from its highest to its humblest departments, the capacity of passing promptly from one subject of consideration to another, without letting the active spring of the intellect run down between the two, is a power far more valuable; and this power women pre-eminently possess, by virtue of the very mobility of which they are accused. They perhaps have it from nature, but they certainly have it by training and education; for nearly the whole of the occupations of women consist in the management of small but multitudinous details, on each of which the mind cannot dwell even for a minute, but must pass on to other things, and if anything requires longer thought, must steal time at odd moments for thinking of it. The capacity indeed which women show for doing their thinking in circumstances and at times which almost any man would make an excuse to himself for not attempting it, has often been noticed: and a woman's mind, though it may be occupied only with small things, can hardly ever permit itself to be vacant, as a man's so often is when not engaged in what he chooses to consider the business of his life. The business of a woman's ordinary life is things in general, and can as little case to go on as the world to go round.

There are other reasons, besides those which we have now given, that help to explain why women remain behind men, even in the pursuits which are open to both. For one thing, very few women have time for them. This may seem a paradox; it is an undoubted social fact. The time and thoughts of very woman have to satisfy great previous demands on them for things practical. There is first, the superintendence of the family and the domestic expenditure, which occupies at least one woman in every family, generally the one of mature years and acquired experience; unless the family is so rich as to admit of delegating that task to hired agency, and submitting to all the waste and malversation inseparable from that mode of conducting it. The superintendence of a household, even when not in other respects laborious, is extremely onerous to the thoughts; it requires incessant vigilance, an eye which no detail escapes, and presents questions for consideration and solution, foreseen and unforeseen, at every hour of the day, from which the person responsible for them can hardly ever shake herself free. If a woman is of a rank and circumstances which relieve her in a measure from these cares, she has still devolving on her the management of the whole family of its intercourse with others—of what is called society, and the less the call made on her by the former duty, the greater is always the development of the latter: the dinner parties, concerts, evening parties, morning visits, letter writing, and all that goes with them. All this is over and above the engrossing duty which society imposes exclusively on women of making themselves charming. A clever woman of the higher ranks finds nearly a sufficient employment of her talents in cultivating the graces of manner and the arts of conversation. To look only at the outward side of the subject: the great and continual exercise of thought which all women who attach any value to dressing well (I do not mean expensively, but with taste, and perception of natural and of artificial *convenance*) must bestow upon their own dress, perhaps also upon that of their daughters, would alone go a great way toward achieving respectable results in art, or science, or literature, and does actually exhaust much of the time and mental power they might have to spare for either. If it were possible that all this number of little practical interests (which are made great to them) should leave them either much leisure, or much energy and freedom of mind, to be devoted to art or speculation, they must have a much greater original supply of active faculty than the vast majority of men. But this is not all. Independently of the regular offices of life which devolve upon a woman, she is expected to have her time and faculties always at the disposal of everybody. If a man has not a profession to exempt him from such demands, still, if he has a pursuit, he offends nobody by devoting his time to it; occupation is received as a valid excuse for his not answering to every casual demand which may be made on him. Are a woman's occupations, especially her chosen and voluntary ones, ever regarded as excusing her from any of what are termed the calls of society? Scarcely are her most necessary and recognized duties allowed as an exemption. It requires an illness in the family, or something else out of the common way, to entitle her to give her own business the precedence over other people's amusement. She must always be at the beck and call of somebody, generally of everybody. If she has a study or a pursuit, she must snatch any short interval which accidentally occurs to be employed in it. A celebrated woman, in a work which I hope will some day be published, remarks truly that everything a woman does is done at odd times. Is it wonderful, then, if she does not attain the highest eminence in things which require consecutive attention, and the concentration on them of the chief interest of life? Such is philosophy, and such, above all, is art, in which, besides the devotion of the thoughts and feelings, the hand also must be kept in constant exercise to attain high skill.

[Chapter 4] Would mankind be at all better off if women were free?

To which let me first answer, the advantage of having the most universal and pervading of all human relations regulated by justice instead of injustice. . . . All the selfish propensities, the self-worship, the unjust self-preference, which exist among mankind, have their source and root in, and derive their principal nourishment from, the present constitution of the relation between men and women. Think what it is to a boy, to grow up to manhood in the belief that without any merit or any exertion of his own, though he may be the most frivolous and empty or the most ignorant and stolid of mankind, by the mere fact of being born a male he is by right the superior of all and every one of an entire half of the human race: including probably some whose real superiority to himself he has daily or hourly occasion to feel; but even if in his whole conduct he habitually follows a woman's guidance, still, if he is a fool, she thinks that of course she is not, and cannot be, equal in ability and judgment to himself; and if he is not a fool, he does worse—he sees that she is superior to him, and believes that, notwithstanding her superiority, he is entitled to command and she is bound to obey. What must be the effect on his character, of this lesson? And men of the cultivated classes are often not aware how deeply it sinks into the immense majority of male minds.

What marriage may be in the case of two persons of cultivated faculties, identical in opinions and purposes, between whom there exists that best kind of equality, similarity of powers and capacities with reciprocal superiority in them—so that each can enjoy the luxury of looking up to the other, and can have alternately the pleasure of leading and of being led in the path of development—I will not attempt to describe. To those who can conceive it, there is no need; to those who cannot, it would appear the dream of an enthusiast. But I maintain, with the profoundest conviction, that this, and this only, is the ideal of marriage; and that all opinions, customs, and institutions which favor any other notion of it, or turn the conceptions and aspirations connected with it into any other direction, by whatever pretences they may be colored, are relics of primitive barbarism. The moral regeneration of mankind will only really commence, when the most fundamental of the social relations is placed under the rule of equal justice, and when human beings learn to cultivated their strongest sympathy with an equal in rights and in cultivation.

Thus far, the benefits which it has appeared that the world would gain by ceasing to make sex a disqualification for privileges and a badge of subjection, are social rather than individual; consisting in a increase of the general fund of thinking and acting power, and an improvement in the general conditions of the associations of men with women. But it would be a grievous understatement of the case to omit the most direct benefit of all, the unspeakable gain in private happiness to the liberated half of the species; the difference to them between a life of subjection the will of others, and a life of rational freedom.

Commentary by *Jo Ellen Jacobs*, Taylor and Mill: Joining Forces to Contest the Subordination of Women

INTRODUCTION

Unlike many of the writers in this book, Taylor and Mill knew each other. In fact, they married just after Taylor completed "Enfranchisement of Women" in the spring of 1851. Their married lives ended in 1858 when Taylor died. Mill did not write *Subjection of Women* until two years later when, in a house overlooking her grave in Avignon, France, he completed a draft that he would not publish until nine years later. These two pieces were known around the world and have been used by feminists as a source of inspiration and argument since they appeared.

RESOURCES

Four resources guided me as I explored these two essays, and you may wish to consult them if you want to explore the ideas in these works further. (Many of the points made below first appeared in these articles.) Alice Rossi's careful 1970 study reawakened interest in these two explorers of the idea of justice for women.[8] In 1977, Julia Annas pointed to some of the differences between Taylor and Mill's positions and suggested that Taylor's argument was more consistent.[9] Richard Krouse examined the way Taylor's position, unlike Mill's, was a more coherent solution to some of the problems in Victorian liberal political theory.[10] It took until 1989, a full 120 years after Mill published *Subjection of Women*, before a book-length study of this seminal work appeared. Gail Tulloch's detailed analysis of the *Subjection of Women* concurred with Rossi, Annas, and Krouse, that Mill's position was more inconsistent than Taylor's.[11] Hundreds of articles and dozens of books had been written about Mill's work on political economy, ethics, and logic, but not one on Mill's feminist philosophy. It is only fitting to ask why this is.

ESSAYS ON MARRIAGE

In order to understand the central claims of each of these articles and the differences and similarities between them we must begin with two essays they each wrote twenty years earlier, in 1832.[12] Near the beginning of their friendship with one another, they agreed to privately exchange their thoughts on marriage and divorce. Given the circumstances in which they found themselves—loving each other while Harriet Taylor was married to John Taylor—it was a delicate choice of topics.

Taylor's writing asserted an extremely radical position: give women access to education, careers, and legal equality and you can eliminate marriage as an institution altogether. Women will choose very carefully whether or not to have children, and if they do, they will be able to support them by themselves, if required. She pinned the core of women's inequality on their inability to own money or work. Given the marriage laws that gave men the right to force sex on their wives, even after beating them or separating from them, and given that divorce was generally illegal, marriage amounted to a kind of prostitution in which women bartered their sexuality for protection and economic power. So, if marriage is to continue as an institution, it must include the right to divorce.

Mill's essay, dedicated to "she to whom my life is devoted," agreed that Victorian marriage was about men's sexuality and that making divorce legal would most benefit women. He reaffirms Taylor's idea that financial independence was indispensable for equality. However, unlike Taylor, Mill claims that, although women should be free to have a career, married women would "naturally" choose not to work. Women's "occupation should rather be to adorn and beautify" life and this task can be "accomplished rather by being than by doing." A wife might "share [her husband's] occupation" but her chief function is to be charming. Further, doubling the number of workers competing in the labor market would be economically unsound. Yet Mill reiterates the point that if women could earn money on their own prior to marriage, then marriage can be voluntary. As it was then practiced, marriage was a lottery. On the other hand, divorce will lead to bitterness and children need two parents, so spouses should wait to have children until they are sure of their marriage commitment. (This would have been very difficult in an age before reliable contraception!)

Already in these essays we begin to see the more radical views of Taylor and the relatively more moderate views of Mill. The article that Taylor would write twenty years later would not include the most radical suggestion that marriage be abandoned, but it would continue to insist that women must have the ability to earn and own money before and after marriage, if they were to gain equality. Mill's book, published nearly forty years later, would continue the tension between a conservative view of the importance of the traditional family and the realization that women's economic independence was needed for equality.

AUTHORSHIP

Taylor and Mill collaborated in varying degrees throughout their relationship. Sometimes Taylor merely suggested ideas and did editing work. On the other end of the spectrum, she coauthored work with Mill.[13] In the case of *Subjection of Women*, the question of coauthorship with Taylor is clear—this work was not coauthored, since Taylor had died before Mill began the work. (However, his collaboration on this piece with Taylor's daughter, Helen, may be less clear.) The authorship of "Enfranchisement of Women" is muddier. Outlines of arguments and ideas used for this work appear in both Mill's and Taylor's handwriting.[14] However, Mill's rejection of some of the central ideas, the parallel to earlier work by Taylor, the attribution by Mill of this article to Taylor, and the separate publication of it by Mrs. Stuart Mill (after its anonymous original publication in the *Westminster Review*), all point to Taylor as the author.

DISSIMILARITIES

I've hinted at the dissimilarity between the ideas in Taylor's and Mill's work. Now it is time to take a closer look. You should look for three issues as you read these articles: the question of nature versus nurture, the importance of careers for married women, and the division of labor within the family. (The nature versus nurture question may be familiar from psychology classes.)

The nature versus nurture question is whether a given characteristic is the result of a natural, even genetic necessity, or the result of environmental stimuli such as parents' discipline or peer pressure. Many people in the Victorian period, as now, looked at differences between genders, races, or classes and claimed the reason a specific group was, for example, dumber, less motivated, more emotional, and so forth was due to natural, inevitable, unchangeable features we might now call "genetic." The justification for why women should vote, have jobs, be on juries, or be educated was often supposed to be their natural inability. Taylor is outraged by this assumption.

What are women naturally able to do or be? Taylor's answer: we don't have a clue, and we will not have a clue until women are educated equally and are able to compete freely with men for careers. Short of a world of true freedom, we will only see women who have been stunted by the confines of a society that tells girls they aren't good at math, are too emotional to be leaders, and need someone to take care of them. Anyone nurtured in this way will grow up unsure, timid, and fearful.

Mill's answer is less consistent. Yes, Mill agrees, "I consider it presumption in any one to pretend to decide what women are or are not, can or cannot be, by natural constitution." However, he cannot resist thinking he does know what women are really like: "But, looking at women as they are known in experience, it may be said of them with more truth than belongs to most other generalizations on the subject, which the general bent of their talents is toward the practical." Women are more practical, more intuitive, while men are more theoretical, more rational. Mill is quick to point out that this practical, intuitive bent is a very good thing and an enormous help to philosophers like him who might get too unrealistic from time to time without the input of an intuitive woman to set them straight. But you see the problem: he can't both say it is a presumption to know what women are really like and then turn around and tell you what women are really like.

Mill makes the same mistake with "nervous susceptibility." This classic attribute of women might, Mill points out, be the result of the way women are reared.

> If a woman is treated as a kind of hothouse plant, shielded from the wholesome vicissitudes of air and temperature, and untrained in any of the occupations and exercises which give stimulus and development to the circulatory and muscular system, while their nervous system, especially in its emotional department, is kept in unnaturally active play; it is no wonder if those of them who do not die of consumption, grow up with constitutions liable to derangement from slight causes, both internal and external, and without stamina to support any task, physical or mental, requiring continuity of effort.[15]

So far, so good, but again, Mill can't resist a "but." "But it is possible, and probable, that the nervous temperature (as it is called) is inherited by a greater number of women than of men." Men, although in few numbers according to Mill, can have a nervous temperament, and both unstable men and women can be successful, particularly in certain careers. So, nervous susceptibility is not complete proof that women can't work. Yet, we see Mill again waffle between "we can't know what women are really like" and "but here's how they are different and isn't it a good thing." (The exact debate between those who claim that there is no essential characteristic of women and those who claim that there is and that it is to be celebrated has continued throughout the history of feminist studies.)[16]

The second major point of contention between Taylor and Mill concerns money and jobs. Taylor is convinced from her earliest writing that women will not have equality until they have economic independence. Therefore, education for real careers and access to jobs are crucial for women to gain the power needed to demand equality. To the argument Mill gave in his 1832 essay on marriage that doubling the number of those seeking jobs would be bad for the economy, Taylor retorts,

> Even if every woman, as matters now stand, had a claim on some man for support, how infinitely preferable is it that part of the income should be of the woman's earning, even if the aggregate sum were but little increased by it, rather than that she should be compelled to stand aside in order that men may be the sole earners, and the sole dispensers of what is earned. Even under the present laws respecting the property of women, a woman who contributes materially to the support of the family, cannot be treated in the same contemptuously tyrannical manner as one who, however she may toil as a domestic drudge, is a dependent on the man for subsistence.[17]

What men didn't seem to understand, according to Taylor, is that money is power. To have to ask for every cent you spend is inevitably going to lead to inequality in the relationship. Even if the result of women having the freedom to work is that both husband and wife make together what the husband made alone before women had the right to work, Taylor says that women would be better off because the power within the marriage would be closer to equal. In addition, if child labor were banned, as it should be, the number of workers would decline, and if birth control were practiced, as it should be, the number of workers would eventually decline even more. So the "doubling of competitors" could be alleviated. Further, even if women entering the workforce caused some to suffer, it is unjust to prevent one-half the population from competing in the free market.

Domestic violence will also be reduced if women have the economic freedom to abandon a man who beats them, Taylor asserts. Even in the twenty-first century the primary reason women stay with abusers is that they believe they are economically dependent. Having the right to work outside the home is not merely a luxury to fight some theoretical power struggle; for many women it is the only means to escape an abusive relationship.[18]

If women are to have economic freedom, they must be educated just as men are. Taylor rejects the "moderate" reformers who want women to be educated enough to be intellectual companions for men. They should know just enough about history, politics, or literature to entertain their husbands, if such reformers had their way. (How similar is this to the kind of education a geisha might receive?) Taylor counterargues that women need to be taught the same kind of critical thinking that men are taught. Women will be attracted to the work of education for the same reasons men are: the intrinsic value of ideas and the practical application of those ideas in a career.

What makes intelligent beings is the power of thought: the stimuli that call forth that power are the interest and dignity of thought itself and a field for its practical application. Both motives are cut off from those who are told from infancy that thought, and all its greater applications, are other people's business, while theirs is to make themselves agreeable to other people. High mental powers in women will be but an exceptional accident, until every career is open to them, and until they, as well as men, are educated for themselves and for the world—not one sex for the other.

Mill, on the other hand, prefers women to stay at home after they are married, just as he did in 1832. Women should have the right to inherit and own money. In fact, according to Mill, economic equality will be the easiest of the laws supporting the subjection of women to be overturned. But (here we are again with a "but"),

> when the support of the family depends, not on property, but on earnings, the common arrangement, by which the man earns the income and the wife superintends the domestic expenditure, seems to me in general the most suitable division of labor between the two persons.[19]

Although Mill doesn't repeat the faux pas of saying that women will "naturally" choose not to work after they marry or that their "occupation should rather be to adorn and beautify" as he did in 1832, the ideal is still the same. The main reason women can't work once they have married is because of all the housework they will be doing.

If, in addition to the physical suffering of bearing children, and the whole responsibility of their care and education in early years, the wife undertakes the careful and economical application of the husband's earnings to the general comfort of the family; she takes not only her fair share, but usually the larger share, of the bodily and mental exertion required by their joint existence. If she undertakes any additional portion, it seldom relieves her from this, but only prevents her from performing it properly.

Whether she works or not outside the home, a wife will still be doing all the work inside the home, because no one else will do it, according to Mill. So, Mill's kindness suggests that women would be better off with only one job: the work inside the house.

Mill is quite aware of the enormous amount of work hidden beneath the term "housework" as he demonstrates in the detailed outline he gives of "women's" work. However, what Mill fails to imagine is the possibility of sharing that housework as well as sharing the work outside the home. Mill knows that "The *power* of earning is essential to the dignity of a woman." Mill is clear that women are capable and willing and should be granted the equality of a career. Yet he seems completely unable to picture a world that will include men who are capable and willing and should be granted the equality of sharing in the work of a family. Mill must be seen as a Victorian man and not judged too harshly for this failure, especially since the data from "Second Shift" and "Halving It All" reveal that this kind of failure of imagination is still quite common and is still having practical consequences.[20]

The third divergence between Taylor and Mill is connected to the question of division of labor within a family. Mill argues that marriage should be like a business partnership with no one legally in control. As in a partnership, who makes the decisions on what issues is decided between the partners either by a prearranged legal contract, or by mutual agreement. Likewise the final power to decide in various aspects of a marriage contract could be "pre-appointed," but must be flexible and reflect individual differences. (Listen for a "but" coming) However, the one with the most age, most wealth, or most intelligence will usually make the decisions. And since husbands are usually older, richer, and better educated, well, you can fill in the blanks. Given that Mill, at his worst, believes that women are more practical and more likely to have "nervous susceptibility" and that they should not work outside the home, guess who gets to make the decisions about the nanny and who decides about finances?

SIMILARITIES

Now for my own "however." Before we become too critical of Mill, we should spend some time on all of the ideas that he and Taylor agreed on. *The Subjection of Women* is much longer than "Enfranchisement of Women" and hence had to be cut much more for inclusion in this volume. I confess that I purposefully included the sections that show the divergence between Taylor's and Mill's ideas. You'll need to read all of the *Subjection* in order to see how frequently they agree on all the ideas listed below.

- Inequality is both unjust and inexpedient.
- Women's legal and social subordination to men is fundamentally unfair and it stunts human development.
- In particular, it prevents human progress by intellectually and morally corrupting both husband and wife in an unequal marriage.
- In a "companionate" marriage men's intellectual development is prevented because he spends his free time with someone who has little education and, hence, little ability to push him to think harder about a subject.
- Inequality leads both men and women to be less moral. Because women have no legal power, they learn to use manipulation and sexuality to control men in immoral ways.
- Men who care about their wives are distracted from public virtues by their companion's whose sole concern is the advancement of their individual family's status.
- Women are trained and educated by society to be subservient and, hence, they do not fight for equality because their subordination has numbed them to the possibility and importance of freedom.[21]
- Families are important agents of moral and political education. Until children are raised in an atmosphere of equality, until girls are taught as boys are, until wives have the same choices husbands have, society will not be as developed as it can be.
- Domestic violence is in part a direct result of women's legal and economic inequality and will not cease until the fundamental causes are eliminated.
- The reason men promote inequality is that they like it. They fail to understand that ultimately they, as well as women, suffer from its continuation.
- The kind of vigorous intellectual equality Taylor and Mill themselves enjoyed is the only means of social advancement.
- What has been the case, what is customary, does not help us understand what women are capable of or how men and women ought to live together.
- We need to open the educational, legal, and economic gates to women and see what happens in order to know what is possible.
- Laws need not prohibit what is unnatural. If women naturally want to stay at home, there is no need for laws banning women's labor.

That inequality is unjust seems fairly obvious, but the argument that Taylor and Mill make that women's subordination is inexpedient is more interesting. Liberal Victorians were intent on eliminating the laws that had prevented the unleashing of human potential. Taylor and Mill seemed to recognize that changing laws alone would be inadequate. The moral and intellectual atmosphere within the family was the key to human development. If other couples could experience what they had—the intellectual give-and-take of argument, in the freedom to travel, retain control of money, and work together, and in the willingness to question each other's moral stances—other partners would push each other into a new era of progress. As long as one-half of the species was forced to be underdeveloped, they would drag everyone down to their level. Men like the privileges their gender enjoyed and they would not be persuaded on the high plain of justice, but perhaps the image of a stultified society that cannot improve further without granting women equality in marriage, jobs, and law would convince them.

For readers unaccustomed to Victorian literature, I must say a word about the unfair and inaccurate way Taylor and Mill think about class. In several places they make disparaging remarks about the aggressiveness and general moral inadequacies of the lower classes. This kind of rhetoric was fairly common in this period. Race, class, and gender were all seen through a lens of bigotry that was very hard to overcome. As we see in Taylor and Mill, just because they saw the unfairness of assumptions about women, does not mean they see the same injustice in their presumptions about class.

REACTIONS

Reactions to both pieces varied widely. In England, on the one hand, the "Enfranchisement" article was welcomed by the radicals like George Holyoake who reprinted it (without permission). On the other hand, Carlyle's misogynist declaration that Taylor was a "silly woman" who might be better off quietly darning socks,[22] parallels Charlotte Brontë's proclamation that the author "had a hard, jealous heart, muscles of iron, and nerves of bent leather; of a woman who longed for power, and had never felt affection."[23] Meanwhile American feminists like Lucretia Mott, Lucy Stone, and Susan B. Anthony rejoiced in the article. Indeed, according to Evelyn Pugh, "reprinted many times in pamphlet form, the 'Enfranchisement of Women' became one of the best-selling tracts of the American women's rights movement."[24]

The reactions in Europe were more mixed. Freud, as you might expect, warned his fiancée of such ideas, and he could not imagine his sweet "girl" competing for jobs, but only envisioned her, as nature had appointed her, secluded in his house.[25] Oddly, Nietzsche studied these works and agreed with their vision of marriage as an intellectual partnership.[26] From home or abroad, the reactions to Taylor's radical vision of equality in marriage, careers, education, and before the law were passionately positive or negative.

Reactions to Mill's piece published eighteen years after Taylor's varied from the extremely negative to the bland approval. Because of Mill's reputation as a scholar, *The Subjection* received critical review, most of it loud and very negative criticism in intellectual circles of England and beyond. Many critics were incensed by Mill's descriptions of domestic abuse. William James was sure that such violence did not occur in America.[27] But even the feminists such as Lucy Stone and Susan B. Anthony who had enthusiastically endorsed Taylor's article were silent on Mill's book, while Elizabeth Cady Stanton openly disagreed with Mill's ideas.[28] (It is important to remember that the Civil War took place between the publication of Taylor's and Mill's work.)

And after the initial vehement philosophical responses—nothing. Few, if any, mentioned the book in classrooms, in commentaries, or in summaries of Mill's ideas. Historians of philosophy buried it until a hundred years later, when in 1970 Alice Rossi published a reprint of both Taylor's and Mill's work on this subject and her commentary on it. Although now Mill's work has become a staple in feminist theory courses, rarely does a history of nineteenth-century philosophy course include either work. And ironically, despite its initial reception by feminists and despite its obvious inconsistencies, *Subjection of Women* is far better known than "Enfranchisement of Women."

Conclusion

Both Taylor's and Mill's work is so far ahead of its time that both pieces still feel fresh and controversial. Certainly these issues still confront us daily. How should we live? How should we live with one another? These are fundamental questions of ethics and political philosophy that philosophers have argued about since the beginning of philosophy. Taylor and Mill made us realize that there is a question of gender hidden in these questions. How should we live together requires us to figure out how men and women should delegate power. How we should live requires us to figure out what role work and family should play in both partners' lives.

Questions for Reflection

Regarding marriage and family life: Do you think family life is an appropriate topic for political philosophy? Do you think Taylor was right in her early essay that we should abandon marriage as an institution? Defend your answer to each question.

Regarding economic equality: Do you agree that women will not have true equality until they have economic equality? Do you think the Mill's are correct in their assertion that domestic violence persists because women are not economically independent? Are there clear examples where women do and women do not have "true equality" and "economic independence" in today's world? Defend your answers.

Do you agree with the argument, defended by both Taylor and John Stuart Mill, that inequality harms men (not just women) both morally and intellectually? Why or why not?

Notes

1. John Stuart Mill, *Autobiography*, in *Collected Works of John Stuart Mill*, vol. 1, ed. J. M. Robson (Toronto: University of Toronto Press, 1963), 239. Cited in Fred Wilson, "John Stuart Mill," *Stanford Encyclopedia of Philosophy* (Fall 2007), ed. Edward N. Zalta, http://plato.stanford.edu/archives/fall2007/entries/mill/.

2. The point is not that motive and duty are irrelevant; rather, their relevance is unpacked in terms of utility—the utility of acting from a certain motive or in accordance with a specific duty.

3. In order to avoid the problem with "the greatest happiness principle" of needing to maximize two independent variables at the same time, many contemporary utilitarians state the principle of utilitarianism in other ways: for example, an act (kind of act, rule) is right if and only if no alternative act (kind of act, rule) produces greater net utility (usually understood as "pleasure minus pain").

4. If, as most contemporary feminist philosophers now agree, Plato was not the first male feminist philosopher, then probably the first was Mill.

5. Dale E. Miller, "Harriet Taylor Mill," *Stanford Encyclopedia of Philosophy* (Summer 2002), ed. Edward N. Zalta, http://plato.stanford.edu/archives/sum2002/entries/harriet-mill/. Miller offers full bibliographical citations on the names of these critics and the source of the quotes excerpted here.

6. Harriet Taylor Mill, "Enfranchisement of Women," in *The Complete Works of Harriet Taylor Mill*, ed. Jo Ellen Jacobs and Paula Payne (Bloomington: Indiana University Press, 1998), 51–73.

7. John Stuart Mill, *Subjection of Women*, in *Essays on Sex Equality*, ed. Alice S. Rossi (Chicago: University of Chicago Press, 1970), 125–242.

8. Rossi, *Essays on Sex Equality*, chap. 2.

9. Julia Annas, "Mill and the Subjection of Women," *Philosophy* 52 (1977): 179–94.

10. Richard W. Krouse, "Patriarchal Liberalism and Beyond: From John Stuart Mill to Harriet Taylor," in *The Family in Political Thought*, ed. Jean Bethke Elshtain (Amherst: University of Massachusetts Press, 1982), 145–72.

11. Gail Tulloch, *Mill and Sexual Equality* (Boulder, CO: Lynne Rienner Publishers, 1989).

12. Rossi, *Essays on Sex Equality*, chap. 2.

13. For more consideration of this topic see Jo Ellen Jacobs, *The Voice of Harriet Taylor Mill* (Bloomington: Indiana University Press, 2002), chap. 3.

14. See Jacobs, *Complete Works of Harriet Taylor Mill*, 27–31.

15. John Stuart Mill, *Subjection of Women*.

16. See, for example, Carol Gilligan, *In a Different Voice: Psychological Theory and Women's Development* (Cambridge, MA: Harvard University Press, 1982); and Monique Wittig, "One is Not Born a Woman," in *Feminist Frameworks*, ed. Alison M. Jaggar and Paula S. Rothenberg (New York: McGraw-Hill, 1993).

17. Harriet Taylor Mill, "Enfranchisement of Women,"

18. Taylor and Mill coauthored a number of newspaper articles around the time this article was written about the horrors of domestic violence and the unfairness of abuse laws. See Jacobs, *Complete Works of Harriet Taylor Mill*, chap. 4.

19. John Stuart Mill, *Subjection of Women*.

20. Arlie Russell Hochschild, *The Second Shift* (New York: Avon Books, 1999); and Francine M. Deutsch, *Halving It All: How Equally Shared Parenting Works* (Cambridge, MA: Harvard University Press, 1999).

21. Their idea is similar to Martha Nussbaum's that a woman in India, for example, might not know that she is suffering just because she is only allowed to eat leftovers after men have eaten. Nussbaum, *Upheavals of Thought: The Intelligence of Emotions* (Cambridge, UK: Cambridge University Press, 2001), 309.

22. See Harriet Blodgett, *Centuries of Female Days: Englishwomen's Private Diaries* (New Brunswick, NJ: Rutgers University Press, 1988), 134.

23. Bronte thought it was the work of a woman with these traits until she mistakenly learned that it was written by Mill. See Jacobs, *The Voice of Harriet Taylor Mill*, 220.

24. Evelyn L. Pugh, "John Stuart Mill, Harriet Taylor, and Women's Rights in America, 1850–1873," *Canadian Journal of History* 13 (1978): 426.

25. Letters of Sigmund Freud, see Jacobs, *The Voice of Harriet Taylor Mill*, 221.

26. Ruth Abbey, "Odd Bedfellows: Nietzsche and Mill on Marriage," *History of European Ideas* 23 (1997): 81–104.

27. Pugh, "Women's Rights in America," 439.

28. Pugh, "Women's Rights in America," 434–35.

CHAPTER 12

Heidegger and Arendt

Introduction by *Karen J. Warren*

Martin Heidegger (1889–1976) and Hannah Arendt (1906–1975) are two very different personalities whose lives are interconnected personally and philosophically by a mutual interest in thinking and a grounding of philosophy in lived experience. This introduction begins with brief biographical remarks, followed by a relatively lengthy philosophical description of Heidegger's main claims in *Being and Time* (1928), and a description of key components of Arendt's writings that is intended to supplement the account of Arendt's life and work in the chapter's commentary.

HEIDEGGER

Heidegger was born into a Catholic family in Messkirch, Germany, and, as a youth, prepared for the priesthood. In 1906, at the age of seventeen, he read Franz Brentano's book *On the Manifold Meaning of Being According to Aristotle*, which inspired his interest in the meaning of Being. In 1913, he completed a doctorate in philosophy at Freiburg University.

His academic career was interrupted frequently during the next ten years, particularly when he began active military duty in 1918. He returned to Freiburg in 1919 as Husserl's assistant and began lecturing on phenomenology, Aristotle, and even a radical reinterpretation of Husserl's phenomenology. In 1923 Heidegger moved to Marburg University where he began teaching.[1] The publication of *Being and Time* earned Heidegger a full professorship at Marburg; subsequently, Heidegger became rector of the university and, in 1933, joined the Nazi party. After the war, he was forbidden by the Allied forces to teach.

From the mid-1940s until his death, Heidegger wrote, lectured, and published prolifically, including "Letter on Humanism" (1947), "The Way to Language" (1959), and "The End of Philosophy and the Task of Thinking" (1964). But unquestionably, the work for which he is best known is *Being and Time*.

Heidegger's *Being and Time* is an answer to the question, "What is the meaning of Being?" According to Heidegger, Western philosophers since Socrates have discussed beings in the world, even the world itself (ontic issues), but not what "being itself" is (ontological issues). In fact, "it was Heidegger's original intention to write a second half of the book, consisting in a *'Destruktion'* of the history of philosophy—a transformation of philosophy by re-tracing its history but he never completed this project."[2]

Heidegger's methodology in *Being and Time* is often described as "hermeneutical phenomenology"—an approach to philosophy that rejects abstract theorizing in favor of uncovering the hidden meanings in our experience. One way this method is described is by analogy to a view of life as a text, where the purpose of our lives—and the challenge to philosophers—is to interpret the text.[3]

I begin with Heidegger's views about the nature of "Being" (*Dasein*) as human being, provided by Heidegger in *Being and Time*. I then proceed in step-like fashion, from Heidegger's starting point views on human beings to Heidegger's culminating views on Being and authenticity. This approach is intended to provide a clear, non-technical understanding of Heidegger's views in a way that starts where Heidegger starts—with Being as human being—without becoming mired in technical terms and deep conceptual issues of interest to Heidegger scholars.

For Heidegger, (1) "Being" may refer either to Being itself or to the ways Being reveals itself through beings in space and time—human beings.[4] The human being is a unique being in several respects. (2) For one thing, a human being is self-aware. Unlike other beings, humans both question Being ("What is Being?") and question our own being ("What is it to be a human being? to be this particular human being?"). The distinctive self-questioning of human beings makes Being aware of its existence as being (as human being). (3) What the preceding implies is that one way humans are distinguished from other beings is that other beings just *are*, while self-questioning humans *"ex-ist."* A human being is a "being-in-the-world," a spatiotemporal being that is the manifestation (or "disclosure") of Being. When Being exists as beings (in the plural and in space and time, as human beings), then human existence is called *Dasein* ("being-there"). (4) A second way human beings are distinguished from other beings and other things that exist is through "negation." As Minnich claims (see glossary): "a tree is not a star, I am not you, the future is not yet." For Heidegger, distinguishing among beings by what they are not means that (and is stated by Heidegger as) negation is intrinsic to beings. Being (existence itself) discloses itself through spatiotemporal beings in terms of this sort of negation. (5) A third way that human beings are distinctive among beings is tied to human self-awareness and awareness of others: "being-in-the-world" involves "being-with-others" in such a way that human beings "care" for other beings and for Being itself. (6) A fourth way human existence is different from the existence of rocks and trees is that beings as Being are aware of possibilities, decisions, and choices (and rocks and trees are not). One possibility is for being to choose to embrace or turn away from Being. When one raises the question, "Why is there something rather than nothing?" the answer reveals the fundamental meaning of Being (*Dasein*): Being is aware that among its possibilities is death (mortality). Heidegger calls this awareness "being-toward-death." With death, "being-in-the-world" becomes (through negation) "no-longer-being-there." Unfortunately, (7) the awareness of *Dasein* as "being-toward-death" causes beings-in-the-world existential *angst* (anxiety or dread) about their own death.

Faced with their own mortality, human beings have two choices: (8) they may try to avoid this *angst* by turning away from Being and ignoring their individuality (for example, by trying to "blend in," "fade undetected into the crowd," no longer be a distinct "I" but be part of a "they"), or (9) they may accept that the meaning of death is inherently within life. Stated in non-Heideggerian language, humans are free to turn away from Being and deny their true selves as mortal, thinking beings. This occurs when humans replace the sort of "thinking for itself," which Heidegger identifies with Socrates ("pure thinking") with conventional, non-reflective or habitual thinking that generates customary ready-made answers. (10) When human beings chose the first option, their existence (the existence of being) is "inauthentic." One might say that an "inauthentic" life is one lived "contrary to one's nature." When human beings ("being") chose the second action, being accepts its mortality and achieves a radical openness to Being—both Being as it reveals itself (being-in-the-world) and as it withdraws (negates) itself (being-toward-death).

Heidegger tries to redirect being (humans) toward authenticity: (11) Human beings can choose the second option—to accept that "being-toward-death" (their mortality) is inherent in "being-in-the-world"—and embrace the *angst* of beings who know they will become "no-longer-being-there." Choosing this option permits humans to rediscover the wonder and puzzlement of genuinely open-ended thinking that asks what is being? (12) This choice leads to an authentic existence—an existence that is an openness to Being, caring for other beings and Being itself—and a return to thinking for itself. Being makes possible such opportunities for being in the world.

ARENDT

Hannah Arendt was born into a German-Jewish family in Hanover, Germany. In 1924, she went to Marburg University to study with Martin Heidegger, with whom she had a love affair, a broken friendship, and a life-long intellectual relationship. She went to Heidelberg University in 1926, where she received a Ph.D. in philosophy under the supervision of Karl Jaspers. Arendt fled Hitler's Germany for France in 1933, working for a number of Jewish refugee organizations, until she immigrated to the United States in 1940, becoming a naturalized citizen in 1951. She held a number of academic positions at various American universities (Princeton, Berkeley, the University of Chicago, Columbia, Northwestern, and Cornell, as well as the graduate faculty in political and social research at the New School) until her death in 1975.

Arendt is best known for three works, *The Origins of Totalitarianism* (1951), a study of the Nazi and Stalinist regimes, *The Human Condition* (1958), a philosophical study of the *vita activa* (the life of labor, work, action), and *Eichmann in Jerusalem: A Report on the Banality of Evil* (1963), written after having attended the trial of Adolf Eichmann in Jerusalem in 1961 as a reporter for the *New Yorker* magazine. In it Arendt explored the startling, troubling thesis that came to her as she listened to Eichmann at his trial: that monstrous evil can be done by people who are themselves petty, banal—radically thoughtless—and so are able to do the unthinkable. At the time of her death in 1975, she had completed the first two volumes of her last major philosophical work, *The Life of the Mind*; *Thinking* and *Willing* were published posthumously in 1978.

Because commentator Elizabeth Minnich discusses Arendt's views in some detail, I comment only briefly on her philosophical work.

Arendt is well known as one of the leading political philosophers of the twentieth century, even though her writing resists traditional categorization. It is more fitting, especially given Arendt's critique of traditional (canonical) approaches to philosophical issues, to describe some of the topics interwoven throughout Arendt's works: for example, totalitarianism; revolution; freedom; thinking and judging; "natality" as "the human condition" for action; "the banality of evil, " and the *vita activa*. These are just some of the topics that are interwoven throughout Arendt's works.

MINNICH'S COMMENTARY

Minnich's commentary begins with important biographical and historical information about Heidegger's and Arendt's intertwined lives, particularly their differences on Nazism. After describing Heidegger's interest in the role of raw, disruptive thinking to the authentic existence of beings-in-the-world, Minnich asks the reader whether a philosopher's actions during her or his lifetime are relevant to understanding and evaluating their philosophical writings. That straightforward question plunges one into the phenomenological world of thinking about concrete experiences to describe the philosophizing at the center of Heidegger's and Arendt's writings.

Minnich's commentary proceeds to discuss similarities and differences between Heidegger and Arendt on several interrelated topics: (1) thinking and its relation to action—and the dangers of thinking removed from action and public life; (2) ontology, understood as what it means to be, and the nature of Being or, in the case of humans, *Dasein;* (3) the phenomenological method of philosophizing; (4) the role of opinion and generalizations in politics; (5) the conflation of meaning and truth; (6) human mortality and "natality" (Arendt's term for the human condition for action); (7) the masculinized nature of the history of Western philosophy; and (8) evil as done by people who have not thought deeply about good and evil. Minnich ends the commentary where it began, with an explanation of why, for both Arendt and Heidegger, Socrates is the example of a thinker, and teacher of thinking, who philosophizes through thinking, rather than thinking in order to come to an end in knowledge.

Excerpts of Writings by Heidegger and Arendt

I. EXCERPTS FROM ARENDT, "THINKING AND MORAL CONSIDERATION: A LECTURE"[5]

To talk about thinking seems to me so presumptuous that I feel I owe you a justification. Some years ago, reporting the trial of Eichmann in Jerusalem, I spoke of "the banality of evil" and meant with this no theory or doctrine but something quite factual, the phenomenon of evil deeds, committed on a gigantic scale, which could not be traced to an particularity of wickedness, pathology, or ideological conviction in the doer, whose only personal distinction was a perhaps extraordinary shallowness. However monstrous the deeds were, the doer was neither monstrous nor demonic, and the only specific characteristic one could detect in his past as well as in his behavior during the trial and the preceding police examination was something entirely negative: it was not stupidity but a curious, quite authentic inability to think. He functioned in the role of prominent war criminal as well as he had under the Nazi regime; he had not the slightest difficulty in accepting an entirely different set of rules. He knew that what he had once considered his duty was now called a crime, and he accepted this new code of judgment as though it were nothing but another language rule. To his rather limited supply of stock phrases he had added a few new ones, and he was utterly helpless only when he was confronted with a situation to which none of them would apply, as in the most grotesque instance when he had to make a speech under the gallows and was forced to rely on clichés used in funeral oratory which were inapplicable in his case because he was not the survivor. Considering what his last words should be in case of a death sentence, which he had expected all along, this simple fact had not occurred to him, just as inconsistencies and flagrant contradictions in examination and cross-examinations during the trial had not bothered him. Clichés, stock phrases, adherence to conventional, standardized codes of expression and conduct have the socially recognized function of protecting us against reality, that is, against the claim on our thinking attention which all events and facts arouse by virtue of their existence. If we were responsive to this claim all the time, we would soon be exhausted; the difference in Eichmann was only that he clearly knew of no such claim at all.

This total absence of thinking attracted my interest. Is evil-doing, not just the sins of omission but the sins of commission, possible in the absence of not merely "base motives" (as the law calls it) but of any motives at all, any particular prompting of interest or volition? Is wickedness, however we may define it, this being "determined to prove a villain," *not* a necessary condition for evil-doing? Is our ability to judge, to tell right from wrong, beautiful from ugly, dependent upon our faculty of thought? Do the inability to think and a disastrous failure of what we commonly call conscience coincide? The question that imposed itself was: Could the activity of thinking as such, the habit of examining and reflecting upon whatever happens to come to pass, regardless of specific content and quite independent of results, could this activity be of such a nature that it "conditions" men against evil-doing? (The very word *conscience*, at any rate, points in this direction insofar as it means "to know with my self," a kind of knowledge that is actualized in every thinking process.) Finally, is not the urgency of these questions enforced by the well-known and rather alarming fact that only good people are ever bothered by a bad conscience whereas it is a very rare phenomenon among real criminals? A good conscience does not exist except as the absence of a bad one.

Let me sum up my three main propositions in order to restate our problem, the inner connection between the ability or inability to think and the problem of evil.

First, if such a connection exists at all, then the faculty of thinking, as distinguished from the thirst for knowledge, must be ascribed to everybody; it cannot be a privilege of the few.

Second, if Kant is right and the faculty of thought has a "natural aversion" against accepting its own results as "solid axioms" then we cannot expect any moral propositions or commandments, no final code of conduct from the thinking activity, least of all a new and now allegedly final definition of what is good and what is evil.

Third, if it is true that thinking deals with invisibles, it follows that it is out of order because we normally move in a world of appearances in which the most radical experience of disappearance is death. The gift for dealing with things that do not appear has often been believed to exact a price—the price of blinding the thinker or the poet to the visible world. Think of Homer, whom the gods gave the divine gift by striking him with blindness; think of Plato's *Phaedo* where those who do philosophy appear to those who don't, the many, like people who pursue death. Think of Zeno, the founder of Stoicism, who asked the Delphic Oracle what he should do to attain the best life and was answered, "Take on the color of the dead."

Hence the question is unavoidable: How can anything relevant for the world we live in arise out of so resultless an enterprise? An answer, if at all, can come only from the thinking activity, the performance itself, which means that we have to trace experiences rather than doctrines. And where do we turn for these experiences?

In brief, I propose to use a man as our model who did think without becoming a philosopher, a citizen among citizens, doing nothing, claiming nothing that, in his view, every citizen should do and had a right to claim. You will have guessed that I intend to speak about Socrates, and I hope that no one will seriously dispute that my choice is historically justifiable.

The first thing that strikes us in Plato's Socratic dialogues is that they are all aporetic. The argument either leads nowhere or it goes around in circles. In order to know what justice is one must know what knowledge is, and in order to know that, one must have a previous, unexamined notion of knowledge. (Thus in *Theaetetus* and *Charmides*.) Hence, "A man cannot try to discover either what he knows or what he does not know." If he knows, "there is no need of inquiry; if he does not know . . . he does not even know what he is to look for" (*Meno* 80). Or, in the *Euthyphro*: In order to be pious I must know what piety is. Pious are the things that please the gods; but are they pious because they please the gods or do they please the gods because they are pious? None of the *logoi*, the arguments, ever stays put; they move about, because Socrates, asking questions to which he does *not* know the answers, sets them in motion. And once the statements have come full circle, it is usually Socrates who cheerfully proposes to start all over again and inquire about the meaning of justice or piety or knowledge.

For the topics of these early dialogues deal with very simple, everyday concepts, such as arise whenever people open their mouths and being to talk. The introduction usually runs as follows: To be sure, there are happy people, just deeds, courageous men, beautiful things to see and admire, everybody knows about them; the trouble starts with our usage of nouns, presumably derived from those adjectives which we apply to particular cases as they *appear* to us (we *see* a happy man, *perceive* the courageous dead or the just decision), that is, with such words as *happiness, courage, justice*, etc., which we not call concepts and which Solon called the "non-appearing measure" (*aphanes metron*) "most difficult for the mind to comprehend, but nevertheless holding the limits of all things:—and Plato somewhat later called ideas perceivable only by the eyes of the mind. These words, used to group together seen and manifest qualities and occurrences but nevertheless relating to something unseen, are part and parcel of our everyday speech, and still we can give no account of them; when we try to define them, they get slippery; when we talk about their meaning, nothing stays put anymore, everything begins to move. So instead of repeating what we learned from Aristotle, that Socrates was the man who discovered the "concept," we should ask ourselves what Socrates did when he discovered it.

The word *house* is something like a frozen thought which thinking must unfreeze; defrost as it were, whenever it wants to find out its original meaning. In medieval philosophy, this kind of thinking was called meditation, and the word should be heard as different from, even opposed to, contemplation. In any event, this kind of pondering reflection does not product definitions and in this sense is entirely without results; it might however be that those who, for whatever reason, have pondered the meaning of the word *house* will make their apartments look a bit better—though not necessarily so and certainly without being conscious of anything so verifiable as cause and effect. Meditation is not the same as deliberation, which indeed is supposed to end in tangible result; and meditation does not aim at deliberation although it sometimes, by no means very often, turns into it.

Socrates, however, who is commonly said to have believed in the teachability of virtue, seems indeed to have held that talking and thinking about piety, justice, courage, and the rest were liable to make men more pious, more just, more courageous, even though they were not given either definitions or "values" to direct their further conduct.

Let us look briefly at the three similes. *First*, Socrates is a gadfly: he knows how to arouse the citizens who, without him, will "sleep on undisturbed for the rest of their lives," unless somebody else comes along to wake them up again. And what does he arouse them to? To thinking, to examining matters, an activity without which life, according to him, was not only not worth much but was not fully alive.

Second, Socrates is a midwife: Here the implication is threefold—the "sterility" I mentioned before, the expert knowledge of delivering others of their thoughts, that is, of the implications of their opinions, and the Greek midwife's function of deciding whether the child was fit to live or, to use Socratic language, was a mere "windegg," of which the bearer must be cleansed. In this context, only the last two of these implications matter. For looking at the Socratic dialogues, there is nobody among Socrates; interlocutors who ever brought forth a thought that was no windegg. He rather did what Plato, certainly thinking of Socrates, said of the sophists: he purged people of their "opinions," that is, of those unexamined prejudgments which prevent thinking by suggesting that we know where we not only don't know but cannot know, helping them, as Plato remarks, to get rid of what was bad in them, their opinions, without however making them good, giving them truth.

Third, Socrates, knowing that we don't know and still unwilling to let it go at that, remains steadfast with his own perplexities and, like the electric ray, paralyzes with them whomever he comes into contact with. The electric ray, at first glance, seems to be the opposite of the gadfly; it paralyzes where the gadfly arouses. Yet, what cannot but look like paralysis from the outside and the ordinary course of human affairs is felt as the highest state of being alive. There exist, despite the scarcity of documentary evidence for the thinking experience, a number of utterances of the thinkers throughout the centuries to this effect. Socrates himself, very much aware that thinking deals with invisibles and is itself invisible, lacking all the outside manifestation of other activities, seems to have used the metaphor of the wind for it: "The winds themselves are invisible, yet what they do is manifest to us and we somehow feel their approach." (The same metaphor, incidentally, is used by Heidegger who also speaks of the "storm of thought.")

The trouble—and the reason why the same man can be understood and understand himself as gadfly as well as electric ray—is that this same wind, whenever it is aroused, has the peculiarity of doing away with its own previous manifestations. It is in its nature to undo, unfreeze as it were, what language, the medium of thinking, has frozen into thought—words (concepts, sentences, definitions, doctrines), whose "weakness" and inflexibility Plato denounces so splendidly in the *Seventh Letter*. The consequence of this peculiarity is that thinking inevitably has a destructive, undermining effect on all established criteria, values, measurements for good and evil, in short on those customs and rules of conduct we treat of in morals and ethics. These frozen thoughts, Socrates seems to say, come so handy you can use them in your sleep; but if the wind of thinking, which I shall now arouse in you, has roused you from your sleep and made you fully awake and alive, then you will see that you have nothing in your hand but perplexities, and the most we can do with them is share them with each other.

Hence, the paralysis of thought is twofold: It is inherent in the *stop* and think, the interruption of all other activities, and it may have a paralyzing effect when you come out of it, no longer sure of what had seemed to you beyond doubt while you were unthinkingly engaged in whatever you were doing. If your action consisted in applying general rules of conduct to particular cases as they arise in ordinary life, then you will find yourself paralyzed because no such rules can withstand the wind of thought. To use once more the example of the frozen thought inherent in the word *house*, once you have thought about its implied meaning—dwelling, having a home, being housed—you are no longer likely to accept for your own home whatever the fashion of the time may prescribe; but this by no means guarantees that you will be able to come up with an acceptable solution for your own housing problems. You may be paralyzed.

This leads to the last and, perhaps, even greatest danger of this dangerous and resultless enterprise. In the circle around Socrates, there were men like Alcibiades and Critias—God knows, by no means the worst among his so-called pupils—and they had turned out to be a very real threat to the polis, and this not by being paralyzed by the electric ray but, on the contrary, by having been aroused by the gadfly. What they had been aroused to was license and cynicism. They had not been content with being taught how to think without being taught a doctrine, and they changed the non-results of the Socratic thinking examination into negative results: If we cannot define what piety is, let us be impious—which is pretty much the opposite of what Socrates had hoped to achieve by talking about piety.

The quest for meaning, which relentlessly dissolves and examines anew all accepted doctrines and rules, can at every moment turn against itself, as it were, produce a reversal of the old values, and declare these as "new values."

What we commonly call nihilism—and are tempted to date historically, decry politically, and ascribe to thinkers who allegedly dared to think "dangerous thoughts"—is actually a danger inherent in the thinking activity itself. There are no dangerous thoughts; thinking itself is dangerous, but nihilism is not its product. Nihilism is but the other side of conventionalism; its creed consists of negations of the current, so-called positive values to which it remains bound. All critical examinations must go through a stage of at least hypothetically negating accepted opinions and "values" by finding out their implications and tacit assumptions, and in this sense nihilism may be seen as an ever-present danger of thinking. But this danger does not arise out of the Socratic conviction that an unexamined life is not worth living but, on the contrary, out of the desire to find results which would make further thinking unnecessary. Thinking is equally dangerous to all creeds and, by itself, does not bring forth any new creed.

However, non-thinking, which seems so recommendable a state for political and moral affairs, also has its dangers. By shielding people against the dangers of examination, it teaches them to hold fast to whatever the prescribed rules of conduct may be at a given time in a given society. What people then get used to is not so much the content of the rules, a close examination of which would always lead them into perplexity, as the possession of rules under which to subsume particulars. In other words, they get used to never making up their minds. If somebody then should show up who, for whatever reasons and purposes, wishes to abolish the old "values" or virtues, he will find it easy enough provided he offers a new code, and he will need no force and no persuasion—no proof that the new values are better than the old ones—to enforce it. The faster men held to the old code, the more eager will they be to assimilate themselves to the new one; the ease with which such reversals can take place under certain circumstances suggests indeed that everybody is asleep when they occur. This century has offered us some experience in such matters: How easy was it for the totalitarian rulers to reverse the basic commandments of Western morality—"Thou shalt not kill" in the case of Hitler's German, "Thou shalt not bear false testimony against thy neighbor" in the case of Stalin's Russia.

To come back to Socrates. The Athenians told him that thinking was subversive, that the wind of thought was a hurricane which sweeps away all the established signs by which men orient themselves in the world; it brings disorder into the cities and it confuses the citizens, especially the young ones. And though Socrates denied that thinking corrupts, he did not pretend that it improves, and though he declared that "no greater good has ever befallen" the polis than what he was doing, he did not pretend that he started his career as a philosopher in order to become such a great benefactor. If "an unexamined life is not worth living," then thinking accompanies living when it concerns itself with such concepts as justice, happiness, temperance, pleasure, with words for invisible things which language has offered us to express the meaning of whatever happens in life and occurs to use while we are alive.

Socrates calls this quest for meaning *erôs*, a kind of love which is primarily a need—it desires what it has not—and which is the only matter he pretends to be an expert in. Men are in love with wisdom and do philosophy (*philosophein*) because they are not wise, just as they are in love with beauty and "do beauty," as it were (*philokalein*, as Pericles called it) because they are not beautiful. Love, by desiring what is not there, establishes a relationship with it. To bring this relationship into the open, make it appear, men speak about it in the same way the lover wants to speak about his beloved. Since the quest is a kind of love and desire, the objects of thought can only be lovable things—beauty, wisdom, justice, etc. Ugliness and evil are excluded by definition from the thinking concern, although they may occasionally turn up as deficiencies, as lack of beauty, injustice, and evil (*kakia*) as lack of good. This means that they have no roots of their own, no essence of which thought could get hold. Evil, we are told, cannot be done voluntarily because of its "ontological status," as we would say today; it consists in an absence, in something that is not. If thinking dissolves normal, positive concepts into their original meaning, then the same process dissolves these negative "concepts" into their original meaninglessness, into nothing. This incidentally is by no means only Socrates' opinion; that evil is a mere privation, negation, or exception from the rule is the nearly unanimous opinion of all thinkers. (The most conspicuous and most dangerous fallacy in the proposition, as old as

Plato, "Nobody wants to do good." The sad truth of the matter is that most evil is done by people who never made up their mind to be either bad or good.)

Where does this leave us with respect to our problem—inability or refusal to think and the capacity of doing evil? We are left with the conclusion that only people filled with this *erôs,* this desiring love of wisdom, beauty, and justice, are capable of thought—that is, we are left with Plato's "noble nature" as a prerequisite for thinking. And this was precisely what we were not looking for when we raised the question whether the thinking activity, the very performance itself—as distinguished from the regardless of whatever qualities a man's nature, his soul, may possess—conditions him in such a way that he is incapable of evil.

Among the very few positive statements that Socrates, this lover of perplexities, ever made there are two propositions, closely connected with each other, which deal with our question.

The two positive Socratic propositions read as follows. The *first:* "It is better to be wronged than to do wrong"—to which Callicles, the interlocutor in the dialogue, replies what all Greece would have replied: "To suffer wrong is not the part of a man at all, but that of a slave for whom it is better to be dead than alive, as it is for anyone who is unable to come either to his own assistance when he is wronged or to that of anyone he cares about" . . . The *second:* "It would be better for me that my lyre or a chorus I directed should be out of tune and loud with discord, and that multitudes of men should disagree with me rather than that I, *being one,* should be out of harmony with myself and contradict *me*" . . . Which causes Callicles to tell Socrates that he is "going mad with eloquence," and that it would be better for him and everybody else if he would leave philosophy alone.

And there, as we shall see, he has a point. It was indeed philosophy, or rather the experience of thinking, that led Socrates to make these statements—although, of course, he did not start his enterprise in order to arrive at them. For it would be a serious mistake, I believe, to understand them as the results of some cognition about morality; they are insights, to be sure, but insights of experience, and as far as the thinking process itself is concerned they are at best incidental by-products.

It is rather as though he said to Callicles: If you were like me, in love with wisdom and in need of examining, and if the world should be as you depict it—divided into the strong and the weak where "the strong do what they can and the weak suffer what they must" (Thucydides)—so that no alternative exists but to either do or suffer wrong, then you would agree with me that it is better to suffer than to do. The presupposition is: if you were thinking, if you were to agree that "an unexamined life is not worth living."

It looks as though what we are tempted to understand as a purely moral proposition actually arises out of the thinking experience as such.

And this brings us to the second statement, which is the prerequisite of the first one. It, too, is highly paradoxical. . . . We call *consciousness* (literally, "to know with myself") the curious fact that in a sense I also am for myself, though I hardly appear to me, which indicates that the Socratic "being-one" is not so unproblematic as it seems; I am not only for others but for myself, and in this latter case, I clearly am not just one. A difference is inserted into my Oneness.

Without this original split, which Plato later used in his definition of thinking as the soundless dialogue (*eme emautô*) between me and myself, the two-in-one, which Socrates presupposes in his statement about harmony with myself, would not be possible. Consciousness is not the same as thinking; but without it thinking would be impossible. What thinking actualizes in its process is the difference given in consciousness.

For Socrates, this two-in-one simply meant that if you want to think you must see to it that the two who carry on the thinking dialogue be in good shape, that the partners be friends. It is better for you to suffer than to do wrong because you can remain the friend of the sufferer; who would want to be the friend of and have to live together with a murderer?

This is not a matter of wickedness or goodness, as it is not a matter of intelligence or stupidity. He who does not know the intercourse between me and myself (in which we examine what we say and what we do) will not mind contradicting himself, and this means he will never be either able or willing to give account of what he says or does; nor will he mind committing any crime, since he can be sure that it will be forgotten the next moment.

Thinking in its non-cognitive, non-specialized sense as a natural need of human life, the actualization of the difference given in consciousness, is not a prerogative of the few but an everpresent faculty of everybody; by the same token, inability to think is not the "prerogative" of those many who lack brain power but the everpresent possibility for everybody—scientists, scholars, and other specialists in mental enterprises not excluded—to shun that intercourse with oneself whose possibility and importance Socrates first discovered. We were here not concerned with wickedness, with which religion and literature have tried to come to terms, but with evil; not with sin and the great villains who became the negative heroes in literature and usually acted out of envy and resentment, but with the non-wicked everybody who has no special motives and for this reason is capable of *infinite* evil; unlike the villain, he never meets his midnight disaster.

For the thinking ego and its experience, conscience that "fills a man full of obstacles," is a side effect. And it remains a marginal affair for society at large except in emergencies. For thinking as such does society little good, much less than the thirst for knowledge in which it is used as an instrument for other purposes. It does not create values, it will not find out, once and for all, what "the good" is, and it does not confirm but rather dissolves accepted rules of conduct. Its political and moral significance comes out only in those rare moments in history when "Things fall apart; the centre cannot hold; mere anarchy is loosed upon the world"; when "the best lack all conviction, while the worst are full of passionate intensity."

At these moments, thinking ceases to be a marginal affair in political matters. When everybody is swept away unthinkingly by what everybody else does and believes in, those who think are drawn out of hiding because their refusal to join is conspicuous and thereby becomes a kind of action. The purging element in thinking, Socrates' midwifery, that brings out the implications of unexamined opinions and thereby destroys them—values, doctrines, theories, and even convictions—is political by implication. For this destruction has a liberating effect on another human faculty, the faculty of judgment, which one may call, with some justification, the most political of man's mental abilities. It is the faculty to judge *particulars* without subsuming them under those general rules which can be taught and learned until they grow into habits that can be replaced by other habits and rules.

The faculty of judging particulars (as Kant discovered it), the ability to say, "this is wrong," "this is beautiful," etc., is not the same as the faculty of thinking. Thinking deals with invisibles, with representations of things that are absent; judging always concerns particulars and things close at hand. But the two are interrelated in a way similar to the way consciousness and conscience are interconnected. If thinking, the two-in-one of the soundless dialogue, actualizes the differences within our identity as given in consciousness and thereby results in conscience as its by-product, then judging, the by-product of the liberating effect of thinking, realizes thinking, makes it manifest in the world of appearances, where I am never alone and always much too busy to be able to think. The manifestation of the wind of thought is no knowledge; it is the ability to tell right from wrong, beautiful from ugly. And this indeed may prevent catastrophes, at least for myself, in the rare moments when the chips are down.

II. EXCERPTS FROM HEIDEGGER'S "LETTER ON HUMANISM"[6]

Soon after Being and Time appeared a young friend asked me, "When are you going to write an ethics?" Where the essence of man is thought so essentially, i.e., solely from the question concerning the truth of Being, but still without elevating man to the center of beings, a longing necessarily awakens for a peremptory directive and for rules that say how man, experienced from ek-sistence toward Being, ought to live in a fitting manner. The desire for an ethics presses ever more ardently for fulfillment as the obvious no less than the hidden perplexity of man soars to immeasurable heights. The greatest care must be fostered upon the ethical bond at a time when technological man, delivered over to mass society, can be kept reliably on call only by gathering and ordering all his plans and activities in a way that corresponds to technology.

Who can disregard our predicament? Should we not safeguard and secure the existing bonds even if they hold human beings together ever so tenuously and merely for the present? Certainly. But does this need ever release thought from the task of thinking what still remains principally to be thought and, as Being, prior to all beings, is their guarantor and their truth? Even further, can thinking refuse to think Being after the latter has lain hidden so long in oblivion but at the same time has made itself known in the present moment of world history by the uprooting of all beings?

Before we attempt to determine more precisely the relationship between "ontology" and "ethics" we must ask what "ontology" and "ethics" themselves are. It becomes necessary to ponder whether what can be designated by both terms still remains near and proper to what is assigned to thinking, which as such has to think above all the truth of Being.

Of course if both "ontology" and "ethics," along with all thinking in terms of disciplines, become untenable, and if our thinking therewith becomes more disciplined, how then do matters stand with the question about the relation between these two philosophical disciplines?

Along with "logic" and "physics," "ethics" appeared for the first time in the school of Plato. These disciplines arose at a time when thinking was becoming "philosophy," philosophy *episteme* (science), and science itself a matter for schools and academic pursuits. In the course of a philosophy so understood, science waxed and thinking waned. Thinkers prior to this period knew neither a "logic" nor an "ethics" nor "physics." Yet their thinking was neither illogical nor immoral. But they did think *physis* in a depth and breadth that no subsequent "physics" was ever again able to attain. The tragedies of Sophocles—provided such a comparison is at all permissible—preserve the *êthos* in their sagas more primordially than Aristotle's lectures on "ethics." A saying of Heraclitus which consists of only three words says something so simply that from it the essence of the *êthos* immediately comes to light.

The saying of Heraclitus (Fragment 119) goes: *êthos anthropoi daimon.* This is usually translated, "A man's character is his daimon." This translation thinks in a modern way, not a Greek one. *Êthos* means abode, dwelling place. The word names the open region in which man dwells. The open region of his abode allows what pertains to man's essence, and what in thus arriving resides in nearness to him, to appear. The abode of man contains and preserves the advent of what belongs to man in his essence. According to Heraclitus's phrase this is *daimon*, the god. The fragment says: Man dwells, insofar as he is man, in the nearness of god. A story that Aristotle reports (*De partibus animalium*, I, 5, 645a 17ff.) agrees with this fragment of Heraclitus.

> The story is told of something Heraclitus said to some strangers who wanted to come visit him. Having arrived, they saw him warming himself at a stove. Surprised, they stood there in consternation—above all because he encouraged them, the astounded ones, and called for them to come in, with the words, "For here too the gods are present."

The story certainly speaks for itself, but we may stress a few aspects.

The group of foreign visitors, in their importunate curiosity about the thinker, are disappointed and perplexed by their first glimpse of his abode. They believe they should meet the thinker in circumstances which, contrary to the ordinary round of human life, everywhere bear traces of the exceptional and rare and so of the exciting. The group hopes that in their visit to the thinker they will find things that will provide material for entertaining conservation—at least for a while. The foreigners who wish to visit the thinker expect to catch sight of him perchance at that very moment when, sunk in profound meditation, he is thinking. The visitors want this "experience" not in order to be overwhelmed by thinking but simply so they can say they saw and heard someone everybody says is a thinker.

Instead of this the sightseers find Heraclitus by a stove. That is surely a common and insignificant place. True enough, bread is baked here. But Heraclitus is not even busy baking at the stove. He stands there merely to warm himself. In this altogether everyday place he betrays the whole poverty of his life. The vision of a shivering thinker offers little of interest. At this disappointing spectacle even the curious lose their desire to come any closer. What are they supposed to do here? Such an everyday and unexciting occurrence—somebody who is chilled warming himself at a stove—anyone can find any time at home. So why look up a thinker? The visitors are on the verge of going away again. Heraclitus reads the frustrated curiosity in their faces. He knows that for the crowd the failure of an expected sensation to materialize is enough to make those who have just arrived leave. He therefore encourages them. He invites them explicitly to come in with the words, *Einai gar kia entautha theous*, "Here too the gods come to presence."

This phrase places the abode (*êthos*) of the thinker and his deed in another light. Whether the visitors understood this phrase at once—or at all—and then saw everything differently in this other light the story does not say. But the story was told and has come down to us today because what it reports derives from and characterizes the atmosphere surrounding this thinker. *Kai entautha*, "even here," at the stove, in that ordinary place where every thing and every condition, each deed and thought is intimate and commonplace, that is, familiar [*geheuer*], "even there" in the sphere of the familiar, *einai theous*, it is the case that "the gods come to presence."

Heraclitus himself says, *êthos anthropoi daimon*, "The (familiar) abode for man is the open region for the presencing of god (the unfamiliar one)."

If the name "ethics," in keeping with the basic meaning of the word *êthos*, should now say that "ethics" ponders the abode of man, then that thinking which thinks the truth of Being as the primordial element of man, as one who ek-sists, is in itself the original ethics. However, this thinking is not ethics in the first instance, because it is ontology. For ontology always thinks solely the being (*on*) in its Being. But as long as the truth of Being is not thought all ontology remains without its foundation. Therefore the thinking that in *Being and Time* tries to advance thought in a preliminary way into the truth of Being characterizes itself as "fundamental ontology." [See *Being and Time*, sec. 3 and 4 above.] It strives to reach back into the essential ground from which thought concerning the truth of Being emerges. By initiating another inquiry this thinking is already removed from the "ontology" of metaphysics (even that of Kant). "Ontology" itself, however, whether transcendental or precritical, is subject to criticism, not because it thinks the Being of beings and thereby reduces Being to a concept, but because it does not think the truth of Being and so fails to recognize that there is a thinking more rigorous than the conceptual. In the poverty of its first breakthrough, the thinking that tries to advance thought into the truth of Being brings only a small part of that wholly other dimension to language. This language even falsifies itself, for it does not yet succeed in retaining the essential help of phenomenological seeing while dispensing with the inappropriate concern with "science" and "research." But in order to make the attempt at thinking recognizable and at the same time understandable for existing philosophy, it could at first be expressed only within the horizon of that existing philosophy and its use of current terms.

In the meantime I have learned to see that these very terms were bound to lead immediately and inevitably into error. For the terms and the conceptual language corresponding to them were not rethought by readers from the matter particularly to be thought; rather, the matter was conceived according to the established terminology in its customary meaning. The thinking that inquires into the truth of Being and so defines man's essential abode from Being and toward Being is neither ethics nor ontology. Thus the question about the relation of each to the other no longer has any basis in this sphere. Nonetheless, your question, thought in a more original way, retains a meaning and an essential importance.

For it must be asked: If the thinking that ponders the truth of Being defines the essence of *humanitas* as ek-sistence from the latter's belongingness to Being, then does thinking remain only a theoretical representation of Being and of man; or can we obtain from such knowledge directives that can be readily applied to our active lives?

The answer is that such thinking is neither theoretical nor practical. It comes to pass before this distinction. Such thinking is, insofar as it is, recollection of Being and nothing else. Belonging to Being, because thrown by Being into the preservation of its truth and claimed for such preservation, it thinks Being. Such thinking has no result. It has no effect. It satisfies its essence in that it is. But it is by saying its matter. Historically, only one saying [*Sage*] belongs to the matter of thinking, the one that is in each case appropriate to its matter. Its material relevance is essentially higher than the validity of the sciences, because it is freer. For it lets Being—be.

Thinking builds upon the house of Being, the house in which the jointure of Being fatefully enjoins the essence of man to dwell in the truth of Being. This dwelling is the essence of "being-in-the-world." The reference in *Being and Time* to "being-in" as "dwelling" is no etymological game. The same reference in the 1936 essay on Hölderlin's verse, "Full of merit, yet poetically, man dwells on this earth," is no adornment of a thinking that rescues itself from science by means of poetry. The talk about the house of Being is no transfer of the image "house" to being. But one day we will, by thinking the essence of Being in a way appropriate to its matter, more readily be able to think what "house" and "to dwell" are.

But now in what relation does the thinking of Being stand to theoretical and practical behavior? It exceeds all contemplation because it cares for the light in which a seeing, as *theoria*, can first live and move. Thinking attends to the clearing of Being in that it puts its saying of Being into language as the home of ek-sistence. Thus thinking is a deed. But a deed that also surpasses all *praxis*. Thinking towers above action and production, not through the grandeur of its achievement and not as a consequence of its effect, but through the humbleness of its inconsequential accomplishment.

For thinking in its saying merely brings the unspoken word of Being to language.

The usage "bring to language" employed here is now to be taken quite literally. Being comes, clearing itself, to language. It is perpetually under way to language. Such arriving in its turn brings ek-sisting thought to language in a saying. Thus language itself is raised into the clearing of Being. Language *is* only in this mysterious and yet for us always pervasive way. To the extent that language which has thus been brought fully into its essence is historical, Being is entrusted to recollection. Ek-sistence thoughtfully dwells in the house of Being. In all this it is as if nothing at all happens through thoughtful saying.

But just now an example of the inconspicuous deed of thinking manifested itself. For to the extent that we expressly think the usage "bring to language," which was granted to language, think only that and nothing further, to the extent that we retain this thought in the heedfulness of saying as what in the future continually has to be thought, we have brought something of the essential unfolding of Being itself to language.

What is strange in the thinking of Being is its simplicity. Precisely this keeps us from it. For we look for thinking—which has its world-historical prestige under the name "philosophy"—in the form of the unusual, which is accessible only to initiates. At the same time we conceive of thinking on the model of scientific knowledge and its research projects. We measure deeds by the impressive and successful achievements of *praxis*. But the deed of thinking is neither theoretical nor practical, nor is it the conjunction of these two forms of behavior.

Through its simple essence, the thinking of Being makes itself unrecognizable to us. But if we become acquainted with the unusual character of the simple, then another plight immediately befalls us. The suspicion arises that [with] such thinking the Being falls prey to arbitrariness; for it cannot cling to beings. Whence does thinking take its measure? What law governs its deed?

Here the third question of your letter must be entertained: *Comment sauver l'élément d'aventure que comporte toute recherché sans faire de la philosophie une simple aventurière?* [How can we preserve the element of adventure that all research contains without simply turning philosophy into an adventuress?] I shall mention poetry now only in passing. It is confronted by the same question, and in the same manner, as thinking. But Aristotle's words in the *Poetics*, although they have scarcely been pondered, are still valid—that poetic composition is truer than exploration of beings.

But thinking is an *adventure* not only as a search and an inquiry into the unthought. Thinking, in its essence as thinking of Being, is claimed by Being. Thinking is related to

Being as what arrives (*l'avenant*). Thinking as such is bound to the advent of Being, to Being as advent. Being has already been dispatched to thinking. Being *is* as the destiny of thinking. But destiny is in itself historical. Its history has already come to language in the saying of thinkers.

To bring to language ever and again this advent of Being that remains, and in its remaining waits for man, is the sole matter of thinking. For this reason essential thinkers always say the Same. But that does not mean the identical. Of course they say it only to one who undertakes to think back on them. Whenever thinking, in historical recollection, attends to the destiny of Being, it has already bound itself to what is fitting for it, in accord with its destiny. To flee into the identical is not dangerous. To risk discord in order to say the Same is the danger. Ambiguity threatens, and mere quarreling.

The fittingness of the saying of Being, as of the destiny of truth, is the first law of thinking—not the rules of logic, which can become rules only on the basis of the law of Being. To attend to the fittingness of thoughtful saying does not only imply, however, that we contemplate at every turn *what* is to be said of Being and *how* it is to be said. It is equally essential to ponder *whether* what is to be thought is to be said—to what extent, at what moment of this history of Being, in what sort of dialogue with this history, and on the basis of what claim, it ought to be said. The threefold thing mentioned in an earlier letter is determined in its cohesion by the law of the fittingness of thought on the history of Being: rigor of meditation, carefulness in saying, frugality with words.

It is time to break the habit of overestimating philosophy and of thereby asking too much of it. What is needed in the present world crisis is less philosophy, but more attentiveness in thinking; less literature, but more cultivation of the letter.

The thinking that is to come is no longer philosophy, because it thinks more originally than metaphysics—a name identical to philosophy. However, the thinking that is to come can no longer, as Hegel demanded, set aside the name "love of wisdom" and become wisdom itself in the form of absolute knowledge. Thinking is on the descent to the poverty of its provisional essence. Thinking gathers language into simple saying. In this way language is the language of Being, as clouds are the clouds of the sky. With its saying, thinking lays inconspicuous furrows in language. They are still more inconspicuous than the furrows that the farmer, slow of step, draws through the field.

Commentary by *Elizabeth Minnich*, Arendt and Heidegger: The Life of the Mind, the Life of Action

INTRODUCTION

Separately and together, Martin Heidegger (1889–1976) and Hannah Arendt (1906–1975) are thinkers whose strikingly original works and intertwined lives arouse intense interest and no little controversy. Each in her and his own way radically rethought once-dominant European traditions that were being shattered in their own times. Each emerged from the ruins with fresh insights that are both influential and debated. Readers argue, for example, about whether Arendt, finding a useful vision of free public life in Athens, nostalgically romanticized the *polis*, overlooking its practices of colonization, slavery, and exclusions of women and laborers from participation. Similarly, Heidegger is suspected by some of romanticizing the hard rural life of premodern Germany, and with it, a hypermasculinized, dangerously nationalistic *êthos* of "soil and blood."[7] Such arguments take on greater intensity because of Arendt's and Heidegger's very different responses to the murderous regime of the National Socialist German Labor Party (the Nazis), differences that seem particularly hard to explain given the intimate relationship between the young Arendt and her then-teacher, Heidegger.

Heidegger, already famous as a professor of philosophy, joined the National Socialist Party on May 1, 1933, and served as rector of the University of Freiburg from April 22, 1933, to April 27, 1934. Exactly what he did and did not do in that role is still the subject of research, but at the very least, his prestige, his impassioned public talks, his role as an educator leant moral intellectual legitimacy to the Nazis. He resigned his post after that one year, retreating from political engagement to a very active and productive life of the mind.

Arendt, on the contrary, early judged Nazism to be a "horrible gutter-born phenomenon."[8] Appalled and quick to realize how extreme the threat they posed, in 1933 she left for France, settling finally in 1941 in the United States. There she remained an engaged critic of all challenges to free, open public life. Her first major book was a sweeping, original historical interpretation of *The Origins of Totalitarianism*.[9] In it, she took up the tasks of both comprehending and warning about political dynamics that arose before, and did not disappear with, the defeat of Nazi and Communist totalitarianism.

Among the many spectators who condemn what Heidegger did, more than a few also find it inexplicable to inexcusable that Arendt did not publicly denounce her former teacher and lover. They also ask why she subsequently worked from the United States to get his writings published in English and even returned to Germany long after the war to visit with him briefly a few times.

If we care about political freedom and moral considerations, should we, then, hold Heidegger's philosophy accountable for his personal failures in political, moral judgment? Is Arendt's political thinking discredited by her choice not to reject him and his works entirely? We could say that the works of thinkers should not be reduced to their life stories. However, for both Arendt and Heidegger the familiar Western elevation of the "pure" life of the mind above the life of action was something to be questioned, not accepted.

Heidegger was interested in "authentic" existence, in "being-in-the-world" and "being-with-others." He also emphasized practical engagement with everyday life, and the moods or dispositions that reveal our relationship with nature and art (among other things). Arendt extended the view that philosophy ought to be returned to the world as humans experience it even further. She set out not to be a professional philosopher, but directly to "think what we are doing."[10] Choosing to focus on the *vita activa* rather than turning from it, as Heidegger did after his disastrous year in public life, she often begins her works by reflecting on a highly contemporary situation. To ignore these thinkers' own lives is, then, arguably to contradict their own teachings and views of philosophical methodologies.

But perhaps what Heidegger did, however culpable, was an "error" from which he thereafter learned. In "Martin Heidegger at Eighty," Arendt wrote that, "Heidegger himself corrected his own 'error' more quickly and radically than many of those who later sat in judgment over him—he took considerably greater risks than were usual in German literary and university life during that period."[11] She then says that, having reflected, he emerged with "his discovery of the will as 'the will to will' and hence as the 'will to power'." He concluded that "the will to power" is "opposed to thinking" and affects it "destructively."[12] *As a thinker*, then, Arendt tells us, Heidegger did try to correct his "error," even if, as a citizen, he persisted in not accepting public responsibility for his past. Should we then exempt his philosophy, if not he himself, from implication with his politics?

Arendt also suggests that Heidegger's "error" reveals a problem that arises not from individual character, but from the doing of philosophy (from a *déformation professionelle*). Looking at philosophers from the perspective of one who took public, political life seriously, she observes that, "The attraction to the tyrannical can be demonstrated theoretically in many of the great thinkers (Kant is the great exception)."[13] And if most philosophers did not turn to "tyrants and Fuhrers" as Plato and Heidegger did, she says that may simply be because they did not act politically, rather than because their philosophizing led to no "attraction to the tyrannical." So, while Arendt did not publicly denounce Heidegger, or other philosophers and intellectuals who have failed in political and moral judgment, she did rethink philosophy's relation to the world.

Arendt considered, for example, how the philosophies of Plato, Hegel, and Marx justified tyrannical orders, and what it was in Kant's thinking that kept him from that *déformation professionelle*. More radically, however, she questioned *the experience of thinking* itself. Arendt interrogated, then, not only Heidegger's thinking in relation to political realities, not only philosophy's relation to action, but also the relation of thinking, as a capacity and experience we all have, to moral considerations and political judgment. Interestingly, by focusing on the experience of thinking, Arendt was independently rethinking what she had found to be most significant in Heidegger's teaching as well as his philosophizing.

Students flocked to Heidegger, Arendt tells us, not to become "trained" in "the old academic disciplines, in which philosophy, neatly divided into its special fields—epistemology, aesthetics, ethics, logic, and the like—was not so much communicated as drowned in an ocean of boredom."[14] They came to him because, "There exists a thinker; one can perhaps learn to think."[15]

For neither Arendt nor Heidegger can we most fruitfully ask, then, what is her or his position on basic questions of epistemology, metaphysics, ethics, logic, and so forth? We need to ask, instead, how did they *think* about the questions philosophizing recurrently encounters when yet again it is awakened by wonder, by puzzlement? Behind that is the question, what did they think about thinking? And then there is our question: How are they similar; how do they differ; and do their differences have something to teach us about any "attraction to the tyrannical" that philosophizing, and more broadly, the experience of thinking in which we all engage, might have?

That last question is particularly interesting because Arendt's most influential and controversial concept is "the banality of evil."[16] She meant that, as a matter of fact, evil is mostly done, not by demonic or insane people, but by people who have never thought much about good and evil at all. She found herself with that concept, she tells us, when she reported on the 1961 trial in Jerusalem of Adolf Eichmann, who is generally called the "engineer of the Final Solution." Faced with the reality of a rather colorless, "banal" bureaucrat "whose only personal distinction was a perhaps extraordinary shallowness" but whose work as a Nazi functionary served "evil deeds, committed on a gigantic scale," she also found herself with a question. If this man's "monstrous deeds" "could not be traced to any particularity of wickedness, pathology, or ideological conviction," and if "the only specific characteristic one could detect" in him "was not stupidity but a curious, quite authentic inability to think," might it be that "our ability to judge, to tell right from wrong . . . is dependent upon our faculty of thought?"[17]

This is startling, given what Arendt also said about the *déformation professionelle* of philosophers. What, then, from the perspective of their political effects, might the preeminently thoughtful profession of philosophy and its opposite, unthinking, shallow conventionality, have in common? How can thinking lead to "an attraction to the tyrannical," and also, perhaps, condition people against evil? To read Arendt and Heidegger together is to encounter such questions every step of the way.

ORIGINS AND EFFECTS OF THINKING

As Plato and Aristotle both said, the activity of thinking that characterizes philosophy begins in wonder, or, in puzzlement. The philosophical systems and other knowledge produced in the form of answers to the questions thinking poses, however, differ greatly, as the history of ideas makes evident. Heidegger, however, wants to return to the original (in time, but also in each of us) seeking that is awakened by wonder rather than to add to any established knowledge. He writes, "all the sciences have leapt from the womb of philosophy . . . And now that they are so apart they can never make the leap back into the source from whence they have sprung . . . only thinking can find them."[18] So Heidegger's thinking is preeminently questioning that is dedicated to refinding the source of any and all knowledge, of language—of Being itself. This is a radical project, and it accounts both for his originality and for the difficulty of reading him. He rarely means what we may first think he does. He is trying to go below, behind, what has become familiar, so he uses words in different ways, forcing us to stop and rethink. Those who are unwilling to do so find his writing too difficult. Significant philosophers (particularly among analytical philosophers, e.g., A. J. Ayer) have doubted whether Heidegger makes sense at all. Others, however, find his language evocative, powerful, and useful in thinking in highly suggestive ways.

Arendt, too, calls on us to recognize "the claim on our thinking attention which all events and facts arouse by virtue of their existence,"[19] rather than prejudging "events and facts" by applying the concepts, definitions, interpretations, explanations we already have from both knowledge and conventions. Being concerned with public life and action more than with professional philosophy, she uses more familiar language than Heidegger's. Nevertheless, her desire to break us free of established conventions of all sorts means that she, too, requires readers to stop and think freshly.

For both Arendt and Heidegger, then, thinking is radical and original. It is the capacity we have to reflect about things, to question, to "wander" and "wonder." As we see in Socrates, *the* example of a thinker for both Arendt and Heidegger, when we are thinking we do not "get somewhere" or produce anything. Socrates never wrote anything; he spent his days questioning people. Every conclusion raises new questions, new perspectives—throws us back into being puzzled.

But thinking is not only ceaselessly active. It is responsive. It is, both Heidegger and Arendt say, aroused by something specific. Heidegger writes, "The point is not to gain some knowledge about philosophy but to be able to philosophize," and, "The *path* of our reflections will take us from certain individual problems to the basic problems."[20] They also agree that thinking is what we need to do to prepare to become responsive. Heidegger tells us that his project of destructuring by interrogating traditions of knowledge does not destroy but revivifies them. Arendt says that thinking dissolves preconceived, or frozen, ideas and prejudices. It "brings out the implications of unexamined opinions [values, doctrines, theories] and thereby destroys them."[21] But she too holds that this is liberatory and renewing, and so not finally destructive.

Arendt, however, emphasizes and persistently works through the political implications of thinking in ways that Heidegger does not. She says, "The purging element in thinking, Socrates' midwifery . . . is political by implication."[22] It is specifically political because, lacking certainty about *what* and/or *who* something/someone I encounter in the real world is, I am faced, as people say today, with "a judgment call." I must find a way to respond that honors "*particulars* without subsuming them under general rules [that have grown] . . . into habits . . ."[23] Of the judgment that thinking prepares us for, Arendt (drawing on Kant's understanding of indeterminate judgment) says that it is "the most political" of our "mental abilities."[24] It is political, as it is moral, because we need it to act not correctly, but appropriately. The capacity for judgment allows us to make decisions the way a good judge in a courtroom does. Such a good judge takes into account both the general law *and* the unique individual, who is never exactly like any other. Thus a just, fair, appropriate verdict can be rendered. For example, a person who is young, homeless, penniless, and hungry and so steals bread should not receive the same penalty as a person who is young, rich, healthy, and steals for the thrill of it. Judgment is political because it is concerned not only with what is true as established in various realms, for example. as "the letter of the law," but with its just application.

Heidegger, by contrast, turns his destructuring questioning back on itself, remaining focused on thinking rather than what it does, or does not do, for acting. What he is seeking is truth about what it means *to be*, to exist, at all—truth that, he is sure, precedes questions of justice or ethics. After all, he says, how can we make ethical judgments if we do not know what something, or someone, *is*?

But if thinking has "a peculiarly destructive or critical" effect on "its own results," might Heidegger be vulnerable to equating intellectual destructuring with actual destruction? And might this lead to seeing violence as justified by a political movement committed to "clearing the ground" for a more vital new order? In Heidegger's case, there is evidence that he did just that. In 1935, in *An Introduction to Metaphysics*, he equates the "violence" inherent in "apprehension" to "man . . . undertak[ing] to govern," and says that in thus "daring, man comes necessarily to evil as well as to the brave and noble."[25] But he also often says that his thinking seeks to open "other vistas," not to choose one that might then be imposed. Thinking, he says, lays paths that go nowhere, leaving only "trail markers."

Still, might he have been so engaged with questioning that no ethical principles remained to constrain action, if not thinking? Asked about ethics, he wrote, "The desire for an ethics presses ever more ardently . . . The greatest care must be fostered on the ethical bond." Nevertheless, he says, an ethical quest does not "release thought from the task of thinking what still remains principally to be thought and, as Being, prior to all beings, is their guarantor and truth."[26] And then he asks, "can we obtain from such knowledge [of Being] directives that can be readily applied to our active lives?" His answer is that "such thinking has no result. It has no effect. It satisfies its essence in that it is . . . For it lets Being—be."[27] So he sets ethical questions aside to be asked, if at all, later. This was written after the Holocaust: how could he keep deferring ethical concerns?

Arendt also posed the "unavoidable" question about thinking: "How can anything relevant for the world we live in arise out of so resultless an enterprise?"[28] But unlike Heidegger, Arendt did not think about thinking for the sake of letting "Being—be." Rather she asked what its effects on action and morality might really be. She concluded that, while thinking gives us no new codes to replace those it has dissolved, it releases the free judgment we need to bridge principles and particulars in a way that honors both.

ONTOLOGY

It is in order to ask ontological questions that Heidegger defers ethical, as well as other (in his view), less basic questions. "Ontology" is the philosophical term for studying meanings of "existence," or the study of what it means *to be*.[29] Heidegger writes, "Being is to be laid hold of and made our theme. Being is always being of beings and accordingly it becomes accessible at first only by starting with some being." His approach to Being through "thematizing" beings is "phenomenological," a method for analyzing how things exist developed by his teacher, Husserl. His method differs from Husserl's, whose analysis of how we *know* what exists (an epistemological approach) moved "from the natural attitude of the human being . . . back to the transcendental life of consciousness." But "for *us*," Heidegger writes, the quest is to find how "a being" can be "unconcealed" as it is in the world, in time, rather than only as a "correlate of consciousness."[30]

The German word Heidegger uses for Being is *Sein*. "Being" is usually capitalized in English to indicate that Heidegger's Sein is a universal (rather as "God" is capitalized). His German *seiendes*, often translated as "beings," refers to particulars, so "beings" is usually not capitalized (as "gods" in, say, "the Greek gods" is not capitalized). *Seiendes*, beings, are entities that have qualities by which we distinguish them (the red ball—or, more basically, the roundness that makes a ball what it is in the first place). Sein, Being, refers to their existence per se. Heidegger calls Being in its expression as human beings *Dasein*, which means "being-there." Translators often leave *Dasein* in the German to encourage readers to stop and rethink meanings of the too-familiar "human being." They capitalize *Dasein* to indicate that, for Heidegger, human being is "exemplary" Being—not Being-Itself, but also not like other beings (rather as, for Christians, Christ is "exemplary" in being both human and God).

Heidegger does not turn only to the knowledge of earlier philosophers concerning ontology, although Duns Scotus and Husserl, for key examples, helped him shift from asking *what* exists, *what* existence is, to *how* existence is and, specifically, how we have *thought* it. Heidegger also values the language and apprehensions of poets, the ancient Greeks, as well as Rilke, and Holderlin in particular. He writes, "Language is the primordial poetry in which a people speaks,"[31] so poets reveal in a special way the historical but also still-present origins that Heidegger always seeks. So, to question what it means to exist as a human being, he starts with us as we exist in the world—our being-with-others (a notion also influenced by Dilthey). He reflected on how we go about our practical lives here and now (remembering Aristotle's "practical wisdom"), and on our moods, or states of mind. It is important, for example, that Heidegger thought about human beings in our relation to instruments, tools, things that are "ready-to-hand," and how these "concern" us, how they are useful with regard to our concerns (our projects). Anthropologists—but rarely philosophers—might agree: humans have been definitionally categorized as "tool users."

Starting with how we *are* in everyday life, Heidegger moves further into his seeking of Being. He observes that *Dasein* is "a being that does not simply occur among other beings." Human being "is distinguished by the fact that in its Being this being is concerned *about* its very Being."[32] What it means to be human is fundamentally to be self-questioning. This is why, and how, human beings are "exemplary." In us, Being reveals itself as "in and for itself"—simultaneously pure Existence, existence questioning Itself, and Existence revealing Itself to itself. The philosophical wonder that there is anything at all, rather than nothing, expresses that primal questioning.

Heidegger's self-questioning being, the exemplary Being, is not Descartes's famous *Cogito, ergo sum*—"I think, therefore I am/exist." It is closer to, "Thinking exists, therefore Existence/Being *is revealing itself* to Itself." Heidegger's thinking/being is also not Husserl's Transcendental Ego, a thinking Ego we find only by disregarding ("bracketing off") supposedly "objective" reality (that which science as well as we daily assume to be real) to get back to its meanings as we "intend" them. For Heidegger, Being reveals Itself as, in, through our many ways of being-in-the-world, rather than more specifically in relation only to our consciousness as it constructs meanings.

Being-in-the-world entails also Being in Time, in history. For Heidegger, history is not factual truths about the dead past. *Dasein*, human being, is concerned with pasts that are still with it, of which we were once projections as we also now project futures. It is typical Heidegger to hold that time is in us, and we are in time—he says the same about Being and about language.

Arendt also thinks and writes about humans as creatures that labor to sustain life, who make things to build an inhabitable, shareable world, and who are, fundamentally, self-questioning. (She cites Augustine's "A question have I become for myself" in this context).[33] And she, too, looks for meanings within history, but in thinking about all these ways of being human, she is not looking for universal truths. She says that history is stories people have made of events and, like stories, there is no necessity to be found in them. Only when, and because, a story is finished does what happened appear to have been necessary. While a story is still unfolding, there remain all sorts of possibilities. Like Heidegger, but always focused on plural humans, she holds that, "In this world . . . *Being and Appearing coincide.*"[34] Appearing presumes an audience; and spectators—rather than any abstraction, Being or History—give reality to the spectacle by seeing it and then telling stories about it. To be abstract and universal means, in fact, *not* appearing: I cannot see Being, but only beings, particular phenomena. If Heidegger's real interest is Being, even though he says it exists as beings in time, Arendt's real interest is in human beings, always firmly in the plural. No unusual capital letters in Arendt's English.

Confusion or conflation of abstract generalizations and universals with real, concrete, unique phenomena can be dangerous. Here we may have a key aspect of the *déformation professionelle* of philosophers as Arendt saw it. The Pragmatist philosopher William James called this "vicious intellectualism."[35] He points out, as Arendt does, that once we have categorized a person (seen her/him as an instance of a generalization), we can become blind to everything else that matters. We see that individual only, say, as Southern or Muslim or poor or disabled or a politician.

Further, Arendt also warns about looking for absolute "laws" working through "History" (like those Marx claimed to have found). Believing that one has found lawlike truths about what will happen, Arendt observes, can lead to claiming, as some Communists did, that it is right to kill people who are of a certain economic class because "history has already condemned them." Similarly, the Nazis "justified" the Final Solution—the genocide of the whole "race" of Jews—by invoking "laws" of eugenics (the "science" of "good breeding") by which some "races" and "kinds" of people were supposedly fated not to survive because they were "less fit" than others.

Persistently, Arendt warned against trying to force reality to conform to abstractions. Abstractions that we distill from concrete existences (e.g., an idea of *humans* that relates all of us while distinguishing us from *vegetables* and *minerals*) are not only useful but essential. The specifically political and moral problem, Arendt says, is that "Generalization is inherent in every thought," even when "that thought is insisting [as Heidegger's ontology does] on the universal primacy of the particular."[36] That is, for Arendt there is a catch-22, a paradoxical relation between generalizations and particulars that can cause trouble if we do not remember their essential differences. For example, while it may be noble to call on people to "love humankind," that should not be taken to substitute for, or be more important than, love of real individuals.

Arendt and Heidegger agree, then, that it is particulars, beings, individuals—"everything that is" *as it is* in time—that can and should draw us into thinking. They agree that thinking is questioning that prepares us to be responsive by dissolving certainties that can block us from seeing what is really before us. They even agree about the "universal primacy of the particular." In Arendt's language, this translates most importantly into "Human plurality is the paradoxical plurality of unique beings."[37] But then a difference appears. Noticing that thinking produces as well as dissolves generalizations, Arendt goes on political alert. "Action," she says, "deals with particulars, and only particular statements can be valid in the field of ethics and politics."[38] Generalizations based on abstractions can lose touch with their subject, as when political theorists forget that political systems are and can only be real, historical phenomena, each one differing in crucial aspects from all others, and all of them dealing with individuals and not just "The Citizen." This appears to be a warning that perhaps Heidegger and Plato, both of whom worked for tyrants in hope of bringing a particular political regime into accord with universal truths, should have heeded.

Interestingly, existentialist philosophers such as Jean-Paul Sartre (whose *Being and Nothingness* is profoundly Heideggerian) and Simone de Beauvoir did take up and stress the ways Heidegger's "being-in-the-world" could and should involve liberatory politics. And Beauvoir, in *The Second Sex*,[39] analyzed ways in which *human being* has been gendered male, thereby both excluding half of humankind and distorting what can be said about "man." Michel Foucault also politicizes Heidegger. His "archaeology" of knowledge,[40] like some other poststructuralist, postmodern "deconstructions," "destructures" it to reveal the workings of power.

TRUTH, OPINION, POLITICS

Thinking about the effect that seeking truth may have on politics, on action, Arendt wrote, "The modes of thought and communication that deal with truth . . . are necessarily domineering: they don't take into account other people's opinions."[41] Opinions—or what Heidegger dismissively called "chatter"—are, from the perspective of truth (and so in most philosophers' views), both uninteresting and characteristically erroneous. But for Arendt, "taking [opinions] into account is the hallmark of all strictly political thinking." In public affairs, Arendt says, "The more people's standpoints I have present in my mind while I am pondering a given issue, and the better I can imagine how I would feel and think if I were in their place . . . the more valid my final conclusions."[42] Crucially, I am then prepared to exercise appropriate judgment. If there is to be political justice, differing opinions must be free not only to be expressed but to be taken into account. Kant, whom Arendt says did not suffer from the *déformation professionelle* of philosophers, also held that learning to think in the place of others is essential to being able to think coherently and consistently.

TRUTH AND MEANING

Arendt, again thinking with Kant, distinguishes between the truths of knowledge, which can be correct even if very few agree (we do not vote on whether $2 + 2 = 4$), and meaning, which arises from thinking and comparing views with other people (as we keep asking, What is the meaning of life?). Here again there is a difference between Arendt and Heidegger, and it is one Arendt took to be very serious. He conflates truth and meaning: she quotes him saying, "'Meaning of Being' and 'Truth of Being' say the same."[43] For example, he says that we come "into affiliation with art," and the meaning of art is "truth happening in the work."[44] (Heidegger became more interested in art as his view of truth became more akin to "disclosure," or "unconcealment," rather than the more usual notion that what is true "corresponds" to what is.)

"'Perceive,'" writes Heidegger, "means the same thing as 'receive,'" but includes "also the active trait of undertaking something . . . We take it up specifically, and do something with it . . . We take it to heart. What is taken to heart, however, is left to be exactly as it is. This taking-to-heart does not make over what it takes."[45] Since this "taking-to-heart" of meaningful "disclosure," as distinct from scientific facts we can know, is for him also how we perceive or receive Nature, some environmentalists, including feminists, have found in Heidegger support for their arguments for a caring, nonexploitative, and mutual relation to Nature. Heidegger's anti-Modern critique of technology that reveals its tendency to take over rather than serve us and our projects further supports such contemporary causes.

None of this, we can observe, sounds like the thinking of a person who could be anything other than repelled by the murderous violence of the Nazis, who certainly did actively try to make over what it means to be human. Arendt describes concentration camps as "laboratories" in which the Nazis set out to remake human beings, as did Dr. Mengele with his medical "experiments" on the little people ("dwarfs" and "midgets"), on twins, and other people from whom he wished to learn in order to use "the laws of nature." This is hardly Heidegger's "letting Being—be."

Questioning understandings of science that allowed it to be so radically misused, as well as the failures of political judgment of Heidegger and other philosophers and intellectuals, Arendt emphasized the Kantian distinction between knowing and its truths, on the one hand, and the meaning we seek when we think, on the other hand. As abstract as it sounds, she was sure this distinction mattered politically. For philosophers or anyone else "to interpret meaning on the model of truth," she says, is to become "committed to the notion that philosophy's 'subject proper' is 'the actual knowledge of what truly is.'"[46] And this is dangerous. "Ideologies," like Nazism, Arendt says, "are known for their scientific character: they combine the scientific approach with results of philosophical relevance and pretend to scientific philosophy."[47] It then no longer matters what other people think. If they disagree, their opinion is discredited as "incorrect."

To seek truth, forgetting the distinguishable claim and need we have for meaning, and then to use knowledge to "correct"—and silence—opinion, is for Arendt to pit oneself against the reality of human plurality, and so to threaten freedom. So when Arendt says that "The latest and in some respects most striking instance" of this anti-political "fallacy," "occurs in Heidegger's *Being and Time*,"[48] it is clear that she seriously differs with him.

MORTALITY AND NATALITY

Heidegger's thought about Being and non-Being (nothingness) also has political implications, revealing the masculinized history of philosophy. Thinking about what *not being*, negation, or as Heidegger often says, "nihilation," can possibly mean goes back in philosophy at least to the pre-Socratic Parmenides (to whom Heidegger often returns). Heidegger also thinks about the *angst*, or anxiety, we feel encountering beings that can also not-be, in several senses. This rock might not be what it appears; it might not be real; it need not have existed at all. Such anxiety, like the destructuring of thinking, reopens us, Heidegger says, to differences and "other vistas." Negation, like destructuring, then, is not necessarily negative; it, too, is a way of opening possibilities.

Arendt also stressed differences, the importance of many perspectives, and particularly human plurality. We exist as *many*, she insisted, not as *one*. We may choose to emphasize our oneness, our similarities, but the unity, or oneness, of humankind, is an abstraction—a fiction, not a reality. If we *were* one, we would not need to *assert* it, or preach it. But while emphasizing many kinds of differences, as Heidegger did, Arendt nevertheless did not take Being/Not-Being to be the primal pair (as it was also for Sartre, as *Being and Nothingness* makes evident). Instead, she remembered that, while humans die (are mortal), they are also born (are natal). And with every birth, a newcomer enters and renews the world.[49] "Man who is mortal" may be existentially alone, burdened with a body that can only die, but humans who are also natal are not.

This was a radical insight in philosophical traditions dominated by males who both gendered *Man* (as Beauvoir established) and proclaimed him universal, "exemplary" of human being. Arendt, having coined the philosophical term "natality," then claims that natality is "the human condition" of action. This, too, is radical: political life was long restricted to males. Females, and with them natality, were privatized. But here is Arendt, saying that, "acting together and appearing" in public, "in company with our peers," we translate natural birth into specifically human lives. We insert "ourselves into the world by word and deed, thus acquiring and sustaining our personal identity and beginning something entirely new."[50] Arendt is referencing Heidegger's notion of Being as a "clearing" in which beings "disclose" themselves, but she is translating it into a real public space in which individuals take on specifically human reality by appearing to other people.

Conclusion: Thinking and Political Considerations

Arendt warns us that when a philosopher takes up thinking as an "abode," as Heidegger did, rather than moving in and out of reflection, pondering, questioning in the course of daily life among other people, that thinker may fail to develop the good judgment both morality and politics require. "In its essential seclusion from the world," she writes, "thinking always has to do only with things that are absent. . . . This remoteness is never more manifest than when thinking ponders [human] affairs, training them into its own sequestered stillness." And then she says, "Thus, Aristotle, with the great example of Plato still vividly in view, has already strongly advised philosophers against dreaming of the philosopher king . . ."[51] or führers ("führer," we should note, was a common German term for "leader" that could apply to a teacher, or a rector of a university, and not only to Hitler).

Are we to conclude then that what we learn about thinking from Heidegger's extreme immersion in it is that, to protect ourselves from becoming politically, morally dangerous, we should *not* think? Hardly: Eichmann, as Arendt saw him, did not think and that allowed him to remain actively a part of the murderous Nazi regime far longer than Heidegger did, and to do far worse things. The "professional deformation" Arendt saw in Heidegger, and many other "intellectuals," had to do not with thinking itself, but with wrongly choosing to "escap[e] from the reality of the Gestapo cellars and the torture-hells of the early concentration camps *into ostensibly more significant regions*"[52] (emphasis added). From such failures of judgment, Arendt learned to understand and never forget the profound significance of public life. If we do not preserve freedom and equality in the real, political world, Arendt concluded, we can lose everything. The life of the mind, as invaluable as it is, turns out, she said, to depend on the life of action so long scorned by "high-minded" people.

Arendt did not turn against thinking itself when she differed with the teacher to whom she had once gone to learn how to philosophize. Instead, she turned to another teacher of thinking—to Socrates. With his story in mind, she asks her question: What effects does thinking have that might condition us against doing, or failing to refuse to do, evil? Socrates, she says, unlike "professional thinkers," can represent "everybody": he himself who "counted himself neither among the many nor among the few, did not aspire to be a ruler of cities or claim to know how to improve and take care of citizens' souls . . . did not believe that men could be wise and did not envy the gods their divine wisdom in case they should possess it; and . . . therefore never even tried his hand at formulating a doctrine that could be taught and learned."[53] Crucially, unlike Heidegger, who took up his "abode" within thinking and, despite his own teaching, tried to turn philosophy into a science, Socrates, we are told, insisted that his wisdom lay in knowing that he did not know. The Socratic insistence on questioning everything and everybody marks him as still more radically different from the thoughtlessly conventional Eichmann. And, Arendt says, Socrates differed from both those who seek Truth alone and those whose conventionality refuses dissent in that he "felt the urge to check with his fellowmen if his perplexities were shared by them."[54] Thus, the figure of Socrates, of whom Heidegger said that he was "the purest thinker of the West,"[55] appeared to Arendt to be a teacher with whom we can learn to think without risking the *déformation professionelle* of philosophy. "The manifestation of the wind of thought," she wrote, using a Socratic metaphor, "is no knowledge; it is the ability [practiced as free judgment] to tell right from wrong, beautiful from ugly."[56]

Questions for Reflection

Do you think a philosopher's actions during her or his lifetime are relevant to understanding and/or to critiquing and evaluating her or his writings? Why or why not? Defend your answer by appealing to Heidegger's and Arendt's actions and writings to support your view.

What do you understand to be the relation of Being and Appearing for Heidegger and for Arendt? What political difference do you think it makes if one distinguishes sharply between Being and appearing, or, on the contrary, if one undoes any sharp division between them? Defend your answer.

Arendt said that philosophers seem to be drawn to "tyrants and führers." What do you think she means by that, and do you think that her view is plausible or not? Defend your answer.

Notes

1. W. J. Korab-Karpowicz, "Martin Heidegger," *The Internet Encyclopedia of Philosophy*, http://www.iep .utm.edu/h/heidegge.htm (2007).

2. Robert C. Solomon, *Introducing Philosophy: A Text with Integrated Readings*, 8th ed. (New York: Oxford University Press, 2005), 308.

3. W. J. Korab-Karpowicz, "Martin Heidegger."

4. In writing my account of Heidegger's notion of Being, I used four main resources, in addition to my lecture notes: Forrest E. Baird and Walter Kaufman, *Philosophical Classics*, vol. 5, *Twentieth Century Philosophy* (Upper Saddle River, NJ: Prentice Hall, 1997), 119–56; Marjorie Greene, "Martin Heidegger," in *The Encyclopedia of Philosophy*, vol. 3, ed. Paul Edwards (New York: Macmillan Publishing Co., 1967), 459–65; Elizabeth Minnich's commentary (this chapter) and glossary entries; Solomon, *Introducing Philosophy: A Text with Integrated Readings*, 308, 313, 362, 372.

5. Hannah Arendt, "Thinking and Moral Considerations: A Lecture," in *Social Research*, vol. 38, no. 3 (Fall 1971): excerpts from 417–46.

6. Martin Heidegger, "Letter on Humanism" (1947), in *Martin Heidegger: Basic Writings: From Being and Time (1927) to The Task of Thinking (1964)*, rev. ed., ed. David Farrell Krell (San Francisco: HarperSanFrancisco/HarperCollins, 1993), excerpts from 255–60 and 262–65.

7. See Heidegger's inaugural address as rector of the University of Freiburg, "Die Selbstbehauptung der deutschen Universistat," 1933; Korn Verlag, Breslau, 34, in Richard Wolin, ed., *The Heidegger Controversy: A Critical Reader* (Cambridge, MA: MIT Press, 1998).

8. Hannah Arendt, "Martin Heidegger at Eighty," in *Heidegger & Modern Philosophy*, ed. Michael Murray (New Haven, CT: Yale University Press 1978), n.3, 302.

9. Hannah Arendt, *The Origins of Totalitarianism* (Cleveland, OH: World Publishing Co./Meridian Books, 1966).

10. Hannah Arendt, *The Human Condition* (Chicago: University of Chicago Press, 1958), 5.

11. Arendt, "Martin Heidegger at Eighty," n3.

12. Arendt, "Martin Heidegger at Eighty," 303.

13. Arendt, "Martin Heidegger at Eighty," 303.

14. Arendt, "Martin Heidegger at Eighty," 294.

15. Arendt, "Martin Heidegger at Eighty," 295.

16. Hannah Arendt, *Eichmann in Jerusalem: A Report on the Banality of Evil*, rev. ed. (New York: Penguin Books, 1994).

17. Arendt, "Thinking and Moral Considerations," 417–18.

18. Martin Heidegger, Fred D. Wieck, and J. Glenn Gray, trans. *What Is Called Thinking?* (New York: Harper Torchbooks/Harper & Row, 1972), 18.

19. Arendt, "Thinking and Moral Considerations," 418.

20. Martin Heidegger, *The Basic Problems of Phenomenology*, rev. ed., trans. Albert Hofstadter (Bloomington: Indiana University Press, 1988), 2.

21. Arendt, "Thinking and Moral Considerations," 446.

22. Arendt, "Thinking and Moral Considerations," 446.

23. Arendt, "Thinking and Moral Considerations," 446.

24. Arendt, "Thinking and Moral Considerations," 446.

25. Heidegger, *An Introduction to Metaphysics*, 172.

26. Heidegger, "Letter on Humanism," 255.

27. Heidegger, "Letter on Humanism," 259.

28. Arendt, "Thinking and Moral Considerations," 426.

29. Ontology is often considered a branch of metaphysics: "The science or study of being; that department of metaphysics which relates to the being or essence of things, or to being in the abstract" (Oxford English Dictionary). The *Cambridge Dictionary of Philosophy* (1995) has an entry for metaphysics but not for ontology: "most generally, the philosophical investigation of the nature, constitution, and structure of reality."

30. Heidegger, *The Basic Problems of Phenomenology*, 21.

31. Heidegger, *An Introduction to Metaphysics*, 171.

32. Martin Heidegger, *Being and Time: A Translation of Sein und Zeit*, trans. Joan Stambaugh (Albany: State University of New York Press, 1996), 10.

33. Hannah Arendt, *The Human Condition*, 2nd ed. (Chicago: University of Chicago Press, 1958), 10.

34. Hannah Arendt, *The Life of The Mind*, vol. 1, *Thinking* (New York: Harcourt Brace Jovanovich, 1971), 19.

35. William James, "Monistic Idealism," in *A Pluralistic Universe* (Cambridge, MA: Harvard University Press, 1977), 32.

36. Arendt, *The Life of The Mind*, 199.

37. Arendt, *The Human Condition*, 176.

38. Arendt, *The Life of The Mind*, 200.

39. See Simone de Beauvoir, *The Second Sex*, trans. and ed. H. M. Parshley (New York: Vintage Books/Random House, 1974).

40. See especially Michel Foucault, *The Order of Things: An Archaeology of the Human Sciences* (New York: Vintage Books, Random House, 1973).

41. Hannah Arendt, "Truth and Politics," in *The Portable Hannah Arendt*, ed. Peter Baehr (New York: Penguin Books, 2000), 556.

42. Arendt, *The Portable Hannah Arendt*, 556.

43. Arendt, *The Life of The Mind*, 15.

44. Heidegger, "The Origin of the Work of Art," in *Basic Writings*, 193.

45. Heidegger, *What Is Called Thinking?*, 203.

46. Arendt, *The Life of The Mind*, 15.

47. Arendt, *The Origins of Totalitarianism*, 468.

48. Arendt, *The Origins of Totalitarianism*, 15.

49. Arendt, *The Human Condition*, cf. 9.

50. Arendt, "Truth and Politics," 574.

51. Arendt, "Martin Heidegger at Eighty," 299–300.

52. Arendt, "Martin Heidegger at Eighty," 302, n.3.

53. Arendt, "Thinking and Moral Considerations," 427.

54. Arendt, "Thinking and Moral Considerations," 432.

55. Heidegger, *What Is Called Thinking?*, 17.

56. Arendt, "Thinking and Moral Considerations," 446.

CHAPTER 13

Dewey and Addams

Introduction by *Karen J. Warren*

This chapter's philosophical pair, John Dewey (1859–1952) and Jane Addams (1860–1935), are advocates of a uniquely American (U.S.) philosophical position called "pragmatism." Fischer's commentary describes classical American pragmatism through extensive and illustrative attention to the writings of Addams and Dewey. In this introduction I will fill in some gaps by providing additional biographical information about this philosophical pair and other aspects of pragmatism relevant to an understanding of this chapter's primary texts.

DEWEY

John Dewey, the third of four sons, was born in Burlington, Vermont. The eldest sibling died in infancy. The remaining three brothers attended the University of Vermont in Burlington. Although Dewey's formal education in philosophy there was limited, his introduction to evolutionary theory had a lifelong impact on Dewey's conception of philosophy, including his ethics, epistemology, aesthetics, philosophical psychology, and philosophy of education.

Dewey taught high school for two years after he graduated from the university in 1879. During this time he became interested in pursuing a career in philosophy. He tested the waters by sending an essay to the *Journal of Speculative Philosophy*, which was accepted for publication. He then decided to pursue graduate work in philosophy at Johns Hopkins University in Baltimore, Maryland.

At Johns Hopkins, Dewey was tutored by Hegelian philosopher George Morris and American experimental psychologist G. Stanley Hall. They impressed upon Dewey the importance of an evolutionary, organic concept of nature, with humans as a part of nature, as well as the value of empirical data to test hypotheses—themes that recur throughout his philosophical work. After receiving his Ph.D. from Johns Hopkins in 1884, he taught at the University of Michigan for nine years, publishing his first two books, *Psychology* (1887) and *Leibniz's New Essays Concerning the Human Understanding* (1888). In 1894, Dewey took a position at the newly founded University of Chicago. It was there that he became interested in the developing American philosophical position known as pragmatism, while continuing to develop his philosophy of education. He founded the experimental Laboratory School and published his first book on the philosophy of education, *The School and Society* (1899), based on his experience with the school. Although his reputation as a philosopher was established, conflicts with the university over the Laboratory School led Dewey to resign in 1904. Subsequently, Dewey joined the Philosophy Department at Columbia University where he spent the rest of his professional life.

While at Columbia, Dewey's scholarship was prolific and his reputation grew. He wrote extensively on epistemology and metaphysics; many of the essays were published in two books, *The Influence of Darwin on Philosophy and Other Essays in Contemporary Thought* (1910) and *Essays in Experimental Logic* (1916). His interest in the philosophy of education was sustained through his teaching at the Teachers College at Columbia, resulting in two influential books, *How We Think* (1910) and *Democracy and Education* (1916). He has also earned a reputation as a philosopher who wrote on contemporary issues—what today is known as a "public philosopher"—and worked on behalf of social reform and social justice causes. Publicly recognized for his work, he gave many speaking engagements that provided wonderful material for his books *Reconstruction in Philosophy* (1920), *Human Nature and Conduct* (1922), *Experience and Nature* (1925), *The Public and Its Problems* (1927), and *The Quest for Certainty* (1929).

Although Dewey retired from teaching in 1930, he continued his political activities. He participated in the Commission of Inquiry into the Charges Against Leon Trotsky Trial in Mexico, and he defended fellow philosopher Bertrand Russell against an attempt by conservatives to remove him from his chair at the College of the City of New York in 1940. Dewey continued to publish books (six from 1934–1939) on logical theory, aesthetics, ethics, epistemology, and democracy. He remained active philosophically and politically until he died at age ninety-two.

Dewey's life spanned a historical period that began with the Civil War and ended during the cold war. During that time slaves were emancipated but white supremacy reigned. Immigrants joined American society but, with the influx of new workers, labor conflicts escalated. Women were granted the right to vote but the glass ceiling limited women's access to educational and economic institutions, placed women in the lowest paying jobs, and denied women equal pay for comparable work. In the traditional home, the gendered-division of labor continued virtually unchallenged. As a society, the United States changed from rural to urban, from an agricultural to an industrial and capitalist economy, and emerged as a major world power.

As his philosophical reputation grew, so did Dewey's belief that traditional (canonical) philosophy was simply inadequate for understanding or resolving real-life issues in the public arena. The stereotypical perception of philosophers as ivory tower intellectuals with their heads in the clouds, divorced from everyday concerns, is one Dewey himself would have challenged. His view was that a new conception of philosophy and philosophical method were necessary if philosophy was to have any practical application in public affairs or social reform movements.

It was within this historical and philosophical context that Dewey became a leading proponent of the American school of thought called "pragmatism," an alternative philosophical perspective to traditional, canonical views. Pragmatism rejected many tenets of modern philosophy: Cartesian dualist metaphysics; a lengthy list of traditionally favored dualisms; the epistemologies of rationalism versus empiricism; the static, abstract nature of philosophical theorizing based on reason alone; and a conception of philosophy as the disinterested, detached, impartial, objective, rational pursuit of Truth. Pragmatism favored a different view: philosophical method as an evolutionary process that viewed knowledge as arising from "the human organism's" interaction with its environment; a conception of philosophy as originating in real-life experiences or predicaments; the view that the primary goal and value of philosophy is to contribute to the on-going renewal of human conduct in order to re-create an inclusive democracy.

Given that Dewey's philosophical work critiqued canonical views of modern philosophy, it is not surprising that it received varied responses from the philosophical community. Some philosophers appreciated what other philosophers rejected about Dewey's epistemological position that there is no separation of the knowing subject from the object known, that "objects of knowledge" could only be understood in the broader context of the interrelationship between the "human organism" and its environment (not in the domain of reason or thought alone). Similarly, philosophers disagreed about Dewey's ethical position that value judgments are tools for the redirection of human conduct when habits or cultural influences are insufficient. The pragmatist's approach requires that the warrant for value judgments be located in human conduct and experience, not in fixed, abstract principles. A pragmatist asks whether the value judgments or ethical norms solved the problem they were designed to solve, have consequences that benefit everyone, or recommend alternative value judgments for consideration.

The influence of Dewey's version of American pragmatism was significant in the early 1900s but receded when other philosophical perspectives and methods, such as analytic philosophy in England and the United States and phenomenology in continental Europe, gained advocates. But recently interest in American pragmatism has been revived by feminist, environmental, and phenomenological concerns that intersect with those of American pragmatism: for example, the role of socially constructed conceptual frameworks in shaping one's perception of the world; a rejection of canonical grand narratives in favor of appeals to concrete experience; defenses of contextual ethics that are neither absolutist nor relativist; recognition of the necessary role played by "moral emotions," such as care and empathy, to ethics and ethical reasoning; new conceptions of theory that reject traditional necessary and sufficient condition accounts; and the need to "re-create democracy" (to use Dewey's phrase) through sympathy and respect for the other members of society. These recent philosophies have renewed interest in Dewey's philosophy and American pragmatism in more than just a casual way.

ADDAMS

Laura Jane Addams was born in Cedarville, Illinois, the daughter of politician and successful mill owner John Addams. The timeline of her birth—ten months after the publication of Darwin's *Origin of the Species*, two months prior to the election of Abraham Lincoln as president of the United States, and seven months prior to the secession of the South from the Union—is important to understanding Addams's pragmatist philosophy.

When Jane was two years old her mother died while giving birth to her ninth child. Subsequently, Addams turned to her father for her emotional and intellectual needs. She was an avid reader as a child, having access to the housing of the town library in the Addams home. Her father supported her desire for higher education and paid for her to attend the all-women's institution, Rockford Seminary (later renamed Rockford College). At Rockford, Addams experienced the empowerment of living in a women-centered environment; her intellectual talents and social activism took hold.

After graduation from Rockford she unsuccessfully pursued a medical degree. Addams spent the next ten years soul searching about what she wanted to do. Marriage and religious options—familiar avenues for women—held no interest for her. She made two trips to Europe; on the second trip she visited Toynbee Hall, a community of young men committed to helping the poor of London by living among them in a settlement house. It was that experience that led her to decide to create a similar community in the United States: Hull House in Chicago. Addams worked with other American pragmatists, including John Dewey and George Herbert Mead, on many social reform projects in Chicago.

Hull House became the venue from which Addams developed her pragmatist public philosophy. In 1899, ten years after founding it, Addams published "The Function of the Social Settlement." The essay was an early statement of what became a central theme of Addams's views about democracy: democracy is both a socially informed way of living together and a framework for the development of morality. In order for a democracy to succeed, its members must engage in sympathetic knowledge for the express purpose of learning how to care and act on one another's behalf. She also argued that epistemological concerns were central to the success of social settlements and democracy. Her basic claim was that settlement houses require that people learn about and from one another across traditional socioeconomic and other cultural divides. To this end, Hull House helped immigrants adjust to their new American culture, and Addams's writing about her experiences with immigrants helped communicate to privileged white people what it meant to be poor, culturally displaced, and politically disenfranchised. The immigrants brought many cultural traditions with them, and Addams thought knowledge of these traditions would enrich American life. She always presented the immigrants as agents and as having rich resources to offer. She argued that this reciprocal, collective knowledge formation was beneficial to both the immigrants and the society at large.

Addams authored or coauthored a dozen books and more than five hundred articles on a major theme of American pragmatism—the role of philosophy in helping one understand the interplay between experience and reflection. A poll taken during this time indicated that Addams was one of the most highly recognized and admired figures in the United States. Addams received the ultimate honor as recipient of the Nobel Peace Prize in 1931. She died of cancer a few years later in 1935. Her passing was eulogized in newspapers around the globe.

Addams has long been recognized as a prominent and highly respected social reformer. But it was not until the late twentieth century that she also gained recognition as a philosopher and a pragmatist. The combination of her gender, social activism, and writing style—one that lacks the abstract nature of traditional philosophy and, as a pragmatist, does not begin from pre-constructed theoretical positions—certainly contributed to the delay in such recognition. But it seems prejudicial to read *Democracy and Social Ethics* and not recognize it as written by a practicing woman philosopher in the philosophical tradition of American pragmatism.

FISCHER'S COMMENTARY

Fischer's commentary practices what American pragmatism preaches: it illustrates what it is trying to show—the nature of American pragmatism as represented (though concrete, everyday life examples from which theoretical considerations emerge). Consider how it does this.

The commentary describes key elements of the writings by Dewey and Addams on two topics—a critique of canonical conceptions of philosophy and an endorsement of an alternative philosophy, American pragmatism. Their writings describe the general goal of American pragmatism to generate conclusions from ordinary life experiences that illuminate the nature and problems of those experiences while creating a more effective and satisfying democracy.

Fischer's commentary uses a "logic of inquiry" (Dewey), based in concrete examples (from Fischer's own experiences and Dewey's and Addams's writings), to generate conclusions that provide a better understanding of ordinary life and, thereby, move one closer to learning how to create a better democracy. Fischer's commentary provides conclusions that sometimes come from Dewey's and Addams's social activism, participation in social movements, or use of pragmatic problem-solving strategies to rethink real-life problems. By employing features of American pragmatism in her own writing style and content, Fischer's commentary enables us to see how Dewey and Addams use pragmatism to help philosophy reach its ultimate goal: to re-create democracy through the "creation of more humane experience in which all share and to which all contribute."

Excerpts of Writings by Dewey and Addams

I. EXCERPTS FROM JANE ADDAMS'S "A MODERN LEAR"[1]

Those of us who lived in Chicago during the summer of 1894 were confronted by a drama which epitomized and, at the same time, challenged the code of social ethics under which we live, for a quick series of unusual events had dispelled the good nature which in happier times envelopes the ugliness of the industrial situation. It sometimes seems as if the shocking experiences of that summer, the barbaric instinct to kill, roused on both sides, the sharp division into class lines, with the resultant distrust and bitterness, can only be endured if we learn from it all a great ethical lesson. To endure is all we can hope for. It is impossible to justify such a course of rage and riot in a civilized community to whom the methods of conciliation and control were open. Every public-spirited citizen in Chicago during that summer felt the stress and perplexity of the situation and asked himself, "How far am I responsible for this social disorder? What can be done to prevent such outrageous manifestations of ill-will?"

If the responsibility of tolerance lies with those of the widest vision, it behooves us to consider this great social disaster, not alone in its legal aspect nor in its sociological bearings, but from those deep human motives, which, after all, determine events.

During the discussions which followed the Pullman strike, the defenders of the situation were broadly divided between the people pleading for individual benevolence and those insisting upon social righteousness; between those who held that the philanthropy of the president of the Pullman Company had been most ungratefully received and those who maintained that the situation was the inevitable outcome of the social consciousness developing among working people.

In the midst of these discussions the writer found her mind dwelling upon a comparison which modified and softened all her judgments. Her attention was caught by the similarity of ingratitude suffered by an indulgent employer and an indulgent parent. King Lear came often to her mind. We have all shared the family relationship and our code of ethics concerning it is somewhat settled. We also bear a part in the industrial relationship, but our ethics concerning that are still uncertain. A comparative study of these two relationships presents an advantage, in that it enables us to consider the situation from the known experience toward the unknown. The minds of all of us reach back to our early struggles, as we emerged from the state of self-willed childhood to a recognition of the family claim.

We have all had glimpses of what it might be to blaspheme against family ties; to ignore the elemental claim they make upon us, but on the whole we have recognized them, and it does not occur to us to throw them over. The industrial claim is so difficult; the ties are so intangible that we are constantly ignoring them and shirking the duties which they impose. It will probably be easier to treat of the tragedy of the Pullman strike as if it were already long past when we compare it to the family tragedy of Lear which has already become historic to our minds and which we discuss without personal feeling.

Historically considered, the relation of Lear to his children was archaic and barbaric, holding in it merely the beginnings of a family life, since developed. We may in later years learn to look back upon the industrial relationships in which we are now placed as quite as incomprehensible and selfish, quite as barbaric and undeveloped, as was the family relationship between Lear and his daughters. We may then take the relationship of this unusually generous employer at Pullman to his own town full of employees as at least a fair one, because so exceptionally liberal in many of its aspects. King Lear doubtless held the same notion of a father's duty that was held by the other fathers of his time; but he alone was a king and had kingdoms to bestow upon his children. He was unique, therefore, in the magnitude of his indulgence, and in the magnitude of the disaster which followed it. The sense of duty held by the president of the Pullman Company doubtless represents the ideal in the minds of the best of the present employers as to their obligations toward their employees, but he projected this ideal more magnificently than the others. He alone gave his men so model a town, such perfect surroundings. The magnitude of his indulgence and failure corresponded and we are forced to challenge the ideal itself: the same deal which, more or less clearly defined, is floating in the minds of all philanthropic employers.

This older tragedy implied maladjustment between individuals; the forces of the tragedy were personal and passionate. This modern tragedy in its inception is a maladjustment between two large bodies of men, an employing company and a mass of employees. It deals not with personal relationships, but with industrial relationships.

Owing, however, to the unusual part played in it by the will of one man, we find that it closely approaches Lear in motif. The relation of the British King to his family is very like the relation of the president of the Pullman Company to his town; the denouement of a daughter's break with her father suggests the break of the employees with their benefactor. If we call one an example of the domestic tragedy, the other of the industrial tragedy, it is possible to make them illuminate each other.

It is easy to discover striking points of similarity in the tragedies of the royal father and the philanthropic president of the Pullman Company. The like quality of ingratitude they both suffered is at once apparent. It may be said that the ingratitude which Lear received was poignant and bitter to him in proportion as he recalled the extraordinary benefits he had heaped upon his daughters, and that he found his fate harder to bear because he had so far exceeded the measure of a father's duty, as he himself says. What, then, would be the bitterness of a man who had heaped extraordinary benefits upon those toward whom be bad no duty recognized by common consent; who had not only exceeded the righteousness of the employer, but who had worked out original and striking methods for lavishing goodness and generosity? More than that, the president had been almost persecuted for this goodness by the more utilitarian members of his company and had at one time imperiled his business reputation for the sake of the benefactions to his town, and he had thus reached the height of sacrifice for it. This model town embodied not only his hopes and ambitions, but stood for the peculiar effort which a man makes for that which is misunderstood.

In shops such as those at Pullman, indeed, in all manufacturing affairs since the industrial revolution, industry is organized into a vast social operation. The shops are managed, however, not for the development of the workman thus socialized, but for the interests of the company owning the capital. The divergence between the social form and the individual aim becomes greater as the employees are more highly socialized and dependent, just as the clash in a family is more vital in proportion to the development and closeness of the family tie. The president of the Pullman Company went further than the usual employer does. He socialized not only the factory but the form in which his workmen were living. He built and, in a great measure, regulated an entire town. This again might have worked out into a successful associated effort, if he had had in view the sole good of the inhabitants thus socialized, if he had called upon them for self-expression and had made the town a growth and manifestation of their wants and needs. But, unfortunately, the end to be obtained became ultimately commercial and not social, having in view the payment to the company of at least four per cent on the money invested, so that with this rigid requirement there could be no adaptation of rent to wages, much less to needs. The rents became statical and the wages competitive, shifting inevitably with the demands of trade. The president assumed that he himself knew the needs of his men, and so far from wishing them to express their needs he denied to them the simple rights of trade organization, which would have been, of course, the merest preliminary to an attempt at associated expression. If we may take the dictatorial relation of Lear to Cordelia as a typical and most dramatic example of the distinctively family tragedy, one will asserting its authority through all the entanglement of wounded affection, and insisting upon its selfish ends at all costs, may we not consider the absolute authority of this employer over his town as a typical and dramatic example of the industrial tragedy? One will direct the energies of many others, without regard to their desires, and having in view in the last analysis only commercial results?

It shocks our ideal of family life that a man should fail to know his daughter's heart because she awkwardly expressed her love, that he should refuse to comfort and advise her through all difference of opinion and clashing of will. That a man should be so absorbed in his own indignation as to fail to apprehend his child's thought; that he should lose his affection in his anger, is really no more unnatural than that the man who spent a million dollars on a swamp to make it sanitary for his employees, should refuse to speak to them for ten minutes, whether they were in the right or wrong; or that a man who had given them his time and thought for twenty years should withdraw from them his guidance when he believed them misled by ill-advisers and wandering in a mental fog; or that he should grow hard and angry when they needed tenderness and help.

Lear ignored the common ancestry of Cordelia and himself. He forgot her royal inheritance of magnanimity, and also the power of obstinacy which he shared with her. So long had he thought of himself as the noble and indulgent father that he had lost the faculty by which he might perceive himself in the wrong. Even when his spirit was broken by the storm he declared himself more sinned against than sinning. He could believe any amount of kindness and goodness of himself, but could imagine no fidelity on the part of Cordelia unless she gave him the sign he demanded.

The president of the Pullman Company doubtless began to build his town from an honest desire to give his employees the best surroundings. As it developed it became a source of pride and an exponent of power, that he cared most for when it gave him a glow of benevolence. Gradually, what the outside world thought of it became of importance to him and he ceased to measure its usefulness by the standard of the men's needs. The theater was complete in equipment and beautiful in design, but too costly for a troupe who depended upon the patronage of mechanics, as the church was too expensive to be rented continuously. We can imagine the founder of the town slowly darkening his glints of memory and forgetting the common stock of experience which he held with his men. He cultivated the great and noble impulses of the benefactor, until the power of attaining a simple human relationship with his employees, that of frank equality with them, was gone from him. He, too, lost the faculty of affectionate interpretation, and demanded a sign. He and his employees had no mutual interest in a common cause.

Was not the grotesque situation of the royal father and the philanthropic employer to perform so many good deeds that they lost the power of recognizing good in beneficiaries? Were not both so absorbed in carrying out a personal plan of improvement that they failed to catch the great moral lesson which their times offered them? This is the crucial point to the tragedies and may be further elucidated.

Lear had doubtless swung a bauble before Cordelia's baby eyes that he might have the pleasure of seeing the little pink and tender hands stretched for it. A few years later he had given jewels to the young princess, and felt an exquisite pleasure when she stood before him, delighted with her gaud and grateful to her father. He demanded the same kind of response for his gift of the kingdom, but the gratitude must be larger and more carefully expressed, as befitted such a gift. At the opening of the drama he sat upon his throne ready for this enjoyment, but instead of delight and gratitude he found the first dawn of character. His daughter made the awkward attempt of an untrained soul to be honest, to be scrupulous in the expressions of its feelings. It was new to him that his child should be moved by a principle outside of himself, which even his imagination could not follow; that she had caught the notion of an existence so vast that her relationship as a daughter was but part of it.

Perhaps her suitors, the King of France or the Duke of Burgundy, had first hinted to the young Cordelia that there was a fuller life beyond the seas. Certain it is that some-one had shaken her from the quiet measure of her insular existence and that she had at last felt the thrill of the world's life. She was transformed by a dignity which recast her speech and made it self-contained, as is becoming a citizen of the world. She found herself in the sweep of a notion of justice so large that the immediate loss of a kingdom seemed of little consequence to her. Even an act which might be construed as disrespect to her father was justified in her eyes because she was vainly striving to fill out this larger conception of duty.

The test which comes sooner or later to many parents had come to Lear, to maintain the tenderness of the relation between father and child, after that relation had become one between adults; to be contented with the responses which this adult made to the family claim, while, at the same time, she felt the tug upon her emotions and faculties of the larger life, the life which surrounds and completes the individual and family life, and which shares and widens her attention. He was not sufficiently wise to see that only that child can fulfill the family claim in its sweetness and strength who also fulfills the larger claim, that the adjustment of the lesser and larger implies no conflict. The mind of Lear was not big enough for this test. He failed to see anything but the personal slight involved; the ingratitude alone reached him. It was impossible for him to calmly watch his child developing beyond the strength of his own mind and sympathy.

Without pressing the analogy too hard may we not compare the indulgent relation of this employer to his town to the relation which existed between Lear and Cordelia? He fostered his employees for many years, gave them sanitary houses and beautiful parks, but in their extreme need, when they were struggling with the most difficult question which the times could present to them, when, if ever, they required the assistance of a trained mind and a comprehensive outlook, he lost his touch and had nothing wherewith to help them. He did not see the situation. He had been ignorant of their gropings toward justice. His conception of goodness for them had been cleanliness, decency of living, and above all, thrift and temperance. He had provided them means for all this; had gone further, and given them opportunities for enjoyment and comradeship. But he suddenly found his town in the sweep of a world-wide moral impulse. A movement had been going on about him and through the souls of his workingmen of which he had been unconscious. He had only heard of this movement by rumor. The men who consorted with him at his club and in his business had spoken but little of it, and when they had discussed it had contemptuously called it the "Labor Movement," headed by deadbeats and agitators. Of the force and power of this movement, of all the vitality within it, of that conception of duty which induces men to go without food and to see their wives and children suffer for the sake of securing better wages for fellow-workmen whom they have never seen, this president had dreamed absolutely nothing. But his town had at last become swept into this larger movement, so that the giving up of comfortable homes, of beautiful surround-ings, seemed as naught to the men within its grasp.

Outside the ken of this philanthropist, the proletariat had learned to say in many lan-guages that "the injury of one is the concern of all." Their watchwords were brotherhood, sacrifice, the subordination of individual and trade interests to the good of the working class; and their persistent strivings were toward the ultimate freedom of that class from the conditions under which they now labor.

The president of this company desired that his employees should possess the indi-vidual and family virtues, but did nothing to cherish in them those social virtues which his own age demanded. He rather substituted for that sense of responsibility to the com-munity, a feeling of gratitude to himself, who had provided them with public buildings, and had laid out for them a simulacrum of public life.

Is it strange that when the genuine feeling of the age struck his town this belated and almost feudal virtue of personal gratitude fell before it?

Day after day during that horrible suspense, when the wires constantly reported the same message, "The president of the company holds that there is nothing to arbitrate," one longed to find out what was in the mind of this man, to unfold his ultimate motive. One concludes that he must have been sustained by the consciousness of being in the right. Only that could have held him against the great desire for fair play which swept over the country. Only the training which an arbitrary will receives by years of consult-ing first its own personal and commercial ends could have made it strong enough to withstand the demands for social adjustment. He felt himself right from the commercial standpoint, and could not see the situation from the social standpoint. For years he had gradually accustomed himself to the thought that his motive was beyond reproach; that his attitude to his town was always righteous and philanthropic. Habit held him persistent in this view of the case through all the changing conditions.

Modern philanthropists need to remind themselves of the old definition of great-ness: that it consists in the possession of the largest share of the common human qualities and experiences, not in the acquirements of peculiarities and excessive virtues. Popular opinion calls him the greatest of Americans who gathered to himself the largest amount of American experience, and who never forgot when he was in Washington how the "crackers" in Kentucky and the pioneers of Illinois thought and felt, striving to retain their thoughts and feelings, and to embody only the mighty will of the "common people." The danger of professionally attaining to the power of the righteous man, of yielding to the ambition "for doing good," compared to which the ambitious for political position, learning, or wealth are vulgar and commonplace, ramifies throughout our modern life, and is a constant and settled danger of philanthropy.

In so far as philanthropists are cut off from the influence of the Zeit-Geist, from the code of ethics which rule the body of men, from the great moral life springing from our common experiences, so long as they are "good to people," rather than "with them," they are bound to accomplish a large amount of harm. They are outside of the influence of that great faith which perennially springs up in the hearts of the people, and re-creates the world. In spite of the danger of overloading the tragedies with moral reflections, a point ought to be made on the other side. It is the weakness in the relation of the employees to the employer, the fatal lack of generosity in the attitude of workmen toward the company under whose exactions they feel themselves wronged.

In reading the tragedy of King Lear, Cordelia does not escape our censure. Her first words are cold, and we are shocked by her lack of tenderness. Why should she ignore her father's need for indulgence, and be so unwilling to give him what he so obviously craved? We see in the old king "the overmastering desire of being beloved, which is selfish, and yet characteristic of the selfishness of a loving and kindly nature alone." His eagerness produces in us a strange pity for him, and we are impatient that his youngest and best-beloved child cannot feel this, even in the midst of her search for truth and her newly acquired sense of a higher duty. It seems to us a narrow conception that would break thus abruptly with the past, and would assume that her father had no part in her new life. We want to remind her that "pity, memory and faithfulness are natural ties," and surely as much to be prized as is the development of her own soul. We do not admire the Cordelia "who loves according to her bond" as we later admire the same Cordelia who comes back from France that she may include in her happiness and freer life the father whom she had deserted through her self-absorption. She is aroused to her affection through her pity, but when the floodgates are once open she acknowledges all. It sometimes seems as if only hardship and sorrow could arouse our tenderness, whether in our personal or social relations; that the king, the prosperous man, was the last to receive the justice which can come only through affectionate interpretation. We feel less pity for Lear on his throne than in the storm, although he is the same man, bound up in the same self-righteousness, and exhibiting the same lack of self-control.

As the vision of the life of Europe caught the sight and quickened the pulses of Cordelia, so a vision of the wider life has caught the sight of workingmen. After the vision has once been seen it is impossible to do aught but to press toward its fulfillment. We have all seen it. We are all practically agreed that the social passion of the age is directed toward the emancipation of the wage-worker; that a great accumulation of moral force is overmastering men and making for this emancipation as in another time it has made for the emancipation of the slave; that nothing will satisfy the aroused conscience of men short of the complete participation of the working classes in the spiritual, intellectual and material inheritance of the human race. But just as Cordelia failed to include her father in the scope of her salvation and selfishly took it for herself alone, so workingmen in the dawn of the vision are inclined to claim it for themselves, putting out of their thoughts the old relationships; and just as surely as Cordelia's conscience developed in the new life and later drove her back to her father, where she perished, drawn into the cruelty and wrath which had now become objective and tragic, so the emancipation of working people will have to be inclusive of the employer from the first or it will encounter many failures, cruelties and reactions. It will result not in the position of the repentant Cordelia but in that of King Lear's two older daughters.

If the workingmen's narrow conception of emancipation was fully acted upon, they would hold much the same relationship to their expropriated employer that the two older daughters held to their abdicated father. When the kingdom was given to them they received it as altogether their own, and were dominated by a sense of possession; "it is ours not yours" was never absent from their consciousness. When Lear ruled the kingdom he had never been without this sense of possession, although he expressed it in indulgence and condescending kindness. His older daughters expressed it in cruelty, but the motive of father and children was not unlike. They did not wish to be reminded by the state and retinue of the old King that he had been the former possessor. Finally, his mere presence alone reminded them too much of that and they banished him from the palace. That a newly acquired sense of possession should result in the barbaric, the incredible scenes of bitterness and murder, which were King Lear's portion, is not without a reminder of the barbaric scenes in our political and industrial relationships, when the sense of possession, to obtain and to hold, is aroused on both sides. The scenes in Paris during the political revolution or the more familiar scenes at the mouths of the mines and the terminals of railways occur to all of us.

The doctrine of emancipation preached to the wage-workers alone runs an awful risk of being accepted for what it offers them, for the sake of fleshpots, rather than for the human affection and social justice which it involves. This doctrine must be strong enough in its fusing power to touch those who think they lose, as well as those who think they gain. Only thus can it become the doctrine of a universal movement.

The new claim on the part of the toiling multitude, the new sense of responsibility on the part of the well-to-do, arises in reality from the same source. They are in fact the same "social compunction," and, in spite of their widely varying manifestations, logically converge into the same movement. Mazzini once preached, "the consent of men and your own conscience are two wings given you whereby you may rise to God." It is so easy for the good and powerful to think that they can rise by following the dictates of conscience by pursuing their own ideals, leaving those ideals unconnected with the consent of their fellow-men. The president of the Pullman Company thought out within his own mind a beautiful town. He had power with which to build this town, but he did not appeal to nor obtain the consent of the men who were living in it. The most unambitious reform, recognizing the necessity for this consent, makes for slow but sane and strenuous progress, while the most ambitious of social plans and experiments, ignoring this, is prone to the failure of the model town of Pullman.

The man who insists upon consent, who moves with the people, is bound to consult the feasible right as well as the absolute right. He is often obliged to attain only Mr. Lincoln's "best possible," and often have the sickening sense of compromising with his best convictions. He has to move along with those whom he rules toward a goal that neither he nor they see very clearly till they come to it. He has to discover what people really want, and then "provide the channels in which the growing moral force of their lives shall flow." What he does attain, however, is not the result of his individual striving, as a solitary mountain climber beyond the sight of the valley multitude, but it is underpinned and upheld by the sentiments and aspirations of many others. Progress has been slower perpendicularly, but incomparably greater because lateral.

He has not taught his contemporaries to climb mountains, but he has persuaded the villagers to move up a few feet higher. It is doubtful if personal ambition, whatever may have been its commercial results, has ever been of any value as a motive power in social reform. But whatever it may have done in the past, it is certainly too archaic to accomplish anything now. Our thoughts, at least for this generation, cannot be too much directed from mutual relationships and responsibilities. They will be warped, unless we look all men in the face, as if a community of interests lay between, unless we hold the mind open, to take strength and cheer from a hundred connections.

To touch to vibrating response the noble fiber in each man, to pull these many fibers, fragile, impalpable and constantly breaking, as they are, into one impulse, to develop that mere impulse through its feeble and tentative stages into action, is no easy task, but lateral progress is impossible without it.

If only a few families of the English speaking race had profited by the dramatic failure of Lear, much heart-breaking and domestic friction might have been spared. Is it too much to hope that some of us will carefully consider this modern tragedy, if perchance it may contain a warning for the troublous times in which we live? By considering the dramatic failure of the liberal employer's plans for his employees we may possibly be spared useless industrial tragedies in the uncertain future which lies ahead of us.

II. EXCERPTS FROM JOHN DEWEY'S *THEORIES OF KNOWLEDGE*[2]

A number of theories of knowing have been criticized in the previous pages. In spite of their differences from one another, they all agree in one fundamental respect which contrasts with the theory which has been positively advanced. The latter assumes continuity; the former state or imply certain basic divisions, separations, or antitheses, technically called dualisms. The origin of these divisions we have found in the hard and fast walls which mark off social groups and classes within a group: like those between rich and poor, men and women, noble and baseborn, ruler and ruled. These barriers mean absence of fluent and free intercourse. This absence is equivalent to the setting up of different types of life-experience, each with isolated subject matter, aim, and standard of values. Every such social condition must be formulated in a dualistic philosophy, if philosophy is to be a sincere account of experience. When it gets beyond dualism—as many philosophies do in form—it can only be by appeal to something higher than anything found in experience, by a flight to some transcendental realm. And in denying duality in name such theories restore it in fact, for they end in a division between things of this world as mere appearances and an inaccessible essence of reality.

In the first place, there is the opposition of empirical and higher rational knowing. The first is connected with everyday affairs, serves the purposes of the ordinary individual who has no specialized intellectual pursuit, and brings his wants into some kind of working connection with the immediate environment. Such knowing is depreciated, if not despised, as purely utilitarian, and lacking in cultural significance. Rational knowledge is supposed to be something which touches reality in ultimate, intellectual fashion; to be pursued for its own sake and properly to terminate in purely theoretical insight, not debased by application in behavior. Socially, the distinction corresponds to that of the intelligence used by the working classes and that used by a learned class remote from concern with the means of living.

Philosophically, the difference turns about the distinction of the particular and universal. Experience is an aggregate of more or less isolated particulars, acquaintance with each of which must be separately made. Reason deals with universals, with general principles, with laws, which lie above the welter of concrete details. In the educational precipitate, the pupil is supposed to have to learn, on one hand, a lot of items of specific information, each standing by itself, and upon the other hand, to become familiar with a certain number of laws and general relationships. Geography, as often taught, illustrates the former; mathematics, beyond the rudiments of figuring, the latter. For all practical purposes, they represent two independent worlds.

Another antithesis is suggested by the two senses of the word "learning." On the one hand, learning is the sum total of what is known, as that is handed down by books and learned men. It is something external, an accumulation of cognitions as one might store material commodities in a warehouse. Truth exists ready-made somewhere. Study is then the process by which an individual draws on what is in storage. On the other hand, learning means something which the individual does when he studies. It is an active, personally conducted affair. The dualism here is between knowledge as something external, or, as it is often called, objective, and knowing as something purely internal, subjective, psychical. There is, on one side, a body of truth, ready-made, and, on the other, a ready-made mind equipped with a faculty of knowing—if it only wills to exercise it, which it is often strangely loath to do. The separation, often touched upon, between subject matter and method is the educational equivalent of this dualism. Socially the distinction has to do with the part of life which is dependent upon authority and that where individuals are free to advance.

Another dualism is that of activity and passivity in knowing. Purely empirical and physical things are often supposed to be known by receiving impressions. Physical things somehow stamp themselves upon the mind or convey themselves into consciousness by means of the sense organs. Rational knowledge and knowledge of spiritual things is supposed, on the contrary, to spring from activity initiated within the mind, an activity carried on better if it is kept remote from all sullying touch of the senses and external objects. The distinction between sense training and object lessons and laboratory exercises, and pure ideas contained in books, and appropriated—so it is thought—by some miraculous output of mental energy, is a fair expression in education of this distinction. Socially, it reflects a division between those who are controlled by direct concern with things and those who are free to cultivate themselves.

Another current opposition is that said to exist between the intellect and the emotions. The emotions are conceived to be purely private and personal, having nothing to do with the work of pure intelligence in apprehending facts and truths—except perhaps the single emotion of intellectual curiosity. The intellect is a pure light; the emotions are a disturbing heat. The mind turns outward to truth; the emotions turn inward to considerations of personal advantage and loss. Thus in education we have that systematic depreciation of interest which has been noted, plus the necessity in practice, with most pupils, of recourse to extraneous and irrelevant rewards and penalties in order to induce the person who has a mind (much as his clothes have a pocket) to apply that mind to the truths to be known. Thus we have the spectacle of professional educators decrying appeal to interest while they uphold with great dignity the need of reliance upon examinations, marks, promotions and emotions, prizes, and the time-honored paraphernalia of rewards and punishments. The effect of this situation in crippling the teacher's sense of humor has not received the attention which it deserves.

All of these separations culminate in one between knowing and doing, theory and practice, between mind as the end and spirit of action and the body as its organ and means. We shall not repeat what has been said about the source of this dualism in the division of society into a class laboring with their muscles for material sustenance and a class which, relieved from economic pressure, devotes itself to the arts of expression and social direction. Nor is it necessary to speak again of the educational evils which spring from the separation. We shall be content to summarize the forces which tend to make the untenability of this conception obvious and to replace it by the idea of continuity.

(i) The advance of physiology and the psychology associated with it have shown the connection of mental activity with that of the nervous system. Too often recognition of connection has stopped short at this point; the older dualism of soul and body has been replaced by that of the brain and the rest of the body. But in fact the nervous system is only a specialized mechanism for keeping all bodily activities working together. Instead of being isolated from them, as an organ of knowing from organs of motor response, it is the organ by which they interact responsively with one another. The brain is essentially an organ for effecting the reciprocal adjustment to each other of the stimuli received from the environment and responses directed upon it. Note that the adjusting is reciprocal; the brain not only enables organic activity to be brought to bear upon any object of the environment in response to a sensory stimulation, but this response also determines what the next stimulus will be. See what happens, for example, when a carpenter is at work upon a board, or an etcher upon his plate—or in any case of a consecutive activity. While each motor response is adjusted to the state of affairs indicated through the sense organs, that motor response shapes the next sensory stimulus. Generalizing this illustration, the brain is the machinery for a constant reorganizing of activity so as to maintain its continuity; that is to say, to make such modifications in future action as are required because of what has already been done. The continuity of the work of the carpenter distinguishes it from a routine repetition of identically the same motion and from a random activity where there is nothing cumulative. What makes it continuous, consecutive, or concentrated is that each earlier act prepares the way for later acts, while these take account of or reckon with the results already attained—the basis of all responsibility. No one who has realized the full force of the facts of the connection of knowing with the nervous system and of the nervous system with the readjusting of activity continuously to meet new conditions, will doubt that knowing has to do with reorganizing activity, instead of being something isolated from all activity, complete on its own account.

(ii) The development of biology clinches this lesson, with its discovery of evolution. For the philosophic significance of the doctrine of evolution lies precisely in its emphasis upon continuity of simpler and more complex organic forms until we reach man. The development of organic forms begins with structures where the adjustment of environment and organism is obvious, and where anything which can be called mind is at a minimum. As activity becomes more complex, coordinating a greater number of factors in space and time, intelligence plays a more and more marked role, for it has a larger span of the future to forecast and plan for. The effect upon the theory of knowing is to displace the notion that it is the activity of a mere onlooker or spectator of the world, the notion which goes with the idea of knowing as something complete in itself. For the doctrine of organic development means that the living creature is a part of the world, sharing its vicissitudes and fortunes, and making itself secure in its precarious dependence only as it intellectually identifies itself with the things about it, and, forecasting the future consequences of what is going on, shapes its own activities accordingly. If the living, experiencing being is an intimate participant in the activities of the world to which it belongs, then knowledge is a mode of participation, valuable in the degree in which it is effective. It cannot be the idle view of an unconcerned spectator.

(iii) The development of the experimental method as the method of getting knowledge and of making sure it is knowledge, and not mere opinion—the method of both discovery and proof—is the remaining great force in bringing about a transformation in the theory of knowledge. The experimental method has two sides. (a) On one hand, it means that we have no right to call anything knowledge except where our activity has actually produced certain physical changes in things, which agree with and confirm the conception entertained. Short of such specific changes, our beliefs are only hypotheses, theories, suggestions, guesses, and are to be entertained tentatively and to be utilized as indications of experiments to be tried. (b) On the other hand, the experimental method of thinking signifies that thinking is of avail; that it is of avail in just the degree in which the anticipation of future consequences is made on the basis of thorough observation of present conditions. Experimentation, in other words, is not equivalent to blind reacting. Such surplus activity—a surplus with reference to what has been observed and is now anticipated—is indeed an unescapable factor in all our behavior, but it is not experiment save as consequences are noted and are used to make predictions and plans in similar situations in the future. The more the meaning of the experimental method is perceived, the more our trying out of a certain way of treating the material resources and obstacles which confront us embodies a prior use of intelligence. What we call magic was with respect to many things the experimental method of the savage; but for him to try was to try his luck, not his ideas. The scientific experimental method is, on the contrary, a trial of ideas; hence even when practically—or immediately—unsuccessful, it is intellectual, fruitful; for we learn from our failures when our endeavors are seriously thoughtful.

The experimental method is new as a scientific resource—as a systematized means of making knowledge, though as old as life as a practical device. Hence it is not surprising that men have not recognized its full scope. For the most part, its significance is regarded as belonging to certain technical and merely physical matters. It will doubtless take a long time to secure the perception that it holds equally as to the forming and testing of ideas in social and moral matters. Men still want the crutch of dogma, of beliefs fixed by authority, to relieve them of the trouble of thinking and the responsibility of directing their activity by thought. They tend to confine their own thinking to a consideration of which one among the rival systems of dogma they will accept. Hence the schools are better adapted, as John Stuart Mill said, to make disciples than inquirers. But every advance in the influence of the experimental method is sure to aid in outlawing the literary, dialectic, and authoritative methods of forming beliefs which have governed the schools of the past, and to transfer their prestige to methods which will procure an active concern with things and persons, directed by aims of increasing temporal reach and deploying greater range of things in space. In time the theory of knowing must be derived from the practice which is most successful in making knowledge; and then that theory will be employed to improve the methods which are less successful.

There are various systems of philosophy with characteristically different conceptions of the method of knowing. Some of them are named scholasticism, sensationalism, rationalism, idealism, realism, empiricism, transcendentalism, pragmatism, etc. Many of them have been criticized in connection with the discussion of some educational problem. We are here concerned with them as involving deviations from that method which has proved most effective in achieving knowledge, for a consideration of the deviations may render clearer the true place of knowledge in experience. In brief, the function of knowledge is to make one experience freely available in other experiences. The word "freely" marks the difference between the principle of knowledge and that of habit. Habit means that an individual undergoes a modification through an experience, which modification forms a predisposition to easier and more effective action in a like direction in the future. Thus it also has the function of making one experience available in subsequent experiences. Within certain limits, it performs this function successfully. But habit, apart from knowledge, does not make allowance for change of conditions, for novelty. Prevision of change is not part of its scope, for habit assumes the essential likeness of the new situation with the old. Consequently it often leads astray, or comes between a person and the successful performance of his task, just as the skill, based on habit alone, of the mechanic will desert him when something unexpected occurs in the running of the machine. But a man who understands the machine is the man who knows what he is about. He knows the conditions under which a given habit works, and is in a position to introduce the changes which will readapt it to new conditions.

In other words, knowledge is a perception of those connections of an object which determine its applicability in a given situation. To take an extreme example; savages react to a flaming comet as they are accustomed to react to other events which threaten the security of their life. Since they try to frighten wild animals or their enemies by shrieks, beating of gongs, brandishing of weapons, etc., they use the same methods to scare away the comet. To us, the method is plainly absurd—so absurd that we fail to note that savages are simply falling back upon habit in a way which exhibits its limitations. The only reason we do not act in some analogous fashion is because we do not take the comet as an isolated, disconnected event, but apprehend it in its connections with other events. We place it, as we say, in the astronomical system. We respond to its connections and not simply to the immediate occurrence. Thus our attitude to it is much freer. We may approach it, so to speak, from any one of the angles provided by its connections. We can bring into play, as we deem wise, any one of the habits appropriate to any one of the connected objects. Thus we get at a new event indirectly instead of immediately—by invention, ingenuity, resourcefulness. An ideally perfect knowledge would represent such a network of interconnections that any past experience would offer a point of advantage from which to get at the problem presented in a new experience. In fine, while a habit apart from knowledge supplies us with a single fixed method of attack, knowledge means that selection may be made from a much wider range of habits.

Two aspects of this more general and freer availability of former experiences for subsequent ones may be distinguished. (i) One, the more tangible, is increased power of control. What cannot be managed directly may be handled indirectly; or we can interpose barriers between us and undesirable consequences; or we may evade them if we cannot overcome them. Genuine knowledge has all the practical value attaching to efficient habits in any case. (ii) But it also increases the meaning, the experienced significance, attaching to an experience. A situation to which we respond capriciously or by routine has only a minimum of conscious significance; we get nothing mentally from it. But wherever knowledge comes into play in determining a new experience there is mental reward; even if we fail practically in getting the needed control we have the satisfaction of experiencing a meaning instead of merely reacting physically.

The theory of the method of knowing which is advanced in these pages may be termed pragmatic. Its essential feature is to maintain the continuity of knowing with an activity which purposely modifies the environment. It holds that knowledge in its strict sense of something possessed consists of our intellectual resources—of all the habits that render our action intelligent. Only that which has been organized into our disposition so as to enable us to adapt the environment to our needs and to adapt our aims and desires to the situation in which we live is really knowledge. Knowledge is not just something which we are now conscious of, but consists of the dispositions we consciously use in understanding what now happens. Knowledge as an act is bringing some of our dispositions to consciousness with a view to straightening out a perplexity, by conceiving the connection between ourselves and the world in which we live.

III. EXCERPTS FROM JANE ADDAMS'S "INTRODUCTION" TO *DEMOCRACY AND SOCIAL ETHICS*[3]

It is well to remind ourselves, from time to time, that "Ethics" is but another word for "righteousness," that for which many men and women of every generation have hungered and thirsted, and without which life becomes meaningless.

Certain forms of personal righteousness have become to a majority of the community almost automatic. It is as easy for most of us to keep from stealing our dinners as it is to digest them, and there is quite as much voluntary morality involved in one process as in the other. To steal would be for us to fall sadly below the standard of habit and expectation which makes virtue easy. In the same way we have been carefully reared to a sense of family obligation, to be kindly and considerate to the members of our own households, and to feel responsible for their well-being. As the rules of conduct have become established in regard to our self-development and our families, so they have been in regard to limited circles of friends. If the fulfillment of these claims were all that a righteous life required, the hunger and thirst would be stilled for many good men and women, and the clew of right living would lie easily in their hands.

But we all know that each generation has its own test, the contemporaneous and current standard by which alone it can adequately judge of its own moral achievements, and that it may not legitimately use a previous and less vigorous test. The advanced test must indeed include that which has already been attained; but if it includes no more, we shall fail to go forward, thinking complacently that we have "arrived" when in reality we have not yet started.

To attain individual morality in an age demanding social morality, to pride one's self on the results of personal effort when the time demands social adjustment, is utterly to fail to apprehend the situation.

All about us are men and women who have become unhappy in regard to their attitude toward the social order itself; toward the dreary round of uninteresting work, the pleasures narrowed down to those of appetite, the declining consciousness of brain power, and the lack of mental food which characterizes the lot of the large proportion of their fellow-citizens. These men and women have caught a moral challenge raised by the exigencies of contemporaneous life; some are bewildered, others who are denied the relief which sturdy action brings are even seeking an escape, but all are increasingly anxious concerning their actual relations to the basic organization of society.

The test which they would apply to their conduct is a social test. They fail to be content with the fulfillment of their family and personal obligations, and find themselves striving to respond to a new demand involving a social obligation; they have become conscious of another requirement, and the contribution they would make is toward a code of social ethics. The conception of life which they hold has not yet expressed itself in social changes or legal enactment, but rather in a mental attitude of maladjustment, and in a sense of divergence between their consciences and their conduct. They desire both a clearer definition of the code of morality adapted to present day demands and a part in its fulfillment, both a creed and a practice of social morality. In the perplexity of this intricate situation at least one thing is becoming clear: if the latter day moral ideal is in reality that of a social morality, it is inevitable that those who desire it must be brought in contact with the moral experiences of the many in order to procure an adequate social motive.

These men and women have realized this and have disclosed the fact in their eagerness for a wider acquaintance with and participation in the life about them. They believe that experience gives the easy and trustworthy impulse toward right action in the broad as well as in the narrow relations. We may indeed imagine many of them saying: "Cast our experiences in a larger mould if our lives are to be animated by the larger social aims. We have met the obligations of our family life, not because we had made resolutions to that end, but spontaneously, because of a common fund of memories and affections, from which the obligation naturally develops, and we see no other way in which to prepare ourselves for the larger social duties." Such a demand is reasonable, for by our daily experience we have discovered that we cannot mechanically hold up a moral standard, then jump at it in rare moments of exhilaration when we have the strength for it, but that even as the ideal itself must be a rational development of life, so the strength to attain it must be secured from interest in life itself. We slowly learn that life consists of processes as well as results, and that failure may come quite as easily from ignoring the adequacy of one's method as from selfish or ignoble aims. We are thus brought to a conception of Democracy not merely as a sentiment which desires the well-being of all men, nor yet as a creed which believes in the essential dignity and equality of all men, but as that which affords a rule of living as well as a test of faith.

We are learning that a standard of social ethics is not attained by fulfilling a sequestered byway, but by mixing on the thronged and common road where all must turn out for one another, and at least see the size of one another's burdens. To follow the path of social morality results perforce in the temper if not the practice of the democratic spirit, for it implies that diversified human experience and resultant sympathy which are the foundation and guarantee of Democracy.

Partly through this wide reading of human life, we find in ourselves a new affinity for all men, which probably never existed in the world before. Evil itself does not shock us as it once did, and we count only that man merciful in whom we recognize an understanding of the criminal. We have learned as common knowledge that much of the insensibility and hardness of the world is due to the lack of imagination which prevents a realization of the experiences of other people. Already there is a conviction that we are under a moral obligation in choosing our experiences, since the result of those experiences must ultimately determine our understanding of life. We know instinctively that if we grow contemptuous of our fellows, and consciously limit our intercourse to certain kinds of people whom we have previously decided to respect, we not only tremendously circumscribe our range of life, but limit the scope of our ethics.

We can recall among the selfish people of our acquaintance at least one common characteristic,—the conviction that they are different from other men and women, that they need peculiar consideration because they are more sensitive or more refined. Such people "refuse to be bound by any relation save the personally luxurious ones of love and admiration, or the identity of political opinion, or religious creed." We have learned to recognize them as selfish, although we blame them not for the will which chooses to be selfish, but for a narrowness of interest which deliberately selects its experience within a limited sphere, and we say that they illustrate the danger of concentrating the mind on narrow and unprogressive issues.

We know, at last, that we can only discover truth by a rational and democratic interest in life, and to give truth complete social expression is the endeavor upon which we are entering. Thus the identification with the common lot which is the essential idea of Democracy becomes the source and expression of social ethics. It is as though we thirsted to drink at the great wells of human experience, because we knew that a daintier or less potent draught would not carry us to the end of the journey, going forward as we must in the heat and jostle of the crowd.

The six following chapters [of *Democracy and Social Ethics*] are studies of various types and groups who are being impelled by the newer conception of Democracy to an acceptance of social obligations involving in each instance a new line of conduct. No attempt is made to reach a conclusion, nor to offer advice beyond the assumption that the cure for the ills of Democracy is more Democracy, but the quite unlooked-for result of the studies would seem to indicate that while the strain and perplexity of the situation is felt most keenly by the educated and self-conscious members of the community, the tentative and actual attempts at adjustment are largely coming through those who are simpler and less analytical.

IV. EXCERPTS FROM JOHN DEWEY'S *CREATIVE DEMOCRACY: THE TASK BEFORE US*[4]

We have had the habit of thinking of democracy as a kind of political mechanism that will work as long as citizens were reasonably faithful in performing political duties.

Of late years we have heard more and more frequently that this is not enough; that democracy is a way of life. This saying gets down to hard pan. But I am not sure that something of the externality of the old idea does not cling to the new and better statement. In any case we can escape from this external way of thinking only as we realize in thought and act that democracy is a personal way of individual life; that it signifies the possession and continual use of certain attitudes, forming personal character and determining desire and purpose in all the relations of life. Instead of thinking of our own dispositions and habits as accommodated to certain institutions we have to learn to think of the latter as expressions, projections and extensions of habitually dominant personal attitudes.

Democracy as a personal, an individual, way of life involves nothing fundamentally new. But when applied it puts a new practical meaning in old ideas. Put into effect it signifies that powerful present enemies of democracy can be successfully met only by the creation of personal attitudes in individual human beings; that we must get over our tendency to think that its defense can be found in any external means whatever, whether military or civil, if they are separated from individual attitudes so deep-seated as to constitute personal character.

Democracy is a way of life controlled by a working faith in the possibilities of human nature. Belief in the Common Man is a familiar article in the democratic creed. That belief is without basis and significance save as it means faith in the potentialities of human nature as that nature is exhibited in every human being irrespective of race, color, sex, birth and family, of material or cultural wealth. This faith may be enacted in statutes, but it is only on paper unless it is put in force in the attitudes which human beings display to one another in all the incidents and relations of daily life. To denounce Nazism for intolerance, cruelty and stimulation of hatred amounts to fostering insincerity if, in our personal relations to other persons, if, in our daily walk and conversation, we are moved by racial, color or other class prejudice; indeed, by anything save a generous belief in their possibilities as human beings, a belief which brings with it the need for providing conditions which will enable these capacities to reach fulfillment. The democratic faith in human equality is belief that every human being, independent of the quantity or range of his personal endowment, has the right to equal opportunity with every other person for development of whatever gifts he has. The democratic belief in the principle of leadership is a generous one. It is universal. It is belief in the capacity of every person to lead his own life free from coercion and imposition by others provided right conditions are supplied.

Democracy is a way of personal life controlled not merely by faith in human nature in general but by faith in the capacity of human beings for intelligent judgment and action if proper conditions are furnished. I have been accused more than once and from opposed quarters of an undue, a utopian, faith in the possibilities of intelligence and in education as a correlate of intelligence. At all events, I did not invent this faith. I acquired it from my surroundings as far as those surroundings were animated by the democratic spirit. For what is the faith of democracy in the role of consultation, of conference, of persuasion, of discussion, in formation of public opinion, which in the long run is self-corrective, except faith in the capacity of the intelligence of the common man to respond with commonsense to the free play of facts and ideas which are secured by effective guarantees of free inquiry, free assembly and free communication? I am willing to leave to upholders of totalitarian states of the right and the left the view that faith in the capacities of intelligence is utopian. For the faith is so deeply embedded in the methods which are intrinsic to democracy that when a professed democrat denies the faith he convicts himself of treachery to his profession.

When I think of the conditions under which men and women are living in many foreign countries today, fear of espionage, with danger hanging over the meeting of friends for friendly conversation in private gatherings, I am inclined to believe that the heart and final guarantee of democracy is in free gatherings of neighbors on the street corner to discuss back and forth what is read in uncensored news of the day, and in gatherings of friends in the living rooms of houses and apartments to converse freely with one another. Intolerance, abuse, calling of names because of differences of opinion about religion or politics or business, as well as because of differences of race, color, wealth or degree of culture are treason to the democratic way of life. For everything which bars freedom and fullness of communication sets up barriers that divide human beings into sets and cliques, into antagonistic sects and factions, and thereby undermines the democratic way of life. Merely legal guarantees of the civil liberties of free belief, free expression, free assembly are of little avail if in daily life freedom of communication, the give and take of ideas, facts, experiences, is choked by mutual suspicion, by abuse, by fear and hatred. These things destroy the essential condition of the democratic way of living even more effectually than open coercion which—as the example of totalitarian states proves—is effective only when it succeeds in breeding hate, suspicion, intolerance in the minds of individual human beings.

Finally, given the two conditions just mentioned, democracy as a way of life is controlled by personal faith in personal day-by-day working together with others. Democracy is the belief that even when needs and ends or consequences are different for each individual, the habit of amicable cooperation—which may include, as in sport, rivalry and competition—is itself a priceless addition to life. To take as far as possible every conflict which arises—and they are bound to arise—out of the atmosphere and medium of force, of violence as a means of settlement into that of discussion and of intelligence is to treat those who disagree—even profoundly—with us as those from whom we may learn, and in so far, as friends. A genuinely democratic faith in peace is faith in the possibility of conducting disputes, controversies and conflicts as cooperative undertakings in which both parties learn by giving the other a chance to express itself, instead of having one party conquer by forceful suppression of the other—a suppression which is none the less one of violence when it takes place by psychological means of ridicule, abuse, intimidation, instead of by overt imprisonment or in concentration camps. To cooperate by giving differences a chance to show themselves because of the belief that the expression of difference is not only a right of the other persons but is a means of enriching one's own life-experience, is inherent in the democratic personal way of life.

Democracy is the faith that the process of experience is more important than any special result attained, so that special results achieved are of ultimate value only as they are used to enrich and order the ongoing process. Since the process of experience is capable of being educative, faith in democracy is all one with faith in experience and education. All ends and values that are cut off from the ongoing process become arrests, fixations. They strive to fixate what has been gained instead of using it to open the road and point the way to new and better experiences.

If one asks what is meant by experience in this connection my reply is that it is that free interaction of individual human beings with surrounding conditions, especially the human surroundings, which develops and satisfies need and desire by increasing knowledge of things as they are. Knowledge of conditions as they are is the only solid ground for communication and sharing; all other communication means the subjection of some persons to the personal opinion of other persons. Need and desire—out of which grow purpose and direction of energy—go beyond what exists, and hence beyond knowledge, beyond science. They continually open the way into the unexplored and unattained future.

Democracy as compared with other ways of life is the sole way of living which believes wholeheartedly in the process of experience as end and as means; as that which is capable of generating the science which is the sole dependable authority for the direction of further experience and which releases emotions, needs and desires so as to call into being the things that have not existed in the past. For every way of life that fails in its democracy limits the contacts, the exchanges, the communications, the interactions by which experience is steadied while it is also enlarged and enriched. The task of this release and enrichment is one that has to be carried on day by day. Since it is one that can have no end till experience itself comes to an end, the task of democracy is forever that of creation of a freer and more humane experience in which all share and to which all contribute.

Commentary by *Marilyn Fischer*, Addams and Dewey: Pragmatism, Expression, and Community

INTRODUCTION

Chicago in the 1890s was home to two remarkable institutions, started by two remarkable activist-philosophers, experimenting with ideas and with social change. The first was Hull House, a social settlement, founded by Jane Addams and Ellen Gates Starr in 1889. The second was the Laboratory School, an experimental school opened in 1896 by John Dewey, along with teachers Katherine Camp Mayhew and Anna Camp Edwards. Interaction was constant between the residents of Hull House and the teachers of the Laboratory School, as the participants learned from and taught each other. Through Hull House and the Laboratory School, Addams and Dewey formulated, tested, and enacted central tenets of classical American pragmatism.

Addams had been excited by her visit in 1888 to Toynbee Hall. A group of Oxford University students and faculty had moved into a poor London neighborhood, seeking to bring education and social reform to their new neighbors in the spirit of friendship. In September 1889, Addams and Starr, rejecting the social expectations placed on young women of their social class, rented a house in a congested Chicago neighborhood full of immigrant families representing eighteen different nationalities. Addams and Starr did not have a preconceived reform agenda. They wanted to be responsive to their neighbors' own perception of their needs. As additional residents moved into Hull House, they established education classes, recreational and social clubs, a daycare and a kindergarten, health clinics, and extensive art, music, and theater programs. Hull House became a center for social reform, as residents and neighbors worked together investigating public health, factory, and sweatshop conditions. Many unions, particularly women's unions, were formed at Hull House and held meetings there. Addams gives a wonderfully readable and reflective account of Hull House's activities and growth in her most well-known work, *Twenty Years at Hull House*.[5]

Newly arrived in Chicago to take a position as chair of the University of Chicago's Department of Philosophy, Psychology, and Pedagogy, Dewey was eager to try out some of his ideas about education. Children should be actively engaged in their own learning, Dewey thought. At the school, six-year-olds, for example, built a model farm; they learned about measurement and simple geometry as they performed the carpentry involved. Cooking was the hook for acquiring knowledge of chemistry, biology, and geography. Through these projects the students acquired academic content while working cooperatively together in a way that simultaneously engaged their minds, emotions, and bodies. Teachers, in addition to knowing material of each academic subject, needed knowledge of child development, a great deal of imagination, and a penchant for teaching by indirection.[6]

Addams and Dewey were intellectual colleagues, fellow social reform activists, and friends. They freely and frequently acknowledged how much they learned from each other. Dewey was a member of Hull House's board of trustees. Addams commented on his performance, "Unlike many trustees, he actually worked on the job."[7] Dewey used Addams's book, *Democracy and Social Ethics*, as a text in his classes and invited Addams to lecture to his students.

Dewey and Addams were activists, working for social reform through countless organizations, locally, nationally, and internationally. They were both founding members of the National Association for the Advancement of Colored People (NAACP) and the American Civil Liberties Union (ACLU). Both spoke and wrote vigorously on public issues, including women's suffrage and educational and workplace rights. Both were prolific scholars. Addams wrote eleven books, published hundreds of articles, and gave thousands of speeches. Dewey's collected works fill thirty-seven volumes.

"Only once in a public crisis did I find my road taking a sharp right angle to the one he recommended," Addams said, referring to her disagreement with Dewey about World War I.[8] Addams maintained her pacifism throughout; Dewey supported the U.S. entry into the war. While Dewey criticized most versions of pacifism, he referred to Addams's version as an "intelligent pacifism."[9]

Finally, Addams and Dewey were good friends. Dewey named his daughter Jane after Addams. Addams gave a eulogy at a memorial service for Dewey's son Gordon, who died when he was only eight. In her biography of her father, Jane Dewey wrote, "Dewey's faith in democracy as a guiding force in education took on both a sharper and a deeper meaning because of Hull House and Jane Addams."[10]

Hull House, the Laboratory School, and all of Addams's and Dewey's writings and activism were pragmatist expressions of their driving philosophical passion: democracy. Working toward democracy in industrial relations is a theme in Addams's essay, "A Modern Lear." The essay itself is a magnificent example of how to do pragmatist philosophy. Dewey's "Theories of Knowledge" lays out basic tenets of pragmatism. Their essays on democracy explain what the point of it all is.

After the Civil War the U.S. economy was largely fueled by the railroads. Industrialist George Pullman founded the Pullman Palace Car Company, specializing in luxury railroad sleeping cars. While most factory workers in Chicago lived in squalid tenements, Pullman built a model town for his employees and their families, providing them with tidy brick houses, nicely kept lawns, shops, a school, a park, a church, and a theater. Pullman owned the town, set prices at the shops, and controlled the rents. In 1893, an economic depression hit the country; in response Pullman cut his workers' wages by 25 percent and laid off 20 percent of his workforce. He did not, however, cut rents in the model town. Although they were not permitted to join unions or strike, his workers called a strike in May 1894. Eugene Debs and his American Railway Union struck in sympathy. Addams, as a member of the Civic Federation of Chicago, tried to arbitrate the strike. She knew George Pullman; he had contributed small amounts of money to Hull House. Addams had visited the town of Pullman and spoken directly with the people living there. As tensions in Chicago mounted, President Cleveland sent in federal troops, who put down the strike after it turned violent.

Dewey moved to Chicago that summer, right in the middle of the strike. In the fall he heard Addams lecture on the labor movement and talked with her afterward. It was an intellectual turning point. Dewey wrote to his wife, Alice, that Addams's talk was "the most magnificent exhibition of intellectual and moral faith I ever saw."[11] Of "Modern Lear," Addams's analysis of the strike, Dewey wrote, "It is one of the greatest things I ever read both as to its form and its ethical philosophy."[12] *Forum, North American Review*, and *Atlantic Monthly* all rejected the essay as too inflammatory. It was finally published in 1912, in *Survey*, a social work journal, eighteen years after the events took place.[13]

In "A Modern Lear," Addams takes a pressing, problematic situation, one in which she is politically and personally invested, and tries to make some sense of it. She begins with the two opposing interpretations that people in Chicago gave to the events. Some argued that Pullman was generous, his workers ungrateful. Others, irritated by Pullman's recalcitrance, put justice on the side of the workers. Addams seeks an alternative interpretation that would be fair to both sides, set the tensions within a larger cultural and philosophical context, and give her some sense of how to proceed.

Addams's strategy is to look to the past and find a story rich enough to set side by side with the current tensions. She finds her resource in Shakespeare's *King Lear*. Lear, eighty years old and awaiting death, wants to divide his kingdom among his three adult daughters. The two oldest, Goneril and Regan, gladly feign declarations of deep devotion to their father to get their shares. But the youngest daughter, Cordelia, newly aware of the world beyond the kingdom, responds honestly and awkwardly that she loves her father "according to my bond." Enraged that her loyalty to him is less than all-consuming, Lear denies Cordelia her inheritance.

Addams places several layers of analysis in the essay. She begins with an analysis of family relations in *King Lear*, makes an analogy between Lear's relation to his adult daughters and Pullman's to his workers, and uses these tensions to craft her own position on ethics and on social reform.

Addams interprets Lear's relation to his daughters as that of a classic patriarch. He is generous to them; he may even love them and want what is best for them. But he clearly holds it as his right and role to define their duties and to be given their obedience and gratitude in return. Lear rewards his older daughters' obedience, hypocritical though it was. Cordelia's honesty, however, cannot make up for her lack of obsequiousness.[14]

ADDAMS'S "A MODERN LEAR"[15]

It is quite a distance from Shakespeare's *King Lear*, written in 1606 and set more than four hundred misty years earlier, to industrial strife in that steamy hot Chicago summer of 1894. Pullman was generous in providing decent living spaces for his workers, but in return he wanted their gratitude and obedience. When they responded to wage cuts and layoffs with unions and a strike, Pullman saw only ingratitude in their actions, not their call for justice. His relationship with his workers was as patriarchal as Lear's to his daughters. Both relations, Addams observes, are barbaric.

Addams does not analyze these conflict-ridden relations in terms of good versus evil, nor in terms of clashes in the parties' self-interest. Instead, she locates the source of the tension by hypothesizing that Lear and Pullman adhere to one moral code, while Cordelia and Pullman's workers are working their way toward another. Lear and Pullman base their actions and expectations on the "family claim," and on "individual virtues and family virtues." Within this code, they have extensive power over persons and property under their control. Cordelia and Pullman's workers are responding to a "larger claim" that extends beyond the family or workplace and embraces "social virtues."[16] The workers, as part of the international labor movement of that time, aimed for universal justice for all workers. They called for egalitarian rather than hierarchical relations, where everyone's participation in decision making is welcomed.

Addams's challenge in "A Modern Lear" is to figure out how to proceed when well-meaning people hold conflicting codes about what are morally appropriate expectations and behaviors. Addams asserts that these "mal-adjusted" codes need to be brought into adjustment. She argues that just as social patterns evolve, so moral codes should evolve to match. Social life in late-nineteenth-century Chicago was densely urban, industrial, and multicultural. People's extended families were in some cases a continent away, while they shared a neighborhood with people of different languages, customs, and beliefs. Economic life was highly interdependent; think of the complex chain of relationships created by industrial production and distribution. Addams calls for an ethics appropriate to this social interdependence and based on equality, participation, and concern for the well-being of all.

Pullman's hopes for patriarchal authority in industry were tragically out of date. While his control over his workers' lives was enormous, he did not know them very well. We hear the poignancy in Addams's remark, "We can imagine the founder of the town slowly darkening his glints of memory and forgetting the common stock of experience which he held with his men. He cultivated the great and noble impulses of the benefactor, until the power of attaining a simple human relationship with his employees, that of frank equality with them, was gone from him."[17]

Toward the end of the essay Addams draws out the implications of her theory for social change and gives a stunning critique of philanthropy in the process. Today, as well as in Addams's time, many generous individuals give time and money to create and sustain the public good. Yet like Lear and like Pullman, they seek to control how "the public good" is defined. Genuine social progress, Addams counters, can only be achieved when all members of the public participate in defining and creating that good.

DEWEY'S "THEORIES OF KNOWLEDGE"[18]

This chapter from *Democracy and Education* gives an excellent summary of Dewey's conception of pragmatism, mixed in with his critique of previous ways of doing philosophy. The chapter is particularly valuable in showing the implications of Dewey's epistemology and metaphysics for education. This linkage was intentional. Dewey wrote, "Philosophizing should focus about education as the supreme human interest in which, moreover, other problems, cosmological, moral, logical, come to a head."[19]

After explaining Dewey's objections to previous ways of doing philosophy, I will describe his conception of pragmatism, summarize the implications Dewey sees for education, and then show how Addams's reasoning in "A Modern Lear," written more than twenty years before *Democracy and Education*, employs the pragmatist method.

In "Continuity versus Dualism," the first section of the chapter, Dewey gives a sweeping critique of philosophical approaches to reality and knowledge that are structured around central divisions, or dualisms. Many of the most influential epistemological and metaphysical theories in the history of philosophy have dualistic divisions at their core. Think of how Plato's divided line separates the physical, changing, imperfect world of everyday experience from the immaterial, unchanging and perfect world of Forms. Remember Descartes's divisions between reason and sense experience, between intellect and emotion, between mind and body. (You might go through each of the dualisms Dewey names in this chapter and see if some of the philosophies you have studied incorporate these dualisms.)

These dualistic philosophies were engaged in what Dewey calls a quest for certainty.[20] The philosophers used dualisms to posit some permanent, fixed order, for example, Plato's Forms, Aristotle's unmoved mover, or the transcendent God of Augustine and Aquinas. Descartes searched for an epistemological equivalent to these realms of perfect order, a method of perfect thinking that could guarantee he would never believe something that was false. Dewey writes, "The conceptions that had reigned in the philosophy of nature and knowledge for two thousand years, the conceptions that had become the familiar furniture of the mind, rested on the assumption of the superiority of the fixed and final; they rested upon treating change and origin as signs of defect and unreality."[21]

For Dewey, the central problem with previous, dualistic philosophies is that they have little connection with actual human experience. Change and chance, becoming and decaying, stability and precariousness, predictability and random chance, and our own fallibility are essential features of life as we experience it. Mixed inseparably together are stability and disorder, predictability and random luck. The kind of perfection and certainty posited by past philosophers is unattainable. Nothing in human experience warrants belief in it.[22]

Why so many dualisms in the history of Western philosophy? Why did previous philosophers place such stock on describing ultimate Truth and Reality in terms so distant from our everyday experience? Dewey interprets such divisions in theories as mirroring hierarchical divisions in the social order. He notes that societies from which Western philosophy emerged were structured by divisions between the powerful and the powerless, between rich and poor, between those who labor with their muscles and those privileged not to, and between men and women. Dualistic philosophies reproduce in thought the hierarchical divisions that exist in social fact.[23] Philosophies throughout the history of Western thought have been profoundly antidemocratic.

In his critique of previous philosophies in "Theories of Knowledge," Dewey sketches out some of the key commitments of classical American pragmatism: that evolutionary process gives an accurate account of human and nonhuman reality, that concrete experience underlies our account of knowledge, and that the experimental method is the appropriate one for doing philosophy.

For Dewey, the publication of Charles Darwin's *On the Origin of Species* made dualistic philosophies untenable. Darwin's evolutionary theory swept away the idea that permanence and fixity underlie and guide change. Instead, order and change in the world both emerge from chance variations, their fate resting upon environmental conditions. Genetic mutations in organisms occur by chance; those that help an organism adapt to a given environment persist; those that do not, disappear. For a given organism, a chance mutation may mean felicitous survival in one environmental context, but death in another.

The implications of Darwin's evolutionary theory for philosophy are vast. Dewey writes, "Philosophy forswears inquiry after absolute origins and absolutes finalities in order to explore specific values and the specific conditions that generate them."[24] Everything—nature, experience, and ourselves—is constantly in process; we come to understand truth by investigating that process. Since chance cannot be eliminated from that process, we must abandon the quest for certainty and remain content with the fact of human fallibility.

Humans and human culture are a part of nature. Humans, like animals and plants, are biological creatures. We change and are changed by adapting to the environment and adapting the environment to us. Humans are not simply in nature; we are a part of nature. Dewey explains, "Human nature exists and operates in an environment. And it is not 'in' that environment as coins are in a box, but as a plant is in the sunlight and soil. It is of them, continuous with their energies, dependent upon their support, capable of increase only as it utilizes them, and as it gradually rebuilds from their crude indifference an environment genially civilized."[25]

The plant lives by incorporating features of the environment and in turn, modifying its environment as it moves into future environmental conditions of uncertainty, such as not knowing whether there will be enough water, or whether it will it be trampled or eaten. Likewise, the most salient conditions of human existence are processes that take place in specific physical and social contexts, in interaction with other human and nonhuman organisms. To understand this evolutionary process, we may find it helpful at times to make distinctions, and sometimes dualistic ones. But these are at best mental tools for reflection, useful for understanding specific dimensions of life's continuous processes for specific purposes. These dualisms do not describe actual, objective divisions in the nature of reality.

Thinking about experience in evolutionary terms, as continuity or process rather than as dualistic, we direct our attention away from universal, highly abstract descriptions and instead focus on experience as local and concrete. We attend to specific conditions, specific changes at specific historical times and locations. Thus, experience and experiencing are always from a particular point of view. Dewey writes, "To be 'objective' in thinking is to have a certain sort of selective interest operative. One can only see from a certain standpoint, but this fact does not make all standpoints of equal value. A standpoint which is nowhere in particular and from which things are not seen at a special angle is an absurdity. But one may have affection for a standpoint which gives a rich and ordered landscape rather than for one from which things are seen confusedly and meagerly."[26]

When we think about experience as continuity or process, it is more accurate to talk about "knowing" rather than "knowledge." "Knowledge" connotes something static and fixed. "Knowing" is an active term that conveys how experience itself is an ongoing process of continuous mutual adaptations of organism and environment. For pragmatists, "knowing" is the activity of reflecting on past experience and making connections between that and present perplexities.

This is where Dewey's notion of "habits" or "dispositions" is important. We often think of habits primarily in a negative sense as ritual behaviors we would like to get rid of, such as procrastinating, smoking, and whining. Dewey defines habits more generally as patterns of behavior, or "dispositions," some of which are unproductive, but many others are vitally important. We need to develop habits that we can apply flexibly and intelligently in light of the current situation. For example, I was grateful when my sixteen-year-old acquired the habit of driving at the speed limit. I was even more grateful when he learned to apply that habit intelligently by adjusting his speed each time to actual traffic conditions. Knowledge for Dewey is our stock of habits as intellectual resources, our supply "of all the habits that render our action intelligent."[27]

Evolutionary theory has implications for how we do philosophy, for how philosophical thinking can and should proceed. Dewey argues that we need to adopt a way of doing philosophy, a "logic of inquiry," as Dewey calls it, that is well suited to exploring experience as process and will yield knowledge as useful habits, intelligently applied. Methods used in the past such as Plato's rational contemplation of universals, Aquinas's scholastic system building, or Locke's dividing sense experience into isolated bits are all ill suited for our post-Darwinian understanding of experience as process.

Dewey proposes the experimental method as an appropriate pattern for philosophical thinking. The model goes like this: a problematic situation arises. We feel anxiety, our old habits or ways of thinking are inadequate. (For example, my healthy habit of eating homemade granola for breakfast every morning works just fine, except for those rare occasions when I open the refrigerator and find that my son used up all the milk for his late night snack.) We redefine the situation as a problem to be solved. We call on past experience and use imagination to formulate hypotheses on how to solve the problem. (I can adjust the environment to my desires by going out and buying milk; I can adjust my desires to the environment by eating leftover pasta salad; or I can just wait until lunch.) We then test our hypotheses in actual fact. Sometimes we solve the problem, giving us more control over the environment, but not always. In an uncertain world there are no guarantees of success; unanticipated variables can always arise. Following this method yields "a reconstruction of experience." Dewey writes, "The function of knowledge is to make one experience freely available in other experiences."[28] We notice patterns, make connections, and make past experience useful by modifying and transforming it in light of current, changed conditions.

Dewey's experimental method may suggest the stereotyped image of a detached, calculating, laboratory scientist. Dewey would say that image is not only unfair to scientists, but it is far too narrow. The experimental method, in fact, is a general pattern for effective thinking. Artists choosing which colors to use, car mechanics diagnosing an odd rattle, and caretakers deciding how to sooth an unusually anxious child employ the experimental method when they intelligently adjust old habits to the a situation. In each case they are thinking, using the same pattern, the same "logic of inquiry" as philosophers.[29]

The stereotyped image of the detached, calculating scientist is also too narrow if we take it to suggest that emotion has no role in the scientific method. Dewey does not discuss the role of emotion in inquiry in "Theories of Knowledge," but he discusses it elsewhere and, like Addams, frequently stresses how important emotional engagement is to gathering data and resolving problems. Used appropriately, emotions sustain commitment to the enterprise, without clouding intellectual clarity. Addams expresses this point well when she writes, "Sympathetic knowledge is the only way of approach to any human problem."[30]

JOHN DEWEY'S CONCEPTION OF PHILOSOPHY

What then, for Dewey, is philosophy? Just as Dewey is against dualisms and divisions, except when they are helpful in solving specific problems in specific circumstances, so he does not give a fixed, precise definition of philosophy that differentiates it strongly from other disciplines. Philosophy is not system building. It has no distinctive subject matter. Instead, philosophy is method; it gives a critical examination of ordinary things and particularly of a culture's most basic and influential beliefs.[31]

How do we know when philosophy has done its job? Dewey tells us, "A first rate test of the value of any philosophy which is offered us: Does it end in conclusions which, when they are referred back to ordinary life-experiences and their predicaments, render them more significant, more luminous to us and make our dealings with them more fruitful?"[32] Philosophy for pragmatists begins with the on-going processes of everyday experience. Its abstractions are warranted if we can then return to everyday experience with a richer, fuller, understanding.

There are connections between theories of knowledge and the educational practices that schools adopt. Dewey's pragmatist conceptions of experience as process and knowing as a form of activity were developed in true pragmatist fashion: through educational experimentation in the Laboratory School.

In "Theories of Knowledge" Dewey makes several explicit connections between his epistemology and his theory of education. First, from a pragmatist point of view, education should not be viewed as the process whereby information, warehoused in books, media, or teachers' minds, is somehow transferred into students' heads. Dewey repeatedly speaks of knowledge as the activity of making connections between the problem at hand and past events, and between the current particular set of circumstances and a more general range of considerations. Brewing a cup of Earl Grey tea, for example, can lead to explorations of India's geography and climate and of Britain's history as a colonial power.

Also, education is a process of acquiring those "habits that render our action intelligent."[33] Dewey's example of physicians' education illustrates this well. The aim is to enable physicians to draw upon what they learned from books, laboratory experiments, and clinical experience, and modify it appropriately for new patients, for sets of symptoms not previously encountered, and for broader issues of public health.

Finally, Dewey claims, education should be "the acquisition of knowledge in the schools with activities, or occupations, carried on in a medium of associated life"[34] By "occupation," Dewey does not just mean wage-earning endeavors. He includes all of those activities through which the community meets its needs. Education should prepare students to be skillful participants in and thoughtful critics of their communities.[35]

PRAGMATISM AND LEAR

After examining Dewey's conception of pragmatism in "Theories of Knowledge," we can now identify how Addams's reasoning in "A Modern Lear" is distinctively pragmatist. First, Addams has an evolutionary theory of ethics, claiming that our understanding of ethical obligations needs to evolve as patterns in economic production and social living change. Ethical practices of a previous generation are a valuable inheritance, but they need to be adapted to current situations. In advocating social morality, Addams does not appeal to timeless, universal principles or to a set of ideal virtues. Instead, social morality is an intellectual, an emotional, and an active stance toward others that can evolve through mutual adjustment of persons to each other in their shared environment.

Next, Addams grounds her analysis in concrete experience. Her knowledge of the case is intimate, local, and deep. She was directly involved in the Pullman strike and was well acquainted with the pain and dislocation her fellow Chicagoans suffered because of industrial tensions. Addams works with the idea that each person has his or her own standpoint on experience. Pullman, she says, "felt himself right from the commercial standpoint, and could not see the situation from the social standpoint."[36] To move conflicting standpoints into adjustment, Pullman and his workers will need to enter sympathetically into the standpoint of the other. Addams speaks of "the justice that can only come through affectionate interpretation."[37] Dewey makes the same point in a 1931 essay when he speaks of "that experience which one makes one's own through sympathetic intercommunication."[38] We enlarge our own experience, and thus our own standpoint, through sympathetic interaction with others.

Finally, in thinking through the events in Chicago in 1894, Addams uses the pragmatist experimental method. The problematic situation was real enough: the troubled relations between Pullman and his workers had spread through Chicago and out into the rest of the country. As a member of the arbitration committee, Addams had tried out various hypotheses on how to resolve the strike. All had failed. She turned to philosophy as a method for coming to understand the situation. She adapted the pattern of past troubled relations in Lear's family to the industrial tensions in Chicago. This led her to critique many basic beliefs of the culture. She examined basic beliefs about power relationships in the economic system, about relations between family responsibilities or workplace loyalties and larger social obligations, and about how social change should proceed.

The essay meets the "first-rate test" Dewey poses for philosophy. We can return from Addams's more comprehensive critique of these basic beliefs to the concrete situation of labor relations in Chicago, now "rendered more luminous," to use Dewey's felicitous phrase.

DEMOCRACY AND PRAGMATISM: ADDAMS'S "INTRODUCTION" TO *DEMOCRACY AND SOCIAL ETHICS* AND DEWEY'S "CREATIVE DEMOCRACY—THE TASK BEFORE US"[39]

Addams's and Dewey's essays on democracy glow with optimism. But they are not flourishes of utopian rhetoric, nor were their authors oblivious to the troubles of the times. In 1902, when *Democracy and Social Ethics* was published, Addams experienced daily the toll taken on her neighbors by industrial exploitation, substance abuse, and political corruption. When Dewey wrote "Creative Democracy" thirty-seven years later, Nazi Germany had conquered much of Eastern Europe and Japan occupied Manchuria and eastern China.

In political theory, "democracy" is often defined in terms of governmental procedures based on creedlike beliefs. "We hold these truths to be self-evident," writes Thomas Jefferson, drawing on John Locke's social contract tradition. People have but to consult reason and natural law to know that equality and liberty are moral rights that should be encoded in constitutions and laws. Addams and Dewey see it differently. At Hull House Addams worked and socialized with people from every social class and from many ethnic and cultural backgrounds. She knew firsthand how inadequate a creedal foundation for democracy was. Her immigrant neighbors, in spite of being equal under the law, faced discrimination every day. Their legal equality paled in significance when placed next to industrial exploitation and social ostracism.

For both Addams and Dewey, democracy is a way of living in association with others. It should extend far beyond political machinery and into workplaces, neighborhoods, and families. In "Creative Democracy" Dewey eloquently describes democracy as a personal way of life. One lives a democratic life when one's character is deeply imbued with faith in the potential of every person to be creative, contributing, and fully participating in society, and one's actions are directed toward bringing this about.

Both Addams and Dewey stress that democratic living is based on equality understood as an active, living reciprocity. Dewey describes "the habit of amicable cooperation," as "a priceless addition to life." In light of contemporary calls for greater appreciation of diversity, it is noteworthy that in the same paragraph Dewey explicitly connects "amicable cooperation" with appreciation for difference and indicates how differences benefit both self and others. He writes, "To cooperate by giving differences a chance to show themselves because of the belief that the expression of difference is not only a right of the other persons but is a means of enriching one's own life-experience, is inherent in the democratic personal way of life."[40] Throughout her writings Addams points out in concrete detail how much people born in the United States could learn from socially ostracized groups. She does not temper her frustration when she exclaims, "All members of the community are equally stupid in throwing away the immigrant revelation of social customs and inherited energy."[41]

For both Addams and Dewey, the aim of democracy is more democracy. Dewey ends his essay stating, "The task of democracy is forever that of creation of a freer and more humane experience in which all share and to which all contribute."[42] Addams has the same conception of democracy in mind when she writes in "A Modern Lear," "Nothing will satisfy the aroused conscience of men short of the complete participation of the working classes in the spiritual, intellectual and material inheritance of the human race."[43]

Addams's and Dewey's essays on democracy reflect pragmatism's emphasis on evolutionary process, concrete experience, and the experimental method. *Democracy and Social Ethics* is primarily addressed to middle- and upper-class Americans whose lives of relative ease and amusement somehow feel trivial and empty. These Americans can see how the needs of poor people, immigrants, and former slaves are exacerbated by discrimination and industrial exploitation. "Each generation has its own test," Addams writes at the beginning of the chapter. Her generation's test is to meet the needs of both groups through crafting a democratic way of life. Addams ends the chapter by noting that "actual attempts at adjustment are largely coming through those who are simpler and less analytical."[44] She bases this statement on her years of experience in the Hull House neighborhood. People from nationalities with historic antagonisms learned to live peacefully as neighbors, working democratically together in labor unions and enjoying the pleasures of Hull House hospitality.

Addams and Dewey used the pragmatist experimental method in their activism. For pragmatists, inquiry is a social pursuit. Hull House and the Laboratory School were both cooperative ventures where participants formulated and tested hypotheses about democratic living and learning. Through such inquiry they learned that democratic results can only be achieved through democratic means. People cannot be coerced into democratic "associated living." These relations arise as people acquire habits of living that express sympathetic understanding and reciprocity. Addams writes, "The cure for the ills of Democracy is more Democracy."[45] Dewey ties method, experience, and democracy together when he says, "Democracy is belief in the ability of human experience to generate the aims and methods by which further experience will grow in ordered richness."[46]

Questions for Reflection

Go through each of the dualisms Dewey names in "Theories of Knowledge" and see if some of the philosophies you have studied in this book incorporate these dualisms.

This commentary gives the example of Dewey using cooking as a hook for studying chemistry, biology, and geography and brewing a cup of Earl Grey tea for studying of India's geography and climate and of the history of British colonialism. How does each example illustrate Dewey's view that knowledge is the activity of making connections between particular or concrete problems (situations, contexts) and general—often philosophical—issues and considerations?

Think of a social group in which you participate such as your family, a social club, sports team, or your workplace. Using Addams's and Dewey's conception of democracy, how democratic is your social group? For what sorts of social groups do you think this conception of democracy is appropriate? Inappropriate?

Notes

1. Jane Addams, "A Modern Lear," *Survey* 29 (November 2, 1912): 131–37.

2. John Dewey's *Democracy and Education* (1916), repr. in Jo Ann Boydston, ed. *John Dewey: The Middle Works*, vol. 9 (Carbondale & Edwardsville: Southern Illinois University Press, 1985), chap. 25.

3. Jane Addams, "Introduction," *Democracy and Social Ethics* (New York: Macmillan, 1902), 1–12.

4. John Dewey, *Creative Democracy: The Task Before Us* (1939), repr. in Jo Ann Boydston, ed. *John Dewey: The Later Works*, vol.14 (Carbondale & Edwardsville: Southern Illinois University Press, 1988), 224–30.

5. Jane Addams, *Twenty Years at Hull House* (Urbana: University of Illinois Press, 1990).

6. For discussions of the Laboratory School placed in the context of Dewey's philosophy of education, see Katherine Camp Mayhew and Anna Camp Edwards, *The Dewey School* (New York: D. Appleton-Century Co., 1936). Also see Louis Menand, *The Metaphysical Club* (New York: Farrar, Straus & Giroux, 2001), 316–31; and Robert B. Westbrook, *John Dewey and American Democracy* (Ithaca, NY: Cornell University Press, 1991), chap. 6. Charlene Haddock Seigfried, in *Pragmatism and Feminism* (Chicago: University of Chicago Press,

1996), discusses how central Dewey's work on education was to the development of his philosophical ideas. See especially chapter 5.

7. Jane Addams, "A Toast to John Dewey," in *The Social Thought of Jane Addams*, ed. Christopher Lasch (New York: Irvington Publishers, 1965), 177. For a thorough discussion of Addams's and Dewey's interactions and influences on each other, see Seigfried, *Pragmatism and Feminism*, 73–79.

8. Addams, "A Toast," 181.

9. John Dewey, "The Future of Pacifism" (1917), repr. in Jo Ann Boydston, ed. *John Dewey: The Middle Works*, vol. 10 (Carbondale & Edwardsville: Southern Illinois University Press, 1980), 266.

10. Jane M. Dewey, "Biography of John Dewey," in *The Philosophy of John Dewey*, ed. Paul Arthur Schilpp (Evanston: Northwestern University Press, 1939), 30.

11. Quoted in Steven C. Rockefeller, *John Dewey: Religious Faith and Democratic Humanism* (New York: Columbia University Press, 1991), 208.

12. Westbrook, *John Dewey and American Democracy*, 89.

13. For an excellent discussion of Addams, Dewey, and the Pullman Strike, see Menand, *The Metaphysical Club*, 289–316. For historical background and analysis on the strike, see Richard Schneirov, Shelton Stromquist, and Nick Salvadore, eds., *The Pullman Strike and the Crisis of the 1890s: Essays on Labor and Politics* (Urbana: University of Illinois Press, 1999).

14. One of the main contentions of contemporary feminist ethics is that families and women's positions in families merit philosophical analysis. Addams begins "A Modern Lear" by doing just that.

15. Jane Addams, "A Modern Lear."

16. In attributing a sense of social morality to Cordelia, Addams takes some creative license with Shakespeare's version of the story.

17. Addams, "A Modern Lear," 134.

18. John Dewey, *Democracy and Education* (1916), repr. in Jo Ann Boydston, ed. *John Dewey: The Middle Works*, vol. 9, chap. 25.

19. Dewey, *Democracy and Education*, ix.

20. John Dewey, *The Quest for Certainty* (1929), repr. in Jo Ann Boydston, ed. *John Dewey: The Later Works*, vol. 4 (Carbondale & Edwardsville: Southern Illinois University Press, 1984).

21. John Dewey, "The Need for a Recovery of Philosophy," (1917), repr. in Jo Ann Boydston, ed. *John Dewey: The Middle Works*, 10:3.

22. See chapter 2 of John Dewey, *Experience and Nature* (1925), repr. in Jo Ann Boydston, ed. *John Dewey: The Later Works*, vol.1 (Carbondale & Edwardsville: Southern Illinois University Press, 1981).

23. Dewey, "Theories of Knowledge," 343.

24. Dewey, "The Need for a Recovery of Philosophy," 10.

25. John Dewey, *Human Nature and Conduct* (1922), repr. in Jo Ann Boydston, ed. *John Dewey: The Middle Works*, 14:204.

26. John Dewey, "Context and Thought," (1931), repr. in Jo Ann Boydston, ed. *John Dewey: The Later Works*, vol. 6 (Carbondale & Edwardsville: Southern Illinois University Press, 1985), 14–15.

27. Dewey, "Theories of Knowledge," 354.

28. Dewey, "Theories of Knowledge," 349.

29. See John Dewey, *Art as Experience* (1934), repr. in Jo Ann Boydston, ed. *John Dewey: The Later Works*, 10:11, 80.

30. Jane Addams, *A New Conscience and an Ancient Evil* (New York: Macmillan, 1912), 11.

31. Dewey, "Context and Thought," 19.

32. John Dewey, *Experience and Nature* (1925), repr. in Jo Ann Boydston, ed. *John Dewey: The Later Works*, 1:18.

33. Dewey, "Theories of Knowledge," 354.

34. Dewey, "Theories of Knowledge," 355.

35. See John Dewey, *The School and Society* (1900), repr. in Jo Ann Boydston, ed. *John Dewey: The Middle Works*, 1:5–11.

36. Addams, "A Modern Lear," 135.

37. Addams, "A Modern Lear," 136.

38. John Dewey, "Context and Thought," (1931), repr. in Jo Ann Boydston, ed. *John Dewey: The Later Works*, 6:21.

39. Jane Addams, "Introduction," *Democracy and Social Ethics* (Urbana: University of Illinois Press, 2002; orig. pub. 1902), 5–9. John Dewey, "Creative Democracy—the Task Before Us," (1939); repr. in Jo Ann Boydston, ed. *John Dewey: The Later Works*, 14:224–30.

40. Dewey, "Creative Democracy," 228.

41. Jane Addams, *Newer Ideals of Peace* (New York: Macmillan, 1906), 79.

42. Dewey, "Creative Democracy," 230.

43. Addams, "A Modern Lear," 136.

44. Addams, "Introduction," 5, 9.

45. Addams, "Introduction," 5.

46. Dewey, "Creative Democracy," 229.

CHAPTER 14

Wittgenstein and Anscombe

Introduction by *Karen J. Warren*

G. E. M. "Elizabeth" Anscombe (1919–2001) is probably Britain's most famous woman philosopher. She wrote on a wide range of topics, from the philosophy of mind, philosophy of action, and philosophy of language, to philosophical logic and ethics, but it is her book *Intention* (1957) for which she is best known. The male philosopher with whom she is paired, Ludwig Wittgenstein (1889–1951), is considered by some the most influential philosopher of the twentieth century. He also wrote on topics as diverse as philosophy of logic and language, perception and intention, ethics and religion, aesthetics and culture. Anscombe and Wittgenstein make a wonderful philosophical pair for many reasons, one of which is that they had a long-term association that ultimately led him to ask her to translate and publish one of his most famous books, *Philosophical Investigations*, which she did in 1953. As a pair, these two philosophers continue canonical philosophy to the extent that they engage with familiar, traditional philosophical problems, but like other philosophers in the twentieth century, they open up new possibilities of ways to think about and do philosophy. Like Addams and Dewey who precede them, and Beauvoir and Sartre who follow them, Anscombe and Wittgenstein offer new, unique challenges to canonical philosophy. As such, these three pairs (constituting the last three chapters) represent three (of many) sorts of positions and methodologies that characterize a fractured philosophy—or multiple, often conflicting, conceptions of philosophy—of the twentieth century.

Since Laine's commentary focuses more on Anscombe than Wittgenstein, this introduction focuses mostly on Wittgenstein. It describes ten features of his philosophy of language and epistemology, and it summarizes Anscombe's action theory in ways that differ from but complement the material covered in Laine's commentary.

WITTGENSTEIN

Ludwig Wittgenstein was born in Vienna, Austria, to a wealthy family well-situated in intellectual and cultural Viennese circles. In 1908, Wittgenstein began his studies at Manchester University in aeronautical engineering, but his interest soon centered on philosophy of mathematics. In 1911, he arranged to study in Cambridge under Bertrand Russell, a philosopher with whom he developed a close, often contentious, relationship. Their conversations raised philosophical problems that troubled Wittgenstein so deeply that, on several occasions, he left England for Norway, where he lived in isolation for months at a tme, pondering ways to resolve those philosophical problems. Wittgenstein joined the Austrian army in 1914, just as World War I (1914–1918) was beginning. Taken captive in 1917, he spent time in prison camp writing notes that were subsequently published in German in 1921 as *Tractatus Logico-Philosophicus*.

Scholars speak of the "early," "middle," and "late" Wittgenstein, to distinguish periods that signify dramatic shifts in Wittgenstein's philosophical positions.[1] The *Tractatus* is the work of early Wittgenstein. After writing it, nine years passed before Wittgenstein returned to Cambridge in1929 to resume a vocation in philosophy. This period marks the middle Wittgenstein whose writing (e.g., *The Blue and Brown Books*) rejected traditional philosophical concerns and even the *Tractatus* itself. The later Wittgenstein wrote *Philosophical Investigations*, published posthumously in 1953. During the late period, Wittgenstein developed his philosophy of language, which involved a rejection of earlier writings, particularly the *Tractatus*. After some traveling, Wittgenstein returned to Cambridge in 1951, where he died of cancer.

What are some of the central characteristics of the later Wittgenstein's philosophy? Consider ten features of his philosophy of language and epistemology, as expressed in *Philosophical Investigations* (or *Investigations*). (1) The meaning of a word depends upon its use in the language, or as Wittgenstein says "meaning is use." The meanings of words occur in the public domain. Thus (2) there are no "private meanings," no "private languages." This is a rejection of Cartesian psychology of mind, according to which the contents of the mind are knowable only to the individual whose mind it is. Wittgenstein's philosophy of language sought to undermine this Cartesian view of the mind and show meaningless private claims about indubitable and knowable internal mental states—claims such as "Only I can know whether or not I'm in pain" or "Only I know what I intended in performing a particular act." (3) The multiplicity of meanings of words cannot be captured in a single, all-inclusive definition; there is no one set of necessary and sufficient conditions that apply to, or capture the essential characteristics (properties, meaning) of, the word (term, concept, name, object) at issue. Wittgenstein offers the example of a game: Although there is no one definition that captures the various uses of the word "game" (e.g., chess and bridge are games; war is a game; people play guessing games), we understand each other when the word "game" is used in these various contexts. How can this be if there is no one unifying, overarching definition of 'game.' (4) For Wittgenstein, the answer has to do with the notion of a "language game." The reason words have different meanings is that people are playing different language games. The reason we can understand these different meanings of a word (like "game") is that there are what Wittgenstein calls "family resemblances" among different uses of the same word.

Pause here a moment. What is a language game and what are "family resemblances" that permit words to be used and understood in different contexts even though they are not definable (in traditional ways)? (5) For Wittgenstein, a language game is an *activity* that is rule governed by conventional uses of words and language; it is not just a grammar or logic In *Investigations* (par. 29), Wittgenstein gives quite specific examples of language games, a list that includes activities like giving orders, making jokes, guessing riddles, praying, and cursing. A language game is an activity that uses words that are often specific to that language game. Religious language, for example, is a chunk of discourse that contains within it specific activities, such as praying and worshiping. They are part of religious language games.

Are there any limitations on how language games are played, or on which activities constitute language games? (6) The boundaries of our use of language lie in what Wittgenstein calls "framework propositions." Framework propositions are presupposed by and necessary for empirical claims to be meaningful at all. For Wittgenstein, statements like "There is a physical world" and "This is a hand" look like empirical claims, but they are not. They are the framework propositions that make possible empirical claims. Without them—that is, unless there is a physical world—one cannot ask questions or make claims about a hand as one's own, or that other people besides one's self exist. Recall "The House" (lead essay). There are "framework propositions"—external and internal—that are the above-ground assumptions, claims, or starting points without which one could neither "frame in" (build) a house nor take seriously certain philosophical problems within a framed-in house. Framework propositions connect Wittgenstein's philosophy of language with his epistemology. (7) For Wittgenstein, the very possibility of knowledge requires that some things are taken for granted; these are the framework propositions that make possible meaningful uses of language and knowledge claims. They are fixed, but not (Cartesian) bedrock claims. To illustrate what Wittgenstein means, consider the "problem of the external world." For Wittgenstein, one cannot justify the existence of the external world in a logical way—one cannot prove the existence of the external world—in a way that does not beg the question, "Is there an external world?" This is because the existence of the external world is presupposed by all that we say and do. It is the necessary assumption (the framework propositions) that makes it possible to state such claims as "I received a phone call from New York" or "These are my shoes." Telephoning New York does not prove that the external world exists; rather, it presupposes that the external world exists. (Similarly with "my shoes.") The existence of the external world is a framework proposition, presupposed by things we say and do but not provable by things we say and do. Framework propositions are necessary to building and having a Canonical House (lead essay); they structure and makes possible the above-ground philosophical claims and positions advanced by different traditional philosophers.

(8) Framework propositions play an epistemological role as well. Wittgenstein offers framework propositions as a challenge to a view of knowledge that makes skepticism possible. Cartesian rationalism provides such a view of knowledge: it makes skepticism possible because it assumes that anything knowable is also doubtable. Descartes assumed that the existence of the external world is doubtable—that it is possible that the material world does not exist. For Wittgenstein, to articulate skepticism (e.g., that one cannot know that the external world exists) one must deny the existence of

the external world—which the skeptic does. But, according to Wittgenstein, it is not possible to deny the existence of the external world; the external world's existence is presupposed (as a framework proposition) by the language we use and empirical claims we assert, deny, or doubt.

So what does Wittgenstein say to the skeptic? (9) Wittgenstein would say that the skeptic is right that one cannot *know* (i.e., give an ultimate justification for) the external world, but wrong that, because one cannot justify the existence of the external world, the existence of the external world can be doubted. It cannot be doubted since it is presupposed by everything we say (our language) and do (our activities, forms of life). Thus, even if one cannot *refute* skepticism, one can *undermine* it; it is undermined because we stop requesting justification *before* we get to doubting the existence of everything, including the external world. Like the child's game Why? the questioning must stop somewhere. And for Wittgenstein that request for justification ends in framework propositions or "forms of life."

(10) The later Wittgenstein's views are a rejection of traditional conceptions and methods of philosophy. As Laine clarifies in her commentary, his view is that philosophy is designed to clear up philosophical confusion. In this respect, it is a therapeutic activity that requires that we look and listen to learn what things mean by hearing how ordinary language is used. And, if correct, Wittgenstein's view of philosophy and what philosophers should/should not do would be very different than canonical views.

ANSCOMBE

Elizabeth Anscombe was born in Limerick, Ireland, where her father served as an officer in the British army. Her undergraduate education consisted of study in classics, ancient history, and philosophy at the University of Oxford. While an undergraduate, two significant life-altering events occurred for Anscombe: she converted to Roman Catholicism (remaining a life-long Catholic) and she read Wittgenstein's *Tractatus*, which transformed her intellectual life. In 1941, she married the distinguished British philosopher Peter Geach, also a convert to Roman Catholicism. They raised seven children.

After graduating from Oxford in 1941, Anscombe was awarded a postgraduate research fellowship at Cambridge (1942–1945), which permitted her to attend Wittgenstein's lectures. In 1946, she received a research fellowship at Somerville College, Oxford, though she continued to travel to Cambridge weekly to attend tutorials with Wittgenstein. Wittgenstein's confidence in Anscombe's understanding of his philosophical views led him to choose her to translate his *Philosophical Investigations*. Toward that end, Wittgenstein "arranged for her to spend an extended time in Vienna to strengthen her German and absorb nuances of his own Viennese dialect."[2] She published an English translation of *Philosophical Investigations* that appeared simultaneously with the original.

Anscombe visited with Wittgenstein many times after he left Cambridge in 1947, and she traveled to Cambridge in April 1951 to visit him on his deathbed. Wittgenstein named her as one of three vested with authority to publish many of his manuscripts and notebooks. In this regard, she translated, edited, or coedited several volumes of selections from his notebooks, including *Remarks on the Foundations of Mathematics* (1956). Anscombe remained at Somerville College from 1946 to 1970. In 1970 she was elected professor of philosophy at Cambridge University, where she served until her retirement in 1986.

In 1956, while a research fellow at Oxford University, Anscombe protested Oxford's decision to grant an honorary degree to Harry S Truman, whom she denounced as a mass murderer for his use of atomic bombs at Hiroshima and Nagasaki. She scandalized liberal colleagues with articles defending the Roman Catholic Church's opposition to contraception in the 1960s and early 1970s, and was arrested twice while protesting outside a legal abortion clinic in Britain.

Even taking into account her translations, editions, and commentaries on Wittgenstein's philosophies, Anscombe's most important work is indisputably *Intention* (1957). The aim of *Intention* is to clarify the character of human action and will through the concept of "intention." Anscombe was the first to clarify that actions are intentional under some descriptions and not others. When asked, 'Why did you do X?" the agent's answer provides the descriptions under which the action is intentional or not. Anscombe articulates the importance of providing a reason and a motive in the explanation of why someone did an act (falling under a particular description) for determining whether or not the act is intentional. Anscombe's criticism of moral philosophy is its double failure to provide an account of what counts as a relevant description of an action and an account of what constitutes an intentional act. (I do not write more about her account here because of the extensiveness of the account given in Joy Laine's commentary.)

LAINE'S COMMENTARY

Joy Laine's commentary provides three interrelated approaches to thinking about this innovative and extremely influential philosophical pair, Anscombe and Wittgenstein: first, to describe the historical, political, and philosophical influences that impacted their lives and writing; second, to present and discuss key features of the philosophical positions for which they are well known; third, to clarify the nature of their influence on the conception, practice, and discipline of philosophy. The result is that one learns from her commentary how Anscombe's account of the distinction between intentional and nonintentional action provides a foundational theory of human action that is necessary to any adequate moral philosophy or philosophy of mind. And one learns enough about Wittgenstein's philosophy of language to understand how it is: a critique of Cartesian foundationalism, a rejection of private language arguments that link direct access to one's own internal mental states with causal explanations of why people behave the way they do, and the basis for a new, unique therapeutic method for doing philosophy. Through extensive use of real-life examples, Laine's commentary invites the reader to join Anscombe and Wittgenstein in thinking through the issues that concern them, which is just how Anscombe and Wittgenstein would want their writings to be read.

◦⟨∞⟩◦

Excerpts of Writings by Wittgenstein and Anscombe

I. EXCERPTS FROM LUDWIG WITTGENSTEIN'S *PHILOSOPHICAL INVESTIGATIONS*[3]

1. "When they (my elders) named some object, and accordingly moved toward something, I saw this and I grasped that the thing was called by the sound they uttered when they meant to point it out. Their intention was shewn by their bodily movements, as it were the natural language of all peoples: the expression of the face, the play of the eyes, the movement of other parts of the body, and the tone of voice which expresses our state of mind in seeking, having, rejecting, or avoiding something. Thus, as I heard words repeatedly used in their proper places in various sentences, I gradually learnt to understand what objects they signified; and after I had trained my mouth to form these signs, I used them to express my own desires" (Augustine, *Confessions*, I. 8).

These words, it seems to me, give us a particular picture of the essence of human language. It is this: the individual words in language name objects—sentences are combinations of such names. In this picture of language we find the roots of the following idea: Every word has a meaning. This meaning is correlated with the word. It is the object for which the word stands. Augustine does not speak of there being any difference between kinds of word. If you describe the learning of language in this way you are, I believe, thinking primarily of nouns like "table," "chair," "bread," and of people's names, and only secondarily of the names of certain actions and properties; and of the remaining kinds of word as something that will take care of itself.

Now think of the following use of language: I send someone shopping. I give him a slip marked "five red apples." He takes the slip to the shopkeeper, who opens the drawer marked "apples"; then he looks up the word "red" in a table and finds a color sample opposite it; then he says the series of cardinal numbers—I assume that he knows them by heart—up to the word "five" and for each number he takes an apple of the same color as the sample out of the drawer. It is in this and similar ways that one operates with words. "But how does he know where and how he is to look up the word 'five'?" Well, I assume that he acts as I have described. Explanations come to an end somewhere. But what is the meaning of the word "five"? No such thing was in question here, only how the word "five" is used.

2. That philosophical concept of meaning has its place in a primitive idea of the way language functions. But one can also say that it is the idea of a language more primitive than ours.

Let us imagine a language for which the description given by Augustine is right. The language is meant to serve for communication between a builder A and an assistant B. A is building with building-stones: there are blocks, pillars, slabs, and beams. B has to pass the stones, and that in the order in which A needs them. For this purpose they use a language consisting of the words "block," "pillar," "slab," "beam." A calls them out;—B brings the stone which he has learnt to bring at such-and-such a call. Conceive this as a complete primitive language.

3. Augustine, we might say, does describe a system of communication; only not everything that we call language is this system. And one has to say this in many cases where the question arises "is this an appropriate description or not?" The answer is: "Yes, it is appropriate, buy only for this narrowly circumscribed region, not for the whole of what you were claiming to describe."

It is as if someone were to say: "A game consists in moving objects about on a surface according to certain rules . . . "—and we replied: You seem to be thinking of board games, but there are others. You can make your definition correct by expressly restricting it to those games.

4. Imagine a script in which the letters were used to stand for sounds, and also as signs of emphasis and punctuation. (A script can be conceived as a language for describing sound-patterns.) Now imagine someone interpreting that script as if there were simply a correspondence of letters to sounds and as if the letters had not also completely different functions. Augustine's conception of language is like such a simple conception of the script.

5. If we look at the example in §1, we may perhaps get an inkling how much this general notion of the meaning of a word surrounds the working of language with a haze which makes clear vision impossible. It disperses the fog to study the phenomena of language in primitive kinds of application in which one can command a clear view of the aim and functioning of the words.

A child uses such primitive forms of language when it learns to talk. Here the teaching of language is not explanation, but training.

6. We could imagine that the language of §2 was the *whole* language of A and B; even the whole language of a tribe. The children are brought up to perform *these* words as they do so, and to react in *this* way to the words of others.

An important part of the training will consist in the teacher's pointing to the objects, directing the child's attention to them, and at the same time uttering a word; for instance, the word "slab" as he points to that shape. (I do not want to call this "ostensive definition," because the child cannot as yet *ask* what the name is. I will call it "ostensive teaching of words."—I say that it will form an important part of the training, because it is so with human beings; not because it could not be imagine otherwise. This ostensive teaching of words can be said to establish an association between the word and the thing. But what does this mean? Well, it may mean various things; but one very likely thinks first of all that a picture of the object comes before the child's mind when it hears the word. But now, if this does happen—is it the purpose of the word?—Yes, it *may* be the purpose.—I can imagine such a use of words (or series of sounds). (Uttering a word is like striking a note on the keyboard of the imagination.) But in the language of §2 it is *not* the purpose of the words to evoke images. (It may, of course, be discovered that that helps to attain the actual purpose.)

But if the ostensive teaching has this effect,—am I to say that it effects an understanding of the word? Don't you understand the call "Slab!" if you act upon it in such-and-such a way?—Doubtless the ostensive teaching helped to bring this about; but only together with a particular training. With different training the same teaching of these words would have effected a quite different understanding.

"I set the brake up by connecting up rod and lever."—Yes, given the whole of the rest of the mechanism. Only in conjunction with that is it a brake-lever, and separated from its support it is not even a lever; it may be anything, or nothing.

11. Think of the tools in a tool-box: there is a hammer, pliers, a saw, a screw-driver, a rule, a glue-pot, glue, nails and screws.—The functions of words are as diverse as the functions of these objects. (And in both cases there are similarities.)

Of course, what confuses us is the uniform appearance of words when we hear them spoken or meet them in script and print. For their *application* is not presented to us so clearly. Especially when we are doing philosophy!

12. It is like looking into the cabin of a locomotive. We see handles all looking more or less alike. (Naturally, since they are all supposed to be handled.) But one is the handle of a crank which can be moved continuously (it regulates the opening of a valve); another is the handle of a switch, which has only two effective positions, it is either off or on; a third is the handle of a brake-lever, the harder one pulls on it, the harder it brakes; a fourth, the handle of a pump: it has an effect only so long as it is moved to and fro.

23. But how many kinds of sentence are there? Say assertion, question, and command?—There are *countless* kinds: countless different kinds of use of what we call "symbols," "words," "sentences." And this multiplicity is not something fixed, given once for all; but new types of language, new language-games, as we may say, come into existence, and others become obsolete and get forgotten. (We can get a *rough picture* of this from the changes in mathematics.)

Here the term "language-game" is meant to bring into prominence the fact that the *speaking* of language is part of an activity, or of a form of life.

Review the multiplicity of language-games in the following examples, and in others:

Giving orders, and obeying them—
Describing the appearance of an object, or giving its measurements—
Constructing an object from a description (a drawing)—
Reporting an event—
Speculating about an event—
Forming and testing a hypothesis—
Presenting the results of an experiment in tables and diagrams—
Making up a story; and reading it—
Play-acting—
Singing catches—
Guessing riddles—
Making a joke; telling it—
Solving a problem in practical arithmetic—
Translating from one language into another—
Asking, thanking, cursing, greeting, praying.

It is interesting to compare the multiplicity of the tools in language and of the ways they are used, the multiplicity of kinds of word and sentence, with what logicians have said about the structure of language. (Including the author of the *Tractatus Logico-Philosophicus*.)

65. Here we come up against the great question that lies behind all these considerations.—For someone might object against me: "You take the easy way out! You talk about all sorts of language-games, but have nowhere said what the essence of a language-

game, and hence of language, is: what is common to all these activities, and what makes them into language or parts of language. So you let yourself off the very part of the investigation that once gave you yourself most headache, the part about the *general form of propositions* and of language."

And this is true.—Instead of producing something common to all that we call language, I am saying that these phenomena have no one thing in common which makes us use the same word for all,—but that they are *related* to one another in many different ways. And it is because of this relationship, or these relationships, that we call them all "language." I will try to explain this.

66. Consider for example the proceedings that we call "games." I mean board-games, card-games, ball-games, Olympic games, and so on. What is common to them all?—Don't say: "There *must* be something common, or they would not be called 'games'"—but *look and* see whether there is anything common to all.—For if you look at them you will not see something common to *all*, but similarities, relationships, and a whole series of them at that. To repeat: don't think, but look!—Look for example at board-games, with their multifarious relationships. Now pass to card-games; here you find many correspondences with the first group, but many common features drop out, and others appear. When we pass next to ball-games, much that is common is retained, but much is lost.—Are they all "amusing?" Compare chess with noughts and crosses. Or is there always winning and losing, or competition between players? Think of patience. In ball-games there is winning and losing; but when a child throws his ball at the wall and catches it again, this feature has disappeared. Look at the parts played by skill and luck, and at the difference between skill in chess and skill in tennis. Think now of games like ring-a-ring-a-roses; here is the element of amusement, but how many other characteristic features have disappeared! And we can go through the many, many other groups of games in the same way; one can see how similarities crop up and disappear.

And the result of this examination is we see a complicated network of similarities overlapping and criss-crossing: sometimes overall similarities, sometimes similarities of detail.

67. I can think of no better expression to characterize these similarities than "family resemblances"; for the various resemblances between members of a family: build, features, color of eyes, gait, temperament, etc. etc. overlap and criss-cross in the same way.—And I shall say: "games" form a family.

And for instance the kinds of number form a family in the same way. Why do we call something a "number?" Well, perhaps because it has a—direct—relationship with several things that have hitherto been called number; and this can be said to give it an indirect relationship to other things we call the same name. And we extend our concept of number as in spinning a thread we twist fiber on fiber. And the strength of the thread does not reside in the fact that some one fiber runs through its whole length, but in the overlapping of many fibers.

But if someone wished to say: "There is something common to all these constructions—namely the disjunction of all their common properties"—I should reply: Now you are only playing with words. One might as well say: "Something runs through the whole thread"—namely the continuous overlapping of those fibers.

143. Let us now examine the following kind of language-game: when A gives an order B has to write down series of signs according to a certain formulation rule.

The first of these series is meant to be that of the natural numbers in decimal notation.—How does he get to understand this notation?—First of all series of numbers will be written down for him and he will be required to copy them. (Do not balk at the expression "series of numbers," it is not being used wrongly here.) And here already there is a normal and an abnormal learner's reaction.—At first perhaps we guide his hand in writing out the series 0 to 9; but then the *possibility of getting him to understand* will depend on his going on to write it down independently.—And here we can imagine, e.g., that he does copy the figures independently, but not in the right order: he writes sometimes one sometimes another at random. And then communication stops at *that* point.—Or again, he makes "mistakes" in the order.—The difference between this and the first case will of course be one of frequency.—Or he makes a *systematic* mistake; for example, he copies every other number, or he copies the series 0, 1, 2, 3, 4, 5, . . . like this: 1, 0, 3, 2, 5, 4, ... Here we shall almost be tempted to say that he has understood *wrong*.

Notice, however, that there is no sharp distinction between a random mistake and a systematic one. That is, between what you are inclined to call "random" and what "systematic."

Perhaps it is possible to wean him from the systematic mistake (as from a bad habit). Or perhaps one accepts his way of copying and tries to teach him ours as an offshoot, a variant of his.—And here too our pupil's capacity to learn may come to an end.

144. What do I mean when I say "the pupil's capacity to learn *may* come to an end here"? Do I say this from my own experience? Of course not. (Even if I have had such experience.) Then what am I doing with that proposition? Well, I should like you to say: "Yes, it's true, you can imagine that too, that might happen too!"—But was I trying to draw someone's attention to the fact that he is capable of imagining that?—I wanted to put that picture before him, and his *acceptance* of the picture consists in his now being inclined to regard a given case differently: that is, to compare it with *this* rather than *that* set of pictures. I have changed his *way of looking at things*.

145. Suppose the pupil now writes the series 0 to 9 to our satisfaction.—And this will only be the case when he is often successful, not if he does it right once in a hundred attempts. Now I continue the series and draw his attention to the recurrence of the first series in the units; and then to its recurrence in the tens. (Which only means that I use particular emphases, underline figures, write them one under another in such-and-such ways, and similar things.)—And now at some point he continues the series independently—or he does not.—But why do you say that? *so* much is obvious!—Of course; I only wished to say: the effect of any further *explanation* depends on his *reaction*.

Now, however, let us suppose that after some efforts on the teacher's part he continues the series correctly, that is, as we do it. So now we can say he has mastered the system.—But how far need he continue the series for us to have the right to say that? Clearly you cannot state a limit here.

146. Suppose I now ask: "Has he understood the system when he continues the series to the hundredth place?" Or—if I should not speak of "understanding" in connection with our primitive language-game: He has got the system, if he continues the series correctly so far?—Perhaps you will say here: to have got the system (or, again, to understand it) can't consist in continuing the series up to *this* or *that* number: *that* is only applying one's understanding. The understanding itself is a state which is the *source* of the correct use.

What is one really thinking of here? Isn't one thinking of the derivation of a series from its algebraic formula? Or at least of something analogous?—But this is where we were before. The point is, we can think of more than *one* application of an algebraic formula; and every type of application can in turn be formulated algebraically; but naturally this does not get us any further—the application is still a criterion of understanding.

147. "But how can it be? When I say I understand the rule of a series, I am surely not saying so because I have found out that up to now I have applied the algebraic formula in such-and-such a way! In my own case at all events I surely know that I mean such-and-such a series; it doesn't matter how far I have actually developed it."

Your idea, then, is that you know the application of the rule of the series quite apart from remembering actual applications to particular numbers. And you will perhaps say: "Of course! For the series is infinite and the bit of it that I can have developed finite."

148. But what does this knowledge consist in? Let me ask: *When* do you know that application? Always? day and night? or only when you are actually thinking of the rule? do you know it, that is, in the same way as you know the alphabet and the multiplication table? Or is what you call "knowledge" a state of consciousness or a process—say a thought of something, or the like?

150. The grammar of the word "knows" is evidently closely related to that of "can," "is able to." But also closely related to that of "understands" ("Mastery" of a technique).

II. EXCERPTS FROM ELIZABETH ANSCOMBE'S *INTENTION*[4]

1. Very often, when a man says "I am going to do such-and-such," we should say that this was all expression of intention. We also sometimes speak of an action as intentional, and we may also ask with what intention the thing was done. In each case we employ a concept of "intention"; now if we set out to describe this concept, and took only one of these three kinds of statement as containing our whole topic, we might very likely say things about what "intention" mean which it would be false to say in one of the other cases. For example, we might say "Intention always concerns the future." But an action can be intentional without being concerned with the future in any way. Realizing this might lead us to say that there are various senses of "intention," and perhaps that it is thoroughly misleading that the word "intentional" should be connected with the word "intention," for an action can be intentional without having any intention in it. Or alternatively we may be tempted to think that only actions done with certain further intentions ought to be called intentional. And we may be inclined to say that "intention" has a different sense when we speak of a man's intentions *simpliciter*—i.e. what he intends to do—and of his intention *in* doing or proposing something—what he aims at in it. But in fact it is implausible to say that the word is equivocal as it occurs in these different cases.

Where we are tempted to speak of "different senses" of a word which is clearly not equivocal, we may infer that we are in fact pretty much in the dark about the character of the concept which it represents. There is, however, nothing wrong with taking a topic piecemeal.

23. Let us ask: is there any description which is *the* description of an intentional action, given that an intentional action occurs? And let us consider a concrete situation. A man is pumping water into the cistern which supplies the drinking water of a house.

Someone has found a way of systematically contaminating the source with a deadly cumulative poison whose effects are unnoticeable until they can no longer be cured. The house is regularly inhabited by a small group of party chiefs, with their immediate families, who are in control of a great state; they are engaged in exterminating the Jews and perhaps plan a world war.—The man who contaminated the source has calculated that if these people are destroyed some good men will get into power who will govern well, or even institute the Kingdom of Heaven on earth and secure a good life for all the people; and he has revealed the calculation, together with the fact about the poison, to the man who is pumping. The death of the inhabitants of the house will, of course, have all sorts of other effects; e.g., that a number of people unknown to these men will receive legacies, about which they know nothing.

This man's arm is going up and down, up and down. Certain muscles, with Latin names which doctors know, are contracting and relaxing. Certain substances are getting generated in some nerve fibers—substances whose generation in the course of voluntary movement interests physiologists. The moving arm is casting a shadow on a rockery where at one place and from one position it produces a curious effect as if a face were looking out of the rockery. Further, the pump makes a series of clicking noises, which are in fact beating out a noticeable rhythm.

Now we ask: What is this man doing? What is *the* description of his action?

First, of course, *any* description of what is going on, with him as subject, which is in fact true. E.g. he is earning wages, he is supporting a family, he is wearing away his shoe-soles, he is making a disturbance of the air. He is sweating, he is generating those substances in his nerve fibers. If in fact good government, or the Kingdom of Heaven on earth and a good life for everyone, comes about by the labors of the good men who get into power because the party chiefs die, then he will have been helping to produce this state of affairs. However, our enquiries into the question "Why?" enable us to narrow down our consideration of descriptions of what he is doing to a range covering all and only his intentional actions. "He is X-ing" is a description of an intentional action if (a) it is true and (b) there is such a thing as an answer in the range I have defined to the question "Why are you X-ing?" That is to say, the description in "Why are you contracting those muscles?" is ruled out if the *only* sort of answer to the question "Why?" displays that the man's knowledge, if any, that he was contracting those muscles is an inference from his knowledge of anatomy. And the description in the question "Why are you generating those substances in your nerve fibers?" will *in fact* always be ruled out on these lines unless we suppose that the man has a plan of producing these substances (if it were possible, we might suppose he wanted to collect some) and so moves his arm vigorously to generate them. But the descriptions in the questions "Why are you making that face come and go in the rockery?," "Why are you beating out that curious rhythm?" will be revealed as descriptions of intentional actions or not by different styles of answer, of which one would contain something signifying that the man *notices* that he does that, while the other would be in the range we have defined. But there are a large number of X's, in the imagined case, for which we can readily suppose that the answer to the question "Why are you X-ing?" falls within the range. E.g. "Why are you moving your arm up and down?"—"I'm pumping." "Why are you pumping?"—"I'm pumping the water-supply for the house." "Why are you beating out that curious rhythm?"—"Oh, I found out how to do it, as the pump does click anyway, and I do it just for fun." "Why are you pumping the water?"—"Because it's needed up at the house" and (*sotto voce*) "To polish that lot off." "Why are you poisoning these people?"—"If we can get rid of them, the other lot will get in and. . . . "

Now there is a break in the series of answers that one may get to such a question. Let the answer contain a further description Y, then sometimes it is correct to say not merely: the man is X-ing, but also: "the man is Y-ing"—if that is, nothing falsifying the statement "He is Y-ing" can be observed. E.g. "Why are you pumping?"—"To replenish the water-supply." If this was the answer, then we can say "He *is* replenishing the water-supply"; unless indeed, he is not. This will appear a tautologous pronouncement; but there *is* more to it. For if after his saying "To replenish the water-supply'" we can say "He is replenishing the water-supply," then this would, in ordinary circumstances, of itself be enough to characterize *that* as an intentional action. (The qualification is necessary because an intended effect just occasionally comes about by accident.) Now that is to say, as we have already determined, that the same question "Why?" will have application to this action in its turn. This is not an empty conclusion: it means that someone who, having so answered "To replenish the water-supply," is asked "Why are you replenishing the water-supply?," must not say e.g. "Oh, I didn't know I was doing that," or refuse any but a causal sense of the question. Or rather, that if he does, this makes nonsense of his answers.

A man can *be doing* something which he nevertheless does not *do*, if it is some process or enterprise which it takes time to complete and of which therefore, if it is cut short at any time, we may say that he *was doing* it, but *did not do* it. This point, however, is in no way peculiar to intentional action; for we can say that something was falling over but did not fall (since something stopped it). Therefore we do not appeal to the presence of intention to justify the description "He is Y-ing"; though in some cases his own statement that he is Y-ing may, at a certain stage of the proceedings, be needed for anybody else to be able to say he is Y-ing, since not enough has gone on for that to be evident; as when we see a man doing things with an array of wires and plugs and so on.

Sometimes, jokingly, we are pleased to say of a man "He is doing such-and-such" when he manifestly is not. E.g. "He is replenishing the water-supply," when this is not happening because, as we can see but he cannot, the water is pouring out of a hole in a pipe on the way to the cistern. And in the same way we may speak of some rather doubtful or remote objective, e.g. "He is proving Fermat's last theorem"; or again one might say of a madman "He is leading his victorious armies." It is easy, however, to exclude these cases from consideration and point out the break between cases where we can say "He is Y-ing," when he has mentioned Y in answer to the question "Why are you X-ing?," and ones where we say rather "He is going to Y." I do not think it is a quite sharp break, e.g. is there much to choose between "She is making tea" and "She is putting on the kettle in order to make tea"—i.e. "She is going to make tea?" Obviously not. And hence the common use of the present to describe a future action which is by no means just a later stage in activity which has a name as a single whole. E.g. "I am seeing my dentist," "He is demonstrating in Trafalgar Square" (either might be said when someone is at the moment e.g. traveling in a train). But the less normal it would be to take the achievement of the objective as a matter of course, the more the objective gets expressed *only* by "in order to." E.g. "I am going to London in order to make my uncle change his will"; not "I am making my uncle change his will."

To a certain extent the three divisions of the subject made in §1, are simply equivalent. That is to say, where the answers "I am going to fetch my camera," and "in order to fetch my camera" are interchangeable as answers to the question "Why?" asked when I go upstairs.

Now if all this holds, what are we to say about all these many descriptions of an intentional action? Are we to say that there are as many distinct actions as we can generate distinct descriptions, with X as our starting point? I mean: We say "Why are you X-ing?" and get the answer "To Y," or "I'm Y-ing," Y being such that we can say "he's Y-ing"; and then we can ask "Why are you Y-ing?" and perhaps get the answer "To Z," and can still say "He's Z-ing." E.g. "Why are you moving your arm up and down?" "To operate the pump," and he is operating the pump. "Why are you pumping?" "To replenish the water-supply" and he is replenishing the water-supply; "Why are you replenishing the water-supply?" "To poison the inhabitants" and he is poisoning the inhabitants, for they are getting poisoned. And here comes the break; for though in the case we have described there is probably a further answer, other than "just for fun," all the same this further description (e.g. to save the Jews, to put in the good men, to get the Kingdom of Heaven on earth) is not such that we can now say: he is saving the Jews, he is getting the Kingdom of Heaven, he is putting in the good ones. So let us stop here and say: are there four actions here, because we have found four distinct descriptions satisfying our conditions, namely moving his arm up and down, operating the pump, replenishing the water-supply, and poisoning the inhabitants?

24. Before trying to answer this, however, we must raise some difficulties. For someone might raise the objection that pumping can hardly be an act of poisoning. It is of course, as the lawyers would say, an act of laying poison, and one might try to reply by saying the man poisons the inhabitants if he lays poison and they get poisoned. But after all we said it was a cumulative poison; this means that no single act of laying the poison is by itself an act of poisoning; besides, didn't the other man "lay" the poison? Suppose we ask "When did our man poison them?" One might answer: all the time they got poisoned. But in that case one might say "His poisoning them was not an action; for he was perhaps doing nothing relevant at any of the times they were drinking the poison." Is the question "When exactly did he poison them?" to be answered by specifying all the numerous times when he laid the poison? But none of them by itself could be called poisoning them; so how can we call the man's present pumping an intentional act of poisoning? Or must we draw the conclusion that he at no time poisoned them, since he was not engaged in poisoning at the times at which they were being poisoned? We cannot say that since at some time he poisoned them, there *must* be actions which we can label "poisoning them," and in which we can find what it was to poison them. For in the acts of pumping poisoned water nothing in particular is necessarily going on that might not equally well have been going on if the acts had been acts of pumping non-poisonous water. Even if you imagine that pictures of the inhabitants lying dead occur in the man's head, and please him—such pictures could also occur in the head of a man who was *not* poisoning them, and *need* not occur in this man. The difference appears to be one of circumstances, not of anything that is going on *then*.

25. A further difficulty however arises from the fact that the man's intention might not be to poison them but only to earn his pay. That is to say, if he is being improbably confidential and is asked "Why did you replenish the house water-supply with poisoned

water?," his reply is not "To polish then off," but "I didn't care about that, I wanted my pay and just did my usual job." In that case, although he knows concerning an intentional act of his—for it, namely replenishing the house water-supply, is intentional by our criteria—that it is *also* an act of replenishing the house water-supply with *poisoned* water, it would be incorrect, by our criteria, to say that his act of replenishing the house supply with poisoned water was intentional. And I do not doubt the correctness of the conclusion; it seems to shew that our criteria are rather good. On the other hand, we really do seem to be in a bit of a difficulty to find the intentional act of poisoning those people, supposing that this is what his intentional act is. It is really not at all to be wondered at that so very many people have thought of intention as a special interior movement; then the thing that marked this man's proceedings as *intentional* poisoning of those people would just be that this interior movement occurred in him. But (quite apart from the objections to this idea which we have already considered) the notion of the interior movement tends to have the most unfortunately absurd consequences. For after all we can *form* intentions; now if intention is an interior movement, it would appear that we can choose to have a certain intention and not another, just by e.g. saying within ourselves: "What I *mean* to be doing is earning my living, and *not* poisoning the household"; or "What I *mean* to be doing is helping those good men into power; I withdraw my intention from the act of poisoning the household, which I prefer to think goes on without my intention being in it." The idea that one can determine one's intentions by making such a little speech to oneself is obvious bosh. Nevertheless the genuine case of "I didn't care tuppence one way or the other for the fact that someone had poisoned the water, I just wanted to earn my pay without trouble by doing my usual job—I go with the house, see? and it doesn't matter to me who's in it" does appear to make it very difficult to find anything except a man's thoughts—and these are surely interior—to distinguish the intentional poisoning from poisoning knowingly when this was nevertheless not the man's intention.

Well, one may say, isn't my proposed criterion in a way a criterion by thoughts? If the answer to the question "Why did you replenish the house supply with poisoned water?" is "To polish them off," or any answer within the range, like "I just thought I would," then by my criterion the action under that description is characterized as intentional; otherwise not. But does this not suppose that the answer is or would be *given*? And a man can surely make up the answer that he prefers! So it may appear that I have supplied something just like the interior movement, which a man can make what he likes; but (perhaps out of an attachment to "verificationism") preferred an external answer (actual or hypothetical) which a man can equally make what he likes—at least within the range of moderately plausible answers. Of course I must mean that the *truthful* answer is, or would be, one or the other; but what sort of control of truthfulness can be established here?

The answer to this has to be: there can be a certain amount of control of the truthfulness of the answer. For example, in the case of the man who didn't care tuppence, part of the account we imagined him as giving was that he just went on doing his usual job. It is therefore necessary that it should be his usual job if his answer is to be acceptable; and he must not do anything, out of the usual course of his job, that assists the poisoning and of which he cannot give an acceptable account. E.g. suppose he distracts the attention of one of the inhabitants from something about the water source that might suggest the truth; the question "Why did you call him from over there?" must have a credible answer other than "to prevent him from seeing"; and a multiplication of such points needing explanation would cast doubt on his claim not to have done anything with a view to facilitating the poisoning.—And yet here we might encounter the following explanation: he did not want the enormous trouble that would result from a certain person's noticing; hoped that since the poison was laid it would all go off safely. All along the line he calculated what looked like landing him personally in least trouble, and he reckoned that preventing anything from being suspected would do that. That is quite possible.

Up to a point, then, there is a check on his truthfulness in the account we are thinking he would perhaps give; but still, there is an area in which there is none. The difference between the cases in which he doesn't care whether the people are actually poisoned or not, and in which he is very glad on realizing that they will be poisoned if he co-operates by going on doing his ordinary job, is not one that necessarily carries with it any difference in what he overtly does or how he looks. The difference in his thought on the subject *might* only be the difference between the meanings of the grunt that he gives when he grasps that the water is poisoned. That is to say, when asked "Why did you either reply 'I couldn't care tuppence' or say 'I was glad to help to polish them off,'" and if capable of saying what had actually occurred in him at the time as the vehicle of either of these thoughts, he might have to say only that he grunted. This is the kind of truth there is in the statement "Only you can know if you had such-and-such an intention or not." There is a point at which only what the man himself says is a "sign" and here there is room for much dispute and fine diagnosis of his genuineness.

On the other hand, if, say, this was not his normal job, but he was hired by the poisoner to pump the water, knowing it was poisoned, the case is different. He can say he doesn't care tuppence, and that he only wants the money; but the commission by the acceptance and performance of which he gets the money is—however implicit this is allowed to be—to pump poisoned water. Therefore unless he takes steps to cheat his hirer (he might e.g. put what he mistakenly thought was an antidote into the water), it is not an acceptable account if he says "I wasn't intending to pump poisoned water, only to pump water and get my hire," so that the forms he adopts for refusing to answer the question "Why did you pump poisoned water?" with an answer in our defined range—e.g. with the answer "to get the pay"—are unacceptable. So that while we can find cases where only the man himself can say whether he had a certain intention or not; they are further limited by this: he cannot profess not to have had the intention of doing the thing that was a means to an end of his.

All this, I think, serves to explain what Wittgenstein says at §644 of *Philosophical Investigations*:

> I am not ashamed of what I did then, but of the intention which I had.
>   And didn't the intention reside *also* in what I did? What justifies the shame?
> The whole history of the incident.

And against the background of the qualifications we have introduced, we can epitomize the point by saying "Roughly speaking, a man intends to do what he does." But of course that is *very* roughly speaking. It is right to formulate it, however, as an antidote against the absurd thesis which is sometimes maintained: that a man's intended action is only described by describing his *objective*.

III. EXCERPTS FROM ELIZABETH ANSCOMBE'S "THE JUSTICE OF THE PRESENT WAR EXAMINED"[5]

1. The Conditions of the Just War

There are seven conditions which must be all fulfilled for a war to be just:

- There must be a just occasion: that is, there must be violation of, or attack upon, strict rights.
- The war must be made by a lawful authority: that is, when there is no higher authority, a sovereign state.
- The warring state must have an upright intention in making war: it must not declare war in order to obtain or inflict anything unjust.
- Only right means must be used in the conduct of the war.
- War must be the only possible means of righting the wrong done.
- There must be a reasonable hope of victory.
- The probable good must outweigh the probably evil effects of the war.

For this present war there is a just occasion; the rights of Poland have been infringed. The war was declared by a lawful authority. There is, so far as we can tell, a reasonable hope of victory. And though we may suspect that war could have been averted by a more intelligent policy up to a very short time before war broke out, yet at the time when war was declared it is possible that the wrong done could not have been righted by peaceful means. But there remain three conditions to be fulfilled: the intentions of our government must be upright, both (1) as to means, and (2) as to ends, and (3) the probable good effects of the war must outweigh the probable evil. If these conditions are not fulfilled, this war is rendered wrong, however just the occasion, however desirable that we should fight a war. Nor, if we know that a war is wrong, may we take part in it without sin, however previous it may seem to stand apart from our fellow countrymen.

We must note that, if we fight a war, it is the government's war, since as we have seen, wars can only be made by sovereign states. Therefore we cannot say: "The government's intentions are *vicious*; but the things *I* am fighting for are just," or "The government intends to use evil means, but *I* shall do nothing unjust." A private person may not make war; and if he joins in a war, he joins in it as justified or vitiated by the just or unjust intentions of the government under which he fights. By "government" we mean the persons holding power in a sovereign state. Another point to note is that a government may succumb to temptation in the course of the war; if this involved departure from any of the seven conditions the justice of the war would be vitiated. But isolated pieces of wickedness, though participation in them would be wrong, would not themselves vitiate the whole war on grounds of intention; the probability of such would simply contribute to the balance of evil effects which must be considered.

4. On Aims

If a war is to be just, the warring state must intend only what is just, and the aim of the war must be to set right certain specific injustices. That is, the righting of wrong done must be a sufficient condition on which peace will be made.

In the present war, we may have grave doubts about our government's sincerity. It may seem that we never cared about Poland, but made the Polish treaty as a pretext for seizing the next opportunity to oppose the German government. Our government was badly frightened; it had been weak; it wanted to take a strong line lest it be utterly discredited; and hence the Polish pact. These beginnings are dubious enough; partly because the injustice done to Poland seems our pretext, not our cause, for entering the war; partly because our government appears to have acted from fear and pride, rather than from a desire for justice. Nevertheless it is not wrong to be afraid of Germany's unjust encroachments and to make war in order to stop them, so long as we feared them because they attacked a just settlement and endangered our just interests. But what is the evidence? After the last war, we made the treaty of Versailles, now condemned by every one. But we have made no attempt to rectify it, even when it became urgently necessary that we should do so. We have not tried to make a just and reasonable settlement with Germany; we have merely set aside portions of the treaty by force, and with grave injustice. Finally, we have clamored to negotiate at the last moment, when otherwise Germany would take by force; and our offers have been rejected. Unjustly, it may be; but the evil done by our enemies does not affect our own condemnation.

Our policy, it might be said, is incomprehensible, except as a policy, not of opposing German injustice, but of trying to preserve the status quo and that an unjust one. Some of us may think the case clear enough; yet such argument is likely to lead us into endless controversy. It may be that we could not prove irrefutably that our government's aims are positively vicious.

Some might say that the government is not clear enough about its aims for them to be vicious. Yet if this is so, the government's intention in fighting the war must still be condemned. For it is a condition of a just war that it *should* be fought with a *just* intention; not that it should *not* be fought with an *unjust* intention. If the government's intentions cannot be known to be unjust because they are vague, that vagueness itself vitiates them. But the case is even clearer than this. For the truth is that the government's professed intentions are not merely vague, but unlimited. They have not said: "When justice is done on points A, B and C, then we will stop fighting." They have talked about "sweeping away everything that Hitlerism stands for" and about "building a new order in Europe." What does this mean but that our intentions are so unlimited that there is no point at which we or the Germans could say to our government: "Stop fighting; for your conditions are satisfied." It is true that our government has said that it will not consider peace negotiations until certain injustices are set right. But it has made this only a necessary and not a sufficient condition; therefore it is nothing against our argument.

There results a tendency to interpret our government's phrases according to various predilections. A socialist will tell you that he is fighting for social justice and free speech, a Catholic that he is fighting for the Church. We should forget our own desires and consider narrowly what can be deduced from our government's actions, coupled with these vague and inevitable catchwords. There can be only one conclusion: we are fighting against an unjust cause, indeed; but not for a just one.

5. On the Morality of Means

Before considering whether or not there are any persons who may not be attacked in war, we must try to elucidate, in however crude a fashion, the doctrine of intention in human acts. For in all actions of rational beings we can distinguish three ends of action: there is the motive or motives of the agent, the proper effect of the act as such, and the completed act itself. These are not always distinct in fact, but they can be; if they do coincide this does not make them less distinct in nature, though the distinction is sometimes subtle. For example, take the action of a carpenter in the stroke of a chisel. His motive may be the glory of God, or the obtaining of wages, or the satisfaction of a completed job, or several or all of these, and more besides. The proper effect of the act as such is the removal of a shaving of wood, and this may also be considered as one of the ends of the agent as well as of the action. The completed act itself is simply the completed successful stroke. Let us apply this analysis to military attack. The motive may be to win the war, or medals, or simply to attack successfully and destroy the enemy who receive the impact of the attack. The proper effect is the weakening, disabling or destruction of those who receive that impact. The completed act itself is the completed attack, or, in the case, let us say, of bombing, the dropping and explosion in the right place of the bomb.

Now as to morals. If an act is to be lawful, it is not sufficient that the motives of the agent should be good, though this is necessary. First, the act itself must not be intrinsically wrong; it must not be such an act as is wrong under any circumstance. Second, the proper effects of the act must be permissible. And unless these conditions are present, the act is wrong. To apply these principles once more in the case of military attack: an attack on men is not intrinsically vicious: is not, that is, a perverted act; it is circumstances that make it right or wrong. The motive of the attackers belongs to a consideration of aims rather than of means; or, if we are considering individual soldiers, it is matter for God at the Last Judgment, not for us here. But what of the proper effects of the completed action? These, as we have seen, consist in the destruction of the persons attacked. If, therefore, the attack is to be lawful, the persons attacked must be persons whom the attackers may legitimately destroy. Our object is to consider whether in warfare these persons include civilians.

6. On Means

(i) *The prospect of attack on civilians*: It is generally recognized that, in certain circumstances, we shall attack civilians from the air; we are already attacking them by blockade. We have no space to prove these facts in detail: for the first, it suffices to recall the answer made by our government to President Roosevelt, when he asked for a promise not to attack civilians. We said that we should adhere to international law on the matter, but that we reserved the right "to adopt appropriate measures" if the Germans should break it. If the right to adopt appropriate measures is a reservation to a promise not to attack civilians, then it can only mean that, given certain circumstances, we should attack civilians. The language is veiled, but it can hardly be interpreted in any other way.

(ii) *On blockade*: As for blockade; it has been pretended, in justification, that the blockade is not a blockade; or that it does not attack civilians. But some people, when they are arguing on another subject, when they are assuring us of victory, *then* they tell us that we cannot but win because the Germans cannot survive the blockade, since it prevents things essential to their national life from reaching them. Others, at this point, say that we could not really be responsible for starving the German people, because they divert the supplies to the fighting forces, and therefore are responsible themselves. But this argument admits that civilians do suffer attack and therefore can be dealt with under that head.

(iii) *The "indivisibility" of modern war and the justification of killing enemies in war:*
It is argued that it is just to attack civilians in war because war is now "indivisible." The civilian population is really as much combatant as the fighting forces, for it is their essential backing. The military strength of a country is its whole economic and social strength. Therefore civilians may be attacked as combatants.

Here we must ask two questions: first what is the justification of killing in war? and, second, in what does the indivisibility of war consist? It is no sin to kill a man in self-defense or in defense of rights, if there is no possibility of appeal to a higher authority. A private person can appeal to the authority of the state, and therefore has no right to choose the death of a man in order to defend his rights; though he commits no sin if his action in resisting attack, at the time of attack, results in the death of the attacker; for such death is accidental. But where there is no higher authority to which to appeal, as in the case of a sovereign state at war, men who are wrongfully attacking rights may be killed in order to defend those rights if they cannot be defended in any other way.

We must notice two things about this doctrine: first that those who are killed are killed as *wrongfully* attacking rights, in virtue of the fact that it is not possible to appeal to any higher authority than the parties in the dispute. In this sense, the justly warring state is "in the stead of a judge," having chosen to inflict death on men for the general good. Those men *must* be *wrongfully attacking* rights, or retaining what they have wrongfully gained; for it is wrong to slay the innocent for the good of the people. But second, though it proceeds from this quasi-judicial position of the justly warring state, that it can give its ministers authority deliberately to kill its enemies, *yet* they may only kill as a means of self-defense or the defense of rights; the judicial power does not permit them to kill purely punitively; for it is not lawful to kill men simply punitively, except after trial. The justly warring state has to judge of the right or wrong done; but it has no power of judgment on personal guilt or innocence. These two points must therefore be maintained: to quote St Thomas Aquinas [*Summa Theologica*],

> it is unlawful for a man to intend to kill any one in order to defend himself, except for one with public authority; and he, intending to kill a man for his own defense, refers this to the general good, as is plain in the case of a soldier fighting enemies, and the minister of a judge fighting against robbers. (2a 2ae. 64, art.7)

We have it, then, that no one may be deliberately attacked in war, unless his actions constitute an attack on the rights which are being defended or restored. To deny this will be to assert that we may attack any one anywhere, whose life in any way hinders the prosecution of the war, or in any way assists our enemies; and such a conclusion is as immoral as to be a reductio ad absurdum in itself.

Now in what does the "indivisibility" of war consist? It consists in this, that it would be impossible for the combatant forces to fight, unless they were backed by the economic and social strength of the nation behind them. Therefore, it is argued, the civil population is a military target. To this there is only one reply. The civilian population behind an army does not fulfill the conditions which make it right to kill a man in war. Civilians are not committing wrong acts against those who are defending or restoring rights. They are maintaining the economic and social strength of a nation, and that is not wrong, even though that strength is being used by their government as the essential backing of an army unjustly fighting in the field.

It has been argued that, as accessories to a murder are by law punished equally with the murderer, so the citizens of an enemy country may be killed equally with the fighting forces. But the analogy is false. An accessory is punished as morally guilty of murder. But we have seen that it is not right to kill merely punitively in war; so whatever the guilt of the enemy nation, we cannot arrogate to ourselves the position of a judge, and execute them. A man cannot be judge in his own suit; and we are one of the parties in the quarrel. In default of a higher authority, we may kill those whose actions are an attack on our rights, in order to defend those rights: but the actions must themselves be wrong. The actions of a great mass of the civilian population are not in themselves wrongful attacks on us. Therefore they may not be killed by us, simply as deserving to die, nor yet because their death would be useful to us.

(iv) *A note on reprisals*: It follows from this analysis that no warring state may claim the right to inflict certain harm on the enemy simply because he has inflicted it on you. The morality of the action itself must be considered before it can be justified.

(v) *On double effect*: It has been argued that it is justifiable to attack civilians because their death is an example of "double effect." But this is no example of double effect, which is exemplified when an action designed to produce one effect produces another as well by accident. If, for example, a military target is being attacked and in the course of the attack civilians are also destroyed, then their destruction is not wicked, for it is accidental. Obviously before their destruction can be passed over on these grounds, it must also be shown that the action is of sufficient importance to allow such grave incidental effects. No action can be excused whose consequences involve a greater evil than the good of the action itself, whether these consequences are accidental or not. Double effect therefore only excuses a grave incidental consequence where the balance of the total effects of an action is on the side of the good.

There is a great distinction between attacking a group of persons directly, and killing them accidentally in the course of attack on others. But yet another distinction must be made. It is a different thing, while making one group of persons a target, to kill others by accident, and to make a group of persons a target, in order—by attacking them all—to attack some members of the group who are persons who may legitimately be attacked. The first case involves no sin; the second involves murder and is not an example of double effect. It has been claimed as such by some who, defending blockade, allow that civilians are not a proper military target, but who argue that attack may be made on a whole group of persons which includes both civilians and combatants. This claim cannot be allowed.

Again, we cannot say with regard to blockade that the starvation of a civilian population by the diversion of supplies to its army is an incidental and unintentional effect of an action intended to demoralize the army. For to do so it would be necessary not only to prove that such an evil effect would in fact be outweighed by the good effects expected, but also that there would be no causal relation between the preceding starvation of a civilian population and the demoralization of an army. This aspect of the problem of double effect is distinct from that treated immediately above. There we were considering whether it is an example of double effect to attack one group of persons as a means of destroying a part of the same group. Both cases are immoral if a group of, or including, civilians, is made a military target; and neither is a case of double effect.

Commentary by *Joy Laine*, Anscombe and Wittgenstein: A Public Voice for Philosophy

ANSCOMBE

Elizabeth Anscombe's philosophical work made major contributions to three distinct traditions of philosophy: the ancient philosophy of classical Greece; the Catholic philosophical tradition; and the twentieth-century tradition of analytical philosophy, particularly the philosophy of language and moral philosophy. In addition to her own work, Anscombe is also well known throughout the English-speaking philosophical world for her long association with Ludwig Wittgenstein, one of the most influential philosophers of the twentieth century. The appearance of her translation of Wittgenstein's *Philosophical Investigations* in 1953 was one of the great publishing events of the twentieth century and had a tremendous impact on the way philosophers thought about language and its relationship to mind and reality.

Shortly after publishing her translation of the *Philosophical Investigations* Anscombe published *Intention* (1957), the philosophical work for which she is best known. Her reputation for being the foundational thinker for contemporary philosophy of action rests largely on this one publication, and understanding its content, genesis, and methodology is key to understanding her career as a whole.

ANSCOMBE AND MORAL PHILOSOPHY

As its title suggests, *Intention* is about a specific type of human action, namely, those actions that are characterized as "intentional actions." Walking to the kitchen to get myself a drink would be an example of an intentional act, whereas the reflex movement my leg makes in response to a doctor tapping on my knee would not. Although we may use the intentional-nonintentional labels to characterize the difference between these two acts, this does not really give us an explanation of what distinguishes them. For that, an adequate account is needed of the intentional-nonintentional distinction itself. Anscombe's search for a satisfactory account of this distinction lies at the core of *Intention*.

In "Modern Moral Philosophy" (1958),[6] a paper that she published shortly after the appearance of *Intention*, Anscombe claimed that an adequate human action theory was a necessary foundation for moral philosophy. In the same paper Anscombe claimed that such a theory was missing in the work of her peers. Her criticism was not that moral philosophers had failed to recognize the relevance of the distinction between intentional and nonintentional acts for developing theories of moral responsibility and free will, since, typically, we are presumed not to be morally responsible for those things we did not or could not have done voluntarily, knowingly, or consciously—that is, intentionally. Rather, Anscombe's criticism of moral philosophy was that it took this distinction for granted, using the distinction without explaining its basis. In *Intention*, she went back to the very foundations of moral philosophy in order to provide an account of the intention-nonintentional distinction.

Furthermore, Anscombe claimed that there are two even more fundamental ways in which a theory of intentional action (action theory) is pivotal for moral philosophy.[7] The first way is that moral philosophy fails to provide an adequate theory of what counts as a relevant description of any particular action. Anscombe is critical of both Kant and Mill, the two foundational thinkers of ethical theory, for their failure to understand the importance of an adequate description and analysis of any particular human action for their ethical positions. Although Kant and Mill are two ethical theorists whose positions are mutually incompatible, Anscombe believed that they shared this fundamental flaw. Against Kant, for example, she argues that his categorical imperative stipulates that one (the individual as rational agent) should act only on those maxims that one could will to be a universal law. But, as Anscombe points out, such universalizable maxims will be "useless without stipulations as to what shall count as a relevant description of an action with a view to constructing a maxim about it."[8] How one characterizes any particular action can be crucial to one's moral evaluation of it.

The second way a theory of intentional action is pivotal for moral philosophy is that the intention with which an action is done is relevant to how one describes an action and, hence, to the moral evaluation of any particular action. In "Modern Moral Philosophy," Anscombe chastises the leading moral philosophers of her day for unanimously disregarding the relevance of the intention with which an action is performed to the moral worth of the action. She rejects the view that "it does not make any difference to a man's responsibility for an effect of his action which he can foresee, that he does not intend it."[9] The ethical position that rejects the intention with which an action is done as relevant to the moral evaluation of the action she dubbed "consequentialism."

Anscombe's appreciation of the need for a theory of intentional acts was not merely theoretical; it grew out of her opposition to Britain's declaration of war against Germany in 1939. Anscombe had been a vocal opponent of this war, fearing (correctly as it turned out) that it would lead to a British policy of intentional civilian killing. It was in this historical context that she first began to think seriously about the distinction between intentional and nonintentional acts. Anscombe's responses to the historical events surrounding World War II give the book a poignancy that otherwise might be missed.

In her first publication (at age twenty), "The Justice of the Present War Examined" coauthored with Norman Daniel at the outset of the war, the authors questioned whether or not the war satisfied the conditions of a just war. The publication of this pamphlet at the beginning of World War II demonstrates considerable moral courage on the part of its authors, since they challenged the morality of Britain's actions in a public climate of widespread support for Britain's war against Germany.[10]

In this pamphlet Anscombe discusses one of the conditions of a just war, namely that only the "right means" may be used in the conduct of the war. According to Anscombe, if a war is to be conducted by right means, then those prosecuting the war are not permitted to engage in acts that are intrinsically wrong. Murder is an intrinsically wrong act. So it is important for those wanting to act in accordance with the conditions and limitations of a just war to know which people it is permissible to kill during a war in order to avoid murderous acts. Who are such persons? In this pamphlet, Anscombe presents an argument that they do not include civilians, since the intentional killing of civilians in the conduct of a war is murder and, therefore, wrong.

Anscombe held other fundamental beliefs about the nature of a just war that are key to understanding her reasoning prohibiting attacks on civilians in a war. In addition to the right means condition, Anscombe claimed that a just war must be an act of self-defense undertaken by a sovereign state on behalf of its citizens. For Anscombe, war is a permissible conflict resolution strategy between states: it may permit states to kill those who wrongfully attack collective human rights, if no other defense is possible. The key to Anscombe's conclusion that civilians may not be legitimately attacked in a war, but that military combatants may, hinges on the premise that civilians are not committing wrong acts against those who are fighting to restore their rights.

Anscombe realizes that if the principle of right means is to have any practical application, it must distinguish between those who may be legitimately killed in a war from those who may not: For Anscombe, that meant "we must try to elucidate, in however crude a fashion, the doctrine of intention in human acts."[11] This statement reveals the beginnings of the philosophical journey that eventually found its full expression in *Intention*. Anscombe's position that a doctrine of intention in human acts is necessary to ascertain who may or may not be justly killed during a war plays a prominent role in the two main arguments against the killing of civilians she gives in "The Justice of the Present War Examined."

The two arguments rest on Anscombe's rejection of "the indivisibility thesis," which claims that there is no distinction between civilians and military combatants in times of war. One argument against the intentional killing of civilians in times of war claims that there *ought* not to be such a distinction; the other denies the claim that as a matter of practical reality there cannot be such a distinction.

In her first argument against the indivisibility thesis, Anscombe demonstrates that the intentional acts of civilians engaged in their normal business cannot be characterized as *wrongful* acts against the warring opposition. Consider the example a farmer plowing his fields while his country is at war with another. The crucial question here is whether his plowing commits any wrongful acts against the opposing army. This is a question that turns on the descriptions under which the farmer's action is characterized, and consequently, whether there is any description of the farmer's could make the actions a wrongful attack on the rights of the warring opposition. A farmer plowing his field is doing many things in addition to plowing. He is walking up and down his fields. He is preparing the soil to plant wheat. He is growing food for his fellow citizens, and he is going about his normal business. But his plowing the field is also contributing to the prosperity of his nation. So, some would argue that since the farmer is making a contribution to the war effort, he is a legitimate military target. In response, Anscombe denies that the farmer is committing a wrongful act against the enemy; hence, to kill him would be to cross the line between self-defense and punitive killing. Certainly, because the farmer's action contributes to the economic prosperity of his nation, the farmer's destruction might be useful to the enemy forces. But contributing to the economic prosperity of one's nation does not by itself constitute a wrongful attack against the rights of another nation; as such, Anscombe concludes that his destruction would be murder.

In this first argument Anscombe is struggling with the problem that any action is open to a plurality of descriptions. Which descriptions properly characterize the intentional actions? This became one of the central questions of *Intention* (discussed later in this commentary).

Anscombe's second argument against the indivisibility thesis is directed to those who might agree with Anscombe's argument that civilians ought not to have the status of combatants in a war, yet lament that in reality civilian death is an inevitable consequence of modern warfare. So the destruction of a munitions factory, for example, may often involve the destruction of innocent bystanders. It is an unfortunate matter of statistical certainty that in modern warfare innocent people will be killed. This might seem to imply that pacifism is the only option for someone committed to the idea that the killing of innocent people in a war constitutes murder.

To counter these claims, Anscombe appeals to an argument based on the principle of double effect, well known in the Catholic tradition as a basis for justifying such deaths. Double effect turns on the distinction between circumstances where the death of civilians is an *accidental effect* of actions whose primary purpose or *intended effect* is something else, in this case to destroy the munitions factory. Keenly aware that the principle of double effect is open to misuse, Anscombe argues that a defense of civilian death based on double effect is legitimate only if the death of the civilians is truly accidental, a genuinely unintended effect. Anscombe argues that if I intentionally attack a group that I know includes civilians in order to destroy noncivilian members of the group (i.e., the death of the civilians is an intended effect), then this is unjust killing and not an authentic example of double effect.

Anscombe insisted that decisions about intention are too important to be left to first-person accounts of the contents of one's own mind.[12] Where the intention of an action is thought to be an interior act of the mind preceding the action, then it would seem that all one needs to do to ensure the moral goodness of an action is to make a little speech to oneself, to direct one's attention in a certain way. Furthermore, her arguments against civilian bombing that used the principle of double effect illustrate the significance of distinguishing between cases where civilian death was due to unintended but foreseen consequences of a military action and cases where civilian death was the intention of a military action. Determining which actions are and are not examples of double effect turns, then, on the intentions with which an action is carried out. How can we determine that? This becomes a central question in *Intention*. But first, consider the effect Wittgenstein's views about language had on Anscombe's theory in *Intention*.

ANSCOMBE AND WITTGENSTEIN

It was while she was preoccupied with questions about the justice of World War II that Anscombe first became associated with Wittgenstein. Anscombe wrote *Intention* within a few years of translating Wittgenstein's *Philosophical Investigations* and it would be fair to say that she found Wittgenstein's philosophical method key to solving her own philosophical puzzles. Famously, Wittgenstein believed that philosophical problems originate from confusions about language; he viewed philosophy as a therapeutic activity directed at clearing up these confusions. Furthermore, since philosophy is therapeutic, his books demand participation from the reader. When we read a work by Wittgenstein he takes us on an intellectual odyssey. In *Philosophical Investigations*, Wittgenstein's technique is to remind his readers of what we say, how we use language in our everyday practices, and to "bring words back from their metaphysical to their everyday use."[13] An imaginary interlocutor haunts the pages of the *Philosophical Investigations*, asking the kinds of confused questions that we the readers might also be tempted to ask. Wittgenstein saw his task as one of delivering his readers from such confusion by clarifying language use.

Anscombe has written about how liberated she felt by Wittgenstein's method of doing philosophy.[14] Anscombe's *Intention* has many of the qualities of Wittgenstein's work. For instance, throughout the book she uses the pronoun "we" and the reader is expected to struggle along with her. Simplistic solutions that a reader might be tempted to offer are brushed aside, and we are constantly reminded of the real-life complexity of the language of intention. Like *Philosophical Investigations*, *Intention* is written as a sequence of fairly short, numbered paragraphs, a presentation particularly suited to a style of philosophy that aims to expose the complicated practices of ordinary language by separating issues about language and language practices into readable paragraphs, thereby avoiding the temptation to reduce such practices to one simple thesis.

In *Philosophical Investigations* Wittgenstein mounts a sustained critique of traditional views about what makes language meaningful. Philosophers such as Locke had argued that the meaning of a word is to be equated with the corresponding idea in the mind of the user. Unfortunately, if none of us is able to access the contents of a mind other than our own, this model leads to a great deal of skepticism about whether or not we really mean the same things by the words that we use.

Wittgenstein offers an alternative model. Speaking a language, he says, is like playing a game: it is something that people do and it forms a seamless whole with other human activities.[15] Since language is used for a multitude of tasks, like a tool box containing different tools,[16] language is a complex entity made up of numerous smaller units that Wittgenstein calls "language games."[17] If we think of an activity that we would ordinarily call a game, basketball for example, we will see that it is essential that the players agree on the rules and how to follow the rules of the game. Analogously, Wittgenstein proposed that words have meaning in virtue of being used in publicly accessible, rule-governed ways, rather than by being associated with some private image in the mind of the user. One cannot follow a rule privately, since rule following is essentially a public activity. Consequently, Wittgenstein's views about language situate the meanings of words in activities that take place in public space rather than the so-called privacy of the individual mind.[18]

It might seem that Wittgenstein's analysis would break down when it comes to language that is specifically about the inner life of the individual. When we speak about our sensations, beliefs, and intentions, for example, it would seem that we are speaking about things, processes, or experiences going on within ourselves—what might be called "private objects." However, a major part of the *Philosophical Investigations* is dedicated to demonstrating that even when we are using language to speak about our inner lives, it is a mistake to think that such language refers to essentially private objects. If this were the way in which such language operated then it would be what Wittgenstein describes as a private language and only the speaker would have access to the referents of such a language. In a private language it would be claimed that only I can know what I am speaking about if I say that I am in pain, for example, since no one else can experience my pain.

Wittgenstein demonstrates that in a so-called private language the conditions that allow for following a rule consistently are absent, whatever seems right will be right, and hence the conditions necessary for using words consistently are absent. *It is the consistent application of rules that give words a use and hence a meaning.* Thus, even for words like "pain," there must be a public context for their use to ensure their meaningfulness.

Wittgenstein's analysis of someone learning to continue a numerical series demonstrates his strategy of grounding language about our mental life in a public arena.[19] If someone is presented with a numerical sequence and asked to continue the sequence, we may ask the question, "Does he know how to continue the series?" Wittgenstein answers this question by linking understanding to performance. Understanding how to continue with the numerical sequence depends upon whether or not we give the right numbers in answer to a point where the audience is satisfied. It doesn't depend on us having the correct formula in our heads, upon being in some requisite brain state or upon having some interior sense of understanding.

Some have interpreted Wittgenstein as a behaviorist, meaning that language is just about human rule–governed behaviors. But such a view misses the point of his analysis. He does not deny, in the case of the numerical sequence for example, that certain formulae occur in our minds or that there are certain sensations connected with thinking that we understand. Rather, his point is that their occurrence is not the basis on which we could say that someone *understands* the numerical series. Whether or not these events are occurring, if we cannot perform the task, then it could not be said that we understood the sequence. We need to distinguish between giving an account of the mental causes leading to our continuing the number sequence, which may involve talk about our inner lives, and giving an account of what constitutes the understanding, which is a public activity. Anscombe employs a similar strategy in her work on intentions. Like Wittgenstein she is no behaviorist, but she is concerned to locate our talk about what we do and why we do it in the arena of public discourse.

ANSCOMBE'S *INTENTION*

All the preceding bears on Anscombe's arguments in *Intention*. Anscombe begins *Intention* by claiming that the word "intention" is not equivocal but does have a complex usage in our language. She lists three ways the words "intention" and "intentional" are employed in our language. First, we may describe an expression in our language as being an expression of intention, as opposed say to an expression of prediction. One and the same grammatical expression, "I am going to fail the exam tomorrow," for example, can be used to make a prediction or express an intention. Anscombe's first task, then, is to ask how we can distinguish between expressions of intention and expressions of prediction, given that their grammatical expressions are often the same. Second, we also speak about actions as being intentional in nature. Her second task in *Intention*, then, is to investigate the basis for classifying some actions as intentional and others as nonintentional. Last, we may ask with what intention a thing was done. Her third task is, therefore, to see how we can determine the intention of any particular action.

Given the need for brevity, here we can only consider some of the arguments that Anscombe presents in *Intention*. In her arguments against Britain's war with Germany,

Anscombe came to understand the importance of distinguishing between the intentional and nonintentional killing of civilians. In *Intention*, she revisits this question more broadly, asking, "What is the basis for characterizing some actions as 'intentional' in nature?" One answer is to say that intentional actions are those things that we do voluntarily, but this would just seem to take the problem back one step. As Anscombe points out, the distinction between voluntary and involuntary actions itself "covers notions of exactly the type that a philosophical inquiry into intention ought to be elucidating."[20] Moreover, if we look at actions that we would characterize as involuntary, we will see that this is itself a mixed group.

Anscombe's thesis is that intentional actions are ones linked to a certain type of response that we would give to the question "Why are you doing X?" A first step in trying to explain here what we mean by "a certain type of response" would be to say that when the appropriate response to the question "Why are you doing X?" is to give a *reason for action*, then we could classify X as an intentional action. This first suggestion may point us in the right direction and is helpful in distinguishing expressions of intention from expressions of prediction. If we are making a prediction when we say "I am going to fail the exam tomorrow," for example, we will give *evidence* for the likelihood of this coming to be true whereas if we are using this sentence to express our intention to fail the exam, we will give a *reason* for doing so. Anscombe, however, will need to explain more specifically what makes something a reason for action, as opposed to a cause, for example. Anscombe's strategy is to devise a series of tests, based on the kind of response that would be given to the question "Why are you doing X?," that allows us to decide whether an action is intentional or not.

One way of answering the question "Why are you doing X?" is to say, "I didn't know that I was doing X." Some of the things that are happening to us we know only on the basis of observation, like the peristaltic movement of the gut. Anscombe is using the term "observation" in a somewhat technical sense here. By observation, Anscombe is referring to phenomena that we come to know only on the basis of something else, as opposed to phenomena known directly. A good example of something known without observation would be the position of one's limbs. This is something that we know but we do not know this on the basis of something else that tells us the position of our limbs. The peristaltic movement of the gut, however, would be something that we would have to learn about from something else, such as books or medical technology. Thus if I ask you why you are making peristaltic movements with your gut it may be appropriate for you to respond "I did not know that I was doing that." When it makes sense to answer the question in this way, it indicates that the action in question falls outside of the class of voluntary actions. According to Anscombe, we have now found a way of demarcating between intentional actions and one type of involuntary action—namely, those actions whose occurrence we know about *only* on the basis of observation. What is important is that this test does not itself depend on us having a prior account of the voluntary-involuntary distinction.

A second way that we might respond to the question "Why are you doing X?" is to conjecture about a possible answer or else admit ignorance as to why. This will be the type of answer that we would give for those actions whose occurrence, unlike the peristaltic movement of the gut, we can know directly (say through experience or sensation) and not on the basis of observation, but whose *cause* we know only on the basis of observation. We know, without having to learn about it, that our bodies sometimes jerk just before we go to sleep. What we do not know, however, without observation, is what causes this to happen. When the cause of an action is known only on the basis of observation, this will also allow us to reject one particular sense of the question "Why are you doing X?" that asks us for a reason. This separates another group of actions from those that we would denote as voluntary. So we now have two kinds of involuntary actions that are not intentional actions: (1) those known only through observation, and (2) those known directly without observation but whose causes are known only through observation.

Anscombe's task is now to distinguish intentional actions from a third group of nonintentional actions—(3) actions whose occurrence and cause are both known without observation. When we know the cause of an action directly, and not on the basis of observation, this is defined by Anscombe as a case of "mental causality." An example of an action that has a mental cause would be my knowing that it was the strange face appearing at the window that caused me to knock the cup off the table.

Anscombe now faces the difficult task of distinguishing between this third group of nonintentional actions from intentional acts such as "I got off the chair to go to the kitchen." This brings us to the central problem of intentional action, namely, how to distinguish between, (3) caused actions, where the cause is known directly by the agent, and, (4) intentional actions (defined below).

Initially, we might think that these two types of action can be distinguished by saying that in the first case I will give the *cause* of my acting in response to the question "Why are you doing X?" whereas in the second case I will give the *reason* for my acting. Anscombe's familiarity with Wittgenstein's work, particularly Wittgenstein's insistence that philosophical descriptions reflect the actual usage of words, makes her wary of accepting such an easy distinction. If we acknowledge how we actually use language, then we will not be tempted by what might initially seem to be a promising solution. We might be tempted to see this reason-cause distinction as being clear and unproblematic. Anscombe casts doubt on there being such clarity. Using her example, if I hang my hat on a peg in response to my host saying "Hang up your hat on that peg" are her words the *reason* why I hang my hat on the peg, or are they the *cause* of my hanging my hat on the peg? Anscombe argues that the assumption that there is always a clear distinction between reason and cause is simply not always true. This does not mean, however, that there is no distinction to be made.

The difference between reason and cause is seen best by looking at clear examples of each. Knocking a cup off the table because of a strange face appearing at the window is a clear case of my action being caused, killing my father out of revenge is a clear case of my acting for a specific reason. Anscombe's suggestion here is that giving a reason is to give a certain *form of explanation* that might involve an interpretation of the action, or mention something in the future, or simply mention an event from the past. Something is established as a reason if one argues against it in such a way as to link it up with motives. If we give this type of answer to the question "Why are you doing X?" then we can determine that the act under question is intentional, (4). Intentional acts are ones for which there is (or one gives) a reason in the form of an explanation that is linked with motives.

Anscombe's analysis of intentional actions is thoroughly Wittgensteinian insofar as she resists the idea that there is some distinctive inner mental event preceding or accompanying the act that gives it its intentional character. This thesis often takes the form that intentional acts are caused by a specific type of mental event, namely, intentions. There are several reasons why someone well versed in Wittgenstein's philosophy of mind and language would object to such a thesis.

First, the thesis as it stands just seems to be wrong. Wittgenstein would often advise his students to "Look and see!" His respect for our everyday practices meant that the gold standard for any philosophical idea is whether or not it accurately describes how we ordinarily use language. In this particular case, if we look we will see that for many actions that we would characterize as being intentional in nature there is in reality no preceding intention causing us to act. Many of our more routine actions, such as driving a car, are like this. I may intentionally stop at a stop sign without being moved by a desire or intention to do so. It is just something that I simply do. I develop habits because of a particular training.

Second, this model that locates the distinguishing feature of intentional acts in an event that takes place in the private mental space of each individual goes against the whole tenor of the *Philosophical Investigations*. Anscombe believes that we make a profound error if we try to distinguish intentional actions on the basis of mental causality. This is not to say that mental causes are absent in the case of such actions; rather, it is to say that the occurrence of such mental causes is not the basis for an action's being intentional. As such, when we ask the question "Why did you do X?" we may be asking for the causal history of the act, the mental causes that led us to do the action. We may be asking what feelings, thoughts, images, and so forth led up to our acting as we did. This kind of question, for example, might be asked by a psychologist, interested in the mental history leading up to a particular action. However, Anscombe argues that if this is so, then the question "Why did you do X?" is a different question from the usual sense in which we ask of someone "Why did you do X?" although the two questions might be related. The normal response to the question would involve giving a reason for doing X. The reason why someone did X involves situating the particular action in the broader context of a person's life. If we ask the farmer, "Why are you plowing your field?" he might reply, "Because I'm preparing the soil to plant my crops." This would be an appropriate answer, yet it might be absent from the farmer's conscious mental life as he goes out to plow his field.

This distinction, between giving reasons for acting and giving an account of the mental life of the agent immediately prior to an action, is particularly important when it comes to dealing with the third question raised in *Intention*, namely, how can we determine for any particular action the intention with which the action was done? Anscombe phrases the question this way: "Is there any description which is *the* description of an intentional action, given that an intentional action occurs?" It might be thought that the answer to this question could be given by giving an account of what occurred in the person's mind immediately prior to acting. Intentions would then be thought of as acts of the mind, taking place prior to and causing the subsequent action. To identify the intention with which an action is performed would be to know the specific content of the mental act of the actor-agent occurring prior to the action. But both her understanding of Wittgenstein's work and her recognition that the ethical consequences of this type of view would be disastrous led her to reject this type of Cartesian psychology.[21]

How then are we to determine the intention of a particular action? Anscombe uses an example of a man pumping water into a cistern that supplies the drinking water for a household. Suppose the water happens to have been systematically contaminated by someone else with the intention of killing all of the inhabitants of the house. Suppose, further, that the reason the person contaminates the water is that the inhabitants are also engaged in a plot to exterminate the Jews. The man pumping the water is obviously doing many things; Anscombe has given us a way of distinguishing those actions of his that are intentional (such as pumping the water) from those that are not (such as producing certain chemical reactions in his neurotransmitters). This will still leave us with a plurality of answers to the question, "What are you doing?" that would characterize the action as being intentional in nature. He might answer in the following ways: "I'm moving my arm up and down." "I'm pumping." "I'm pumping the water supply to the house." This plurality of answers reflects an important feature of an intentional act, namely, that it can fall under numerous descriptions. What we may be doing intentionally under one description we may not be doing intentionally under another description.

The question to ask in the case of the man pumping the water is whether or not the description of his act as "poisoning the inhabitants of the house" is correct and an appropriate description of the man's intention. Again, Anscombe rejects the temptation to answer the question by reference to some interior event going on within the man himself, claiming "The idea that one can determine one's intentions by making such a little speech to oneself is obvious bosh." Whether or not the man is intentionally poisoning the inhabitants of the house is not determined solely by giving a mental history of the man's inner life. Anscombe argues that we can tie the truthfulness of an answer to the question "What are you doing?" to the man's behavior. If we see the man pumping the water also attempt to distract the attention of others nearby in order to prevent them from finding out that the water supply is contaminated, then this information is relevant to what we say about his intentions. Anscombe is arguing against the privacy of intention and for the relevance of "circumstances" (including a person's own comments about an action) to the correct description of an action.

Anscombe's engagement with Wittgenstein's philosophy, particularly his work in the philosophy of language and mind, contributed to what she accomplished in *Intention*. Wittgenstein was a highly abstract thinker whose philosophical positions were often difficult to interpret. Anscombe's deep understanding of his work allowed her to make connections between Wittgenstein's philosophy and the political turmoil in which she lived and worked. Unlike Wittgenstein, Anscombe lived the life of a public intellectual who frequently wrote about the important social and political events of her time. Through such writings she demonstrated the value of "public philosophy" that hitherto had been largely known to only a small group of professional philosophers

Conclusion

Elizabeth Anscombe has become an almost legendary figure in the history of twentieth-century philosophy. This legendary status rests not just on her published work but also on who she was and how she chose to live her life. The connections she makes between concrete, personal, and historical circumstances and the abstract world of traditional philosophy is one that is widely accepted by today's intellectual community. In retrospect we can see that she was a pioneer in bringing about these changes.

Questions for Reflection

Why do you think the movement my leg makes when a doctor taps on my knee isn't an intentional action? How does Anscombe conclude that this isn't an intentional action?

Anscombe believed that the intentional killing of civilians was wrong. Yet she also accepted that the killing of civilians during the prosecution of a modern war is inevitable. What criteria does Anscombe give for discriminating between the intentional and nonintentional killing of civilians? Are these good criteria? Can you think of an alternative set of criteria that could be used instead? (It might be helpful to use a specific example to help you answer these questions.)

Locke states that in their primary and immediate signification words stand for nothing but the ideas in the mind of the user. Why did Wittgenstein reject this view of language? According to Wittgenstein, what makes the words that we use meaningful? Which account do you think is correct, Locke's or Wittgenstein's?

Notes

1. Most of my exposition on Wittgenstein's philosophical views is taken from my lecture notes, which include contributions by my colleagues, professors Janet Folina and Joy Laine (from occasions when they guest lectured on Wittgenstein in my courses. I thank them for what they taught me about Wittgenstein. Any mistakes in descriptions and interpretations of Wittgenstein's views are mine, not theirs.

2. This comment is taken from John Dolan's obituary on Anscombe, "G. E. M. Anscombe: Living the Truth," *First Things* (May 2001): 11–13.

3. Ludwig Wittgenstein, *Philosophical Investigations:* 3rd ed., trans. G. E. M. Anscombe (London: Basil Blackwell & Mott, Ltd, 1958), par. 1–6, 11–12, 23, 65–67, 143–50, 163–65; pp. 2–5, 6, 7, 11–12, 31–32, 56–59, 163–65.

4. G. E. M. Anscombe, *Intention* (Oxford: Basil Blackwell, 1957). Reprinted as G. E. M. Anscombe, *Intention* (Ithaca, NY: Cornell University Press), par. 1, 6–16, 23–27; pp. 1, 11–25, 37–49.

5. G.E.M. Anscombe and Norman Daniel, "The Justice of the Present War Examined," in *Collected Philosophical Papers* (Oxford: Oxford University Press, 1939), 73–79.

6. G. E. M. Anscombe, "Modern Moral Philosophy," in *Philosophy* 33 (1958), repr. in her *Collected Philosophical Papers*, vol. 3, *Ethics, Religion and Politics* (Minneapolis: University of Minnesota Press, 1981), 26–42.

7. Anscombe, "Moral Philosophy," 27.

8. Anscombe, "Moral Philosophy," 35.

9. Anscombe, "Moral Philosophy," 35.

10. Anscombe did not see herself to be a pacifist and felt that in some circumstance war might be justified. She argues that pacifism's unilateral opposition to all killing collapses important moral distinctions, and makes the killing of children, for example, morally the same as the killing of combatant soldiers. She fears that pacifism weakens the arguments that she wants to make that war can be conducted on a moral basis.

11. Anscombe, "Justice of Present War," 75.

12. Anscombe argues that such an acceptance of Cartesian psychology has allowed for the frequent abuse of the principle of double effect: "the principle has been repeatedly abused from the seventeenth century up till now. The causes lie in the history of philosophy. From the seventeenth century till now what may be called Cartesian psychology has dominated the thought of philosophers and theologians. According to this psychology, an intention was an interior act of the mind that could be produced at will. Now if intention is all important—as it is—in determining the goodness or badness of an action, then, on the theory of what intention is, a marvelous way offered itself of making any action lawful. You had only to direct your intention in a suitable

way. In practice this means making a little speech to yourself: 'What I mean to be doing is. . . . '" Quotation from G. E. M. Anscombe, "War and Murder" in *Collected Philosophical Papers*, 58–59.

13. Wittgenstein, *Philosophical Investigations*, par. 116, 48.

14. Anscombe writes about this in the preface of *Collected Philosophical Papers*, viii–ix.

15. Wittgenstein, *Philosophical Investigations*, par. 23, 11.

16. Wittgenstein, *Philosophical Investigations*, par. 11, 6.

17. Wittgenstein, *Philosophical Investigations*, par. 65–67, 31–32.

18. Wittgenstein, *Philosophical Investigations*, par. 199–202, 80–81. "Privacy" here refers to the privacy associated with a Cartesian view of the mind. The Cartesian mind is private in the sense that its contents are knowable only to the individual whose mind it is. Those who hold such a view of the mind would say things like, "Only I can know whether or not I'm in pain." Wittgenstein's philosophy of language seeks to undermine this Cartesian psychology.

19. Wittgenstein, *Philosophical Investigations*, par. 143–150.

20. Anscombe, *Intention*, 12.

21. See notes 2, 18, and the glossary.

CHAPTER 15

Sartre and Beauvoir

Introduction by *Karen J. Warren*

The best-known philosophical pair of existential philosophy is Jean-Paul Sartre (1905–1980) and Simone de Beauvoir (1908–1986). Lifelong partners and intellectual companions, their existentialist positions challenge key features of canonical Western philosophy—for example, essentialism, the mind-body dualism, the distinction between self and other, and the nature of philosophical methodology. In this chapter, the topic of conversation is the notion of the self. Both Sartre and Beauvoir offer a notion of the self that is characterized by four distinct features—intersubjectivity, atemporality, embodiment, and the nature and role of the Other—even though they frequently offer very different positions on each feature. This introduction provides biographical and philosophical information about Sartre and Beauvoir that is intended to do two things: to enable a more informed understanding of the primary texts, and to draw attention to the unique accessiblity and illuminating nature of Fullbrook and Simons's commentary.

SARTRE

Sartre is commonly considered the father of French existentialist philosophy. His writings on psychology, ethics, politics, ontology, and the philosophical dimensions of literature helped shape the nature and direction of philosophy and philosophical methodology after World War II. His lifelong companionship and intellectual engagement with Beauvoir is part of the story of who Sartre was.

Sartre was born in Paris to Jean-Baptiste Sartre, an officer of the French Navy, and Anne-Marie Schweitzer, a cousin of German Nobel prize laureate Albert Schweitzer. When Sartre was fifteen months old, his father died of a fever. His mother and maternal grandfather, a high school teacher, raised him. His grandfather taught Sartre mathematics and, when Sartre was quite young, introduced him to classical literature.

As a teenager, Sartre became attracted to philosophy when he read Henri Bergson's *Essay on the Immediate Data of Consciousness*. He studied in Paris at the elite École Normale Supérieure, where he was influenced by the philosophies of several key Western philosophers, particularly the work of Kant and Hegel. (Sartre did not study Heidegger until the 1930s.) In 1929, he met his lifelong companion, Simone de Beauvoir, who was studying at the Sorbonne. After Sartre graduated in 1929, he served as a conscript in the French Army from 1929 to 1931.

From 1933 to 1934 Sartre attended the French Institute in Berlin where he was introduced to phenomenology. He was particularly drawn to Husserl's notion of the intentionality of consciousness (understanding the objects of consciousness) and Heidegger's notion of humans as beings in the world (Heidegger's *Dasein*) that are neither Cartesian detached, disembodied thinking things whose existence is independent from other beings, nor Kantian phenomenal selves—things-as-they-appear—in the world of sense perception (in contrast to "really real" noumenal selves—things-in-themselves—in a posited nonsensory noumenal world). One appropriate question to ask, then, is what is Sartre's notion of the self? (The commentary addresses this question in some detail.)

In Sartre's most famous work, *Being and Nothingness*, subtitled a "Phenomenological Ontology," Sartre distinguishes two irreducible kinds of being: the in-itself (*en-soi*) and the for-itself (*pour-soi*). (Later in the book Sartre adds a third kind of being, the for-others or *pour-autrui*, not discussed here.) Being-in-itself and being-for-itself have mutually exclusive features, yet humans are a combination of both. The in-itself is passive; it simply is—what Sartre calls a "facticity." The for-itself is active, dynamic; it is what Sartre calls "transcendence." Humans exist "in situations" and the "givens" of our situation (e.g., our language, our environment, our previous choices) are our facticity. But as conscious individuals, we do or can transcend this facticity in (of) our situation. So, we are always beings in situation, a mixture of facticity and transcendence that makes our futures indeterminate.

This distinction between two kinds of beings is connected to Sartre's ethic of responsibility, a familiar theme of his existentialist philosophy. His ethic is based on two seemingly inconsistent claims: humans are at the same time both radically determined (by their facticity) and radically free (by their transcendence). Humans are born without a Cartesian or Platonic essence and without a set of values or ethical principles already in place. Instead, humans are born radically free—free to create their own values at every moment of their existence. The givenness (facticity) of the situation is that a human is born "radically determined" or destined to make ethical choices; we have no choice about that. So, our situation is one of total freedom and total determinism. For Sarte, an ethically responsible life is an "authentic life"—one where a human accepts both its passive facticity and its active transcendence. A self "falls into bad faith" (is not authentic) when it deceives itself into believing that it is either only a body-as-object—facticity without freedom—or a body-as subject—freedom without facticity—when one is really both.

There are two more biographical pieces of information about Sartre that may be of interest in light of his existentialism (discussed in the primary texts and commentary). The first is that, following the publication of an autobiography of his childhood, *The Words* (1964), Sartre was offered the Nobel Prize for Literature. Sartre "characteristically refused along with its substantial cash grant lest his acceptance be read as approval of the bourgeois values that the honor seemed to emblemize."[1] The second is that Sartre, who had lost the use of one eye in childhood, became almost totally blind at the end of his life. He continued writing with the help of a tape recorder. After his death, tens of thousands joined his funeral cortège in a memorable tribute to his respect and esteem among the public at large. As the headline of one Parisian newspaper lamented: "France has lost its conscience."[2]

BEAUVOIR

Simone de Beauvoir (Simone-Ernestine-Lucie-Marie Bertrand de Beauvoir) was born in Paris in 1908. Her father was a conservative man, a legal secretary by occupation, who married a devout, Catholic woman, Françoise Brasseur. Beauvoir was an intellectually curious, independent child. Her father encouraged her to read and provided her with selections from great literature. Beauvoir's earliest proclivities were to become a writer and teacher. Until she was seventeen Beauvoir was educated in a private Catholic school for girls. But at age fourteen she rejected religion and became an atheist for the duration of her life. Beauvoir's atheism was an on-going source of conflict with her mother.

As an undergraduate, Beauvoir decided to pursue and teach philosophy. She passed the *baccalauréat* exams in mathematics and philosophy in 1925. She then studied mathematics and languages at two different schools, passing exams in 1926 for Certificates of Higher Studies in French literature and Latin. She began her study of philosophy in 1927 at the Sorbonne. The same year Beauvoir passed exams for Certificates in History of Philosophy, General Philosophy, Greek, and Logic, and in 1928 she received Certificates in Ethics, Sociology, and Psychology. She wrote the equivalent of a doctoral dissertation (a graduate *diplôme*) on Leibniz, and in 1929 she earned second place in the highly competitive philosophy *agrégation* exam, barely losing to Jean-Paul Sartre who took first in his second attempt at the exam. At twenty-one years of age, Beauvoir was the youngest student ever—not the youngest woman student—to pass the *agrégation* in philosophy and youngest philosophy teacher in France.

In 1929, Beauvoir met Sartre and studied with him for the public oral examination component of the *agrégation*. For the rest of their lives, they were to remain lovers, friends, and philosophical companions until Sartre's death in 1980. Although Sartre proposed to her in 1931, they never married. They are buried side-by-side in the Montparnasse Cemetery in Paris.

In 1932, Beauvoir taught advanced literature and philosophy classes at the Lycée Jeanne d'Arc. Her criticisms of women's subordinate status and her public pacifism during the time the Nazis occupied Paris (1940) led to Beauvoir's dismissal from her teaching by the Nazi government. Another dismissal from a high school teaching position occurred in 1943, instigated by a disgruntled parent's complaint that Beauvoir was corrupting a female student. Beauvoir never taught again.

Beauvoir's novel, *She Came to Stay*, was written from 1935 to 1937 and was read by Sartre in manuscript form before he began writing *Being and Nothingness*; it was published in 1943. Initially, during the 1940s, *She Came to Stay* was treated publicly in France as a philosophical work by none less than Merleau-Ponty and, during the 1950s, by Hazel Barnes, the English translator of *Being and Nothingness*. But from the early 1960s through the 1980s, this reading of *She Came to Stay* was suppressed. Some refer still to *Pyrrhus et Cinéas* (1943) as Beauvoir's first philosophical work. Her second book on ethics, *The Ethics of Ambiguity* (1947), is generally viewed as one of the best elucidations of an existentialist ethics.

In 1949, Beauvoir published her two-volume work on woman's oppression, *Le Deuxième Sexe* (*The Second Sex*)—a book that investigates the nature and solutions to women's oppression. It soon became a feminist classic, broadening Beauvoir's reputation to include "leading feminist author of the twentieth century," even though Beauvoir had never called herself a feminist before publication of this book. It was a highly controversial book that was attacked by critics at both ends of the political spectrum, yet it did not deter Beauvoir from continuing her active involvement in demonstrations, public speeches, and writing on behalf of women's equality.

Prior to the 1940s, Beauvoir was unknown and Sartre nearly so. Beauvoir continued to travel—one of her passions—embarking on a lecture tour in the United States in 1947 and a trip with Sartre to Communist China in 1955. She also continued to write, publishing a four-volume autobiography, articles against the French war in Algeria, and a study of the oppression of older people (1970). When Sartre died in 1980, Beauvoir wrote about his passing in *Adieux: A Farewell to Sartre* (1981). The same year Beauvoir officially adopted her companion, Sylvie le Bon, as her literary executor. Beauvoir died of a pulmonary edema in 1986.

Beauvoir was publicly regarded as a philosopher in France and North America, as evidenced by the reception to her lecture tour in the 1940s. But during the second half of her life Beauvoir was unfairly and incorrectly criticized on two grounds: she was not a philosopher and any philosophical views she advanced were not original but "Sartrean." Unfortunately, Beauvoir contributed to these mistaken views by sometimes (others not) appearing to agree with them (despite her status as the youngest student ever to pass the *agrégation* in philosophy).

Scholars have begun to explore reasons why Beauvoir came to be falsely viewed as neither an original thinker nor a philosopher.[3] Certainly her use of the metaphysical novel as a method of doing philosophy, her rejection of traditional conceptions of philosophy as system building, and her gender were contributing factors. Are there additional reasons for so describing and assessing Beauvoir and her intellectual contributions?

FULLBROOK AND SIMONS'S COMMENTARY

In their commentary Edward Fullbrook and Margaret Simons argue that the most current scholarly discussions of the writings by Sartre and Beauvoir *do* offer compelling reasons to rethink both views, especially regarding the proper authorship of the notion of the self that Sartre articulates in *Being and Nothingness* (1943): They argue that this notion, which is viewed as a key Sartrean (not Beauvoirean) contribution to philosophy, is, in fact, authored by Beauvoir, not Sartre. The case they made undermines the view that Beauvoir was neither an original thinker nor philosopher.

In their discussion of Beauvoir's and Sartre's notion of the self, Fullbrook and Simons consider four ideas: embodiment, temporality, the Other, and intersubjectivity. They carefully distinguish the different meanings of each and explore the role that gender plays in understanding the differences between Sartre's and Beauvoir's positions. After situating their discussion of Sartre and Beauvoir in the context of their mutual rejection of a Cartesian view of the self, their commentary provides an illuminating description of their individual views. Based on the most current scholarly assessment of the contributions of Sartre and Beauvoir, they argue that Beauvoir was both a philosopher and the proper author of the so-called Sartrean notion of the self. It is left to the reader to decide not only the merits of the Fullbrook–Simons argument, but also how history should describe, interpret, and assess the writings of Beauvoir and Sartre.

Excerpts of Writings by Sartre and Beauvoir

I. EXCERPTS FROM JEAN-PAUL SARTRE'S *BEING AND NOTHINGNESS*[4]

Chapter 1: The Existence of Others

I. The Problem

We have described human reality from the standpoint of negating conduct and from the standpoint of the cogito. Following this lead we have discovered that human reality is for-itself. Is this all that it is? Without going outside our attitude of reflective description, we can encounter modes of consciousness which seem, even while themselves remaining strictly in for-itself, to point to a radically different type of ontological structure. This ontological structure is mine; it is in relation to myself as subject that I am concerned about myself, and yet this concern (for-myself) reveals to me a being which is my being without being-for-me.

Consider for example shame. Here we are dealing with a mode of consciousness which has a structure identical with all those which we have previously described. It is a non-positional self-consciousness, conscious (of) itself as shame; as such, it is an example of what the Germans call Erlebnis, and it is accessible to reflection. In addition its structure is intentional; it is a shameful apprehension of something and this something is me. I am ashamed of what I am. Shame therefore realizes an intimate relation of myself to myself. Through shame I have discovered an aspect of my being. Yet although certain complex forms derived from shame can appear on the reflective plane, shame is not originally a phenomenon of reflection. In fact no matter what results one can obtain in solitude by the religious practice of shame, it is in its primary structure shame before somebody. I have just made an awkward or vulgar gesture. This gesture clings to me; I neither judge it nor blame it. I simply live it. I realize it in the mode of for-itself. But now suddenly I raise my head. Somebody was there and has seen me. Suddenly I realize the vulgarity of my gesture, and I am ashamed. It is certain that my shame is not reflective, for the presence of another in my consciousness, even as a catalyst, is incompatible with the reflective attitude; in the field of my reflection I can never meet with anything but the consciousness which is mine. But the Other is the indispensable mediator between myself and me. I am ashamed of myself as I appear to the Other.

By the mere appearance of the Other, I am put in the position of passing judgment on myself as on an object, for it is as an object that I appear to the Other. Yet this object which has appeared to the Other is not an empty image in the mind of another. Such an image, in fact, would be imputable wholly to the Other and so could not "touch" me. I could feel irritation, or anger before it as before a bad portrait of myself which gives to my expression an ugliness or baseness which I do not have, but I could not be touched to the quick. Shame is by nature recognition. I recognize that I am as the Other sees me. There is however no question of a comparison between what I am for myself and what I am for the Other as if I found in myself, in the mode of being of the For-itself, an equivalent of what I am for the Other. In the first place this comparison is not encountered in us as the result of a concrete psychic operation. Shame is an immediate shudder which runs through me from head to foot without any discursive preparation. In addition the comparison is impossible; I am unable to bring about any relation between what I am in the intimacy of the For-Itself, without distance, without recoil, without perspective, and this unjustifiable being-in-itself which I am for the Other. There is no standard here, no table of correlation. Moreover the very notion of vulgarity implies an inter-monad relation. Nobody can be vulgar all alone!

Thus the Other has not only revealed to me what I was; he has established me in a new type of being which can support new qualifications. This being was not in me potentially before the appearance of the Other, for it could not have found any place in the For-itself. Even if some power had been pleased to endow me with a body wholly constituted before it should be for-others, still my vulgarity and my awkwardness could not lodge there potentially; for they are meanings and as such they surpass the body and at the same time refer to a witness capable of understanding them and to the totality of my human reality. But this new being which appears for the other does not reside in the Other; I am responsible for it as is shown very well by the education system which consists in making children ashamed of what they are.

Thus shame is shame of oneself before the Other; these two structures are inseparable. But at the same time I need the Other in order to realize fully all the structures of my being. The For-itself refers to the For-others. Therefore if we wish to grasp in its totality the relation of man's being to being-in-itself, we can not be satisfied with the descriptions outlined in the earlier chapters of this work. We must answer two far more formidable questions: first that of the existence of the Other, then that of the relation of my being to the being of the Other.

IV. The Look

This woman whom I see coming toward me, this man who is passing by in the street, this beggar whom I hear calling before my window, all are for me objects, of that there is no doubt. Thus it is true that at least one of the modalities of the Other's presence to me is object-ness. But we have seen that if this relation of object-ness is the fundamental relation between the Other and myself, then the Other's existence remains purely conjectural. Now it is not only conjectural but probable that this voice which I hear is that of a man and not a song on a phonograph; it is infinitely probable that the passerby whom I see is a man and not a perfected robot. This means that without going beyond the limits of probability and indeed because of this very probability, my apprehension of the other as an object essentially refers me to a fundamental apprehension of the other in which he will not be revealed to me as an object but as a "presence in person." In short, if the Other is to be a probable object and not a dream of an object, then his object-ness must of necessity refer not to an original solitude beyond my reach, but to a fundamental connection in which the Other is manifested in some way other than through the knowledge which I have of him. The classical theories are right in considering that every perceived human organism refers to something and that this to which it refers is the foundation and guarantee of its probability. Their mistake lies in believing that this reference indicates a separate existence, a consciousness which would be behind its perceptible manifestations as the noumenon is behind the Kantian Empfindung. Whether or not this consciousness exists in a separate state, the face which I see does not refer to it; it is not this consciousness which is the truth of the probable object which I perceive. In actual fact the reference to a twin upsurge in which the Other is presence for me is to a "being-in-a-pair-with-the-Other," and this is given outside of knowledge proper even if the latter be conceived as an obscure and unexpressible form on the order of intuition. In other words, the problem of Others has generally been treated as if the primary relation by which the Other is discovered is object-ness; that is, as if the Other were first revealed—directly or indirectly—to our perception. But since this perception by its very nature refers to something other than to itself and since it can refer neither to an infinite series of appearances of the same type—as in idealism the perception of the table or of the chair does—nor to an isolated entity located on principle outside my reach, its essence must be to refer to a primary relation between my consciousness and the Other's. This relation, in which the Other must be given to me directly as a subject although in connection with me, is the fundamental relation, the very type of my being-for-others.

Nevertheless the reference here cannot be to any mystic or ineffable experience. It is in the reality of everyday life that the Other appears to us, and his probability refers to everyday reality. The problem is precisely this: there is in everyday reality an original relation to the Other which can be constantly pointed to and which consequently can be revealed to me outside all reference to a religious or mystic unknowable. In order to understand it I must question more exactly this ordinary appearance of the Other in the field of my perception; since this appearance refers to that fundamental relation, the appearance must be capable of revealing to us, at least as a reality aimed at, the relation to which it refers.

I am in a public park. Not far away there is a lawn and along the edge of that lawn there are benches. A man passes by those benches. I see this man; I apprehend him as an object and at the same time as a man. What does this signify? What do I mean when I assert that this object is a man?

If I were to think of him as being only a puppet, I should apply to him the categories which I ordinarily use to group temporal-spatial "things." That is, I should apprehend him as being "beside" the benches, two yards and twenty inches from the lawn, as exercising a certain pressure on the ground, etc. His relation with other objects would be of the purely additive type; this means that I could have him disappear without the relations of the other objects around him being perceptibly changed. In short, no new relation would appear through him between those things in my universe: grouped and synthesized from my point of view into instrumental complexes, they would from him disintegrate into multiplicities of indifferent relations. Perceiving him as a man, on the other hand, is not to apprehend an additive relation between the chair and him; it is to register an organization without distance of the things in my universe around that privileged object. To be sure, the lawn remains two yards and twenty inches away from him, but it is also as a lawn bound to him in a relation which at once both transcends distance and contains it. Instead of the two terms of the distance being indifferent, interchangeable able, and in a reciprocal relation, the distance is unfolded starting from the man whom I see and extending up to the lawn as the synthetic up-surge of a univocal relation. We are dealing with a relation which is without parts, given at one stroke, inside of which there unfolds a spatiality; which is not my spatiality; for instead of a grouping toward me of the objects, there is now an orientation which flees from me.

Of course this relation without distance and without parts is in no way that original relation of the Other to me which I am seeking. In the first place, it concerns only the man and the things in the world. In addition it is still an object of knowledge; I shall express it, for example, by saying that this man sees the lawn, or that in spite of the prohibiting sign he is preparing to walk on the grass, etc. Finally it still retains a pure character of probability: First, it is probable that this object is a man. Second, even granted that he is a man, it remains only probable that he sees the lawn at the moment that I perceive him; it is possible that he is dreaming of some project without exactly being aware of what is around him, or that he is blind, etc. Nevertheless this new relation of the object-man to the object-lawn has a particular character; it is simultaneously given to me as a whole, since it is there in the world as an object which I know (it is, in fact, an objective relation which I express by saying: Pierre has glanced at this watch, Jean has looked out the window, etc.), and at the same time it entirely escapes me. To the extent that the man-as-object is the fundamental term of this relation, to the extent that the relation reaches toward him, it escapes me. I can not put myself at the center of it. The distance which unfolds between the lawn and the man across the synthetic upsurge of this primary relation is a negation of the distance which I establish—as a pure type of external negation between these two objects. The distance appears as a pure disintegration of the relations which I apprehend between the objects of my universe. It is not I who realize this disintegration; it appears to me as a relation which I aim at emptily across the distances which I originally established between things. It stands as a background of things, a background which on principle escapes me and which is conferred on them from without. Thus the appearance among the objects of my universe of an element of disintegration in that universe is what I mean by the appearance of a man in my universe.

The Other is first the permanent flight of things toward a goal which I apprehend as an object at a certain distance from me but which escapes me inasmuch as it unfolds about itself its own distances. Moreover this disintegration grows by degrees; if there exists between the lawn and the Other a relation which is without distance and which creates distance, then there exists necessarily a relation between the Other and the statue which stands on a pedestal in the middle of the lawn, and a relation between the Other and the big chestnut trees which border the walk; there is a total space which is grouped around the Other, and this space is made with my space; there is a regrouping in which I take part but which escapes me, a regrouping of all the objects which people my universe. This regrouping does not stop there. The grass is something qualified; it is this green grass which exists for the Other; in this sense the very quality of the object, its deep, raw green is in direct relation to this man. This green turns toward the Other a face which escapes me. I apprehend the relation of the green to the Other as an objective relation, but I can not apprehend the green as it appears to the Other. Thus suddenly an object has appeared which has stolen the world from me. Everything is in place; everything still exists for me;

but everything is traversed by an invisible flight and fixed in the direction of a new object. The appearance of the Other in the world corresponds therefore to a fixed sliding of the whole universe, to a decentralization of the world which undermines the centralization which I am simultaneously effecting.

But the Other is still an object for me. He belongs to my distances; the man is there, twenty paces from me, he is turning his back on me. As such he is again two yards, twenty inches from the lawn, six yards from the statue; hence the disintegration of my universe is contained within the limits of this same universe; we are not dealing here with a flight of the world toward nothingness or outside itself. Rather it appears that the world has a kind of drain hole in the middle of its being and that it is perpetually flowing off through this hole. The universe, the flow, and the drain hole are all once again recovered, reapprehended, and fixed as an object. All this is there for me as a partial structure of the world, even though the total disintegration of the universe is involved. Moreover these disintegrations may often be contained within more narrow limits. There for example, is a man who is reading while he walks. The disintegration of the universe which he represents is purely virtual; he has ears which do not hear, eyes which see nothing except his book. Between his book and him I apprehend an undeniable relation without distance of the same type as that which earlier connected the walker with the grass. But this time the form has closed in on itself. There is a full object for me to grasp. In the midst of the world I can say "man-reading" as I could say "cold stone," "fine rain." I apprehend a closed "Gestalt" in which the reading forms the essential quality; for the rest, it remains blind and mute, lets itself be known and perceived as a pure and simple temporal, spatial thing, and seems to be related to the rest of the world by a purely indifferent externality. The quality "man-reading" as the relation of the man to the book is simply a little particular crack in my universe. At the heart of this solid, visible form he makes himself a particular emptying. The form is massive only in appearance; its peculiar meaning is to be in the midst of my universe, at ten paces from me, at the heart of that massivity—a closely consolidated and localized flight.

None of this enables us to leave the level on which the Other is an object. At most we are dealing with a particular type of objectivity akin to that which Husserl designated by the term absence without, however, his noting that the Other is defined not as the absence of a consciousness in relation to the body which I see but by the absence of the world which I perceive, an absence discovered at the very heart of my perception of this world. On this level the Other is an object in the world, an object which can be defined by the world. But this relation of flight and of absence on the part of the world in relation to me is only probable. If it is this which defines the objectivity of the Other, then to what original presence of the Other does it refer? At present we can give this answer: if the Other-as-object is defined in connection with the world as the object which sees what I see, then my fundamental connection with the Other-as-subject must be able to be referred back to my permanent possibility of being seen by the Other. It is in and through the revelation of my being-as-object for the Other that I must be able to apprehend the presence of his being-as-subject. For just as the Other is a probable object for me-as-subject, so I can discover myself in the process of becoming a probable object for only a certain subject. This revelation can not derive from the fact that my universe is an object for the Other-as-object, as if the Others look after having wandered over the lawn and the surrounding objects came following a definite path to place itself on me. I have observed that I can not be an object for an object. A radical conversion of the other is necessary if he is to escape objectivity. Therefore I can not consider the look which the Other directs on me as one of the possible manifestations of his objective being; the Other can not look at me as he looks at the grass. Furthermore my objectivity can not itself derive for me from the objectivity of the world since I am precisely the one by whom there is a world; that is, the one who on principle can not be an object for himself.

Thus this relation which I call "being-seen-by-another," far from being merely one of the relations signified by the word man, represents an irreducible fact which can not be deduced either from the essence of the other-as-object, or from my being-as-subject. On the contrary, if the concept of the Other-as-object is to have any meaning, this can be only as the result of the conversion and the degradation of that original relation. In a word, my apprehension of the Other in the world as probably being a man refers to my permanent possibility of being-seen-by-him; that is, to the permanent possibility that a subject who sees me may be substituted for the object seen by me. "Being-seen-by-the-Other" is the truth of "seeing-the-Other." Thus the notion of the Other can not under any circumstances aim at a solitary, extra-mundane consciousness which I can not even think. The man is defined by his relation to the world and by his relation to myself. He is that object in the world which determines an internal flow of the universe, an internal hemorrhage. He is the subject who is revealed to me in that flight of myself toward objectivation. But the original relation of myself to the Other is not only an absent truth aimed at across the concrete presence of an object in my universe; it is also a concrete, daily relation which at each instant I experience. At each instant the Other is looking at me. It is easy therefore for us to attempt with concrete examples to describe this fundamental connection which must form the basis of any theory concerning the Other. If the Other is on principle the one who looks at me, then we must be able to explain the meaning of the Other's look.

Every look directed toward me is manifested in connection with the appearance of a sensible form in our perceptive field, but contrary to what might be expected, it is not connected with any determined form. Of course what most often manifests a look is the convergence of two ocular globes in my direction. But the look will be given just as well on occasion when there is a rustling of branches, or the sound of a footstep followed by silence, or the slight opening of a shutter, or a light movement of a curtain. During an attack men who are crawling through the brush apprehend as a look to be avoided, not two eyes, but a white farmhouse which is outlined against the sky at the top of a little hill. It is obvious that the object thus constituted still manifests the look as being probable. It is only probable that behind the bush which has just moved there is someone hiding who is watching me. But this probability need not detain us; for the moment; we shall return to this point later. What is important first is to define the look in itself. Now the bush, the farmhouse are not the look; they only represent the eye, for the eye is not at first apprehended as a sensible organ of vision but as the support for the look. They never refer therefore to the actual eye of the watcher hidden behind the curtain behind a window in the farmhouse. In themselves they are already eyes. On the other hand neither is the look one quality among others of the object which functions as an eye, nor is it the total form of that object nor a worldly relation which is established between that object and me. On the contrary, far from perceiving the look on the objects which manifest it, my apprehension of a look turned toward me appears on the ground of the destruction of the eyes which "look at me." If I apprehend the look, I cease to perceive the eyes; they are there, they remain in the field of my perception as pure presentations, but I do not make any use of them; they are neutralized, put out of play; they are no longer the object of a thesis but remain in that state of "disconnection" in which the world is put by a consciousness practicing the phenomenological reduction prescribed by Husserl. It is never when eyes are looking at you, that you can find them beautiful or ugly, that you can remark on their color. The Other's look hides his eyes; he seems to go in front of them. This illusion stems from the fact that eyes as objects of my perception remain at a precise distance which unfolds from me to them (in a word, I am present to the eyes without distance, but they are distant from the place where I "find myself") whereas the look is upon me without distance while at the same time it holds me at a distance—that is, its immediate presence to me unfolds a distance which removes me from it. I cannot therefore direct my attention on the look without at the same stroke causing my perception to decompose and pass into the background. There is produced here something analogous to what I attempted to show elsewhere in connection with the subject of the imagination. We can not, I said then, perceive and imagine simultaneously; it must be either one or the other. I should willingly say here: we can not perceive the world and at the same time apprehend a look fastened upon us; it must either be one or the other. This is because to perceive is to look at, and to apprehend a look is not to apprehend a look-as-object in the world (unless the look is not directed upon us); it is to be conscious of being looked at. The look which the eyes manifest, no matter what kind of eyes they are is a pure reference to myself. What I apprehend immediately when I hear the branches crackling behind me is not that there is someone there; it is that I am vulnerable, that I have a body which can be hurt, that I occupy a place and that I can not in any case escape from the space in which I am without defense—in short, that I am seen. Thus the look is first an intermediary which refers from me to myself. What is the nature of this intermediary? What does being seen mean for me?

Let us imagine that moved by jealousy, curiosity, or vice I have just glued my ear to the door and looked through a keyhole. I am alone and on the level of a non-thetic self-consciousness. This means first of all that there is no self to inhabit my consciousness, nothing therefore to which I can refer my acts in order to qualify them. They are in no way known; I am my acts and hence they carry in themselves their whole justification. I am a pure consciousness of things, and things, caught up in the circuit of my selfness, offer to me their potentialities as the proof of my non-thetic consciousness (of) my own possibilities. This means that behind that door a spectacle is presented as "to be seen," a conversation "to be heard." The door, the keyhole are at once both instruments and obstacles; they are presented as "to be handled with care"; the keyhole is given as "to be looked through close by and a little to one side," etc. Hence from this moment "I do what I have to do." No transcending view comes to confer upon my acts the character of a given on which a judgment can be brought to bear. My consciousness sticks to my acts, it is my acts; and my acts are commanded only by the ends to be attained and by the instruments to be employed. My attitude, for example, has no "outside"; it is a pure process of relating the instrument (the keyhole) to the end to be attained (the spectacle to be seen), a pure mode of losing myself in the world, of causing myself to be drunk in by things as ink is by a blotter in order that an instrumental-complex oriented toward an end may be synthetically detached on the ground of the world. The order is the reverse of causal order. It is the end to be attained which organizes all the moments which precede it. The end justifies the means; the means do not exist for themselves and outside the end.

Moreover the ensemble exists only in relation to a free project of my possibilities. Jealousy, as the possibility which I am, organizes this instrumental complex by transcending it toward itself. But I am this jealousy; I do not know it. If I contemplated it instead of making it, then only the worldly complex of instrumentality could teach it to me. This ensemble in the world with its double and inverted determination (there is a spectacle to be seen behind the door only because I am jealous, but my jealousy is nothing except the simple objective fact that there is a sight to be seen behind the door)—this we shall call situation. This situation reflects to me at once both my facticity and my freedom; on the occasion of a certain objective structure of the world which surrounds me, it refers my freedom to me in the form of tasks to be freely done. There is no constraint here since my freedom eats into my possibles and since correlatively the potentialities of the world indicate and offer only themselves. Moreover I can not truly define myself as being in a situation: first because I am not a positional consciousness of myself; second because I am my own nothingness. In this sense—and since I am what I am not and since I am not what I am—I can not even define myself as truly being in the process of listening at doors. I escape this provisional definition of myself by means of all my transcendence. There as we have seen is the origin of bad faith. Thus not only am I unable to know myself, but my very being escapes—although I am that very escape from my being—and I am absolutely nothing. There is nothing there but a pure nothingness encircling a certain objective ensemble and throwing it into relief outlined upon the world, but this ensemble is a real system, a disposition of means in view of an end.

But all of a sudden I hear footsteps in the hall. Someone is looking at me! What does this mean? It means that I am suddenly affected in my being and that essential modifications appear in my structure—modifications which I can apprehend and fix conceptually by means of the reflective cogito.

First of all, I now exist myself for my unreflective consciousness. It is this irruption of the self which has been most often described: I see myself because somebody sees me—as it is usually expressed. This way of putting it is not wholly exact. But let us look more carefully. So long as we considered the for-itself in its isolation, we were able to maintain that the unreflective consciousness can not be inhabited by a self; the self was given in the form of an object and only for the reflective consciousness. But here the self comes to haunt the unreflective consciousness. Now the unreflective consciousness is a consciousness of the world. Therefore for the unreflective consciousness the self exists on the level of objects in the world; this role which devolved only on the reflective consciousness—the making-present of the self—belongs now to the unreflective consciousness. Only the reflective consciousness has the self directly for an object. The unreflective consciousness does not apprehend the person directly or as its object; the person is presented to consciousness in so far as the person is an object for the Other. This means that all of a sudden I am conscious of myself as escaping myself, not in that I am the foundation of my own nothingness but in that I have my foundation outside myself. I am for myself only as I am a pure reference to the Other.

Nevertheless we must not conclude here that the object is the Other and that the Ego present to my consciousness is a secondary structure or a meaning of the Other-as-object; the Other is not an object here and can not be an object, as we have shown, unless by the same stroke my self ceases to be object-for-the-Other and vanishes. Thus I do not aim at the other as an object nor at my Ego as an object for myself; I do not even direct an empty intention toward that Ego as toward an object presently out of reach. In fact it is separated from me by a nothingness which I can not fill since I apprehend it as not being for me and since I apprehend it as not being for me and since on principle it exists for the Other. Therefore I do not aim at it as if it could someday be given me but on the contrary in so far as it on principle flees from me and will never belong to me. Nevertheless I am that Ego; I do not reject it as a strange image, but it is present to me as a self which [sic] I am without knowing it; for I discover it in shame and, in other instances, in pride. It is shame or pride which reveals to me the Other's look and myself at the end of that look. It is the shame or pride which makes me live, not know the situation of being looked at.

Now, shame, as we noted at the beginning of this chapter, is shame of self; it is the recognition of the fact that I am indeed that object which the other is looking at and judging. I can be ashamed only as my freedom escapes me in order to become a given object. Thus originally the bond between my unreflective consciousness and my Ego, which is being looked at, is a bond not of knowing but of being. Beyond any knowledge which I can have, I am this self which another knows. And this self which I am—this I am in a world which the Other has made alien to me, for the Other's look embraces my being and correlatively the walls, the door, the keyhole. All these instrumental-things, in the midst of which I am, now turn toward the Other a face which on principle escapes me. Thus I am my Ego for the Other in the midst of a world which flows toward the Other. Earlier we were able to call this internal hemorrhage the flow of my world toward the Other-as-object. This was because the flow of blood was trapped and localized by the very fact that I fixed as an object in my world that Other toward which this world was bleeding. Thus not a drop of blood was lost; all was recovered, surrounded, localized although in a being which I could not penetrate. Here on the contrary the flight is without limit; it is lost externally; the world flows out of the world and I flow outside myself. The Other's look makes me be beyond my being in this world and puts me in the midst of the world which is at once this world and beyond this world. What sort of relations can I enter into with this being which I am and which shame reveals to me?

II. EXCERPTS FROM SIMONE DE BEAUVOIR'S *THE SECOND SEX*[5]

The Introduction

If her functioning as a female is not enough to define woman, if we decline also to explain her through "the eternal feminine," and if nevertheless we admit, provisionally, that women do exist, then we must face the question: what is a woman?

To state the question is, to me, to suggest, at once, a preliminary answer. The fact that I ask it is in itself significant. A man would never get the notion of writing a book on the peculiar situation of the human male. But if I wish to define myself, I must first of all say: "I am a woman"; on this truth must be based all further discussion. A man never begins by presenting himself as an individual of a certain sex; it goes without saying that he is a man. The terms *masculine* and *feminine* are used symmetrically only as a matter of form, as on legal papers. In actuality the relation of the two sexes is not quite like that of two electrical poles, for man represents both the positive and the neutral, as is indicated by the common use of *man* to designate human beings in general, the singular meaning of the word "*vir*" being assimilated to the general meaning of the word "*homo*"; whereas woman represents only the negative, defined by limiting criteria, without reciprocity. In the midst of an abstract discussion it is vexing to hear a man say: "You think thus and so because you are a woman"; but I know that my only defense is to reply: "I think thus and so because it is true," thereby removing my subjectivity from the argument. It would be out of the question to reply: "And you think the contrary because you are a man," for it is understood that the fact of being a man is no singularity. A man is in the right in being a man; it is the woman who is in the wrong. It amounts to this: just as for the ancients there was an absolute vertical with reference to which the oblique was defined, so there is an absolute human type, the masculine. Woman has ovaries, a uterus; these singular conditions imprison her in her subjectivity. It is often said that she thinks with her glands. Man superbly ignores the fact that his anatomy also includes glands, such as the testicles, and that they secrete hormones. He thinks of his body as a direct and normal relation with the world which he believes he apprehends in its objectivity, whereas he considers the body of woman as a hindrance, a prison, weighed down by everything specific to it. "The female is a female by virtue of a certain *lack* of qualities," said Aristotle; "we should regard women's character as afflicted with a natural defectiveness." And St. Thomas for his part pronounced woman to be an "imperfect man," an "incidental" being. This is symbolized in Genesis where Eve is depicted as made from what Bossuet called "a supernumerary bone" of Adam.

Thus humanity is male and man defines woman not in herself but relative to him; she is not regarded as an autonomous being. Michelet writes: "Woman, the relative being. . . ." And Benda is most positive in his *Rapport d'Uriel*: "The body of man makes sense in itself quite apart from that of woman, whereas the latter seems wanting in significance by itself. . . . Man can think of himself without woman. She cannot think of herself without man." And she is simply what man decrees; thus she is called "the sex," by which is meant that she appears essentially to the male as a sexual being. For him she is sex, thus she is sex absolutely. She is defined and differentiated in relation to man and not he in relation to her; she is the inessential confronting the essential. He is the Subject, he is the Absolute—she is the Other.

The category of the *Other* is as primordial as consciousness itself. In the most primitive societies, in the most ancient mythologies, one finds the expression of a duality—that of the Same and the Other. This duality was not originally attached to the division of the sexes; it was not dependent upon any empirical facts. It is revealed in such works as that of Granet on Chinese thought and those of Dumézil on the East Indies and Rome. The feminine element was at first no more involved in such pairs as Varuna-Mitra, Uranus-Zeus, Sun-Moon, and Day-Night than it was in the contrasts between Good and Evil, lucky and unlucky auspices, right and left, God and Lucifer. Alterity is a fundamental category of human thought.

Thus it is that no collectivity ever defines itself as the One without immediately positing the Other opposite itself. If three travelers chance to occupy the same compartment, that is enough to make vaguely hostile "others" out of all the rest of the passengers on the train. In small-town eyes all persons not belonging to the village are "others" and suspect; to the native of a country all who inhabit other countries are "foreigners"; Jews are "others" for the anti-Semite, Blacks for the American racists, indigenous peoples for the colonists, the proletariat for the propertied classes.

Lévi-Strauss, at the end of a profound work on the various forms of primitive societies, reaches the following conclusion: "Passage from the state of Nature to the state of Culture is marked by man's ability to view biological relations as systems of oppositions; duality, alternation, opposition, and symmetry, whether under definite or vague forms, constitute not so much phenomena to be explained as fundamental and immediately given data of social reality." These phenomena would be incomprehensible if human reality were simply a *mitsein* based on solidarity and friendship. Things become clear, on the contrary, if, following Hegel, we find in consciousness itself a fundamental hostility toward every other consciousness; the subject poses himself only in opposing—he asserts himself as the essential and constitutes the other as inessential, as object.

But the other consciousness opposes to him a reciprocal claim. The native traveling abroad is shocked to find himself in turn regarded as a stranger by the natives of neighboring countries. As a matter of fact, wars, potlatchs, trading, treaties, and contests tend to deprive the concept *Other* of its absolute sense and reveal its relativity; whether they like it or not, individuals and groups are required to recognize the reciprocity of their relations. How is it, then, that this reciprocity has not been posited between the sexes, that one of the terms could assert itself as the sole essential, denying any relativity in regard to its correlative and defining the latter as pure alterity? Why is it that women do not contest male sovereignty? No subject will readily and spontaneously posit himself as the inessential; it is not the Other who, in defining himself as the Other defines the One. He is posited as the Other by the One in positing himself as the One. But if the reversion of the Other to the One is not to proceed, he must submit to this alien point of view. Whence comes this submission in the case of woman?

There are other cases in which a certain category has succeeded in absolutely dominating an Other for a time. Very often this privilege is conferred by a numerical inequality—the majority imposes its rule on the minority or persecutes it. But women are not a minority, like the American Blacks or the Jews; there are as many women as men on earth. Again, the two groups concerned have often been originally independent; they may have been formerly unaware of each other's existence, or perhaps they recognized each other's autonomy. An historical event has resulted in the subjugation of the weaker by the stronger. The Jewish diaspora, the introduction of slavery into America, the colonial conquests are dated facts. In these cases, there was a *before* for the oppressed; they possessed in common a past, a tradition, sometimes a religion, a culture.

In this sense, the parallel drawn by Bebel between women and the proletariat would be the best founded in that neither ever formed a numerical minority or a separate collectivity. And instead of a single historical event, it is in both cases a historical development that explains their existence as a class and accounts for the membership of these individuals in that class. But proletarians have not always existed, whereas there have always been women. They are women in virtue of their physiological structure. Throughout history, they have always been subordinated to men, and their dependency is not the result of an event or an evolution—it was not something that *occurred*. The reason why alterity in this case seems to be an absolute is in part that it evades the accidental character of historical facts. A situation created at one time can be defeated at another time, as the Blacks of Haiti among others have proved; but it might seem that a natural condition defies change. In truth, however, nature is no more an immutable given than historical reality. If woman discovers herself as the inessential that never reverts to the essential, it is that she herself has not brought about this reversal. Proletarians say "we"; Blacks also. Positing themselves as subjects they thus change the bourgeois or the Whites into "others." But women do not say "we," except at some meetings which remain abstract demonstrations; men say "women," and women use the same word in referring to themselves. They do not posit themselves authentically as Subject. The proletarians have accomplished the revolution in Russia, the Blacks in Haiti, the Indochinese are battling for it in Indo-China; but the women's action has never been anything more than a symbolic agitation. They have gained only what men have been willing to grant; they have taken nothing, they have only received.

It is that women do not have the concrete means to organize themselves into a unity which could posit itself in opposing. They have no past, no history, no religion of their own; and they have no such solidarity of work and interest as that of the proletariat. There is not even this special promiscuity that makes a community of the American Blacks, the ghetto Jews, or the workers of Saint-Denis and the Renault factories. They live dispersed among the men, tied by housing, work, economic interests, and social condition to certain men—fathers or husbands—more firmly than to other women. Bourgeois women feel solidarity with the bourgeois and not with proletarian women; white women with white men and not black women. The proletariat can propose to massacre the ruling class; a fanatical Jew or Black might dream of getting sole possession of the atomic bomb and making humanity wholly Jewish or black; but woman cannot even dream of exterminating the males. The bond that unites her to her oppressors is not comparable to any other. The division of the sexes is a biological given, not a moment of human history. Their opposition has taken shape in the heart of an original *mitsein* and woman has not broken it. The couple is a fundamental unity with its two halves riveted together, and the cleavage of society along the line of sex is impossible. Here is to be found the fundamental characteristic of woman: she is the Other in the heart of a totality of which the two terms are necessary to one another.

From a chapter in The Second Sex *on "Myths"*

We have seen that there were not at first free women whom the males had enslaved nor were there ever castes based on the division of the sexes. To assimilate woman to the slave is an error; there were women among the slaves, but there always existed free women, that is, women endowed with a religious and social dignity. They accepted man's sovereignty and he did not feel menaced by a revolt that could transform him in turn into the object. Woman thus appears as the inessential who never returns to the essential, as the absolute Other, without reciprocity. This conviction is dear to the male, and every creation myth has expressed it, among others the legend of Genesis, which, through Christianity, has been kept alive in Western civilization. Eve was not fashioned at the same time as the man; she was not fabricated from a different substance, nor of the same clay as was used to model Adam: she was taken from the flank of the first male. Not even her birth was independent; God did not spontaneously choose to create her as an end in herself and in order to be worshipped directly by her in return for it. She was destined by Him for man; it was to rescue Adam from loneliness that He gave her to him, in her mate was her origin and her purpose; she was his complement in the mode of the inessential. Thus she appeared as a privileged prey. She is nature elevated to the translucence of consciousness, she is a naturally submissive consciousness. And therein lies the wondrous hope that man has often put in woman: he hopes to accomplish himself as being in carnally possessing a being, but at the same time being confirmed in his freedom by a docile freedom. No man would consent to be a woman, but every man wants women to exist. "Thank God for having created woman." "Nature is good since she has given women to men." In such phrases man once more asserts with naïve arrogance that his presence in this world is an ineluctable fact and a right, that of woman a mere accident—but a very happy accident. Appearing as the Other, woman appears at the same time as a plenitude of being in contrast to that the existence the nothingness of which man senses in himself; the Other, being posited as object in the eyes of the subject, is posited as in itself, thus as being. In woman is incarnated in positive form the lack that the existent carries in his heart, and it is in seeking to rejoin himself through her that man hopes to realize himself.

Perhaps the myth of woman will some day be extinguished; the more women assert themselves as human beings, the more the marvelous quality of the Other will die out in them. But today it still exists in the heart of every man.

A myth always implies a subject who projects his hopes and his fears toward a transcendent sky. Women do not posit themselves as Subject and hence have created no virile myth in which their projects are reflected; they have no religion or poetry of their own; they still dream through the dreams of men. Gods made by males are the gods they worship. Men have shaped for their own exaltation great virile figures: Hercules, Prometheus, Parsifal; woman has only a secondary part to play in the destiny of these heroes. No doubt there are conventional figures of man caught in his relations to woman: the father, the seducer, the husband, the jealous lover, the good son, the wayward son; but they have all been established by men, and they lack the dignity of myth, being hardly more than clichés. Whereas a woman is defined exclusively in her relation to man. The asymmetry of the categories—male and female—manifests itself in the unilateral form of sexual myths. We sometimes say "the sex" to designate woman; she is the flesh, its delights and dangers. The truth, that for woman, man is sex and carnality has never been proclaimed because there is no one to proclaim it. The representation of the world, like the world itself, is the operation of men; they describe it from their own point of view, which they confuse with absolute truth.

III: EXCERPTS FROM SIMONE DE BEAUVOIR'S *SHE CAME TO STAY*[6]

Part 1, Chapter 7

Slowly, Paula's arm came to life, the slumbering machine was beginning to operate. Little by little the rhythm accelerated, but Françoise saw neither the driving rod, nor the rotating wheels, nor any of the motions of steel. She saw only Paula. A woman of her own age, a woman who also had her past, her work, and a life of her own; a woman who was dancing without giving Françoise a thought; and when, a little later, she would smile at her, it would only be to one among many other spectators. To her, Françoise was no more than a piece of scenery.

If only it were possible to calmly prefer oneself to all others, thought Françoise with anguish. At that moment, there were thousands of women all over the world listening breathlessly to the beating of their own hearts; each woman to her own heart, each woman for herself. How could she believe that she was the center of the world? There were Paula, and Xavière, and so many others. She could not even compare herself with them.

Françoise slowly ran her hand down the length of her skirt.

Just what am I? she wondered. She looked at Paula. She looked at Xavière whose face radiated shameless admiration. She knew what these women were. They had their own special memories, tastes, and ideas which distinguished them, and well-defined personalities that were expressed in their features. But in herself Françoise could not see any clear-cut shape. The light that had flashed through her a short while before had revealed nothing but emptiness. "She never looks at herself," Xavière had said. It was true. She never gave her face a thought except to take care of it as a foreign object. She searched her past for landscapes and people, but not for herself; and it was not her ideas and her tastes that made her face what it was. That face only reflected the truths that had revealed themselves to her, and they no more belonged to her than the bunches of mistletoe and holly that hung from the flies.

I am no one, she thought. Often she had taken pride in not being enclosed like other people in narrow individual boundaries, as on that night, not so very long ago, at the Prairie, with Elisabeth and Xavière. She thought of herself as a consciousness naked before the world. She touched her face: to her it was no more than a white mask. And yet all these people saw it; and, whether she liked it or not, she too was in the world, a part of this world. She was a woman among other women, and she had permitted this woman to grow at random without shaping her. She was utterly incapable of passing any judgment on this unknown woman. And yet Xavière had judged her, had compared her with Paula. Which of them did she prefer? And Pierre? When he looked at her what did he see? She turned her eyes toward Pierre, but Pierre was not looking at her.

Part 2, Chapter 2

Françoise felt as if her heart were drowning in misery. Did Xavière always hate her? She had been amiable throughout the afternoon, but only in a superficial way, because the weather was heavenly and the flea-market enchanted her; it meant absolutely nothing. *And what can I do if she does hate me?* thought Françoise. She lifted her glass to her lips and noticed that her hands were trembling; she had drunk too much coffee during the day, and impatience was making her jittery. She could do nothing, she had no real hold on this stubborn little soul, not even on the beautiful body of flesh and blood protecting it; a warm, lithe body, accessible to masculine hands, but which confronted Françoise like a rigid suit of armor. She could only wait quietly for the verdict that would acquit or condemn her; and she had now been waiting for ten hours.

It's sordid! she thought suddenly.

She had spent the day watching Xavière's every frown, listening to every intonation; at this moment, she was still exclusively absorbed in this despicable anguish, separated from Pierre, and from these pleasant surroundings reflected by the mirror, separated from herself.

And if she hates me, what then? she thought defiantly. Was it possible to consider Xavière's hatred face to face, exactly as she did those cheese cakes lying on a plate? They were a beautiful pale yellow, decorated with pink arabesques; she might have almost been tempted to eat one, had she not known their sourish, new-born-baby taste. Xavière's small, round head did not occupy much more space in the world, one glance encompassed it; and if those fumes of hatred issuing from it could only be forced back into their container, then one could have them at one's mercy as well. One word, and the hatred would thunderously collapse, dissolving into a cloud of smoke that would exactly fill Xavière's body, becoming as harmless as the familiar taste hidden under the yellow cream of the cakes; Xavière felt that she existed, but that hardly mattered. She was writhing in contortions of rage all in vain; one could just barely make out a few faint eddies, passing over her defenseless face, as unexpected and orderly as clouds in the sky.

They're simply thoughts in her head, Françoise thought.

For a moment she thought the words had taken effect, for only the faintest vignettes were now flitting in disorder beneath that blond head; if she took her eyes off them, even for an instant, they were no longer to be seen.

Part 2, Chapter 4

Xavière was no longer watching the woman; she was staring into space. She was holding a lighted cigarette which had burned down to the point where the lighted end was almost touching her fingers, without her apparently being aware of it; she seemed to be in the grip of an hysterical ecstasy. Françoise passed her hand across her forehead, she was dripping with perspiration. The atmosphere was stifling, and her thoughts burned like fire. This hostile presence, which had betrayed itself earlier in a mad smile, was approaching closer and closer; there was now no way of escaping this terrifying disclosure. Day after day, minute after minute, Françoise had fled the danger; but the worst had happened, and she had at last come face to face with this insurmountable obstacle, which she had sensed, under vague forms since her earliest childhood. Behind Xavière's maniacal pleasure, behind her hatred and jealousy, the abomination loomed, as monstrous and definite as death. Before Françoise's very eyes, yet apart from her, existed something like a hopeless condemnation: free, absolute, irreducible, a foreign consciousness was rising. It was like death, a total negation, an eternal absence, and yet, by a staggering contradiction, this abyss of nothingness could make itself present to itself and make itself exist for itself with plenitude. The entire universe was engulfed in it, and Françoise, forever excluded from the world, was herself dissolved in this void, the infinity of which no word, no image could encompass.

"Look out!" said Pierre.

He bent over Xavière, and lifted the red-hot stub from her fingers. She stared at him as if having been awakened from a nightmare, then looked at Françoise, and abruptly took each of them by the hand. The palms of her hands were burning. Françoise shuddered when she came in contact with these feverish fingers which tightened on hers; she wanted to withdraw her hand, turn her head away, talk to Pierre, but she was now unable to move. Riveted to Xavière, she contemplated in amazement this body which allowed itself to be touched, and this beautiful face behind which an abominable presence was concealed. For a long time Xavière had been only a fragment of Françoise's life, and suddenly she had become the only sovereign reality, and Françoise had no more consistency than a pale reflection.

Why should it be she rather than I? thought Françoise, with anger. She need only have said one word, she need only say, "It is I." But she would have had to believe it; she would have had to choose herself. For many weeks Françoise had no longer been able to dissolve Xavière's hatred, affection, or thoughts into harmless vapors. She had let them bite into her; she had turned herself into a prey. Freely, through her moments of resistance and revolt, she had been busy destroying herself. She was witnessing the course of her own life like an indifferent spectator, without ever daring to affirm herself, whereas Xavière, from head to foot, was nothing but a living affirmation of herself. She made herself exist with so sure a force that Françoise, spellbound, had let herself be charmed into preferring Xavière to herself, thus obliterating herself. She had begun to see everything through Xavière's eyes—places, people, and Pierre's smiles. She had reached the point of no longer knowing herself, except through Xavière's feelings for her, and now she was trying to merge with Xavière. But in this hopeless effort she was only succeeding in annihilating herself.

The guitars kept up their monotonous thrumming and the air felt like a fiery sirocco. Xavière's hands had not let go their prey; her set face was expressionless. Pierre had not moved either. It was as if the same spell had transformed all three of them into marble. Pictures kept flashing through Françoise's mind—an old jacket, a deserted glade, a corner of the Pôle Nord where Pierre and Xavière were carrying on a mysterious tête-à-tête far removed from her. She had felt before, as she did this night, her own being dissolving itself in favor of other inaccessible beings; but she never had realized with such perfect lucidity her own annihilation. If only there were nothing left in her; but there still remained, among an infinity of deceptive will-o'-the-wisps, a faint phosphorescence hovering over the surface of things. The tension that had held her in its grip all evening suddenly snapped and she burst into silent sobs.

"You'll laugh at me," [Françoise] said, with a weak smile. There was a glimmer of hope; perhaps if she managed to enclose her anguish in words she might be rid of it. "It's because I discovered that she has a consciousness like mine. Has it already happened to you to feel the consciousness of the other as though from inside?" Again she was trembling. The words were not releasing her. "It's intolerable, you know."

Pierre was looking at her a little incredulously.

"You think I'm drunk," she said. "In a way I am, that's true, but it makes no difference. Why are you so astounded?" She rose suddenly. "If I were to tell you that I'm afraid of death, you would understand. Well, this thing is just as real and just as terrifying. Of course, we all know we're not alone in the world; we say these things, just as we say that we'll die some day. But when we begin to believe it."

Part 2, Chapter 5

"You're amazing. You're the only living being I know who's capable of shedding tears on discovering in someone else a consciousness similar to your own."

"Do you consider that stupid?"

"Of course not," said Pierre. "It's quite true that everyone experiences his own consciousness as an absolute. How can several absolutes be compatible? The problem is as great a mystery as birth or death, in fact, it's such a problem that philosophers break their heads over it."

"Well, then, why are you amazed?"

"What surprises me, is that you should be affected in such a concrete manner by a metaphysical situation."

"But it is something concrete," Françoise said. "The whole meaning of my life is at stake."

"I don't say it isn't," said Pierre. He surveyed her with curiosity. "Nevertheless, this power you have to live an idea, body and soul, is exceptional."

"But to me, an idea is not theoretical. It can be experienced or, if it remains theoretical, it doesn't count." She smiled. "Otherwise, I wouldn't have waited for Xavière's arrival to suddenly realize that my consciousness is not unique in the world."

Pierre ran his finger thoughtfully over his lower lip. "I can readily understand your making this discovery apropos of Xavière," he said.

"Yes," said Françoise. "With you I've never been troubled, because I barely distinguish you from myself."

"And besides, between us there is reciprocity," said Pierre.

"How do you mean?"

"The moment you recognize a consciousness in me, you know that I recognize one in you as well. That changes everything."

"Perhaps," said Françoise. She stared in momentary perplexity at the bottom of her glass. "In short, that is friendship. Each renounces his pre-eminence. But what if either one refuses to renounce it?"

"In that case, friendship is impossible," said Pierre.

"Well, then, what can be done about it?"

"I don't know," said Pierre.

Xavière never renounced herself. No matter how high she placed you, even when she cherished you, one remained an object for her.

Commentary by *Edward Fullbrook and Margaret A. Simons*, Beauvoir and Sartre: The Problem of the Other

INTRODUCTION

Simone de Beauvoir and Jean-Paul Sartre struggled for the whole of their philosophical careers against one of modern Western philosophy's most pervasive concepts, the Cartesian notion of self. A notion of self is always a complex of ideas; in the case of Beauvoir and Sartre it includes the ideas of embodiment, temporality, the Other, and intersubjectivity. This essay will show the considerable part that gender, especially Beauvoir's position as a woman in twentieth-century France, played in the development, presentation and reception of the couple's alternative formulation. We begin by looking briefly at the history of the tradition against which Beauvoir and Sartre rebelled. (See also chapter 5.)

CARTESIAN HERITAGE

René Descartes began his famous metaphysical deliberations (*Discourse on Method*, 1637; *Meditations*, 1641)[7] at a historical crossroads. It was a time when secularized conceptions of the self were undermining religious ones, thereby destroying the certainty about one's self and place in the world that had been a common birthright in the West for centuries. Caught up in this historical flux, Descartes suffered what today we would call existential despair. Even his own existence fell for him within "the sphere of the doubtful." He resolved to regain his lost certainty of self. For this he invented a philosophical method—a "method of systematic doubt":

> I thought it necessary . . . to reject as if utterly false anything in which I could discover the least grounds for doubt, so that I could find out if I was left with anything at all which was absolutely indubitable.[8]

What became so significant for the history of philosophy and eventually for the philosophical ambitions of Beauvoir and Sartre was that Descartes counted as doubtable anything revealed by our senses, memory, logical reasoning and, astonishingly, the existence of his own body. Descartes wrote, "I shall consider myself as having no hands, no eyes, no flesh, no blood, nor any senses, yet falsely believing myself to possess all these things."[9] Only his existence as an incorporeal thinking being survived his program of radical doubt. As he says in *Discourse on Method*, "I am thinking, therefore I exist."

Descartes's conception of himself as a disembodied being initiated the idea of a thinker-observer who is completely detached from the external world, existing independently of time, place, and other human beings. "I am a substance," he wrote in *Discourse on Method* (Part IV), the whole nature or essence of which is to think, and which for its existence does not need any place or depend on any material thing." This phantom of perfect nongendered, nonembodied self-consciousness and independence from the world was reified by succeeding generations and became the intellectual ideal of philosophical thought in Western society. Even British empiricism, contrary sometimes to popular belief, founded itself on Descartes's notion of a completely autonomous self, separate from place, time, materiality, and society, and therefore self-identical over time.[10]

Through the past five centuries, then, the inward-looking line of thought begun by Descartes became a worldly and pervasive force not only in philosophy but in society as well. The Cartesian view of human reality, both in Europe and in the English-speaking world, shaped the way we think, especially the way we theorize, about all aspects of social and personal existence. Descartes's disembodiment of human thought created a conceptually unbridgeable gap between the observer and the observed, the knower and the known, the subject and the object, thereby ascribing to each individual two separate planes of existence, an inside and an outside: one where we are the observer, the knower, the thinker, the perceiver, and the subject, the other where we are the observed, the known and the object of thought and perception. Under these Cartesian dualisms, especially the mind-body dualism, the body came to be thought of as a mere capsule, with windows called sense organs, in which human consciousness lived, cut off from the immediacy of the world around it and forever secure from the possibility of intersubjectivity. This led to the tradition of conceptualizing the "nature" of human beings abstractly, as outside and beyond society, thereby erasing their complex and ongoing development as historically located, embodied, gendered social beings.

The commitment to intrasubjective philosophy initiated by Descartes was renewed with the advent of the analytical movement in philosophy, sometimes called "logical positivism," at the beginning of the twentieth century. In *The Problems of Philosophy*, effectively the movement's manifesto, Bertrand Russell cajoles and enjoins fellow philosophers to embrace Cartesian fundamentals. He calls for recruits who

> will see as God might see, without a here and now, without hopes and fears, without the trammels of customary beliefs and traditional prejudices . . . [and who] will value more the abstract and universal knowledge into which the accidents of private history do not enter, than the knowledge brought by the senses, and dependent, as such knowledge must be, upon an exclusive and personal point of view and a body whose sense-organs distort as much as they reveal.[11]

Russell's notion of the ideal philosopher, which was and remains so extraordinarily influential, helps us to understand and appreciate Simone de Beauvoir because, in effect, she defined herself (and selves generally) as its antithesis.[12] She rejected the Cartesian disembodied, ahistorical, and intrasubjective self (as well as the Kantian noumenal self), both as her ultimate unit of analysis and as the supposed basis of her performance as a philosopher. From her recently discovered early diaries we know that in her student days, from 1926 to 1929, Beauvoir had already settled upon her radical approach to philosophy.

BEAUVOIR, *DIARY OF A PHILOSOPHY STUDENT 1926–1927*

The philosophical precocity displayed in Beauvoir's recently released student diaries, especially her commitment to the philosopher's life and her dogged determination to think through philosophy's big questions for herself, is impressive. Reading her diaries exhilarates, first because they draw us into this young woman's extreme, almost preternatural, passion for life and, second, because we see already emerging some of the originality of not only Beauvoir's mature philosophical thought but also Sartre's. She dedicates herself to developing "my philosophical ideas" and going "deeper into the problems that have appealed to me."[13]

We also see her developing her method, the intermingling of the personal with the philosophical, done with a logical hardheadedness that even the young Descartes or the mature Hume might have envied. And just as Descartes's method of eliminating from philosophical consideration all aspects of himself that were epistemologically (rather than psychologically) certain and fixed had the consequence of defining a permissible field of inquiry, so also are Beauvoir's philosophical method and concerns inextricably intertwined.

In her *Diaries*, Beauvoir, like Descartes in his *Meditations*, is concerned with the nature of her self. But she moves in the opposite direction from Descartes, seeking to bring back into philosophical illumination all those aspects of the human self blanked out by his radical reduction of selves to mental beings, disembodied thinking substances. This means examining the human self as an entity that exists not in seclusion but in-the-world. The Western philosophical tradition as commonly conveyed did not support such a project. However, that did not stop Beauvoir in 1927, still a teenager, from committing herself to this pursuit. Attracted to works by Henri Bergson and Gottfried Leibniz (an unlikely duo), she culled ideas from them which, when combined with her own, formed the first foundation of what became the basis of her mature thought. We should, therefore, look closely at the diaries of this girl-woman because, regardless of what prejudice may say, they document a series of mental events important in shaping twentieth-century continental philosophy.

Already in her 1926 diary, Beauvoir, age eighteen, began to identify and formulate "the problem of the Other," which in various forms became the preeminent philosophical concern and focus of both her and Sartre's philosophical careers. It is particularly interesting to observe the role of gender in the epistemological nature of Beauvoir's philosophical interest in and formulation of the problem in her diaries. They are characterized by three primary dimensions. First, they are fine examples of a late teenage girl's diaries, one of the oldest and commonest of all literary genres. Beauvoir's diaries reveal heartthrob, self-doubt, and general mental tumult. Second, her diaries are examples of a serious philosophy student's journal, not a common genre but one with pedigree. It calls for the student to write down his or her bright ideas, usually gleamed from lectures. Third, Beauvoir's diary writing does the most improbable thing: it links the first two and not, as one might expect, by applying philosophical ideas to an analysis of personal experiences. The link works in the opposite direction. This is Beauvoir's innovation as a diarist and accounts in the main for her student diaries's philosophical originality. She describes her experiences at coping, or not, with life's contingencies and then, sometimes over a period of weeks or months, distills from them general philosophical questions and insights. For example, consider how Beauvoir came to her formulation of the problem of the self and the other. Early in her 1926 diary she considers how one must serve both one's self and others, the one posing the temptation of egoism, the other the temptation of self-abnegation. She writes: "[It's] very difficult, because turning in on oneself readily turns into egoism; while on the other hand, when one goes out of oneself, it's indeed rare that one does not go too far and that one is not diminished. What I'm proposing is to achieve this equilibrium."[14] This reflective musing, based on her own in-the-world experience, shows a certain wisdom without rising above the level of advice dispensed by a good professional counselor. Later in the same year's diary, however, she translates her empirical observation into a bold and anti-Cartesian philosophical proposition. She makes an ontological distinction between "two parts in my existence: one for others [*pour autrui*]," "the links that unite me with all beings," and another "part for myself [*pour moi-même*]."[15]

One cannot help but notice the similarity between Beauvoir's and Descartes's predicaments that led them to radical philosophical reflection. They both faced an existential crisis. Hers arose from her loss of her childhood faith in God and from the development of her critical consciousness:

> What has this year brought me intellectually? A serious philosophical forma-
> tion that has . . . sharpened my critical spirit, alas! . . . I have everywhere noted
> only our powerlessness to establish anything in the realm of knowledge as in
> that of ethics.[16]

The frustrated yearning for an absolute justification for her life threatens her, as it did Descartes, with despair. But her response is the opposite of his: she chooses the phenomenal world in preference to the noumenal one. Moreover, she fails to find "being" anchored to a self in her consciousness. "These miserable efforts for being!" she writes in her diary entry for May 19, 1927, "at its very base, masked by these daily diversions, the same void!"[17] Against the Cartesian tradition, she takes her self to be an entity that will be constructed in the course of life and thus an object of consciousness rather than its subject that resides ready made in it:

> I know myself that there is only one problem and that it does not have
> a solution, because perhaps it has no sense. . . . I would like to believe in
> something—to encounter total exigency—to justify life; in brief, I would like
> God. Once this is said, I will not forget it. But knowing that this unattainable
> noumenal world exists where alone could be explained to me why I live, in the
> phenomenal world (which is not for all that so negligible), I will construct my
> life. I will take myself as an end.[18]

Philosophically, this was a doubly radical position to take since Beauvoir was rejecting not only the Cartesian self, but also Henri Bergson's proposed alternative, which was to identify with one's memories, that is with one's past. Thinking of Bergson in 1927, Beauvoir wrote: "My past is behind me like a thing gone from me; on which I can no longer act and which regard with the eyes of a stranger, a thing in which I have no part at all."[19] Her view is that one's self, that is one's being, is continually in the making, haunted by a nothingness.

Beauvoir's view of the self became fundamental both to Beauvoir's and, more famously, to Sartre's mature thought in *Being and Nothingness* (1943).[20] Quite important, the idea is invariably attributed to Sartre, but the fact is that, in her diary in 1927, Beauvoir introduced and discussed the notion of "the nothingness of everything human."[21]

Beauvoir's phenomenological turn not only set her apart from the modern mainstream, analytic, positivist, philosophical tradition, but also presented her with new methodological imperatives and possibilities for doing philosophy. By committing herself to the pursuit of philosophical truth in the phenomenal world she had to find a way to get beyond the philosopher's traditional *a priorism*. She was already doing this through her diaries. But a vague suggestion from Henri Bergson pointed her toward another way of doing philosophy, one through which gender difference would in time have a profound impact on her and Sartre's philosophical careers. In *Time and Free Will* Bergson gestures at the possibility of "some bold novelist"[22] who reveals the phenomenological realities of selfhood masked by philosophical terminology. The teenage

Beauvoir grabbed hold of and began to flesh out this idea, declaring her intention to write philosophy in fictional form:

> I must . . . write "essays on life" which would not be a novel, but philosophy, linking them together vaguely with a fiction but the thought would be the essential thing, and I would be searching to find the truth, not to express it, to describe the search for truth.[23]

And she knew which philosophical problems she would undertake in search for the truth.

> I must rework my philosophical ideas . . . go deeper into the problems that have appealed to me . . . The theme is almost always this opposition of self and other that I felt at beginning to live.[24]

How often in the history of philosophy has there been a philosopher so precocious as Beauvoir? She was only nineteen, but had already:

- rejected the standard notion of the self of traditional Western philosophy, as well as the one ready-made alternative on offer (viz., Bergson's), in favor of her own analysis;
- broadly formulated a new notion of self as an ongoing intersubjective construction;
- committed herself to pursuing the reorientation of philosophy from the study of the noumenal world to the phenomenal world;
- set about developing a new philosophical method, namely using first person narrative and fiction to develop her philosophy;
- identified being and nothingness as her central theme;
- settled upon the opposition of self and other as the primary philosophical problem that she sought to resolve.

It is important to note here that Beauvoir was still two years away from meeting Sartre. So her ideas listed above *were her own, not Sartrean,* as so many scholars have tended to generalize about and characterize Beauvoir's philosophy. Meanwhile Sartre also read (April 1925, age twenty) and took inspiration from Bergson in his first year as a university student. After reading *Time and Free Will* Sartre opted decisively for philosophy as his area of study: Bergson had shown him the possibility of connecting philosophy with psychology and thus to personal experience. This way of approaching philosophy fit his prior and continuing intention to become a novelist.[25]

Thus, although Beauvoir and Sartre took the same book both as their starting point for philosophical exploration and as their rationale for connecting philosophy and fiction, they did so independently of one another and for opposite reasons. Sartre initially looked to philosophy as a means for enhancing his fiction, whereas Beauvoir envisioned fiction as her means for developing new philosophy.

Although perhaps initially unaware, Beauvoir's idea of using fiction as the literary form in which she would do philosophy was profoundly significant to her precisely because she was a woman. Her commitment to give her life to the pursuit of philosophical truth, when interpreted as a career aspiration and placed in the social context of her time and place, was, without her methodological innovation, patently absurd. Philosophers were male. The very idea of a great or original philosopher who was a woman was, like a round square, perceived as an oxymoron. Women did not write philosophy books, or if they did, they were not published as such or authored under their own name. Women did, however, even if not with the frequency of men, write and publish short stories and novels.

BEAUVOIR AND SARTRE TOGETHER

Beauvoir and Sartre met in 1929 in the final weeks of their student days, immediately commencing a philosophical dialogue that continued until Sartre's death in 1980. Soon they became lovers as well as colleagues. In October 1929, on a stone bench in the shadows of the Louvre, they took an oath of mutual allegiance. Their agreement, which allowed them each to have other sexual partners, remained the primary framework for both their lives until Sartre's death. We mention these personal facts not for their color but because an appreciation of Beauvoir and Sartre's relationship is essential to understanding their working lives as professional philosophers and to how gender entered, directly and indirectly and in complex ways, into the making of their philosophies.

The meeting of Beauvoir and Sartre was the beginning of long apprenticeships for both of them, especially Beauvoir. She would not break into print until 1943, yet all the while writing almost continually, turning out a succession of practice novels and stories, honing her technique. Sartre also scribbled incessantly, essays as well as fiction. They critiqued each other's efforts mercilessly. During these years they worked as lycée philosophy teachers (similar to high school teachers in the United States), first in the provinces, later in Paris.

Beauvoir continued to be fascinated with the problem of otherness and the concept of the Other. Sartre also had an intellectual interest in other people but, as Beauvoir explained in *The Prime of Life*, his interest was mainly psychological, whereas hers was attuned to philosophical, especially ontological, questions.[26] His first published work, *The Imagination* (1936), was mainly a psychological work that does not enter into the sort of questions that fascinated Beauvoir. In fact, throughout the whole of the 1930s, and in retrospect this seems remarkable, Sartre appears not to have shared Beauvoir's primary philosophical concern.

However, during these years they did pursue together other philosophical problems. Most notable of these was how to explain a whole range of human behavior without appealing to the existence of an unconscious, a concept of psychological determinism inconsistent with their emerging notion of human freedom. Instead of positing an unconscious, they attributed these behaviors to a form of self-deceit that they called "bad faith." By systematically observing themselves and people around them, they identified various types and patterns of self-deceit, gradually building up an ever more powerful system of analysis that became central to their shared philosophy, as well as providing the basis for a non-Freudian branch of psychoanalysis.

By 1930 the question of contingency versus determinism in human action was a fashionable topic in French philosophy, and soon after Sartre finished his formal studies, he began a "lengthy, abstract dissertation on contingency."[27] But his first draft left Beauvoir unimpressed. She set about convincing him that he could and should turn his essay into a novel. He agreed and over a period of several years wrote many drafts of what was to become *Nausea*, the most celebrated of all his novels. Beauvoir read and meticulously critiqued each draft. As she has explained: "I knew exactly what he was after, and I could more nearly put myself in a reader's place than he could when it came to judging whether he had hit the mark or not. The result was that he invariably took my advice."[28]

Nausea was published in 1938 to both instant acclaim and recognition of its philosophical dimension. Subsequently it became part of the canon of existential philosophy. Arthur Danto, an eminent American analytical philosopher, regards *Nausea* as Sartre's second most important philosophical work after *Being and Nothingness*. Danto begins his excellent book on Sartre's philosophy as follows:

> Sartre's great philosophical novel, *Nausea*, is a sustained reflection on the relationships and ultimately the discrepancies between the world and our ways of representing it; and each of its major characters is defined through his deep belief that reality has the structures which, he comes to realize, instead belong to the several ways he organizes it.[29]

THE METHODOLOGY OF EXISTENTIALISM

But how, you may ask, is sustained philosophical reflection possible in a novel? Consumerist culture encourages us to mistake form for content and thus confuse the means of expression with the ideas expressed. So to be on safe side, we want to elaborate further, because it is so crucial to an appreciation of Sartre and Beauvoir as philosophers and of their working relationship, on how the nature of their philosophical pursuits enabled and at times required them to write and create new philosophy by using, in addition to the essay, the novel, the short story, and the diary.

Remember that in her student days, Beauvoir rejected the idea that philosophers had special universal access to the world, that, as Russell put it, they could "see as God might see, without a *here* and *now*." Moreover, as working philosophers, she and Sartre inverted the universalist presumption. In 1946, Beauvoir published an essay, "Literature and Metaphysics," explaining the philosophical method used by Sartre in *Nausea* and herself in *She Came to Stay* (as well as in other works). If the world can be viewed only from a particular (historically located, not abstract) point of view, Beauvoir argued, then the philosophical enterprise must begin with particular and concrete descriptions of subjects' relations with the world and with other consciousnesses. Beauvoir believes people's lives are full of metaphysical experiences, such as "one's presence in the world, one's abandonment in the world, one's freedom, the opacity of things, the resistance of foreign consciousnesses." "To make" philosophy, she says, is "to be" philosophical in the sense of sensitizing oneself to these individual metaphysical experiences and then describing them. If other people recognize these particular statements as true, then in a manner suggestive of empirical science, they can be used to generate general statements. For Beauvoir, and subsequently Sartre, good philosophical practice began not with *a priorism* but with accurate descriptions of an individual's metaphysical relations with the world, something for which fiction, as Bergson had suggested, was ideally suited. Beauvoir explains it as follows:

> In the real world the sense of an object is not a concept knowable by pure understanding: it is the object in that it unveils itself to us in the global relation

that we maintain with it and in that it is action, emotion, sentiment; one asks
of the novelists to evoke this presence of flesh and bone whose complexity,
singular and infinitely rich, overflows all subjective interpretation.[30]

Mary Warnock, another eminent analytical philosopher who has found much to admire in existential philosophy, explains its method in this way: "The methodology of Existentialism . . . consists in a perfectly deliberate and intentional use of the concrete as a way
of approaching the abstract, the particular as a way of approaching the general."[31] And:

> The existential philosopher, then, must above all describe the world in such
> a way that its meanings emerge. He cannot, obviously, describe the world as
> a whole. He must take examples in as much detail as he can, and from these
> examples his intuition of significance will become clear. It is plain how close
> such a method is to the methods of the novelist, the short-story writer.[32]

SHE CAME TO STAY AND BEING AND NOTHINGNESS

The ultimate exemplification of the use of fiction as a vehicle for philosophical discovery
is Beauvoir's first published novel, *She Came to Stay* (1943). Sartre's *Being and Nothingness*, a conventional philosopher's essay on which his philosophical reputation in the
main rests, was also published in 1943. Beauvoir, however, had drafted her novel before
Sartre began his essay. And it could not have been otherwise because Sartre had read
Beauvoir's primary research from *She Came to Stay*; it lies behind the more abstract *Being
and Nothingness*.

The relation between these two works, both in the process of their creation and in
their public reception, is fascinating, complex, and heavily influenced by gender. Space
does not permit a broad survey of the philosophical content of *She Came to Stay*, so we
will focus primarily on its complex concept of self, before showing how Sartre later used
this and other material from Beauvoir's novel in *Being and Nothingness*. Finally we will
consider the part gender played in determining the couple's division of philosophical
labor and the public's response to these two books.

She Came to Stay takes place in the bohemian Paris of the late 1930s and is centered
on the lives of five young people variously involved in the arts. Most of the narrative takes
the point of view of Françoise, who is thirty and an aspiring writer. The book opens with
Françoise personifying the Cartesian self: she regards her consciousness as independent
both of her body and other consciousnesses and her self as self-identical over time. (In
traditional philosophy, this would be understood as saying that Françoise is addressing
the "other minds problem" and "the problem of personal identity.") Françoise then undergoes a series of lived situations that test these and other hypotheses, the metaphysical
drama of the novel being coextensive with the philosophical argument. The events of
the first half of the book falsify the traditional positions, while the second half develops
Beauvoir's own theories, with constant testing against the characters' experiences.

She Came to Stay shows individuals divided not between mind and body, but between their situation or, as she calls it, "facticity"—aspects that resemble inert objects
(for example, the past, social circumstance, and body-as-object) and elements of freedom (for example, projects, values, and the body-as-subject). Its characters fall into bad

faith when they fail to coordinate these two dimensions of their reality; that is, bad faith occurs when they pretend that they are facticity without freedom or freedom without facticity. This split in human being makes self-identity an illusive goal: our freedom keeps our sense of self, including even how we see our past, from ever being complete and final. Through her characters Beauvoir demonstrates that one is always separated from one's "self" by one's freedom to do, imagine, or believe differently. Furthermore, as with all objects of consciousness, the possible points of view one may adopt toward one's "self" are unlimited.

By letting go of the traditional Cartesian views of consciousness as disembodied and of the self as a fixed entity residing *in* consciousness, and, instead, putting in their place the ideas of embodied consciousness and of the self as an object *of* consciousness and an ongoing project, Beauvoir was opening the philosophical door to the possibility that the self could be fundamentally influenced by other people. This was part of her groundwork for solving her "problem of the other" with which, as a teenager, she had so passionately begun her life as a philosopher.

But this problem ("the problem of other minds"), which figures so large in *She Came to Stay*, was not only a personal and experiential one; it also tied up with one of the oldest problems in philosophy: How do we know that other people are, like ourselves, conscious beings? We can observe "other people from without, through the shape of words, gestures and faces," but we cannot observe that they have thoughts and sensations like ourselves.[33] From one's individual experience of being conscious one can argue from analogy that other people are conscious too, but as a philosophical argument this inductive leap barely makes the grade. Nor does it provide any ontological foundation for creating a theory of intersubjectivity. Even those, like Hegel and Heidegger, who might have wished to do so, could not provide a direct relation between concrete individual consciousnesses.

But Beauvoir did and did so by borrowing an old trick from Descartes. His cogito, "I am thinking, therefore I am," offers no proof or argument that he exists. Instead he identifies a fundamental experience, thinking, that leads him to believe beyond all doubt that he exists and that is, he presumes, a part of everyone's experience. Similarly, Beauvoir ignored the problem of proving the existence of other minds, in favor of asking: What universal experience leads us all to believe other people to be conscious beings like ourselves? She answers that it is the phenomenological event of experiencing oneself as the object of another's look. To be conscious of being looked at or judged by another person can actually cause a metamorphosis in someone's consciousness: they are made aware that they have another self, an "objective" one that exists only for the Other. In *She Came to Stay*, Pierre peeking at lovers though a keyhole and imagining himself being caught illustrates the experience.[34] *She Came to Stay* shows individuals divided not between mind and body, but between his self-for-the-other revealed to him as an awareness that the Other has an image of him as an object in a world whose center of reference is no longer his consciousness. This experience of being an object entails the Other-as-subject: only another consciousness could cause this decentering of his sense of self.

She Came to Stay is structured in part around six modes of Being-for-Others, (namely, masochism, love, sadism, hate, desire, and indifference) and provides numerous illustrations and extensive analysis of each. For Beauvoir, the philosophical significance of these common experiences is that they all presume a direct or internal relation between consciousnesses. For example, the flush of embarrassment one undergoes when caught, like Pierre, in an unseemly act is not founded on an analogy that probabilistically induces the existence of other consciousnesses; rather, it manifests itself instantaneously as the consequence of a causal relation internal to one's own consciousness and the Other's. The person's embarrassment arises from a sudden transformation in the mode of their consciousness, from one where they experienced themselves wholly as subject, that is, as the point of view around which the world is organized, to a mode where they are an object in a world organized by the Other. This asymmetrical subject-object relation so extensively explored in *She Came to Stay* provides the ontological basis of Beauvoir's theory of intersubjectivity, which, when extended to groups as well as to individuals, provided the analytical framework of her most famous work, *The Second Sex*.[35]

Long ago it was pointed out by the English translator of Sartre's *Being and Nothingness*, Hazel Barnes, that much of its philosophical content is also found in *She Came to Stay*. For example Barnes writes:

> As with all of de Beauvoir's early fiction, the reader of *She Came to Stay* feels that the inspiration of the book was simply de Beauvoir's decision to show how Sartre's abstract principles could be make to work out in "real life."[36]

But we know now that the real work sequence between the couple was the reverse of the one suggested by Barnes. Sartre's biographers divide over when Sartre began to write *Being and Nothingness*. Some say he did so in late July 1940; others say it was the autumn of 1941. But—and this is what is so significant—both these dates come *after* Beauvoir had finished the first and most, if not all, of the second draft of *She Came to Stay*.[37] In addition, it is also now known that in February 1940 Sartre, while on leave from the army, closely read Beauvoir's manuscript. Sartre scholars agree, from a study of the diaries that he kept in this period (*War Diaries*) that his flowering as a philosopher with new ideas took place in the weeks immediately following his reading of Beauvoir's novel.[38]

In and of itself there is nothing scandalous or indecent about Sartre's debt to Beauvoir for so many of the ideas and insights that he wove together in his great treatise. It merely reflected how the couple came to work together as philosophers. But it is important, especially in the context of this book, to appreciate the social origins of their professional relationship and that the initial originator of a notion of the self that Beauvoir and Sartre later developed was Beauvoir. So to close this essay we are going to return briefly to Beauvoir's student days and diaries.

A DIVISION OF LABOR

Early in her student days Beauvoir became a close friend and colleague of Maurice Merleau-Ponty, whom she also let study *She Came to Stay* long before it was published, and who became not only an existential philosopher like Sartre but also his closest rival. In 1927, Merleau-Ponty came third in the philosophy exams at the Sorbonne behind two women, Simone Weil and Beauvoir. Following encounters with him and other male students who expressed irritation with these results, Beauvoir wrote as follows in her diary:

> And so, my friends, you do not like girls but consider that not only do they have a reason to satisfy but a heavy heart to restrain—and in that respect I

want to remain a woman, more masculine yet in the brain, more feminine in sensibility.[39]

And a few pages further on Beauvoir expands on these thoughts about how gender differences differentiate her and Merleau-Ponty's approach to philosophy:

> "Aristocrat" he calls me? It's true. I can't get rid of this idea that I am alone, in a world apart, being present at the other as at a spectacle. . . . Dreams are forbidden him. Ah! As for me I have riches there that I do not want to get rid of. Drama of my affections, pathos of life. Certainly, I have a more complicated, more nuanced sensibility than his and a more exhausting power of love. These problems that he lives with his brain, I live them with my arms and my legs. . . . I don't want to lose all of that.[40]

These words, after the fact, resound with irony because Merleau-Ponty became famous for practicing philosophy in the phenomenological manner, with the emphasis on embodiment that Beauvoir had already been advocating and doing in her writing. But sixteen years later and now a convert, he published an article on *She Came to Stay* titled "Metaphysics and the Novel." It includes a cogent explanation of the significance of Beauvoir's philosophical method. "Classical metaphysics," he writes, "could pass for a speciality with which literature had nothing to do because metaphysics operated on the basis of uncontested rationalism, convinced it could make the world and human life understood by an arrangement of concepts."[41] But, Merleau-Ponty continues:

> Everything changes when a phenomenological or existential philosophy assigns itself the task, not of explaining the world or of discovering its "conditions of possibility," but rather of formulating an experience of the world, a contact with the world which precedes all thought *about* the world. After this, whatever is metaphysical in man cannot be credited to something outside his empirical being—to God, to Consciousness. Man is metaphysical in his very being, in his loves, in his hates, in his individual and collective history.[42]

In less sophisticated prose, these views, sentiments, and passions are found in Beauvoir's teenage diaries. As a young woman she hung on to and extended the nuanced sensibility that as a girl she so prized. When in maturity Beauvoir coupled it with her writer's craft, she, as Merleau-Ponty acclaimed, succeeded in unveiling pretheoretical layers of experience, in seeing the world as immediate and thus as metaphysical experience.

As the years and decades went by, Beauvoir became even more persuaded that her untraditional and "feminine" way of doing philosophy, if not the only valid way, was in any case essential for providing real insights upon which system builders, like her beloved Sartre, could do legitimate work. She continued to believe that the universalist presumption of male philosophers was delusory, egomaniacal, and only apparently tenable when claimed from their position of masculine privilege. Likewise, to the end of her life she insisted on the philosophical relevance of individual human experience. More than once, she expressed the view that system building in philosophy was a form of male madness. But we know that, at the very least, she did heavy editing on *Being and Nothingness*. It must have been immensely satisfying, even thrilling, for Beauvoir to see her discoveries and ideas incorporated in "Sartre's system" and in consequence ingested by intellectuals around the world.

Beauvoir and Sartre were bound together not only by immense love but also by a division of labor. Beauvoir carried out most of the primary research and its distillation. Together, often in the cafes of Paris, they did the refinement. And Sartre did most of the system making. But ethically it was a double-edged division of labor. On the one hand it came about through the different roles, opportunities, and expectations that the couple's society gave the two sexes. On the other, for fifty-one years, it gave Beauvoir and Sartre a working life in a sort of philosopher's paradise. Inevitably accounts of Beauvoir and Sartre's working relationship have been corrupted, often grotesquely so, by sexism. This is a great pity. In the whole of philosophy there is no story of collaboration more inspiring than the true story of the gendered philosophical partnership of Beauvoir and Sartre.

Questions for Reflection

In what respects does Beauvoir's experience of being dismissed as Sartre's philosophical follower reflect the experience of woman as the Other described in *The Second Sex*? Be specific in your answer. What is Beauvoir's description of the Other in your answer? Have you ever experienced yourself as a (Beauvoirian) Other?

In *She Came to Stay*, how is Françoise's sense of self transformed by her experiences? How has your own sense of self been transformed by your own experiences? Considering both Françoise's and your own sense of self, how might you describe your self in a Beauvoirian way—as haunted by nothingness, or as a spiritual union with God, or perhaps as a material girl who lives to shop, or as . . . ?

Beauvoir and Sartre both describe the metaphysical experience of the look of the other. What do they say, what do they each mean, and how and why does someone make another person the Other? What can one do to prevent making another an Other? Defend your answer.

Notes

1. Thomas Flynn, "Jean-Paul Sartre," *The Stanford Encyclopedia of Philosophy (Spring 2008 Edition)*, Edward N. Zalta (ed.), URL = <http://plato.stanford.edu/archives/spr2008/entries/sartre/>.

2. Thomas Flynn (tflynn@emory.edu), "Jean Paul Sartre," *The Stanford Encyclopedia of Philosophy*, April, 2004, at http://plato.stanford.edu/entries/sartre/.

3. Personal conversation with Peg Simons on April 18, 2002.

4. Jean-Paul Sartre, *Being and Nothingness: An Essay on Phenomenological Ontology*, trans. Hazel E. Barnes (New York: Philosophical Library, 1953), chap. 1, esp. pp. 221–23, 252–61.

5. Simone de Beauvoir, *The Second Sex*, trans. H. M. Parshley (New York: Knopf, 1952), xxi–xxvi, 156–57.

6. Simone de Beauvoir, *She Came to Stay* [1943], rev. and trans. Yvonne Moyse and Roger Senhouser (Cleveland, OH: World Publishing Company, 1954); revised trans. by Margaret A. Simons and Edward Fullbrook.

7. René Descartes, *A Discourse on Method and Other Works* (1637), trans. E. S. Haldane and G. R. T. Ross (New York: Washington Square Press, 1965).

8. Descartes, *Discourse on Method and Other Works*, Part IV, 9.

9. Descartes, *Discourse on Method and Other Works*, First Meditation, 19.

10. John Locke (1632–1704) broke with rationalism by declaring that all our ideas were derived from experience (*An Essay Concerning Human Understanding*, 1690). But he saw knowledge as a product of reason working out the connections between those ideas, and he insisted upon Descartes's phantom as the agent who carries out this process of reason. Locke made a distinction between "person" and "man," and, by extension, between personal identity and a man's identity. The identity of a man, he wrote, is "participation of the same continued life, by constantly fleeting particles of matter, in succession vitally united to the same organized body" (*An Essay Concerning Human Understanding*, II, xxvii, 6). But the identity of a person is that of "a thinking intelligent being, that has reason, and reflection, and can consider itself as itself, the same thinking thing in different times and places" (II, xxvii, 9). Locke's thinker is not his concept of "man" but rather his Cartesian concept of "person," who, out of ideas, creates knowledge independently of time, place, and society, and who became for British philosophers, no less than for Continentals, their imaginary, ideal persona.

11. Bertrand Russell, *The Problems of Philosophy* (New York: Oxford University Press, 1971–1972), 160.

12. An example of where the Cartesian-Russellian self continues its prominence in philosophy is John Rawls's immensely influential *A Theory of Justice* (Boston, MA: Harvard University Press, 1971). He explains the foundational presuppositions of his work as follows.

> The essential point is that we need an argument showing which principles, if any, free and equal rational persons would choose . . . My suggestion is that we think of the original position as the point of view from which noumenal selves see the world . . . The description of the original position interprets the point of view of the noumenal selves, . . . 255–56.

For philosophers, this notion that some individuals, nearly always male, possess the means to "see as God might see," to attain "the original position" so that their point of view should then outweigh and invalidate all others holds a powerful attraction, capable of seducing the best minds, even Bertrand Russell's.

13. Barbara Klaw, Sylvie Le Bon de Beauvoir, and Margaret Simons, eds., *Diary of a Philosophy Student*, vol. 1, *1926–1927* (Urbana: University of Illinois Press, 2007), 95.

14. Klaw, Beauvoir, and Simons, *Diary*, 95.

15. Klaw, Beauvoir, and Simons, *Diary*, CA2 1.

16. Klaw, Beauvoir, and Simons, *Diary*, CA26 53.

17. Klaw, Beauvoir, and Simons, *Diary*, 11.

18. Klaw, Beauvoir, and Simons, *Diary*, 55.

19. Klaw, Beauvoir, and Simons, *Diary*, 62.

20. Klaw, Beauvoir, and Simons, *Diary*, 18.

21. Klaw, Beauvoir, and Simons, *Diary*, 160.

22. Henri Bergson, *Time and Free Will: An Essay on the Immediate Data of Consciousness*, trans. F. L. Pogson (New York: Macmillan, 1913), 133.

23. Klaw, Beauvoir, and Simons, *Diary*, CA27 54.

24. Klaw, Beauvoir, and Simons, *Diary*, CA27 95.

25. Kate Fullbrook and Edward Fullbrook, *Simone de Beauvoir and Jean-Paul Sartre: The Remaking of a Twentieth-Century Legend* (London: Harvester, 1993), 28.

26. Simone de Beauvoir, *The Prime of Life: The Autobiography of Simone de Beauvoir*, trans. Peter Green (Harmondsworth, Middlesex, England: Penguin, 1962), 124–26.

27. Beauvoir, *The Prime of Life*, 106.

28. Beauvoir, *The Prime of Life*, 106.

29. Arthur C. Danto, *Sartre*, 2nd. ed. (London: Fontana, 1975), 5.

30. Simone de Beauvoir, "Littérature et Métaphysique," in *Existentialisme et la Sagesse des Nations* (Paris: Nagel, 1946), 105–6.

31. Mary Warnock, *Existentialism* (Oxford: Oxford University Press, 1984), 133.

32. Warnock, *Existentialism*, 136.

33. Beauvoir, *She Came to Stay*, 307–10.

34. Hazel Barnes, *The Literature of Possibility: A Study in Humanistic Existentialism* (London: Tavistock, 1961), 121–22.

35. The documentary evidence for this assertion is voluminous, diverse, and incontrovertible. It consists of the diaries and of letters of Beauvoir and Sartre during this period, which were not available to scholars when Barnes was writing.

36. Ronald Hayman, *Writing Against: A Biography of Sartre* (London: Trafalgar Square, 1986), 149; Kenneth A. Thompson, *Sartre: Life and Works* (New York: Facts On File, 1984), 43; Thomas R. Flynn, "Sartre and the Poetics of History," in *The Cambridge Companion to Sartre*, ed. Christina Howells (Cambridge, UK: Cambridge University Press, 1992), 213–60, 215; William L. McBride, *Sartre's Political Theory* (Bloomington: Indiana University Press, 1991), 32; Anna Boschetti, *The Intellectual Enterprise: Sartre and Les Temps Modernes*, trans. Richard C. McCleary (Evanston, IL: Northwestern University Press, 1985), 55; Leo Fretz, "Individuality in Sartre's Philosophy" in *The Cambridge Companion to Sartre*, ed., Christina Howells (Cambridge, UK: Cambridge University Press,1992), 67–102, 70, 77, 71.

37. Klaw, Beauvoir, and Simons, *Diary*, 106–7.

38. Klaw, Beauvoir, and Simons, *Diary*, 126.

39. Klaw, Beauvoir, and Simons, *Diary*, 27–28.

40. Klaw, Beauvoir, and Simons, *Diary*, 126.

41. Maurice Merleau-Ponty, (1945), "Metaphysics and the Novel," in *Sense and Non-Sense*, trans. Hubert L. Dreyfus and Patricia Ann Dreyfus (Evanston, IL: Northwestern University Press, 1964), 27.

42. Merleau-Ponty, "Metaphysics and the Novel," 27–28.

Appendix A

SOME WOMEN PHILOSOPHERS[1]

I. 600 B.C.E.–400/500 C.E.: ANCIENT PHILOSOPHY

Name	Date
Hippo	ca. twelfth century B.C.E.
Themistoclea	sixth century B.C.E.
Theano	sixth century B.C.E.
Chilonis	sixth century B.C.E.
Cleobulina of Rhodes	ca. 570 B.C.E.
Arignote	sixth–fifth century B.C.E.
Myia	sixth–fifth century B.C.E.
Damo	sixth–fifth century B.C.E.
Sara	sixth–fifth century B.C.E.
Diotima of Mantinea	fifth century B.C.E.
Aspasia of Miletus	ca. 470–445 B.C.E.
Perictione I	ca. 449 B.C.E.
Arete of Cerene	fifth or fourth century B.C.E.
Aesara of Lucania	ca. 425 B.C.E.–100 C.E.
Theano II	ca. 425 B.C.E.–100 C.E.
Perictione II	ca. 425 B.C.E.–100 C.E.
Nicarete	fourth century B.C.E.
Lasthenia of Mantinea	347 B.C.E.
Timycha	ca. fourth century B.C.E.
Themista of Lampsacus	306 B.C.E.
Leontium	fourth–third century B.C.E.
Theophilia	fourth–third century B.C.E.
Hipparcia the Cynic	365–285 B.C.E.
Asclepigenia of Athens	ca. 375 B.C.E.
Axiothea of Philius	347 B.C.E.

Name	Date
Batis of Lampsacus	306 B.C.E.
Echecratia	third century B.C.E.
Phintys of Sparta	second century B.C.E.
Porcia	Died 42 B.C.E.
Pamphila	first century C.E.
Caerellia	first century C.E.
Ban Zhao	ca. 35–100 C.E.
Fannia	56–107 C.E.
Anteia	70–79 C.E.
Arria the Elder	death 42 C.E.
Arria the Younger	66–107 C.E.
Clea	first–second century C.E.
Eurydice	first–second century C.E.
Julia Domna	170–217 C.E.
Ptolemais	second–third century C.E.
Magnilla	second to third century C.E.
Arria	third century C.E.
Geminae	third century C.E.
Salonina Cornelia	260–268 C.E.
Saint Catharine of Alexandria	Died in 307 C.E.
Sosipatra	327–379 C.E.
Makrina the Younger	ca. 330–379 C.E.
Hypatia of Alexandria	370–415 C.E.
Asclepienia	ca. 375 C.E.
Ampliclea	fourth century C.E.
Eudocia-Athenais	ca. 401–460 C.E.
Anthusa	fifth century C.E.

II. 400/500–1600: MEDIEVAL, RENAISSANCE, AND ENLIGHTENMENT PHILOSOPHY

Name	Date
Hrosvith of Gandersheim	935–1101
Lady Murasaki Shikibu	978–1014
Eudocia	eleventh century
Anna Comnena	1083–1148
Hildegard of Bingen	1098–1179
Heloise	1101–1164
Herrad of Hohenbourg	1130–1195
Beatrice of Nazareth	1200–1268
Mechtild of Magdeburg	ca. 1207–1282
Hadewijch of Antwerp	thirteenth century
St. Birgitta of Sweden	1303–1373
Juliana of Norwich	ca. 1342–1413

Name	Date
St. Catherine of Siena	1347–1380
Christine de Pisan	1364–1431
Battista de Montefeltro Malatesta	1383–1450
Dorotea Bucca (Bocchi) of Bologne	ca. 1390s–1430s
Panypersebasta	fourteenth century
Novella	fourteenth century
Catherine of Bologna	1413–1463
Ginevra Nogarola	1417–1461
Isotta Nogarola	1418–1466
Cecilia Gonzaga	1425–1451
Costanza Varano	1426–1466
Cassandra Fedele	1465–1558
Laura Cereta of Brescia	1469–1499
Beatrix Galindo	1474–1534
Margaret Roper	1505–1544
St. Teresa of Avila	1515–1582
Fulvia Olympia Morata	1526–1555
Lady Jane Grey (La Latina)	1537–1554
Tarquinia Molza of Modena	1542–1617
Olivia de Nantes Barrera Sabuco	1562–1625
Marie le Jars de Gournay	1565–1645
Margherita Sarrocchi	1569–1618
Lady Deborah Moody	1586–1659
Madame de Rambouillet (née Catherine de Vivonne)	1588–1655
Marquise de Sablé (née Madeleine de Souvré)	1599–1698

III. 1600–1900: MODERN PHILOSOPHY

Name	Date
Anna Maria van Schurman	1607–1678
Madeleine de Scudéry	1607–1701
Anne Bradstreet	1612–1672
Elisabeth of Bohemia, Princess Palatine	1618–1680
Duchess de Longueville (born Ann de Bourbon)	1619–1679
Margaret Cavendish, Duchess of Newcastle	1623–1673
Cristina Wasa, Queen of Sweden	1626–1689
Madame de Sévigné (née Marie de Rabutin-Chantal)	1626–1696
Anne Finch Conway, Viscountess	1631–1679

Name	Date
Madame de LaFayette (born Marie Madeleine Priochede la Vergne)	1634–1692
Madame de Maintenon (Françoise d'Aubigné)	1635–1719
Madame de Grignan	1646–1705
Aphra Behn	1640–1689
Elena Cornaro	1646–1684
Sor Juana Ines de la Cruz	1651–1695
Madame Dacier (born Anne Lefebrve)	1654–1720
Lady Mary Lee Chudleigh	1656–1710
Damaris Cudworth Masham	1659–1708
Mary Astell	1666–1731
Catherine Trotter Cockburn	1679–1749
Caroline of Brandenburg-Ansbach	1683–1787
Lady Mary Wortley Montagu	1689–1762
Emilie du Châtelet	1706–1749
Laura Maria Caterina Bassi	1711–1778
Maria Gaetana Agnesi	1718–1799
Mercy Otis Warren	1728–1814
Catharine Sawbridge Macaulay	1731–1791
Hannah More	1745–1833
Judith Sargent Murray	1751–1820
Marie-Jeanne Philipon (Madame Roland)	1754–1793
Mary Wollstonecraft	1759–1797
Madame de Condorcet	1764–1822
Mme Germaine de Staël	1766–1817
Lady Mary Shepherd	1777–1847
Frances Wright	1795–1852
Catharine Ward Beecher	1800–1878
Harriet Martineau	1802–1876
Sarah Helen Whitman	1803–1878
Harriet Hardy Taylor Mill	1807–1858
Jenny Poinsard d'Hericourt	1809–1875
Margaret Fuller	1810–1850
George Eliot (Marian Evans)	1819–1880
Edna Dow Cheney	1824–1904
Antoninette Brown Blackwell	1825–1921
Clemence Royer	1830–1902
Julie Velten Favre	1834–1896
Lady Welby Victoria	1837–1912
Eliza Sunderland	1839–1910
Marietta Kies	1853–1899

IV. 1900–PRESENT: CONTEMPORARY PHILOSOPHY

Name	Date
Juliette Lambert la Messine Adam	1836–1936
E. E. Constance Jones	1842–1922
Christine Ladd-Franklin	1847–1930
Sophie Willock Bryant	1850–1922
Clara Marie Hitchcock	1853–1933
Helen Magill White	1853–1944
Julia Henrietta Gulliver	1856–1940
Eliza Richtie	1856–1933
May Preston Slosson	1858–1943
Anna Julia Cooper	1858–1964
Charlotte Perkins Gilman	1860–1935
Helen Dendy Bosanquet	1860–1925
Jane Addams	1860–1935
Lou Andreas-Salomé	1861–1937
Elizabeth S. Haldane	1862–1937
Mary Whiton Calkins	1863–1930
May Sinclair	1863–1946
Caroline Miles Hill	1866–1951
Alice Julia Hamlin Hinman	1867–1934
Ellen Bliss Talbot	1867–1968
Blanche Zehring	1867–1950
Emma Goldman	1869–1940
Beatrice Edgell	1871–1948
Evelyn Underhill	1875–1941
Ivy MacKenzie	1877–1959
Grace Mead Andrus de Laguna	1878–1978
Nina Hirschensohn Alderblum	1882–1974
L. Susan Stebbing	1885–1943
Katherine Everett Gilbert	1886–1952
Helen Huss Parkhurst	1887–1959
Hedwig Conrad-Martius	1888–1966
Sister Mary Patricia Garvey	1888–1952
Karin Costelloe Stephen	1889–1953
Marjorie Silliman Harris	1890–1976
Edith Stein	1891–1942
Phyllis Ackerman	1893–1977
Dorothy Wrinch Nicholson	1894–1976
Susanne K. Langer	1895–1985
Gerda Walther	1897–1977
Ruth Lydia Saw	1901–1983
Ayn Rand	1905–1982
Cornelia Johanna de Vogel	1905–1986
Alice Ambrose	1906–2001

Name	Date
Hannah Arendt	1906–1975
Margaret MacDonald	1907–1956
Simone de Beauvoir	1908–1986
Simone Weil	1909–1943
Margaret Masterman Braithwaite	1910–1986
Elizabeth Anscombe	1919–2001
Iris Murdoch	1919–1999
Veda Cobb-Smith	1948–1989
Iris Marion Young	1949–2006

Note

1. This is a highly selective list; it only includes women philosophers through the twentieth century who are deceased. The names of these women philosophers are generated primarily from the "recovery books" cited in the Lead Essay, note 3.

Appendix B

2,600 YEARS OF GENDER-EXCLUSIVE PHILOSOPHY: ENOUGH IS ENOUGH!

A STUDENT PERSPECTIVE BY THE BOOK'S RESEARCH ASSISTANT *AUDUN SOLLI*

When Dr. Warren asked me to assist her with this project, I was unaware of all that would open up to me in the process. I was a beginning philosophy student for whom English is a second language. As a student who represented the intended audience of the book, Professor Warren gave me an initial set of responsibilities, including reading and commenting on the fifteen commentaries for the book. She provided me with a basic set of questions to ask myself while reading the commentaries. These questions included: "Were the commentaries clear, informative, and suitable for an audience of beginning philosophy students like me? Did they identify the field of philosophy and positions of each philosopher in the chapter? Did they discuss similarities and dissimilarities between the two philosophers in the 'pair?' Did I learn anything I thought was important about philosophy by the inclusion of women and considerations of gender in the writings of the philosophical pairs in the commentaries?" Answering these questions gave me an opportunity not only to recommend changes to the commentaries to make them better suited for introductory students and history of (Western) philosophy courses; they also prompted me to think often and deeply about issues of gender by reading the traditional male philosophers *paired* with women philosophers—whom I had never heard of before I began work on the book.

Professor Warren gave me full reign. I focused on four main areas: First, and most important, I read the initial draft of each commentary and wrote detailed, sometimes negatively critical, comments and revision suggestions from my perspective. Second, I took responsibility for the nonsubstantive administrative tasks, including the tedious and time-consuming process of obtaining copyright permissions that became a four-year endeavor. Third, I facilitated most of the correspondence with the commentators. I was responsible for preparing the initial rough draft, including primary texts. I kept specific charts on word counts on texts and diagrams to be included to keep to word-count limitations.

My fourth contribution was my suggestion to Professor Warren that the book include a glossary. The need for a glossary became obvious to me as I read the initial drafts. Studying philosophy is in itself a challenging enterprise. This is especially true for beginning students, or students for whom English is a second language. We often encounter textbooks suitable for graduate students that assume that the reader is familiar with basic philosophical concepts and expressions. In my written reviews of each commentary, I provided a list of terms or concepts, whose meanings were unclear to me. For instance, I doubt that most beginning philosophy students know the difference between Plato, Platonists, Neoplatonists, and Cambridge Platonists. Without clearly identified meanings, an entire perspective or point may be unnecessarily lost on the student. Professor Warren made the decision to add a glossary of terms and asked the commentators to provide definitions of terms and concepts used by them or their philosophical pair. She said she would provide definitions for more generic philosophical terms or references.

Professor Warren specifically sought feedback from me, as well as other members of the two history of women philosophers classes she taught, on how we would answer the questions raised in the commentaries—especially the "questions for reflection" at the end of each commentary—and what we would like to learn about the particular women selected for inclusion in the book. Just asking us these two questions, from class to class, affected how we all viewed the inclusion of women in the history of philosophy and how gender considerations continually changed our understanding of the nature of philosophy. Her hope was that by receiving my (and other students') feedback on the writings and biographies of some women philosophers during the last 2,600 years, this anthology would really be written in a way that would appeal to a newcomer to philosophy—be user friendly—and also provide a scholarly contribution to the history of Western philosophy by its *inclusion of women.*

With these guidelines, I wrote specific questions about the role of gender in my revision comments to each commentator. I later learned that the commentators were genuinely grateful for the feedback and typically revised their commentaries to explicitly address relevant questions concerning gender.

By working on this anthology, I came to truly believe that studying philosophy without women is a serious mistake. I understand now how it misrepresents the history of Western philosophy as primarily for and by men. It has given me a better understanding of what a gender-inclusive philosophy is or could be. I feel fortunate to have had the opportunity to participate in the creation of this volume. By undertaking the roles and activities I did, I proudly contributed to the ongoing "recovery and inclusion project." I am confident that beginning philosophy students and other persons interested in the history of Western philosophy will benefit in similar ways from reading this book.

To conclude this essay, I want to acknowledge several people whose assistance and support contributed to my four years working on this book. I want to thank all the commentators who worked so closely with me on the project, and my friends Sumeet Kaur Atul and Matti Erpestad for valuable and substantive assistance with my use of English in this essay. While in my home country of Norway, I needed to communicate by e-mail with Professor Warren, which was difficult since I do not have Internet access at home. Tore Lahn at the Glomdal Museum graciously let me use his office and computer for this purpose. My good friends Viggo Oppegård, Mari Vold Lexander, and Øistein Steineide Refseth also helped when I had dozens of e-mails to send. But most important, I want to thank Professor Warren for giving me the opportunity to be her research assistant and work on this book. As a student of German literature and international studies, it has been an extremely interesting experience and I am grateful she had faith in my ability to work independently on my tasks and valued my concerns and feedback so highly. It has been an honor to work with such an energetic, intelligent, and dedicated scholar. I can honestly say it is the most important intellectual undertaking I experienced as an undergraduate student.

Glossary

akrasia (chapter 2): A term used by Aristotle for weakness of the will: acting against one's own better judgment. Plato shares the Socratic position that *akrasia* is impossible, since no one does wrong knowingly (contrast with *akrteia*).

akrateia (chapter 2): A term used by Plato to denote a lack of self-control in general.

amicitia (chapter 4): Love characteristic of a strongly committed friendship.

amor (chapter 4): Love characterized by passion and desire, or a term that refers to the person toward whom the emotion is felt.

analytic (chapter 10): In Kant, one of two divisions of logic, the other being Dialectic.

analytic claim (chapters 7 and 10): A claim that is demonstrably true by virtue of either its logical form or the definitions/meanings of the component words (e.g., All men are men, all bachelors are male, where the definition of "bachelor" is unmarried male).

analytical philosophy (Lead Essay; chapter 14): The school of twentieth-century philosophy that is characterized by a critical concern with language and meaning, conceptual analysis, and rigorous argumentative proof. In the 1930s analytical philosophy was particularly associated with the anti-metaphysical stance of the movement known as logical positivism.

angst (chapters 12 and 15): Anxiety or dread that, according to French existentialists, is what humans experience when they become aware of their mortality (see "existentialism").

apeiron (chapter 2): A Pythagorean term meaning "unlimited" or "indefinite." Limit (*peiras*) and the unlimited (*apeiron*) are basic metaphysical principles for Pythagoreans: All order is analyzed as the demarcation of limit in the unlimited.

apodeictic (chapter 10): Something asserted as necessary.

a posteriori (chapters 7 and 10): A term applied claims that originate in or are arrived at (verified) by appeal to sensory experience and information not available through reason alone. An *a posteriori* claim is one about sensory data or sensory experience (e.g., It is raining today).

appearing (chapter 12): For Arendt and Heidegger, truth and reality are not necessarily hidden; they are to be sought through thinking in the world as the world is for us.

Arendt holds that our sense of our own reality depends on our appearing to and being recognized by others, and on others confirming what we see. Consequently, she is concerned with worldly "public spaces," arguably thereby translating Heidegger's "clearing of Being" in political, rather than ontological, terms.

a priori (chapters 7 and 10): A term Kant applies to all judgments, statements, claims, and principles whose justification is independent of and not confirmed by appeal to sense impressions or human experience. An *a priori* claim is one arrived at or known through reason alone.

architectonic (chapter 10): Structural design of a philosophical system (e.g., Kant's "architectonic" system rests on distinctions of logic).

aretaic ethics (chapter 2): Aristotelian term referring to virtue ethics or character-based ethics.

arête (chapter 2): Aristotelian term meaning "excellence." Every living thing has an *arête*. The *arête* of being human is to have two kinds of excellence: moral excellence (or understanding) and practical wisdom.

argument: A set of at least two declarative sentences or statements (sentences that are true or false), one of which (the conclusion) is alleged to follow necessarily (in deductive arguments) or probably (in inductive arguments) from the other statements (the premises).

authentic existence: For existentialists, humans live an "authentic" life by accepting their radical freedom ("freedom without facticity") and also their mortality ("facticity without freedom"). Inauthenthic life is living in denial or self-deceit, trying to avoid one's mortality. To live an inauthentic life is "bad faith," (see also "existentialism").

autonomous (Lead Essay; chapter 10): Humans are autonomous ("self-legislating," auto + *nomos*): As rational beings (rather than as particular individuals) humans can regard themselves as the authors of the moral law. Paradoxically, autonomous actions—actions done in accordance with reason, preserve one's freedom by one's submission to moral law.

bad faith (chapter 15): A form of self-deceit, where one either denies something one is conscious about or chooses to live "inauthentic" lives. Selves "fall into bad faith" when they pretend that they are "body-as-object"—facticity without freedom—or body-as-subject—freedom without facticity, when they are really both (see also "existentialism").

Beauty (chapter 1): As used by Plato, Beauty (or, The Beautiful)—beauty with a capital B—refers to a perfect and eternal essence, a Platonic Form, which is the ultimate cause and explanation of why beautiful things are beautiful.

Being (chapter 12): The English verb "to be" commonly asserts or, in the negative, denies that something or someone exists (as in "I am," "The Golden Age is no more"), or asserts or denies a description of something (such as "The ball is—or is not—red"). Heidegger is interested in the meaning of *Being* itself, which he understood as an answer to the question "Why is there something rather than nothing?" Being is capitalized in English translations of Heidegger (e.g., "the Being of beings," to indicate that "being" refers both to what is fundamental—Being—when "being" is capitalized, and to how Being discloses itself in time and space—as beings (including human beings). The term is analogous to "The Truth of all truths" or "History that is revealed through histories."

being-for-itself (chapter 15): In French existentialism, this is the being (or self) of human consciousness, which is fluid (not fixed, not a given "facticity") and freely chooses its nature and future at every moment of its existence.

being-in-itself (chapter 15): This is the being of things simply as they are, without meaning, consciousness, or purpose, such as the being of trees and rocks.

Cambridge Platonism (chapters 7 and 8): A group of seventeenth-century English philosophers, including Henry More, Ralph Cudworth, John Smith, and Anne Conway, who rejected scholasticism in favor of rationalism and a neoplatonic metaphysics. Their work attempted to integrate insights from Plato and Plotinus with those inspired by scientific resolution (while rejecting scientific mechanism). They believed in a suprasensible reality, innate ideas, the compatibility of human reason with faith, and that faith was a reliable source of truth.

canonical philosophy, The Canon (Lead Essay): The "Western philosophical canon," as used in this text, refers to: (i) the philosophical tradition traceable to ancient Greece; (ii) those male philosophers and texts that are commonly read in History of Western Philosophy courses throughout the English-speaking Western world; (iii) a focus on distinctively "philosophical questions"; (iv) a set of common assumptions, concepts, values, beliefs, definitions, and distinctions (including dualisms); (v) a concern with age-old "problems of philosophy"; and (vi) an argument-based style of analysis.

caritas (chapter 4): A loving emotion characterized by caring about another, being concerned for another.

Cartesian principles: Principles derived from the philosophy of Réne Descartes.

Cartesian psychology (chapter 14): The mind is viewed as "private" in the sense that its contents are knowable only to the individual whose mind it is. Those who hold such a view would say things like, "Only I can know whether or not I'm in pain." Wittgenstein's philosophy of language, like much of contemporary philosophy of mind, sought to undermine this Cartesian view of the mind.

categories (chapter 10): The basic general concepts of thought, language, or reality. Kant's term (borrowed from Aristotle) for those most basic *a priori* concepts of human knowledge (e.g., causality, substance).

cause (chapter 2): Anything responsible for change. Aristotle identified four causes: the *material* cause (the matter or stuff out of which something is made, such as the marble that will be used to make a statue); the *formal* cause (the essence of a thing, that which it strives to be, such as the actual statue that is only a potential statue in the marble itself until the artist/sculpture actualizes the potentiality of the marble); the *efficient* cause (the force or event that brings about the change, such as the sculptor chipping the marble or shaping the clay); the *final* cause (the purpose or *telos* of a thing, such as to beautify the courthouse in Athens).

clarity and distinctness (chapter 5): Descartes's principle of indubitable truth that "whatever I perceive clearly and distinctly is true," based on his reflection of the epistemological certainty of "I [Descartes] exist." Clear perceptions are "present and accessible." Distinct perceptions are "sharply separated" from other perceptions and contain only what is clear. The principle is offered as known *a priori*.

Cogito; ergo, sum (chapter 5): Descartes's famous "I think; therefore, I am." "The *cogito*" is offered as the epistemologically certain truth (like an axiom in mathematics) that is the basis for establishing his essence as a thinking thing, for deriving the rest of his philosophy and the basic truths of philosophy.

cognitive theories of emotion (chapter 2): Emotions are intentional, which means they have an object, typically a belief that something is good or bad (e.g., anger as the belief that one has been done an injustice).

common will (chapter 9): A central concept in Rousseau's philosophy, interpreted in different ways, refers to the power of the people as the ultimate authority.

community (chapter 13): A central theme in classical American pragmatism. For Addams and Dewey, the community is the social environment in which individuals interact and change. Pragmatists do not see the individual and the community as opposed to each other; rather, they see the community as an essential setting for fostering individuality.

concrete experience (chapter 13): For Dewey and Addams, this refers to the hands-on, day-to-day experience that people, as biological and social beings, have. Concrete experience always involves interaction and change between individuals and their biological and social environments. For pragmatists, philosophical ideas and theories need to be tested in light of concrete experience.

covenant (chapters 6, 7, and 9): A pact, a binding agreement. Used throughout the book in connection with "social contract" theories.

Dasein (chapter 12): Dasein ("being there") is Heidegger's term for the meaning of Being. Heidegger's Dasein refers to human being, or the being of humans.

deduction (chapter 10): The inference in an argument whereby a conclusion is alleged to follow necessarily from one or more given premises. (Kant would describe valid deduction as a necessary analytical inference.)

déformation professionelle (chapter 12): Arendt's use of a common French phrase referring to quirks and even distortions that can come to characterize members of professions. Thus a trial lawyer may come to consider anything other than winning or losing in court irrelevant; a psychologist may become unable to think of people in anything other than clinical terms. Arendt claimed that a passion for arriving at or establishing certain truths that are evident in confusions of philosophy with science, and—most of all—of meaning with truth, created a philosophical déformation professionelle that made even its best thinkers vulnerable to admiration of tyranny.

democracy (chapter 13): For Addams and Dewey, "democracy" is not just a term for a particular set of governmental procedures. Instead, democracy is a form of associated living that should extend to communities, workplaces, and other cultural institutions, as well as the political sphere. Democratic forms of living are characterized by high levels of cooperation and participation, a willingness to learn from all other members of the community, and a commitment to fostering every member's creative potential.

dilectio/diligo (chapter 4): Indicates a chosen loved one, or a love that is characterized by a decision, intention, or choice rather than an irresistible emotion.

Doctrine of the Mean (chapter 2): Aristotle's doctrine that morally appropriate action and emotional responses must avoid the extremes of excess and defect. Virtue (moral excellence) is a state of character, or settled disposition, to choose and achieve the "mean."

dualisms: "Either-or" dichotomies that traditionally are assumed to identify mutually exclusive options, concepts, assumptions, or descriptions of realities. Some of the more common are: reason (rationality) versus emotion; mind versus body; mental versus physical; culture versus nature; objective versus subjective; absolutism versus relativism; universal versus particular; human versus nonhuman (animals); essential versus accidental properties; public (polis) versus private ("the domestic sphere"); empiricism versus rationalism; realism versus idealism; factual claim versus value claim ("is versus ought"); subject versus object; self versus other (or, sometimes, Other).

dualisms (chapter 13): Dewey criticized many philosophical theories because they incorporated faulty dualisms such as mind from body, reason from emotion, and the transcendent reality from the earthly world. Dewey claims that these dualisms lead us to misunderstand and devalue concrete experience, by elevating one "disjunct" (mind, reason, transcendence) that should be the basis for all philosophizing.

empiricism (chapters 7 and 10): The position that all knowledge of the sensory world is derived from experience and known *a posteriori,* through sensory and empirical data (see also Rationalism).

epistemology: The study of knowledge (including theories about what knowledge is, what can be known, how something is known, and the nature of the knower)

Eros (chapter 1): Ancient Greek term referring to sexual love and desire; also used as a proper name of a mythical being supposed to be the child of the goddess of love, Aphrodite.

essence (Lead Essay; chapters 1 and 2): The defining characteristic(s) of a thing; what makes a thing what it is rather than something else; the core reality or true definition of any given thing or concept. For Plato, forms provide the essence of different kinds of objects—mathematical, particulars, and representations of particulars. Knowledge of essences is the only true knowledge. For Aristotle, "essence" is what remains throughout change of a thing from potentiality to actuality.

"essence precedes existence." (chapter 15): An expression used by Sartre regarding humans which claims that all things and beings other than humans have an essence—a set of properties that makes them what they are before they are born or created. For humans, the converse is true, "existence precedes essence": humans are born totally free, with no essential nature or essence. Humans create who they are, what they value by the choices they make.

essentialism (Lead Essay; chapter 1): *Conceptual* essentialism refers to the position that there is a set of properties (characteristics) that make something (a person, thing, or concept) what it is and not something else. *Strategic* essentialism refers to the position that, for practical or political reasons, it may be helpful and appropriate to use a word or concept (such as women), make an assumption or generalization (about women) as if there were some meaningful concept or essence of woman *simpliciter,* some set of properties that all and only women have. Strategic essentialism allows one to make true generalizations (e.g., about women earning less for comparable work than men) without being committed to conceptual essentialism (about "women").

ethical theories: Traditionally, there are three categories of ethical theories: (a) consequentialist theories (e.g., ethical egoism, ethical altruism, utilitarianism); (b) non-consequentialist theories (e.g., Kantian ethics of duty, the divine command theory, rights-based theories); and (c) virtue or character-based ethics. In addition, there are positions that challenge the existence of "absolute" or "cross-culturally valid" ethical theories: (d) ethical relativism (ethics is whatever the beliefs or conventions of a society permit), (e) ethical nihilism (there is no value, no right or wrong), (f) ethical skepticism (there is no way of knowing whether there are absolute ethical principles, whether an action is right or wrong). Some contemporary ethics (e.g., some feminist ethics and environmental ethics) challenge these categories and offer alternative accounts of ethics (e.g., ethical contextualism, an ethic of care, environmental pragmatism, environmental phenomenology).

ethics (traditional): Ethics may refer to: (a) descriptive ethics (observational accounts of the values people, societies, cultures actually have; (b) normative ethics (theories of moral obligation that provide accounts of what makes actions and kinds of actions right or wrong; and (c) meta-ethics (theories about the meaning of ethical terms, what constitutes a proof in ethics, whether moral judgments can be proven).

eudaimonia (chapter 2): For Aristotle, the "flourishing" or well-being (sometimes translated "happiness") that is the *arête*, "excellence or virtue of individual selves and a just state."

evolutionary process (chapter 13): classical American pragmatists adapt Darwin's evolutionary framework for their philosophizing. All human acting and thinking takes place within biological and social environments in which the individual and the environment constantly shape and modify each other. "Reality" and "truth" are thus always subject to change; no fixed or permanent reality or truth can be identified.

"existence precedes essence": See entry "essence precedes existence."

existentialism (chapter 15): A twentieth-century philosophy that emphasizes the primacy of freely chosen individual existence. There are different versions (e.g., between theist and atheist existentialists), but French existentialists generally agree that the fact of one's existence as a human being entails both radical freedom (since one is not born with a fixed essence) and radical responsibility (since one has no alternative to making choices). (See also *angst*, bad faith, authentic existence.)

extended body (chapter 5): For Descartes, there are two kinds of substance; bodily sustance (*res extensa*) has the property of spatial magnitude, considered to be an essential attribute of matter.

extension (chapter 5): Physical space considered as a single continuum.

facticity (chapter 15): For French existentialitsts, the situation of a person's life that cannot be changed, aspects which resemble inert objects (for example, the past, social circumstance, and body-as-object) and humans' bodily existence; humans are always "in situation" and free to choose (for example, projects, values, and the body-as-subject).

family resemblance (chapter 14): A term Wittgenstein uses for the way in which expressions apply to things or kinds of things (e.g., games) that do not share a common defining property, but an interrelated complex of likenesses.

feeling: See entry on Aristotle's usage of the term *pathos*.

feminism: There are many feminisms, and they disagree about fundamental issues. But as used in this book, "feminism" involves basic claims: sexism exists, is wrong, and must be changed; women deserve the same legal rights, educational opportunities, economic independence, equal pay, and access to jobs as men; one must eliminate various forms of "male-bias" (e.g., in the concept of reason/rationality, canonical dualisms, views about women, main assumptions of traditional philosophy, in social institutions).

framework propositions (chapter 14): Wittgenstein's terminology for those things that must be taken for granted—fixed but not bedrock claims—and that make possible meaningful uses of language and knowledge claims. The existence of the external world is a framework proposition, presupposed by things we say and do but not provable by things we say and do.

habits (chapter 13): A central concept in Dewey's philosophy, habits are organized patterns of acting and thinking that function as skills or tools which make higher level acting and thinking possible. For example, musicians' or athletes' collections of tech-niques, or "habits," free them to perform at higher levels of sophistication. Dewey also thinks of character traits as "habits" which we develop over time and then use in our decisions and actions.

harmonia (chapter 2): A Pythagorean principle of harmony that applies to the cosmos and everything in it. The word comes from a verb, *harmzon,* which means "fit together." The term has applications to musical harmony, cosmic order, and what is morally "fitting."

hedonism: The nonmoral value theory that obtaining pleasureis the only intrinsically good thing or end worth pursuing.

House, The Canonical House (Lead Essay): A visual image and metaphor for the Western philosophical tradition, which captures the (six) key features of the Western "philo-sophical canon."

human condition (chapter 6): A phrase used to describe humanity as good or evil (or both), and our struggle to understand what it is to be human.

human nature (chapter 6): What makes a being human; the specific characteristics com-mon to all human beings. Some view humans as "thinking things" or rational animals who are basically good (or basically evil).

idealist metaphysics (chapter 8): An account of reality that claims that, ultimately, only spirit is real.

immutable principle (chapter 6): A fixed or unchanging rule or code of conduct.

individual ethics (chapter 13): Addams's term for an approach to ethics characterized by social hierarchy, where one person or group decides what is good for others. Philan-thropy and capitalism embody individual ethics. Addams argues that this makes them undemocratic, and thus not suitable for the high degree of social interdependence found in urban, industrial societies.

inference (chapter 10): Process of reasoning from a proposition accepted as true to an-other proposition whose truth is alleged to be implied or to "follow" ("necessarily," in deductive arguments and "probably," in inductive arguments).

intencio (chapter 4): The act of the will in forming an intention as a result of the delibera-tions of *ratio*; what is willed or intended.

intention (chapter 14): For Anscombe, determining whether or not an act is intentional requires providing a reason and a motive in the explanation of why someone did an act (where acts always fall under a particular description).

intentionality: The feature of emotions, mental and linguistic states that they have an object or content, that they are about something.

intersubjectivity: The denial of the Cartesian notion of mental substances as intrasub-jective but, cut off from the immediacy of the world, incapable of direct, concrete relationships between individual consciousnesses—incapable of the possibility of intersubjectivity between selves. Beauvoir establishes intersubjectivity between selves through the phenomenological event of experiencing oneself as the object of another's look—being conscious of being looked at or judged by another person—makes selves aware that they have another self, an "objective" one which exists only for the Other.

judgment (chapter 12): In the context of Arendt, it means the free act of mind by which we relate a principle to a particular while honoring both. We have judges to interpret the law, and value good judgment in general, precisely because, while the law, or a principle, may "cover" a kind of situation or act, the individual(s) involved are always unique, and situations always differ. Today, we say we had to "make a judgment call" when we cannot be certain, but must decide what to do—make judgments—anyway.

Kabbalah (chapter 8): The mystical Judaic doctrine defined and set out in the "Zohar."

language game (chapter 14): Wittgenstein's expression for an activity that is rule-governed by conventional uses of words and language, not just a grammar. It includes such activities as giving orders, making jokes, guessing riddles, praying.

leviathan (chapter 6): Term used by Thomas Hobbes for the entity—either a single man or an assembly of men—that has been given the power necessary to provide the peace and defense of the community.

Light (and Living Light) (chapters 3, 5, and 10): Terms used variously to refer to illuminations from God, or the light of God (revealed through Jesus), or "natural light of reason."

logical positivism (Lead Essay; chapter 14): The twentieth-century philosophical position that claimed that the only meaningful claims of philosophy were those based in/derived from scientific and empirical data or proven by rules of logic. Knowledge is based on only these two sources. They claimed that metaphysics and aesthetics (for example) are not just false but are meaningless (and hence not legitimate areas or topics of philosophy).

the look (chapter 15): The existential notion of Beauvoir and Sartre of the self-as-object to other human beings. The Look is when the Other transforms or objectifies the self into the object of its gaze.

materialism (chapter 5): The doctrine that nothing exists except matter, physical or extended body, and its movement and modifications.

medieval (or, monastic) (chapters 4 and 10): The curriculum that focused on the seven liberal arts, divided into: the *trivium* (three subjects) of liberal arts—classical Latin language, literature (grammar and rhetoric), and Aristotelian logic ("dialectic")—and the *quadrivium* (four subjects) of arithmetic, music, geometry, and astronomy. The study of theology, canon law, and medicine presupposed this rigorous course of study.

metaphysical dualism (Lead Essay; chapters 5, 8, 10, 13, 14, 15): The view, most notably associated with Descartes, that there exists two different kinds of substances in the world: minds (*res cogitans*, thinking substances) and bodies (*res extensa*, extended, spatiotemporal substances).

metaphysics: (1) An area of philosophy that is the study of what is real, what constitutes reality, in what reality consists. (2) The study of the world beyond experience to establish first principles as a foundation for other knowledge (chapter 10).

modes (chapter 10): Manners of thinking.

monads (chapter 8): For Leibniz, monads are simple, nonmaterial substances that are without parts and do not causally interact with each other. When Conway writes of "monads," or the barest units, as a monistic vitalist she is denying Leibniz's notion of monads as nonmaterial substances: there is no unit of matter that is not itself (save God) a complex mingling of both matter and spirit.

monistic vitalism (chapter 8): Conway's view that the universe is composed of a mixture of spirit and matter, differing in the proportions of each with regard to various individuals (in contrast to Leibniz's materialism).

moral philosophy (chapter 6): The philosophical study of human values and conduct (see "ethics, traditional").

mortality (versus natality) (chapter 12): Mortality is death—the inescapable "given" that what lives eventually dies. Natality is birth—the "given" of living. Natality is the view that newcomers are always arriving among us, that there is a recurrent need for historical new beginnings to revive deadening intellectual, social, political conventions in order to revivify humankind. Arendt saw natality as the "human condition" for action, which she defines as starting something new, as when we speak up publicly rather than "behaving ourselves" such that nothing surprising breaks through settled conventions.

necessary (chapter 10): A claim that is "forced" by the premises of a valid deductive argument. A proposition is "necessary" if its denial involves or implies a contradiction.

negation, nihilation (chapter 12): If Being *is* as beings, in the plural and in time, then everything that exists can be differentiated from other things through negation: a tree is *not* a star, I *am not* you, the future *is not yet*. And if negation is intrinsic to beings, the fundamental Being that discloses itself as or through beings (including human beings) must itself entail fundamental negation, or Nothingness. Heidegger writes of nihilation, or annihilation, then, not as nihilism, but as clearing the ground for Being as beings to appear. Facing our own death can lead to existential anxiety and cynicism, but through such "moods," we can, on the contrary, be recalled to "care" for beings that are always also what they are not. Realizing that the meaning of death is within life, we can achieve a radical openness to Being as it both reveals and withdraws (negates and/or nihilates) itself. Arendt, more simply, reminds us that "God is dead" is self-contradictory: what has "died" is the old (Cartesian) two-world schema in which the true and eternal were radically divided from the real and temporal. We are then freed to think about humans and our worlds as they really appear to us.

nominalism: As opposed to realism, for which universals are required to explain how general terms apply to different particulars, nominalism is the position that the only feature that particulars falling under the same general term have in common is that they are covered by the same term. For nominalism, language, rather than independent reality, underlies perceived likenesses between general terms.

noumena; noumenal world (chapters 10 and 15): For Kant, the nonsensory "really real world" beyond phenomena of space and time.

noumenal self (chapters 10 and 15): Kant's notion of the real self, the self as a "thing-in-itself," an "end-in-itself," which exists not in the phenomenal world of sense experience but in the nonspatial noumenal world.

ontology: (1) A description, analysis, and reflection on the nature or construction of reality *per se*—of being, of existence—and so also of entities deemed to exist, to be real. A philosopher's ontology is a description or account of the sorts of things that philosophers countenance as real and their status vis-à-vis each other. (2) For Heidegger (chapter 12), philosophical efforts to comprehend what existence is, or Being itself—ontologies—are themselves manifestations of Being in time. Specific historical ontologies are both analyses of Being, and, more basically, Being reflecting on itself in differing ways through history. When Heidegger reflects about traditional philosophical ontologies, he is doing meta-ontology. But Heidegger's project was to think Being itself in a way that calls "man" back to "his" "primordial" relationship with the ontological, with the Being of beings. Such a relationship is more poetic than analytic, more life craft (doing, making) than science; it holds us *within* and *open* to Being as it is for us, as we are in the world that is present to and for us. This effort to call us back into relation with being-in-the-world is his fundamental ontology.

other-as-object (chapter 15): The existential notion of one's own awareness that another, "the Other," exists for oneself as an object in the world.

other-as-subject (chapter 15): The existential notion of another consciousness that experiences one's self as an object.

pantheism (chapter 8): An account of reality that claims that the divine principle (for some God) is immanently contained in all things, including the nonhuman natural world. The divine principle and essence is not found in some abstract, independent, transcendent principle or being.

pathos: For Aristotle, feeling, includes appetite (*epithumia*) and emotion (*thumos*). For Aristotle, feelings (emotions) have a cognitive aspect. Appetite includes, but is not confined to, desires such as hunger and thirst or those involving other bodily needs (e.g., an "appetite" for health or learning)To have an appetite for something is to regard it as pleasant. In the case of emotions, the cognitive aspect involves a belief that something is good or bad (see Cognitive Theories of Emotion).

phenomenal self (chapter 10): Kant's term for the self as it appears or exists in the external world, in contrast to the "noumenal self."

phenomenology: For Hegel, the study of the dialectical development of Spirit towards self-conscious freedom; for Husserl, a philosophical method based on the study of consciousness, focused on the intentionality of mental states. Husserl attempted to draw a sharp boundary between phenomenology and psychology. Other writers, especially Heidegger, use the term very differently.

phenomenon (chapter 10): Kant's term for events, experiences, objects in the sensible, external world ("the phenomenal world").

philosophy (chapter 1): In its etymology, "philosophy" is linked to two Greek terms meaning "love of wisdom" or "the search for wisdom." From *philein*, verb meaning "to love," "to seek after," and *sophia* the noun meaning "wisdom."

philosophy as experimental method (chapter 13): For pragmatists like Dewey and Addams, philosophy is a method for solving problems, rather than a search for eternal truths. Pragmatists emphasize observation and experiment, testing their ideas with concrete experience. Dewey believes that philosophy should be social criticism, devoted to pressing social problems.

philosophy of mind (chapter 14): A sub-field of philosophy that deals with questions about the place of mind in the natural, material world (this is the mind/body problem). Important questions include the problem of consciousness (specifically the relationship between consciousness and matter); the problem of mental causation (how a mental event, such as the desire for a drink, can cause a physical event, such as walking to the fridge to get a drink); and problems relating to intentionality (mental states such as beliefs and desires about something). This capacity of the mind is known as intentionality and problems relating to intentionality include giving an account of what constitutes the essential features of intentionality (what makes a desire the specific desire that it is, for example) and trying to understand intentionality in terms of the biological features of the organism.

phronesis (chapters 2 and 10): It is "practical wisdom." According to Aristotle, this intellectual excellence is related to moral excellence. Practical wisdom is knowing how to achieve "the mean" in practice. (See "Doctrine of the Mean.") A practically wise person is morally perceptive, able to recognize the morally relevant factors in concrete situations, exhibiting the excellence of *phronesis*.

political/moral inequality (chapter 9): This is the position that some people or classes of people do not (or should not) have the same political or moral standing as others and thus would not have the same rights or have a claim to be accorded the same treatment as others.

political philosophy: A subfield of philosophy concerning the arrangements of our collective life, in particular political institutions. Its central question historically has been, "When do authorities (e.g., governments) have a right to rule and citizens have a (correlative) duty to obey? What makes a government legitimate?"

postmillennialism (chapter 6): The view or belief that there is a divine plan for a gradual improvement in human nature and society leading to a time of perfection on earth signaling the Second Coming of Christ.

power (versus force, violence, authority) (chapter 12): For Arendt, power springs up among people who, gathered to talk, are sometimes persuaded to act together to achieve some goal. Power is not the same as force, by which one or many use their greater strength to coerce others. Power is also not the same as violence, which does greater harm than force, and usually requires instruments (e.g., guns) that allow weaker people to dominate stronger ones, and a few to dominate many. Nor is power the same as authority, which may invoke a source of legitimacy that renders differing opinions invalid, or irrelevant (e.g., when a scholar cites a text as "authoritative").

pragmatism, classical American (chapter 13): An American (U.S.) approach to philosophy developed in the late nineteenth and early twentieth centuries (e.g., by Peirce, Dewey, James, Addams), which places experience within an evolutionary context of change and development; it tests ideas and theories in light of concrete experience, rather than seeking fixed, permanent truths.

problems of philosophy: In canonical philosophy, there are many. Some of the most common are: (a) *the mind-body problem*: if minds and bodies are two different kinds of substances (thinking things and extended things, respectively), then how are they "connected" as one self and how is causal interaction between them possible? (b) *the problem of the existence of the external world*: how does one establish the independent existence of the sensory world, especially if one's starting point is "I exist" as a mental being? (c) *the problem of solipsism* (or, "the egocentric predicament): how does one establish that there is more than one's ideas and perception; how does one get "beyond" one's own existence to the existence of other things or beings? (d) *the problem of appearance versus reality*: how does one know what is real, in what reality consists, if one's direct, immediate, unmediated experience is only of things-as-they-appear through sensory impressions and data? (e) *the problem of other minds*: given one's own existence as a mind or thinking thing, how does one prove there are "other minds," other thinking beings? (f) *the problem of identity* (including personal identity): what makes something (a self) the same thing (self) through the passage of time? (g) *the problem of evil*: if God is all-good, all-powerful and all-knowing, then why is there evil (natural or moral evil)? (h) *the free will versus determinism problem*: how is human freedom of choice (free will) compatible with biological predispositions and a scientific world governed by material and physical laws?

propaedeutic (chapter 10): Providing introductory instruction.

proposition (chapter 10): Whatever is asserted, denied, contended, assumed or maintained in or by a declarative sentence; the meaning ("sense") of a claim or statement (where a statement is a sentence that is either true or false).

pseudepigrapha (chapter 2): A Pythagorean term meaning "spurious" or "fictional" writings. Work thought not to be written by the authors to whom they are attributed. Late Pythagoreans had a tradition of attributing their works to early Pythagoreans, even to Pythagoras himself.

ratio (chapter 4): The rational mind; the deliberative actions of the faculty of reason; the outcome or conclusions reached by reason.

rationalism (chapters 7, 8, and 10): In contrast to empiricism, the position that genuine knowledge, proof of fundamental claims, or legitimate philosophical issues are derived from reason, not from sensory, empirical, or experiential evidence. With Kant's terminology and endorsement of synthetic *a priori* truths—truths about the sensible world that are arrived at, proven, or known through reason alone, sometimes rationalism may be understood as the position that, unlike empiricism, accepts synthetic *a priori* knowledge.

realism: A variety of doctrines about the existence of different entities or facts—all contested. These include: the reality of Platonic Forms (and their status as the most real entities); the reality of universals (in addition or contrast to particulars); the reality of numbers; the reality of moral facts in ethics; the reality of time in metaphysics. In contrast to different forms of "realism" are such positions as: nominalism, idealism, reductionism, conventionalism, constructivism, relativism, and anti-realism. Kant argued for both empirical realism and transcendental idealism.

republic (chapter 6): Government in which the supreme authority is invested in the people. Also, a specific use of the term for the government that existed in England between the execution of Charles I in 1649 and the Restoration in 1660.

rhetoric (chapters 1 and 4): The study and creation of formal set speeches on various themes, rhetoric is also a discipline which flourished in the classical period (fifth–fourth centuries B.C.E.) in ancient Greece. Socrates, in Plato's dialogues, is often critical of rhetoric as a legitimate practice or object of interest.

rhetorical reasoning (Lead Essay; chapters 1, 2, and 4): A form of persuasive reasoning that involves the use of logic (*logos*) and emotion (*pathos*) to establish or appeal to an ethical position or orientation (*êthos*).

royalist (chapter 6): A person who supports a king, or who supports government by monarchy.

scepticism (chapters 10 and 14): Commonly understood as the view that one cannot know or prove that a given proposition is true. Some also understand it as a method of intellectual caution, a proposition about the limits of knowledge.

scholasticism (chapter 10): Scholasticism is a name derived from the cloister schools in France extending from the ninth through the fifteenth centuries. The logic of this period, shaped by Aristotle, engaged in metaphysical and theological disputes such as those advanced by Pierre (or Peter) Abélard in the twelfth century in his *Sic et Non*, and the views of Thomas Aquinas in the thirteenth century in his *Summa Theologiae*.

self-for-itself (chapter 15): The existential concept of the self-as-subject, *pour moi-même*, is one's experience of oneself as subject of another's look. To be conscious of being looked at or judged by another person; the awareness that one has another self, an "objective" one which exists only for the Other (the self-for-the-other).

self-for-the-other (chapter 15): The existential concept of the "self-for-others," *pour autrui*, is the existential awareness that the Other has an image of one's self as an object in a world whose center of reference is not one's own consciousness (but that of the Other); experiencing oneself as the object of another's look.

social contract (chapters 6, 7, and 9): An agreement, implicit or explicit, whereby all members of civil society agree to abide by the laws of the state/government to maximize human safety, survival, or bring about the common good. According to Locke, humans agree to give up some of their natural rights in return for protection; for Hobbes, humans in a state of nature are in a "war against all," where fear of mutual violence and the inability to the protect one's own life make people agree to turn over all their rights to an artificially created "leviathan" in exchange for protection of one's life. For Rousseau, who believes "man is born free," it is a means of bringing about the basic goodness of humans. Social contract theory, based on the consent of the subject-as-citizen, often is offered as the moral basis for the legitimacy of a government (its right to rule) and the duty of citizens to obey.

social Ethics (chapter 13): Addams's term for an approach to ethics that is democratic, characterized by equality of all, reciprocity, and high levels of participation. Addams uses "social ethics" and "democracy" as synonymous terms.

sovereign (chapter 6): For Thomas Hobbes, the sovereign is an alternative name or referent for the Leviathan—the person or group of people authorized to act on behalf of the community.

state of nature (chapters 6, 7, and 9): Human life without civil authority; a precivil society in which humans live in state of conflict with each other. For Hobbes, it is a precivil society in which life is "solitary, poor, nasty, brutish and short." For Rousseau, "state of nature" had various meanings. Some view it as referring to an idea/ideal; others that it refers to an actual historical state.

substance (chapters 2, 5, 8, and 10): Something that can exist by itself. It has various meanings: e.g., the "substratum" underlying the existence of other things (pre-Socratics); the subject of which other things are predicated, which can be matter and/or form (Aristotle); two kinds of substances, minds and bodies (Descartes); monads are simple substances (Leibniz); a corpuscular substrate with primary qualities (Locke).

syllogism (chapter 10): Arguments consisting of three and only three propositions, expressed in standard categorical subject-predicate form; with four logical forms for constructing the propositions into standard syllogistic form.

sympathetic knowledge (chapter 13): For Addams and Dewey, sympathetic knowledge is an essential part of coming to understand any person or social situation. Both emotional engagement and empirical data are needed for genuine understanding.

synthetic (chapter 10): A judgment relating a subject concept with a predicated concept not included within the subject proper. In contrast to an analytic claim (such as All A are A), a synthetic claim is about the sensory world (such as "it is snowing.").

tabula rasa (chapters 7 and 9): This expression is used to describe the human mind as a "blank slate," a mind prior to the possession of any ideas or impressions. The notion is offered by Locke to refute the existence of innate ideas.

telos (chapter 2): *Telos* means end or goal. Aristotle's approach to ethics is teleological (goal- or purpose-oriented) rather than deontological (a nonconsequential ethics). For Aristotle, the *telos* of human life is *eudaimonia* (human flourishing, or happiness).

Theory of Forms (chapter 1): Plato's doctrine that the most real objects are Forms (Ideas) that are differentiated from other less real objects: mathematical objects (triangularity), particular objects that are individuals (e.g., particular triangles), and particular objects that are images, copies or representations of individuals (paintings of triangles). Forms are also the "essences" and causes of the existence of these other objects. The traditional view is that Forms exist in a nonspatial, nontemporal, changeless, nonsensory world, in contrast to the sensory world of particulars.

things-as-they appear (chapter 10): See "phenomena."

things-in-themselves (chapter 10): See "noumena."

thinking (chapter 12): For Arendt and Heidegger, thinking is most like questioning: it opens up what was settled, discloses what was not seen, but does not solve anything or arrive at conclusions. Heidegger speaks of thinking as being like laying trails or paths that open ways, but do not arrive anywhere. Thinking is not calculating or problem-solving, nor is it deduction or induction (it is not logical: it does not follow rules). It wanders and wonders freely, and so it is always "out of order." For Heidegger, Socrates is the exemplar of thinking; his thinking "discloses" Being and construes thinking as care, as poetic, as piety/Arendt emphasizes thinking as a public activity.

time and space (chapter 12): The *when* and *where* that both bind and ground human lives; they can be understood as facts, like dates, specific places, and/or scientific abstractions, but these do not exhaust their meanings. Arendt claims that they both relate and hold people separate (like a table around which we gather). Her interest in time is in the way we make stories of what has happened in order to make sense of it in and as providing new material for future stories. She also says that when we are thinking, we "leap above" the past that presses us from "behind" as the future "in front" of us presses us back, thereby clearing a "space" that allows us to judge what is going on (we thereby "gain perspective"). Heidegger depicts thinking as "in" neither lineal time nor linear space—like those moments when we see it all at once, as if space and time were no longer extended and sequential.

transcendent (chapter 1): Surpassing the level of ordinary experience. Used to describe a realm of reality referred to by Plato as the only truly existing and knowable level of existence—the world of Forms—and contrasted it with the world of sense experience and material things.

transcendental (chapter 10): Kant's name for his *a priori* science of pure reason. Transcendental knowledge is possible, but transcendent (that which is beyond the senses) knowledge is not.

truth, opinion (chapter 12): Both Arendt and Heidegger were as concerned about "popular opinion" as they were about the deadening effects of conformity, of "good behavior." They valued the unique, and feared the standardizing effects of what Arendt called "the social" and Heidegger called *das Man*, or the They (as in, "We can't do that: they won't approve"). But Arendt, unlike Heidegger, valued informed individual opinions (statements about which we properly say, "It seems to me . . .") It is because opinions can only invite agreement and cannot force it that Arendt insists that in public life even a truth must appear as an opinion. Otherwise, those who differ will be silenced, at cost of freedom and equality. Heidegger also spoke against logical necessity: his truth of being was to be revealed, not deduced. Nevertheless, he had little but scorn for what he called "chatter," and so also for public life.

"two-world" schemas (chapter 12): Hannah Arendt describes classic Western "two-world" schemas in terms of a basic distinction between whatever is not given to the senses—God or Being or the First Principles or Platonic Forms or Causes—as more real, more truthful, more meaningful, not beyond sense perception but above the world of the senses. Heidegger and Arendt both argue against hierarchical ontologies. For Arendt, ideas have meaning as abstractions from real experiences, including conceptual experiences.

universal (Lead Essay; chapter 10): That term which can be applied throughout the universe. In ethics principles of right act, duty, or virtue are universal if and only if they apply to all humans.

valid (chapter 10): A deductive argument or inference is said to be valid if and only if it is not possible for the premises to be true and the conclusion false. It is a formal property of arguments (i.e., the validity of an argument is about its structure or form, not about the truth or falsity of the premises and conclusion). Inductive arguments are strong or weak, not valid or invalid.

vita activa (chapter 12): Arendt uses the classic Latin phrase to invoke a richer meaning for "politics"—a life of action, a public life.

About the Contributors

Eve Browning is an associate professor in the Department of Philosophy at the University of Minnesota, Duluth (UMD). She earned a Ph.D. in philosophy in 1979 at the University of California, San Diego. Prior to joining the UMD faculty, she held university appointments at the University of California, Riverside, in 1979–1980, Ohio State University 1980–1983, and the University of Denver 1983–1984. She specializes in ancient philosophy and also has lively interests in feminist philosophy, ethics, classical studies, including classical mythology, philosophy of art, and environmental issues.

Jane Duran is a Fellow in philosophy and lecturer in Humanities at the University of California at Santa Barbara. She is the author of numerous articles on epistemology, feminist theory, and women philosophers. Her latest books are *Worlds of Knowing* and *Eight Women Philosophers*.

Therese Boos Dykeman is an independent scholar with interdisciplinary interests in rhetoric and philosophy. She is an adjunct professor at Fairfield and Sacred Heart Universities in Fairfield, Connecticut, and author of *American Women Philosophers, 1650–1930: Six Exemplary Thinkers* and *The Neglected Canon: Nine Women Philosophers, First to the Twentieth Century*. She recently coedited a six-volume *Republication of the Social, Political and Philosophical Works of Catharine E. Beecher*.

Marilyn Fischer is professor of philosophy at the University of Dayton where she is actively involved in interdisciplinary and collaborative teaching. She is the author of *On Addams*, and co-editor with Judy D. Whipps of a four-volume set of Addams's writings on peace. She published *Ethical Decision Making in Fund Raising*, in which she draws on Addams's and Dewey's ethics in constructing an ethical decision-making model for philanthropic fundraisers. She is currently writing on Addams's theories on peace and international understanding. Formerly a symphony violinist, Marilyn now fiddles with a bluegrass band.

Lois Frankel taught in various universities for ten years, during which time she published several articles, primarily on early modern philosophy. After publishing and perishing, she lives on in her reprints and occasional new work (such as her chapter in this volume). She now works for a not-for-profit company that has connections to education. When not at work, she collects antique sewing machines and uses them, as well as modern sewing machines, to make fiber art.

Edward Fullbrook, with Kate Fullbrook, is the author of a dozen essays on Beauvoir's philosophy and two books, *Simone de Beauvoir and Jean-Paul Sartre: The Remaking of 20th Century Legend* and *Simone de Beauvoir: A Critical Introduction*. He is also an economist whose most recent book, *The Crisis in Economics*, was published by Routledge in 2003. He is a member of the School of Economics of the University of the West of England.

Catherine Villanueva Gardner is associate professor of philosophy and women's studies at the University of Massachusetts-Dartmouth. She has written on ecofeminism, as well as the history of women philosophers. She is author of *Rediscovering Women Philosophers: Genre and the Boundaries of Philosophy*.

Vicki Lynn Harper is associate professor of philosophy at St. Olaf College in Minnesota, where she has been teaching since 1979, and earned her Ph.D. in classical philosophy from Harvard University. She has published entries on Greek and Roman women in philosophy in the *Oxford Classical Dictionary* and translations and commentaries on women in classical philosophy in *A History of Women Philosophers*, vol. 1, edited by Mary Ellen Waithe (Martinus Nijholf 1987).

Jo Ellen Jacobs is chair of the Philosophy Department at Millikin University. In addition to editing *The Complete Works of Harriet Taylor Mill* with Paula Harms Payne and writing *The Voice of Harriet Taylor Mill*, Jacobs has written a number of articles on this feisty woman.

Joy Laine, chair of philosophy at Macalester College, is currently engaged in research on personal identity and Hindu/Buddhist debates in the eleventh century. She is writing a book about the treatment of personal identity in the philosophical tradition. Her key publications include "Indian Philosophy of Mind," *Routledge Encyclopedia of Philosophy* (1998); "Some Remarks on the *Gunagunibhedabhanga* in Udayana's *Atmatattvaviveka*," *Journal of Indian Philosophy* 21 (1993); and "Udayana's Refutation of the Buddhist Thesis of Momentariness in the *Atmatattvaviveka*," *Journal of Indian Philosophy* 26 (1998).

Kate Lindemann is professor emerita of philosophy at Mount Saint Mary College in Newburgh, New York. Her research and publications include works in liberating pedagogy, philosophy of liberation, ethics, especially the ethics of receiving, and several pieces about women philosophers. Currently she is the coordinator and chief editor of an Internet project on women philosophers; the site is located at www.Women-Philosophers.com.

Elizabeth Minnich is core professor at the Graduate College for Interdisciplinary Arts & Sciences, the Union Institute & University. She is the author of *Transforming Knowledge*, coeditor of *Reconstructing the Academy*; series editor for *The New Academy*, with articles in textbooks, anthologies, and referred journals. Special appointments include Visiting Scholar at the Getty Institute for the History of Art & the Humanities; the Whichard Visiting Distinguished Professor of Humanities & Women's Studies; and the Hartley Burr Alexander Chair for Public Philosophy. Her Ph.D. in philosophy is from the New School University, where she was Hannah Arendt's teaching assistant.

Andrea Nye is professor emeritas at the University of Wisconsin-Whitewater. Throughout her books and articles, Nye has explored ways feminists have critically engaged the Western philosophic tradition (*Feminism and the Philosophies of Man*, *Words of Power*, *Feminism and Philosophy*, *Philosophia*). A special interest of Nye's has been to revive the work of women philosophers, especially Diotima, Heloise, Simone Weil, and Princess Elisabeth of the Palatine. English versions of all of Elisabeth's letters, along with further biographical and philosophical commentary, are available in her book, *The Princess and the Philosopher: The Letters of Elisabeth of the Palatine to René Descartes*.

Margaret A. Simons, professor of philosophy at Southern Illinois University, Edwardsville, is the author of *Beauvoir and The Second Sex*. She is currently coediting, with Sylvie Le Bon de Beauvoir, a seven-volume series of Beauvoir's works in English translation, forthcoming from the University of Illinois Press, a project supported by a collaborative research grant from the National Endowment for the Humanities.

Audun Solli, Karen J. Warren's research assistant for *An Unconventional History of Western Philosophy* during his four years at Macalester College, graduated with majors in German literature and international studies. His academic interests range from globalization theories to writers such as Franz Kafka, Emine Sevgi Özdamar, Feridun Zaimoglu, Edward Said, and Simone de Beauvoir. Audun is now a master's student in international studies at Stellenbosch University in South Africa and is currently doing an integrated semester at the International Peace Research Institute in Oslo, Norway, his native country.

Judith Chelius Stark, Ph.D., is a professor of philosophy at Seton Hall University in South Orange, New Jersey. In addition to her work on Augustine, she conducts research in feminist theories, environmental ethics, and ecotourism. With Joanna Vecchiarelli Scott, she edited *Hannah Arendt, Love and Saint Augustine* (University of Chicago Press 1996), the critical edition of Hannah Arendt's dissertation on Augustine. Stark is the editor of the volume on Augustine, *Feminist Interpretations of Augustine*, for the series *Re-Reading the Canon* (Penn State Press). In her leisure time, she enjoys ocean swimming, birding, and sea kayaking.

Mary Ellen Waithe completed her Ph.D. at the University of Minnesota. She is the editor of the four-volume series *A History of Women Philosophers*, and author of many chapters in that series, including one on Heloise. Her most recent publication is a translation of Oliva Sabuco's 1587 work *New Philosophy of Human Nature*. She teaches philosophy at Cleveland State University.

Karen J. Warren, Ph.D., is professor of philosophy at Macalester College, is a pioneer of ecofeminist philosophy. She has edited six books on philosophical dimensions of ecofeminism and written *Ecofeminist Philosophy: A Western Perspective on What It Is and Why It Matters* (2000). In 1972, Warren established one of the first high school philosophy programs in the United States. She has received four teaching or educator awards, occupied an endowed chair (Marquette University, 2004) and been the Ecofeminist Scholar-in-Residence at Murdoch University (Western Australia, 1995).

Henry R. West is professor emeritus of philosophy at Macalester College. His areas of specialization are ethics, political philosophy, and the history of Western philosophy. He has written or edited three books: *An Introduction to Mill's Utilitarian Ethics* (Cambridge 2004), *The Blackwell Guide to Mill's Utilitarianism* (Oxford 2006), and *Mill's Utilitarianism: A Reader's Guide* (2007). An article on Mill's *On Liberty* is included in an anthology on Mill to be published by Cambridge University Press. In 2003 he co-taught ancient and medieval philosophies, with Karen J. Warren. It was the first time women philosophers were included in that course.